Am-MC-I-37,2

PEASANTS AND POVERTY

Lund Economic Studies Number 18

PEASANTS AND POVERTY

A STUDY OF HAITI

MATS LUNDAHL

CROOM HELM   LONDON

© 1979 Mats Lundahl
Croom Helm Ltd, 2-10 St John's Road, London SW11

British Library Cataloguing in Publication Data

Lundahl, Mats
   Peasants and poverty.
   1. Haiti – Economic conditions
   I. Title
   330.9'7294   HC157.H2
   ISBN 0-85664-602-4

Printed in Great Britain by
Redwood Burn Limited
Trowbridge & Esher

CONTENTS

Preface

Map of Haiti

1. Introduction and Summary   11
   Appendix: The Literature of the Haitian Peasant Economy   31
2. The Peasant Economy   37
   Appendix: Disguised Unemployment   86
3. The Cumulative Process: Falling Rural Incomes   91
4. Poverty and the Market   121
   Appendix: Transportation: the Main Obstacle to Competition   180
5. Erosion   187
   Appendix 1: The Composition of Peasant Output   235
   Appendix 2: Agricultural Involution in Java and Haiti   250
6. Land Reform   255
   Appendix: The Choice of Capital   293
7. The Passive Government   297
8. Haitian Public Finance   365
   Appendix: Total Government Expenditure   404
9. Malnutrition and Disease   409
10. The Role of Education   453
11. Problems of Rural Credit   503
12. Resistance to Innovation   557

Epilogue   623

Bibliography   649

Index   685

TABLES

2.1	Dependence of Mean Temperature on Altitude	39
2.2	The Distribution of Tenant Farmers in 1950	49
2.3	The Average Size of Landholdings in 1950	51
2.4	The Average Size of Landholdings in 1971	51
2.5	Number of Plots per Farm and Size of Plots 1971	53
2.6	Population Density in Some Caribbean and Central American Countries 1970	56
2.7	Percentage of the Population Living in Urban Areas in Some Latin American Countries 1975	56
2.8	Extension of Soils in Haiti According to the OAS Classifications	58
2.9	Topographical Characteristics of Haiti	59
2.10	Some Estimates of the Arable Area	59
2.11	Rural Population in Relation to Arable Area in Some Caribbean and Central American Countries	60
2.12	Agricultural Implements in the Marbial Valley in the Late 1940s	63
2.13	Seasonal Distribution of Rainfall in Port-au-Prince	64
2.14	Female Participation in the Labor Force	72
2.15	Occupational Distribution of the Labor Force 1950 and 1971	75
2.16	Land/Man Ratios in Latin American Agriculture	76
2.17	Yields per Hectare for Selected Crops 1972	80
A2.1	Distribution of the Agricultural Labor Force 1950	88
3.1	Underdeveloped Countries with Declining Real Per Capita Incomes 1950-74	98
3.2	Underdeveloped Countries with Declining Food Production Per Capita 1961-74	99
3.3	Real Gross Domestic Product Per Capita 1954/55-1971/72	103
3.4	Real Agricultural Product Per Capita of Total Population 1954/55-1971/72	104
3.5	Production per Rural Inhabitant of Some Important Crops in 1950 and 1970	105
3.6	Surveys of Average Daily Outlay on Food in Rural Areas 1957-65	107
3.7	Malnutrition among Preschool Children 1958 and 1974/75	108

3.8	Malnutrition among Preschool Children 1964/65 and 1974/75	109
4.1	Categories of Peasant Products in Haiti	126
4.2	Estimates of the Marketed Percentage of Selected Peasant Crops	126
4.3	Number of Coffee Speculators and Volume of Coffee Sold by District 1972-3	135
4.4	The Degree of Concentration among Coffee Exporters	138
4.5	Relative Positions of Leading Coffee Exporters	138
4.6	Shares in f.o.b. Prices of Haitian Coffee 1950-7 and 1964-70	140
4.7	Distribution of Returns on Coffee Exports 1975-6	142
4.8	Margins in Vegetable Marketing	154
A4.1	The Transport Sector 1952-73	182
5.1	The Population of Saint-Domingue 1775-89	190
5.2	Projection of the Haitian Population 1970-85	192
5.3	Natural Growth Rate of the Haitian Population 1824-1973	193
5.4	Mahogany Exports 1835-64	197
5.5	Logwood Exports 1818-1952	197
5.6	Consumption of Wood for Fuel Purposes 1953 and 1968	199
5.7	Oil Price Increases 1965-74	202
5.8	Production of Selected Agricultural Products 1950-70	206
5.9	Production of Selected Agricultural Products 1950-72	206
5.10	Estimates of Good Arable Soil 1938-70	212
5.11	F.o.b. Prices and Prices to Producer of Haitian Raw Sisal 1951/52-1972/73	217
5.12	International Cocoa Prices 1950/51-1971/72	217
5.13	Price Indices for Port-au-Prince for Some Important Subsistence Crops 1953-71	219
A5.1.1	Labor Requirements per Hectare for Selected Crops with Traditional Techniques	236
6.1	Saint-Domingue Exports of Four Agricultural Products 1789 and 1795	260
6.2	Exports of Four Agricultural Products in 1802 and 1804	262
6.3	The Establishment of American-owned Plantations in Haiti 1915-27	267
6.4	Average f.o.b. Price of Raw Sisal 1929/30-1951/52	284
7.1	Expenditures of the Department of Agriculture 1922/23-1929/30	301
7.2	Expenditures of the Department of Agriculture 1930/31-1940/41	304

7.3	Expenditures of the Department of Agriculture 1941/42-1945/46	305
7.4	Expenditures of the Department of Agriculture 1946/47-1949/50	306
7.5	Regular Budgetary Expenditure of the Department of Agriculture 1950/51-1956/57	308
7.6	Planned and Realized Expenditure in the Agricultural Sector Development Plans (1968/69-1970/71)	312
7.7	Planned and Realized Public Investments in the Agricultural Sector 1971/72-1973/74	313
8.1	Estimated Annual Rate of Increase in Money Supply 1843-69	368
8.2	Amount of Cash Balance at the End of Fiscal Years 1924-30	371
8.3	The Haitian Public Debt 1938-46	374
8.4	Percentage of Public Expenditure Going to the Armed Forces 1933/34-1949/50	380
8.5	Percentage of Budget Expenditures Going to the Armed Forces and to the Department of the Interior 1950/51-1956/57	381
8.6	Government Spending on Army and Police 1960-7	382
8.7	Wages and Salaries Expenditures of the Service Technique 1925/26-1929/30	384
8.8	Wages and Salaries Expenditures of the Service National de la Production Agricole et de l'Enseignement Rural 1933/34-1939/40	385
8.9	Wages and Salaries Expenditures of the Haitian Government 1959/60-1971/72	386
8.10	The Shares of Import and Export Duties in Public Revenues 1837-1957	393
8.11	The Shares of Import and Export Duties in Fiscal Revenues 1959/60-1970/71	394
8.12	Coffee Export Taxes in Percent of Peasants' Potential Coffee Incomes 1964-71	397
A8.1	Total Government Expenditure 1922/23-1951/52	404
A8.2	Total Government Expenditure 1952/53-1971/72	405
A8.3	Real Government Expenditure Per Capita	406
A8.4	Total Government Expenditure in Percent of GDP in Central America and the Caribbean 1970-4	406
9.1	Weight of Preschool Children in Fond-Parisien, June 1964	414
9.2	Surveys of Average Daily Calorie and Protein Intakes in Rural Areas 1951-65	418

9.3	Public Health Facilities in 1952 and 1973	429
9.4	Percentage of Physicians Graduated in Haiti 1928-68 Practising Abroad	430
10.1	Financial Aspects of the Haitian School System 1924-9	468
10.2	Rural Primary Education 1933-46	470
10.3	Rural Primary Education 1959-71	476
10.4	Adult Alphabetization 1961-6	477
10.5	Official Illiteracy Estimates for 1950 and 1971	478
10.6	Rural Primary Education 1971-5	479
10.7	Enrolment by Grade in Public Rural Primary Schools 1974-5	492
11.1	Some Reasons for Indebtedness in the Marbial Valley in the Late 1940s	510
11.2	Maximum Interest Rates that Borrowers May Be Willing to Pay	518
11.3	Estimates of Interest Rates that Lenders Would Have to Charge to Compensate for Defaults	525
11.4	Amounts Loaned under the IDAI Supervised Credit Program 1962-73	538
11.5	Authorized and Advanced Credits under the IDAI Supervised Lending Scheme, 1968-73	539
11.6	The Costs of Technical Assistance under the IDAI Supervised Credit Scheme 1972-3	550
12.1	Unit Values of US Coffee Imports 1821-1914	565
E.1	Estimated Legal Migration from Haiti to Cuba 1915-29	625
E.2	Increase in Urban Population 1950-61	629
E.3	Increase in Urban Population 1950-71	630
E.4	Population and Growth Rates for Selected Caribbean and South American Cities	631
E.5	Increase in Active Population 1950-71	634
E.6	Absorption of Labor outside the Agricultural Sector 1950-71	634

For Maja, Hanna, and Sara

PREFACE

The present study is the result of an eight-year love affair with Haiti and its people and of five longer or shorter visits to the country between 1969 and 1976. My interest in Haiti was first awakened by Bo Södersten who suggested that I should undertake a study of its economy. Then, I read James G. Leyburn's truly outstanding *The Haitian People*, and of course, there was no way back. The book began its life as an undergraduate paper in 1970 and turned into a major effort in 1974. Thereafter, most of my time and mental energy have been absorbed by work on the book.

An additional reason for selecting Haiti for the study has been that Haiti represents an extreme case of poverty and deprivation. It is the poorest country in the Western Hemisphere and one of the poorest in the world. A study of how extreme poverty arises might, if successful, represent a way of uncovering some of the intricate mechanisms which keep economies underdeveloped.

Many times during the course of writing the present book I have felt the loneliness of the long-distance runner. However, I have then had the privilege to benefit from the friendly support and good advice of a number of colleagues who in one way or another have made their impact on the final result. My greatest debt of gratitude is to Bo Södersten who initiated the study, who closely followed the course of my work from the first draft page to the last, and who generously and constantly provided intellectual encouragement and inspiration in difficult moments. Christopher K. Clague, Wolf Donner, Sidney W. Mintz, Gérard Pierre-Charles, Eskil Wadensjö and Roland Wingfield all read substantial portions of the manuscript and contributed with innumerable constructive suggestions along the way. Morgan Åberg, Tom Alberts, Arne Bigsten, Anders Borglin, Gunilla Bornmalm-Jardelöw, Harald Dickson, René Dorville, Alberto García-Munevar, Jan Gunnarsson, Mohinder Guron, Antonio Handal, Göte Hansson, Lennart Hjalmarsson, Bengt Höglund, Rogelio Imable, Bengt Jönsson, Lars Jonung, Charlie Karlsson, Michel S. Laguerre, Millard F. Long, Marianne Lundahl, Gustav F. Papanek, Inga Persson-Tanimura, Erling Petersson, Lennart Petersson, Paul N. Rosenstein-Rodan, Robert I. Rotberg, Bo Sandelin, Daniel M. Schydlowsky, Lars Söderström, László Somogyi Björn Thalberg and Bo Walfridson struggled with drafts of varying quality and improved them by numerous comments.

I owe special thanks to Peter Stenkula for providing office space, logistic services and a minimum of duties at the Department of Economics at the University of Lund, to Paul N. Rosenstein-Rodan for generously extending to me the stimulating environment at the Center for Latin American Development Studies at Boston University during 1975, to Michel Montoya Maquin for inviting me to spend the summer of 1976 with the Inter-American Institute of Agricultural Sciences at Port-au-Prince, and to José Luís Barreiro for necessary support during my stay with IICA.

Alan Harkess and Richard Tanimura undertook the difficult task of straightening out my English. Lena Somogyi typed the final version of the manuscript with incredible speed and accuracy. Agnetta Kretz drew all the figures amidst a host of other duties, Maj-Britt Mondélus lent her excellent French to the translation of all quotations in that language. To all these goes my ample gratitude.

The work has been financed by grants from the Swedish Council for Social Science Research and from the Swedish Agency for Research Cooperation with Developing Countries (SAREC). This support is gratefully acknowledged.

Needless to say, all the usual disclaimers apply. The responsibility for the faults and defects of the present work and for all opinions expressed therein is entirely my own.

Mats Lundahl

Lund
24 June 1978

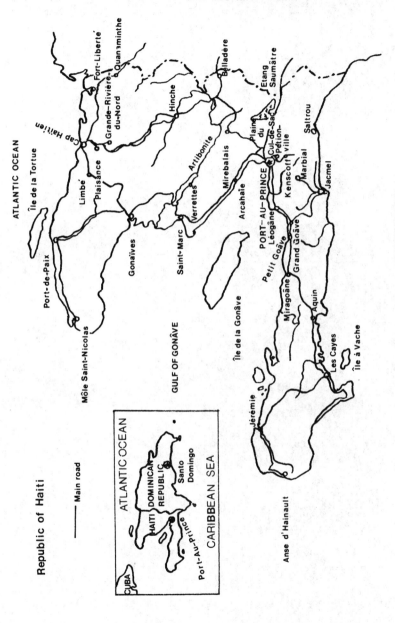

1 INTRODUCTION AND SUMMARY

Haiti is a country which with few exceptions has remained outside the focus of world interest and outside the important international historical currents during its entire existence as a free nation. At best, Haiti has been a 'pawn' in the game of international politics. Often, it has been an 'outcast'.[1] The decisive period in Haitian history, the period when the Haitian institutions, the class structure, the political tradition and the economic system were shaped, was the nineteenth century. During most of this period, the country was isolated, left to itself. Haitian society developed without much contact with the industrialized or industrializing nations of the world, and indeed, without much contact with its immediate neighbors. In the course of less than a century of relative isolation, Haiti became a peasant nation.

Basically, it remains so today. During the 1950s and 1960s, agriculture accounted for approximately one-half of the gross domestic product. This figure fell during the first half of the 1970s, but still, the share of the agricultural sector exceeds 40 percent.[2] At the beginning of the 1950s, 95 percent of the value of Haiti's exports derived from agricultural products. Subsequently, as other exports increased (bauxite, copper, essential oils,* light manufactures) the percentage of agriculture declined, but 45 percent in the mid-1970s still represents an important share.[3]

Most of the agricultural production comes from small peasant farms. Around 80 percent of the Haitian population lived in rural areas in 1971, and the same year, according to official statistics, almost 75 percent of the labor force were occupied in the agricultural sector.[4] The importance of the peasants to the national economy is high. However, the peasants only derive a meager living out of their cultures. The per capita income in the agricultural sector in 1971 only amounted to US $63.5 according to official statistics.[5] The exact figure is impossible to determine, but for the great majority of peasants, real incomes probably lie well under US $100.[6]

The present work analyzes the Haitian peasant economy and its problems, mainly from the early 1950s to the early 1970s, but often the time perspective has been extended backwards, since a full

---

*The raw material for these, however, comes from agriculture.

comprehension of today's problems requires thorough acquaintance with events that took place during the nineteenth century and in certain instances during the colonial period.

The book deals with the secular tendency of rural per capita incomes to decline and offers a number of explanations as to the causes of this decline. The core of the argument is advanced in economic terms. We have attempted in the main to rely on traditional economic analysis. However, it is not possible to understand Haiti's plight fully without venturing outside the scope of economics proper. Account must be taken of a number of political and social factors as well. Therefore, when the need has arisen, additional considerations have been introduced. Hence, much of the book is interdisciplinary in character.

Methodologically, our work relies almost exclusively on written sources — published and unpublished. No major or minor field study to gather primary material has been undertaken. The reason lies in the state of economic research on Haitian agriculture. Contrary to what may be thought, the material on Haiti is abundant.[7] The main problem is that it is not systematized. On the one hand, the concentration of most students of Haitian life has not been on the economy. 'For each anthropological paper on peasant economy, for instance, there must be at least a hundred on *voudoun*, folklore, music, and dance,' writes Sidney W. Mintz.[8] On the other hand, it is not possible rigorously to separate the material on for example folklore from the material dealing with economic questions. Hence, anybody looking for material regarding the economy must be prepared to read a huge amount of sociological, anthropological, cultural and political material as well, to find the necessary facts. The economic data, especially for earlier periods, are often scattered in a wide variety of sources. Frequently, important information is to be found where *a priori* one would not expect to find it. To systematize and synthesize this written material is a major task in itself, and this task has to be undertaken before field studies to gather supplementary material to confirm or refute the hypotheses emanating from the study of the written sources can be successfully attempted.

The present work represents an effort to create what I hope amounts to a coherent picture of the peasant economy out of some of the available written material. Few major monographs dealing with the peasant sector are available, and none has been published where systematic use has been made of principles of economic theory in the interpretation of the empirical material. The contribution of the present work, if any, lies precisely here — in the interpretation of existing data in the light of the findings of economic theory to understand the causes of stagnation

Introduction and Summary

and retrogression in the Haitian peasant sector. Ideally, this study should point to a number of areas where fruitful empirical research may be undertaken to fill the gaps of our knowledge of the peasant economy. The book is intended as a starting point rather than as a summary.

Peasants and Peasant Economies

The subject matter of our study is the Haitian peasant in his capacity as an economic agent and the stagnation of the Haitian peasant economy. What then constitutes a peasant, or what is a peasant economy? Sometimes it has been claimed that peasants and peasant economies are specific economic or historical categories which must be analyzed with the aid of a conceptual and theoretical apparatus which differs from the one to be applied, for example, to the study of farmers in industrialized nations.[9] Without going to these methodological extremes it may still be useful to list some of the most commonly adduced economic characteristics of peasants and hence also of peasant economies. The characteristics should be read, and this must be emphasized, keeping in mind that it is not possible to draw up any clear limits between peasants and other similar groups. As always in the social sciences, it is difficult to make a rigorous separation of categories. The borderlines between peasants, tenants, farmers, etc. are often floating in practice.

The first requirement is that a peasant must be an agriculturalist.[10] He must derive his main subsistence and his main cash income from crop-raising. This does not exclude supplementary activities such as livestock-raising, hunting, gathering, fishing, trading, processing or handicrafts, but the bulk of the income of a peasant family must come from crop production. Whatever other incomes the family has must be secondary to that deriving from agriculture.

The requirement that a peasant must be an agriculturalist excludes certain groups who do not rely on cultivation of crops for their main living. Raymond Firth has suggested that the concept of peasant can be extended to encompass groups like fishermen or rural craftsmen as well as agriculturalists because of similarities in other respects than their main occupation.[11] Most definitions of peasants and peasant economies, however, exclude these groups, for example 'because the economic and cultural implications...are sufficiently different from those of agriculture to warrant separate treatment'.[12]

The second characteristic of a peasant is that he somehow controls the land which he is cultivating.[13] The peasant does not have to pay dues to outside landowners who supply him with land. This feature distinguishes peasants from tenants or sharecroppers whose access to land is controlled by others and who have to pay rents in cash or in kind to these groups. Peasant control of land does not exclude part-time tenancy or sharecropping. As in the case of occupation, we only require that the *main* portion of the land they cultivate should not be subject to control by outside groups.

Thirdly, production in a peasant economy is carried out with the aid of simple capital equipment only.[14] Sophisticated machinery is ruled out but not simple plows, animal traction, etc. Often, however, hand-tools constitute the most typical capital inputs.

The fourth characteristic of peasants and peasant economies is that the predominant unit of production is the small family farm.[15] Typically, peasant societies contain mostly minifundia holdings, exclusively or side by side with larger units. A common pattern, for example in Latin America, is that family farms and large plantations or latifundia can be found together. The second part of the requirement is that these farms should be cultivated mainly with the aid of family labor. Outside labor, in the form of wage labor, collective work teams or otherwise may complement the picture, but the owner family provides most of the labor input required. The size and the family labor requirement distinguish the peasant farm from commercial farms, plantations, latifundia, collective farms, etc.

Peasant production aims mainly at consumption, not so much at reinvestment and expansion of activities.[16] This establishes the dividing line between peasants and farmers. The latter regard agriculture as a business enterprise which in principle does not differ from any other type of business in, for example, the manufacturing sector. The net income obtained by a farmer goes partly to consumption of goods and services but is used to cover amortization as well and perhaps also to expand the scope of the business enterprise. Not so with the peasant. The latter's basic aim is to provide his family with goods and services to be consumed either for the purpose of subsistence or to enhance the peasant's social status in the community, while investment considerations usually play a very minor role, if any at all.

A word of caution is in order here. The peasant must not be thought of in terms of a more or less pure subsistence economy where only a minuscule fraction of the goods produced enters the market. Some peasants mainly cultivate to fulfill subsistence requirements. Others are heavily involved in the market economy. The peasants cannot produce everything they need themselves but grow a number of cash crops to obtain goods of urban origin. Subsistence crops often form the basis of peasant production but just as often the peasants are linked to consumers outside the peasant community by means of a market network, and frequently money is the predominant means of exchange.[17]

> We are sure to go astray if we try to conceive of peasant economies as exclusively 'subsistence' oriented and to suspect capitalism wherever the peasants show evidence of being 'market' oriented. It is much sounder to take it for granted, as a starting point, that for ages peasant economies have had a double orientation towards both. In this way, much fruitless discussion about the nature of so-called 'subsistence' economies can be avoided.

So writes Daniel Thorner.[18] Usually, peasants have a double orientation when it comes to production. Cash crops and subsistence crops are both grown on the same farm, and often the difference between the two is one of degree rather than one of kind. The same types of crops that are consumed by the peasant households are also sold to bring in cash incomes. (In addition, the peasants may grow crops that have no place at all in the rural consumption pattern but whose only function is to secure monetary incomes.)

Want of 'urban' goods is not the only reason why the peasants produce a surplus over what they consume themselves. One of the most important characteristics of a peasant society is that it is involved in a relationship with a wider world, regionally, nationally or internationally. This world is urban and for it to exist, the peasants must produce a surplus that somehow can be appropriated by the outside. This characteristic has been very heavily stressed by Eric R. Wolf who points out that it is only when cultivators become subject to some type of demands and sanctions from an external power that we may speak of a peasantry.[19] It is this feature which distinguishes a peasant economy from the primitive tribal cultivators. The latter may participate in a wider economy to a considerable extent,[20] but the character of the involvement is fundamentally different from that of the peasants. These have to turn some of their surplus over to a group of outside power-holders who employ this surplus both to further its own standard of living and to redistribute to those groups in society who do not cultivate the soil.[21] These outside groups usually constitute some kind of elite, socially, politically, religiously, etc. and appropriate the peasant surplus, e.g. by means of taxation in cash, in kind, or otherwise. The demands by outside groups frequently force the peasants into the wider circuit of exchange and production. Here they differ from the tribal cultivators. The latter are not subject to outside demands and powers, at least not to the same extent as the peasants.*

Related to the appropriation of peasant surplus by outside groups is our seventh and final characteristic of a peasant economy. The peasants have no power of their own to determine the conditions which draw the lines within which the rural economy has to operate.[22] The basic decisions are made by the outside power-holders to whom the peasants hand over their surplus. The larger region or nation makes and enforces the laws governing rural life. The peasant is in an underdog position against which he rarely rebels.

The Literature

Haiti is a nation of peasants. The majority of the population lives in an economy which presents all the characteristics enumerated in the foregoing section. A great deal has been written about the Haitian peasant. The appendix to the present chapter briefly surveys the most important works from the post-1935 period which in one way or another relate to the economic aspects of the peasantry.

The overall impression left by a reading of the material in this brief survey is that there is no dearth of descriptive material regarding the Haitian peasant economy, while quantitative data are more scarce. Analyses in anthropological and sociological terms are also available, while very little has been achieved in the field of economic analysis of peasant problems and hardly any economic theory has been applied. The present study represents an attempt to fill some of this gap.

The two best comprehensive works dealing with the Haitian peasant are James G. Leyburn's *The Haitian People*,[23] published in 1941, and Paul Moral's *Le paysan haïtien*,[24] which appeared exactly 20 years later. Reading these two books gives the best introduction to the problems facing the peasant economy. Leyburn analyzes the rise of peasant agriculture in Haiti and deals extensively with the important events of the nineteenth century. His main interest, however, does not lie in economic matters but in explaining the cleavage of Haitian society into a tiny elite and a mass of peasants. Still, for students of economics as well, the Leyburn book makes indispensable reading.

The Moral book is different. The emphasis is on economic geography, including geology and long descriptions of different Haitian regions, but

---

*Cf., however, Herskovits (1952), Chapter 19 which contains a review of taxation in primitive economies. However, Herskovits does not make any sharp distinction between peasant economies and primitive cultivators. (The word 'peasant' does not appear in the index of the book.)

in addition Moral manages very perceptively to deal with matters of agrarian structure, rural commerce, export production, etc., so as to draw up a detailed picture of today's main problems viewed in a historical perspective.

Neither the Leyburn nor the Moral book resorts to use of economic theory to explain the patterns of the Haitian peasant economy. The best 'theoretical' approach to purely economic problems is found in two chapters by Christopher K. Clague in Robert I. Rotberg's *Haiti: The Politics of Squalor*,[25] where a variety of issues are discussed. Clague's analysis remains limited, however, in so far as it forms part of a larger, mainly non-economic work where peasant questions are not allowed to dominate. Hence, there is great need for a full-length monograph dealing with the peasant economy where use is made both of the abundant descriptive material and of principles of economic theory.

Summary of the Present Work

The Peasant Economy

Chapter 2 presents some basic facts about the peasant sector especially with regard to products, agrarian structure and methods of production. Two types of crops are raised: export crops and subsistence crops. Coffee is the main export crop and the cash crop *par excellence* of the peasant economy. The other traditional export crops are sugar cane, sisal, cocoa, cotton and bananas. The last two are no longer exported, but recently essential oils and beef have been added to the list of agricultural exports instead. A wide variety of subsistence crops (also sold on the domestic market) are grown: corn, sorghum, rice, manioc, sweet potatoes, yams, plantains, peas, beans and fruits of various kinds.

Most Haitian peasants have access to land which they regard as their own, although as a rule this land is not secured by any written deeds. In addition, they may take some land on lease against fixed rents or against a share of the future crop. The majority of Haitian farms are minifundia holdings which are often scattered in two or more non-contiguous plots. These characteristics in turn mean that Haiti does not need a land reform in the conventional sense and, more important, that the peasants are not exploited by a class of landowners, either in the land or in the labor market.

Peasant techniques are labor-intensive. Land is a scarce factor in Haiti. The population density is among the highest in the Caribbean area, and the scarcity of land becomes even more pronounced when one takes into account the fact that much of the soil is in mountainous terrain or of low fertility. Hardly any capital at all is employed in the peasant sector. Traditional, unimproved seed and plant varieties and simple hand-tools are as a rule the only capital inputs to be seen. Labor, on the other hand, is abundant. Women, children and old people participate in rural work to an unusually high extent, and it is difficult to find gainful employment in urban areas. Simple production methods dominate. Yields per hectare are low.

The appendix to Chapter 2 discusses the possibility of disguised unemployment in the peasant sector.

The Cumulative Process: Falling Rural Incomes

Chapter 3 begins with a short historical review of the use of cumulative processes in analyses of economic development and underdevelopment. The modern concept of cumulation is traced back to the monetary analysis of Knut Wicksell, whose ideas were later developed by Gunnar Myrdal and employed in discussions of racial problems in the United States and in studies of economic underdevelopment in the Third World.

The principles of cumulation are discussed next, and it is pointed out that cumulative processes sooner or later must come to a halt because of the existence of certain counteracting forces which slow the processes down and eventually make them settle in some stable equilibrium.

Stagnating or falling real per capita incomes are common in the less developed world, and stagnation in the agricultural sector appears to be one of the common reasons for this. Evidence with respect to *rural* per capita incomes is scarce, but presumably, agricultural stagnation is coupled with declining incomes for the rural population in a number of developing countries. The central theme of the present work is that Haiti is one of these countries. The Haitian peasant sector is caught in a downward spiral of circular and cumulative causation which slowly depresses the standard of living among the peasants. The existence of vicious circles or cumulative processes has been noted by some students of the Haitian economy, but no systematic attempt has so far been made to analyze the retrogression of the peasant sector in terms of cumulative interdependence.

The second part of Chapter 3 presents the available evidence with respect of falling real incomes among the peasantry. The average GDP per capita fell in real terms from the mid-fifties to the early seventies, and so did agricultural output per capita of the total population. An examination of the production per rural inhabitant of the major crops conveys the same impression.

The picture with respect to rural nutrition is less clear-cut. Figures for average daily outlays on food and for malnutrition among preschool children (nutritionally the most vulnerable group) reveal no distinct trends. However, the best evidence — calculations of average calorie intake in the countryside — points to a declining standard of living at least since the early 1960s.

A third indication, of a more tentative character, is provided by the changing character of co-operative agricultural work. Traditionally, a *coumbite* involves not only purely productive activities but also social ones, i.e. consumption. The tendency today is that production gradually dominates. A plausible explanation is that social activities are a luxury good, e.g. in comparison to food, so that when per capita incomes decline in rural areas, the social activites connected with co-operative work tend to disappear.

Poverty and the Market

Chapter 4 reviews the argument which attributes the poverty of the Haitian peasant mainly to the exploitation by monopolist and monopsonist intermediaries in the commodity markets. It is concluded that this argument lacks relevance, and that those commodity markets in which the peasants are involved are basically competitive.

The Haitian peasants participate in a market economy where money is used in the transactions. The extent of this involvement is such that monopoly or monopsony tendencies in the markets where the peasants buy and sell could have serious consequences for the standard of living in rural areas. After defining monopsonistic and monopolistic exploitation, the marketing of coffee, subsistence goods and peasant consumption goods is examined to see whether any exploitation takes place in these markets.

Coffee is marketed via a network for intermediaries *(spéculateurs)* and exporters. The number of intermediaries in this marketing process is sufficiently high at all stages of this chain to exclude exploitation. Administration and supervision costs generally preclude the concentration of coffee marketing to a few hands only. The profit margins prevailing at all stages are not higher than is compatible with competitive conditions. The prices obtained basically reflect supply and demand conditions in the world market and cannot be influenced by the Haitian intermediaries.

Subsistence crops are sold through a network of market-places extending across the entire country, through which the goods flow as a result of the transport and marketing efforts of itinerant market women.

The available evidence regarding profit levels at various stages of this marketing process clearly shows that what these intermediaries receive is mainly a remuneration for their labor expended and not a profit.

The peasants are generally free to choose between different channels of sales (and purchases), and it is as a rule possible to omit one or more of the steps involved from the producer to the final consumer of the product. There is freedom of entry in marketing. The price is set by the interaction of demand and supply, and monopolies or monopsonies are not likely to arise. Both buyers and sellers are usually well informed with respect to actual demand and supply conditions. Haggling procedures compensate for deficiencies with respect to quality and measures. Finally, competition goes on, not only in terms of price, but in other ways as well.

The marketing system for both coffee and subsistence and peasant consumption goods exhibits a high degree of static technological efficiency in that, given the limitations of transportation etc., it makes goods flow from producer to consumer at a very low real cost to the economy. Information regarding market conditions, especially, appears to be very efficiently created and diffused in this system.

The role of transportation as an obstacle to competition is dealt with in the appendix to Chapter 4.

Erosion

In spite of the static technological efficiency exhibited by the market system, per capita incomes appear to be declining in the rural economy. Static efficiency does not guarantee that an economy does not retrogress. This is clearly seen in Chapter 5, which analyzes the cumulative process destroying the natural resource base of the peasant sector. The interaction between population growth, composition of peasant output and erosion is discussed, and the reasons for the absence of erosion control are analyzed.

The chapter begins with a sketch of the demographic history of Haiti, where it is shown that the rate of population growth appears to have increased since the nineteenth century. Next, the components of the erosion process are analyzed. Population growth in two ways may lead to increased erosion. In many instances deforestation of steep hillsides is caused by a need for firewood (and during the nineteenth century by exportation of precious woods at a tremendously high rate). The peasants have no economic alternatives to using firewood and charcoal, e.g. for cooking purposes, particularly after the rise of oil prices at the beginning of the 1970s.

Introduction and Summary 21

The second mechanism leading to erosion is when the labor intensity of cultivation increases on steep mountainsides. As the population grows, so does the labor force, and in the absence of sufficient urban employment, this increase has to be absorbed by the agricultural sector. At a constant relative price of export and subsistence crops, the output of the former will be reduced and that of the latter will be increased. (Subsistence crops are relatively labor-intensive in comparison to export crops, and the Rybczynski theorem may be applied.) With the technology available to the Haitian peasant, this also means that the rate of erosion will increase, since by its nature, cultivation of subsistence goods exposes the soil more to the tropical rains than does cultivation of export goods. Thus, the supply of available land will shrink at an increasing rate in a process of circular and cumulative causation where erosion becomes self-sustaining and accelerates as time elapses. Rural per capita incomes tend to fall.

In principle, this shift into production of subsistence goods away from export goods could be counteracted by a rise in the price of export goods in terms of subsistence goods. During the 1950-70 period, however, this was not the case, but due to the demand and supply conditions prevailing in the world market for the most important Haitian export goods, due to shifts in domestic taxation and due to domestic demand shifts provoked by the growth of the population, the relative price of export goods fell instead. Thereby the erosion process may have received additional impetus.

The last part of Chapter 5 deals with the absence of erosion control. The latter is only rarely practiced in Haiti. Quite probably, the individual peasant is caught in a 'prisoner's dilemma', where due to the presence of externalities it does not pay him to undertake any control measures unless other peasants do likewise. Also, the peasants are likely to perceive the benefits of erosion control as distant and uncertain and will therefore discount them heavily in relation to the costs of control, which arise in the present. In this perspective, erosion control does not appear as an attractive alternative. Neither has the government attempted any comprehensive attack on the erosion problem. Haiti possesses an elaborate legislation which rigorously prohibits tree-felling under certain conditions etc., but this legislation is not enforced, the main reason being that the government does not perceive any positive benefits emanating from anti-erosion control.

Appendix 1 to Chapter 5 spells out the algebraic model underlying the discussion of erosion in the main text, and Appendix 2 discusses whether Haiti may be said to constitute a case of agricultural 'involution' in the same sense as, for example, Java.

Land Reform

In Chapter 6 we begin an analysis of the political component of economic stagnation and retrogression in the peasant sector. This chapter serves as a preliminary to Chapters 7 and 8, but also casts some light on why Haiti had a land reform already during the early nineteenth century and on why large-scale agriculture has not managed to return.

The colonial economy of Saint-Domingue was based on large-scale plantations. Sugar, the main export crop, required comparatively large concentrations of capital and labor. After the wars of liberation, this structure broke down in spite of strong efforts by the early Haitian rulers to maintain the plantation economy. In 1809, Alexandre Pétion began the first redistribution of land and was followed in this by most of his successors in office during the nineteenth century. By the turn of the century, Haiti was already a minifundia peasant country and subsequent efforts to reintroduce large estates have for the most part failed.

The reasons behind the redistribution of land were both political and economic. Pétion needed the redistribution to maintain internal peace and to resettle army veterans. Far more fundamental, however, was that neither the capital nor the labor needed for large-scale cultivation could be obtained. There was plenty of land for the free Haitians to squat on, and the production apparatus of the eighteenth century had by and large been destroyed by the wars of independence, not to be re-built again.

Demand conditions played their role as well. The price of sugar fell, and Haiti may also have been cut off from important export opportunities by the Napoleonic wars. Property rights in land could not be enforced by the weak nineteenth-century administrations. This gave ample opportunities to squatters. Finally, the inheritance laws gave equal rights to all children.

The latter factor continues to operate to keep farm size small today. Also, in a situation where labor is the abundant factor of production, incentives for installation of capital equipment connected with economies of scale are lacking. The general poverty precludes savings. The market situation, finally, for both sugar and sisal – the most important large-scale products in the twentieth century – has generally been such as to discourage the expansion of cultivations during the past 60 years.

The appendix to Chapter 6 describes a model originated by Amartya K. Sen which is used to analyze the choice of capital in the main text.

Introduction and Summary

The Passive Government

Chapter 7 deals with the reasons for government passivity in the agricultural sector. The first part of the chapter describes the lack of intervention in agriculture and shows that with the exception of the American occupation of the country (1915-34) little has been attempted with respect to changes in the living conditions of the masses. On average, the agricultural sector has received less than 10 percent of total government expenditures. Most of the development measures have been *ad hoc* undertakings or have been connected with outside, windfall opportunities. No comprehensive efforts have been made to develop agriculture.

To understand the reasons for government passivity, the political structure is examined. It is shown that the peasants and the governing groups differ in most important characteristics: wealth, occupation, location, education, language, religion, family organization, culture, etc. The dominant feature of Haitian society has always been this cleavage of the population into a small elite and near-elite and a mass of peasants.

The reasons behind this cleavage are traced back to the slave society of Saint-Domingue and to the developments that took place during the nineteenth century. Here, the land reform played an important role. The upper-class groups had taken over the large estates and derived their incomes from these. When the land reform put an end to large-scale agriculture, this was no longer possible. The landowners instead turned into competition for government with the main purpose of filling their pockets. A soft state developed in Haiti during the nineteenth century where corruption was ubiquitous in the administration. Particularly the turn of the century, up to the American occupation in 1915, was characterized by a never-ending series of revolutions and counter-revolutions to conquer the treasury for more or less private purposes.

The American occupation attempted to set higher standards of honesty and to purge the administration but failed. After the withdrawal of the American forces in 1934, the old pattern of clique rule was resumed again, although in a slightly different form. This pattern, with a few changes, continues to be valid today.

During this process, the peasants were politically marginalized. When their desires for freedom and land had been satisified by the land reform, they withdrew to cultivate their plots and minimized the extent of their contacts with official representatives. The government, in turn, did nothing to educate the masses politically. In addition, the peasantry has always been governed in a military fashion. This authoritarian regime, finally, is supplemented and reinforced by the structure of informal community leadership, notably by the voodoo clergy, who interpret the environment in supernatural terms and act as an obstacle to change and modernization.

Haitian Public Finance

Chapter 8 examines the economic consequences of the non-identification of the governing cliques with the peasants. The structure of government and revenues is examined. It is seen that public outlays have been concentrated on debt service, army and police and wages and salaries for the administration, while much of the revenues derive from taxes levied on products produced or consumed by the peasants.

The first foreign debt was contracted as a result of the wars of liberation — as an indemnity to be paid to France for the recognition of national sovereignty. Later, however, a good record of interest and amortization payments was spoiled by a number of 'consolidations' of this debt. To obtain funds for obscure purposes, new loans were taken in 1874, 1875, 1896 and 1910 — loans which left little for the treasury to spend on development.

During the American occupation, the foreign debt was consolidated into American hands, and a tightly supervised repayment policy was begun. Haiti managed to handle interest and amortization payments even during most of the Depression years, when all other Latin American governments defaulted, but could not obtain outside development finance to any noticeable extent. In terms of debt management the governments of Haiti followed the conventional conservative wisdom, but without results. By having squandered the previously borrowed funds, the foreign debt led not to an expansion of development resources, but to an additional drain on the treasury and the economy instead. In 1947, finally, the last of this foreign debt was paid off.

The second important expenditure category has been that of maintaining a large army and police. Haiti has always been an overmilitarized country — mostly because both army and police have been used for political purposes. This has constituted a severe drain on funds which could otherwise have been used for developing the economy.

The third and last expenditure category analyzed is that of wages and salaries. With clique infighting for political power followed a spoils system which has been carried to extremes, where government jobs are regarded mainly as a reward for political loyalty and which has been conducive to extremely low administrative standards.

The selfish view of politics and the widespread corruption has also determined the structure of government revenues. The governments

Introduction and Summary 25

have attempted to maximize public revenues within the constraints set by their reluctance to impose taxes on incomes and by the general inefficiency of the tax administration. This has led to a situation where the main revenues have been derived from duties on exports and imports of such goods that are either produced or consumed by the peasants and which hence permit shifting of some of the tax burden to the poorer segments of the population.

The appendix to Chapter 8 examines total government expenditures.

Malnutrition and Disease

Chapter 9 examines whether the cumulative process depressing rural per capita incomes has been counteracted by any health changes among the rural population in the 1950s, 1960s and early 1970s. First, the extent of malnutrition and diseases in the countryside is reviewed to see whether any definite trends are discernible. The group which is worst off nutritionally are the preschool children who show what appears as a high incidence of protein-calorie malnutrition and who also experience deficiencies with respect to Vitamin B_2 and iron. Nutrition appears to be fairly adequate as long as the children are breast-fed whereas it deteriorates rapidly when weaning begins.

Malnutrition exists among adults as well. Both calorie and protein consumption appears on average to be grossly deficient, and the situation is complicated by vitamin and iron deficiencies. As indicated in Chapter 3, the average nutritional standard appears to be deteriorating.

A number of diseases are prevalent in rural Haiti. At the time of the American occupation, yaws, malaria, intestinal parasites and tuberculosis constituted the main threats. Few changes in this picture took place until the beginning of the 1950s when yaws was eradicated by penicillin treatment on a mass scale. A number of anti-malaria campaigns have been less successful. The disease still has a tendency to flare up with epidemic force. For preschool children, the situation is somewhat different, with tetanus neonatorum and nutritionally related gastrointestinal diseases constituting the most severe problems. The availability of medical and public health facilities is very low in rural districts. Popular herbalists and voodoo priests are the main 'doctors' resorted to by the peasant population.

In the second half of the chapter an effort is made to discuss the economic impact of yaws eradication and increasing malnutrition in the human production factor. Due to the lack of empirical data, most of the discussion is carried out in principle only for effects on rural population growth and agricultural output. It is concluded that we cannot be certain of the net direction and magnitude of the changes but that we cannot rule out the possibility that the net effect has been to make agricultural production per capita of the rural population decline as a result of the changes in health conditions.

The Role of Education

Chapter 10 examines whether changes in education have been able to counteract the tendency of rural incomes to fall by contributing to an increased formation of human capital in the countryside. After an examination of how this accumulation of human capital could take place in the agricultural sector and of what purposes it could serve, the Haitian rural educational record is scrutinized.

During the nineteenth century, little education was received in rural areas. Illiteracy rates ranged well above 90 percent at the beginning of the occupation. The main emphasis in the schools lay on humanities. The Americans attempted to create a vocationally-oriented rural school system instead and systematically starved the traditional Haitian system of funds. The attempt failed due to the lack of co-operation by the Haitian authorities who opposed the racist attitudes and contempt for Haitian culture among the Americans which was clearly visible in the educational policy pursued.

After the end of the occupation, the school system slowly reverted to the traditional patterns and things remained fairly stationary during the 1930s and the 1940s. The 1950 census revealed that the illiteracy rate still lay above 90 percent in the countryside. In principle, this situation has continued also after 1950. The efforts undertaken in primary and adult education have not been strong enough to increase the percentage of literates more than marginally up to the beginning of the 1970s.

The main role of education, however, has not been that of human capital formation. The rural educational system exhibits a number of discriminatory features which makes it virtually impossible for a rural child to complete his primary education. Of course, to some extent this is dependent on conditions connected with the general poverty prevailing in the countryside, but in addition, the children have to struggle with instruction in a foreign language, with low quality teachers, schools and pedagogic material as well as with a strong emphasis on examinations. Taken together, these factors act as a filter which efficiently prevents rural children from obtaining any education. The rural educational system constitutes one of the main instruments whereby the governing cliques dominate the peasants.

Introduction and Summary 27

Problems of Rural Credit

Chapter 11 discusses some of the problems connected with capital formation in peasant agriculture. The chapter opens with an examination of rural savings patterns where it is seen that the Haitian peasant when able to save as a rule attempts to buy animals and eventually land instead of letting his savings take the form of an addition to his production capital. The reason probably is to be found in the low level of technology prevailing. In this situation, acquiring land may be the best way of protection against a future decline in real incomes. However, most peasants presumably save little. Often they have to borrow instead in the informal rural credit markets. This borrowing generally does not take place for production purposes, but the most common pattern appears to be that of taking a loan for a short period while waiting for the harvest to come.

These loans often carry a comparatively high rate of interest. The low absolute incomes and the time-shape of the income stream make the rate of time preference high among the peasants in the short-term perspective, and when it is remembered that sale and repurchase of certain assets, notably land, are connected with high transaction costs, it is understandable that the peasants are prepared to pay a high rate of interest on these loans. Long-term production loans, on the other hand, are infrequent. The rate of time preference is lower in a long-term perspective, while the rates asked by the lenders are higher due to a higher perceived risk. (Viewed from the lender side, risk is the most important determinant of the rate of interest asked also in short-term transactions.)

Chapter 11 also examines whether the peasants are exploited by the lenders in the informal credit markets. The number of potential borrowers in relation to the number of potential lenders in these markets is calculated. A comparatively low figure emerges. Potential causes of monopoly are discussed, and it is concluded that monopolistic exploitation is not likely to be an important issue.

The last part of the chapter examines the record of organized rural credit in Haiti. On average, less than 1 percent of the peasant population has been touched by such ventures. For several reasons formal agricultural credit has foundered. Credit is not likely to be any good given the traditional low-yielding technology. Some credit schemes entail compulsory technological change, which, however, for reasons analyzed in Chapter 12, is a difficult matter. The peasants distrust government officials. They may jeopardize their chances of obtaining a consumption loan from their traditional informal credit sources, if at the same time they borrow from official lending agencies. The government lacks resources (both financial and manpower) to extend credits other than to a limited number of peasants. Production loans do not meet the demand of the peasants which is mainly for consumption credit. Government lending agencies presumably have a strong tendency to attract bad risks and have hence restricted the scope of their operations. Finally, in schemes incorporating technological change, extension costs have sometimes been very high in relation to the benefits emanating from the schemes.

Resistance to Innovation

Chapter 12 analyzes why innovations are resisted in the peasant sector. The production technology today closely resembles that of more than a century ago, and it has also proved very difficult to introduce new crops in the peasant sector.

The nineteenth century probably witnessed a genuine technological retrogression take place in agriculture. Labor efficiency had been high during the colonial period due to the stern discipline upheld in the slave gangs and to the realization of economies of specialization and scale on the plantations. After the land reform, work discipline was relaxed. Most of the plantation capital equipment was destroyed or decayed for lack of maintenance, and the size of farms declined considerably. American attempts to introduce new technologies during the occupation failed, and so did almost every other subsequent effort.

In principle, population growth could act as an inducement to innovation in agriculture. When per capita incomes fall too much, the technology could change and new crops could be introduced to reverse this trend. This has not taken place in Haiti, however, for a number of reasons. First, technological change is an inherently difficult process in agriculture. Cultivation consists in manipulation of organic matter, and this reduces man to an imitator of nature. Secondly, agricultural production in Haiti is governed by natural precipitation. The most important operations take place immediately before the rains come, which in turn reduces the scope for innovations. Thirdly, Haiti is an extremely mountainous country. This greatly reduces the utility of the plow in most of the country, for example. Transportation takes more time than on flat land, and transportation difficulties may limit the extent of the market, and hence also the scope for specialization.

Relative factor prices play an important role. Many innovations imply an intensive use of material inputs, but such innovations are not profitable in a situation where the price of capital is high in terms of labor, especially not if indivisibilities are present as well. Indivisibilities may also preclude technological change if money to finance the innovation must be borrowed at interest rates which are higher than the financial yield of the innovation in question. The plow represents a special case of indivisibilities. The size of most Haitian farms is too small to make the use of the plow profitable. This could in principle be overcome by co-operative purchase of plows but *dirigisme,* illiteracy and lack of innovative informal leadership has made the co-operative movement less successful in rural districts.

A peasant can never be certain that a new technology or a new crop will perform well under local conditions. All innovations are risky, and this poor peasants are ill-prepared to meet. Risk may also be important in another form. Written land titles generally do not exist in Haiti. Hence, profitable innovations increasing the value of peasant land may easily jeopardize the rights of the peasants.

Malnutrition and disease may preclude the physical and mental efforts required in connection with innovative activities. Lack of information and education makes peasant search for new crops and methods inefficient, and the extension efforts by the government have been inadequate compensation for this.

Epilogue

The first part of the epilogue points to the consequences of rural poverty in the form of migration from the countryside — to urban areas and out of the country, temporarily or permanently. The second half sums up the most important results of the study and points to three important development issues in connection with Haitian agriculture: erosion, anti-peasant bias and politics. It is concluded that government attitudes constitute a main bottleneck in the development process.

Notes

1. Cf. Logan (1941), Chapters 3-7.
2. IHS (1971), pp. 267-71; IHS (1976), p. 20.
3. IHS (1971), pp. 210-22; IHS (1976), p. 29.
4. Cf. below, Chapters 2 and 3.
5. IHS (1974), pp. 121, 214; IHS (1973), p. 1.
6. See Zuvekas (1978), pp. 30-59 for a discussion of income levels and standards of living in the countryside.
7. Cf. e.g. the bibliography contained in Zuvekas (1977), which *only* deals with the agricultural sector and which with a few exceptions only covers material written since 1950.
8. Mintz (1975), note, p. 482.
9. Notably by Chayanov (1966) in the 1920s. Cf. also Thorner (1962) and Kerblay (1971).

10. Wolf (1955), p. 503; Thorner (1962), p. 203; Shanin (1966), p. 240; (1971), p. 15; Foster (1967), p. 6; Pearse (1971), p. 69.
11. Firth (1946).
12. Wolf (1955), p. 503.
13. Ibid.; Kerblay (1971), p. 151; Pearse (1971), p. 69.
14. Firth (1946), p. 22; Shanin (1966), p. 240.
15. Thorner (1962), p. 205; Shanin (1971), pp. 14-15; Kerblay (1971), pp. 150-51; Reynolds (1975), pp. 2-4.
16. Wolf (1955), p. 504.
17. Thorner (1962), pp. 206-7; Shanin (1971), pp. 71-2; Saul & Woods (1971), p. 109.
18. Thorner (1962), p. 207.
19. Wolf (1966), Chapter 1. The idea goes back to Kroeber (1948), p. 284.
20. The classic example is furnished by Malinowski's 1922 study of the *Kula* circuit of the Western Pacific (Malinowski (1961)).
21. A modern formulation in economic terms of mechanisms whereby urban groups appropriate the surplus created by the rural economy is given by Lipton (1977).
22. Wolf (1966), Chapter 1; Foster (1967), pp. 3, 8; Shanin (1971), p. 15; Pearse (1971), pp. 69-70.
23. Leyburn (1966).
24. Moral (1961).
25. Rotberg & Clague (1971).

APPENDIX: The Literature on the Haitian Peasant Economy[1]

A number of articles and books have been written about the Haitian peasant and the rural economy. Here we will briefly survey some of the major works. The survey will be limited to the most influential literature and will cover only the post-1935 period.

The first 'modern' social scientist to deal with the Haitian peasant was the eminent anthropologist Melville J. Herskovits, who in 1937 published *Life in a Haitian Valley*[2] – the first modern classic on Haiti. Four years later, in 1941, an even more important work appeared, sociologist James G. Leyburn's *The Haitian People*[3], a book which brilliantly analyzed the development of the Haitian class system and which provided the first account of how peasant Haiti evolved.

An article by George Eaton Simpson, *Haitian Peasant Economy*[4] (1940) represents the first, albeit unsystematic effort to analyze rural economic problems. A later paper by Giles A. Hubert, *Some Problems of a Colonial Economy: A Study of Economic Dualism in Haiti*[5] (1950), in the spirit of Dutch economist J.H. Boeke[6] attempts to analyze the Haitian economy in terms of the side-by-side existence of a 'capitalistic' and a 'non-capitalistic' sector. Abundant factual evidence on the rural economy is found in United Nations' *Mission to Haiti*[7] (1949). A full factual picture of the Haitian economy during the 1940s is also provided by the PhD thesis by Robert S. Folsom, *Haitian Economy*[8] (1945, updated 1954).

The UNESCO pilot project on rural education in the Marbial valley at the beginning of the 1950s yielded two important and complementary studies following the Herskovits tradition and with abundant observations with regard to the peasant economy: Alfred Métraux and associates: *Making a Living in the Marbial Valley (Haiti)*[9] and Rémy Bastien: *La familia rural haitiana*,[10] both published in 1951. The Métraux volume in particular contains much material which still is pertinent for students of the peasant economy.

A paper by anthropologist Charles John Erasmus, *Agricultural Changes in Haiti: Patterns of Resistance and Acceptance*[11] (1952) is the point of departure for any study of technological change in rural areas, and still remains the most important work in the field. Three years later the first book dedicated to Haitian agriculture, *Agriculture in Haiti,* by agronomist Marc Aurèle Holly,[12] was published. Unfortunately, the book is uneven. Good observations are mixed with lengthy, undigested material from agricultural treatises. An overlooked source of factual material is Marie V. Wood's *Agricultural Development and Rural Life in Haiti, 1934 to 1953*[13] (PhD thesis, 1955).

An original, but often unreliable, interpretation of the Haitian peasant economy is made by Maurice de Young in *Man and Land in the Haitian Economy*[14] (1958). Three unpublished essays by William B. Gates, Jr.: *Some Observations on Economic Development and Haiti*,[15] *The Haitian Coffee Industry*,[16] and *The Haitian Cotton and Cotton Textile Industry*[17] (all three dating from 1959) represent the first, unfinished attempt to apply economic reasoning to Haitian development problems. The same year, a most important work was published by French economic geographer Paul Moral: *L'économie haïtienne*[18] which, mainly based on 1950 census data, combines description and analysis, but without resort to theory. This book was two years later expanded into what still remains the best comprehensive study of the economic aspects of peasant life, *Le paysan haïtien*[19] with emphasis on geographic aspects but employing a historical perspective as well. Geographic (and botanic) contemporary and historical considerations also dominate John M. Street's *Historical and Economic Geography of the Southwest Peninsula of Haiti*[20] (1960).

In the late 1950s and early 1960s a number of pioneering papers by anthropologist Sidney W. Mintz on the rural marketing system appeared: *International Market Systems as Mechanisms of Social Articulation*[21] (1959), *Peasant Markets*[22] (1960), *A Tentative Typology of Eight Haitian Marketplaces*[23] (1960), *Le système du marché rural dans l'économie haïtienne*[24] (1960), *Pratik: Haitian Personal Economic Relationships*[25] (1961), *Standards of Value and Units of Measure in the Fond-des-Nègres Market Place, Haiti*[26] (1961), and *The Employment of Capital by Market Women in Haiti*[27] (1964). A summary of the earlier literature on rural marketing is given by Frances W. Underwood in *The Marketing System in Peasant Haiti*[28] (1960).

A good interpretation in Marxist terms of the Haitian economy and its evolution is Gérard Pierre-Charles' *La economía haitiana y su vía de desarrollo*[29] (1965, French version 1967[30]) which contains important sections on the rural economy. Of related interest is the 'underground' classic by Gérald Brisson: *Les relations agraires dans l'Haïti contemporaine*[31] (1968), which makes use of a more orthodox Marxist framework. (Brisson, however, erroneously asserts that the agrarian structure in Haiti is dominated by large estates.) A broad, somewhat impressionistic perspective of Haitian development problems with emphasis on the sociological aspects but covering economic topics as well (with particularly good sections on migration) is taken in Roland Wingfield's *Haiti, A Case Study of an Underdeveloped Area*[32] (PhD thesis, 1966). Richard P. Schaedel's *An Essay on the Human Resources of Haiti*[33] (1962) contains much original field data and an anthropological analysis of a number of rural communities.

A few major works on Haiti were published at the beginning of the 1970s. Historian Robert I. Rotberg's Haiti, *The Politics of Squalor*[34] (1971) contains a very good section on economic problems written by Christopher K. Clague, and puts considerable emphasis on economic matters throughout the book. A work dealing exclusively with the economy is O. Ernest Moore's *Haiti. Its Stagnant Society and Shackled Economy*[35] (1972). The emphasis of the book is on historical description. The same year, the Organization of American States published a major survey of the economy: *Haïti: Mission d'assistance technique integrée*[36] which, however, does not contain any systematic analysis of the problems of agriculture. The relations between peasantry and elite are analyzed by Ulrich Fleischmann in a manner reminscent of Leyburn in *Aspekte der sozialen und politischen Entwicklung Haitis*[37] (1971).

Enquête sur le développement[38] (1974) by Jean-Jacques Honorat and *Contribution à l'élaboration d'une politique agricole en Haïti*[39] (1972) by Jean-Robert Estimé are recent, although somewhat unsystematic, Haitian contributions to the study of the peasant sector. More important, the Inter-American Institute of Agricultural Sciences (IICA) of the OAS carried out a series of analyses of the marketing system for rural products in the mid-seventies, building on the previously mentioned efforts by Mintz. The most important of these studies, which have considerably increased our knowledge of rural trade are Gerald F. Murray & Maria D. Alvarez: *The Marketing of Beans in Haiti: An Exploratory Study*[40] (1973), Uli Locher: *The Internal Market System for Agricultural Produce in Port-au-Prince*[41] (1974), Verdy Duplan & Jerry LaGra: *Analyse du système de taxation des produits agricoles dans les marchés haïtiens*[42] (1974), Bernard Fatton: *Eléments d'information sur la production et la commercialisation du sisal en Haïti*[43] (1975), Jerry LaGra, Wesner Charleston & Guy Fanfan: *Prix des produits agricoles dans les marchés haïtiens*[44] (1975), and *Les marchés publics d'Haïti*[45] (1975), and Christian Girault & Jerry LaGra: *Caractéristiques structurelles de la commercialisation interne des produits agricoles en Haïti*[46] (1975). Of related interest also are a number of commodity studies undertaken by the JWK International Corporation, notably *Agricultural Policy Studies in Haiti: Coffee*[47] (1976).

Appendix

Among the most recent additions to the list of studies of rural Haiti are two detailed geographical and anthropological micro-studies of land use and land tenure: Ernest Charles Palmer: *Land Use and Landscape Change along the Dominican-Haitian Borderlands*[48] (PhD thesis, 1976) and Gerald F. Murray: *The Evolution of Haitian Peasant Land Tenure: A Case Study in Agrarian Adaptation to Population Growth*[49] (PhD thesis, 1977).* Finally, an interesting anthropological analysis of rural co-operative work, Michel Laguerre's *Les associations traditionelles de travail dans la paysannerie haïtienne*[50] (1975), and an extremely valuable survey by economist Clarence Zuvekas, Jr, *Land Tenure, Income, and Employment in Rural Haiti*[51] (1978) should be noted.

Notes

1. The reader should consult Zuvekas (1977), for a detailed bibliography.
2. Herskovits (1971).
3. Leyburn (1966).
4. Simpson (1940).
5. Hubert (1950).
6. Boeke's main work is Boeke (1953).
7. UN (1949).
8. Folsom (1954).
9. Métraux *et al.* (1951).
10. Bastien (1951).
11. Erasmus (1952).
12. Holly (1955).
13. Wood (1955).
14. DeYoung (1958).
15. Gates (1959:1).
16. Gates (1959:2).
17. Gates (1959:3).
18. Moral (1959).
19. Moral (1961).
20. Street (1960).
21. Mintz (1959).
22. Mintz (1960:1).
23. Mintz (1960:2).
24. Mintz (1960:3).
25. Mintz (1961:1).
26. Mintz (1961:2).
27. Mintz (1964).
28. Underwood (1960).
29. Pierre-Charles (1965).
30. Pierre-Charles (1967).
31. Brisson (1968).

*These two studies were not available to me at the time of writing of the present work and their results could hence not be incorporated.

Appendix

32. Wingfield (1966).
33. Schaedel (1962).
34. Rotberg & Clague (1971).
35. Moore (1972).
36. OEA (1972).
37. Fleischmann (1971).
38. Honorat (1974).
39. Estimé (1972).
40. Murray & Alvarez (1973).
41. Locher (1974).
42. Duplan & LaGra (1974).
43. Fatton (1975).
44. LaGra, Charleston & Fanfan (1975).
45. LaGra, Fanfan & Charleston (1975).
46. Girault & LaGra (1975).
47. JWK (1976:1).
48. Palmer (1976).
49. Murray (1977).
50. Laguerre (1975).
51. Zuvekas (1978).

2 THE PEASANT ECONOMY

In Chapter 3 we will present the theoretical approach used in the present study — that of circular and cumulative causation — but before we go into that approach, it is necessary to present the main characteristics of the peasant sector. In an empirical study, the theoretical approach always needs to be firmly rooted in the institutional reality, and this institutional reality in turn, may to a certain extent be explained by the theoretical approach.

The central theme of this book is that the Haitian peasant economy is caught in a process of circular, cumulative causation which tends to depress rural per capita incomes. The driving force behind this process is the interaction of population and labor-force growth with soil exhaustion and erosion via *inter alia* changes in the composition of peasant output. When the rural population grows, the output of land-intensive products (export goods) falls and the output of labor-intensive goods (subsistence products) expands. The soil is then cultivated more intensively than before, and the result is increased exhaustion and erosion. The first part of this chapter introduces the reader to the main crops within each of the two categories of export and subsistence goods as a background to the subsequent analysis in Chapter 5. A study of the composition of peasant output is important in order to get a firm grasp of Haitian realities, and an analysis of the changes in this composition is an essential ingredient when it comes to understanding the cumulative process in the agricultural sector. The distinction between export and subsistence crops is also important for the analysis of agricultural marketing in Chapter 4, since the subsistence crops are sold in the market-places, while the export crops reach their final destination via entirely different channels.

The second feature presented in this chapter is the system of land tenure, i.e. the agrarian structure. The predominant system of tenure is that of peasant-owned smallholdings. Haiti does not conform to the standard Latin American pattern of heavy concentration of land in the hands of a minority of latifundistas who exploit a majority of peasants, tenant farmers, or landless agricultural workers. The Haitian peasant owns his land, and most of the agricultural land is held in small family farms. The low standard of living of the majority of the Haitian population cannot be explained in terms of exploitation of the peasants by a landowning class. Rather, the explanation must be sought in the mechanisms that work within the peasant economy itself (and in the absence of positive action by successive Haitian governments).

The small size of the majority of the Haitian farms is the outcome of a land redistribution process which took place during the nineteenth century. We will analyze this redistribution in Chapters 6 and 7, with two purposes in mind. The first is to explain why the redistribution actually took place and why very few large-scale plantations subsequently managed to penetrate the agricultural sector. The second is to bring out how the redistribution in combination with some other factors explains the lack of positive interest in the agricultural sector on the part of the government — one of the potentially most important checks on the downward cumulative process in the rural sector.

The stagnation and retrogression of the agricultural sector is intimately connected with the factor combination and techniques employed by the peasants. The methods of cultivation have undergone few changes since the nineteenth century. In Chapter 12 we will attempt to explain why technological change has been conspicuously absent from Haitian agriculture. The last two sections of the present chapter furnish the appropriate background to that analysis. First, the characteristics of the land, labor and capital employed by the peasants are given, and the combination in which these factors are used is described, while the last part of the chapter describes the methods resulting from this factor mix.

The Natural Setting

The Haitian climate presents few difficulties as to the range of crops that can be cultivated in the country. The intensity of sunlight is high, and the variation in daylight is minimal throughout the year.[1] The average temperature lies somewhere between 24° and 27° C,[2] with only slight variations across the year, of perhaps 5° C between the averages for the hottest and coolest months.[3] (Variations between day and night, on the other hand, are generally as high as 10° to 12° C.)[4]

The natural vegetation of the country is subtropical,[5] but fruits and vegetables typical of the temperate zone can be cultivated at higher altitudes. Haiti is an extremely mountainous country, and due to this topographical feature temperatures for geographically close points sometimes differ considerably. The mean temperature decreases very regularly by some 0.75° C for each 100 meters of elevation.[6] Compare for example the averages for Port-au-Prince, Pétionville and Kenscoff in Table 2.1. The geographical distance between Port-au-Prince and

The Peasant Economy 39

Pétionville is 8 kilometers and the distance between Pétionville and Kenscoff is 9 kilometers.

Table 2.1 : Dependence of Mean Temperature on Altitude

	Altitude (meters)	Mean temperature (°C)
Port-au-Prince	40	26.3
Pétionville	400	24.7
Kenscoff	1,450	18.5

Source: Moral (1961), p. 109.

These differences in temperature, caused by the topography, lie behind the important distinction in Haitian agriculture between 'hot' and 'cool' lands — *tè cho* and *tè frèt*. Generally speaking, *tè frèt* begins at an altitude of 700 to 800 meters,[7] but the contrasts between hot and cool lands are often locally determined. Within the same mountain range it is possible to find hot, humid valleys and cool, wind-swept hillsides geographically very close to each other. Vegetation and cultivation become different on hot and cool lands. Coffee, vegetables and fruit trees of the temperate zone get more room on *tè frèt* while plants requiring higher temperatures disappear.*

The Purpose of Peasant Production

Schematically, the Haitian peasant may be said to cultivate his lands with two goals in mind. He wants to feed himself and his family, and he wants to sell part of his crop in order to buy certain commodities that he cannot produce himself. Conversely, the urban sector in Haiti views the peasant as a supplier of staple food crops and certain export crops. The peasant is heavily engaged in the monetary economy,[8] and these relations with the outside world have consequently shaped his production pattern. Peasant output can be divided into three parts: one which may be designed as a pure subsistence part, and which never leaves the *habitation* (farm) but is consumed there by the family; another, consisting of the same types of products as the subsistence part, that is sold for ultimate consumption within Haiti, in the countryside

---

*The two concepts *tè cho* and *tè frèt* also have a second meaning. *Tè cho* then denotes the best lands, those used for growing the most important crops, above all the subsistence crops, while *tè frèt* often means less valuable, eroded soils, used for secondary crops that give comparatively low yields.

or in urban areas; and finally one which in the main is designed for ultimate export with lesser quantities being consumed within the country.[9] In the following, crops designed for the peasant families themselves or for other domestic consumption will be termed *subsistence crops* and the crops leaving the country will be called *export crops*. Up to the present, the most important past and present export products deriving from the peasant sector are coffee, sugar cane, sisal, cocoa, cotton, bananas,* essential oils and beef, while corn, sorghum, rice, plantains, peas and beans, manioc, sweet potatoes, yams and fruits are the main subsistence crops.**

The Export Products[10]

Coffee

Coffee is the most important export crop and by far the most typical cash crop in the peasant economy. From time to time other crops, like bananas, sugar, sisal and cotton have competed with it as a source of export revenues, but none of these products has been able to seriously challenge the position of coffee.†

The coffee plant (which in Haiti is of the *Arabica* variety) was introduced around 1725 in the northern part of the island,[11] and the north quickly became the most important coffee-growing area of French Saint-Domingue. Production increased rapidly, so that on the verge of the French Revolution Saint-Domingue supplied no less than 60 percent of the world's coffee.[12] At that time, sugar was still the dominant crop in the colony, but when the large estates were broken up after the wars of independence, coffee became the leading export crop and remains so today. In the process the southern part of the country progressively came to overshadow the traditional growing centers in the north. The northern plantations had been severely hit by the war. The south was excellently suited for coffee production and had the advantage of being close to the emerging national capital, Port-au-Prince. Finally, when the first rulers of independent Haiti tried to re-establish the plantation system, emphasizing sugar production, this process went on longer

---

*Cotton and bananas are no longer exported.
**It is not possible to separate the two types of crops rigorously, since some of the traditional export crops no longer leave the country. The division has been made mainly as a prelude to the discussion of Chapter 5.
†In 1973-4, coffee accounted for 33.5 percent of total export revenues, while essential oils, sisal and sugar accounted for 9.5, 6.5 and 2.5 percent, respectively (IHS (1976), p. 29).

in the north than in the south, so that when finally the subdivision of the northern properties began, the hegemony of the south was already established.[13] Today, the southern part of the country continues to be the most important coffee-producing area. Peasant production dominates the industry completely, and rarely does a coffee 'plantation' exceed 5 hectares.[14]

Sugar Cane

The position of Saint-Domingue as the most lucrative colony in the world was to a very large extent the result of its sugar exports. The cultivation of sugar cane during colonial days (the sugar cane was introduced from the Canaries during the first years of the sixteenth century)[15] was a large-scale venture. When the French were forced to abandon their colony after the wars of independence and the large estates were gradually dismembered, sugar cane cultivation rapidly declined in importance. Exports came to a complete stop and were not resumed until the latter part of the nineteenth century. With the advent of the large Haitian American Sugar Company (HASCO) in 1915 and the establishment of some large plantations in the neighborhood of the capital, sugar exports acquired a new momentum, and sugar continues to be an export product today, although the relative importance of the domestic market is increasing.

The main contemporary growing areas are the plains of Cul-de-Sac and Léogâne, near Port-au-Prince — both dominated by the operations of HASCO — the Cayes plain, and the Plaine du Nord. Cultivation basically takes two forms. On the one hand we have the large plantations, mainly HASCO, which employ outside, hired labor and use irrigation, and on the other hand we find a large number of mostly small-scale cultivators that treat sugar cane essentially as a part of the overall, mixed pattern of cultivation which is typical for the peasant sector in general. In the late 1960s about two-thirds of the production was believed to come from plots measuring less than 3 hectares.[16]*

---

*There is, however, no water-tight division between the two modes of cultivation. In the early sixties, HASCO had at its disposal some 11,000 hectares of sugar cane, less than 40 percent of which were cultivated by the company itself (Moral (1961), p. 288). The rest came from independent producers selling to HASCO. In 1969, the area directly cultivated by the company had fallen by 1,500 hectares to 2,600, and more than 70 percent of the total amount of sugar cane used by the company was bought from independent (mainly peasant) producers (OEA (1972), p. 620). However, almost one-half of the cane bought by HASCO in the plain of Léogâne appears to come from less than 30 producers (Larose (n.d.), note, p. 9).

Sisal

Even though sisal has been known in Haiti since pre-Columbian times and was exported during parts of the nineteenth century, its real importance as a cash crop is of more recent origin. In 1926 and 1927, during the American occupation of Haiti, the Haitian American Development Corporation ('Plantation Dauphin') and the Haitian Agricultural Corporation (HACOR) purchased vast land areas in the dry plains around Fort-Liberté in the northern province, and in 1942 the *Société Haitiano-Américaine de Développement Agricole* (SHADA) began sisal cultivation on the west coast.

Rising sisal prices in the world market after the Second World War made sisal the most important export crop after the pre-eminent coffee and attracted a lot of smaller, non-plantation growers to the industry, spreading cultivation to more and more arid or semi-arid areas. Beginning in 1951, the sisal market collapsed, however. Prices fell drastically. This caused a radical change in the mode of production. From being the most typical representative of large-scale monoculture in Haiti, sisal has today been converted into just a marginal part of the peasant cultivations. While in 1954 approximatively 24,300 hectares of sisal were grown under the plantation system and only 4,000 by peasants, at the end of the 1960s 12,000 hectares were cultivated by peasants and only 7,500 by the plantations. In 1968-9, peasant production of sisal amounted to 60 percent of the total output in the industry.[17] The Fort-Liberté section has lost its predominance. Today, the most important sisal district is the Miragoâne-Côtes de Fer-Jacmel triangle on the southern peninsula.

Cocoa

Cocoa, a typical small-scale, peasant crop, was never of more than ephemeral interest in pre-independence days, and it was not until the middle of the nineteenth century that rising world demand for cocoa began to stimulate its cultivation. From the 1890s until the First World War, cocoa became one of the leading export crops of Haiti, and the country earned a reputation in Europe for the high quality of the beans. Cocoa continued to be important well into the 1920s when the Haitian cocoa market crashed due to the increased competition and modernization of cultivation in Latin America and Africa. Neither a subsequent rise in cocoa prices following the Second World War nor domestic efforts to stimulate production have had much effect on the volume of output which has remained fairly stationary since the mid-1930s. Cocoa has been relegated to becoming nothing but 'a humble appendix to coffee production'.[18] The most important cocoa-producing areas today are the Dame-Marie and Jérémie districts on the western tip of the southern peninsula and the Port-de-Paix and Cap-Haïtien areas in the north.

Cotton

Cotton was an export crop of the French Saint-Domingue colony. The wars of liberation, however, wiped out the cotton plantations almost entirely, and for some 25 years following independence hardly any cotton at all was exported. Subsequently, with improved world market prices production slowly increased, only to experience a new period of decline during the last quarter of the nineteenth century. It was not until after the First World War that cotton once more became important as an export crop, soon ranking second to coffee. In the mid-1930s, however, cotton production met with new difficulties in the form of an insect: the Mexican boll-weevil. Simultaneously the European markets (France and Britain) were largely lost because of trade and exchange regulations following the Depression.

The cotton grown in Haiti during the 1930s was of the perennial Sea Island variety. Perennial cotton is very susceptible to the boll-weevil, so various efforts were made to substitute annual varieties for the traditional one,[19] but little success was achieved until the *Institut de Développement Agricole et Industriel* (IDAI) in 1962 started to promote the planting of a cotton known as Stoneville 7-A, which already by 1970 accounted for as much as 37 percent of total cotton production.[20] The introduction of annual cotton has, however, not sufficed to stop the declining trend in cotton exports. In 1964-5 exports ceased altogether, and today what production there is, is absorbed by the domestic market, while, in addition, imports have to be resorted to by Haitian cotton mills.

Bananas

Bananas were introduced in Hispaniola at the beginning of the sixteenth century and were soon extended across the entire island. There are two species of bananas in Haiti: *Musa sapientum* (Creole: *figue-banane*), henceforth referred to as bananas — which may be eaten raw — and *Musa paradisiaca*, plantains — which must be cooked before eaten. The latter constitute an important part of the peasant diet, while the former are the bananas of commerce, out of which the *Gros Michel* variety has been exported.

The rise and fall of the banana-exporting industry is a fairly recent event in Haitian agricultural history. Apart from some minor exports of plantains, from the turn of the century onwards, no foreign trade in bananas took place until the beginning of the 1930s. In 1935, however, a boom began in the banana industry, and the countryside experienced a period of relative prosperity due to *la figue-banane salvatrice*[21] during the first two-thirds of the 1940s, in spite of the transport difficulties caused by the war. However, this prosperity soon came to an abrupt end, due to political manipulations, and the peasantry reduced their cultivation of bananas in favor of plantains and other crops. Governmental efforts to revitalize the industry led to nothing, and by the mid-1950s the volume of banana exports had fallen almost to zero.

Essential Oils

Another relatively recent Haitian export article is essential oils which are used for the manufacture of perfumes, soaps, flavoring extracts, etc. and sometimes also as ingredients in medicinal products. The main raw materials for essential oils that are grown in Haiti are vetiver, lemongrass, lime, amyris, petit-grain, neroli, sweet basil and citronella. Cultivation started as a peasant venture within the traditional mode of production at the beginning of the 1940s and in spite of frequent claims that the structure of production has been transformed into large plantations[22] still continues to be largely a peasant enterprise.[23]

Due to the absence of quality control among peasants and insufficient demand in the world market, exports in recent years have been concentrated to only three products: vetiver, lime and amyris. Still, at the beginning of the 1970s essential oils ranked next to coffee among the agricultural exports. The most important single product within the group is vetiver.

Beef

Haiti is a country where the domestic animals are few and poverty makes the peasant feel that at times there is direct competition between men and animals in terms of the land used to feed both. (Consequently, domestic animals are mostly left to feed themselves as they can.) In spite of this, beef has been an export product since the beginning of the 1960s, following an agreement between the Haitian government and the Haitian Meat and Provision Company (HAMPCO). The contract, which was signed in 1958, conferred an abattoir monopoly for Port-au-Prince and its surroundings to HAMPCO.* Recently, however, the company has

---

*For an account of the extra-legal manipulations in connection with HAMPCO's entry into the lucrative American and Puerto Rican markets see Rotberg & Clague (1971), note, p. 211.

The Peasant Economy

experienced difficulties in obtaining a regular supply of animals for its operations, since it appears that peasants prefer to sell their animals to small, clandestine slaughterhouses, where there is no quality control, instead of to HAMPCO.[24]

The Subsistence Crops[25]

Corn

Corn is a plant which is native of the Americas and which was cultivated in Hispaniola long before the European discovery of the island. Today, it constitutes the mainstay of the peasant diet for the greatest part of the year, and there are few Haitian peasants who do not cultivate their own patch of corn.

Corn generally thrives best where the soil is fertile and the rainfall is adequate, but in Haiti it is grown under a variety of circumstances, often on dry, infertile steep hillsides as well as at sea level. In certain areas (where the precipitation permits) two crops are taken each year, but as a rule the peasant has to be content with one. The majority of cultivations employ indigenous varieties.

While in the 1940s corn even used to be exported in small quantities to some of the neighboring West Indian islands, in recent years production has not been large enough to cover domestic demand, so that imports have taken place to cover the deficit.

Sorghum*

Where there is not enough moisture to grow corn, sorghum is generally substituted for it, since sorghum is a very hardy plant which can be advantageously cultivated on dry plains or rocky hillsides with poor soils. Sorghum is considered a poor man's food,** which makes it less interesting to market than for example corn. It is therefore mainly used for consumption directly by the producer. In this respect it is interesting to compare the situation in Haiti with the situation in the neighboring Dominican Republic, which is a comparatively richer country with considerably less population pressure on the land. The type of land areas which in the Dominican Republic are used for grazing lands

---

*The Creole expression for sorghum is *piti mi*, a term which in Haiti designates various varieties of both sorghum proper *(Sorghum vulgare)* and millet *(Pennisetum typhoideum)* the former being the quantitatively more important variety.
**Métraux *et al.* (1951), p. 41, mention how some very poor peasants even make soup from the waste and dust left at the bottom of the sifter when separating the grain from the sorghum ears.

in Haiti have to serve for sorghum cultivation.

The most important sorghum-producing areas are to be found in the Plateau Central, around Cayes, and around Gonaïves.

Rice

Two varieties of rice are grown in Haiti, the mountain rice *(Oryza montana)* and the swamp rice *(Oryza sativa)*. The latter is a typical cash crop, sold mainly for urban consumption, grown in irrigated areas in the Artibonite valley (which is the most important rice-producing area of the country), in the Plaine du Nord, in some areas on the southern peninsula and between Port-au-Prince and Léogâne, while the mountain rice is more of a pure subsistence crop grown all over Haiti.

Compared to corn and sorghum, rice is an expensive cereal and is therefore consumed chiefly in urban areas. Traditionally, domestic rice production has not been able to keep pace with demand, and consequently Haiti used to have to import rice. In the 1940s imports declined considerably and some exports even took place.* Rice exports came to an end in 1948, however, and while during the past two decades the country normally has been self-sufficient in rice, imports have recently had to be resumed.

Root Crops

The most common root crop in Haiti is manioc, of which both the sweet and bitter variety are grown. In general the latter is preferred to the former since it gives a higher yield. Manioc is used for the preparation of cassava meal — one of the most common foods of the peasants — or bread and for making starch and flour. (The latter has at times been exported.) Although manioc can be found almost everywhere in Haiti — being a hardy plant that does not require much humidity — the most important cultivations are those in the Plaine du Nord and in the Cayes plain.

Following manioc in importance among the root crops is the sweet potato, of which numerous varieties are grown in Haiti. Although sweet potatoes in principle require a warm climate, often cultivation takes place also in *tè frèt,* where it takes longer for the tubers to ripen and yields are inferior to yields in *tè cho*. Other root crops grown in Haiti are yams and malanga *(Xanthosoma terviride)*.

---

*The cessation of imports was probably not due only to increased domestic production but also to decreasing purchasing power among the peasants (Holly (1955), p. 95).

Plantains

Plantains were grown as one of the staples of the peasant diet when the export of bananas began in the 1930s. Then, peasants switched some of their cultivation into the profitable export crop, which did not require any excessive efforts since the techniques for growing the two are essentially the same. This also made it possible for the peasants to adjust easily — going back to plantains anew — when the banana boom was over. Plantains are boiled and often roasted before being eaten, or a flour is made out of them, which is eaten mixed with water or milk. The most important production zones are those of Archaie, Cul-de-Sac, Grand'Anse and the northwest.

Peas and Beans

In certain areas of the country, mainly in the Massif de la Selle and in temperate mountain regions, beans and peas are among the most important crops. Many different varieties are grown (all of which are known as *pois* in Creole) and it is possible to take up to three crops a year in humid areas. Recently production has been insufficient, however, and imports have taken place. Most important is the red bean, which is the one that is mixed with rice to form one of the most popular dishes in Haiti. Red beans are mainly cultivated in irrigated areas or areas with an adequate natural rainfall. Other common varieties are cow peas, pigeon peas and black or white beans.

Fruits

The Haitian climate is excellently suited to most tropical fruits, and a wide variety of fruits are also produced and sold locally. By far the two most important ones are mangoes and avocados.* Mango trees are usually the only ones that are spared as plains or mountain sides are cleared for cultivation. They are found all over the country, principally along roads and close to the *habitations*. Mangoes are consumed in great quantities when in season and have, as Alfred Métraux and his collaborators aptly remark, 'more than once spared poor families the pangs of hunger.'[26] Avocado trees are generally found in open fields or serve as protection for coffee plants. Some other fruits that are commonly picked or cultivated and consumed in Haiti are pineapples, papaya, guava, oranges, grapefruits, melons and star apples.

The distinction between export and subsistence products is a fundamental one for our analysis. During the 1950-70 period an important

---

*Mangoes are exported to the USA. (Cf. JWK (1976:5), p. 12.)

shift in the composition of peasant production took place in Haiti. The output of export crops fell in absolute terms while the production of subsistence goods increased. This shift was important, not only in terms of Haitian export revenues, but also in terms of rural per capita incomes. In Chapter 5 we will demonstrate how the shift from export to subsistence crops has given an increased impetus to soil erosion so as to lower the production capacity of the peasant sector and thereby presumably also to reduce incomes per head in the Haitian countryside.

The Agrarian Structure

The 1950 census indicated that some 85 percent of all Haitian peasants 'owned' the land they cultivated.[27]* On the other hand, regional surveys from the Ouest and Artibonite departments gave figures of slightly over 50 percent.[28] As Paul Moral has pointed out, the resolution of this apparent paradox quite probably lies in the fact that in popular usage 'property' is a synonym for 'cultivated land', so that the term tends to lost its significance altogether. A *propriétaire* is nothing but a person who for a long time has cultivated a particular plot.[29] Even though land transactions ought to be carried out by a deed which is executed and authenticated by a notary so that they can be registered, few peasants are in the situation where they could present any titles to the land they claim as theirs. No cadastral survey has ever been undertaken in the country, but historical possession of a given piece of land for successive generations within the peasant community takes the place of written deeds. 'The proof is in the reputation,' as Paul Moral expresses it.[30] Legally, 20 years of uninterrupted possession without deeds theoretically establishes an undisputed right to the land in question.**

The impression of a predominance of peasant ownership of agricultural land is strengthened by two more recent surveys, one made on a nationwide basis in 1970 and one covering 7,355 farms in the *arrondissement* of Cap-Haïtien, taken in 1974. The former classified 60 percent of all 'parcels' as being cultivated by owner-cultivators,[31] and the latter indicated that 75 percent of the agricultural land in the Cap region belonged to the peasants.[32]†

---

*The census did, however, not indicate what percentage of *land* was owned (Zuvekas (1978), p. 9.).
**Moral (1961), pp. 181-2. Exceptions to this rule may, however, be found if the value of the land increases. In Chapter 12 we will give examples of how technical progress has led to increased insecurity of holdings.
†Cf. also Zuvekas (1978), p. 13, who lists 12 different studies indicating that from 56 to 100 percent of all peasants own at least part of their land.

The Peasant Economy

The fact that the majority of the Haitian peasants own their farms is very important. A common pattern in underdeveloped economies, particularly in Latin America, is that the cultivator and the owner is not the same person. Such a system bears within it the seed of exploitation, and the seed is only too easily brought to germination and fruition.[33] In Haiti this potentially disastrous situation has not arisen since the peasants work on their own land. No exploitation of the peasants can be deduced from the characteristics of the Haitian system of land tenure.*

Tenant Farming and Sharecropping

Often peasants with only small plots find it difficult to make a living for themselves and their families without access to more land and hence decide to take additional land on lease. Neither do all peasants own land (with or without deeds).[34] Alfred Métraux and his colleagues found that about one-third of all peasants in the Marbial valley towards the end of the 1940s were wholly or partly tenant farmers, leasing from 0.06 to 6 carreaux,** with an average of 1.32 carreau.[35] The 1950 census on the other hand revealed the distribution shown in Table 2.2 of peasants who did not own the land they worked.

Table 2.2: The Distribution of Tenant Farmers in 1950 (percent of all farmers)†

Lease from government	1.90
Lease from private landowners	2.90
Sharecroppers	3.47
Total	8.27

†It should be observed that the figures in the table only refer to peasants that do not own any land, not to part-time tenants.
Source: Pierre-Charles (1965), pp. 85-6.

Other surveys also tend to give contradictory results. Thus, in a sample of 540 farms it was found that around 30 percent of all peasants were

---

*In this connection it should be noted that the number of landless rural workers is believed to be low. A review of the scanty evidence is given by Zuvekas (1978), pp. 86-7. Other forms of possible exploitation — via the marketing process and via the rural credit system — are analyzed in Chapters 4 and 11, respectively.
** 1 carreau = 1.29 hectares.

tenants only, while another 19 percent supplemented their own holdings by leasing more land, while in another sample of 372 farms only 6 percent of the surveyed peasants were tenants and only 2.5 percent combined ownership and tenant status. A survey in 25 rural *sections* led to the conclusion that 170,000 hectares — almost 20 percent of the cultivated area — in the entire country should be under leasehold.[36] Newer figures are scarce. The results of the 1971 census are not yet available at the time of writing. The above-mentioned 1970 survey, however, classified only 14 percent of all 'parcels' as being cultivated by tenant farmers (excluding sharecroppers), [37] and the 1974 Cap survey showed that only 8 percent of the agricultural land was leased out under fixed rents.[38]

A special form of land lease is the *de moitié* system (sharecropping), where the landlord provides the land and the lessee provides seeds, plants and labor. When the harvest comes the crop is shared between the two according to some formula agreed upon in advance.* As with fixed rent tenancy, it is difficult to know the exact incidence of sharecropping in Haiti. The 1950 census (Table 2.2) indicated a low figure of 3.5 percent (of all peasants) while the Métraux team found that over 50 percent of all Marbial peasants were sharecroppers (partly or solely).[39] Only 14 percent of all 'parcels' in 1970 were cultivated by sharecroppers,[40] and in the Cap-Haïtien district in 1974 only 6 percent of the land was leased out under crop-sharing arrangements.[41]

The Size of Holdings

The 1950 census indicated that an absolute majority of Haitian farms were minifundia holdings. Thirty-six percent of all rural families were found to work on less than one carreau and 68 percent on less than two. Only 6 percent of all holdings were larger than 5 carreaux.[42] Paul Moral has criticized these figures, however, on the ground that the likely method of computation has been to add the areas declared to be occupied by various crops. This procedure does not take into account that the incidence of mixed cultivation is very high in Haiti and will therefore give an upward bias.[43] Five local surveys from various parts of the country (quoted by Moral) give lower estimates, and Moral concludes that the most likely average for 1950 would be a figure of

---

*In spite of the term, *de moitié* does not necessarily mean that the harvest needs to be shared on a fifty-fifty basis. According to the law, however, the sharecropper is entitled to a minimum of 50 percent (Labour and Welfare Department (1961), art. 471).

The Peasant Economy

slightly more than one hectare, as shown in Table 2.3.

Table 2.3: The Average Size of Landholdings in 1950

Department	Cultivated area (hectares)	Number of farms	Average size of farms (hectares)
Nord	110,000	98,000	1.12
Nord-Ouest†	26,000	30,000	0.87
Artibonite†	120,000	117,000	1.03
Ouest	215,000	185,000	1.16
Sud	170,000	150,000	1.13
Entire country	641,000	580,000	1.10

†Figures for Nord-Ouest and Artibonite have been recalculated so as to be consistent.

Source: Moral (1961), p. 186.

The 1971 census gives somewhat larger averages, but still the average for Haiti as a whole is as low as 1.40 hectares per farm, as Table 2.4 indicates.* Thirty-three percent of all land was found to be holdings of 1 carreau or less and 59 percent holdings of 2 carreaux or less, while only 14 percent consisted of farms in excess of 5 carreaux.[44]

Table 2.4: The Average Size of Landholdings in 1971

Department	Cultivated area (hectares)	Number of farms	Average size of farms (hectares)
Nord	169,650	106,400	1.59
Nord-Ouest	67,080	30,100	2.22
Artibonite	196,170	140,000	1.40
Ouest	200,800	177,060	1.13
Sud	229,830	163,150	1.41
Entire country	863,530	616,710	1.40

Sources: Computations based on IHS (1973), pp. 37, 40.

*The problem of mixed cultivation has been accounted for in the 1971 census (IHS (n.d.:1), p. 45).

However, the 1971 census (and the 1950 census as well) understates the area occupied by large landholdings. For example, it states that not more than 10,600 hectares consist of holdings larger than 20 carreaux, which is slightly more than 1 percent of the total cultivated area.⁴⁵ This is clearly wrong. The most important large landholdings are those of HASCO and Plantation Dauphin, which in the early 1960s together controlled around 30,000 hectares.⁴⁶ HASCO alone was reported to own 11,000 hectares as of 1969.⁴⁷ Hence, the 1971 census figure must be adjusted upwards to some (unknown) extent. However, even if such adjustments were made, the basic picture would probably not be changed, but the distribution of land in Haiti would still be much less unequal than in most Latin American states.⁴⁸* The largest single landowner is the Haitian government, but since no cadastral survey has taken place in Haiti it is not known with any degree of accuracy how much of the land is government property. Guesses run as high as one-third of total area of the country.⁴⁹ Most of the government-owned land is cultivated by tenants or by squatters who due to the general confusion regarding land titles do not pay any rent.

Scattered Landholdings

Often the Haitian peasant does not dispose of a single, unified piece of land. Instead his holding is split up into two or more scattered plots, often at a considerable distance from each other. Thus, in 1950, only 28 percent of all farms consisted of a single, contiguous plot, around the *caille* (hut), while 25 percent were unified holdings at some distance from the hut, and 47 percent were non-contiguous plots.** This pattern has been confirmed by later investigations. Harold A. Wood in the *Département du Nord* found that 'many individuals have two plots, some as many as four or five, separated from one another by distances of up to about four miles,'⁵⁰ and a study in the Gonaïves area found

---

*Casimir (1964), pp. 41-6, Brisson (1968), Chapter 1, Pierre-Charles (1969:1), pp. 132-3, and Jean (1974), pp. 32-4, maintain, however, that agricultural land is concentrated in very few hands. According to Casimir it is very probable that more than one-half of the acreage consists of holdings exceeding 20 carreaux, while the other authors contend that 67 percent of the arable land consists of farms in excess of 10 carreaux. However, this claim appears too strong. (Cf. Zuvekas (1978), p. 25.)

**Moral (1961), p. 187. Cf. the situation in the Marbial valley: 'There are few peasants, today, who own 2 car. of land all in one piece. Even in the case of poorer farmers the average size of the gardens owned is 1 "carreau". One owner of 12 different plots estimated their total surface area at 2 "carreaux"...' (Métraux et al. (1951), p. 31).

that the average farm consisted of two plots.[51] In 1971, the situation was as shown in Table 2.5. Recent local and regional surveys point to yet higher figures, ranging from 2.2 to 5.4 parcels.*

Table 2.5: Number of Plots per Farm and Size of Plots 1971

Department	Number of farms	Number of plots	Plots per farm	Average size of plots (hectares)
Nord	106,400	200,400	1.9	0.85
Nord-Ouest	30,100	53,430	1.8	1.25
Artibonite	140,000	246,600	1.8	0.55
Ouest	177,060	312,100	1.8	0.65
Sud	163,150	305,700	1.9	0.75
Entire country	616,710	1,118,230	1.8	0.75

Source: IHS (1973), pp. 37, 40.

A very common division is the one indicated at the beginning of this chapter, where the peasant has got one plot in *tè cho*, at lower altitude, and another in *tè frèt*, higher up on the hillsides.

Hence, while it is not possible to contend that Haiti needs land reform in the conventional sense of the term — that of a subdivision of latifundia holdings into smaller units — the need for a geographical unification of holdings certainly exists, as we will find in Chapter 12. The fact that most peasants own more than one plot makes technological progress in agriculture a difficult matter. No Haitian government has dared to attack these problems, because no government has been administratively strong enough and because no government has been interested in the matter, as we will see in the part of this book which deals with government *vis-à-vis* the peasants.

Sidney W. Mintz gives a good summary of the land tenure situation in Haiti:

> Haiti does not have a 'land problem' as that phrase is conventionally applied to Latin America. It does, it is true, suffer from a land shortage, inasmuch as too little land is worked at too low a level of productivity and must feed too many mouths. But a very substantial portion of the rural masses owns land or has regular access to it. It is

*This is mentioned in 7 of 9 surveys summarized by Zuvekas (1978), pp. 16-17.

true that most of the land is held in small plots and without clear title. But those persons who own no land or who lack land to work are perhaps fewer than in any country in Latin America...and 'land reform' in the conventional sense – the breaking-up of large estates and the creation of a class of small landholders – is nearly irrelevant to Haiti's needs.[52]

One cannot emphasize sufficiently the significance of the Haitian agrarian structure. The destruction of the French plantations and the rise of the minifundia system during the nineteenth century was one of the most decisive events of Haitian history. On the one hand, the predominance of peasant-owned smallholdings saved Haiti from sharing the fate of most other Latin American countries: a concentration of the best lands in the hands of an oligarchy coupled with the creation of strong patterns of dependence of peasants and landless workers on the *haciendas*.* On the other hand, the creation of a minifundia system had some perverse effects, not normally associated with land reforms, on the pattern of Haitian politics. As we will show in Chapters 6 and 7, the destruction of the plantations was responsible to a very large extent for the chaotic course subsequently taken by the political and administrative system of the country and also for the more or less total lack of interest in agriculture shown by virtually every single Haitian government from the mid-nineteenth century up to the present time.

The Factor Combination of Peasant Agriculture

The first part of the present chapter gave an account of the most important crops produced by the Haitian peasants. Now, let us turn our attention to how these crops are produced, i.e. to which inputs are and are not used and to how these inputs are combined to yield the methods of cultivation. The input combination and production methods obviously determine the productivity of the agricultural sector, and since the capacity of the peasant sector to feed the increasing population appears to be decreasing, it is essential to have a full knowledge of exactly how the Haitian peasant produces his output.

Maurice de Young has described Haitian peasant farming as *horticulture,* by which is meant a type of farming which uses land in small units and where capital is used only to a very limited extent, while labor is used extensively. The use of animals (except for marketing the

---

*Often, monopolization of land at the same time creates a monopsony in the rural labor market. (Cf. e.g. Griffin (1969), pp. 70-74.)

The Peasant Economy

produce) is precluded in horticulture as well as the use of the plow.* This is a very accurate description, for the techniques employed in the peasant sector are of a labor-intensive type, and very little capital equipment, except for a few simple tools, is generally used.

Land

Land is a scarce factor in Haiti. Its price in terms of labor (or goods) is high. As early as in the 1930s Melville J. Herskovits, in his classic account of life in the Mirebalais valley, heavily stressed the struggle among the peasants to obtain land:

> ...as one resident of Mirebalais remarked, 'Because of a few feet of land a peasant will, if necessary, spend a thousand gourdes at court.' ...there are few, among the peasants at least, who do not seek by all means to add to their heritage, for among those folk the ambition to obtain more and more land is a dominating one. To this end the peasant skimps and saves, depriving himself even of his important needs, until at the proper time some choice parcel of ground comes on the market...Thus the drive to obtain property is an obsession with the Haitian peasant.[53]

This situation still persists today. As the population grows and erosion spreads, agricultural land becomes increasingly scarce. Very few students of Haitian agriculture have failed to stress this fact.[54]

Underlying the land scarcity is the population density. The latest available official estimate of 4,833,000 persons (for 1978) gives a population density of 174 persons per km^2. For 1970 (according to official figures) the density was 153, which is among the higher figures for the Caribbean area as may be seen in Table 2.6.[55]

Haiti is predominantly rural. According to the 1950 census only 12 percent of the population lived in urban areas — the lowest proportion of any Latin American country. However, the urban proportion appears to have increased during the past 25 years. According to the census, the urban share was as high as 20 percent in 1971.[56] Still, the rurality of Haiti is overwhelming. Table 2.7 compares the percentage of the population living in urban areas in a number of Latin American

---

*De Young (1958), p. 2. When animal traction and plows are used on an extensive basis de Young names this practice *agriculture*, which in Haiti is relevant only for a few large plantations.

countries. The lowest figure by far is that of Haiti.*

Table 2.6: Population Density in Some Caribbean and Central American Countries 1970

Country	Persons per km^2	Country	Persons per km^2
Barbados	595	Guatemala	47
Trinidad and Tobago	209	Costa Rica	33
Jamaica	182	Mexico	26
El Salvador	165	Honduras	23
Haiti	153	Panama	19
Dominican Republic	89	Nicaragua	15
Cuba	75		

Sources: Statistical Abstract of Latin America (1970), p. 56. For Haiti see text.

Table 2.7: Percentage of the Population Living in Urban Areas in Some Latin American Countries 1975

Country	Percentage of population in urban areas	Country	Percentage of population in urban areas
Argentina	82.5	Jamaica	52.9
Barbados	45.0	Mexico	61.2
Bolivia	30.9	Nicaragua	52.1
Brazil	61.5	Panama	50.4
Colombia	66.8	Paraguay	36.1
Costa Rica	42.2	Peru	63.5
Chile	80.5	Dominican Republic	46.3
Ecuador	42.0	Trinidad and Tobago	56.6
El Salvador	39.8	Uruguay	80.8
Guatemala	31.4	Venezuela	82.6
Haiti	22.0		
Honduras	32.5	Latin America	61.8

Source: BID (1975), p. 423.

*The Table needs to be interpreted with some caution, since the definition of 'urban' may vary from country to country.

The scarcity of land becomes more pronounced if we allow for the fact that a large portion of the Haitian territory is unsuitable for cultivation due to low soil fertility or excessive ruggedness. In the late 1960s the Organization of American States (OAS) made a tentative classification of the Haitian soils according to agricultural productivity and potential use, following a system used by the US Department of Agriculture which identified the following eight soil categories:[57]

> I: Cultivable soils, suitable for irrigation; plain topography without any limiting factors; high productivity, with good management not requiring conservation measures.
> II: Cultivable soils, suitable for irrigation; plain or slightly rugged topography, limiting factors not severe and may be compensated for by more or less intensive management. High productivity with good management; require some moderate conservation measures.
> III: Cultivable soils, suitable for irrigation only with very profitable cultures; plain or slightly rugged topography with somewhat severe limiting factors; average productivity with intensive management practices. Require intensive conservation measures.
> IV: Soils of limited use, unsuitable for irrigation except under special circumstances and with very profitable cultures; mainly suited for grazing or permanent cultures; plain or rugged topography; severe limitations requiring very intensive management, low or mediocre productivity. Regarding conservation, permanent cultures requiring little labor are to be preferred.
> V: Soils unsuitable for agriculture; good only for rice cultures; without restrictions for grazing; severe limitations especially as far as drainage is concerned; high productivity in grazing or rice cultivation with very intensive management methods (especially drainage). Soils included in this category for reasons of low fertility require intensive use of fertilizers.
> VI: Soils unsuitable for agriculture, suitable mainly for forestry and grazing; severe limitations especially from topography, profundity and rockiness. Without restrictions for forestry; considerable restrictions for grazing.
> VII: Unsuitable for agriculture; suitable only for forestry. Severe limitations for cultures. In those parts where the effective depth of the soil and the slope permits it is possible to develop tree-crops, coffee, and fruits, and in some instances grazing lands.
> VIII: Unsuitable for agriculture; without restrictions for national parks or zones of fauna conservation and recreation.

The extension of each of these soils is given in Table 2.8.

Table 2.8: Extension of Soils in Haiti According to the OAS Classification

Classes	Area in hectares	Percent
I	--- (+)	--- (+)
II	225,750	8.37
III	297,189	11.01
IV	247,725	9.18
V	74,150	2.75
VI	371,422	13.76
VII	1,381,048	51.18
VIII	101,213	3.75

(+) Negligible

Source: Giles (1973), p. 9.

The majority of the Haitian population depends for its existence on soils of type VI and VII.[58] The principal problem of both categories, the limiting factor as far as agricultural use is concerned, is their topography. The mission stressed that terracing is necessary if any agricultural use is to be made of type VI soils, and in principle the type VII soils should be reafforested immediately to stop the ongoing erosion resulting from excessive cultivation of these lands.

Three major and several minor mountain ranges traverse Haiti from west to east. Interspersed between these ranges are seven principal and fifteen secondary plains, which, however, do not together cover more than 21 percent of the total area of the country. Around 40 percent of the area consists of lands at an altitude exceeding 500 meters, and approximately 20 percent of the country lies above 800 meters.[59] From Table 2.9 it can be seen that more than one-half of the total land area consists of hills or mountains with a slope exceeding 40 percent.

The highly rugged character of the Haitian terrain renders at least half of the area of the country worthless for agricultural use, unless exceptional measures are resorted to. Some estimates of the arable or cultivable area of Haiti are presented in Table 2.10.*

---

*The reader is advised to take all these estimates *cum grano salis* since their origins are very obscure. It is not clear upon what they are based. Paul Moral points out that very often the procedure has been to collect old, obsolete data —

Table 2.9: Topographical Characteristics of Haiti

Slope (%)	Area (hectares)	Percent of all land†
0 – 10	782,874	29
10 – 20	195,258	7
20 – 40	252,155	9
more than 40	1,451,009	54
Total land	2,681,296	100
Water	17,200	
Total area	2,698,496	

†Due to rounding percentage figures do not add up to 100 percent.
Source: PNUD (1971), p. 2.

Table 2.10: Some Estimates of the Arable Area

Source	Year	Hectares
Marc A. Holly	1957	1,161,000
Paul Moral	1961	700,000 – 1,000,000
OAS/ECLA/IDB	1962	1,400,000
CONADEP/DARNDR	1969	1,407,800
Rotberg & Clague	1971	637,100
OAS	1972	1,339,780
IHS	1975	1,170,000

Sources: Holly: Holly (1955), p. 31; Moral: Moral (1961), p. 121; OAS/ECLA/IDB: OEA/CEPAL/BID (1962), pp. 15-16, CONADEP/DARNDR: P & D, No. 2, 1969, p.20 Estimé (1972), p. 28; Roberg & Clague: Rotberg & Clague (1971), p. 12; OAS: OEA (1972), p. 612; IHS: République d' Haïti (1975), p. 1.

sometimes going as far back as colonial days, when the situation was entirely different from the present one! (Moral (1961), p. 121.) The methods of estimation are nowhere given explicitly and are by all probability very rough. Nowhere is the term 'arable' or 'cultivable' defined. These terms in principle could mean anything. The crucial factors involved are the agricultural techniques employed and the real cost of these techniques. It is for example not self-evident that the procedure should be to depart from the existing state of arts and postulate that this will continue for ever. On the one hand, the Dutch have reclaimed parts of the North Sea and the Israelis have made agricultural use of the Negev desert. On the other hand, Haitian peasants often cultivate practically vertical slopes, using ropes to stop them falling off their lands, with the clearly detrimental effects that this kind of cultivation has on soil fertility. Hence, arbitrarily postulating today's techniques could err on either side of the 'true' figure – however this is to be defined. Another problem concerns the frequent inclusion of pastoral lands in the estimates. The productivity of these lands is largely unknown, since much of the area is quite inaccessible (Lebeau (1974), p. 12).

If we use the rural population figure according to the 1971 census — 3,434,920[60] — and put this in relation to the 1972 OAS estimate of the arable area, we arrive at a rural population density per hectare of arable land of 2.56 persons. From the comparison in Table 2.11 we can see that this is one of the higher ratios in the Caribbean and Central America.* This figure must be taken as a minimum estimate of the population pressure on the available resources, since it includes grazing lands in the computations[61] and there is doubt concerning the extent to which these lands can actually be developed.[62] Large parts of the pastoral area are virtually inaccessible and extremely steep, and it is quite probable that the economic return from such land in agriculture proper falls short of what can be obtained by keeping it as grazing land.[63] To this must be added another consideration, namely that some of the arable land is in fallow at any one time.[64]

Table 2.11: Rural Population in Relation to Arable Area in Some Caribbean and Central American Countries

Country	Year	Rural persons per hectare
Barbados	1960	8.49
Jamaica	1965	5.11
Cuba	1964	3.47
Haiti	1971	2.56
El Salvador	1961	2.38
Dominican Republic	1960	1.99
Guatemala	1964	1.90
Honduras	1963	1.75
Costa Rica	1963	1.41
Panama	1961	1.12
Nicaragua	1963	1.04
Mexico	1960	0.72

Sources: *Statistical Abstract of Latin America* (1970), p. 56. For Haiti see text.

*Robert I. Rotberg contends that 'Haiti is saddled with the most densely packed rural population in the Western Hemisphere and, next to Java and the Egyptian delta, in the world. Although her estimated 4.6 million...average out to about 430 per square mile, far less than Mauritius (1961), Martinique (769), the United Kingdom (583), Puerto Rico (777), and Barbados (1,365) — but more than the neighboring Dominican Republic (199) and El Salvador (316) — over half of Haiti's population lives on the 23 percent of the land mass which is arable... Overall, the rural share of the population has remained at about 89 percent — the

The Peasant Economy

Rural Haiti is very densely populated. At least 75 percent of all Haitians live in rural areas and hence depend directly on agriculture for both food and cash incomes. The natural base of their subsistence is narrow indeed, however, as the present sections should have made clear. Good, flat, arable land is extremely scarce in Haiti. The full significance of this fact will not be brought out until Chapter 5, where the process of soil destruction is analyzed. The resource base is shrinking as a result of the actions of the peasants. Each year new areas are lost for ever for cultivation.

Capital

The second production factor which is scarce, in the sense that it commands a high price in terms of goods or labor, is capital. In the model developed in Chapter 5 where we analyze the erosion process, we assume that the peasants employ no capital but that export and subsistence goods can be produced with the aid of land and labor alone. Although this is known to be a realistic assumption for small family farms in most underdeveloped economies,[65] its use in each individual case requires empirical justification. This will be provided in the present section. A presentation of the relative lack of capital inputs in peasant production is important also from another point of view, namely that it is intrinsically bound up with the low level of the technology which we will return to in Chapters 11 and 12.

The lack of capital inputs is a striking feature of Haitian agriculture. In the main, the peasants employ only the minimum amount of circulating capital necessary – in the form of plants and seeds – and likewise, stick to employing fixed capital only in the form of a few, simple hand tools, while irrigation works, pesticides and insecticides, fertilizer,

---

highest in the Western Hemisphere. In terms of rural persons per square mile of arable land, Haiti's dire position is even more marked: the figure for Haiti is 1,600, only slightly less than the most crowded parts of central Java and the Egyptian delta; in Peru, 515; the Dominican Republic 516; El Salvador, 617, Barbados, 839; and Jamaica 945.' (Rotberg & Clague (1971), pp. 12-13.) 1,600 rural persons per square mile of arable land corresponds to 6.18 rural persons per hectare. This figure is based on a far lower estimate of the arable area than the official government figures. The total area of the republic of Haiti is 10,694 square miles (2,770,000 hectares). If the arable land is taken to be 23 percent of the total area we arrive at a figure of 2,460 square miles (637,100 hectares). Conversely, the rural population figure presumably employed by Rotberg – 4,094,000 – is far higher than the one obtained in the 1971 census – 3,434,920. (The former figure gives a rural density of 1,664 persons per square mile of arable land – 6.43 per hectare.)

storage facilities, plows and animal or mechanical traction are notable by their absence.

Seeds and Plants

As a rule, plant species and seeds are of unimproved qualities, and although efforts have been made several times to make peasants change to high-yielding or otherwise superior varieties, the success has been very limited, except in the case of cotton and, to a lesser extent, rice.[66]

Only the crudest forms of plant and seed selection have been used, if any. A good example is coffee, which is not even sown or planted by the peasants. Instead, reproduction is taken care of by rodents like mice and rats. The coffee berry consists of two seeds embedded in sweetish pulp. At harvest time, some berries fall to the ground where the pulp is eaten by the rodents, who in doing so drop the seeds, which in turn give rise to new coffee seedlings. Thus, there is nothing to guarantee that only the best berries are used, and only by pure chance may the quality of the coffee trees be improved.* Neither do the peasants bother to get rid of old low-yielding trees. Theoretically, a coffee plantation cannot produce efficiently for more than some twenty years without replanting the trees. This principle is generally violated in Haiti, however.

Tools

Very few tools and implements are encountered in the peasant sector. As a rule, the peasant tool kit consists only of two general-purpose hand tools, the most important of which is the machete, which is used for a very wide variety of purposes — even for clearing the ground and for digging when the terrain is too rocky or too steep to allow other tools to be used. Second in importance is the long, broad-blade hoe, which is, however, not seen everywhere and which often has to be borrowed.[67]

An idea of the lack of implements and the relative frequency of different tools may be given by two surveys made in the 1950s. On 540 farms in the Saltrou region 1,135 agricultural implements were found — 342 machetes, 173 hoes, 35 picks, and 585 'others', and in four *sections* of the lower Artibonite on the average less than 60 tools were found per 50 hectares — 31 hoes, 23 machetes, and 4 'others'.[68] As shown in Table 2.12, the number of tools generally increases with farm size but the degree of sophistication remains low. The plow and the harrow are

---

*The coffee obtained by the described process in Haiti is known as *café-rat*.

The Peasant Economy

virtually unknown to the great majority of peasants,* and so is the wheelbarrow.** Wheel carriages are seldom seen in the Haitian countryside. Burdens are generally loaded on donkeys or carried by the men and women themselves.

Table 2.12: Agricultural Implements in the Marbial Valley in the Late 1940s

Land farmed	Number of families	Average number of tools†
Less than 1.50 car.	71	2
1.50-4 car.	50	4
at least 4 car.	26	7

†2 tools: a hoe and a bill-hook, 2 bill-hooks, a hoe and a machete; 4 tools: hoe, machete, bill-hook, and pick; 2 hoes, machete, bill-hook; hoe, 2 bill-hooks, machete; 7 tools: 1 or 2 hoes, machete, 1 or 2 bill-hooks, dibble, pick, and iron bar.

Source: Métraux et al. (1951), p. 184.

The lack of sufficiently sophisticated tools is directly detrimental to the growth and yielding capacity of the plants. The hoe, for example, only penetrates 10-15 centimeters into the ground which is insufficient to ensure adequate development of the root system.[69]

Manure and Fertilizers

The peasants do not generally manure their fields. The relatively low number of domestic animals in Haiti obviously precludes extensive use of dung, and composting of crop residues, weeds, household refuse etc. is not a common practice. Instead straw, chaff and other crop residues are usually burned. Green manuring is hardly ever encountered.

As for chemical fertilizers the total use in 1968-9 was estimated to be as low as 1 kilo per hectare of cultivated land,[70] most of which presumably was used by the larger estates so that the figure for peasant

---

*Henry Christophe tried to introduce the plow in Haiti in the early nineteenth century, but was never successful. Today it may be seen in the Plateau Central and in the Cayes district, but even there the number of plows is low and the practice is not generally accepted (OEA (1972), p. 630; Rotberg & Clague (1971), p. 289).
**Selden Rodman contends that Haiti probably is the only country in the Western Hemisphere where neither the plow nor the wheelbarrow are in general use (Rodman (1961), p. 36).

agriculture in fact must have been even lower. Beginning in 1968, the *Institut Haïtien de Promotion du Café et des Denrées d'Exportation* (IHPCADE) has been distributing fertilizers to peasants, either free or at one-half the commercial price, actually reaching a figure of 600 tons a year.[71] Total fertilizer use in 1973 amounted to 3,000 tons, or somewhat more than 3 kilos per hectare of cultivated land.[72] Its use was however, largely limited to rice, sugar cane, coffee, cotton and vegetables.

Irrigation: Precipitation

Rainfall in Haiti is very unevenly distributed throughout the year. Almost the entire country is subject to longer or shorter periods of relative drought. Spring and fall constitute the rainy seasons, while winter and summer are relatively dry. In the capital, Port-au-Prince, we have the seasonal distribution of rainfall shown in Table 2.13. This seasonality, with local variations, is typical for the entire country.[73]

Table 2.13: Seasonal Distribution of Rainfall in Port-au-Prince

Spring (April-June)	80 days – 455 mm average	57 mm/10 days
Summer (June-July)	40 " – 100 " "	25 "
Fall (August-October)	90 " – 496 " "	55 "
Winter (November-March)	150 " – 285 " "	19 "

Source: Moral (1961), p. 110.

The yearly rainfall in different regions is seen in Figure 2.1.[74] Four regions have a precipitation of less than 1,000 millimeters per year. The largest area extends in an s-shaped line from Port-de-Paix in the north, across the northwest peninsula, via the lower Artibonite and the island of Gonâve across the Cul-de-Sac plain east of Port-au-Prince. The other three are the Fort-Liberté area in the far northeast and the Saltrou and Aquin regions on the southern coast.*

In tropical and subtropical agriculture, where frosts rarely occur and temperatures remain fairly uniform across the year, variations in timing and amount of precipitation is a key factor in the determination of the agricultural possibilities of a region.[75] Timing and duration of precipitation assume special importance, and any displacement of the wet seasons may easily have fatal consequences:

---

*Approximatively one quarter of Haiti consists of areas with an annual precipitation of less than 1,200 mm (Moral (1961), p. 106).

The Peasant Economy

[The] rhythm [of peasant agriculture] is disturbed by the irregularities of the climate, especially those of rainfall, by too early or too late spring and fall rains, and by the duration and rigor of the dry seasons. Most marked are the uncertainties concerning the beginning of the spring rain season. An accentuated drought in March which persists abnormally long, until mid-April, leads to famine in the plains. In the mountains it threatens the second blooming of the coffee bushes. The summer drought too may be very devastating if it begins already in mid-June and continues until August. The planting made in the spring fails, the rice planted in March is lost, the peas and beans produce no yield, the coffee bushes of the lowlands are 'burned'. The cultivators of the plains have to procure provisions from the more or less unaffected highlands while they wait for the September rains.[76]

Figure 2.1

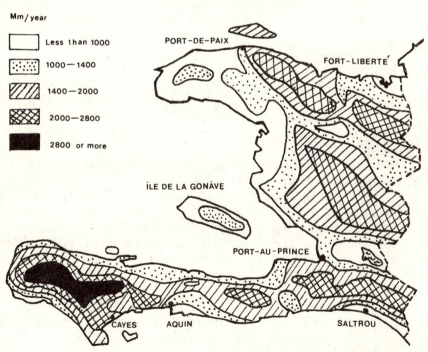

Source: Anglade (1974), p. 13.

Irrigation Systems

Together with soil quality, the amount and timing of the natural precipitation constitute the most important climatological constraint on Haitian agriculture. Strong and unpredictable seasonal variations in rainfall, as well as permanent semi-aridness of certain areas call for the use of irrigation, which, however, is not always a simple affair. The Haitian rivers are comparatively short, and their water content varies considerably over the year. Some of the rivers never reach the sea except under extremely favorable circumstances. Their water is lost into the subsoil. Even the largest river, the Artibonite, loses most of its water during the dry seasons. The average flow for the entire year is 99 m^3 per second, but in March this figure falls to 24 m^3 per second and it becomes possible to ford the river. In October, on the other hand, the average flow increases to 196 m^3 per second.[77] The river is then dangerous to cross, even in a boat, and often floods. Smaller rivers may dry up entirely during certain periods while they become tumultuous torrents during the rainy seasons. Thus, the rivers display the same seasonal variations as does precipitation. This fact makes it difficult to use them for irrigation purposes.

The biggest lake, the Etang Saumâtre, unfortunately contains brackish water, but the smaller freshwater lakes like the Etang de Miragoâne, which waters the Petit-Goâve plain of the southern peninsula, can be used for irrigation. However, the water content of this lake varies considerably between dry and rainy seasons. Some of the plains like those of Cul-de-Sac, Archaie, Gonaïves and Cayes have larger supplies of groundwater.[78]

In spite of these difficulties, Haiti possessed a well developed system of irrigational facilities for the plantations during the colonial period. This system fell into decay after the liberation, however, and today it is estimated that less than 10 percent of the cultivated area is under irrigation (other than natural precipitations). The *Conseil National de Développement et de Planification* (CONADEP) for the year 1969 gives a figure of 70,000 hectares,[79] which is slightly lower than the figure given by the OAS mission for the same time — 75,000 hectares, the majority of which are government-run.*

The existing irrigation systems show several deficiencies.[80] Drainage systems do not generally work efficiently, and this, in the absence of natural drainage, leads to salinization of the soil. Sedimentation is also a common problem. Dams and canals are easily filled with alluvial silt,

---

*Government 71,700 ha, HASCO: 3,500 ha (OEA (1972), pp. 572, 588, 566).

which often is the result of a lack of adequate installations at intake points from rivers, which in time leads to blocking of water courses. Very often no work at all is undertaken to clean dams, canals or screens at intake points. The sedimentation problem is likely to assume further importance in the future, with the advance of water erosion. Often masonry lining is lacking in longer canals or when the irrigated areas are large, with seepage as a consequence. Finally, there are no instruments to indicate the amount of water consumption, so that almost all existing systems are serving larger areas than can be advantageously done, with a consequent loss of efficiency.

Given the vast importance of a sufficient and regular water supply to agriculture, construction and maintenance of irrigation works is one of the most urgent tasks to be carried out in the peasant sector. Still, in actual practice only one-tenth of the cultivated area is under irrigation, while the existing irrigation systems slowly decay for want of maintenance. In Chapter 12 we will analyze why technical progress (e.g. in the form of increased use of irrigation) is conspicuously absent in Haitian agriculture, and in Chapters 6-8, which deal with government passivity with respect to the agricultural sector, it will become apparent why the existing facilities are left to decay.

Pesticides and Insecticides

Peasant cultivations are frequently haunted by diseases or insects. Coffee is attacked by a fungus known as *oeil brun*, which makes the leaves fall off the trees prematurely and makes the berries degenerate. It is also plagued by various lice, crickets and ants.[81] Bananas have been subject to attacks from beetles and from the Panama and Sigatoka diseases.[82] In 1935, the Mexican boll-weevil struck Haitian cotton plantations and contributed to the disappearance of cotton from the list of Haitian exports.[83] In the thirties the Witch's Broom disease also affected the cocoa plantations.[84]

Subsistence crops are also attacked. Cultivation of corn offers many problems from the point of view of pests and diseases:

> Corn is attacked by various insect pests and is subject to various diseases. Some regions in Haiti are so infested by fungus diseases that any attempt to grow corn there is doomed in advance to complete failure. These places are designated by the peasants by the name of *maïs gâté*, which means 'spoiled corn areas'. The predominant disease in these regions is perhaps anthrax or *charbon* caused by [a] fungus...against which no treatment is yet known.[85]

Sweet potatoes are also subject to diseases and attacks from rats.[86] Coconuts, finally, are often destroyed by coconut bud rot and by a pest which attacks the roots of the trees.[87] Against these insects and diseases the peasants have few or no means of defense. The quantities of pesticides used in the peasant sector are negligible.*

Not only insects and diseases threaten the cultivations. Domestic and wild animals constitute another problem:

> Growing crops are endangered by the inroads of domestic animals such as cows, horses, goats, pigs and poultry which, in a very short time, may cause great damage. Fields are therefore protected by live hedges...or by enclosures of bamboo or stakes...There are other dangers, too, to which the crops are exposed. Sometimes wild guinea-fowl invade a recently sown field; flocks of parrots may attack the maize, or 'tchits' or 'Madame Sarahs' the millet. The only remedy against these pests is to post children in the gardens, to scare them off with shouts and other noises. The peasant has no cast-off clothing with which to make scarecrows, and he does not in [the Marbial valley] as in other parts of Haiti, mount a horse's or ox's skull on the end of a pole to frighten off the birds.
>
> During the 'dead season' it often happens that dogs — which are mostly half starved — try to eat off the ears of the maize growing on irrigated land. The remedy here is to wrap each ear up in the leaves of its supporting stalk.[88]

Storage

Storage facilities are either lacking or primitive and inefficient. Only the well-to-do can afford the installations required for an efficient storage and protection of the crops. This means that the peasants run a considerable risk that their crops will be damaged by rats or humidity for example.

The storage methods commonly used are quite inadequate. Marc A. Holly gives an account of the problems connected with storing corn:

> Weevils are the chief enemies of storage corn, and cause great damage in Haiti. In fact, they constitute the main factor in the acute problem of grain conservation...They bore into seeds, chiefly into the embryos, eat the starch and other food, and move on, destroying the seeds and reducing their value. The primary attack on the grain takes

---

*Pesticides are little used outside cotton production (Lebeau (1974), p. 58).

place in the field, and as the crop is stored, the insects multiply and so extend their work of destruction...When left on the cobs, corn can remain in good condition for a much longer time than when the shucks are removed and the grain taken off. Rats, however, are very fond of the cereal, and great precautions must be taken to prevent their attacks. The peasant stores corn by handing the cobs with the enclosing shucks to very high trees or poles, whose trunks are encircled with a ring of tin sheeting to prevent the rats from climbing up. The crop is sometimes covered with palm leaves to protect it from rain.[89]

This storing practice of course does not prevent the crop from being blown down by the wind, from being eaten by birds, or from being stolen. Other cereals, like sorghum, are generally stored in the house, which makes them a far easier prey for the rats. Only the more wealthy peasants can afford to build small lofts on piles, around which collars of sheet iron are put to keep the rats out.[90]

In the case of root crops, the most common practice is to delay harvesting until the roots are to be consumed or sold. Only a small quantity is taken out of the ground at each time, and the rest can be left for months without injury. This is often a necessary procedure. Manioc, for example, must be prepared very soon after the tubers are dug up, since otherwise they will become inedible in 24 to 48 hours (using peasant storage methods).

On the whole, there are no silos, granaries and warehouses,[91] so that the peasants often have to sell or consume the crop rapidly, before it is destroyed. This is unfortunate, since it often leads to the peasants being without seed later, at sowing time, which in turn forces them to buy seeds at a higher price than the one prevailing at harvest time.

The high price of capital (in terms of labor) is amply borne out by the preceding sections. As we will see in Chapter 12 when dealing with technical progress, in some cases complementarities and indivisibilities further complicate the picture, but even where the latter are insignificant, as in the case of insecticides or tools for example, the relative price of these material inputs appears to be so high as to preclude the use of all but the most rudimentary and necessary forms: traditional, unimproved seeds and plants and simple general-purpose hand tools.[92] We will come back to the price of capital in Chapter 12 when we analyze the absence of innovations, since one of the main vehicles of technical progress is precisely its embodiment in capital.

Labor

The final production factor to be discussed is the relatively abundant one — labor. The shadow price of labor is low. Alfred Métraux and his associates found that it was always possible to find people who were willing to take a day's job for 0.60 – 0.75 gourde* in the Marbial valley in the late 1940s,[93] and Marie V. Wood in 1955 estimated the average earnings of a fully employed unskilled laborer to be less than 250 gourdes per year.[94] The situation today is similar. Although the minimum daily wage in 1969 was 3.50 gourdes per eight-hour day, labor was available for road construction in the provinces for as little as 0.50 gourde per day plus food.[95] Estimating the food cost to be another 0.50 gourde,[96] the total daily wage would be 1 gourde.[97] Recently (1974), the nominal wage of agricultural labor appears to have increased to between 2 and 3 gourdes,[98]** but if we adjust for the increase in the cost of living during the same period by recalculating both the 1969 and the 1974 wages (1974 = 2.5 gourdes) in 1955 prices the difference narrows considerably (1969: 0.83 gourde, 1974: 1.16 gourde).[99]

The Working Population

To understand the reasons underlying the low wages we must examine the size and composition of the working population in Haiti. The working or active population of a country is traditionally defined as the population between 15 and 64 years.[100] In less developed countries, where child labor is often prevalent and where people within the conventional age range (generally women) for reasons of customs, attitudes and institutions may voluntarily abstain from work, even when such is available, the traditional definition, however, loses much of its meaning.[101] The age structure, the ratio of child participation and the ratio of female participation become the most important determinants of the size of the working population.[102]

The age structure of the Haitian population is heavily tilted toward young age groups. In 1950, around 40 percent of the total population was below 15 years of age.[103] The 1971 census gave virtually the same figure, and this percentage is expected to be valid also for 1980.[104]

A high percentage of the children under 15 years belong to the labor force:

---

*Since 1919, 1 gourde = 20 US cents by law.
**Similar figures are reported in most recent surveys. For a summary, see Zuvekas (1978), p. 91.

Children slip into their work roles at an early age. Boys and girls as young as three or four may be seen carrying small tins of water on their heads, on their way from the springs, usually in groups with older girls or women. Young girls assume woman's work as soon as they can handle it; lighter work first, heavier work later. Small boys tend cattle and help the men in the fields.[105]

Especially during the peak seasons in agriculture, when the entire family is put to work, the contribution of the children is needed to help sustain the family. The 1950 census indicated that less than 5 percent of all children under 15 belonged to the labor force,[106] but this is probably a gross underestimate. The quality of the census is known to be low,[107] and a demographic survey made by the *Institut Haïtien de Statistique* in 1972 gave a figure of almost 25 percent.[108]

Also in the highest age group, that over 64, the extent of economic activity is high. There is no retirement age proper for the majority of the Haitian population. It is estimated that more than 70 percent of those over 64 have to continue their attempts at making a living after reaching that age.[109]

Women take part in all kinds of economic activities. They nurse the children, run the household, perform much agricultural work except for the hard toil of preparing the fields for planting, and perhaps most important of all: they handle most of the retail trade in Haiti outside the stores of the cities. James G. Leyburn emphatically points out that 'practically every Haitian peasant woman has her experience of going to market to sell the vegetables, trinkets, or other wares her family may produce, and to buy necessities.'[110] A considerable number of Haitian peasant women at least during some period of their lives become professional ambulant vendors — *Madam Sara* — who constantly travel back and forth between town and countryside to act as intermediaries between peasants and townspeople.[111]

In 1950, 56 percent of the total population was stated to be included in the working population. The figure was slightly higher for men (59 percent) than for women (54 percent).[112] The figures for 1972 were virtually the same. The labor force as a percentage of the total population was unchanged at 56 percent, the male figure was 58 percent and the female figure 55 percent.[113]

The Haitian ratio of female participation in the labor force appears to be high when seen in an international perspective. Some comparisons are made in Table 2.14. This table needs to be interpreted with utmost care, since very much depends on factors such as when during the agricultural year the surveys or censuses were taken, how the labor force was defined, to what extent unpaid female family workers were included etc., in each particular instance.[114]

Table 2.14: Female Participation in the Labor Force
(percent of total female population)

Country	Year	Percentage	Country	Year	Percentage
Haiti	1950	54	Panama	1970	18
"	1972	55	Argentina	1970	19
Africa			Brazil	1970	13
Algeria	1966	2	Chile	1970	13
Botswana	1964	45	Colombia	1964	12
Burundi	1965	51	Ecuador	1962	11
Ghana	1970	34	Paraguay	1962	14
Lesotho	1966	57	Peru	1972	12
Liberia	1962	29	Uruguay	1963	19
Libya	1964	3	Venezuela	1971	13
Morocco	1971	8	*Asia*		
Nigeria	1963	16	Bahrain	1971	3
Sierra Leone	1963	30	Brunei	1971	10
Swaziland	1966	28	Cambodia	1962	37
Togo	1970	31	Hong Kong	1971	29
Tunisia	1966	3	India	1971	12
Cameroon	1965	48	Indonesia	1971	22
Tanzania	1967	41	Iran	1966	8
Zambia	1969	17	South Korea	1970	23
Latin America			Kuwait	1970	5
Costa Rica	1963	12	Nepal	1971	25
Cuba	1970	12	Philippines	1970	19
El Salvador	1971	22	Singapore	1970	19
Guatemala	1964	8	Sri Lanka	1963	14
Jamaica	1970	20	Syria	1970	9
Mexico	1970	11	Thailand	1970	46
Nicaragua	1963	12	Turkey	1965	34

Sources: For Haiti see text. Rest of table: UN (1976), Table 20.

Of all the countries in the table, only Lesotho shows a higher female participation ratio than Haiti, and the Haitian figures are significantly higher than those of most other countries. Part of this is of course spurious, for the reasons mentioned above, but it is still hard to escape the conclusion that female participation must be comparatively high in Haiti, for a good explanation of such a pattern is easy to find.

The high female participation ratio in Haiti goes way back in time.[115] The roots of the tradition may perhaps be found in Africa, the homeland of the Haitian Negro slaves, where often the greatest part of the responsibility for both fieldwork and marketing rested with the women.[116] Similar features soon developed in Haiti. Women were employed in the field work by the French planters, and the same practice continued during the days of forced labor, under Toussaint, Dessalines and Christophe. The predominance of women in marketing is of a somewhat later origin. Although markets where the slaves could exchange their surplus produce from the small plots alloted to them by the plantation owners appear to have been a well-established feature in colonial Saint-Domingue,[117] it was not until after independence that it became an accepted division of labor that marketing was a predominantly female activity.[118] The *corvée* system employed by Toussaint and his two immediate successors absorbed the men into the army as soldiers or into the reactivated plantations as laborers, and the women took care of the marketing. When the *corvée* days were over new factors emerged:

> From 1843 on through most of the century there was an additional reason why peasant men would not go to the market towns: recruits were needed, both for the army and whatever revolutionary coup might be brewing; a man who did not relish fighting did better to stay out of sight in the hills. In fact, this has even been called the chief reason for which women assumed a larger part of the agricultural work in the early days of the century: to keep their husbands indoors during the hours of daylight.[119]

During the nineteenth century, the Haitian man obviously developed a strong preference for leisure. From the 1820s until the end of the century a steady stream of books and pamphlets dealing with Haiti emphasized the differences in industriousness between the Haitian woman and her male companion. While the women were constantly striving to make an existence for the family, the men were portrayed as spending their time drinking or napping in the shade.[120] Much of this of course could be explained away as being the work of white foreigners seeking evidence for the inferiority of the Negro race or of elite representatives who thought that the only reason for the existence of black peasants was hard work, but as Leyburn remarks, not even friendly authors could abstain from such comments. Therefore Leyburn concludes that there is some truth in the assertion and also tries to explain why the Haitian man during the nineteenth century had such strong preferences for leisure.

According to Leyburn, the essential explanation lies in the fact that Haiti during the entire nineteenth century was an overmilitarized country. A large number of men were lured into the regular army or into guerilla forces[121] which besides depriving the countryside of parts of its regular labor force also had psychological consequences:

> To be drawn away from the land at the very moment of physical maturity was to predispose a youth against humdrum field work. As a soldier he traveled, knew excitement, was fed and clothed, and could loaf, except during battle. So schooled, upon retirement from the army a man was hardly disposed to settle down to steady labor.[122]

Thus, the development of a high participation ratio among Haitian women is the logical outcome of a system which has strong traditions of female labor. When this system was confronted with a situation where male labor for reasons stated above was available only in limited quantities, the natural response was to increase the economic importance and responsibility of the women.

Today, few students of Haitian life would be prepared to state that the Haitian man is lazy. The high participation ratios referred to above indicate that there does not appear to be any binding constraints affecting the willingness to work that stem from cultural or institutional arrangements. In Chapter 8 we will see how the American occupation of Haiti between 1915 and 1934 put an end to the old army and instead created a modern efficient constabulary and how this constabulary in turn was destroyed in the 1960s. Peasant boys are no longer being drawn away from field work into the idle life fostering negative attitudes towards work. The Haitian peasant toils as strenuously as his female companion to make a living for the family.[123]

The supply of labor is abundant in Haiti. The labor force includes not only the 15-64 age group, but also percentages of the younger and older groups as well. Another reason for the abundant labor supply is that the participation ratio for women appears to be unusually high. To understand why the going wage rate in agriculture is low, it is not

The Peasant Economy

sufficient to examine the supply side, however, but we must also take demand into account. We will therefore now go on to see which employment alternatives the Haitian masses face.

The Employment Situation

Table 2.15 shows the distribution of the labor force between different occupations in 1950 and 1971.* The picture conveyed by the table is that outside of agriculture there are very few places to go. In 1950, more than 85 percent had to be absorbed in the rural sector. According to the census figures, this percentage in 1971 had fallen to 73,** but still an overwhelming majority of Haitians have to make their living as peasants or agricultural workers.

Table 2.15: Occupational Distribution of the Labor Force 1950 and 1971 (percent)

	1950	1971
Agriculture	85.3	73.3
Construction	0.6	0.9
Manufacturing	5.0	6.2
Commerce	3.6	10.1
Transport & communications	0.6	0.6
Services	4.7	5.2
Others	0.2	3.7
Total	100.0	100.0

Source: CONADEP (1976), Table A-6.

The concentration of the labor force in the agricultural sector in combination with the scarcity of capital and land has resulted in a labor-intensive type of agriculture. In Table 2.16 land/man ratios for Haiti and some other Latin American countries are presented. Among all the countries represented in the table Haiti has the lowest land/man ratio in its agriculture.† Even though the crude ratios in the table do not take into account that the work duration and the amount of work performed per unit of time might differ between various countries, these figures

---

*The table excludes those reported as unemployed (1950:40,000, 1971:100,000).
**We will come back to these figures in Chapter 5 and in the epilogue.
† The figures refer to the entire agricultural sector, not only to peasant agriculture.

still are a strong indication of the relative labor intensity of Haitian peasant agriculture.* To get a clearer picture of what exactly the high labor intensity implies, we must now take a look at how the most important agricultural operations are performed.

Table 2.16: Land/Man Ratios in Latin American Agriculture

Country	Year	Land/Man Ratio in Agriculture (hectares under cultivation per person in agriculture)
Haiti	1971	0.6
Mexico	1960	3.7
El Salvador	1961	1.0
Guatemala	1964	1.3
Nicaragua	1963	2.6
Dominican Republic	1960	1.2
Argentina	1960	13.8
Bolivia	1950	3.1
Brazil	1960	1.8
Chile	1965	3.7
Ecuador	1954	1.7
Paraguay	1961	2.2
Peru	1961	1.3
Venezuela	1961	2.4

Sources: Haiti: Cultivated area: IHS (1973), p. 40. Labor force in agriculture CONADEP (1976): Table A-6 (15 years or more). All other countries: *Statistical Abstract of Latin America* (1970), p. 191.

Agricultural Operations

The first tasks to be attended to during the agricultural cycle are the clearing and hoeing of the fields. This is done immediately before the rains come in spring and fall.

> If a field is to be made out of hitherto unworked land, or ground which has lain fallow for several years is to be cultivated again, the work is begun by cutting down the trees. The twigs are heaped preparatory to burning them, and the larger branches and the tree-trunks

---

*The appendix to this chapter discusses the possibility of disguised unemployment in the rural sector.

The Peasant Economy

are used to make fences. After the dried leaves and branches have been burned, the field is cleared of small brush, and is then ready for its initial hoeing, which, according to the crops to be planted, is sometimes delayed until some months later. Usually, however, after two or three rains have cooled and softened land that has been burned over, work continues on it.[124]

Clearing and hoeing is heavy work and is generally performed by men. The task of preparing the ground for sowing requires a concentrated effort during a comparatively short period of time and is therefore sometimes done with the aid of neighbors and friends, either in the traditional, collective work team known as the *coumbite*[125] or using other types of hired labor. The Métraux group has given a good description of a *coumbite* moving across a field:

> The team of workers, once on the scene of operations, clear the land in 'portions'....The farmers form rank with about a foot's distance between them, and, directed by the leaders, advance slowly or quickly, as the case may be, until the end of a 'portion' has been reached. When they all have arrived, they rest for a few moments, retrace their steps, form rank again and clear another 'portion' of the field.
>
> As the clearers go forward, throwing behind them the weeds they have hoed out, they kick away, more or less mechanically, the earth still adhering to the roots, so as to lay these bare and prevent the weeds taking hold again in the soil.[126]

When the field is cleared the weeds are picked up (usually by women) and piled for burning which then takes place, and when the rainy season sets in, the peasants begin to sow. Cereals and leguminous plants are put in holes or seed pockets dug with a hoe (on rocky ground with a pick or bill-hook). The digging is done by the men who are followed by the women who in turn drop the seeds into the holes and cover them with earth. Tubers, like manioc and sweet potatoes, are planted in earth mounds or ridges of about a foot in height.

Interplanting is the common practice. A given field usually carries more than one crop at the time. In the Marbial valley, 'maize and cowpeas are sown simultaneously over the greater part of a field, and millet will be added ten or fifteen days later. Sesame, which is sown in small quantities, is usually mixed with beans and maize, though not with millet.'[127] The same applies to other crops and other regions.[128] A single field may hold five or more different crops at the same time.[129] Once the seeds or plants are in the ground most of the care of the growing crops is left to nature. As a rule only one or two weedings (depending on the type of crop and on local customs) take place before the harvest.[130] Thus, coffee plantations are weeded only once, just before the harvest, to make the picking of the berries easier, and one single weeding is the general practice also as far as cotton is concerned. Pruning (e.g. of coffee or cocoa) seldom if ever takes place.*

Hence, the labor effort is not evenly distributed throughout the year but is concentrated in the periods of planting and harvesting. Harvesting is carried out entirely by hand with the aid of the simple hand tools at the disposal of the peasants. Tubers are unearthed using a hoe or a machete.** Corn, sorghum and beans are gathered by hand. Coffee beans should be picked selectively by hand so that only the red, ripe berries are harvested, but very often all the berries, ripe as well as unripe, are pulled down the branches with a single movement of the hand. Also the cocoa harvesting method is defective. The pods should be cut off carefully, but frequently this is not done. Instead the pods are pulled or twisted off, tearing away some of the eyes which should produce the next crop from the base of the stalks. Often *coumbites* have to be used during the harvest, so as to make sure that the crop is off the field and stored or sold before it is time to clear and plant the field again.

Fallow and Crop Rotation Practices

Few peasants have access to a land area which is large enough to permit any elaborate fallow practices. Only the more wealthy peasants are in a position to use this practice.[131] Otherwise the land is cultivated year after year under the intense system of mixed cropping until the soil is close to total exhaustion. Only then is it left fallow. As the Métraux team observed, this is a curative measure, not a preventive one.[132] This state of the art is not as much due to a lack of knowledge as to a relative scarcity of land:

---

*Métraux *et al.* tall the following incident: 'Most peasants are very averse [to] pruning their coffee shrubs. We heard of one who after having reconciled himself to doing so, began to tremble violently just as he was about to begin. After cutting the first branch, he collapsed in a semi-faint' (Métraux *et al.* (1951), note, p. 54).

**The digging up of tubers is a delicate operation, and great care must be taken not to injure the tubers.

The Peasant Economy

The peasants know that land showing signs of exhaustion must be rested. A poor farmer who has only one plot or a very small number of plots must exploit them until their yield falls to an impossibly low level. He must then become a tenant-farmer [or] a share-cropper ...so as to give his own land a rest. The large landowner is in quite a different situation. He can exploit different areas of land in turn, operating a rotation system so far as fallow land is concerned. The rhythm is naturally dictated by the richness or otherwise of the soil.[133]

Once the soil is exhausted, it is left fallow for two to five years, and then only serves as grazing land. No other measures to restore fertility (such as planting of leguminous crops) are usually taken, but the land is left to itself.[134]

Neither is crop rotation practiced systematically by small farmers. It has been observed that

the Haitian farmer does not practise any formal rotation of crops, but continues to plant a given crop in the same field until the harvest becomes perceptibly smaller than in former years, when a change is made to another type of produce. Later, when the same phenomenon is again observed, a third crop may be planted, but sooner or later the land is 'put to rest', in which case it is either allowed to lie fallow or is planted with cotton, which is not thought of in the same category as other crops, but is held to be a tree, and like other trees that of themselves spring up in a fallow field, is believed to give strength to the exhausted earth. A field of this kind remains outside cultivation as a 'fallen garden' for four or five years and the animals are allowed to enter freely and graze in it until it has become a 'new garden' again.[135]

This was written in the 1930s but is as true today as it was then. Peasants know that some plants, like manioc and corn, exhaust the soil and that others, like leguminous crops, restore its fertility, but this does not imply that any balanced crop rotation takes place. Rather, the primary consideration underlying existing crop rotation procedures is the need for the peasants to produce food for themselves and their families.

The above should have provided the reader with some insights into the production techniques employed by the Haitian peasants. The principal thesis in the present work is that the peasant sector is stagnating and even retrogressing in terms of its capacity to provide a living for the rural masses. One of the main causes is to be found in the lack of capacity for technological change in agriculture. The methods employed by today's peasants and the type of inputs among which they may choose very closely resemble those employed a century or more ago. In an economy characterized by population growth these methods have become outdated. As we will show in Chapters 3 and 9, the yields are too low to feed the population adequately. In an international perspective the efficiency of Haitian agriculture ranks low. Table 2.17 compares yield figures per hectare in Haiti and underdeveloped areas in general for a number of crops. In 50 percent of the cases presented the Haitian figures are lower than the averages for the Third World. The table actually understates the problem, however. It is only by also relating production capacity to the size of the rural population, as we will do in Chapter 3, that the significance of the inefficient production methods can be fully brought out. In any case, given this lack of efficiency it becomes important to analyze why the agricultural technology does not change. This is dealt with in Chapters 11 and 12.

Table 2.17: Yields per Hectare for Selected Crops 1972 (kilos per hectare)

Crop	Under-developed areas	Africa	Latin America	Near East	Far East	Asia	Haiti
Coffee	515	437	556	280	528	334	250
Cocoa	315	297	353	–	594	–	323
Sugar cane	50,186	57,517	52,900	89,906	44,880	66,553	59,322*
Cotton	801	452	1,089	1,819	549	935	242
Corn	1,225	1,091	1,333	2,336	965	2,640	1,076
Rice	1,783	1,326	1,719	3,753	1,779	3,038	2,118†
Sorghum	705	733	1,735	945	460	899	981
Millet	560	612	815	1,434	464	759	
Beans	447	414	627	1,314	281	701	520
Yams	9,539	9,669	11,352	3,000	4,357	–	5,000
Manioc	9,600	7,812	13,868	5,000	9,588	8,308	4,000

*The saccharine content of Haitian sugar cane is extremely low, however. According to Honorat (1974), pp. 91-3, 267-8, it is the lowest in the world.
†Estimé (1972), p. 37 gives a rice yield of 1,000-2,000 kilos/hectare.

Sources: Haiti: yams and manioc: Estimé (1972), p. 37, other crops: CONADEP (1976), Table A-13. Rest of table: FAO (1972), Tables 14, 16, 19-20, 26-8, 45, 68, 81-2.

Conclusions

This chapter has presented the basic facts of Haitian peasant agriculture. An extensive account of products, agrarian structure, inputs and cultivation practices has been given, which may be summarized in the following points:

1. The Haitian peasant sector is an economy where basically two different groups of outputs are produced: export products and subsistence crops. The most important export crop is coffee.

2. Peasant-owned family minifundia with an average size of 1 hectare dominate the agrarian structure. Latifundia and large-scale plantations are few in number and occupy a comparatively small percentage of the agricultural land. Hence, the patterns of exploitation of smallholders by large landowners, which are typical of Latin America and which are based on monopolization of farm land, are not found in Haiti.

3. Farm land is scarce due to high population pressure and due to an extremely rugged topography. Landholdings are generally not contiguous but scattered.

4. The use of capital inputs in the sector is negligible. Basically, the farm capital employed consists only of unimproved seeds and simple general-purpose hand tools.

5. Labor is an abundant factor of production. The participation ratios of children, old people and women are high. Since the employment opportunities outside the agricultural sector are very limited, almost 75 percent of the population is concentrated in rural areas.

6. The production techniques employed are simple and labor-intensive. Each plot as a rule carries several different crops at the same time. Work efforts are concentrated in the periods of planting and harvesting. The primitive methods employed result in low yields per hectare.

These conclusions should be kept in mind throughout the rest of the book. We must return to them in order to understand the hypothesis of Chapter 3: namely that rural per capita incomes are falling, in order to analyze the marketing process in Chapter 4, in order to see how the interaction between population pressure and production methods leads to erosion which progressively destroys the resource base of the agricultural sector (Chapter 5), in order to find out how the minifundia system developed and what effects this had on politics and government economic action (Chapters 6-8), in order to see why the quality of the human factor appears to have undergone few changes (Chapters 9-10) and finally, in order to analyze which structures and mechanisms that

82 *The Peasant Economy*

ban capital formation and technological progress from the Haitian countryside (Chapters 11-12).

Notes

1. Holly (1955), pp. 22-4. Cf. OEA (1972), pp. 470-4.
2. OEA (1972), p. 468.
3. Holly (1955), p. 18.
4. Ibid., pp. 18, 20. Cf. OEA (1972), pp. 460, 468.
5. OEA (1972), pp. 558 ff.
6. Ibid., p. 468.
7. Moral (1961), p. 110.
8. Cf. De Young (1959), p.2; Moral (1961) pp. 200-1; Beghin, Fougère & King (1970), p. 43, and Rotberg & Clague (1971), pp. 274-6.
9. Cf. Mintz (1966:1), p. xxvii.
10. Descriptions of the export crops can be found in Folsom (1954), pp. 195-245; Holly (1955), Chapter 4; Wood (1955), pp. 25-31; Street (1960), pp. 234-337; Moral (1961), Chapter 12; Moore (1972), Chapter 12, and OEA (1972), pp. 618 ff. Cf. also Gates (1959:2), Gates (1959:3), US/AID (1974), Fatton (1975), JWK (1976:1), JWK (1976:2), JWK (1976:3) and JWK (1976:4) for studies of individual products.
11. Moral (1961), pp. 262-3.
12. Rotberg & Clague (1971), p. 29.
13. See Chapter 6.
14. Moral (1961), p. 276. Cf. OEA (1972), p. 623.
15. Moral (1961), p. 282.
16. OEA (1972), p. 620.
17. Ibid., p. 622.
18. Moral (1961), p. 306.
19. Cf. Rotberg & Clague (1971), pp. 284-6 and Holly (1955), p. 80.
20. OEA (1972), p. 625.
21. Moral (1961), p. 311.
22. E.g. Moore (1972), p. 155.
23. OEA (1972), p. 626.
24. Honorat (1974), p. 96; JWK (1976:4), p. 46.
25. Descriptions of the subsistence crops may be found in Métraux *et al.* (1951), pp. 39-53; Folsom (1954), pp. 245-53; Holly (1955), pp. 90-124; Wood (1955), pp. 31-4; Street (1960), pp. 231-7; Moral (1961), pp. 200-3; Moore (1972), pp. 157-61 and OEA (1972), pp. 627-30.
26. Métraux *et al.* (1951), p. 48.
27. Pierre-Charles (1965), pp. 85-6. Cf. also Moral (1961), p. 178.
28. Moral (1961), p. 179.
29. Ibid., p. 181.
30. Ibid.
31. IHS (1975:1), p. 41.
32. Saint Clair & Dauphin (1975), p. 40.
33. See e.g. Griffin (1969), Chapter 1 and Feder (1971), passim, for good accounts of the situation in most Latin American countries.
34. Cf. Pierre-Charles (1965), pp. 87-8.
35. Métraux *et al.* (1951), p.17.
36. Moral (1959), p. 52.
37. IHS (1975:1), p. 41.

38. Saint Clair & Dauphin (1975), p. 40.
39. Métraux et al. (1951), p. 19.
40. IHS (1975:1), p. 41.
41. Saint Clair & Dauphin (1975), p. 40.
42. Moral (1961), p. 183.
43. Ibid., pp. 183-5.
44. IHS (1973), p. 39.
45. IHS (1973), p. 40.
46. Pierre-Charles (1965), p. 99.
47. Zuvekas (1978), note, p. 27.
48. Ibid., p. 27.
49. Pierre-Charles (1965), p. 95.
50. Wood (1961), p. 10.
51. OEA (1972), p. 630.
52. Mintz (1966:1), pp. xxvi-xxvii.
53. Herskovits (1971), pp. 131, 134, 135.
54. For a sample see Herskovits (1971), p. 131; Simpson (1940), p. 515; Leyburn (1966), p. 199; Métraux et al. (1951), p. 30; Hubert (1950), p. 11; Moral (1959), pp. 180-3; Moral (1961), pp. 318-24; Courlander (1960), p. 115; Courlander (1966), p. 6; Logan (1968), p. 23; Mintz (1966:1), p. xxvi; Despeignes (n.d.), p. 74; Wingfield (1966), p. 39; Wood (1963), p. 21; CIAP (1968:1), p. 11; Rotberg & Clague (1971), pp. 12-13; OAS (1972), p. 612; Anglade (1974), p. 14.
55. Population figures: IHS (n.d.:2). Area figures: IHS (1971), p. 6.
56. IHS (1973), p. 1.
57. OEA (1972), pp. 552-5 and Carte 3: Sols et vocations de la terre.
58. Ibid., p. 554.
59. Moral (1959), p. 6.
60. IHS (1973), p. 1.
61. Cf. ibid., p. VI.
62. Cf. Métraux et al. (1951), p. 2.
63. Cf. Lebeau (1974), p. 12.
64. Ibid., p. 11; Wood (1963), pp. 15-16; Dorville & Dauphin (1974), pp. 23-4.
65. Cf. Reynolds (1975), p. 4.
66. Lebeau (1974), p. 57. Cf. Holly (1955), pp. 80-82 and Rotberg & Clague (1971), pp. 284-6 for accounts of failure to introduce new varieties.
67. OEA (1972), p. 631.
68. Moral (1961), p. 190.
69. Dorville (1975:2), p. 17.
70. CONADEP (1968-69), p. 40.
71. Lebeau (1974), p. 41.
72. Brummit & Culp (n.d.), p. 11.
73. Cf. OEA (1972), pp. 447-52, for the distribution of rainfall in different locations.
74. See also ibid., p. 455
75. McPherson & Johnston (1967), p. 189.
76. Moral (1961), p. 199.
77. Ibid., p. 113.
78. For a more detailed description and for summaries for different regions see OEA (1972), pp. 490-513. The extent of groundwater resources is largely unknown, however.
79. P & D no. 2, pp. 20-21.
80. Cf. OEA (1972), pp. 571-2.
81. Moral (1961), p. 277; Holly (1955), p. 59.
82. Holly (1955), p. 72.
83. Ibid., pp. 76 ff.

84. Moral (1961), p. 307.
85. Holly (1955), p. 103.
86. Ibid., p. 108.
87. Ibid., pp. 123-4.
88. Métraux et al. (1951), pp. 60-61.
89. Holly (1955), pp. 103-4. Cf. Métraux et al. (1951), p. 40 and Schaedel (1962), p. 79.
90. Métraux et al. (1951), p. 41.
91. Some improved storage techniques are discussed in Dorville (1974).
92. Direct data are sadly lacking, but cf. the indications in Brummit & Culp (n.d.), p. 25 and Duplan (1975:2), p. 60.
93. Métraux et al. (1951), p. 86.
94. Wood (1955), p. 234.
95. OEA (1972), p. 631.
96. According to Beghin, Fougère & King (1970), p. 80, the average outlay on food in rural areas in the late sixties was 0.45 gourde per day and person.
97. Cf. also Latortue (1969), p. 504: 0.40-0.50 gourde per 13-14 hour day.
98. Dorville & Dauphin (1974), p. 26. Cf. also Laguerre (1975), p. 33 who gives a figure of 1.50 gourdes per day.
99. The cost of living index for Port-au-Prince was 120.4 in 1969 (IHS (1971), p. 422) and 215.8 in 1974 (IHS (1976), p. 32).
100. Petersen (1969), pp. 67-8.
101. Myrdal (1968), pp. 1014-15.
102. Cf. Turnham & Jaeger (1971), pp. 23-5.
103. Saint Surin (1962), p. 11.
104. CONADEP (1976), Tables A-1, A-2.
105. Courlander (1960), pp. 113-14. Cf. Wood (1955), pp. 246-7.
106. IHS (1971), p. 52; Brand (1965), pp. 25-6.
107. Cf. Saint Surin (1962), pp. 4-5.
108. République d'Haïti (1975), p. 31.
109. IHS (1971), p. 52; Brand (1965), p. 26; République d'Haïti (1975), p. 31.
110. Leyburn (1966), p. 196.
111. See Chapter 4, for an analysis of their activities.
112. Brand (1965), pp. 30-31.
113. République d'Haïti (1975), p. 31.
114. Cf. Hartman (1977), pp. 350-51. For more figures regarding female participation ratios, see ILO (1958), p. 256 and Turnham & Jaeger (1971), p. 24.
115. Cf. Leyburn (1966), pp. 201-6.
116. Especially marketing is often dominated by women. For some African cases see the articles in Bohannan & Dalton (1962).
117. Mintz (1960:1), pp. 112, 114.
118. Leyburn (1966), p. 202.
119. Ibid., pp. 202-3.
120. Cf. ibid., pp. 203-6 for a sample of quotations.
121. See Chapter 8 for a more detailed account.
122. Leyburn (1966), p. 205.
123. Cf. ibid., p. 206; Courlander (1960), p. 113; Moore (1972), p. 143.
124. Herskovits (1971), p. 69.
125. The *coumbite* is described and analyzed in Chapter 3.
126. Métraux et al. (1951), pp. 57-8.
127. Ibid., p. 59.
128. Moral (1961), pp. 196-7; Street (1960), pp. 225-6; Dorville (1975:1), pp. 23-5.
129. Métraux et al. (1951), p. 65; Dorville (1975:1), p. 24; Street (1960). p. 226.

130. OEA (1972), p. 631.
131. Moral (1961), p. 194.
132. Métraux *et al.* (1951), p. 65.
133. Ibid., p. 62.
134. OEA (1972), p. 631.
135. Herskovits, p. 69. Cf. Wood (1955), p. 241.

APPENDIX: Disguised Unemployment

The Haitian active population is heavily concentrated in agriculture. This immediately raises one of the most controversial issues in the field of economic development: Is there disguised unemployment in Haitian agriculture, i.e. can any part of the rural labor force be removed without any decrease in agricultural output?[1]

Antonio Giles has made an attempt to quantify the magnitude of disguised unemployment in the rural sector. He assumes that 300 days per year constitutes full employment for a person.[2] With a rural labor force of 1,700,000 persons[3] the total supply of agricultural labor is 510,000,000 man-days. Against this we have a total demand of 108,808,300 man-days,[4] which leads Giles to conclude that the total agricultural production could be carried out with approximately 20 percent of the available labor supply.

This estimate cannot be taken at face value, however, since it rests upon the tacit assumption that there are no seasonal variations in agriculture.* This is of course not a legitimate assumption. Seasonal idleness is inherent in agriculture. The production process in itself involves certain peak periods to be followed by periods of less intense activity.

The agricultural cycle in Haiti may be said to start in February when the land is prepared for the first round of sowing which takes place before the spring rains in April. The summer months of June and July constitute a less busy period with harvesting of subsistence crops that were sown or planted in March and April on tè cho. In August and September the land is once more prepared and sown before the autumn rains. The end of the fall again is dedicated to harvesting food crops on tè cho and somewhat later on tè frèt. The coffee harvest starts to gain momentum in October and November (on higher altitudes).** The

---

*It also implicitly assumes that it is possible to employ the excess rural labor force in the non-agricultural sectors and that the 20 percent remaining in agriculture would actually be willing to work 300 days a year in agriculture, both of which are doubtful assumptions.
**Already towards the end of August the coffee harvest starts in the lowlands. There, coffee blooms only once, in January. Practically all the coffee ripens at the same time so that the harvest becomes concentrated in the months of September and October. At higher altitudes, except in January, coffee also blooms in March and July which leads to an extension of the harvest from August to April. During this period coffee may be collected two or three times.

harvest of other cash crops starts in December with cotton in the central region and sugar cane in the plains. The winter months, finally, constitute another period of comparative rest from agricultural work. Regional and local differences in climate affect the exact timing of sowing, planting and harvesting, respectively.[5]

To a certain extent, the seasonal variations in agricultural employment are reduced by diversifying the structure of output and by supplementing agriculture with animal husbandry and gathering activities:

> As can be seen from the annual cycles of crops [the peasant] has enough variety to be either harvesting or planting or clearing at any time of the year...The devices resorted to by farmers to 'keep busy' are impressive. We have seen the four rice crop rotation in the Torbeck area, as well as the use of short and long corn harvest. The alternation of the bean crops and the root crops also follow rather sophisticated patterns. In dry areas the farmers tend to charcoal production, goat raising, artisanry and gathering firewood. Gathering in Haiti is a field of economic activity largely underestimated. Aside from the various medicinal leaves that are the pharmacopeia of the rural area, the peasants gather Spanish moss for stuffing mattresses, mangrove for tanning, certain tree saps for glue and a varied list of plants and leaves for fibre making that can readily be turned to extra cash.[6]

Artisan crafts are widespread throughout the countryside. As a rule one encounters a diversified artisanry based on traditional techniques. Some regions, however, are more specialized, and their products are sold throughout the country.[7] Other complementary occupations are fishing (along the coast) and retail trade, the latter mainly being pursued by women. Peasant incomes rarely derive just from agriculture but should rather be viewed as the result of an extensive list of activities. According to Paul Moral, the Haitian peasant is always prepared to leave his farming activities if a 'job' opportunity should present itself.[8]

As can be seen from Table A2.1 most of the labor force in agriculture consists of family labor. Regular hired labor is a phenomenon that is largely limited to the big, export-oriented plantations. Thus the Haitian peasant most of the time is aided only by his wife and children. During the peak seasons when field work becomes more intensive, however, the demand for labor may increase:

> for this purpose he must have considerable manpower at his disposal

at the necessary periods, which recur several times during the year. He must also overcome an obstacle which is characteristic of tropical countries: shortage of time. The rainy seasons are brief, and the various phases of agricultural work follow each other in rapid succession. Clearing operations, for instance, are confined to a relatively short period, the beginning and end of which vary from year to year. If the ground is cleared too early, the weeds will come back in force; if clearing is too long delayed, the heavy downpours of the rainy season will hamper the work, and the peasant will lose valuable weeks...The more rapidly the peasant works, the greater his likelihood of obtaining a good crop, for 'the spring' may last only a short time and give a bad yield unless the plants enjoy the two months' rain that they need.[9]

Viewed against the seasonal pattern of Haitian agriculture and against the host of complementary activities that support agricultural incomes during the slack periods, it is clear that the Giles estimate of an 80 percent excess labor force in the rural sector must be revised downwards. The seasonal variations must not be underestimated. What needs to be undertaken is a study that, month by month, calculates the need for labor in agriculture and in complementary activities in the countryside.[10] Only when such a study has been made will it be possible to state how much, if any, of the existing rural labor force can actually be removed, given the willingness of the remaining workers to reorganize and increase their work efforts and given that a surplus could actually be employed outside of agriculture.

Table A2.1: Distribution of the Agricultural Labor Force 1950 (percent)

Cultivators with hired labor	1.4
Cultivators without hired labor	44.1
Family labor	48.4
Labor hired by private enterprises	5.9
Labor hired by government or other official bodies	0.1
No indication	0.1
Total	100.0

Source: Latortue (1969), p. 500.

Appendix

Notes

1. For a survey of the general discussion of disguised unemployment see Sen (1975) especially Chapter 4 and the literature referred to there.
2. Giles (1973), p. 6. For a survey of other estimates, see Zuvekas (1978), pp. 78-86.
3. Ibid.
4. Ibid., p. 14. For the calculations see pp. 4 and 111.
5. Cf. Métraux *et. al.* (1951), pp. 33-4; Moral (1961), p. 198; Herskovits (1971), pp. 76-7; Schaedel (1962), p. 39 and Laurent & Alphonse (1956), p. 15, for agricultural calendars.
6. Schaedel (1962), p. 78. Cf. Métraux *et al.* (1951), pp. 188 ff.
7. Cf. Cantave (1969), pp. 198-9.
8. Moral (1961), p. 207. See also Pierre-Charles (1965), p. 81.
9. Métraux *et al.* (1951), p. 67.
10. For such a study, dealing with southern Italy, see Rosenstein-Rodan (1957).

3 THE CUMULATIVE PROCESS: FALLING RURAL INCOMES

Chapter 2 introduced some of the most important characteristics of Haitian peasant agriculture viewed mainly from a static perspective. In the present chapter we will widen the scope so as to adopt a dynamic view. The framework employed will be one that has been frequently and successfully used in development economics: that of circular and cumulative causation. With the aid of this framework the central thesis of the study will be presented: that the forces at work in the peasant sector generate a tendency for per capita incomes to stagnate and fall in agriculture.

After some general observations on the nature and principles of cumulative causation at the beginning of the chapter, we will go on to formulate our hypothesis and to give some empirical evidence in support of the view that rural per capita incomes are falling.

Interdependence and Cumulative Causation in Economic Analysis

Perhaps the finest contribution of the neoclassical school of economists was that it drew attention to the fact that all parts of an economic system are intimately and interdependently related to each other, and that in an interdependent system it is generally not possible to separate causes and effects rigorously. Interdependent systems have to be analyzed by methods capable of dealing with simultaneity. Neoclassical theorizing and analysis, however, was by and large limited to statics and comparative statics, i.e. to the investigation of equilibria and displacement of equilibria leading to new equilibria. Little attention was paid to disequilibrium situations, with one significant exception: Knut Wicksell, who in a celebrated passage in his *Lectures on Political Economy* showed how a self-sustained cumulative process leading to changes in the price level could be created by a discrepancy between the 'natural' and 'money' rates of interest.[1]

Wicksell's contribution inspired Gunnar Myrdal, who after a criticism of Wicksell's cumulative process in the thirties[2] put the principle to work in a radically different context: the analysis of the racial issue in the United States.[3] In *An American Dilemma* Myrdal vigorously attacked the notion of stable equilibrium and stressed the need for emphasizing dynamic social causation chains. Three different factors

91

interact to create a racial problem:

1. the standard of living of the black community,
2. black standards of intelligence, ambition, health, education, decency, manners and morals,
3. discrimination by whites.

White prejudice and discrimination lead to low economic standards among blacks which in turn result in deficient health conditions, education, ambitions etc., and this, finally, reinforces the patterns of prejudice and discrimination. If we assume that the three components (accidentally) balance each other in an equilibrium, a change in any of the components will lead to changes in the other two which in turn feed back and reinforce the original change, so that the entire system cumulatively moves in one direction or the other. This feedback is the essential feature of a cumulative process. The equilibrium position described is inherently instable. Any random shocks to the system trigger off movements *away from* the equilibrium, and there are no forces in the system which automatically ensure that the original equilibrium is reinstated.

The cumulative movements may be either upward or downward. Any improvement in the standard of living will lead to positive changes in health, education, manners etc., which in turn reduce white prejudices etc., while a decreasing material standard of living will set a downward process in motion. A corollary of this reasoning is that it becomes possible in principle to change a downward (negatively valued) process into an upward one by altering any one of the three components. A rational policy, however, cannot always rely on affecting single variables only, but the efforts should often be spread (between the factors and over time) to achieve the maximum impact on the system.

Circular, cumulative causation chains constitute one of the methodological cornerstones of Myrdal's works.[4] The analysis and policy prescriptions of *An American Dilemma* anticipated the development debate of the 1950s, when a number of authors popularized the notion of vicious circles in underdevelopment and when the ideas of balanced growth were in vogue. Various authors stressed the interaction — with or without cumulation — of a number of factors which kept the standard of living in underdeveloped economies low.[5] Myrdal himself expanded his ideas and finally presented his synthesis of them in *Asian Drama*.[6]

From the methodological viewpoint, *Asian Drama* presents an

The Cumulative Process: Falling Rural Incomes

important novel feature as compared to *An American Dilemma*. The social system, as described in the former, is disaggregated, and analyzed in a manner which explicitly takes into account the possibility that certain forces exist which may counteract the cumulative process or preclude its generation altogether. In *Asian Drama,* Myrdal distinguishes six components of the social system:

1. output and incomes,
2. conditions of production,
3. levels of living,
4. attitudes toward life and work,
5. institutions,
6. policies.

The basic assumption is that the causal relationships between these components or conditions are circular and unidirectional. When one of them changes, the rest of them change in the same direction as well, as a result of circular and cumulative interaction between the six categories.[7] This is the same assumption as that made in *An American Dilemma*. The assumption needs some qualifications, however, for it might lead to the belief that social systems regularly move in one direction or the other as a result of unidirectional cumulation. Myrdal is very careful to point out that this is not the case — and it is here that *Asian Drama* differs from the earlier work — for 'The great bulk of historical, anthropological, and sociological evidence and thought suggests that social stability and equilibrium is the norm and that all societies, and underdeveloped societies in particular, possess institutions of a strongly stabilizing character.'[8]

Attempts by development planners to start an upward cumulative process may prove abortive because counteracting forces which are strong enough to wipe out the positive impact may be generated. These forces may arise either spontaneously — without relation to the efforts of the planners — or as a direct result of the policy changes. In addition, it is probable that all development efforts may have to face a number of 'thresholds' which must be overcome if a positive, upward cumulative movement is not to lose its momentum at an early stage. Small changes may not be sufficient to set the social system in sustained motion towards the desired goals. Some type of 'big push' may be necessary. Mutual causation is not enough to trigger off a cumulative process. It is only when the reinforcing feedback effects are strong enough to overcome thresholds, autonomous counteracting forces, or such counteracting changes that are generated by the primary change itself that actual cumulation in the same direction as the initial change results.

A cumulative process, once it has been set in motion, will usually not go on for ever, but sooner or later the counteracting forces will become strong enough to slow the process down and bring it to a halt. This fact is illustrated in Figure 3.1. Let us, for the sake of simplicity, assume that there are only two sets of interacting factors. One set contains everything which is included in what somewhat vaguely may be labeled the 'level of development' or the 'standard of living'.[9] The other set contains all factors that promote development or underdevelopment. Ideally, it should be possible to construct an index of all the factors in the second set to obtain a net excess of development-promoting factors over those promoting underdevelopment. In practice, this is of course a formidable task, but for the sake of reasoning we will in the following assume that we have such an index of the 'forces' as well as one for the standard of living.[10]

Figure 3.1

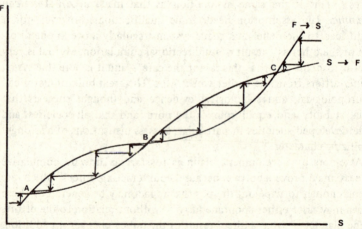

Figure 3.1 portrays the interaction between the net standard-raising forces and the standard of living itself. On the vertical axis we have the net standard-raising forces, and on the horizontal axis we measure the standard of living. The diagram contains two curved lines which show how the forces and the standard of living interact. The F → S curve portrays the influence of the standard-raising forces on the standard of living, and the S → F curve indicates how the standard of living influences the forces. Both these relationships are assumed to be positive,

The Cumulative Process: Falling Rural Incomes

i.e. the higher the level of the forces, the higher the standard of living, and vice versa.

The two curves intersect each other three times, yielding three equilibrium points: two which are stable (A and C) and one which is unstable (B). This may be seen in the following way. At all points to the left of the F →S curve the standard of living is lower than the standard which would be generated by the level of the forces at the point in question. Hence, the standard of living must rise, which in terms of the diagram signifies a rightward movement. By the same token, any point to the right of the F → S curve indicates a higher standard of living than the one compatible with the level of the forces. Hence, the standard of living must fall. The same reasoning applies to the S → F curve. Points above the curve indicate a level of the forces that is too high given the standard of living, and points below the curve are positions where the forces fall short of the level corresponding to the standard of living in the points.

Given the above facts, the two curves interact. If we begin to the left of point A we find that any departure from A will generate a rightward-upward movement back to A. Similarly, a move to the right from A will be counteracted by a leftward-downward movement, which re-establishes the former equilibrium. Hence, A is stable. In the same fashion we find that point C is also stable. B, on the other hand, is unstable, since a movement to the left from the equilibrium will trigger off a cumulative process which (if left to itself) will not end until point A has been reached, while a movement to the right will lead to an upward-rightward spiral ending in a new equilibrium at C.

Experience teaches up that upward or downward cumulative processes cannot go on indefinitely. To quote Paul Streeten:

> It is not difficult to think of reasons why the sensitivity of both functions should be low for both low and high values, and high for intermediate values. At low levels [S] will not have much effect on F because tradition has a strong hold, the forces of resistance are strong, it will be difficult to squeeze out even a moderate investment ratio, the market will be small, ignorance and imperfections will prevail, etc. F in turn will have small effects on [S] because population growth will wipe out a large part of any increase in income per head. Similarly, one may speculate, that, at high values, people get tired of the effort required by growth, the third generation has less vigour, opposition and destructive criticisms grow...For intermediate values responsiveness will be high, both because the obstacles to development

will have been overcome successfully, particularly population pressure, and because the higher income level makes it much easier to do all kinds of things conducive to faster development.[11]

This necessarily leaves us with the multiple equilibrium situation in Figure 3.1. Presumably, point A represents some kind of quasi-Malthusian equilibrium with a standard of living at or very near the biological subsistence level. If the per capita income falls short of A, death rates will increase due to starvation and the equilibrium at A will be restored, and if income rises above A, forces like those indicated by the quotation from Streeten above or other mechanisms may come into play and push incomes back to the subsistence level. The transition from B to C as well as C itself are also covered by the Streeten quotation. It is far harder to think of any suitable description of the unstable equilibrium point B. What perhaps first springs to mind is the Schultzian traditional society:

> There is...a large class of poor agricultural communities in which people have been doing the same things for generations. Changes in products and factors have not crowded in on them. For them neither consumption nor production is studded with new gadgets. The factors of production on which they depend are known through long experience and are in this sense 'traditional'. While the communities in this class differ appreciably one from another in the quantity of factors they possess, in what they grow, in the arts of cultivation, and culturally, they have one attribute in common: they have for years not experienced any significant alterations in the state of the arts. This means simply that farmers of this class continue year after year to cultivate the same type of land, sow the same crops, use the same techniques of production, and bring the same skills to bear in agricultural production...
>
> It should be made clear that not all poor agricultural communities have the economic attributes of traditional agriculture. Some are excluded on the ground that they have been subject to change. Any community that has experienced a significant alteration to which it has not had time to adjust fully is excluded. When a new road or railroad is built, as a rule it takes some years for the communities affected to adapt to it. The economic routine of the affected communities is also disturbed by a new large dam, irrigation canals, structures to control floods and to reduce soil erosion. A serious adversity of nature — a flood or a drought followed by famine — can

be a source of disequilibrium. Some poor agricultural communities must be excluded because they have been subject to large political changes, for example by partition, by recruitment of many men into the armed services, or by the destruction of both human and non-human resources by war. Large changes in relative prices of products because of outside developments affecting the terms of trade can also upset the quiet economic life of particular communities. In modern times the most pervasive force disturbing the equilibrium of agricultural communities is the advance in knowledge useful in agricultural production.[12]

These are tremendous requirements which are not likely to be fulfilled in many societies. Still, one could perhaps visualize some kind of (inherently unstable) equilibrium in those societies that have not yet experienced any population explosion, where land is plentiful enough to permit cultivation to expand with constant techniques as the population grows, where the rate of erosion is not yet excessive, where the contacts with the outer world are few, and where production is concentrated on food and other subsistence products. This type of economy may be a candidate for unstable equilibrium, which is easily disrupted by population growth, increased erosion, integration into a larger national or international economy, etc.

The Hypothesis

Stagnating or falling real per capita income is a common feature in the less developed world. Table 3.1 lists 31 countries which all experienced negative growth rates during some part of the 1950-74 period. In a majority of these countries agriculture is the most important sector, both in terms of employment and in terms of contribution to GDP. If we look at Table 3.2 we also find that the stagnation and decline of the agricultural sector appears to have been behind at least part of the overall decline in many countries. The table also shows something else, namely that no less than 85 out of the 111 underdeveloped countries for which data were available for the 1961-74 period saw their domestic production of foodstuffs fall in per capita terms during either the 1960s or the 1970s. Many of the comparatively high rates for the 1970-74 period can be explained by the worldwide drought during this period, but even if we restrict our attention to the 1960s we find that food production per capita declined in 49 underdeveloped countries. In some cases this decline was due to increased industrialization and deliberate changes in the structure of output, but for many countries a more likely explanation is the stagnation or decline of the production capacity of the agricultural sector in combination with rapid population growth.

Table 3.1: Underdeveloped Countries with Declining Real Per Capita Incomes 1950-74

Country	Annual average growth of GDP per capita† (percent)		
	1950-60	1960-70	1970-74
Uruguay			− 1.7
Bolivia	− 2.1		
Chile			− 0.6
Honduras			− 0.1
Haiti		− 1.6	
Barbados			− 1.7
Algeria		− 0.8	
Morocco	− 0.8		
Sudan		− 1.0	− 0.4
Burundi	− 3.4	− 5.0	
Chad		− 2.4	− 3.8
Madagascar			− 1.0
Rwanda	− 2.0		− 0.9
Somalia		− 0.4	
Zaire		− 0.1	
Central African Republic		− 1.0	− 0.1
Cameroon	− 0.5		
Mali		− 2.0	− 4.6
Niger			− 6.0
Senegal		− 1.4	− 2.0
Uganda		− 4.5	− 0.5
Equatorial Guinea			− 6.1
Ghana		− 0.8	
Guinea		− 1.0	
Cyprus			− 0.1
Syria	− 0.4		
Democratic Yemen		− 5.5	− 1.7
Bangladesh	− 0.6		− 0.5
India			− 0.8
Laos	− 0.4		
South Vietnam			− 0.8

†Only negative values are included in the table.

Source: UNCTAD (1976), pp. 342-5.

Figures dealing directly with rural per capita incomes are much harder to obtain. Statistics appear to be available only for a few countries. We will not attempt to be systematic here, but a few examples will have to

Table 3.2: Underdeveloped Countries with Declining Food Production Per Capita 1961-74

Country	1961-70	1970-74	Country	1961-70	1970-74
Argentina		− 0.2	Kenya		− 2.2
Mexico		− 1.8	Uganda		− 3.3
Paraguay	− 0.1	− 2.5	Tanzania		− 2.6
Uruguay		− 1.3	Angola		− 1.4
Chile		− 3.4	Equatorial		
Colombia	− 0.4	− 0.3	Guinea	− 1.2	−11.1
Ecuador	− 0.2	− 4.7	Ethiopia		− 3.1
Peru		− 3.9	Ghana	− 0.4	− 0.7
El Salvador	− 0.1		Guinea		− 3.2
Guatemala		− 0.5	Lesotho	− 1.4	
Honduras		− 1.1	Liberia	− 0.8	
Nicaragua		− 2.7	Nigeria	− 1.4	− 4.8
Cuba	− 0.3	− 3.9	Reunion	− 1.6	
Dominican			Sierra Leone		− 0.2
Republic	− 0.9		Rhodesia	− 1.7	
Haiti	− 1.1		Cyprus		− 0.4
Panama		− 0.7	Iran		− 1.1
Puerto Rico	− 3.6	− 3.2	Iraq		− 0.5
Barbados	− 0.2	− 4.6	Jordan	− 8.5	
Guyana	− 0.1	− 0.1	Syria	− 2.9	
Trinidad			Yemen	− 3.8	
and Tobago		− 0.4	Democratic Yemen	− 0.4	
Guadeloupe	− 2.1	− 3.4	Afghanistan	− 0.6	
Jamaica	− 1.2	− 0.5	Indonesia	− 0.3	
Martinique	− 2.7		Philippines	− 0.1	
Surinam		− 0.6	Bangladesh	− 0.3	− 1.7
Algeria	− 1.9	− 4.5	Burma	− 0.8	− 0.9
Morocco		− 3.5	Cambodia		−26.3
Tunisia	− 0.4		Hong Kong	− 4.1	− 4.9
Egypt		− 1.2	India	− 0.1	− 2.0
Sudan		− 0.4	South Korea		− 1.4
Benin		− 0.6	Laos		− 1.0
Chad	− 2.2	−11.5	Nepal	− 1.0	− 2.3
Madagascar		− 1.8	Pakistan		− 1.0
Rwanda		− 4.6	South Vietnam	− 1.5	
Togo		− 8.9	Sri Lanka	− 0.3	− 0.6
Central African			British Solomon		
Republic	− 1.3	− 0.3	Islands	− 1.1	− 4.0
Congo	− 4.0		Fiji		− 6.1
Cameroon		− 0.6	French Polynesia	− 3.5	− 9.1
Mali	− 0.9	− 9.1	New Hebrides	− 0.9	− 6.5
Mauritania	− 0.1	−11.4	Tonga	− 1.1	
Niger		− 9.7	North Korea	− 0.5	
Senegal	− 2.4	− 1.3	Mongolia	− 3.7	
Upper Volta		−12.6	North Vietnam	− 1.9	− 0.2

†Only negative values are included in the table.
Source: UNCTAD (1976), pp. 378-82.

suffice. For example, rural incomes appear to have fallen in Pakistan during the 1950s, in the Peruvian Sierra and in Argentina during the latter half of the decade,[13] and in Java in the late 1960s.[14] Presumably, a number of the other countries included in Table 3.2 have experienced similar developments.

The main thesis of the present study is that one of these countries is Haiti. In 1963, Juan Bosch, then president of the Dominican Republic, coined the term 'haitianization' for the process whereby the development of some countries in [Latin]America had come to a halt and [the countries] after a short stagnation had begun to retrogress.'[15] Bosch was thinking in broader terms than those of just the agricultural sector, but his statement fits agriculture well. *The Haitian peasant sector is caught in a downward process of circular cumulative causation which slowly leads the standard of living to deteriorate in rural areas.* The theory which was outlined in the preceding section should be eminently applicable to the Haitian case. In terms of Figure 3.1 the peasant sector should be somewhere between points B and A heading towards what may turn out to be some type of Malthusian equilibrium in A as a result of the interaction between a number of forces which act so as to depress the standard of living in the sector. The task of this book is to identify these forces and analyze how they interact as well as to identify possible counteracting forces which may slow the process down and, if possible to find out something about the relative strength of these forces and the forces of the cumulative process itself.

The existence of a process of circular causation in the Haitian economy was first noted by Gérard Pierre-Charles in 1965. Pierre-Charles presents the economic relationships shown in Figure 3.2. However, these relationships are derived from one of the standard textbooks of development economics and are only indirectly based upon empirical investigation of the Haitian economy.[16]

Pierre-Charles also, from a Marxist position, criticizes the idea that circular causation of the type indicated by Figure 3.2 should constitute the main obstacle to Haitian development. He stresses that one has to add, 'outside the realm of pure economics, a variety of social, political, and cultural relations; all of which depend on the precapitalist structure of the economy.'[17] It is precisely this precapitalist mode of production 'reinforced by the ties of imperialist penetration in the core of the Haitian economy,'[18] which, according to Pierre-Charles, ultimately conditions the structure of circular causation illustrated in Figure 3.2.[19]

A second, independent interpretation of the Haitian society in terms of circular causation or vicious circles has been made by Roland

Wingfield. In Wingfield's view the factors responsible for Haitian underdevelopment are that

> historically the country never got off the ground; ecologically it suffers from mediocre resources and overpopulation; culturally it presents a picture of archaic social institutions on one side and anarchy on the other; and with respect to the mentality factor, the Haitian personality has adjusted to the climate of insecurity and by doing so has reinforced dysfunctional elements in the social system.[20]

Wingfield takes a broad perspective and analyzes all the elements included in the quotation. Very many aspects of the Haitian society are covered. However, the approach is basically sociological. The emphasis is on the social and political system, and the economy is not dealt with in much detail.

Figure 3.2

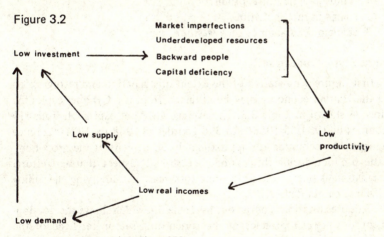

Source: Pierre-Charles (1965), p. 252.

A third work which mentions the existence of vicious circles in Haiti is that of Robert I. Rotberg and Christopher K. Clague:

> Haiti has for long been caught in a vicious circle of poverty; she stagnated not only because she was too poor to save or because population growth automatically absorbed increases in real income. Rather, Haiti failed to save because the quality of her government was poor, and, in turn, the extent of Haiti's poverty impeded the

development of political institutions capable of maximizing the potentialities for economic growth.[21]

Neither the Rotberg-Clague book nor the works of Pierre-Charles or Wingfield use the notion of circular cumulative causation systematically. The fact that such mechanisms may exist is noted, but the analysis is not explicitly cast in these terms. Besides, Wingfield, and to a lesser degree Pierre-Charles and Rotberg and Clague basically analyze a static vicious circle rather than a cumulative process proper.

In Chapter 5 we will discuss cumulation explicitly to explain how the standard of living in rural districts is depressed by soil erosion. Before we do that, however, we will present some primary factual evidence to indicate that rural per capita incomes and living standards are slowly deteriorating. This evidence is found under the following three headings:

1. trends in agricultural production,
2. trends in rural nutrition,
3. changing character of the *coumbite*.

Agricultural Production

A first, indirect indication of the extent of stagnation and retrogression in the Haitian economy may be obtained from the GDP per capita figures, as shown in Table 3.3. The average GDP per capita fell from 419 gourdes in 1954/55-1958/9 to 396 gourdes in 1968/69-1971/72. Since agriculture accounted for approximately 50 percent of the gross domestic product during this period, one should suspect that agricultural stagnation is one of the most important reasons underlying the falling GDP per capita figures.

This presumption is borne out by Table 3.4 which shows the development of the real product of the agricultural sector per head of the entire population. From an average of approximately 207 gourdes during the first five years of the period the per capita product in agriculture fell to an average of 192 gourdes in 1968/69-1971/72. Discounting animal husbandry, forestry, apiculture, hunting and fishing, i.e. everything except agriculture proper, the same trends can be observed. The gross product per capita (of the entire population) fell from an average of 185 gourdes to one of 171.

From Table 3.4 it appears as if the production capacity of the Haitian agricultural sector is falling in per capita terms. However, to an important extent, this conclusion may be more apparent than real. The

The Cumulative Process: Falling Rural Incomes

source from which both Table 3.3 and Table 3.4 are taken assumes domestic consumption of agricultural goods to increase *pari passu* with the population. Livestock production, apiculture, forestry, hunting and dishing are treated in a similar manner. Industrial use of agricultural products is taken to be a constant percentage of industrial production in the relevant branches. Losses and inputs are calculated as constant factions of gross production in the sector. The only realistic attempt to measure output is made for exports, where adjustments have been undertaken to account for the changing composition of export production during the period.

Table 3.3: Real Gross Domestic Product Per Capita 1954/55-1971/72 (1954-55 prices)

Fiscal year	Total GDP (million gourdes)	Population (1,000s)	GDP per capita (gourdes)
1954-55	1,386	3,355	413
1955-56	1,507	3,407	442
1956-57	1,399	3,460	404
1957-58	1,532	3,514	436
1958-59	1,419	3,568	398
1959-60	1,523	3,623	420
1960-61	1,478	3,679	401
1961-62	1,595	3,736	427
1962-63	1,564	3,793	412
1963-64	1,539	3,852	399
1964-65	1,572	3,912	402
1965-66	1,563	3,972	393
1966-67	1,530	4,035	379
1967-68	1,578	4,098	385
1968-69	1,639	4,163	394
1969-70	1,649	4,235	389
1970-71	1,756	4,315	407
1971-72	1,773	4,368	406

Source: IHS (1974), p. 225.

Still, the same conclusion applies if we go on to examine trends for individual products. Table 3.5 compares the production of a number of agricultural products per rural inhabitant in 1950 and 1970. Both estimates convey the same picture. The output of agricultural products per rural inhabitant fell between 1950 and 1970. The crops included in Table 3.5 comprise 70-85 percent of the value of agricultural production (excluding subsidiary activities). Using the values in Table 3.4 (and similar values for 1950),[22] and comparing the list of products in Table 3.5 with the account given in Chapter 2 we see that very few important crops (with the possible exception of fruits) are not included in the table. Hence, the actual percentage covered by Table 3.5 is probably even higher.

Table 3.4: Real Agricultural Product Per Capita of Total Population 1954/55-1971/72 (1954-55 prices)

Fiscal year	Total product in agricultural sector (million gourdes)	Total product per capita of total population (gourdes)	Product of agriculture proper (million gourdes)	Agricultural product per capita of total population (gourdes)
1954-55	682	203	611	182
1955-56	732	215	659	194
1956-57	693	200	619	179
1957-58	759	216	685	195
1958-59	708	199	632	177
1959-60	753	208	676	187
1960-61	724	197	646	176
1961-62	783	210	702	188
1962-63	776	205	693	183
1963-64	767	199	682	177
1964-65	775	198	691	177
1965-66	794	200	708	178
1966-67	776	192	687	170
1967-68	793	194	705	172
1968-69	804	193	715	172
1969-70	806	190	716	169
1970-71	838	194	745	173
1971-72	832	191	737	169

Sources: Production figures: IHS (1974), p. 121. Population figures: Table 3.3.

Finally, a few local surveys have been made that point in the same direction as the evidence on the national level:

Several researchers have asked farmers to compare past and present living standards. In the Northwest, 88 percent of the 243 families interviewed reported lower production from their plots compared with 5 years earlier, and 76 percent reported lower living standards ...most people in Belladère felt that their living standards were declining and saw little hope for improvement...farmers in Plaisance, in the North, regarded the 1920s as the high point of economic activity in that area.[23]

Table 3.5: Production per Rural Inhabitant of Some Important Crops in 1950 and 1970 (1972)

Products	IDB estimate (kilos, bananas and plantains: stems)		CONADEP estimate (1,000 1954-55 gourdes)	
	1950	1970	1950	1972
Coffee	12	11	39.8	31.6
Sugar cane	1,410	1,033	21.2	17.2
Sisal	11	5	4.8	2.3
Cocoa	1.0	0.5	3.1	2.5
Bananas	6	–	–	–
Cotton	2	1	1.7	1.0
Corn	69	69	–	–
Sorghum	59	44	10.3	10.6
Plantains	9	12	15.7	13.6
Peas and beans	12	12	33.3	34.6
Rice	14	15	20.2	16.4
Sweet potatoes	27	21	4.8	3.4
Manioc	35	38	0.9	1.0
Pigeon beans	–	–	17.2	13.7
Peanuts	–	–	0.38	0.33

Sources: Production estimates: BID (1974), p. 142; CONADEP (1976), Table A-14. Number of rural inhabitants: Brand (1965), p. 30; IHS (1973), p. 1. (The latter source gives the 1971 rural population as 79.6 percent of the total population. We have here assumed that the rural population in 1970 and 1972 amounted to 80 percent of the total figures given in Table 3.3 above.)

Even the most casual observations seem to suggest that a genuine deterioration in the standard of living is taking place in rural Haiti. 'Any old peasant can tell you that in his youth he ate more plentifully than his grandchildren [today],' emphasizes Roland Wingfield.[24] Cases like the following (described by Harold Courlander) are probably typical for the situation of most Haitian peasants:

> The Haitian habitant (the peasant) is poorer and hungrier today than he was fifty years ago, or even twenty years ago. In 1955 I visited a number of peasant families I had known since 1932, and with hardly an exception I found them worse off than they had been before. Their tiny landholdings had shrunk. Some land that had been lush had dried up and eroded. Little groves of trees had disappeared. Clothes had become shabby, and many of the men could no longer afford to wear the inexpensive traditional blue denim costume that was once so common. In the cities there is evidence that some of the elite have improved their life. But in a large part of the countryside the peasants are finding that the old system that served them for a hundred and fifty years can no longer feed them adequately.[25]

The production figures presented in this chapter are very uncertain indeed. The margins of error are probably quite high. Nevertheless, the only possible interpretation of them that can be made is that they seem to indicate that rural per capita incomes are slowly falling. This impression is not contradicted if we go on to examine the available nutritional statistics.

Rural Nutrition

Beginning in the 1950s a number of budget studies and nutritional surveys have been carried out in rural Haiti. Table 3.6 shows the average daily nominal and real outlays for food encountered in rural surveys between 1957 and 1965. The table possibly indicates a slight decline in real outlays per person, but it is also possible that the 1964-65 surveys are not representative of rural Haiti in general. Fond-Parisien and Ganthier are both presumably somewhat poorer than the average agricultural district.[26]

A number of studies of malnutrition among preschool children have been carried out at different times, mainly in rural districts. A nationwide study was undertaken by Derrick and Patricia Jelliffe in 1958, and in 1974-5 a similar survey was made for the American Federation for the Overseas Blind. The results of the two studies are somewhat difficult to interpret, since a lot may depend on what is actually compared. The Jelliffe study employed the bodyweight of Jamaican children as the standard to compare their Haitian data with. Malnutrition was classified according to the so-called Gómez criteria, where a body weight of

Table 3.6: Surveys of Average Daily Outlay on Food in Rural Areas 1957-65

Locality	Year	Nominal outlays	Food price index† (1948 = 100)	Real outlays
Whole country	1957	0.45	106.2	0.42
Whole country	1962	0.52	95.6	0.54
Port-Margot	1962	0.39	95.6	0.41
Fond-Parisien	1964	0.39	114.2	0.34
Ganthier	1964	0.43	114.2	0.38
Guérin	1965	0.41	111.8	0.37

Average daily outlay on food per person (gourdes)

†For lack of other indices the food price index of Port-au-Prince has been used.

Sources: Nominal outlays: Beghin, Fougère & King (1970), p. 79; Food price index: IHS (1971), p. 421.

90 percent or more of the standard weight of the age group in question is considered as an indication of normal nutrition, a percentage of 75 to 89 as first degree malnutrition, and percentages of 60 to 74 and below 60 as second and third degree malnutrition, respectively.* If the same standard is applied to the 1974-5 survey we obtain the figures presented in Table 3.7 which indicate that the incidence of child malnutrition appears to have decreased since 1958.

It is probable, however, that the comparison should not be taken too *ad notam*. Several factors render the two studies not strictly comparable:

> First of all, the Jelliffe survey was conducted in June-July, while the [1974/75] survey was carried out between December and February. Possible seasonal differences in food intake, food availability, incidence of parasitic infections and parental working patterns, all of which affect nutritional status of the child, should be taken into account. Also, since the study populations in the surveys were selected by entirely different methods, it is possible that the two survey samples are not comparable. In the [1974/75] survey, home selection by rigid statistical technique followed by home visits was

---

*Usually all cases of edema, irrespectively of body weight are classified as third degree malnutrition. This is not done in Table 3.7, however. An evaluation of the reliability of the Gómez criteria is found in Jelliffe & Jelliffe (1961), pp. 36-7.

employed whereas in the Jelliffe survey, sites were established within villages and mothers brought their children to the sites voluntarily.[27]

Table 3.7: Malnutrition among Preschool Children 1958 and 1974/75 According to the Gómez Criteria

	1958	1974/75
Age of children	0-72 months	0-72 months
Number of children surveyed	2,132	1,143
Normal	47%	55%
1st degree malnutrition	32%	28%
2nd degree malnutrition	19%	12%
3rd degree malnutrition	2%	5%

Sources: 1958: computed from data in Jelliffe & Jelliffe (1961), pp. 10, 11, 21, 22. 1974/75: Gédéon, Lamothe & Haverberg, (1976), Table IV.

Especially, it needs to be stressed that June and July (the 1958 survey) constitute the 'dead season' in Haitian agriculture and consequently also the time of the year when food intake should be lowest, while the period between December and February comes during and right after the coffee harvest which in turn, is the period when rural incomes reach their peak. Hence, *a priori* one should expect any survey taken during the latter period to yield a better result in terms of nutrition than one conducted during the dead season.

While the 1958 data, as given by the Jelliffes, do not permit any conversion into percentages of American weight norms, which have been extensively used in a number of Haitian studies, and which may be as appropriate as the Jamaican norms, the 1974-5 study does provide such data, as does another recent study, which was carried out in three villages in the Northwest province. Table 3.8 compares these two surveys with studies made in Fond-Parisien, Ganthier and Guérin ten years earlier. The result of this comparison is that the nutritional standard of Haitian children has not necessarily improved. The figures in the table are highly inconclusive on this point. It should also be kept in mind, when reading the table, that the two latest observations include children under one year of age and children between four and six years, which is likely to bias the results of these surveys 'upwards', i.e. in the direction of an understatement of the extent of malnutrition. The 1958 survey clearly showed that the 1-3 age group is nutritionally worse off than both the 0-1-year-olds (mainly due to breastfeeding) and the older children.[28]

While data on child malnutrition lead to no definite conclusions, other evidence seems to support the hypothesis of a falling standard of nutrition, however. In 1969, King, basing his statement on hospital experience, suggested 'that kwashiorkor, nutritional edema in infants fed a reasonable amount of calories but very little protein, is becoming less frequent while marasmus, total starvation, is increasing. This shift from kwashiorkor towards marasmus appears to be occurring in other parts of the world as the sustained high birth rate aggravates an already inadequate supply of food.'[29]

Table 3.8: Malnutrition among Preschool Children According to the Gómez Criteria, 1964/65 and 1974/75†

	Fond-Parisien 1964	Ganthier 1964	Guérin 1965	Whole country 1974/75	Northwest 1976
Age of children	1-4 years	1-4 years	1-4 years	0-6 years	0-6 years
Number of children surveyed	366	105	129	1,143	551
Normal	16%	23%	9%	18%	34%
1st degree malnutrition	53%	52%	39%	31%	42%
2nd degree malnutrition	19%	23%	35%	35%	21%
3rd degree malnutrition	12%	2%	17%	18%††	3%††

†American weight standards.
††Does not automatically include edema cases.
Sources: 1964/65: Beghin, Fougère & King (1970), p. 153; 1974/75: Gédéon, Lamothe & Haverberg (1976), Table IV; 1976: Lamothe & Haverberg (1976), p. 5.

Beghin, Fougère and King in 1962 calculated the average calorie intake and arrived at a figure of 1,880 calories per day and person.[30] A similar calculation in 1966 gave a lower figure — 1,700 calories.[31] Although the sources of information used for the 1962 calculations were not strictly comparable to those of 1966, the authors conclude that 'We cannot, however, escape from the impression that there has been a real decline in calorie consumption, which was already insufficient in 1962.'[32] However, both these estimates appear to be underestimates. The 1966 figure, and presumably also that for 1962, build on the population estimates made by Jacques Saint Surin which when compared with the 1971 census results seem to be too high.[33] Assuming the total population to be 4.2 million in 1962 and 4.7 million in 1966[34] gives a total supply of 7,900 and 7,990 million calories per day for these two years. If instead of the above population figures those based on the 1971 census (see Table 3.3) are used, we obtain a daily calorie intake per person of 2,140 for 1962 and 2,000 for 1966. However, this recalculation only strengthens the conclusions drawn by Beghin, Fougère and King. The figures are known 'to bear in particular on the rural population of middle or low economic level.'[35] This means that they may be compared with a later figure. In 1975, a mission from the Canadian International Development Agency recalculated the average calorie intake using the same methodology as Beghin, Fougère and King and obtained a figure for rural areas of 1,450 calories per day and person[36] — a decline of more than 25 percent in comparison to the 1966 figure. Hence, the evidence based upon food availability suggests a declining trend in the field of nutrition.

It is not entirely clear what has happened to the nutritional situation in Haiti over the past 15 years. What scanty evidence there is from the 1960s points to a gradual decline of nutritional standards. A comparison between the 1958 and 1974-5 nationwide surveys rather seems to indicate that the standard is going up, but differences in timing may invalidate this result, while a comparison between mid-sixties and mid-seventies data does not provide any conclusive results. Finally, calculations based upon the availability of food products suggest that the nutritional standard is falling. More evidence is needed before anything very definite can be stated, but taking into consideration the many problems connected with survey studies (as indicated above), especially those which arise from comparing different studies made with different selection principles at different times of the year or in different localities, it seems that, for the time being, more importance should be given to the indirect methods, i.e. to the calculations of food availability made. Hence, with due caution, it can be concluded that we are actually witnessing a real decline in calorie intake in rural areas.

The Coumbite

In most circumstances the Haitian peasant cultivates his land with only the aid of his wife and family. The typical family unit in Haiti, however, is small — five or six persons. This number may be too low during the busy seasons, especially if heavy work like forest or land clearing or preparation of the ground for sowing is to be performed. A common device for coping with these difficulties is the use of a co-operative labor team most commonly known as the *coumbite*.*

In his classic account of Haitian peasant life Melville J. Herskovits gives a vivid description of the way the *coumbite* could be held in the 1930s:

> When a man or a woman needs help in preparing a field...a request is made of key-men in the district informally called *chefs d'esquade*. They have the reputation of being those to whose call a number of men, perhaps a dozen, perhaps two or three times that many will respond and come to give the aid that is desired. There is no requirement in either law or custom to respond to the call for communal work, and the larger landowners, who usually reside in the towns, rarely participate in a *combite*. So great is the pleasure derived from work of this sort, however, that a man hesitates before he refuses to take part in a *combite* to which he has been summoned...
>
> The scene in a field where a large *combite* is at work is an arresting one. The men form a line, with a drummer in front of their hoes. The *simidor,* who leads the singing as he works with the others, adds the rhythm of his song to the regular beats of the drum, thus setting the time for the strokes of the implements yielded by the workers. This drum not only beats the time for the hoes, but notifies all concerned that the *combite* is under way. The size of the *combite* is judged by the number of drums and *lambi*, or conch-shell horns used, for where two or three of either are required, an especially large group of workers is usually assembled...
>
> The preparation of the food is the work of the women of the household giving the *combite,* aided by their female relations and the wives of friends and neighbors. This is no small task, for goats and even a bullock may be killed to feed a large *combite,* while in addition other dishes to go with the meat must be cooked...While the food is being cooked, the real object of the *combite,* the clearing of the field, is being pursued. A *chef d'esquade*, usually with a small group, begins the afternoon's labor, and, being a fast worker, he himself sets the pace. As more men arrive, he walks about, encouraging

---

*Probably from the Spanish *convidar* = invite. (For other interpretations see Laguerre (1975), pp. 3-4.) The word *coumbite* is used in two different senses in the literature on Haiti. It is often used as the common denomination of all types of co-operative work in Haiti, but, as we will point out later in the present chapter, it actually refers to a special kind of collective work group only (cf. the criticism in Laguerre (1975), pp. 2-3).

the constantly increasing number of men in their efforts, seeing to it that the tempo originally set is continued, and when necessary picking up a hoe to restore a lagging rhythm. Occasionally the *chef d'esquade* will stand in front of the men to make sure that all keep together, and if the lazy cannot be roused to work by direct order or through ridicule, he will drive them away.

The work progresses with incredible speed as the line moves down the field. In one case a *combite* of between fifty and seventy-five men completely cleared a field of several acres in a single afternoon, and this without undue effort or what appeared to be the expenditure of much energy. The flashing of the hoes in the brilliant sunlight accentuates the color of the scene; each implement is to be raised high above the head of the one who wields it, to be brought down at the proper instant and in almost perfect accord with the hoes of all other men in line. Pauses are frequent, and men often drop out of the line for a longer period of rest...and these, for the time being, join the singing with added verve. During the periods of rest, realignments are made and, if necessary, the direction of the line is changed; after a short time, however, the cry of the *simidor* rings out, the initial statement of a song is sounded, and as the chorus swings into melody, the hoes rise again, the beat of the drum is begun, the plaintive notes of the *lambi* are heard, and the workers once more move down the field.[37]

The origin of the *coumbite* is somewhat obscure. Herskovits contends that the practice is largely West African.[38] James G. Leyburn, however, raises some objections. First, the same kind of co-operative work is found in the United States, in Europe and in South America. Furthermore the practice, if it were of West African origin, was certainly not upheld during the slave days and during the first forty to fifty years of the free nation. In fact, not a single book written by visitors to Haiti from 1818 to 1843 mentions the practice. Not until the middle of the nineteenth century was the *coumbite* established in Haiti. By then, no one in Haiti had direct contact with West Africa. Even so, the *coumbite* bears a striking resemblance to Dahomean practices as described by Herskovits. A possible reconciliation of these seemingly contradictory facts is given by Leyburn:

> If one concludes that the *coumbite* did not become peasant practice until the mid-nineteenth century, all possibility of contact with Negroes familiar with Dahomean routine has disappeared. What

remains is the verbal handing down of recollections, one of the most natural things in the world and one congenial to Haitian peasants. Every region, every village, has its accomplished storytellers. The phenomenal resemblances in detail of the *coumbite* to Dahomean cooperative work may be due therefore to this verbal tradition.[39]

To this it may be added that during the French period as well as during the regimes of Toussaint, Dessalines and Christophe, collective labor (although of a forced kind) was a general practice. Thus, collective working practices had not disappeared altogether. Seen against this background it is easier to understand how the West African system could be transplanted to the Haitian environment despite the lack of continuity.

Collective work groups are not used for all kinds of agricultural operations. As we have noted, only especially demanding tasks that have to be performed during a relatively short time interval make use of the labor team. The most important of these tasks is the clearing of the ground before sowing. The critical moments in the Haitian agricultural calendar are the rains.[40] With regional and local variations these come during relatively short periods in spring (April to June) and fall (September to November).

Clearing, hoeing, sowing and planting must all take place immediately before the spring and autumn rainy seasons since

> disadvantages are enhanced if the soil is left bare for any length of time, so that soil temperatures are raised and rainfall impact... destroys structure, sealing the surface and increasing the risk of run-off and erosion. It is therefore important to provide vegetative cover and to put in any necessary soil conservation works as soon as possible after clearing. The crop, whether annual or perennial, should be planted with a minimum of delay, and with tree crops it is desirable to establish a cover crop as quickly as possible. If shade plants are needed as they may be, for example, with cocoa, coffee or tea, they too should be planted as soon as possible after clearing.[41]

There are other reasons as well behind the necessity of timing:

> In regions of alternating dry and wet seasons, weed growth is naturally minimal or absent in the dry season, but once the rains break weeds grow rapidly and luxuriantly and are difficult to control. It is, therefore, desirable to prepare land before the rains break, in

order to obtain a clean seedbed under dry weather conditions, and thus to reduce weed competition during the early stages of crop growth. Early land preparation is also desirable because numerous experiments, in many parts of the tropics with a variety of annual crops, have shown that early planting generally gives the highest yields. As a rule, yields are markedly and progressively reduced the longer planting is delayed after the onset of the rains. Apart from suffering less weed competition, early sown crops benefit by receiving the full season's rainfall, and because the soil nitrate content is high at the beginning of the rains, whereas later it is reduced by the slower rate of humus decomposition and by leaching.[42]

The advent of the rains in spring and fall is the axis around which the entire Haitian peasant economy rotates. Peasants are eager to get seeds and plants into the ground before it is too late. One way of getting this done in a short time is to arrange a *coumbite*. A labor team is also usually employed during the harvest.[43]

Three types of collective labor teams can be distinguished in Haiti:[44] (1) the *coumbite* proper; (2) the *escouade;* (3) the *société*. A *coumbite* proper consists of a group of peasants who meet on a given day to perform a given task which does not last more than one day. The labor team is not fixed in advance but is formed on the spot for the occasion.[45] There is no obligation for anybody to participate in this type of work. The *coumbite* is based on the principle of reciprocity. Those who help in the *coumbite* can count on the person they help if they organize a *coumbite* of their own. Alternatively, they may receive payment in kind (especially during the harvest season) or some other favors. Money, however, is never used to remunerate the participants in a *coumbite*.* The *coumbite* basically consists of a number of friends, relatives and neighbors who gather to form a labor team. The number of people involved may be fairly high. According to Michel Laguerre, the average size of a *coumbite* is around 50 persons.[46] In addition to those who work, a *coumbite* also attracts a number of hangers-on who only come to eat and have a generally good time, for during the work *clairin*** and some food is distributed.

The second type of labor team is the *escouade*. This is a seasonal or permanent association for mutual help where everybody benefits from

---

*Money enters the *coumbite* only when it simultaneously involves an *escouade*, and then only as payment for the *escouade* (Laguerre (1975), p. 24).
**A cheap white rum.

the work of the others. The *escouade* rotates its services among the members, and each member has one day which 'belongs' to him. This type of labor team basically consists of members who are of equal social and economic standing and who have exactly the same type of rights and obligations within the *escouade*. Everybody must be able to do a day's work. No idleness is tolerated. The *escouade* as a rule is much smaller than the *coumbite* and only counts some 5-15 members.[47] In addition to performing agricultural work for its members, the *escouade* also generally sells its services against money to peasants not belonging to the association.

The largest collective labor team are the *sociétés de travail*. These are stable associations like some *escouades* but differ from the latter in mainly two respects. The first is size. While the *escouade* is a small group, *sociétés* of up to 180 members have been identified.[48] The second difference is that the *sociétés* are not egalitarian. The bulk of the members work, but in addition the *sociétés* contain a number of honorary dignitaries who perform no manual work. The operations of the *sociétés* take place according to more or less fixed, often quite elaborate and complicated rules. There are rules for summoning the *société*, for going to the field, for the carrying out of the field, for dealing with shirkers, for the relations between the *société* and the employer, etc.[49] Only those who work get paid, not the dignitaries. The *société* rotates among the working members in the same way as the two other labor teams. The dignitaries can have their day of work if they need one but are generally not included in the systematic rotation of services. The *société* as well as the *escouade* can sell its services to people not belonging to the *société* themselves.

The character and extent of the co-operative labor in the Haitian countryside has changed over the years. To a large extent the *sociétés* and the *coumbites* seem to be disappearing. Thirty to forty years ago it was still a common occurrence in the Haitian countryside to see labor teams encompassing perhaps three or four dozen people, all of whom had to be fed by the employer when the day was over, the employer giving a regular feast with a lavish distribution of food and drinks to the members of the team. Today, collective work tends to mean that five or six, perhaps ten neighbors work together during a morning or an afternoon. Much of the agricultural work, however, is done without any collective work at all, by the peasant and his family alone or, when labor requirements are especially demanding, with the aid of a few hired hands or some neighbors in return for similar services. The tendency among the *sociétés* is to avoid having more than 20 members and to reduce the number of people who are included in the honorary category and who do not work, while the simpler and smaller *escouade* has gradually been substituted for both the *société* and the *coumbite*.[50] Today the *escouade* is without doubt the most common labor team in rural Haiti.

The gradual disappearance of the larger and more elaborate forms of co-operative work is probably a sign of increasing general poverty in rural areas. To understand why, we have to introduce one aspect of co-operative labor which so far we have only touched on indirectly.

In primitive or underdeveloped economies the borderline between work proper, social activities, and leisure is often flexible.[51] Observable events often contain elements of all these kinds. A number of authors have in various ways drawn attention to the social significance of the *coumbites* and *sociétés:*

> Though strenuous physical effort is involved in the work of the *combite,* for the Haitian it symbolizes recreation and enjoyment — the stimulus of working with friends, and the partaking of the feast which marks the climax of the day. All this makes the occasion one to be anticipated and enjoyed, and no one witnessing ten or fifteen men on horseback, each with a hoe over his shoulder, shouting and laughing as they clatter by at full gallop, can fail to sense their eager desire to arrive at their destination, a near-by *combite.*[52]

> Co-operative group work enables its organizer to increase his prestige and to win fresh authority by showing himself a generous host, grudging no expense. If he does things handsomely, he will be spoken of with respect, and he will always be able, henceforth, to rely on his neighbours' goodwill...
>
> It is not sufficient to have enough for everybody; some must be left over, as a sign of the host's prosperity and generosity. Nothing flatters a peasant more than to have it said of his labour team that: 'The rows of people stretched as far as one could see. There was that much food left on the ground. He's a man who does things properly...' The host's reputation will suffer if the portions are too strictly calculated, or if there are complaints about the quantity or quality of the food. All those present must be able to gorge themselves, and some will even expect to take scraps home in their *makout* [bags].[53]

> Almost the entire social life of the members is found within the society. During working hours singing, drinking, and general good fellowship prevails. It is certain that more labor per man is obtained

with these stimuli than would ever be the case otherwise. Meals and liquid refreshments are served by the host at the end of each day's work. Frequently a barbecue and dance are held that night by the member whose field has been worked. The celebration of Saints' days, funerals, 'placements', and other events keep the program of social engagements full.[54]

The festive part of *coumbites* and *sociétés* is still important. A *coumbite*, for example, not only provides labor for its organizer but also offers an occasion, for the participants to meet friends from the neighborhood, to chat, gossip and hear news. It is 'a rural feast to which one comes to eat and drink to saturation.'[55] Undoubtedly, the *coumbite*, along with funeral wakes, voodoo ceremonies and marriages even today is one of the most popular social occasions in the Haitian countryside.[56] Still, both the *coumbite* and the *société* are on their way out of the rural picture, and the simpler *escouade* is taking their place. Presumably this is a sign of declining per capita incomes in rural districts. In the late 1940s, Alfred Métraux found that the Marbial valley was in what certainly appeared to be a state of relative depression or at least declining opulence. Métraux saw that there was a link between this fact and the fact that the traditional *coumbite* was disappearing:

> Nothing points more clearly to the economic decadence of the Marbial region than the decline in the number of these working parties. Peasants who can afford to organize them are becoming fewer and fewer; and whereas in the old days they were glad to help a neighbour in return for a good meal, their chief wish nowadays is to get money with which to buy seed or pay their debts.[57]

During the 1950s and the 1960s the same process has been operating throughout the entire country.[58] To understand how the process works we may look at Figure 3.3. The different types of co-operative labor may be arranged along a scale which has at one extreme the situation where only a feast is held (and no work is performed) and at the other that which consists only of work (without any festive parts). The *escouade* is close to the latter end point, while the *société* and the *coumbite* entail both productive work and social activities. Another way of expressing this is by saying that *coumbites* and *sociétés* involve not only production but also *consumption* of social activities. During the past 20-30 years a rightward movement on the scale of Figure 3.3 has taken place. Co-operative work today entails comparatively more production and comparatively less consumption than during the 1930s or the 1940s, and this decline in consumption of social activities may be a sign of falling rural per capita incomes. Social activities of the type involved in a *coumbite* or *société* may be regarded as luxury goods in the sense that the consumption of them is very sensitive to changes in incomes. When per capita incomes fall in the countryside, the peasants may adjust their consumption patterns so as to consume relatively less of social activities and relatively more of other goods (mainly food).

Figure 3.3

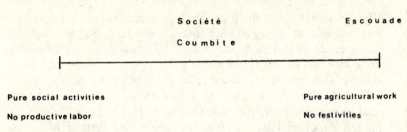

Conclusions

The hypothesis of the present chapter is that per capita incomes are slowly falling in rural areas in Haiti. We have advanced three different pieces of evidence to support this view. The available production statistics directly indicate a downward trend. Nutrition statistics tend to show that the average calorie intake in the countryside is falling. Some of the most important traditional social activities are slowly dying, probably because of the increasing problems of maintaining them in the face of falling real incomes. Taken separately, each of the above pieces of evidence is not convincing. Taken together, on the other hand, they appear to form part of a definite pattern. The individual margin of error may be large, but when we put the pieces together our case is strengthened.

The task of the remainder of this book is to investigate the nature of the mechanisms underlying the decreasing incomes and to find out whether there are any counteracting forces at work which may check or mitigate the tendency for incomes to fall.

Notes

1. Wicksell (1935), pp. 175-208.
2. Myrdal (1939).
3. Myrdal (1944). See especially pp. 75-7, 207-9, 1065-70.
4. Cf. e.g. Myrdal (1957) and Myrdal (1968).
5. For a selection see Myrdal (1968), notes pp. 1844-5.
6. Ibid. See especially Appendix 2.

The Cumulative Process: Falling Rural Incomes 119

7. For details see ibid., pp. 1859-64.
8. Ibid., p. 1871.
9. This type of diagram was first used by Kaldor (1940) in his analysis of the trade cycle. Similar models were later applied by Leibenstein (1957), especially Chapters 3 and 8, in his development of the critical minimum effort thesis of economic development (cf. also Leibenstein (1954) and Nelson (1956)), by Swan (1962) in a criticism of Myrdal's *An American Dilemma* and by Streeten in various development contexts (e.g. (1967) and (1972), Chapter 5).
10. For a discussion of the practical problems of constructing such indices, see Streeten (1972), pp. 63-4. As a 'rough-and-ready index' Streeten uses the income per head.
11. Ibid., pp. 67-8.
12. Schultz (1964), pp. 36-8.
13. Griffin (1969), pp. 26-7, 59, 61.
14. King & Weldon (1977), p. 709.
15. Bosch (1969), p. 12.
16. Meier & Baldwin (1957), p. 320.
17. Pierre-Charles (1965), p. 252.
18. Ibid., p. 253.
19. Traces of circular causation can be found also in Pierre-Charles (1969:2) and Pierre-Charles (1971).
20. Wingfield (1966), p. 321.
21. Rotberg & Clague (1971), p. 273.
22. An estimate of the 1950 production is found in IHS (1964), p. 98.
23. Zuvekas (1978), note, p. 39.
24. Personal communication, dated 22 August 1976.
25. Courlander (1960), p. 114. Cf. Zuvekas (1978), pp. 31, note, p. 39, 41, 43, 47.
26. Beghin, Fougère & King (1970), p. 74; Fougère & King (1975), p. 245.
27. Gédéon, Lamothe & Haverberg (1976), p. 5.
28. Jelliffe & Jelliffe (1961), pp. 11, 23.
29. King (1969), pp. 355-6. Cf. Palmer (1972), p. 15, for worldwide trends.
30. Beghin, Fougère & King (1970), p. 77.
31. Ibid., p. 107, where the methodology of the calculations is also explained.
32. Ibid., p. 77.
33. Ibid., p. 107. Saint Surin's population estimates are found in Saint Surin (1962), p. 21.
34. Saint Surin gives a figure for 1960 of 4.155 million and for 1965 of 4.66 million (Saint Surin (1962), p. 21).
35. Beghin, Fougère & King (1970), p. 76.
36. CRN (1975), pp. 60, 65.
37. Herskovits (1971), pp. 71-3. Cf. Courlander (1960), pp. 117-18.
38. Herskovits (1971), pp. 259-60. Cf. also pp. 23-4 where the Dahomean counterpart to the *coumbite* – the *dokpwe* – is described.
39. Leyburn (1966), pp. 200-1.
40. This is a general feature of tropical agriculture. Cf. McPherson & Johnston (1967), pp. 189-90.
41. Webster & Wilson (1966), p. 134.
42. Ibid., pp. 137-8.
43. Paul (1959), p. 2.
44. This division is due to Michel Laguerre. See Laguerre (1975), passim.
45. A discussion of various types of invitations to a *coumbite* is made in ibid., pp. 10-15.
46. Ibid., p. 10.

47. Ibid., p. 39.
48. Bastien (1951), p. 130.
49. An excellent description of a *société* in the Marbial valley is given by Métraux *et al.* (1951), pp. 73-86. Cf. also Hall (1929), passim; Wirkus & Dudley (1931), pp. 215-18; Laguerre (1975), pp. 55-60.
50. Laguerre (1975), pp. 37, 39, 49, 65.
51. Cf. Turnham & Jaeger (1971), p. 15.
52. Herskovits (1971), p. 70. Cf. also Herskovits (1952), p. 101.
53. Métraux *et al.* (1951), pp. 69-70.
54. Hall (1929), p. 692.
55. Laguerre (1975), p. 33.
56. Ibid., p. 35.
57. Métraux *et al.* (1951), pp. 70-71.
58. Cf. Laguerre (1975), pp. 37, 39, 70; Moral (1961), p. 193.

4 POVERTY AND THE MARKET

A frequent and often powerful explanation of peasant poverty in underdeveloped economies is the one which runs in terms of exploitation by monopsonistic or oligopsonistic middlemen who control the marketing of peasant produce. For one reason or another, bargaining power in the commodity markets is sufficiently unequally distributed as to confer all or most advantages on the intermediaries leaving the peasant producers in a situation where they receive less for their product than they would in a market characterized by competition. The same type of situation may also prevail in the markets for those goods the peasants cannot produce themselves but which have to be procured from outside. The sellers in these markets (who are often identical with the buyers in the markets for peasant goods) are either outright monopolists or else oligopolists who work in close collaboration and collusion, fixing a higher price for the peasant consumer than he would otherwise have paid in a competitive market.[1]

The thesis that the Haitian peasants are subject to exploitation by the intermediaries in the commercial chain has been advanced by a number of authors.[2] According to this view, the peasants receive a very small benefit from the sale of their products and have to pay dearly for what they buy, while large profits are taken by the middlemen. The following quotation is typical:

> The 'commodity speculators' dominate the commercial activity of the rural small-towns. They are licenced intermediaries who, on behalf of a large trading firm in the city, buy different export commodities from the peasants...The commodity speculator...[is] an important person in the Haitian economy and society, since he combines his official business with retail trade and even with a certain amount of processing of the goods. The regulation of the commerce in the countryside has above all been made for his benefit...
>
> The commerce that takes place in rural areas is spread out over an infinite number of small transactions, where sales and purchases, gains and disbursements are almost simultaneous. From these operations the peasant only receives a miserable benefit. Like the 'grappillage'* itself,

---

*The term *grappillage* is probably of colonial origin. During the eighteenth

commerce is improvised and follows the rhythm of the former. The most unfavorable effects on the family economy must also be taken into consideration. In the first place, when it is time for him to sell his crops, the 'habitant' almost always finds himself facing a recently contracted, heavy debt. The usual source of funds in the countryside is the speculator, who himself is in severe financial obligation to the exporter in town, and hence sometimes submits the small producer to onerous conditions. Those advances which he grants the peasant, for two or three months, carry an exorbitant rate of interest (25% and more) and are to be repaid at the beginning of the harvest, when prices are clearly unfavorable for the 'habitant'. The latter, pressed to sell, every year sees most of his profit tied up in the liquidation of debts which are in arrears, or used for careless purchases in the shop next to the speculator's office...[3]

Secondly, the frequency of retail and even micro retail trade considerably increases the price of the commodities coming from the city: matches in small packages, cigarettes individually, lard by the spoonful, cloth in small pieces, soap in fractions of bars, oil in small flasks, etc.....If we add to this the credulity of the 'habitant', the traditional frauds when the products are weighed, the hasty deliveries before the prices have been firmly established and the purchases of seed in March at the worst time of the year, we see how the meager revenues of the family farm are further jeopardized by the organization of the transactions. Thus, in general, the peasant has only very small sums of money at his disposal.[4]

Other students of the Haitian marketing system take the opposite view, namely that within the obvious limitations imposed by the topography and the bad transportation system the marketing process is fairly efficient and does not contain any important exploitative elements:

> The technical level of marketing services in Haitian society seems low, but society pays a low price all the same for what the market system provides. This low price is guaranteed not by the high productivity of those participating but rather by their numbers. The

---

century it was used to designate the fourth indigo harvest, the one with the lowest quality. It was also applied to the last coffee harvest. Nowadays, *grappillage* notably means the coffee harvest, but also peasant agriculture in general, 'discontinuous and without amplitude...where gathering activities to satisfy the most immediate needs continue to play a decisive role' (Moral (1961), p. 189).

price is raised by such considerations as shockingly poor roads, high import duties on vehicles and fuels, backward and poorly capitalized agriculture resulting in poor yields and relatively high production costs, and onerous taxation of the activities of distributive intermediaries. These problems, however, do not originate with the market woman. And though she communicates demand to potential producers, relates new producers to the market, stimulates improvement in agriculture and closer ties between the producer and his market, she cannot solve the problems that beset the economy.[5]

In this chapter we will show that it is the latter of the two quotations which comes closest to the truth and that the view which holds that the Haitian peasants are subject to monopsonistic or monopolistic exploitation by the intermediaries does not appear to be compatible with the available empirical evidence. We will begin with an examination of the degree to which peasant products are actually sold in the market. Thereafter, efficiency and exploitation will be defined, and the evidence available for export and subsistence crops will be examined. In the appendix to the present chapter, the role of transportation problems as an obstacle to competition will be discussed.

We will find that the Haitian economy is essentially a market economy and that the marketing system works smoothly and efficiently as far as the middlemen are concerned — both with respect to export products, subsistence goods and peasant consumption goods. The system operates under conditions which closely resemble those of the textbook models of perfect competition. Both buyers and sellers are numerous. No collusion appears to take place among the intermediaries. Entry and exit into the system are virtually free, and market information is produced at a low real cost to the economy. It is not possible to find any plausible sources of monopoly or monopsony power, and the profit levels prevailing convey the impression of being perfectly compatible with competitive conditions.

A Market Economy

Even to the most casual observer one of the most striking characteristics of Haitian everyday life is the ubiquity of market-places and traders. The market possesses a long tradition in Haiti. Maurice de Young has observed that it is quite possible that the Tainos formed part of a wider system of commodity exchange, although it does not seem possible to prove this proposition strictly,[6] and that from the earliest European settlement on the western third of Hispaniola, the economy was governed by impulses emanating from the market.[7] The market system was well established in Europe by this time, and the slaves also brought with them a cultural background where the market system played an important role: that of West Africa.[8]

The French colonial economy of Saint-Domingue was based on the market system, since it was an export economy, but also at the domestic level the market was an important factor in economic life. Slaves were usually given small plots of land where they could cultivate food crops to supplement their rations or such products that they could sell in town.[9] Thus, a considerable volume of commerce developed between country and city blacks. Moreau de Saint-Méry in his monumental work on colonial Saint-Domingue describes the Negro market in Cap-Français where up to 15,000 slaves traded on market day,[10] and other contemporary sources also indicate that the principle of buying and selling in the market-place was firmly established during the French period.[11]

Nevertheless, the development of the market system was incomplete. The bulk of commercial activity was concentrated in the export ports, and the number of days when market transactions could take place between slaves was also limited by laws and decrees.[12]

After independence, the market system gradually developed and expanded geographically. Up to around 1840, the Haitian governments continued to restrict the freedom of internal trade, but with the transition from plantations to small farms and the expansion of the latter across the Haitian territory new market-places were created in rural areas to permit an increasing exchange of goods to take place between the peasants. This process was not entirely painless, for with the development of purely rural market-places the interests of the town and city merchants were threatened. This conflict between rural and urban interests continued during the present century. Periods of free rural trade alternated with periods of severe restrictions on the functioning of the rural market-places, and it was not until 1952 that the survival of the latter was finally legally assured.[13]

Today, in Haiti the importance of the market system for agricultural products is established beyond doubt. Although the peasants to a large extent consume the crops they produce, the country and the agricultural sector can by no means be regarded as a subsistence economy. The peasants do not consume all that they produce themselves nor do they produce all that they consume. Many of the goods needed cannot be produced by the peasants themselves but have to be purchased from outside. The metal tools used in agriculture come from urban areas as do many other necessities, like cloth, kerosene, oil, flour, and all the

Poverty and the Market

minor items that in Haiti are labeled *kêkay*, like 'soap, matches, cigarettes, star anise, cinnamon, Jamaican pimento, sulphur, blueing, asafoetida, bicarbonate of soda, students' notebooks, needles and thread, nails, resin, tailors' wax, buttons, cloves, dried thyme, candles [and] catechisms.'[14] Frequently these are imported products. At any rate, to purchase them the peasant must obtain cash, which can be done both by selling export and subsistence crops. Besides, even when it comes to food products the peasants have to purchase some items on the market, since production and cropping patterns vary, and since the timing of the harvest differs slightly from one part of the country to another and the peasants are unable to store their products properly once they are harvested. In Chapter 2 we made the distinction between 'hot' and 'cool' lands, according to altitude and temperature, and we found that the two types of lands have different agricultural cycles and that different agricultural products are grown. This in turn creates commerce in agricultural products between peasants from neighboring yet differing localities.[15]

The percentage sold in the market varies with the nature of the crop. René Dorville has divided those peasant products which are consumed domestically into five groups according to who the principal user is. This division is shown in Table 4.1.* If we compare that table with Table 4.2, which shows the percentage marketed for a few crops, we find that the percentage sold on the market increases as we move from the peasant staples to those products that are designed mainly for urban use. No estimates for groups 4 and 5 exist, but given the fact that the principal users are located in urban areas, the percentage passing through the marketing system should at least lie in the same range as that of group 3.

In such regions where 'urban' crops are grown, the tendency to market most of the harvest is very pronounced, even when the peasant has the option of consuming the crop himself. Gerald F. Murray and María D. Alvarez quote a typical case. In a study of bean-growing peasants in the Cul-de-Sac plain they found that most of the time the peasants purchased what they ate and sold their beans. The reason was that beans were an expensive source of calories and protein in relation to other products. Therefore, the Cul-de-Sac peasants exchanged their beans for cheaper foodstuffs like cornmeal and millet in the market. In all of the cases encountered, the larger part of the crop was sold, unless

---

*Mintz (1959), p. 21, estimates that more than one-half of the value of the subsistence commodities is consumed by 'members of the same class as the producers.'

the harvest had failed to the point of only leaving a few pounds of beans. This trend became even more evident as the poverty of the peasant increased.[16]

Table 4.1: Categories of Peasant Products in Haiti

Group†	Principal users	Products
1	peasants	sorghum, sweet potatoes, yams, manioc, malanga, bread fruit, peas
2	peasants and town-dwellers	corn, mangoes, avocados, citrus fruits, plantains
3	town-dwellers	beans, rice
4	prosperous town-dwellers	meat, milk, eggs, chicken, onions, tomatoes, carrots, potatoes, lettuce, etc.
5	industries	sugar cane, cotton, tobacco

†Our categories 2 and 3 correspond to Dorville's numbers 3 and 2, respectively.
Source: Dorville (1975:1), pp. 4-10.

Table 4.2: Estimates of the Marketed Percentage of Selected Peasant Crops

Crop	Group	Percentage sold in the market
Sorghum	1	10
Corn	2	50
Plantains	2	66
Beans	3	75
Rice	3	90

Source: Dorville (1975:1), p. 12.

The Haitian peasants produce not only to feed their families but also to sell in the market in order to bring in the cash which is needed for buying those necessities (and luxuries for that matter) which cannot be produced on the farm. The Haitian peasant economy is a market economy and a monetary economy where the choice of crops to a very large extent is governed by relative prices, and has been so for a long time. The importance of the market in rural Haiti is definitely of such a magnitude that the existence of monopsony, oligopsony, monopoly or oligopoly in the markets for those commodities the peasants sell and buy can have very serious consequences for the standard of living in rural areas. An investigation of the organization of these markets therefore is of paramount importance when it comes to determining the possible causes of the low peasant standard of living and the changes in this level over time.

The Efficiency of Perfect Competition

Perfect competition is said to prevail in a market when the following conditions are satisified:[17]

1. From the buyer's point of view there must be no special advantage connected with purchasing from a particular seller and vice versa. In equilibrium, all buyers and sellers must face the same price.
2. Both buyers and sellers must possess perfect information regarding the price prevailing in the market.
3. All buyers and sellers must be 'small' enough so that no single buyer or seller can affect the market price or the conditions whereunder the sales take place. No collusion must take place between buyers or sellers.
4. Entry into and exit from the market must be free for both buyers and sellers.

In addition, it is assumed that there are no externalities in production or consumption, no collective goods, no indivisibilities and no increasing returns, that all sellers (including intermediaries) seek to maximize their profits and that all final consumers attempt to maximize their utility (in terms of goods purchased).

It is a standard result of economic theory that an economy which operates under these conditions will exhibit certain desirable features with respect to efficiency. All firms and industries will be *technologically* efficient in the sense that the allocation of factors and outputs within each firm and industry is such that the production of a given output is achieved at a minimum expenditure of productive resources, or the production of a maximum output is achieved given the quantity of productive factors.[18] The *economy* as a whole will be technologically efficient in the sense that it will not be possible to increase the output of any commodity without simultaneously reducing the output of at least one other good,[19] but it will also be *economically* efficient, i.e. the output and the factor use will exhibit 'conformity to the community's wishes'[20] in the sense that it will be impossible to make any consumer better off without at the same time making someone else worse off.[21] In other words, the economy will be at a Paretian optimum.

In the present chapter we will be concerned with two closely related problems: first, with the efficiency of the markets in which the peasants buy and sell their products, and secondly, with the efficiency of the marketing organization itself. As will be shown in the section below, market imperfections could result in technological inefficiencies as well as in exploitation of the peasants. However, real peasant incomes will also be affected by the efficiency of the marketing system. Given the commodity market form, the price received by the peasantry for a product will usually be higher, the lower the cost added by the marketing system. Similarly, the price of the products bought by the peasants will usually be lower, the lower the marketing costs are. Thus the two problems are interrelated and will be dealt with below in an integrated manner.

We will be concerned with technological efficiency only. The reason for not going into the question of economic efficiency is that we simply cannot analyze every single market in the economy. An economically efficient allocation of the resources is achieved only if perfect competition prevails in *all* markets, and an investigation of whether this is actually the case in Haiti is impossible from the practical point of view. It also falls outside the scope of the present work, since we are not interested in the total efficiency of the economy. For our purpose, efficiency and inefficiency are interesting concepts only to the extent that market conditions affect *peasant* incomes and welfare.

The Meaning of Exploitation

In the present chapter attention will be focused on the performance of the marketing system, i.e. on the network of intermediaries who on the one hand ensure that the peasants are supplied with those goods they require but cannot or do not want to produce themselves and on the other hand buy the commodities produced by the peasants and ensure that they are exported or that they reach their final consumers if the goods in question are consumed within the country.

For the marketing system to be technologically efficient, i.e. for the system to handle the distribution of goods at a minimum expenditure of productive resources, it is sufficient that perfect competition prevails in those commodity and factor markets which involve the marketing system.[22] We saw at the beginning of the chapter that the marketing system has frequently been accused of being inefficient. These accusations have concentrated on alleged imperfections in the commodity markets (both for the products consumed by the peasants and for the products sold by them), while no similar statements appear to have

Poverty and the Market

been made with respect to the markets for those factors which the intermediaries employ in the marketing process. Hence, we will in the following concentrate on the commodity markets, assuming that there are no important imperfections in the factor markets.

Figures 4.1 and 4.2 are well known to all students of economics. Figure 4.1 illustrates the situation where a monopsonist takes over a hitherto competitive industry.* If competition prevails among buyers, the equilibrium price (P_C) and quantity (Q_C) will be determined by the intersection of the market demand and supply curves in point B. Assuming instead that a single buyer (a monopsonist) or a consortium of oligopsonistic buyers who act in close collusion takes over, the equilibrium position will no longer be determined by the intersection of the demand and supply curves. Being the only buyer, the monopsonist cannot take the price of the commodity as given, but any increases in the purchases of the monopsonist will also increase the price. The supply curve, which is identical to the marginal cost curve of the competitive industry, differs from the marginal cost curve of the monopsonistic buyer. The marginal cost of the monopsonist will exceed the price, since by increasing his demand, the monopsonist also drives up the market price. Hence, the monopsonist's marginal cost curve must lie above the supply curve, and the equilibrium is determined by the intersection of this curve and the monopsonist's marginal utility curve which, under competitive conditions, would be identical to the market demand curve. Both the price (P_X) and the quantity (Q_M) thus determined will be lower than under conditions of competitive equilibrium. This is a well-known result.

We now clearly see the impact on peasant incomes of monopsony in the market for peasant products, and we may define monopsonistic (oligopsonistic) exploitation as the reduction in peasant incomes resulting from dealing with a monopsonistic buyer (intermediary) instead of with a competitive market. The effect, as is easily seen in Figure 4.1, is to decrease both the volume sold by the peasants and the price they receive, and thereby also peasant incomes.**

Monopolistic (oligopolistic) exploitation may be treated in an analogous manner. Figure 4.2 illustrates the losses incurred by the peasants in

---

*For the sake of simplicity, all relationships are taken to be linear.
**The present analysis assumes that the peasants cannot shift to other crops, but the effects of monopsonistic exploitation depend on the alternatives open to the peasants. The fall in the real incomes of peasant producers will be lower the more easily resources can be shifted into production of goods sold in competitive markets and/or production of crops which can be consumed on the farm.

their capacity of consumers when they face a monopolistic seller or a number of oligopolistic sellers practicing collusion. Under competitive conditions, the equilibrium price (P_C) and quantity (Q_C) would have been determined by the intersection of the market demand and supply schedules. If a monopolist takes over the industry, a higher equilibrium price (P_M) will result instead and a lower quantity (Q_M) will be consumed by the peasants, for the monopolist is able to influence the price prevailing in the market. His marginal revenue is no longer equal to the price (as it would have been under competitive conditions), but as the monopolist expands his sales he simultaneously drives down the price he receives. The demand curve facing him slopes downward, and hence, the marginal revenue curve lies below the demand curve. The monopolist maximizes his profits by equating marginal costs and revenues in point E — leaving the consumers (in our case the peasants) with a higher price to pay and a lower quantity to consume than under competitive conditions. The consumers are subject to monopolistic (oligopolistic) exploitation.*

Figure 4.1

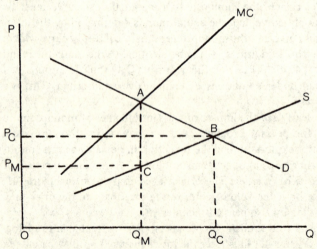

Under conditions of monopsony or monopoly, technological inefficiency may arise, e.g. if the monopsonist or monopolist applies discriminatory pricing practices. If, for example, the monopsonist pays a higher price

---

*We assume, as before, that the consumers do not shift their consumption to other products.

to producer A than to producer B for a homogeneous product, then producer A will expand production to a limit where his marginal cost will be higher than B's marginal cost. The total cost of producing the product in question will then not be minimized. Technological inefficiency ensues. In addition, given the demand schedule facing the monopsonist, lowering the price paid allows the monopsonist to waste more resources on the marketing process than would have been the case in a competitive situation and still charge the same price. Similarly, if a monopolist sells an agricultural input, for example, at different prices, different peasants will face different factor prices and once again the total cost of producing agricultural commodities will not be minimized. Also, in analogy to the monopsony case, charging a price to the peasants which is higher than the price which would have ensued under competitive conditions allows the monopolist to incur higher costs in marketing than those arising had marketing been characterized by competition.

Figure 4.2

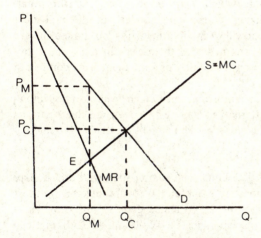

Sources of Monopsony or Monopoly Power

Imperfections in the marketing system may affect the standard of living of the peasants in two different ways, depending on the nature of the imperfections. Monopsony power among the middlemen may lower the incomes received and monopoly power may force the peasants to consume less and to pay a higher price than under perfect competition. It then becomes interesting to see under which circumstances monopsony or monopoly may arise in an economy of the Haitian type. Clifton R. Wharton, Jr, in a study of Malayan rubber smallholdings has identified seven classes of sources of such power:[23]

1. Legal power, i.e. when (in our case) a middleman (or a number of middlemen) is given a license or an exclusive right to buy or sell a certain product.
2. Illegal power, i.e. use of force, threats, coercion etc. to achieve a monopsony or monopoly position.
3. Economic power, e.g. by control of one or more inputs which are essential to the peasants, like land or credit. Other possible controls may be those over transport or processing facilities.
4. Technical or natural power, as typically exemplified by telephones, gas, etc., but also by physical isolation or other natural barriers to communication and information.
5. Cultural power, in the form of such social relationships which prevent the peasants from switching their business to other buyers or sellers due to e.g. family or other socio-cultural relationships.
6. Psychological power, which may range from outright brainwashing and propagandizing to spontaneous fear of the individual (peasant) of losing the goodwill of the intermediary. This type of power may operate among the intermediaries themselves in the form of unwritten laws or codes of conduct which prevent them from competing with each other.
7. Informational or educational power, which leads to poor knowledge of the available alternatives among the peasants. Such barriers may arise by themselves or may be deliberately created by the middlemen.

Each of the above categories, alone or in combination with others, may create monopoly or monopsony situations. We will, however, not deal with all of them in the following. Available data do not allow us to check whether illegal or psychological power is present. All that can be said is that we have not come across any indications of such power. Likewise, cultural power may be removed from our list at once. No evidence of such power has been found. Technical or natural power such as gas and the telephone may be excluded since the nature of the products involved is not such as to make it possible for this type of power to arise. One form of economic power has been dealt with already in Chapter 2, where we found that the access to land is not being controlled by any minority. Another type of possible economic

Poverty and the Market

power — monopolization of the supply of credit — will not be discussed until Chapter 11, where we will conclude that no such monopolization appears to exist.

This leaves us with legal power, possible control over transport or processing facilities, and possible barriers to physical access and market information, all of which will be discussed during the course of the present chapter, directly and indirectly. In this analysis we will make a distinction between export and subsistence crops, since the marketing processes for the two types of crops differ in that subsistence crops are sold via the system of market-places while export crops (except for those quantities that are consumed within Haiti) are handled by a chain of intermediaries who operate outside the market-places. It should also be pointed out that we will not deal separately with the middlemen in their capacity as sellers to the peasants, since as we will see, the same middlemen who buy from the peasants also to a very large extent supply them with goods, and therefore it is preferable to discuss their two capacities jointly. Let us begin with the marketing of export crops.

The Marketing of Export Crops

The only export crop for which enough data are available to permit any conclusions to be drawn is coffee, but since no other export crop has ever come close to coffee as a source of cash incomes for the peasants, we can presumably get a good idea about what the Haitian peasant gains from export cultivation by an examination of the case of coffee.

The Coffee Marketing Chain

Figure 4.3 depicts the marketing chain for coffee. There are an estimated 384,000 coffee-growing peasants in Haiti.[24] They harvest their coffee and either dry and process the beans to yield natural coffee or sell it as cherries to the factories for preparation according to the wet method.* The peasants deal with middlemen at many different levels.

---

*Once harvested, coffee is processed in two different ways in Haiti. Most common is the preparation by the peasants themselves of natural coffee by what is known as the dry process. The coffee beans are dried in the sun for two or three weeks, sometimes on a *glacis*, a concrete slab, on which the beans are spread out. The dried pulp is pounded off the beans with a mortar and a pestle *(café pilé)*, or decorticated in a simple machine, owned by a middleman *(café décortiqué)*, and the beans are again dried in the sun, before they are cleaned and sacked. The wet process whereby washed coffee is produced cannot be handled by the peasants themselves, but washed coffee is produced in local factories, where the cherries are poured into cement tanks filled with water where they are sorted and, to a certain extent, fermented, before they go through a depulping machine. After the

The most important middlemen are those known in Haiti as *spéculateurs*. The speculators are either licensed *spéculateurs en denrées* or operate illegally (*'sous-marins'*, *'bafonneurs'*, *'zombis'*, *'spéculateurs marrons'*, etc.). The operations of the licensed speculators are regulated by law. To become a speculator one must have a *patente* which allows the speculator to deal with coffee after paying the appropriate fees. The legal speculators are only permitted to operate 'within the limits of speculation', i.e. in the cities, towns and *bourgs,* and can only carry out business in their own shop.[25] In most cases the licensed speculators are at the same time small coffee growers, and often own a shop where the peasants can buy goods of imported or urban origin as well.[26]

Figure 4.3

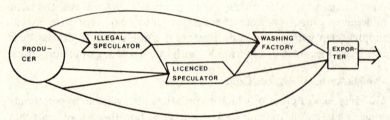

Many speculators hire agents to buy on their behalf. These agents, in so far as they are going to operate legally, must be licensed, exactly like the speculators themselves, but do not have to own an establishment or to pay some of the taxes levied on the speculator group.

The peasants bring their coffee to the speculation posts in the *bourgs,* since the licensed speculators cannot legally operate outside the designed marketing centers, but they also deal with illegal speculators who go directly into the rural areas themselves and assemble the crop there to resell it to a licensed speculator or perhaps, in the case of cherries, to a washing factory.* The latter is fed also by legal speculators who buy cherries either from their illegal counterparts or from the peasants who may themselves in turn be dealing directly with the factories.

The final link in the chain of intermediaries is the exporter, who

---

pulp has been removed, the beans are fermented for 18 to 24 hours in water basins (to loosen up their seed coats). Then the beans are dried, mechanically or on a *glacis* in the sun. When the beans have dried they are deparched, i.e. their seed coat is removed. Finally, they are cleaned and sacked.

*Legally, speculators are not allowed to buy coffee cherries, but since they are often growers as well the restriction is easy to get around (JWK (1976:1), p. 37).

Poverty and the Market

may be dealing with either of the groups mentioned with the exception of the illegal speculators. The exporters are concentrated in the major ports of the county.

In spite of the legal regulations pertaining to the coffee trade, no legally enforced monopsony power that disturbs the efficiency of the marketing system has arisen.* As indicated by Figure 4.3, the peasants are not tied to any particular buyer or type of buyer, but have a very real opportunity to skip one or two links of the chain. Besides, there is a large number of intermediaries to choose from at all stages. In 1972-3, there were a total of 113 coffee marketing centers with some 830 licensed speculators in Haiti.[27] Table 4.3 shows the regional division of centers and speculators. The average number of speculators per speculation post was 7 in the country as a whole, with a range from 2 to 14, and the number of centers ranged from 2 to 20. With the exception of Saint-Marc no buying district had fewer than 29 speculators.**

Table 4.3: Number of Coffee Speculators and Volume of Coffee Sold by District 1972-3

Districts	Speculation centers	Speculators		Volume of coffee sold	
		Number	Average per center	No. of 60 kg. sacks	Average no. of sacks per speculator
Port-au-Prince	11	88	8	30,292	344
Croix-des-Bouquets	17	51	3	19,028	373
Cap-Haïtien	20	125	6	74,752	598
Port-de-Paix	4	59	14	26,952	457
Gonaïves	4	29	7	11,619	400
Saint-Marc	4	7	2	3,187	455
Jacmel	6	77	12	30,995	402
Petit-Goâve	13	93	7	14,755	158
Jérémie	21	216	10	63,351	293
Cayes	13	85	5	43,737	514
Total	113	830	7	318,068	383

Source: JWK (1976:1), p. 45.

*No economic monopsony resulting from possible monopolization of processing facilities, i.e. washing factories, has arisen either, since washing is not a compulsory operation.
**In 1972-3 Saint-Marc only accounted for 1 percent of the total production, however (JWK (1976:1), p. 31).

The number of speculators has varied considerably since the 1920s. By the end of that decade the number lay around 700. In order to become a speculator a fee of 25 gourdes per season had to be paid. In the beginning of the 1930s, this tax was reduced, and the number of speculators swelled to over 5,000 in 1933-4. (An additional reason for the multiplication of traders reportedly was the difficulty to sustain a decent income after the onset of the Depression.) The reduction of the speculation fee was accompanied by other liberalization measures. Hitherto, the speculators had been permitted to operate only in the major coffee centers, but this clause was now relaxed and the intermediaries could go into a larger number of rural districts than before. Competition increased among the speculators.

Subsequently, the number of licensed speculators fell again. William B. Gates, Jr, reports a figure of 1,500 to 2,000 from the late 1950s,[28] and Paul Moral mentions a number of 1,100 for the same period.[29] Still, at that time it was felt that the number of speculators was far too high, and that in addition to fragmentation of coffee holdings, and hence increased gathering problems, it reflected a lack of other opportunities of gainful employment rather than the needs of producers and consumers.[30] From the early fifties to the mid-seventies the coffee market shrank and the price of coffee fell. The number of speculators was reduced even further. Ever since the thirties there also appears to have been another trend at work which indicates strong competition (and possibly some increasing concentration) in the industry. At the beginning of the thirties many speculators operated fairly independently, with their own capital,[31] but since then an increasing number of speculators have lost their financial independence and have been reduced to being mere agents for the exporters who at the beginning of the buying season advance the necessary funds.[32] Today the great majority of the speculators are agents.

Going back to Table 4.3, we find yet another indication of competition among the licensed speculators. The average number of coffee sacks bought per year is low — not more than 383. (This, however, does not mean that all speculators operate on a small scale. A recent, thorough study of the coffee industry reports for example that one of the largest speculators in the Cap-Haïtien area buys no less than 150 sacks per week during the peak season.[33])

A third indication of strong competition among speculators is the *sous-marins*.* The licensed speculators cannot rely on the peasants to

---

*Their number remains unknown.

Poverty and the Market

bring in their harvest to the speculation posts, but the peasants have a great deal of freedom of choice. They can choose among the speculators, and they can also bypass the speculators entirely and sell directly to washing factories (in the case of cherries) or exporters. Gates reports an amusing incident with respect to this freedom of choice:

> I will have difficulty forgetting the sight of a peasant woman marching away from a coffee washing plant with a few bidons* of cherries because she was obliged to stand in line longer than seemed appropriate. The incident was climaxed when an important official of a leading coffee house dashed after her to keep those bidons from walking off to a competitor a few miles down the narrow, soggy road.[34]

Competition among speculators is not carried out in terms of price, since, as we will soon see, the speculators are not in the position where they can influence the coffee price. Instead, they try to tie the peasants to them by extending credits before the harvest against delivery of the crop when harvested.[35] They also try to maintain good relations with the peasants throughout the year to assure that the latter will patronize them when the harvest comes.[36] Sometimes, these relations develop into formal *pratik* relationships.[37] On the other hand, speculators who do not offer the going market price easily lose business, since the peasants appear to be very sensitive even to very small price differences. Word of such differences spreads rapidly during the harvest season,[38] and the peasants react strongly. Reportedly, they will transport coffee for up to 12 kilometers to take advantage of a one-cent-a-pound difference in the price given by two competitors.[39] Hence, no informational power barriers which may lead to monopsony generally exist.

The number of exporters is much lower than that of speculators. Gates in his investigation of the coffee industry in the 1950s lists around 35 companies,[40] and the most recent study lists 28 exporters.[41] Table 4.4 shows that the degree of concentration among exporters has changed very little since the 1950s. The four largest companies handle more than 50 percent of the exports, with the following six accounting for around 25 percent. On the face of it, this opens strong possibilities for collusion among the leading exporters to obtain pricing agreements, but in practice competition seems to be as strong among exporters as among speculators.

---

*The *bidon* is the standard measure for Haitian coffee when sold by the peasants. It is a can holding 3.5-6 kilos of cherries (JWK (1976:1), p. 47).

138 Poverty and the Market

Table 4.4: The Degree of Concentration among Coffee Exporters

	Percentage of total exports	
	1951/52-1956/57	1972/73
First four firms	54 - 62	54
Following six firms	23 - 28	26
Others	12 - 20	20

Sources: Gates (1959:2), p. 27; JWK (1976:1), p. 50.

Table 4.5 lists the eight most important exporters in 1951/52, their relative positions and their shares of total coffee exports for some later years for which data are available. The table shows that neither the relative position of the exporters nor their respective shares of total exports are given — either in the long or in the very short run.

Table 4.5: Relative Positions of Leading Coffee Exporters

	1951/2		1952/3		1953/4		1954/5		1955/6		1956/7		1957/8		1974/5	
	Rank	%	Rank	%	Rank	%	Rank	%	Rank	%	Rank	%	Rank	%	Rank	%
Mantèque	1	16.7	1	17.6	1	17.0	3	14.7	2	16.0	3	13.4	4	10.0	1	18.1
Madsen	2	14.7	3	14.4	3	12.4	4	13.9	1	17.7	4	11.6	2	15.1	3	13.0
Wiener	3	14.0	2	15.9	2	15.5	2	14.9	4	13.6	2	16.6	3	14.6	2	15.3
Blanchet	4	8.5	5	6.9	5	7.6	5	6.7	7	4.2	5	6.1	6	5.9	—	—
Reinbold	5	7.0	4	8.3	4	10.1	1	15.3	3	14.0	1	20.3	1	16.2	—	—
Dufort	6	6.7	6	5.8	6	4.2	6	5.6	5	6.4	8	3.6	5	6.2	4	6.9
Vital	7	5.0	7	4.6	7	4.1	7	4.2	6	4.6	7	5.1	7	4.7	8	3.9
Novella	8	3.6	8	3.9	10	2.4	—	—	—	—	—	—	10	2.6	6	5.5

Sources: Gates (1959:2), p. 27; DARNDR (1974-5), Table 14.

Pricing agreements in fact do exist from time to time among exporters and were more or less formalized a few years ago when the *Association des Exportateurs de Café* (ASDEC) was formed to guide exporter pricing.[42] Such agreements — formal or informal — have, however, proved to be without effect. As a rule they do not last beyond the first few weeks of the buying season, whereafter they break down under the pressure of competition among the exporters.[43]

It appears as if one of the main reasons behind the intense competition (which is reported to have been virtually cut-throat at times) is the existence of diseconomies of scale in administration and supervision. The main problem is how to supervise the activities of the speculators so as to assure that these actually deliver the coffee to the exporters that have financed their buying. The very act of advancing money is no guarantee, since slight price differences between exporters make the speculators prefer the higher bidders, and loans can be repaid regardless of who gets the coffee.[44] In addition, the exporter has to make sure that he does not advance money to speculators who are likely to default. Not only the speculators have to be supervised, but also the final cleaning, drying and sorting process which takes place after the exporter has received the coffee (as well as the washing process in those cases where the exporter owns a washing factory), in order to minimize theft and to maintain the good quality of the final product in order to bring in as much as possible when the coffee is sold. According to Gates, the diseconomies of large scale set in approximately when the exporter reaches an export volume of some 90,000 60-kilo sacks.[45] Small and medium-size exporters give the impression that they can compete efficiently with their bigger colleagues, and that competition among the 'big four' may be at least as intense was seen when one of them during the fifties had to fight to regain its position at the top, as well as during the sixties when exports fell and many exporters lost money almost to the point of actual bankruptcy. The ASDEC and the efforts to establish a formal pricing agreement was a direct outcome of this fight for market shares.[46]

All the evidence examined so far indicates that coffee marketing is highly competitive and hence also technologically highly efficient. No legal monopsony or oligopsony due to legal power resulting from the requirement that middlemen be licensed has been proved to exist, but a large number of illegal intermediaries operate without licences. No economic power due to monopolization of washing facilities exists, since washing is not a compulsory operation. No barriers to the spread of market information have been found. Instead, we have seen that the number of middlemen is high at all stages of the commercial process (except maybe for the exporter level). Furthermore, we have seen that the coffee-growing peasant is not tied to any particular intermediary or even to any particular *kind* of intermediaries, but he can easily skip one or more stages in the commercial process, should the conditions for the transactions be unsatisfactory at the level at which he usually trades. In sum, all types of intermediaries appear to compete very actively with each other (including the exporters). This result runs contrary to some of the conventional wisdom (which, however, is not shared by all students of the coffee industry). It is therefore important to check the conclusion in some way, and this may be done by an examination of some figures for the middlemen's profit margins.

Middlemen's Profit Margins

Table 4.6 shows the changes in the division of coffee export incomes between producers, intermediaries and taxes from the early fifties to

Table 4.6: Shares in f.o.b. Prices of Haitian Coffee 1950-7 and 1964-70 (US dollars per 100 kilos; percent)

Year	f.o.b. Export Price	Taxes Amount	Share	Intermediaries Amount	Share	Producer Amount	Share
1950	102.00	16.40	16%	11.60	11%	74.00	73%
....							
1952	104.00	16.80	16%	13.20	12%	74.00	72%
1953	108.00	17.40	16%	17.60	16%	73.00	68%
1954	137.00	33.00	24%	25.60	19%	78.40	57%
1955	117.00	31.20	27%	16.60	14%	69.20	59%
1956	107.00	28.40	27%	18.20	17%	60.40	56%
1957	114.00	30.80	27%	15.20	13%	68.00	60%
....							
....							
1964	80.00	25.82	32%	14.18	18%	40.00	50%
1965	84.00	26.82	32%	23.18	28%	34.00	40%
1966	85.00	26.82	32%	23.18	27%	35.00	41%
1967	79.00	26.82	34%	20.18	25%	32.00	41%
1968	74.00	26.82	36%	16.18	22%	31.00	42%
1969	72.00	26.48	37%	17.72	24%	28.00	39%
1970	95.80	27.25	29%	21.37	22%	47.18	49%
1971	87.30	28.30	32%	26.70	31%	32.00	37%
1972	86.00	27.30	32%	21.70	25%	37.00	43%
1973	107.85	28.40	26%	24.60	23%	55.00	51%
1974	131.00	30.83	24%	33.17	25%	67.00	51%
1975	105.54	27.96	26%	36.04	34%	42.00	40%
1976	170.13	36.17	21%	28.96	17%	105.00	62%

Sources: 1950, 1952-3, 1964-70: CIAP (1972), p. 52; 1954-7: Gates (1959:2), p. 24; 1971-6: Information from Section des Statistiques, Institut Haïtien de Promotion du Café et des Denrées d'Exportation.

the mid-seventies. The share of the middlemen rose from an average of 16 percent in the 1952-56 period to 23 percent 1967-71 and 25 percent

1972-76. Taken at face value, this could perhaps be interpreted as a sign of increased concentration and price fixing on the part of the intermediaries to the disadvantage of the peasants, but in reality this is less likely to be true. Probably most of the increase is due to increased transport costs, for example. Coffee often used to be transported by sea from provincial harbors to the export ports. The most important item for the Haitian cabotage was imported wheat flour, but when substitution of domestic grains for the latter began, coastal shipping declined, and coffee, which was only a marginal cargo, instead had to be transported on rough and increasingly deteriorating roads.[47] This of course means that the entire increase cannot be treated as an addition to intermediary profits.

The profits shown in Table 4.6 are gross, not net profits. Unfortunately, the data upon which the table is based do not allow a computation of any net figures, but if we go on to Table 4.7 we may get a clearer idea of intermediary costs in relation to profits in the coffee industry. We see that 15 percent of the f.o.b. price consists of gross intermediary profits, and that another 15 percent consists of exporter costs. From the gross figures we have to subtract some costs to arrive at the net margins. The speculators, whose gross profits average 3 percent, often have to pay for transportation of the coffee from their speculation posts to the warehouse of the exporter. To this we have to add the rent for buying and storage premises, the yearly cost of capital (*glacis*, weighing scale) and taxes, license fees, *patente*, etc. Most speculators also hire one or two people who help them handle the coffee. Taken altogether, these costs reduce the average net profit of the speculators to some $0.50-$0.75 per bag, or less than 1 percent of the f.o.b. price.[48] Thus, the level of speculator profits is virtually zero. The speculators receive only compensation for their work, and profits in the sense of a reward exceeding what the speculators could earn in alternative employments[49] are practically absent at this level of the coffee marketing system.

Some of the exporter costs are indicated in Table 4.7. Most important are the weight losses due to humidity which appear to have increased in recent years because of relaxed controls. (In some districts they are reported to be as high as 20 percent.) Second in importance is the loss due to sorting (*triage*). Stones, trash, improperly dried beans, and beans that have been subject to improper processing and handling must be sorted out. This loss is not a net loss, however, since some of the *triage* coffee can be sold on the domestic market or can be exported at reduced prices. A third cost is that of bags. The exporters are required to purchase only government-manufactured sisal bags. Transportation, finally, is another important cost for the exporter. He sometimes has to pay for moving the coffee from the growing areas to the provincial towns, and in addition for moving it to the export ports.

Table 4.7: Distribution of Returns on Coffee Exports 1975-6

		US$ per 60-kilo sack	Percent
	Price to producer	34.61	45
+	Gross speculator profit	2.47	3
=	Price to speculator	37.08	
+	Exporter costs	11.45	15
+	Gross exporter profit	8.82	12
+	Taxes	18.90	25
=	f.o.b. price	76.25	100

Source: JWK (1976:1), p. 55. (The table presented there has been corrected for a mistake in average gross exporter profit.)

Subtracting the above costs from the price that the exporters receive leaves an average gross profit of 12 percent, as seen in Table 4.7, with an estimated range of 4 to 18 percent.[50] To arrive at the net profit of the exporters some more cost items have to be taken into account. Exporters are subject to various license fees and taxes: *patente,* revenue taxes, banking fees, property taxes, business taxes, etc. In addition they have to face depreciation of capital assets, uncollectable loans to speculators, administrative overhead costs, interest, labor costs, costs related to utilities, etc. Deducting all these costs cuts the net profit to less than one-half of the gross margin — to 4 or 5 percent of the f.o.b. price per bag, which is believed not to be excessive in comparison to what alternative investments yield. (Very many exporters have actually diversified their portfolios by establishing other business and reducing the share invested in coffee marketing.[51])

The strong competition among intermediaries in the coffee trade means that the middlemen are not in a position to influence the price paid to the producers. This price instead is an outcome of two things: the export taxes on coffee (which will be dealt with in Chapter 8) and the competitive process. The price of Haitian coffee on the world market essentially follows that of Santos 'B' on the New York coffee exchange and the prices established on the London Arabica terminal.[52] The exporters in Haiti in turn keep in daily contact with price movements on these two markets through private news and wire services, and relate their offer prices accordingly.

Figure 4.4 shows the monthly fluctuations in the price of Haitian coffee between 1970 and 1973. The f.o.b. price fluctuated considerably during this period, and as the figure reveals, during the period the price received by the farmers generally followed the export price and the price received by the exporters (after export taxes have been deducted) reasonably well.

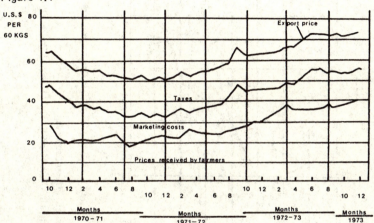

Figure 4.4

Source: JWK (1976:1), p. 63.

The results of the analysis of monthly time series data are corroborated by a look at the annual data. Such series are shown in Figure 4.5 for the period from 1933 to 1974. Here, as in the case of monthly data, the prices received by the producers appear to follow those received by the exporters fairly closely.

To sum up: the net profit levels of the exporters appear to be somewhat higher than those of the speculators, but neither group of intermediaries reaches the profit level where it becomes appropriate to speak of monopsony profits. From the gross profit levels of 3 percent (speculators) and 12 percent (exporters) of the f.o.b. price, a number of costs must be deducted before the net profit levels are arrived at, and once this operation is performed, the profit levels are reduced – in the case of speculators virtually to zero and in the case of exporters to a level of around 5 percent of the f.o.b. price. The price received by the peasant

Figure 4.5

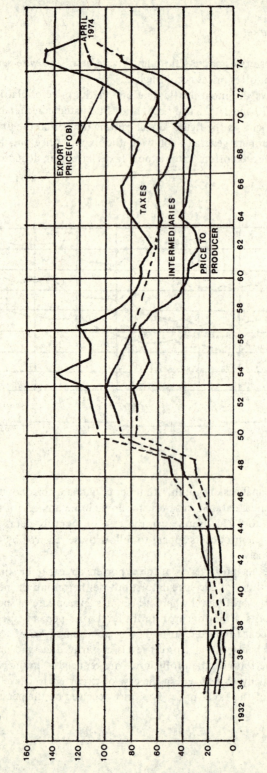

US $ PER 100 KGS

The figure does not quite correspond to Table 4.6 which is partly based on different sources.
Sources: 1933/34-1948/49, 1953-57 (intermediaries): based upon figures in Gates (1959:2), p. 24, rest of figure: US/AID (1974), p. 17.

for his product moves in fairly close harmony with those prevailing in the world market. In terms of net profits, the exporters and the speculators convey a picture of a coffee marketing system which appears to operate very close to the technical efficiency frontier. The costs are held at a minimum (given the obstacles posed by the transportation system — which will be dealt with in the appendix to this chapter).

The competition which takes place between the intermediaries of the coffee marketing chain approaches perfect competition. The product is not homogeneous but this is compensated for by differences in price according to the quality level so that at a given stage of the marketing process for a given quality there is a strong tendency for the price to be uniform. Sellers and buyers alike appear to have a good knowledge of the going market price. Entry into the market seems to be relatively free as indicated by the low levels of profits both among speculators and among exporters, and the number of buyers (and sellers) finally, is presumably high enough to preclude any monopsonistic influences on the price received by the peasants. No sources of monopsony power have been found, and as we will see in the second half of this chapter, the coffee middlemen are probably not in the situation where they can monopolize sales to the peasants either. It is therefore difficult to avoid the conclusion that the marketing system for coffee is relatively technologically efficient and that the peasants are not being exploited by monopsonistic or oligopsonistic middlemen. The marketing of coffee is not likely to be an important reason for peasant poverty in Haiti.

The Marketing of Subsistence Crops

In the remaining part of this chapter we will devote our attention to an analysis of the marketing system for those crops which do not enter international trade, i.e. those crops we have chosen to call subsistence crops. This system also handles the distribution of those goods of urban origin that the peasants consume. We will begin with a description of the intermediaries in the marketing chain, and, after a short discussion of the system of market-places, we will examine the available evidence with respect to collusion and competition among the intermediaries.

The Intermediaries

Subsistence crops are grown on more than half a million small peasant farms, and after the harvest whatever commercial surplus the peasant family may possess is marketed. The basic choice for the family is then whether the crop should be brought to a market-place or whether it should be sold to an intermediary in the home of the peasant. If brought to the market-place the crop is sold at the going retail price, but if a home transaction with an intermediary is made, it is a wholesale deal, and the price received by the peasant is slightly lower.[53] Against this difference in prices the peasant must weigh at least two other factors. One is the cost of transporting the goods to the market-place, which is avoided if a home transaction is made. The other has to do with the fact that many agricultural commodities are very perishable. If the market-place happens to be glutted with the crop that the peasant wants to sell, turnover may be very slow so that the goods may have to be taken back home unsold, and the peasant may have to wait up to one week before another attempt at marketing can be made, and in the meantime the product may be partly or wholly destroyed. Until 11 September 1974 the peasants also had to pay a market tax each time they visited a market-place as sellers, which in turn, was an additional reason why home transactions should be preferred.[54]

In the case where the peasants choose to bring their products to the market-place the transactions are generally handled by the women. The Haitian men do basically only farm work while their women see to it that the crops are sold. This sexual division of labor is a rule with rather few exceptions. (Men usually sell coffee and cattle — neither of which enter the regular market-places — and also charcoal and wood in bulk.*)

Nearly every peasant woman during the course of her life acquires a considerable amount of trading experience. At one time or another, several try their luck as professional tradeswomen. Often this begins (on a minor scale) at a very early age. Sidney W. Mintz has described a typical start:

> Girl children learn how to trade from their mothers, aunts, older sisters and other female relatives and ritual kinfolk. They customarily accompany some older women, first to the local marketplaces and the market-like gatherings for cockfights, wakes, etc. Later they will be taken to the large regional marketplaces, the town marketplaces, and even the great marketplaces of the capital. They are taught to buy and sell, to calculate value and to recognize currency, to measure and to judge quantity and quality, to assess various products, as matter-of-factly as boys are taught to plant, cultivate

---

*The sexual division of trading activities is not entirely rigid but subject to e.g. regional variations (Underwood (1960), p. 5). In principle, however, everywhere in Haiti the women do most of the trading.

and harvest. It is usual for a little girl to receive a small gift of cash from a relative or godparent to enable her to undertake business on her own, under the supervision of an older woman. The first marketing activities a young girl undertakes with the hope of profit are likely to be small-scale bulk-breaking (for instance, the retailing of small quantities of sugar or soap) or commission selling. These are low-profit, 'safe' operations. While doing these things, the child learns about bulking, processing, wholesaling and other ways to make a profit in marketing. Above all, she has a chance in the marketplace to see how trade is done, and those older than her have a chance to see if she is quick and zestful in trade.[55]

If the young girl is successful in her operations she may continue on her own, usually with a very small capital in her first operations — given to her by relatives, amassed by the family's farming activities, gathered by taking a loan or by taking stock on credit. With skill the girl may move up the social hierarchy of tradeswomen, finally to acquire her own store in town. Before she reaches this goal, however, she has for some time been a *Madam Sara,* a traveling intermediary.

Madam Sara* is the most strategic person in the marketing system for subsistence goods. She is the agent that establishes the contact between urban consumers and rural producers and vice versa. She constantly travels back and forth between rural and urban districts, between the larger cities and their hinterland, sometimes covering vast geographical areas. To do so she does not rely on carrying her stock or loading it on donkey back, which are the prevalent modes of transportation with the peasants, but instead travels with the regular network of truckers that operate continuously between most major centers in Haiti. *Madam Sara* usually is a woman of peasant origin. In the vast majority of cases she has begun her activities on a very small scale in a

---

*The word comes from the name of a migratory bird that 'flies from place to place and never fails to find its food wherever it might be' (Murray & Alvarez (1973), p. 28). The term also carries somewhat derogatory connotations, since this bird is known to pillage the peasant's crops (Métraux *et al.* (1951), p. 122). The terminology with respect to female traders is a little bit confusing. Many different terms are used to denote professional female traders. Three of the most common are *revendeuses, pacotilleuses* and *Madam Sara.* The exact meaning of the words varies from author to author. In the present study we will adopt the meaning of *Madam Sara* and *revendeuse* used in the market studies carried out recently under the auspices of IICA (Inter-American Institute of Agricultural Sciences). (See e.g. Murray & Alvarez (1973); IICA (1974:2); and Dorville (1975:3).)

manner resembling the one described above, gradually establishing herself as a *revendeuse,* a retailer. When enough capital has been amassed, the first trading expedition out of the local area is launched. The successful *Madam Sara,* reinvesting her profits, slowly manages to develop a network of complex operations:

> The following may give some idea of the complicated nature of the ...transactions [of the *Madam Sara*]. A woman of Jacmel bought avocadoes, poultry, pork and syrup in the Marbial market. She sold this produce at Jacmel; there, she was careful to buy oranges, rice, maize and large beans which she went to sell at Port-au-Prince. In the capital she obtained the local blue cloth for clothing, Siamese cloth, trousers, blouses, dresses, soap and hardware or haberdashery articles, which she disposed of in the 'mornes'; after which she recommenced the whole series of purchases and sales.[56]

Often, the *Madam Sara* specialize in their trading activities, limiting their sphere of action to a particular geographic route to establish close contacts with buyers, sellers and truckers so as to obtain better and safer terms on which to carry out their transactions, or by handling a limited number of goods, usually with one crop as the main item and the others as sidelines that can be expanded if demand or supply of the main good should contract.

Madam Sara is essentially a wholesale dealer who only under exceptional circumstances turns her attention to retailing. The latter type of commerce is handled by the *revendeuses* who either obtain their stock from the family farm or buy it from other peasants or from *Madam Sara.* The borderline between the *revendeuse* and *Madam Sara* is sometimes floating, however. Many *revendeuses* travel to the capital, for example, to buy products that are not locally available, bringing agricultural commodities with them to make the trip worthwhile, but these trips are much less frequent and more irregular than those of the *Madam Sara.* Generally, a *revendeuse* buys wholesale and sells retail to local, rural *habitants* or to town-dwellers (depending on her location) in market-places or streets or on other public occasions.[57]

The last link in the commercialization chain for subsistence goods that will be described here is that of the depots. A depot is a 'secure storage [area] where space is rented to intermediaries dealing primarily in the wholesale trade.'[58] The depot system has been developed almost exclusively in the capital* and is concentrated in a single area. Still, in a

---

*Some depots are found in Cap-Haïtien but the system there is not nearly as well

sense, it plays an important role in the commercial process. Most *Madam Sara* when arriving in Port-au-Prince are dropped by the truckers in the downtown depot district where they rent space from a depot owner to store their produce. Usually they can also conduct their selling business in the depot and even sleep there at night.

Murray and Alvarez make a distinction between two types of depots: the *dépôt publique* and the *dépôt personnel*. In the former the owner merely rents storing, trading and sleeping space to his customers, and is responsible for the security of the merchandise, while in the *dépôt personnel* he is himself engaged in commerce and hence purchases some of the stock brought in by the *Madam Sara*, to resell it to the city retailers himself.[59]

At the depots bulk-breaking of agricultural products and bulking of urban goods both take place. As soon as the *Madam Sara* get off the trucks, their regular customers gather, and frequently most of their stock is sold within a few hours of their arrival in Port-au-Prince.[60] The *revendeuses* know exactly where and when to find what they are looking for in the depot area, and in the case of going to a *dépôt personnel* the owner of the place is quick to pick out what he needs. What is not sold the first evening is disposed of during the course of the next few days, and during this time *Madam Sara* also buys and bulks whatever stock she wants to bring back into the rural section — part of it right in the depot district.[61]

The Network of Market-places

Before we go on to examine the extent of competition between the intermediaries involved in the marketing of subsistence products and city goods we will give a short description of the second important element in the marketing of these goods — the system of market-places.

At the very simplest level, market-places are totally unorganized. Whenever there is some kind of activity going on that may attract a crowd there is also a potential market. This is the *ti maché* described by Frances W. Underwood:

> Roadside gatherings of women venders offering small amounts of foodstuffs, cooked food, or drinks are to be seen every day throughout Haiti...They are frequent within the towns when there is no

developed as in the capital and the depots appear to be without much practical importance (Werleigh & Duplan (1975), pp. 35-7).

market day and operate outside them on market days to avoid the market tax...Pralines, maize puddings, coconut puddings, small dishes of cooked goat meat or rice and beans, cassava cakes, candies, and fresh fruits are standard items, as are cola, rum drinks, cigarettes, and tobacco. Tomatoes, mangoes, oranges, and *caimitos* are arranged in little piles or heaped in small half calabashes. Sweetmeats and 'bread' (rolls) are regularly arranged on trays, while tobacco is sold in small packets. Cola and rum drinks are offered in small quantities (glass or cup) poured by the trader from a quart bottle.

In addition, such dry goods as thread, matches, combs, and needles; staples such as coffee, beans, sugar, and spices; cooking substances such as lard; and craft items such as woven hats, sandals, or belts may be hawked alongside the roadways...

The term 'small market' is also applied to the group of women traders which gathers at cockfights, dances, 'wakes' for the dead, or communal celebrations to sell trays of refreshments — drinks, rolls, sweets, cigarettes, and occasionally cooked meats.[62]

Far more important than these unorganized trading activities, however, are the state-controlled markets. A survey made by the Inter-American Institute of Agricultural Sciences (IICA) in 1975 identified 519 such market-places, the geographical distribution of which is shown in Figure 4.6.*

On the lowest level we find the semi-rural markets.[63] This is the most common type of organized market in Haiti. No less than 426 of the markets in the IICA survey were classified as semi-rural.[64] These markets only touch the immediate localities where they are situated. Their radius of action is limited to one or two kilometers. The trade that takes place there is either between peasant women from the local community or between peasant women and traveling *Madam Sara* that are bulking foodstuffs to be brought into urban areas. The latter also dispose of peasant necessities of urban or imported origin in these markets.

Moving another step up the ladder we find the regional marketplaces. Their influence extends over a wider area than that of the town markets, in extreme cases across almost the entire country. Larger and more varied quantities of goods are bought and sold here. Staples come

---

*LaGra, Fanfan & Charleston (1975), p. 3. This study explicitly excluded all markets with a presence of less than 50 persons on a normal market day, and the authors state that it is possible that some larger markets were excluded as well.

Poverty and the Market

in from different regions, some of which is bulked by the large number of *Madam Sara* usually present to be taken into the largest cities, and yet another part is broken to be resold to the local communities on town markets and local markets. Some consumers may also buy directly in these markets to take advantage of the wide range of goods displayed there.

Figure 4.6

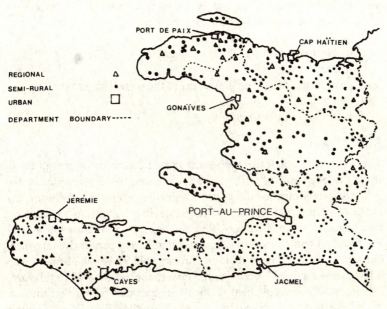

Source: LaGra, Fanfan & Charleston (1975), Carte 1.

On the highest level in the hierarchy of market-places, finally, we find the urban markets — the large sea ports and the department capitals. These are the points of final consumption for much of the peasant produce. The transactions that take place in this type of market are mostly between consumers and middlemen and between different categories of middlemen before the goods reach the final consumer. These markets, if situated on the sea, are also the points where imported peasant necessities reach the country and undergo the first bulk-breaking operations.

The Degree of Competition among Intermediaries

We have now gathered enough factual knowledge about the system of intermediaries and market-places involved in the trade with subsistence goods and peasant consumer goods of urban origin to go on to examine whether this system is as efficient as the coffee marketing system or whether it contains any important monopsonistic or monopolistic features.

Cases of genuine collusion among intermediaries are hard to find. No combines of middlemen are known to exist at any level of the marketing system for subsistence goods, and students of this system generally put strong emphasis on its purely competitive nature.[65] Evidence of this competition may be found under five headings:

1. profit margins among the intermediaries,
2. freedom of entry,
3. possibilities of making short-cuts in the marketing chain,
4. determination of prices,
5. non-price competition.

Profit Margins

The scanty available evidence regarding middlemen profit margins confirms the existence of stiff competition among the intermediaries. No systematic investigation of these margins has ever been made for any category of intermediaries, but the scattered observations available by and large convey a picture of slim net returns. On the lowest level of the trading hierarchy the profits generated barely permit the intermediaries to stay alive. Home retailing, for example, rarely yields more than a few pennies a day.[66] Whatever incomes that are generated in this manner are merely a supplement to incomes generated from other sources. Alfred Métraux and his staff in the Marbial valley found that a couple of families doing some part-time trading added less than 1 percent to their total income.[67] Due to the abundance of time available during most of the year and due to the lack of other economic opportunities peasant women are always ready to engage in part-time trading at virtually no profit. The capital at their disposal as a rule is very small which means that the absolute size of the profits generated is tiny, but with an opportunity cost of labor which is close to zero except during the agricultural peak seasons, trading with very small amounts still makes sense. The Métraux team provides some good illustrations of this point:

> Little profit comes...from petty trade. To us, the small profits for which the peasants are prepared to make sustained efforts are almost inconceivable. We have come across peasants who have gone 9 miles

or so to buy maize at 0.20 gourde the 'godet' (standard container), whereas they could have obtained it where they were at 0.45 gourde for two 'godet'. Typical of this, too, was another scene we witnessed. A woman was trying to persuade a *revendeuse* to sell her maize semolina at the current price, but to let her use her own measuring apparatus, which would have assigned her a very slightly larger quantity of semolina than would that of the reseller; but it was this imperceptible difference in quantity that was to constitute the latter's profit. The bargaining, which was about an amount of less than 0.05 gourde lasted a good hour and was extremely lively. Each week, peasant women go to Port-au-Prince with an immense load on their heads, which makes the climbing of steep mountains, under a baking sun a formidable task indeed. After being away for three or four days, they return home, having made a profit of 3 or 4 gdes.[68]

Perhaps the most typical case of small-scale trading at extremely small profit margins is that of selling in the *ti maché*:

> The women who sell cola, 'clairin', candies and biscuits are constantly on the move. They go to any place in the valley where for any reason a group of people are gathered together — for a service, a marriage, a political meeting, etc. 'Wakes' for the dead — by relatives and friends, an occasion for festivity and entertainment — are a godsend to these traders. As soon as they learn that someone in some *kay* has died, they proceed thither at any hour of the day or night, carrying their heavy trays on their heads. They also go from market to market, in the sole hope of making a few pence of profit. Their wandering existence is a specially hard one, and the slightest accident — a theft, a fall or an illness — may permanently destroy their small trading concern.[69]

The situation of the regular *revendeuses* appears not to be much better. Métraux states that the female traders always strive to make a profit of 0.20 gourde on each gourde invested, but that competition often forces them to accept a margin of 10 percent or less,[70] and Mintz mentions that for a *revendeuse* to walk 30 miles in a day to acquire or dispose of stock is not unusual, and that distances nearly twice as long may have to be covered if particular market-places are to be reached.[71]

Murray and Alvarez followed a *Madam Sara* on the route between Lascahobas and Port-au-Prince, a distance of 90 kilometers. The woman, who was mainly selling beans, made a net profit of about 10 percent on her original investment on that trip. The same woman on a later trip netted 7 percent on her investment. Murray and Alvarez conclude that 10 percent seems to be 'a fairly "normal" profit for the traveling intermediary'.[72]

René Dorville presents similar figures for vegetable marketing. As shown in Table 4.8, between 25 and 40 percent was added to the price between Bellevue de la Montagne in the Kenscoff region and Port-au-Prince (a distance of 27 kilometers, although with a considerable difference in altitude). The figure indicates gross, not net margins, however, so that the costs of the intermediaries have to be deducted to arrive at the 'true' profits realized. Even so, we see that at least for the retailers the margins must be very small. The same is probably true also for the *Madam Sara*, since their gross margins contain the entire cost of transporting the vegetables to the capital and storing them in the depots there, and all the products shown in Table 4.8 are fairly bulky items.

Table 4.8: Margins in Vegetable Marketing

	Potatoes	Cabbage	Carrots	Onions
Producer	60%	60%	75%	75%
Madam Sara	25%	30%	20%	20%
Revendeuse	15%	10%	5%	5%
Total	100%	100%	100%	100%

Source: Dorville (1975:3), p. 45.

That the profit of the *Madam Sara* as a rule is not excessive becomes even more evident if the services that these women provide are taken into account. The margins discussed in the preceding paragraphs are not net of the cost of the labor supplied by the *Madam Sara* themselves and their agents. One of the main problems of marketing agricultural produce in Haiti is that production is very dispersed. There are more than 600,000 farms in the country, most of which produce only small quantities.[73] Besides, few areas are specialized on one or just a few products. Under such circumstances bulking becomes a very labor-intensive activity. The *Madam Sara* have to buy small quantities from a large number of suppliers, which is very time-consuming, and if they cannot amass enough volume their often very extensive trips do not yield any profit. The effort involved in bulking is often so great that agents have to be employed to supplement the efforts of *Madam Sara* herself.

Not only do the traveling intermediaries bulk agricultural goods but the same bulk is later broken in the urban centers, which further increases the number of small-scale transactions that the *Madam Sara* have to handle, since the retailers purchase mostly in only limited quantities. With this mode of operation the claims on *Madam Sara's* time increase correspondingly. Bulking and bulk-breaking also work in the opposite direction. Before going back into the rural districts, the tradeswomen gather goods of urban or imported origin which they later have to break before selling them to the country-based *revendeuses*. For those *Madam Sara* who do some of the retailing themselves the labor input required is even greater.

The third service provided by the traveling intermediaries is that of moving the goods physically from one place to another, which is done by using the existing network of more or less regularly running trucks. Given the deplorable state of the Haitian roads (which we will come back to in the appendix) spending the entire day on the road is very common.*

Other services provided are those of storing the goods, gathering information about demand, supply and prices in different markets, money-lending, supply of credit, packing of the merchandise, etc.

Seen in the light of this information, the margin of 20-30 percent shrinks considerably. Most of this margin consists of costs incurred in the process of amassing, transporting, storing and bulk-breaking of the goods etc., and what is left in the form of a net profit after subtracting these costs plus the implicit wage accruing to *Madam Sara* for providing her service probably does not represent a higher return on the money put into trading than the prospective return from alternative forms of investment.

Our examination of profit data for the intermediaries handling the marketing of subsistence goods indicates that competition is strong at all levels. On the petty trade level the profits generated do not suffice to ensure the existence of the intermediaries but must be regarded as nothing but a marginal addition to other incomes. The *revendeuses* are in a similar situation. Their net profit margins appear to be reduced to a level which does not allow us to speak of profits proper but only of a return to the labor expended. The information regarding the profits of *Madam Sara* finally indicates that the operations of the *Madam Sara*

---

*Often, when a truck has to be repaired, they spend two or three days on the road.

do not yield much more in the form of profits than other types of investment would have done.

Freedom of Entry

The comparatively low profits accruing to the intermediaries are a consequence of the large number of people engaged in the trading sector.[74]

It is not known with any accuracy how many intermediaries are involved in the marketing of subsistence crops in Haiti. In principle, all intermediaries must pay a fee to obtain a *patente*: the license which entitles them to carry on trading operations. In the late 1950s there were approximately 2,000 intermediaries with a *patente* in the entire country.[75] In practice, however, it appears as if the authorities bother to control only the itinerant *Madam Sara* who are charged according to how far they propose to travel. The great majority of Haitian tradeswomen, those operating on a small retail basis, generally possess no license.[76] Paul Moral in the late 1950s estimated that more than 50,000 women (and 15,000 men) could be classified as 'traders'.[77] Even this estimate probably gives a wrong idea about the numbers really involved, however, since it does not take into account the children under fourteen years of age engaged in petty trade nor the part-time intermediaries who slip in and out of trade as the profitability of marketing changes.[78] At any rate, the number is high enough to preclude any legally founded monopsony or monopoly tendencies among the middlemen. 'The unique feature of [the Haitian] market system is the vast number of persons it engages.'[79] Throughout most of the year there exists in the countryside a large pool of labor that is underemployed. One of the few productive outlets for these people lies in the marketing of subsistence goods and peasant consumer goods at various stages of the commercial chain.

There is very little to prevent entry among intermediaries. In the higher echelons of the trading hierarchy some capital is needed. A *Madam Sara* as a rule is financially independent. Few traveling wholesalers operate on a borrowing or credit basis.[80] Murray and Alvarez state that at least $60 is required to be a *Madam Sara*, and that a person with only that amount would be nothing but a very small wholesaler indeed.[81] This statement is confirmed by other observations. Sidney W. Mintz interviewed twenty female onion wholesalers who all had a capital exceeding $100, and all of them, with only a single exception, held the opinion that it would not be possible to carry out their trades with lesser amounts.[82] It is of course not very meaningful

Poverty and the Market 157

to try to establish any average sums, especially since *Madam Sara* usually keeps her working capital a secret which is not be revealed to her competitors, but sums ranging from $200 to $500 do not appear to be uncommon.[83]

To say that a *Madam Sara* requires a minimum capital of, say $60 does not imply that this sum acts as a barrier to entry. There are always *revendeuses* who have managed to build up a sufficient capital to take off on their first expeditions to urban areas that are ready to step in as soon as they perceive a possibility of making a profit. On average, however, the working capital of the *revendeuses* is smaller than that of a *Madam Sara* – in the case of bean retailers $50 against the suggested minimum of $60 for the wholesalers.[84] *Revendeuses* frequently resort to borrowing or to taking stock on credit to finance their operations.

In the same way as the successful *revendeuses* constantly push to become *Madam Sara*, there are always a number of young girls who are making the first efforts to become *revendeuses*:

> A young girl, the daughter of landed peasants, may initiate her career in commerce with no more stock than several hands of ripe bananas coming from her parents' land. No cash outlay is calculated in the acquisition and resale of this stock. She will try to sell it to other retailers at the mouths of paths leading to the market road, thus avoiding the payment of taxes or market fees. By repeating this manoeuvre, she may be able to acquire enough capital to begin buying hard goods such as soap or matches to sell in local markets; or to buy fowls in her rural district to resell to poultry merchants from the town. Idle capital can go into small livestock or into the planting of fast-maturing legumes, such as the ever-popular red, black and congo beans.[85]

Competition is keen at all levels. Tradeswomen are often heavily engaged in social climbing, and successful climbing becomes possible when transfer from one trading category to a superior one is completed. This of course also means that the trading system contains some downward social mobility. There is not room for everyone in marketing. Many are forced to leave trading altogether. Others move down the ladder, permanently or temporarily. *Madam Sara* in times of strong competition sometimes turn to retailing instead of wholesaling.[86] Conversely, when profit opportunities are favorable, people who normally do not dedicate themselves to trade enter into competition. Thus, during periods of scarcity of agricultural produce many Port-au-Prince depot owners actively compete with the *revendeuses* and very energetically try to persuade the *Madam Sara* to sell to them instead of dealing with the retailers.[87]

Another example is provided by the weekend commerce in Port-au-Prince. On weekends the demand for agricultural commodities always goes up, but prices generally do not increase. Thousands of part-time intermediaries (*revendeuses*) enter the market and compete with the full-time market-women. In addition, the *Madam Sara* usually plan their trips so that they arrive in Port-au-Prince on Friday or Saturday so that the increased demand for agricultural products is matched by an increase in supply. A sample taken in eleven market-places in the capital revealed a 25 percent increase in the number of market-women between Wednesday and Saturday, a figure that corresponds to an estimated total increase of more than 2,800 in twenty-three markets (not counting street retailing between market-places).[88]

There is great freedom of entry (and exit) in the marketing of subsistence goods and peasant consumer goods. Large numbers of intermediaries operate at all stages of the marketing process, and there is strong mobility (both upwards and downwards) between the stages. There are always enough people around with an amount of capital equal to or close to the 'critical' level required to trade at a certain stage. These people will enter the market as soon as the profit level rises above its equilibrium level creating a long-run tendency for profits to fall to zero.

Shortening the Marketing Chain

At most stages of the marketing process one or more steps can easily be bypassed by producers, intermediaries or consumers. This puts a squeeze on the middlemen to compete efficiently and renders monopsonization or monopolization very difficult. Three case histories neatly show the validity of this proposition. All three of them are concerned with how the merchandise gets all the way from the producer to the final consumer in the capital.

The marketing chain for beans is described in Figure 4.7.[89] The producer is faced with no less than four different choices of buyer. It is possible that he will sell directly to the local consumer, but this is not likely to be the case, since beans are a high-price foodstuff that not many local *habitants* will consider. His second choice is to call a buyer to his home and make a transaction there. Two types of buyers will then be considered: local *commerçants*, who operate independently,

Poverty and the Market 159

with their own capital or on credit, and *sékrétè* working as agents for the *Madam Sara*. The peasant may also let his wife bring the beans into the local market-place, which in turn, gives three options: selling to a town-dweller who buys for consumption on the local market, selling to a *sékrétè* (mainly on the way to the market-place), and finally selling to *Madam Sara* herself.

Figure 4.7

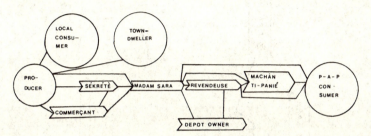

Both the *commerçants* and the *sékrétè* resell their beans to a *Madam Sara* (the *commerçants* perhaps via the *sékrétè*), who then bulks the beans and transports them to the capital by truck. After her arrival in Port-au-Prince *Madam Sara* also has a choice of four different categories of buyers. She may sell to a depot owner who is himself trading actively in beans; she may (most likely) sell to a *revendeuse*; she may sell to a 'little basket merchant' (*machân ti-panié*) who resells the beans on her rounds in the city neighborhoods; finally she may opt for selling directly to the consumers, which, however, is the least likely of her courses of action. Her buyers, in turn, directly or indirectly supply the Port-au-Prince consumers with beans.

Figure 4.8 gives a summary view of the commercialization process for rice.[90] The production of rice is concentrated in the Artibonite valley. In the first step most of the harvest is sold to local *Madam Sara* who operate only inside the valley. These intermediaries in turn sell the rice to a rice mill where it is polished. The polished rice is resold either to traveling *Madam Sara* who bring it into the depots of the capital or to Port-au-Prince-based wholesalers who supply the supermarkets of the capital and its suburbs. Some of these dealers also buy directly from the producers to avoid the intermediaries, have the rice polished and then sell it to the supermarkets.

In Figure 4.9 we illustrate the marketing chain for vegetables.[91] The peasants have three alternatives of selling: directly to the consumers in Port-au-Prince, to a *revendeuse* or to a *Madam Sara*. The

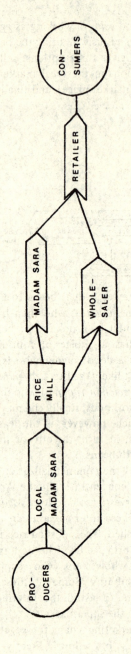

Figure 4.8

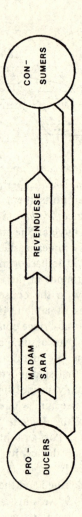

Figure 4.9

Poverty and the Market 161

latter, in turn, can choose between selling to a *revendeuse* or directly to the consumer.

Within Port-au-Prince there is an even wider range of choices for both intermediaries and consumers. After the merchandise has been unloaded in the depots it may change hands several times before reaching the final consumer. Uli Locher states that six times is not an uncommon figure. As the diagram in Figure 4.10 shows, the goods may even move 'backwards' in the commercialization chain, and presumably also change hands on the same level. Locher quotes extreme instances where no less than ten different transactions have been completed before the good in question even moved out of the depot area![92] This long chain is by no means a necessary one, however. Figure 4.10 also clearly illustrates the fact that the consumer can step in at any stage of the process and buy, or the intermediaries may jump one or more steps in the chain.

Figure 4.10

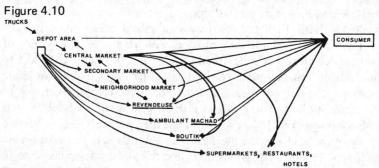

Source: Locher (1973), p. 16.

Locher also shows how the intermediaries sometimes try to avoid using the Port-au-Prince depots. Many *revendeuses* go into direct competition with the *Madam Sara* and buy produce in some of the large rural markets in the neighborhood of the capital. In this way agricultural products frequently reach the Port-au-Prince consumers without having passed more than one intermediary on its way from the producer.*

---

* Large-scale execution of such operations is difficult, however. On the one hand, if the number of *revendeuses* trying to avoid dealing with the *Madam Sara* increases the peasants are likely to raise their prices, and on the other hand, if a single *revendeuse* tries to expand the scale of her operations she will after a while inevitably run into a storage problem which, however, is most easily solved by resorting to the depots which means increased expenses (Locher (1973), pp. 20-21).

As in the case of coffee marketing, there are many possibilities from which the peasants can choose regarding the type of middleman with whom they want to deal when selling their subsistence crops. There is a large degree of flexibility with respect to which level in the marketing process that will make the first transactions. The same type of flexibility extends all the way through the chain. This flexibility increases the degree of competition among the intermediaries and hence also the efficiency of the marketing system. Any tendencies to price fixing by the middlemen at a particular level can be overcome simply by avoiding this level, going directly to the following one.

Setting the Price

A fourth way of checking the efficiency of the marketing system for subsistence goods and peasant consumer goods is to examine how prices are determined in the network of market-places. The price-setting process is complicated by two factors both of which could lead to inefficiency. First, agricultural products generally are of a very uneven quality in Haiti. High and low grades are mixed indiscriminately most of the time.[93] Second, the situation with regard to the system of measures employed in agricultural commerce is in a sense chaotic.* In the individual market-place considerable order reigns. Sidney W. Mintz examined the units of measure in the Fond-des-Nègres market, one of the largest regional market-places in Haiti, and found that both buyers and sellers were well informed as to what they were receiving in relation to the price paid despite the fact that different sets of measures are employed for different goods, and that this order also spilled over to the smaller market-places within the zone of influence of Fond-des-Nègres.[94] As we move from one market region to another, problems arise, however, since the same term may apply to different measures and one and the same measure may be known under various names in different regions. Paul Moral in *L'économie haïtienne* lists no less than 160 different measures of volume and weight.[95] Hence, when

---

* Much of the disorder may be due to the fact that for subsistence products the measures employed are volume, not weight measures (Comhaire-Sylvain (1964), p. 399; Mintz (1961:1), p. 23; Murray & Alvarez (1973), p. 22). Hence, the buyers get widely varying weights when buying the same volume, due to differences e.g. in water content. Sometimes sellers even deliberately immerse their products in water to make them bulkier (and heavier) (Métraux et al.(1951), p. 122). It should be noted, however, that scales are usually not efficient in a market situation unless there is an absolutely fool-proof system for their inspection. To replace measures of volume by measures of weight without providing the buyer with a means to check on the honesty of the seller is simply to concentrate more information in the hands of the sellers.

buyers and sellers from geographic locations at some distance from each other meet they must somehow make certain that both parties involved understand the relation between prices and measures.

Both the quality problem and the problem connected with measurement are resolved by resorting to a process of bargaining or haggling. This process usually entails the enactment of quite a little comedy:

> Purchases are always the subject of long bargaining. Here is a scene actually witnessed. The buyer asks the price of two red herrings, and the seller quotes her 45 centimes. The conversation then proceeds as follows: 'Your final price?' The saleswoman hesitates and then says: 'I'll give you them for 40', 'You ask a good deal; do you think people eat up money like that? I'll give you 35', 'You're not serious'. Thereupon the buyer, with an air of indifference, makes as if to take herself off. After a few steps, she turns back and, in a conciliatory tone, says: 'Go on, give them me for 35 centimes; if I had 40, I'd give them you'. The seller, simulating a high degree of indignation, exclaims: 'Now, gossip, be off with you'. Disappointed, the buyer moves away, this time for good. She has gone quite some distance, when the saleswoman calls her back and says: 'All right, take them'.

> The byplay engaged in by both parties is as expressive as their words. A seller wishing to show that the prices offered by her customers are an insult will cover up her wares; so as to show that she does not propose to sell anything to people so lacking in seriousness. She adopts a pouting air, and, turning her head away, gives vent to her wrath in sudden, violent vituperation. All the bystanders are called upon to witness the insult to which she has been subjected.

> The buyers, when examining wares, often put on a disdainful expression, and choose each article with calculated deliberation. Sometimes, having felt and weighed in their hand every piece of fruit or tuber in a pile marked at 0.10 gde each, they will move away complaining. When it comes to paying, other little comedies are enacted. The price has been agreed; but the buyer, as if paralyzed, cannot find her money. She hesitates a long time and then, with a show of great unwillingness, begins to pay over her 'sous' one by one. Occasionally she stops, in the vain hope that the seller will be satisfied with what has been so far paid or that the question of the price can be reopened. The seller, however, in a hard and impatient tone, exacts what is due, or threatens to

withhold the articles that have been chosen. Once she has been paid, she counts the sum over again, in accordance with the saying *lajâ fèt pou kôté* (money is made to be counted).[96]

Due to problems of quality and/or measurement no single equilibrium price prevails in the market. Instead there is a price range which is considered 'acceptable' by buyers and sellers alike. Where exactly within this range the final price will fall is determined by the relative skill and strength of the two parties. However, the haggling process does not normally start within the acceptable price range. Buyers and sellers have bidding and asking ranges which they consider normal, and within these limits the serious haggling procedure takes place. As the bargaining proceeds the range usually narrows down, first to the acceptable range and finally to a price agreed upon by both parties.*

With all its picturesque details haggling serves very real economic purposes. When qualities and measures are not homogeneous the possibilities for the intermediaries to cheat the suppliers and/or the customers increase. This homogeneity problem is solved by the haggling process. The capacity of the process to perform this function is in turn guaranteed by the relative ease whereby buyers and sellers can inform themselves of demand and supply conditions in the marketplace. Usually, most sellers of a particular product cluster in one or a few limited areas in the market-place.[97] In Port-au-Prince especially, the depot system establishes contacts between a very large number of buyers and sellers. Every *revendeuse* knows exactly where to go to find the products she wants.[98] The concentration of supply maximizes the exposure of the produce, which is very important in the bargaining situation, since the latter as a rule involves comparison of products with those of other sellers, consultations with friends and bystanders, and thorough examination of each item. As a result, the information at the disposal of both buyers and sellers is more or less perfect, and cheating becomes very difficult.[99]

Haggling also builds upon another important factor. The process of discussing, comparing and examining is very time-consuming. *Revendeuses* may spend the entire day selling products that have a total

---

* Uchendu (1967), pp. 39-41. Cf. Scitovsky (1971), pp. 14-15. Frequently, the seller or the buyer will try to quote a price which lies outside the normal asking or bidding range. What will happen in such a situation is uncertain. If the price quoted is considered unreasonable, no transaction may take place, but often such offers are made as tests of the counterpart's market knowledge or as outright jokes which are appreciated by both parties.

value of only a few gourdes,[100] and haggling typically takes place over the price of every agricultural commodity, no matter how small it happens to be,[101] but time is the most abundant resource in the Haitian economy, so judged from this point of view the marketing of subsistence goods represents a very efficient allocation of resources, making an intensive use of time and saving scarce capital.

A related point is that haggling is consistent only with small economic units, not with large ones. Personal contacts are harder to maintain when the economic units grow in size,[102] and this is very much due to the central role of time in bargaining. Since haggling is a time-intensive activity, a seller who has to deal with a large number of buyers (or vice versa) soon reaches a point where it becomes too costly to haggle in comparison to the benefits generated by it. Haggling disappears. Measures and qualities are standardized, and uniform prices will prevail.

The haggling process is a very efficient procedure when quality is uneven and measurement practices vary. In any market-place a uniform price is established each day. This equilibrium price is established within the course of only a few hours:

> Prices for particular items take place in a fashion surprisingly reminiscent of the textbook examples. The seller knows at what price a particular item sold on the previous market day; she also knows at what price she has risked buying. She sets her opening price in line with her expectations. If demand is steady and uncomplaining, she will raise her price but she rarely has to do this, since the asking price usually adjusts downward by small concessions until it becomes stabilized. If demand is slack (and customers voluble in their disdain), and other sellers are doing business at a lower price, she will reluctantly but quickly come down. What is worth remarking is the speed with which these adjustments are made, not over time or uniformly, but for a given and particular situation. If there are a dozen sellers of cornmeal or red beans in a given market at ten o'clock in the morning — by which time the market has been in progress and prices have been finding their levels for several hours — it will be difficult to find a single seller whose price varies as much as a penny a unit for the stock in question.[103]

Summing up: Price determination in the Haitian market-places has to overcome two different problems. In the first place there is no control over the quality of the products, but this varies considerably from peasant to peasant. Second, widely different measures are employed for the transactions in different parts of the country. Both these factors can easily lead to inefficiency in the marketing process in the sense that different prices are paid for the same quality and quantity of a given good by different buyers. These potential disturbances are neutralized by the widespread practice of haggling before a transaction is concluded. The haggling process provides buyers and sellers with ample opportunity to examine and discuss the quality and quantity of each particular item and to make comparisons with the offers and bids of their competitors. A single equilibrium price (adjusted for quality differences) is thereby established for a given, uniform quantity in each market-place on every market day. The haggling procedure ensures that neither quality differences nor differences in measurement units disturb the efficiency of the marketing system.

Non-price Competition

The strong competition which confronts all the intermediaries involved in the marketing of subsistence goods and peasant consumer goods has created devices which are designed to mitigate the effects of competition. In various ways the intermediaries attempt to protect themselves against their rivals. The most commonly employed measures are those of creating *pratik* relations and of avoiding the market-places.

Sidney W. Mintz quotes the following eloquent definition of *pratik*: 'It means that you are selling. I come to buy from you each day. I need credit; you sell to me (on credit); the money is "content" that you sell to me. I always buy from your hand; I pay you well. That means "*pratik*".'[104]

Pratik may be classified as an institutionalized personal secret relationship between any two parties involved in the marketing process. These two parties do not have to be buyers and sellers, but *pratik* ties can be formed with anyone who in any way influences the transactions taking place. A *Madam Sara*, for example, may make *pratik* with the peasants she buys from, with the agents employed by her to procure the merchandise, with the truck driver carrying her and her goods back and forth,* with the tax collectors checking rural commerce,** with the Port-au-Prince or Cap-Haitien depot owner with

---

* Most *Madam Sara* try to use the same truck all the time to get a lower fare for themselves and their merchandise (Murray & Alvarez (1973), p. 36).
** This of course was to avoid paying market taxes or to avoid paying them in full. These taxes were abolished on 11 September 1974, however.

whom she stores her goods, with the *revendeuses* or other customers she sells to, with the merchants supplying her with urban or imported goods, etc.

The *pratik* relationship builds on mutual concessions from the two contracting parties and usually takes one or more of the three following forms:

1. lower prices for the same quantity of goods when selling or higher prices when buying,
2. greater quantities of goods when selling or lesser quantities when buying,
3. provision of credit with or without interest.

Besides these three main forms *pratiks* may grant each other different kinds of services or gifts, very commonly by conceding economic opportunities that cannot be exploited for lack of time, capital or for other reasons. The beginning of a *pratik* relation usually is a small concession in price or quantity that serves a basis of discussions and negotiations and to create a friendly, trustworthy atmosphere in general, while credit giving is saved for later stages — for strengthening and maintaining existing, well-functioning relations.[105]

To establish a *pratik* relationship essentially means that immediate gains are traded for benefits of a more long-run nature by the party making the concession. For example for a *Madam Sara* this is important in more than one way. First and foremost she thereby ensures that she will not be without merchandise if the market becomes tight. *Pratik* relationships are always carefully observed, so that a seller who has *pratik* with a buyer will refuse to sell the part reserved for this particular buyer until after consulting with the latter and obtaining his or her sanction of the deal.[106] In this way the intermediary with good *pratik* never risks being caught without any stock to sell when the supply is scarce and profit chances hence are good unless the situation is really exceptional. The vagaries and hazards of the market are partly neutralized. A second advantage, that may be of almost equal importance to the intermediary, is that forming *pratik* agreements saves her a lot of search activities. *Madam Sara* as a rule cannot waste too much time in searching out the suppliers and haggling with them. Most of the time agricultural goods have to be procured in very small quantities from a large number of individual sellers. Overhead costs must be kept low enough so as not to squander the profit to be made from the difference in prices between rural and urban markets. This problem is neatly solved by entering into *pratik* agreements with the sellers so that they come to the intermediary instead of vice versa. The same principle applies when *Madam Sara* sells her products, both agricultural goods and urban or imported merchandise. To make enough profit to subsist on, her outlets must be assured, and as a rule most of these outlets only buy small quantities.[107] Some observers go so far as to state that it is not possible for a traveling intermediary to amass enough business unless she uses *pratik* arrangements rather extensively.[108]

The employment of *pratik* is backed by strong social sanctions. The agreements must be scrupulously kept. A person who breaks a *pratik* relation or cheats a *pratik* without very special reasons not only gets talked about but will also soon find that she (or he) has trouble finding new *pratik* and even obtaining such little favors that are normally supplied by all traders for free.*

All types of transactions that one finds in the market-places normally also take place on the paths and roads leading to and away from the markets. To buy outside the market-place itself is often stated to be the preferred mode of buying of the *Madam Sara*.[109] There are at least three reasons for this. First of all, catching the peasant women on their way to the market-place always entails the possibility that these women cannot assess the prevailing market price correctly so that buying in this manner may yield an extra profit. Second, before 1974 a market tax had to be paid when dealing in the market-place, and this tax could be evaded by making the transactions outside. Third, the market-places are considered to be poor places for buying wholesale. Competition is keen among the *Madam Sara* and the intermediaries always risk ending up with small quantities only. Murray and Alvarez give a good example from bean trading:

> If a peasant producer or a small rural bulker arrives in the market-place where a lot of *madam sara* are on the lookout for stock, there may be a noisy altercation for the seller's stock, and the result is inevitably that the *madam sara* ends up with only a few *gro-marmit* of beans. The seller will be forced to distribute her stock not only if she has *pratik* relationships with the would-be buyers. Even if she knows none of the buyers, the women will aggressively push the

---

* Mintz (1964), p. 263. One typical favor is the practice of heaping the container when selling by *ti-marmit* or *gro-marmit*. This practice is known as *dégi* or *tiyô*, both meaning 'extra', but the expressions actually convey a false impression, since heaping is the normal practice (Mintz (1961:2), pp. 28-9).

sack of the competitive buyer out of the way after the latter has been given nine or ten *gro-marmit*, claiming that it is now their turn. If a fight ensues, it is known that the authorities will side with the women who wanted to share the stock against the woman who was trying to get it all for herself. Thus in the market place the woman will get only small quantities in times of scarcity.[110]

Another device employed by the *Madam Sara* to avoid the keen competition of the market-place is the use of agents to procure the goods for her directly from the peasants. This practice also saves the time of the intermediaries. In spite of the fact that time is an abundant resource in the Haitian economy, due to the necessity of going through the haggling process every time a transaction is concluded, time for *Madam Sara*, who needs to handle a fairly large volume of business to make enough profit to make her trips worthwhile, is limited. Most of her stock comes from a large number of small producers, and to solve this dilemma she employs the services of a *sékrètè* and/or a *koutché* who procures the merchandise during her absence. Usually the *sékrètè* who is entrusted with money by the *Madam Sara* attempts to buy the stock from the local *habitants* outside the market-place, since this makes it possible for them to buy at a lower price than in the market-place itself. Out of this differential the *sékrètè* makes a profit. The *koutché* is not entrusted with money but merely traces the stock for the *Madam Sara*.

Both *pratik* and the procurement of goods outside the market-places by means of agents could be interpreted as imperfections in the marketing system, as practices which serve the purpose of carving out a monopsony or monopoly position for the intermediary. This interpretation is difficult to sustain, however, because it runs contrary to the fact that *both* sides involved in the *pratik* relations and in the transactions taking place outside the market-places seem to derive tangible benefits from these practices. Not only the intermediaries, but also the peasants are protected from some of the inherent uncertainties involved in transactions which rely solely upon price competition and upon transactions within the confines of the market-places. They know they always have a buyer (or seller) to turn to and they receive some price or quantity concessions in return for granting the same security to the intermediaries. The realistic interpretation of both *pratik* and procurement of goods outside the market-places is instead that these practices are an outcome of competition itself. In a situation where competition in terms of price is as intense as it appears to be in the

Haitian marketing system for subsistence products and peasant consumption goods, it is only natural that there should be a tendency for competition to take on novel forms. Price competition in a perfect market leaves sellers and buyers indifferent as to whom they trade with, but this indifference assumes certainty to be able to sell and buy the desired quantities. In practice, nobody can be perfectly sure that his or her needs are met, and therefore it becomes desirable somehow to secure the planned transactions, and it is precisely here that the *pratik* relations and the transactions outside the market-places come into the picture.

Our examination of the marketing of subsistence goods and peasant consumption goods leads us to the same conclusion as in the case of coffee marketing. Essentially the marketing system is technologically efficient. Net profit levels are low. There are no barriers to entry. Peasants and intermediaries alike have real possibilities of making short-cuts in the marketing chain should monopoly or monopsony tendencies manifest themselves at any level. The prices prevailing in the market are essentially the outcome of a haggling process which adjusts for differences in quality and measurement practices. Finally, competition is carried on, not only in terms of price, but the peasants are offered added advantages, e.g. by entering *pratik* relationships with the intermediaries.

Nowhere have we found any monopsony or monopoly tendencies. No power deriving from legal sources that can violate competition has been detected. None of the products sold or bought by the peasants are processed in any special way which could create an exclusive position for any middleman or group of middlemen. The information with respect to prices and qualities in a given market-place was found to be virtually perfect. We have not explicitly studied to what extent the same is true with respect to the transfer of information between market-places, because no direct data appear to exist. Still, given the difficulties posed by the deficient state of the transportation system which will be discussed in the appendix, one can probably assume that the spread of information works reasonably well also on this level This is because the *Madam Sara* constantly travel back and forth between different market-places with small time intervals, and whatever differences in information there may exist should consequently be counteracted by these movements, especially since the number of *Madam Sara* is high so that it should hardly be possible for any of the traveling intermediaries to hide information except under very special circumstances.

The fact that intense competition appears to be the rule in the marketing system for subsistence goods and peasant consumer goods necessarily means that the intermediaries involved in coffee marketing cannot exploit the peasants as monopolists in the cases where they not only buy from the peasants but sell to them as well. There would always be the option for the peasants to turn to one of the middlemen in the subsistence goods chain instead.

Competition and Information

One of the prime requirements for competition is market information. Without sufficient information competition cannot survive but monopolies, monopsonies and collusive oligopolies or oligopsonies will dominate the market. For competitive conditions to prevail it is essential that both buyers and sellers be able to make comparisons with respect to the prices, quantities and qualities offered by different parties. If insufficient information is created and diffused, competition easily breaks down and the marketing process will exhibit a number of exploitative features.

The Haitian marketing system undoubtedly creates and diffuses sufficient quantities of information for the system to work competitively. This process operates at all levels of the system. The most obvious example is the one which we have already discussed: the haggling procedure to establish the price in the individual market-place, where the goods are exposed in such a fashion as to facilitate to the utmost the comparison of prices and qualities. In a given market-place a uniform price is quickly established for each type of quality of a given good.

The information created in the individual market-place is diffused to nearby markets by the itinerant *Madam Sara* during their travels. Their journeys are of comparatively short duration which means that the information they possess and use is relatively accurate all the time. They travel from market to market, perceive the price differences and take advantage of them in their transactions. The information does not work unilaterally to their advantage, however. The *Madam Sara* are generally not in a position where they can exert any influence over the price they pay or at which they sell the goods. The reason for this is simply the large number of competitors who also travel and who therefore possess virtually the same information. Profit opportunities are quickly taken advantage of in the sense that competitive bidding begins. As we have seen, this bidding is likely to drive profits down to a level where it is no longer appropriate to talk about profits proper but only of a return to the labor invested in the marketing process. The intermediaries are always eager to reach the peasant women before the latter enter the market-place, i.e. before they have arrived at a correct evaluation of the current bidding situation.

The constant travels of the *Madam Sara* ensure that a sufficient amount of information is spread from market-place to market-place. In the marketing of coffee the function of the *Madam Sara* is fulfilled by the speculators and their agents, and as we saw earlier in this chapter, during the harvest season the word of differences in the prices offered by speculators or agents spreads rapidly.

Thus, it cannot be doubted that the marketing system creates and disseminates enough information to ensure the competitive nature of the system, but due to the large number of people involved in the marketing process it is often suggested that the marketing system entails a 'considerable waste of produce, energy, time and money'[111] to the economy. The number of intermediaries is high. The time *Madam Sara* has to spend on the road is long, and in the market-places 'an endless bargaining'[112] between buyer and seller makes each and every transaction inefficiently time-consuming. The information necessary to prevent exploitative elements from taking over can, according to this view, only be obtained by dedicating a disproportionately large part of the human resources of the economy to marketing.

However, the view which holds that the marketing system absorbs an excessive share of the labor resources of the nation is mistaken. It is definitely true that the collection and dissemination of market information (as well as all other functions performed by the intermediaries) entails a large human effort. The most casual acquaintance with Haitian marketing is bound to reveal – even to the untrained eye – that marketing in Haiti means that large numbers of people have to meet. One of the most striking characteristics of Haitian everyday life is the ubiquity of market-places and traders. In urban and rural areas alike virtually around the clock, the traveler can be almost certain to meet peasant women busily walking or riding or professional market women transporting goods to or from one of the more than 500 important public markets. The market-place itself is seething with activity when buyers and sellers meet:

> On market days in Haiti the towns and the country market-places gather thousands of peasants for hours of busy and noisy activity. The people come for gossip, courtship and the playing-out of

personal rivalries, to visit a clinic or to register a birth; but above all they come for business — to sell the tiny surpluses of their little farms and to buy necessities. They press together in the ragged lanes among the stalls and the heaps of produce spread on the ground, inspecting and handling the displays of textiles, hardware, spices, soap and cooking oils, buying, selling and chaffering. Children push by hawking trays of sweets; farmers pull produce-laden animals through the crowds, calling loudly for the right of way. Trucks back up and turn around, their drivers honking horns, apparently oblivious of the people and the great piles of goods. There are vigorous arguments, sometimes ending in blows and arrests. In the very intensity of color, sound and smell the outsider is overwhelmed with an impression of confusion and disorder.[113]

Picturesque scenes like this one are apt to be deceptive, however. The apparent disorder does not necessarily mean that the process of marketing is inefficient. The essential point to keep in mind is that the cost entailed in marketing is one of essentially time and human effort only (excepting transport costs), and that this cost is likely to be extremely low throughout most of the year. Due to the inherently seasonal nature of agricultural production, there is an excess of man-hours available for other activities except during peak periods. The employment alternatives available for this labor are extremely few, as we saw in Chapter 2.

The 'modern' sector of the Haitian economy is small and the rate of its expansion has not yet reached such proportions as to exert an upward influence on rural wages. The most realistic alternative would rather be idleness, meaning that an abundant substitution of labor for scarce capital in the marketing process, far from being a 'waste', must be considered as a highly technologically efficient allocation of resources.

The cost of a labor-intensive process of spreading market information in an economy of the Haitian type is low indeed. Failure to understand this fact can only be ascribed to a confusion of 'efficiency' with 'capital intensity'. Quite naturally, there is a tendency for superficial observers — especially for Occidentals — to notice that the methods employed are 'primitive' in the sense that extremely little capital is involved, but the superficiality in the procedure which equates this lack of apparent sophistication with inefficiency becomes perfectly clear once we consider what the 'modern', capital-intensive method would look like. In a country where labor is abundant and capital is scarce, it does not make much sense to invest in e.g. a nationwide telephone system which would permit instantaneous comparisons of market prices between different locations. The functions that such a system could fulfil can be handled more efficiently by the existing system, given the relative real cost of the two alternatives. Efficiency in information gathering and spreading in Haiti goes hand in hand with employment, not with capital investment. By adapting itself to the existing relative factor prices in the economy, the marketing system minimizes the transaction costs involved in running the system.

Conclusions

Haiti is a market economy where the peasants produce not only to feed their own families but with a view to selling their produce in the domestic and international markets as well. The peasants cannot produce everything they need for maintaining their way of life but must also buy a number of products originating in the urban sector of the Haitian economy or even abroad.

In this situation there is a real possibility that the market mechanism may work to the net disadvantage of the peasants, or rather that the intermediaries with whom the peasants have to deal may deprive the peasants of the fruits of their labor. This is a very common pattern in many Latin American economies. Perfect competition among the intermediaries, on the other hand, ensures that the marketing system becomes technologically efficient. The goods move from producer to consumer at the minimum cost and the market is not affected by exploitative elements.

One of the most commonly advanced explanations of peasant misery in Haiti is precisely that the peasants are being exploited and cheated by the middlemen. In the present chapter we have examined what evidence there is to support such a view, by analyzing the structure of the markets for peasant produce and peasant consumption goods.

Virtually all the available evidence points in the same direction. The poverty of rural Haiti is not primarily a result of the behavior of the intermediaries. Strong competition prevails at all stages of the marketing process for all products which the peasants buy and sell, and there does not seem to be any important exceptions to this rule. The marketing system (within the limitations imposed by the transportation difficulties) operates under conditions which resemble those of perfect competition. The products for all practical purposes may be regarded as homogeneous, since in the cases where homogeneity is lacking mechanisms like the haggling process come into play and adjust for the lack of homegeneity by translating the differences in quality or quantity into price differences. The number of both buyers and sellers is high enough to make it impossible for any single agent or group of agents to have a decisive influence on the price. Entry and exit are free at the most modest levels of trade, and as we move 'upwards' we always encounter enough potential entrants with enough capital at their disposal to ensure that supernormal profits do not arise other than very temporarily. Besides, the peasants can always choose the link in the chain of intermediaries with which they want to deal. They are usually not tied to any particular middleman or even category of middlemen, but tendencies towards exploitation at one stage can always be counteracted and neutralized simply by entirely bypassing that stage. The information at the disposal of buyers and sellers, finally, is sufficiently adequate to preclude the creation of monopoly or monopsony conditions except under very special circumstances. The traveling intermediaries, the speculators and their agents gather and spread information regarding the market conditions in different regions.

The competitive character of the marketing system is borne out by the information available with respect to profit levels. As a rule the competition is strong enough to depress profits to levels where it is more appropriate to speak of a return to the labor effort expended by the middlemen instead of to speak of profits in the usual sense.

The fact that the marketing system operates under competitive conditions not only guarantees that no exploitation of the peasants takes place. It also means that the marketing system is technologically efficient, i.e. that it fulfils the function of joining demand and supply at a minimum cost. Too many students of the Haitian economy have not understood this. Within the limits posed by transportation difficulties no other form of market organization would probably do a better job than the existing one in ensuring that a minimum of resources is lost in the physical distribution of goods and in the spread of relevant information regarding market conditions. Consequently, out of the various reforms that have been put forward to improve the efficiency of Haitian agriculture, a break-up of the agricultural marketing system is not likely to be the best one. On the contrary, the best way of improving the marketing process is likely to be found in the improvement of transport facilities, for as we will show in the appendix, it is precisely in the state of the road network that the main *impedimenta* to more efficient marketing are to be found.

Presumably, the factor that has led a number of analysts astray is that the marketing system truly involves large numbers of people. Walking on foot or traveling by *camions* which look ready to break down at any moment may on the face of it appear as a very inefficient way of transporting goods. A lot of time and human effort is lost that way which, runs the argument, could be put to better use elsewhere. In practice, the opposite is more likely to be true. In an economy of the Haitian type, time is an abundant resource most of the year. In consequence, a marketing technology which involves intensive use of time and effort and which economizes scarce capital actually represents a highly efficient allocation of the available resources.

Furthermore, the Haitian marketing system presumably has been the victim of preconceived notions regarding the role of intermediaries in underdeveloped countries. We began this chapter by pointing out that explanations of peasant poverty which run in terms of monopolistic or monopsonistic exploitation are often very powerful tools for examining underdeveloped economies, but this does not mean that such explanations possess universal validity. On the contrary, this validity must be established anew in every single case. One cannot proceed by analogy. The analogy can serve only as a means of formulating the hypothesis, and the hypothesis must be tested against hard facts. In the Haitian case the exploitation hypothesis appears to be false. The peasants are poor, but we cannot place the guilt on the intermediaries. In order to determine the causes of the general poverty of the Haitian countryside and in order to see how this poverty has changed over time we must look for other explanations than this alleged exploitation.

Notes

1. See Wharton (1962) for a good example of how monopsony power may arise. Cf. also Abbott (1967), pp. 368-70 and the literature quoted there and Griffin (1969), p. 74.
2. See e.g. Moral (1961), pp. 245-7; Pierre-Charles (1965), pp. 154-5; Brisson (1968), pp. 47-51; Tanzi (1976), pp. 70-71.
3. The role of credit as a possible means for exploitation is discussed in Chapter 11.
4. Moral (1961), pp. 245, 247.
5. Mintz (1964), p. 285; Cf. Métraux *et al.* (1951), p. 125; Mintz (1959), p. 24; Underwood (1960), p. 32; Rotberg & Clague (1971), p. 281.
6. De Young (1958), pp. 4-7.
7. Ibid, pp. 2, 8-10.
8. Herskovits (1971), p. 257. A penetrating study of the market system in contemporary West Africa is that of Bauer (1964).
9. James (1963), p. 11.
10. Moreau de Saint-Méry (1958), pp. 433-7.
11. See Moral (1961), p. 239.

12. Ibid.
13. Comhaire-Sylvain (1964), p. 397.
14. Mintz (1964), pp. 274-5. Cf. Mintz (1960:2), p. 47 and Underwood (1960), p. 4.
15. Métraux et al. (1951), pp. 117-22; De Young (1958), p. 60.
16. Murray & Alvarez (1973), pp. 3-17.
17. The descriptions vary somewhat in the literature, but the points quoted below appear to be common for most presentations. Cf. e.g. Henderson & Quandt (1958), pp. 86-7; Stigler (1952), pp. 12-14; Cohen & Cyert (1965), pp. 49-51; Baumol (1965), pp. 311-12; Scitovsky (1971), pp. 15-18.
18. Scitovsky (1971), p. 155.
19. Nath (1969), p.13.
20. Scitovsky (1971), p. 155.
21. Ibid., p. 58.
22. Ibid., pp. 159, 183.
23. Wharton (1962), pp. 28-30.
24. JWK (1976:1), p. 44.
25. Département de la Justice (1963), pp. 40-41.
26. Moral (1959), pp. 70-71.
27. JWK (1976:1), p. 44.
28. Gates (1959:2), p. 7.
29. Moral (1961), p. 245.
30. Gates (1959:2), p. 7.
31. Ibid., pp. 46-7.
32. JWK (1976:1), p. 44.
33. Ibid.
34. Gates (1959:2), p. 31.
35. The strength of this hold is discussed in Chapter 11.
36. JWK (1976:1), p. 46.
37. See below.
38. Gates (1959:2), p. 31.
39. JWK (1976:1), p. 46.
40. Gates (1959:2), p. 27.
41. JWK (1976:1), p. 50.
42. Ibid., pp. 51-2.
43. Ibid., p. 52; Gates (1959:2), p. 26.
44. JWK (1976:1), p. 51.
45. Gates (1959:2), P. 28.
46. JWK (1976:1), p. 51.
47. IBRD (1972), p. 8.
48. JWK (1976:1), p. 53.
49. Cf. e.g. Stigler (1952), p. 180.
50. JWK (1976:1), p. 57.
51. Ibid.
52. Ibid., p. 59.
53. Murray & Alvarez (1973), p. 25.
54. For an analysis of these taxes see Duplan & LaGra (1974).
55. Mintz (1964), pp. 282-3.
56. Métraux et al. (1951), p. 123.
57. IICA (1974:2), p. 28.
58. Locher (1974), note, p. 24.
59. Murray & Alvarez (1973), p. 46.
60. IICA (1974:2), p. 50.
61. Ibid., p. 51.

62. Underwood (1960), pp. 8-9.
63. We follow here the IICA classification of the system of market-places. Alternative, but similar classifications can be found in Moral (1959), pp. 74-8; Moral (1961), pp. 241-7; Mintz (1960:2), pp. 51-3; Wood (1963), pp. 130-40; Johnson (1970), p. 83-92.
64. LaGra, Fanfan & Charleston (1975), p. 7.
65. See e.g. Mintz (1961:1), p. 61; (1960:1), p. 118; (1959), p. 24; Murray & Alvarez (1973), p. 49.
66. IICA (1974:2), p. 4.
67. Underwood (1960), note, p. 4.
68. Métraux et al. (1951), p. 3.
69. Ibid., p. 127.
70. Ibid., p. 125.
71. Mintz (1961:1), p. 55.
72. Murray & Alvarez (1973), p. 39.
73. IHS (1973), p. 37.
74. Cf. Mintz (1964), p. 285.
75. Moral (1961), p. 243.
76. Murray & Alvarez (1973), p. 35.
77. Moral (1959), p. 84.
78. Mintz (1961:1), p. 54.
79. De Young (1958), p. 60.
80. Murray & Alvarez (1973), pp. 30, 34.
81. Ibid., p. 29.
82. Mintz (1964), p. 271.
83. Murray & Alvarez (1973), p. 34; Mintz (1964), p. 281.
84. Murray & Alvarez (1973), pp. 29, 52.
85. Mintz (1964), p. 270.
86. Murray & Alvarez (1973), pp. 33-4. Cf. also Mintz (1964), pp. 267-8.
87. Murray & Alvarez (1973), p. 49.
88. Locher (1974), p. 83.
89. Murray & Alvarez (1973), pp. 17-22.
90. Girault & LaGra (1975), pp. 35-7.
91. Dorville (1975:3), pp. 35-8.
92. Locher (1973), p. 17.
93. Holly (1955), p. 277; Dorville (1975:3), p. 40.
94. Mintz (1961:2).
95. Moral (1959), pp. 79-81. Cf. also especially the list in Duplan (1975:1) pp. 8-17, but also Murray & Alvarez (1973), pp. 22-5, and Mintz (1961:2), pp. 25-31.
96. Métraux et al. (1951), pp. 121-2.
97. Locher (1974), pp. 71-2; Mintz (1960:1), p. 116; Mintz (1960:2), p. 21.
98. Locher (1974), p. 39.
99. This does not mean that cheating is never attempted. Cf. e.g. Murray & Alvarez (1973), p. 37.
100. Werleigh & Duplan (1975), p. 69.
101. Underwood (1960), p. 14.
102. Scitovsky (1971), p. 19. Cf. Uchendu (1967), p. 46.
103. Mintz (1961:1), p. 59.
104. Ibid., note, p. 62.
105. Mintz (1964), p. 262.
106. Mintz (1961:1), p. 61.
107. Ibid., pp. 7-8, 20.
108. Mintz (1964), p. 262.
109. Mintz (1960:2), pp. 21-2; Murray & Alvarez (1973), p. 33; IICA (1974:2), pp. 17, 38.

110. Murray & Alvarez (1973), p. 33.
111. Holly (1955), pp. 270-71.
112. Ibid., p. 274.
113. Mintz (1960:1), p. 112.

APPENDIX: Transportation: The Main Obstacle to Competition

In the main text of the present chapter we have dealt with how competition among the intermediaries manifests itself. The exposé would not be complete, however, without a discussion of the state of public transportation, since the latter constitutes the main obstacle confronting the competing intermediaries.

When the Americans began their occupation of Haiti in 1915 they found that the entire country did not possess more than some 340 kilometers of roads that were passable even in the *dry* season. There were only three cars worthy of the name and most of the time merchandise had to be carried on trails and paths to reach marketplaces and urban areas.[1]

The occupation soon changed this state of affairs. By the end of 1923 it was reported that 'the main arteries of the country, with the exception of the road to Jacmel,' were completed, and when the constructive period of the occupation ended in 1929, more than 1,600 kilometers of roads that were passable by car had been built.[2] By that year, Haiti had 3,000 registered motor vehicles.[3] In addition to the work on the main highways a substantial amount of work was put into the improvement of trails and paths, since it was realized that the latter were of supreme importance to the economy.[4]

After the end of the occupation, the road system began to deteriorate once more for lack of maintenance. Virtually all the roads constructed by the American forces were unpaved, and with a lack of maintenance, time and weather soon took a heavy toll. James G. Leyburn in 1941 complained about the state of the communication system:

> Transportation from one part of the country to another is far from easy. There are no railroads — unless one counts the short line running north a few miles from Port-au-Prince to nowhere in particular, and the equally short line coming west into Cap-Haitien from the fields of the northern plain. Roads built by the American Marines make automobile travel between the main towns possible, if one does not mind dust, ruts, and a steady succession of bumps. To travel in the average hired car, driven by a Haitian, is one of the

Appendix 181

grim experiences of life. The driver speeds as if pursued by a demon, while the peasant pedestrians leap for safety into the ditches; the unfortunate passenger is moved to close his eyes to avoid seeing the inevitable crash which does not come. The most comfortable means of travel if one is going only to towns is by ship, for practically all of Haiti's towns are seaports.[5]

In 1948, only the road between the capital and Cap-Haitien was negotiable along its entire length at all times and mountain trails and tracks still played the most important role for transport of merchandise from farms to markets, and the most common means of transport were to carry the goods either on donkey back or on head.[6]

The United Nations mission that visited Haiti in 1948 recommended that all the major roads be reconstructed and paved,[7] and these recommendations were later followed by the Magloire government. Long stretches of the roads connecting the principal cities were covered with asphalt, but inadequate construction and renewed lack of maintenance rapidly broke up the covering and left the roads in a state that was probably even worse than it would have been without covering. A World Bank loan of $2.6 million for the establishment of a repair and maintenance service was obtained in 1956 but never left any patent results.[8] In 1962, this loan was supplemented by a $350,000 credit from the IDA,[9] and a $3.4 million loan for the construction of a highway across the southern peninsula, from the capital to Cayes and Jérémie, was granted by the US Agency for International Development.[10] Shortly thereafter, in late 1962, US aid to Haiti was suspended, however, and in 1963 this was followed by a formal curtailment of all US assistance to Haiti. The Duvalier government then announced that the southern highway was 'a great symbol of the capacity of the Haitian nation to realize its national goals by its own efforts and sacrifices', and it was decided that the project would be carried out with domestic funds only.[11] A few kilometers outside Port-au-Prince were actually paved, but thereafter the project more or less fell into oblivion.

The development of that part of the transport sector which concerns us in the present context is shown in Table A4.1. This table reveals that at least during the 1960s stagnation and gradual deterioration dominated the picture. The total road mileage passable by motor vehicles contracted between 1959 and 1969. Part of the pavement deteriorated and was not replaced, and the number of trucks and buses, which are the most important means of transportation for the *Madam*

Sara, declined.*

Table A4.1: The Transport Sector 1952-73

Year	All roads for motor vehicles (kilometers)	Paved roads (kilometers)	Number of trucks and buses
1952	2,980	193	—
1954	—	—	2,232
1959	3,065	500	1,981
1962	—	554	1,551
1969	3,157	370a	1,307
1973	—	—	1,880

a. 203 listed to be in good condition, 167 in bad condition.
Sources: Road statistics: Rotberg & Clague (1971), p. 332; number of trucks and buses 1954-69; IHS (1971), p. 317; 1973: BTS, *Supplement Annuel 1973*, p. 18.

With the first penetration of the truck into the countryside in the early 1950s commercial practices began to change. The itinerant tradeswomen could then cover larger areas than before and transport larger volumes of goods, and conversely, the peasants could more easily reach town where the supply of goods was more plentiful and where merchandise of urban or imported origin was cheaper than in the countryside. In addition, new market-places arose along the truck routes and in particular at road junctions leading to important regional markets.[12] With the deterioration of the transport system during the 1960s the integration between urban and rural areas is likely to have suffered at least a partial setback, the extent of which, however, is unknown.

Since the beginning of the 1970s some improvements have taken place. As Table A4.1 shows, the number of trucks and buses has once more increased.** A new road from Port-au-Prince to Jacmel has been built with French assistance,† the work on the road across the

---

* It should be observed that not all the 1,307 buses and trucks were at the disposal of the traveling intermediaries in 1969. Most of them were used for other purposes, and the estimated truck fleet for public transportation was no larger than 225 vehicles (Locher (1974), p. 6).
** The number of trucks for public transportation during this period is believed to have risen to 300 (Locher (1974), p. 6).
† The quality of this road appears to be dubious, however, since it is often blocked by landslides, even in the dry season.

Figure A4.1

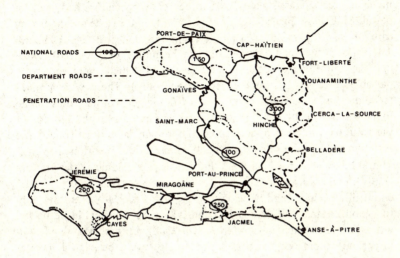

Source: Anglade (1974), p. 217

Figure A4.2

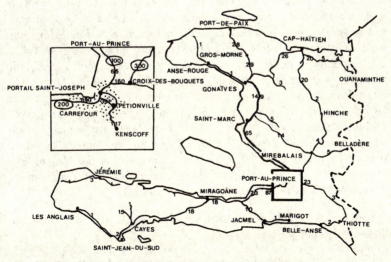

The figures refer to the number of motor vehicles passing per day.
Source: Anglade (1974), p. 219.

southern peninsula has been resumed,* and the road between Port-au-Prince and Cap-Haitien has been improved considerably (both projects involving foreign assistance). All three roads, when finished, will be paved. Still, these projects can only be considered as a beginning taking care of just the most pressing needs in the transport sector. Figure A4.1 shows the road network at the beginning of the 1970s, with only a handful of decent roads (most of which, however, were passable under good weather conditions only). These were limited to connecting the capital with a few of the larger, coastal cities, while there was a lack of good roads which penetrated into the interior of the country and which connected the provincial cities. Today, the situation remains the same with the three exceptions mentioned above.

The state of the road network influences the volume of traffic and goods flowing through it. Figure A4.2 shows the results of a traffic count in November and December 1969, and it is clearly seen that only the good stretches of routes 100 and 200, those that could be passed with ordinary cars without four-wheel drive, etc. sustained any important volume of motorized traffic. Not even the capital itself is reached or left by more than a few dozen trucks and buses each day,[13] and the total number of buses and trucks that can be utilized by the *Madam Sara* is not more than a few hundred† — quite probably a reflection of the poor road conditions. The above-mentioned IICA survey of the system of market-places checked the condition of the roads leading to all the 519 markets included in the study and came up with some rather depressing findings. 187 of the market-places were not served by any road that could be passed by a motor vehicle, but were connected with towns and other markets only by paths or trails, 223 could be reached only on roads that lacked pavement and that were not in the least maintained, 65 were served by 'normal' roads, i.e. non-surfaced roads that were well kept up or paved roads that had begun to deteriorate, and only 44 benefited from paved, well-maintained roads. Most of the latter markets actually were to be found in the capital.[14] Only 159 of the 519 markets could be reached by truck at all.[15] This in practice means that the *Madam Sara* could reach only 30 percent of the market-places with a number of buyers and sellers exceeding 50 persons.

* The benefit-cost ratio of this road is presumably low, however (Rotberg & Clague (1971), pp. 334-7).

† Competition appears to be as strong among the truck drivers as among any other participants in the marketing process. Most of the trucks serving the *Madam Sara* are owned by small-scale entrepreneurs who usually own just one truck and who do at least part of the driving themselves (Locher (1971), pp. 7-8).

Appendix

For the peasants and for the intermediaries, the alternatives to road transportation are few and unsatisfactory. The only railroad that the country possesses is the one run by HASCO in the Léogâne and Cul-de-Sac plains which is used only for transporting sugar cane into the HASCO sugar refinery on the outskirts of the capital. Coastal shipping during the present century has undergone a steady decline due to the competition of road transportation. In the 1880s, 400 to 500 small boats could arrive every Friday and Saturday in the capital, loaded with merchandise from nearby places like Archaie, Léogâne and la Gonâve only,[16] while in the early 1970s, the entire country possessed a scanty total of no more than 400 sailboats and 15 motor vessels serving coastal trade.[17] These boats mainly serve to connect the islands of Gonâve, Tortue and Vache with the main part of the country, and only in special cases like the traffic on the western tip of the southern peninsula where the roads are especially deficient, does coastal shipping assume any importance on the main island itself.[18] Only 49 of the 519 markets in the IICA survey got part of its merchandise by boat.[19] The rivers of Haiti, finally, cannot be used for shipping more than during very short periods of the year (if at all) since they generally dry out during the dry season and are turned into rapid torrents during the wet seasons.

Because of the deficient road network that does not permit the trucks to reach the majority of the market-places and because of the shrinking coastal shipping a substantial volume of agricultural goods must be transported on human heads or on the backs of donkeys into those market-places that are within the range of operations of the *Madam Sara*. In no less than 516 of the markets included in the IICA survey transportation by human beings or donkeys was the most common way of getting the merchandise into the market-place.[20]. This on the one hand is a very time-consuming affair since only small volumes can be carried by single humans or animals so that a substantial amount of labor has to go into transportation. On the other hand, in the light of the large amount of rural unemployment and the scarcity of capital, this mode of transporting goods represents an efficient allocation of resources.

In spite of the relative efficiency of making intensive use of human labor in the process of transporting merchandise, the dismal state of the road system still must be said to constitute the main obstacle to increased competition among the intermediaries. The latter have to spend comparatively long hours on the road, and as a result of this the time they can spend looking for buyers and sellers in rural areas is limited, since they have to get back into the urban districts while their knowledge of market conditions remains fresh. Part of this problem is solved by the employment of agents procuring the goods for the intermediaries, but the agents cannot be of help in solving the second big problem connected with transportation: that of overcoming the limited number of trucks and hence of transport space. It is probably safe to state that the strong competition among the intermediaries is carried on in spite of rather than thanks to the state of the transport system, and that the gradual improvement of the road system which seems to be under way at present will increase competition among the traveling intermediaries even beyond the degree which it has reached today.

Notes

1. Moore (1972), p. 209.
2. Millspaugh (1931), p. 158.
3. Spector (1961), note, p. 213.
4. Millspaugh (1931), p. 159.
5. Leyburn (1966), pp. 294-5.
6. UN (1949), pp. 201-2.
7. Ibid., pp. 203-5.
8. Rotberg & Clague (1971), p. 333.
9. Moore (1972), p. 212.
10. Ibid., p. 213.
11. CONADEP (1963), p. 8.
12. Moral (1961), pp. 248-50.
13. Locher (1974), p. 6. Cf. OEA (1972), pp. 216-17. Detailed studies of the transportation of agricultural goods into Port-au-Prince and Cap-Haïtien are available in Duplan & LaGra (1975) and LaGra & Duplan (1975), respectively.
14. LaGra, Fanfan & Charleston (1975), p. 25.
15. Ibid., p. 18.
16. Moral (1961), p. 249.
17. OEA (1972), p. 245.
18. LaGra, Fanfan & Charleston (1975), p. 18.
19. Ibid.
20. Ibid.

5 EROSION

But the earth's just like a good woman: If you mistreat her, she revolts. I see that you have cleared the hills of trees. The soil is naked, without protection. It's the roots that make friends with the soil, and hold it. It's the mango tree, the oak, the mahogany that give it rainwater when it's thirsty and shade it from the noonday heat. That's how it is — otherwise the rain carries away the soil and sun bakes it, only the rocks remain. That's the truth. It's not God who betrays us. We betray the soil and receive his punishment: drought and poverty and desolation. (Jacques Roumain: *Masters of the Dew*).

When we dealt with the efficiency of the marketing system in Chapter 4, efficiency was defined in a static technological sense. The marketing system for export goods, subsistence goods and peasant consumption goods was deemed efficient in that it appears to provide its services at a minimum expenditure of productive resources, given certain constraints within which the system has to operate. Technological, static efficiency in the marketing system does not, however, guarantee that per capita incomes will not fall in peasant agriculture. Although the conditions for *both* technological *and* economic efficiency may prevail throughout the economy in such a manner that it is not possible to increase the production of any single good without having to reduce the production of some other good, and in addition the economy produces goods and services in quantities compatible with the preferences of the consumers of the economy, it is still not possible to guarantee that peasant incomes will not fall. In order to satisfy this condition, *dynamic* efficiency may be required as well.

We define dynamic efficiency in an analogous manner to the static concept, i.e. as consisting of:

1. dynamic *technological* efficiency, i.e. adoption of new superior methods of production (and development and introduction of new products) at a rapid rate;
2. dynamic *economic* (or allocative) efficiency, i.e. the accumulation of resources (especially capital) at an optimal rate, given the technology and the consumption path of the economy, plus the attainment of the desired consumption path.[1]

Dorfman, Samuelson and Solow have demonstrated that static technological efficiency is a necessary, but not sufficient, condition for inter-temporal efficiency (defined as attainment of the maximum growth rate, given the technology and the consumption path of the economy).[2] Attainment of this type of inter-temporal efficiency does not, however, guarantee that technological change takes place at the desired pace.[3]

The discussion in Chapters 2 and 4 has shown clearly that in Haitian peasant agriculture a statistically efficient marketing system exists side by side with some types of mechanisms which tend to depress peasant per capita incomes as time elapses. We must now identify these mechanisms. Much of the remainder of the book will be devoted to the lack of dynamic efficiency in the peasant sector. In Chapter 12 we will analyze the lack of technological change, i.e. the lack of technological efficiency, in the peasant sector, in Chapter 11 we discuss some of the obstacles to capital accumulation, and in Chapter 9 we deal with the failure to attain what presumably is the most important consumption goal: full stomachs. In the present chapter we will discuss another dynamic aspect, namely how *de*cumulation of land resources results from the growth of the population and the labor force.

The most important change operating in the Haitian peasant economy is a result of the continuous growth of population. Demographic growth constitutes the decisive force behind the downward process of circular cumulative causation which was briefly sketched in Chapters 2 and 3 and which will occupy us in some detail in the present chapter. In the absence of capital formation and technological change, the increasing population density manifests itself essentially as an increasing pressure on the available forest and land resources. As the population grows, the demand for firewood and charcoal – the cheapest sources of energy, and hence also those preferred by the majority of the Haitian population – increases. Every year more trees are cut down for fuel purposes. The rate of erosion increases. The same process also is one of increasing pressure for intensified cultivation. Once the natural forest cover is gone, pastoral lands take over, and after a while the latter have to leave room for export and subsistence crops.[4] Gradually, cultivation is intensified on marginal lands – with fatal consequences. Marginal lands in Haiti are mountain lands. Every year, cultivation of food crops pushes other crops and pastoral lands higher and higher up the *mornes*, and every year, the steepness of the cultivated plots increases. As a consequence of tree-felling and intensification of cultivation, a tremendous problem of soil erosion has been created. The interaction between population growth and soil erosion is undoubtedly the most important element in the process that tends to depress peasant incomes further every year. It forms the very basis of the process and will continue to make living conditions deteriorate towards some kind of Malthusian equilibrium unless something is done to check and control erosion.

In the present chapter we will provide a detailed analysis of the interaction between demographic growth and soil exhaustion and erosion. We will begin with an account of the population history of Haiti. Thereafter, we will show how the growth of the population, the need for energy and the intensification of cultivation in combination with wood exports has led to progressive destruction of the Haitian forests. The third section examines the availability of energy resources other than wood and charcoal. In section four we analyze how increasing population pressure leads to an extension of the cultivation of labor-intensive crops, how this gradually destroys the soil, and how changing relative prices of agricultural goods may have added momentum to the erosion process. (A formal model of this process is given in Appendix 1 to the present chapter). Finally, an explanation of the lack of erosion control is given. A second appendix questions the validity of a suggested application of the term 'involution' to the development of Haitian agriculture.

The Demographic History

Any attempt to trace the demographic history of Haiti by necessity must remain very sketchy, and too much attention should not be paid to individual figures, which taken in isolation at best could be considered as informed guesses, giving only an approximate idea of the size of the population for the year in question. Censuses have been taken very irregularly in the past (except for during a short period of the colonial era) and their quality, at least before the most recent one (1971), is known to have been poor. Between the censuses we only have guesses to fall back upon.

Moreau de Saint-Méry, the colonial historian of Hispaniola, estimated that the indigenous population of the island when it was discovered by Columbus in 1492 lay around 1 million[5] (a figure which, however, is believed to be too high).[6] The Indians were rapidly decimated by forced labor, diseases and outright slaughter by the Spaniards, and within a century of the European discovery they were practically extinct.[7] Beginning in 1502, Negro slaves were imported from Africa to make up for the declining indigenous population. The slave traffic gradually reached considerable proportions. Moreau de Saint-Méry mentions an average figure of 33,000 slaves per year arriving in Haiti during the French colonial period.[8] This led to an increase in the dwindling population. In 1730, the total number of inhabitants was estimated to be around 119,000 and a 1753 census showed a population of some 183,000.[9]

Towards the end of the colonial period, a census was taken every year. Some figures based upon these censuses are shown in Table 5.1. We find that a considerable increase had taken place since the middle of the century due to migration of Europeans and the importation of slaves. During the last two years before the French Revolution the population increase appears to have been higher than 10 percent per year.*

Table 5.1: The Population of Saint-Domingue 1775-89

Year	Population
1775	288,000
1787	408,000
1788	455,000
1789	520,000

Sources: 1775-88: Victor (1944), pp. 25-6; 1789: Moreau de Saint-Méry (1958), p. 28.

As a result of the wars of emancipation and the expulsion of the French, the population fell between 1791 and 1805. In the latter year a census was taken, which gave a population figure of 380,000.[10] The census figure is probably an underestimate, however, and it seems more probable that the true figure should be around 400,000.[11] Once again, the population began to grow. In 1824, the total number of people in Hispaniola was estimated to be 700,000, with a probable figure for Haiti of 600,000.[12] In 1842, the figure given was 880,000.[13] An 1864 census in turn, showed a population of 1,100,000.[14]

During the remainder of the nineteenth century and until the American occupation of the country, only exceedingly rough and highly varying guesses were made, all of which are of little help.[15] In 1918 and 1919 the Dartiguenave government carried out a census, with very disappointing results. Thus, the *Département du Nord Ouest* which is the smallest and least populated of the five Haitian departments, was claimed to have more inhabitants than the *Département de l'Ouest*,

---

* Census figures are known to have been underestimates, however, since they served as a base for a tax on slaves (Victor (1944), pp. 26-7; Laguerre (1973:2), p. 32).

Erosion 191

which includes the capital, and which was known to be the one with the highest population.¹⁶ Hence, these census figures cannot be used. According to Arthur C. Millspaugh, the 'general estimate' of the Haitian population for 1922 was 2 million,¹⁷ an estimate that has also been used by Rotberg and Clague.¹⁸ Assuming this to be a reasonably correct figure,* an average growth rate between 1824 and 1922 of 1.24 percent emerges — a comparatively low figure.¹⁹

In 1950 another census was held, which was more accurate than the one taken in 1918-19, but which still left much to be desired. The official census population for 1950 was 3,097,000,²⁰ but this is known to have been an underestimate. The quality of the census was checked by the Haitian demographer, Jacques Saint Surin, and was found to be very unsatisfactory. The problem with the 1950 census was the inaccurate age structure, which Saint Surin undertook to readjust. It was apparent that there had been an under-representation of children and of men between 18 and 35 years. There was also a preference, especially among women, for ages ending with zero, five and even figures.** These deficiencies were corrected by Saint Surin who arrived at a population figure 9 percent higher than the official one: 3,380,000.²¹ This result in turn, means that the growth rate presumably had increased in comparison to the first half of the century, since if the readjusted 1950 population figure and the Millspaugh estimate for 1922 are used, a growth figure is obtained of approximately 1.9 percent per annum for the 1922-50 period.²²

A census planned for 1960 was never held because of the uneasy political conditions prevailing at the end of the 1950s.²³ Hence, only indirect evidence is available with regard to the situation in the 1960s. A field survey in rural areas made by the Department of Population Sciences at Harvard in the late 1960s pointed toward birth rates of about 35 per mille and death rates of about 15 per mille,²⁴ giving a growth rate of around 2 percent per annum, which was 0.5 percent lower than expected.²⁵†

* The figure could be an underestimate, however. According to the official journal of the Catholic clergy in Haiti, which listed the number of Catholics in the country every year, this number was 2,150,000 in 1919 (Victor (1944), p. 44).
** Saint Surin (1962), p. 5. Brand ascribes the under-representation of children to the fear of their mothers that an 'evil eye' might fall upon them and the under-representation of men to the fact that the census was a *de jure* census leaving out men without fixed residence and to the fear of the records being used for taxation or conscription purposes (Brand (1965), p. 20).
† The estimate considered to be most reliable at that time was the projection made by Saint Surin which indicated a growth rate of 2.5 percent per annum (Saint Surin (1962), p. 16).

In 1970, the *Institut Haïtien de Statistique* made a sample survey of the Haitian population, since it was felt that the 1950 figures were no longer an adequate base for extrapolations, and since it had by then not yet been determined whether or not there would be any census in 1971. The survey (known as the *Enquête socio-économique*)[26] gave an even lower population figure than the one indicated by the Harvard field survey: 4,271,000.[27] This figure in turn, was confirmed by the 1971 census which arrived at a total population of 4,315,000.[28]

At the present time of writing (1978), only preliminary census results are available in a very condensed form, and it has therefore not yet been possible to pass any definite judgment on the quality of the census. We cannot, however, *a priori* exclude the possibility that pitfalls of the same type as those present in the 1950 census have led to a recurrence of under-reporting in 1971. As in 1950, the 1971 census was a *de jure* census, not a *de facto* census, which means that persons without fixed domicile may never have been counted. Nor is there any reason to assume that the other sources of bias which distorted the 1950 results were not present during the 1971 census as well.

The natural growth rate of the population is believed to be around 2.0 percent in the early 1970s,[29] a figure that corresponds well with the result of the Harvard field survey (even birth and death rates are the same), but migration lowers the actual (net) growth rate to 1.60 percent per annum.[30] Some population projections based on the 1971 census are given in Table 5.2.

Table 5.2: Projection of the Haitian Population 1970-85

Year	Population
1970	4,235,000
1975	4,584,785
1980	5,009,000
1985	5,502,000

Source: IHS (n.d.: 2), p. 2.

We will deal with migration in the epilogue. Migration is important since it can be viewed as the result of the cumulative process, but at the present time we are more interested in the natural population growth, since it is that, not population growth net of migration, which is the main factor behind the cumulative process. Table 5.3 shows that the natural growth rate of the population has probably been higher during the twentieth century than during the nineteenth, and today, the natural growth rate in rural areas (the most important figure for our purposes) is equal to the national average: 2 percent.[31]

Table 5.3: Natural Growth Rate of the Haitian Population 1824-1973

Period	Growth Rate
1824-1922	1.24 %
1922-1950	1.9 %
1970-1973	2.0 %

Sources: See text.

What will happen to the (natural) rate of population growth in the future is not at all clear. A study of attitudes towards family size made in 1964 indicated no explicit preferences. According to the survey, family size was something that was largely beyond the scope of human decisions.[32] Only 10,000 women were wearing intra-uterine devices in 1969,[33] and two later studies of attitudes towards family planning indicated that only slightly less than one-half of the women interviewed were in some vague sense positive in their attitudes to family planning.[34]

The rate of population growth in Haiti has increased since the nineteenth century. The net figure at the beginning of the 1970s is believed to be 1.6 percent, and the natural growth rate (both for the country as a whole and for rural areas) was estimated at around 2.0 percent. Internationally, 2.0 percent is not a high figure. The average for less developed countries in 1970-73 is believed to have been 2.5 percent and the average for Latin America was still higher: 2.8 percent.[35]
However, these figures are not strictly comparable. To render them comparable we must take into account that the rural population is higher in Haiti in relation to the arable area than in most other Latin American countries, and that in addition, as we found in Chapter 2, the Haitian terrain is exceedingly rugged. Clearly, under these circumstances a 2 percent increase in the Haitian population may be much more detrimental to the soil than a 3 percent increase in a country where the supply of flat, arable land is more abundant. It will become evident from the following that (in the Haitian case) 2 percent

must be considered a high figure.

A Summary of the Erosion Process

The process whereby the growth of the rural population leads to destruction of the Haitian soil takes place in steps. A typical sequence is outlined in Figure 5.1. Initially, the land in question is covered with forest. Let us assume that the population begins to grow. It is probable that this will ultimately lead to the forests being cleared — for either of two reasons. The first reason is that an expanding population needs more wood for burning and for making charcoal, and the second is that there is a growing need to expand food production. Both factors appear to play an important role in Haiti.*

Figure 5.1

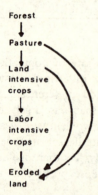

Bush and grass vegetation usually appears when the forest cover disappears, and the land is accordingly used for pastoral purposes. Population pressure is sufficiently heavy to prevent forest regeneration. Either the new trees are cut prematurely — to be burned — or the process goes one step further due to the increased need for crop land. The latter works in the following way: when the population increases and no technological change takes place[36] (as we will show later in the present chapter) there is a strong tendency for relatively labor-intensive crops to expand at the expense of less labor-intensive ones (more land-intensive ones). Subsistence crops expand at the expense of export crops, the latter encroach upon the lands hitherto used as pastures, and pastures take the place of forests. A given plot gradually

---

* Historically, a third factor — exportation of precious woods — has also led to a diminution of the Haitian forest reserves. Cf. below.

undergoes the development shown in Figure 5.1*

For each step in the sequence the danger of erosion increases, as more and more of the vegetative cover is removed. First, the trees disappear, and thereafter the bushes and the grass are replaced by crops. The preparation of the soil for planting and sowing periodically deprives it of its vegetative cover, a process which unavoidably coincides with the arrival of the heavy tropical rains. Layer after layer of the soil is peeled off by precipitation and run-off, and finally the soil's fertility is lost altogether. The land is eroded and becomes worthless for agricultural purposes.

Now that we have an intuitive grasp of the steps in the erosion process we may go on to outline the sequence in more detail and to seek some of the explanations behind the sequence as well as to point to some of the cumulative elements involved in the process. The logical starting point is the deforestation process.

Deforestation

Deforestation began mainly with French colonization.[37] The population grew rapidly, and needed both wood and agricultural land. However, the heaviest fuel requirement derived from the expansion of sugar cultivation. Demand was so great that in addition to the trees growing on land cleared for cane cultivation, lumber and firewood had to be brought in from the mountains. In the late eighteenth century lumber for construction purposes was even imported from North America.[38] Exports of forest products also began during the colonial epoch. The forests of the island of Tortue had achieved contemporary fame. All the valuable species, notably mahogany, grew there, and exploitation of these now started, albeit only on a small scale.[39] Mahogany, lignum vitae and logwood accounted for about 1 percent of the value of Saint-Domingue's exports in 1775 and 1789.[40]

Towards the end of the colonial period Moreau de Saint-Méry described the deforestation process:

> In general, the French Part is warmer and more exposed to dry spells, which one sees becoming both more frequent and longer since, because of an avidity which places no value on the future,

---

* A given land area does not necessarily have to go through all these 'stages', but jumps or omissions are quite conceivable. The figure also represents a simplification of the real world in that it does not pay any attention to the fact that as the population grows, and the intensity of cultivation increases, the soil gradually loses its fertility. After a while, the land has to be rested in fallow, i.e. it typically reverts to pasture for some time before cultivation is resumed.

and which is frequently mistaken as to the value of the present time, people have felled the trees which covered those high points, which brought them fruitful rains, and which retained abundant moisture and a humidity, the useful influence of which was prolonged by the forests . . . Entire forests were cut down to leave their place to the bushes which seem to have taken over all the mountains of the colony.[41]

Deforestation presumably proceeded at a very rapid pace during the colonial period, for by 1780 the forest reserves had been substantially reduced to some isolated areas, basically the same as those containing the actual reserves.[42] The situation in southern Haiti around 1789 is shown in Figure 5.2.

Figure 5.2

 FOREST

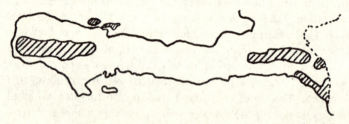

Source: Street (1960), Map VI.

Woodcutting seems to have accelerated after 1804. According to Paul Moral it was of two different kinds:

1. a 'parasitary' deforestation which was of urban origin and which was primarily designed to meet the needs of exportation of precious woods.
2. a 'fundamental' deforestation caused by the peasant needs for construction material, firewood and charcoal.[43]

Exportation of mahogany, logwood, Brazil wood and fustic took place on a large scale. Tables 5.4 (mahogany) and 5.5 (logwood) give an idea of the pace of depletion of the reserves of precious woods.[44]

Erosion

Table 5.4: Mahogany Exports 1835-64

Year	Exports (millions of board feet)	Year	Exports
1835	5.41	1845	7.90
.	.	.	.
.	.	.	.
.	.	.	.
1838	4.88	1859	2.69
1839	5.90	1860	2.26
.	.	1861	1.66
.	.		
1842	4.10	1862	2.44
.	.	1863	2.02
.	.	1864	2.37

Source: Rotberg & Clague (1971), pp. 387-8.

Table 5.5: Logwood Exports 1818-1952

Years	Exports (metric tons)	Years	Exports
1818-1822	11,300	1897/98-1901/02	218,800
1823-1827	12,000	1902/03-1906/07	262,100
1828-1832	35,100	1907/08-1911/12	204,800
1833-1837	31,500	1912/13-1916/17	249,700
1838-1842	63,400	1917/18-1921/22	318,200
.	.	1922/23-1926/27	137,900
.	.	1927/28-1931/32	124,100
.	.	1932/33-1936/37	69,400
.	.	1937/38-1941/42	25,700
1887/88-1891/92	419,300	1942/43-1946/47	16,500
1892/93-1896/97	295,600	1947/48-1951/52	6,100

Source: Benoit (1954:1), pp. 54-5.

While the 'parasitary' woodcutting derived from the international demand for forest products, the 'fundamental' peasant-caused deforestation was a result mainly of the combination of a growing population and a weak political administration. During the nineteenth century, land was plentiful in relation to the population. When the latter grew, it was easy to extend the cultivated area. The forests were gradually cleared to make room for the increasing population, and as the plots under cultivation lost their fertility it was easy to move from one area to another.

Squatting was a simple matter given the political conditions during the nineteenth century. Once the redistribution of land[45] had begun, no administration proved strong enough to prevent the peasants from spreading across the territory. The plantations were abandoned and taken over by peasant squatters. The latter needed not only land but also wood for burning and construction purposes, and wood could be cut on anybody's land without sanctions. The lack of administrative power at the central and local levels opened the way for an external diseconomy resulting from woodcutting: the peasants felled the trees and took the wood, while those who owned the land had to bear the consequences.[46]

The decline of wood exports possibly led to a slight reduction in the urban drain on the forest reserves, but did not bring it to an end. Wood is still needed as raw material for charcoal, for fabrication of lime, for construction (45 percent of all houses in Port-au-Prince in 1949 were made of wood and another 22 percent were made of wood and masonry),[47] for preparation of *clairin* in the *guildives**, for artisanry, etc. In addition, we have to take account of the similar needs of the peasantry. Throughout the twentieth century the forest reserves have continued to contract, and the area under cultivation has gradually expanded.

Today, the forest reserves are small. A study from 1862 describes the Ile de la Gonâve as clad with beautiful forests. Exploitation of these reserves after 1900 quickly ruined them.[48] The same development took place in the rest of the country. Brown and Woodring in 1924 pointed out that what little forests there were left were generally confined to mountainous areas: 'Probably none of the forests anywhere represents the beauty and the extent of those that existed before the discovery of the island. . .virgin forests, if they occur at all, are found only in the most remote and inaccessible localities.'[49] The comparison of Haiti and the neighboring country is striking. The border with the Dominican Republic is clearly seen from the air, with a more or less conserved forest vegetation on the Dominican side and an almost totally denuded landscape in the Haitian part of the island. An FAO forestry specialist in 1954 estimated that the total forest reserves of Haiti were in the order of 200,000 hectares, or 7 percent of the total area of the country,

---

*Primitive rural distilleries.

Erosion

75,000 of which was pine forest.[50] A comparison with Figure 5.3, which provides a tentative estimate of the extension of forest lands in the southern peninsula in 1952-3, conveys a similar impression. Very little forested area was left by the early 1950s.

Figure 5.3

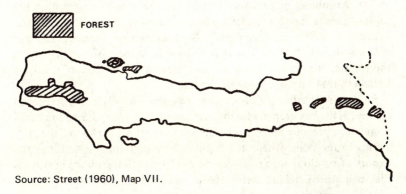

Source: Street (1960), Map VII.

Exactly how much is left today is not known. At the beginning of the 1960s Moral stated that in the Haitian part of Hispaniola there were no more than 20,000 to 30,000 hectares 'which one could call almost untouched forest' in the Massif de la Selle, the Massif de la Hotte and in the Cerca-la-Source region in the east.[51] Moral's definition of forest is, however, likely to differ from that used by Burns in 1954, so it is doubtful whether a comparison of the two figures is meaningful. Still, it would be very surprising if the extent of the forest-clad area has not diminished. An indication of these trends can be found in Table 5.6, which shows the annual consumption of wood for fuel purposes in Haiti in 1953 and 1968. The figures presented in the table are highly approximate, since it is not known how much was consumed by factories in 1968. However, even if factory consumption had fallen to

Table 5.6: Consumption of Wood for Fuel Purposes 1953 and 1968

	1953	1968
Households	8,408,000m^3	12,500,000m^3
Factories	461,000m^3	625,000m^3
Total	8,869,000m^3	13,125,000m^3 [a]

a. This figure was calculated by assuming the same ratio of factory to household consumption as in 1953.
Sources: 1953: calculated from BTS, no. 11, 1953, pp.7-10; 1968: Rotberg & Clague (1971), p.294.

zero, more wood was still consumed for fuel purposes in 1968 than in 1953.* It should also be stressed that Table 5.6 only contains figures for *fuel* consumption, which in 1953 amounted to approximately 75 percent of all wood consumption.[52] Assuming this relationship to have remained constant would give us a total consumption figure for 1968 of 17.5 million cubic meters (against 11.8 million m^3 in 1953). Assuming, in addition, a constant fuel wood consumption per capita, gives a figure of total wood consumption for 1977 of approximately 20 million cubic meters.** Reafforestation programs exist, but it is not known to what extent they have been successful in preserving the forests: for reasons given towards the end of this chapter, it is hard to believe that very much has been achieved.

It is evident from the above that ever since the days of the French colony, Haiti has been gradually stripped of its forests, due to increased population pressure and (in the nineteenth century) exports of precious woods to the point where at present hardly anything is left. Today the export of precious wood has ceased and population growth constitutes the main force behind deforestation. Sooner or later, as population expands, cropping has to be intensified and more wood, mainly for fuel purposes, is needed. We will shortly analyze intensification of cropping and how this leads to erosion, but before that we will examine the other component in the erosion process: the increased need for fuel as the population grows.

Alternative Energy Sources

The main reason why the growth of the Haitian population results in an increased need for firewood (and charcoal) is that no economically feasible alternative energy sources exist for the peasants. Hence, when the rural population grows, so does the demand for firewood. Burning wood and charcoal has always been the cheapest way of obtaining the heat necessary for cooking and other purposes. A number of possible

---

* This is not likely, however. CONADEP for 1969 gives a figure of 13 million cubic meters (without indicating what is included in this figure), which corresponds fairly well to our estimate here (P & D, no. 2, 1969, p. 20).

** This figure is computed as $\frac{12,500,000}{4,100,000} \times 4,700,000 \times \frac{100}{95} \times \frac{4}{3}$, where 4,100,000 is the 1968 and 4,700,000 the 1977 population (IHS (n.d.:2) pp. 1-2), where the share of industry in fuel wood consumption is taken as 5 percent and where the share of fuel wood of total wood consumption is taken as 75 percent.

substitutes for firewood and charcoal have, however, been discussed:

1. petroleum products;
2. coal;
3. biological waste;
4. gravitational energy;
5. geothermal energy;
6. wind energy;
7. nuclear energy;
8. solar energy

Let us examine each one of these in turn.

At the present time Haiti is totally dependent on imports for obtaining petroleum products. Oil deposits do exist in the country, however. A geological survey in the 1920s established the existence of favorable geological conditions in the Plateau Central,[53] and between 1944 and 1947 series of test drillings were undertaken that confirmed the geological results, while a series of drillings in the Ile de la Gonâve in the mid-1950s were less successful. In the Azua region of the Dominican Republic, which presents geological conditions very similar to those of the Haitian Plateau Central, oil has been found.[54] Hence, petroleum reserves no doubt exist in Haiti, but their extent is not known.

The major problem with petroleum as an alternative to wood and charcoal is of course its price. Technically, there are no difficulties. The petroleum derivative which could be used by the peasants is kerosene. A cheap kerosene stove is already being manufactured,[55] and in 1959, the Haitian government wrote a circular letter to the major petroleum companies in the country to find out what the possibilities were for kerosene to compete with charcoal and wood. It was then discovered that due to the tariff on imported kerosene, charcoal and wood were more economical for the majority of the Haitian population.[56] Today, the superiority of wood and charcoal is even more marked. With the multiplication of world market oil prices in the 1970s (see Table 5.7), kerosene is no longer in a position where it could conceivably compete with charcoal or wood.*

Coal is a fuel which is not used by the peasants. Since Haiti does not produce any coal, this would have to be imported at a price which is

---

* Also, peasants complained that their food did not taste 'smokey' but 'oily' when the cheap kerosene stove was used (Roland Wingfield, personal communication, dated 8 June 1978).

Table 5.7: Oil Price Increases 1965-74

	Posted prices. Arabian light crude (34° gravity) f.o.b. Ras Tanura (in dollars per barrel)
December 1965	1.80
December 1970	1.80
June 1971	2.29
January 1972	2.48
January 1973	2.59
October 1973	5.12
January 1974	11.65

Source: Darmstadter & Landsberg (1976), p. 26.

high in relation to that of firewood or charcoal. Presumably, coal mining within the country would also result in a comparatively high price. Haiti does not have any coal deposits with a high carbon content but seems to possess the most extensive deposits of lignite to be found in the West Indies.[57] These lignite deposits have not yet been exploited commercially. One of the reasons for this is precisely that the fuel value is comparatively low. The Haitian lignite contains a high proportion of ash which makes complete combustion difficult.

Methane gas can be derived from garbage and sewage slime, and the use of such a process in Haiti has been suggested.[58] Technically, the process is not too difficult, given the availability of raw materials. The main problem with utilizing biogas instead is that utilization would have to take place on a large scale, which presumably requires systematic co-operation between fairly large groups of peasants.[59] More promising is the possibility of burning *bagasse* (waste which is left when the sugar cane has been processed in the sugar mills). The residual, if dried in the sun for a few days, can be used as fuel, a possibility which hitherto has been utilized only by HASCO.[60] Interestingly enough, current *bagasse* production appears to be large enough to cover almost four times the current commercial energy consumption of the country (1975-76), but presumably a lot of the *bagasse* is simply allowed to go to waste.[61] However, *bagasse* would not suffice to cover the needs of the population (estimated to be thirteen times as high as the total commercial consumption of energy).[62]

Gravitational energy may come from three sources: waterfalls, tides or waves. The first one of these is already an important source of energy in Haiti. At Péligre in 1971-73 three 15.7 MW turbo-alternator groups were installed which together gives a capacity of more than 47,000 kW.[63] This, however, supplies only the capital and some of its suburbs. The needs of the capital alone are already outgrowing the capacity of the Péligre hydroelectric dam, so that none of the hydraulically generated energy will be used to supply provincial cities and towns and rural districts, unless other existing reserves are put to use. It is doubtful, however, whether exploitation of these sources, other than Péligre, is economically viable.[64] The uneven water content of the Haitian rivers would make construction of costly reservoirs necessary. Besides, and even more important, the peasants cannot use hydro-electric energy at all until the countryside is electrified, which would constitute a further considerable addition to the above costs.

The other two sources of gravitational energy, tides and waves, have not been explored at all in Haiti (or in the rest of the West Indies). Tides do not offer much hope in the West Indian context, since the variations between ebb and flood are small, and as far as ocean waves are concerned, their tapping for energy lies entirely in the future.[65]

Haiti also possesses a number of hot springs.[66] The energy that can be extracted from these sources is presumably minor, however, since geothermal fields in general produce steam at relatively low pressures, so that the energy generating units will have to be smaller than these using for example fossil fuel.[67] So far, no attempts to use geothermal energy have been made in Haiti.

Haiti lies in the belt of the northeast trade winds, with prevailing winds from the northeast or east. Due to the mountainous character of the country, wind is not a source of energy that can be used everywhere, however, and up to the present time only HASCO has used wind energy systematically,[68] but it is believed that there is scope for an economic utilization of wind power plants up to 100 or 200 kW.[69] Wind power does not constitute any solution to the problem of the peasants, since it would have to be transferred into electrical power before it could be used for heating purposes.

In a long-term sense, nuclear power may be the solution to Haiti's energy problem, since the necessary technology already exists, but its possible use lies entirely in the future and would presuppose a quite different level of economic development. It goes without saying that nuclear power has no relevance whatsoever for today's problems.[70]

Recently, solar energy has received a great deal of attention as an alternative to nuclear power and fossil fuels, since in comparison to the latter two, solar energy is of infinite duration and in addition nonpolluting. In Haiti, with its high intensity of solar radiation, utilitization of the rays of the sun, if technologically possible, would be an excellent power source. Some commercial applications, mainly water and space heating, are already available. Hence, it appears possible that some of the simple needs of the Haitian peasants could be covered by using solar energy in the future — first and foremost water heating and cooking — but today none of the applications of solar power is cheap enough to be able to compete with wood or charcoal.[71]

From the foregoing it should be perfectly clear that no economic substitute for charcoal and wood will become available in the near future. Legislation may be able to force manufacturing industry to use fuels other than wood and charcoal,* but for peasant households, the situation is totally different. We will return to the legislative measures that have been undertaken to combat erosion. Suffice it here to say that none of them has been very efficient. Taxation or regulation of peasant woodcutting is hardly a feasible proposition in Haiti. In the absence of substitutes therefore charcoal and wood will continue to be the most important sources of fuel for the majority of the households, i.e. tree-felling for burning purposes will continue to pave the way for increased erosion.

Erosion and the Composition of Output: Cumulation at Work

The second cause of erosion is continuing intensification of cultivation. Forest tracts are turned into pastures. Pastures have to bear land-intensive crops. Plots hitherto used for land-intensive crops are instead employed for the cultivation of labor-intensive crops. For each successive step in this process, the exposure of the soil to wind and water increases, and with that the risk of erosion. Each year a portion of the soil is lost forever for productive purposes.

The Growth of the Rural Labor Force

The factor which triggers off the sequence outlined above is the growth of the rural population. Between 1950 and 1971, the rural population probably increased by more than 700,000 people.[72] If this is a reasonably correct figure, we should also expect that the rural labor force increased during the same period. However, this expectation is not confirmed by official figures. According to the available data, the

---

* Such legislation has already been applied to the essential oil industry, which however represents only a minor fraction of the industrial wood use (Rotberg & Clague (1971), p. 294).

population working in the agricultural sector fell by between 20,000 and 30,000 between 1950 and 1971.[73] However, as we will see in the epilogue, such a decrease appears highly unlikely, since few new opportunities of gainful employment in urban areas appeared during this period.

The explanation of the official figures presumably is to be found in the classification of women. Official census figures indicate that the *male* labor force in agriculture increased by approximately 110,000 persons from 1950 to 1971, while the female agricultural labor force according to the same source should have experienced a net decrease of no less than 147,000. The employment of women in the commercial sector is stated to have increased by 127,000.[74] It is well known that classification of female activities in agricultural societies presents formidable difficulties to census takers.[75] Therefore, the enormous differences in the Haitian figures come as no surprise. Against the background of the analysis of competition among female traders in Chapter 4, a net increase of 127,000 in the commercial sector appears to be entirely out of the question. It has simply proved too difficult a task to obtain comparability and consistency between the classification of female activities in 1950 and in 1971. Against the combined background of the overall rural population increase, the increase in the male agricultural labor force and the unavailability of work in urban areas it can therefore safely be assumed that the total agricultural labor force increased almost *pari passu* with the rural population in the 1950s and the 1960s.

The Changing Structure of Output

The growth of the rural labor force has had a definite impact on the composition of output in the peasant sector. Between 1965 and 1970 there appears to have been a marked trend away from export crops towards subsistence crops instead,* as shown in Tables 5.8 and 5.9.

All estimates of agricultural production in Haiti are notoriously uncertain, so too much attention should not be paid to the absolute magnitudes shown in the two tables. However, the trends are supported by direct observation. In very many areas the peasants have been seen

---

* This is not true for vetiver oil, the output of which increased following rising world market prices after 1966 (Lebeau (1974), p.25). Essential oils are today second only to coffee as an export product. However, since their importance was negligible during most of the 1950-70 period, they have not been included in the present chapter.

Table 5.8: Production of Selected Agricultural Products 1950-70. IDB Estimate (thousands of metric tons; bananas and plantains: millions of stems)

Export products	1950	1960	1970
Coffee	34.9	38.9	36.7
Sugar cane	4185.0	4952.0	3500.0
Sisal	33.7	26.6	18.0
Cocoa	3.2	3.9	2.0
Bananas	18.6	16.7	—
Cotton	5.6	3.5	4.0
Subsistence products			
Corn	205.8	226.9	235.0
Sorghum	173.9	182.7	150.0
Plantains	25.3	32.5	39.0
Peas and beans	34.2	37.0	40.0
Rice	41.8	50.4	50.0
Sweet potatoes	79.4	83.3	70.0
Manioc	104.3	109.6	130.0

Source: BID (1974), p. 142.

Table 5.9: Production of Selected Agricultural Products 1950-72. CONADEP Estimate (thousands of 1954/55 gourdes)

Export products	1950	1960	1972
Coffee	118,126	131,702	110,448
Sisal	14,309	11,319	7,863
Sugar cane	62,775	74,280	60,000
Cocoa	9,197	11,209	8,909
Cotton	5,156	3,153	3,640
Subsistence products			
Peas and beans	98,782	108,907	120,960
Rice	59,900	72,331	57,360
Sorghum	30,441	31,983	36,925
Manioc	2,817	2,960	3,618
Sweet potatoes	14,280	15,004	11,880
Cow peas	51,067	55,230	47,712
Plantains	46,520	41,765	47,500

Source: CONADEP (1976), Table A-14.

to uproot their coffee trees, substituting subsistence crops for coffee.[76]

The main explanation for the changing structure of output advanced by official Haitian organizations states that the reduction of export production was the result of recurrent hurricanes and droughts during the period. The country was severely hit by hurricanes in 1954 (Hazel), 1963 (Flora), 1964 (Cleo) and 1966 (Inez), and three major droughts took place: in 1956, 1958-9, and 1966-9, so it is true that nature was unfavorable to Haiti, but while it is undeniable that agricultural output was affected by hurricanes and droughts, this argument does not explain more than a minor part of the change in output composition. For one thing, both subsistence and export crops were hurt. Second, the argument can explain why for example coffee production fell during the four to five years following for example a hurricane − the gestation period of the new plants which were substituted for the destroyed ones − but it cannot explain why replanting took place only to a lesser extent nor can it explain why coffee trees that were actually producing were uprooted. Clearly, other explanations are needed.

A better explanation is based on the growth of the rural labor force. A growing supply of labor affects the composition of peasant output in two ways. It leads to a shift away from land-intensive products towards labor-intensive crops at given relative commodity and factor prices, and it contributes to a change in these prices themselves, which in turn leads to new changes in production. In the following, we will examine both these types of changes and their impact on erosion. We will begin with the shift from land-intensive to labor-intensive crops at constant prices.

Output and Erosion at Constant Prices

In Appendix 1 to the present chapter we give a rigorous demonstration of how the composition of peasant output changes when relative commodity prices are held constant, and of the dependence of output changes on erosion. The reader is referred to the appendix for details. Here we will describe the model in verbal terms.

If we assume that the production functions for both export and subsistence products are linearly homogeneous, i.e. that no economies of scale exist, and we want to maintain a fixed price of export goods in terms of subsistence products, relative factor prices (between land and labor) must also remain constant, since if the factor prices are altered, the relative cost of producing the two types of goods is changed so that it becomes relatively more expensive to produce the goods which use the factor whose relative price increases intensively (provided that factor reversals do not occur). With linearly homogeneous production functions, there is also a one-to-one correspondence between relative factor prices and factor intensities in the two lines of production. Hence, constant relative factor prices also imply constant factor proportions and vice versa.

Assume now that the rural labor force grows, and that we want to maintain a fixed relative price of export goods. In Appendix 1 we show that export products use relatively less labor in relation to land as compared to subsistence goods, i.e. that export production is land-intensive and subsistence production is labor-intensive. Assume also that this is true for all relative factor prices (i.e. that factor reversals do not occur). In order to keep factor proportions (and hence also relative factor and commodity prices) constant when the labor force grows, we must reallocate resources from the land-intensive to the labor-intensive line of production, i.e. from export to subsistence production. The entire addition to the labor force must be allocated to the labor-intensive line of production, but if factor proportions are not to change in subsistence production, some land must be added as well. This land can be taken only from export production and only together with some labor as well. Otherwise, factor proportions would be altered in export production. The production of subsistence goods must increase at given relative commodity prices while the production of export goods must contract. The opposite is not possible. If we allocate the additional labor to export production, i.e. to the land-intensive line, it would not be possible to keep factor proportions constant, for taking land and labor out of subsistence production would always leave us with more additional labor in relation to land than the labor/land ratio in export production to be put into the latter line of production. Factor proportions would change, and with them relative commodity prices.

Neither can we allocate some of the new labor to export production and some to subsistence production. If no land is reallocated the labor/land ratio would increase in both lines of production. If land is taken out of subsistence production (while labor is added) to re-establish the original factor proportions in export production, the labor/land ratio would rise even further in the former sector, and if land is taken out of export production (while at the same time new labor is added) to keep subsistence factor proportions constant, the ratio increases in the export line of production. The only possibility of keeping relative commodity prices unaltered is to allocate the entire increase in the labor force to subsistence production and to reallocate some of the land and labor formerly used in export production to the subsistence sector as well. The output of subsistence goods must increase and the output of export goods must fall.

The forces just described are well-known mechanisms. Together they represent what in the theory of international trade is known as the Rybczynski theorem,[77] which states that with linearly homogeneous production functions, an increase in the supply of one of the factors will lead to an absolute increase of the output of the good which uses the growing factor intensively, while the production of the other good will decrease absolutely and relatively.

In the present context, the Rybczynski theorem achieves a special significance. If for a moment we go back to Figure 5.1, the theorem may be applied to the entire chain of changes shown in the figure. Forest production is less labor-intensive than pastoral activities, which in turn are less labor-intensive than production of land-intensive crops, etc. As the rural labor force increases, there is a series of shifts in the peasant sector towards the labor-intensive end of the chain. Labor-intensive crops take over some of the coffee lands. Coffee is grown where the animals used to graze, and forests are turned into pastures.

As we move towards more labor-intensive utilization of the soil, the risk of erosion increases. Trees can mobilize and store far greater quantities of nutrients per unit area than grass,[78] but in Haiti as a rule only isolated mango and avocado trees are spared in the process of deforestation. Stands of pine trees, for example, once they have been cut down, are usually not allowed to regenerate, and when the density of surviving trees is reduced below the critical level needed for recolonization, the grass vegetation takes over (if not crops).

Grass vegetation *per se* is not necessarily conducive to soil exhaustion and erosion. Grass (at least under humid conditions) can make the soil accumulate sufficient nutrients to permit an active soil life to develop which will protect the soil from erosion.[79] The problem with grass vegetation in Haiti is that it is used as pastures and that the animals grazing on these pastures are mainly sheep and goats, who can easily remove the grass cover. The soil crumb structure is then destroyed and the risk of wind or run-off erosion increases.

Planting trees or bushes frequently facilitates the cultivation of tropical soils for longer periods without too drastic reductions of yields,[80] and traditionally, the Haitian mountain sides have been used for the cultivation of coffee which is a tree crop and which provides some protection against wind and rain for the soil. When we move into cultivation of subsistence crops, however, most of the permanent vegetation disappears. Besides, crops like manioc, yams, malanga, beans, plantains and corn all provide *less* cover for the ground than for example coffee, and they do not provide the dense and intertwined root system of natural grass which serves to prevent the soil from being carried away by wind and water.[81]

All this is conducive to a higher rate of erosion. Depriving the land of its natural vegetation increases the likelihood of its rapid destruction by wind and water. From the erosion point of view, the most critical part of the agricultural year is the end of the dry season, after the harvest and just before the onset of the rains, which is when the peasants clear the land and turn the soil over to be ready for sowing and planting as soon as the rainy season begins. This exposes the humus layer to winds and rains. In Haiti the rains generally have the character of torrential downpours which have fatal consequences for the soil.

A heavy tropical downpour hitting an unprotected soil literally acts like 'thousands of little hammers'.[82] The soil becomes compact. The pores are closed, and the soil rapidly begins to dissolve and forms a mud cover which prevents the rain water from penetrating into the ground. The permeability of the soil is lost and the run-off is high. If the soil is covered by vegetation the raindrops do not hit the soil as directly or as heavily as when the latter is completely exposed. The water can penetrate into the ground through the undamaged pores. The difference in run-off between protected and unprotected soils is considerable. Schiller Nicolas quotes experiments showing that for example if on clay soil protected by a forest cover the run-off from an 800 mm rain is 0.7 percent, burning the forest cover increases the run-off to almost 40 percent.[83] In turn, a heavy run-off, especially when it takes place on a steep mountain slope, carries the topsoil away:

> The eroding capacity of the water begins as soon as the surface of the soil is oversaturated. Water in motion has a tremendous pulverization power, a power which varies with the square of its velocity. Therefore, a river with a velocity of 4 kilometers per hour is 16 times more active than one with a velocity of only 1 kilometer per hour. Its propulsive force varies in relation to the fifth power of its velocity. It is therefore that of these two water courses, one has an eroding capacity which is 824 times larger than the capacity of the other one. The size of the particles carried varies in relation to the sixth power of the velocity. The first river can transport sediments 2,396 times larger than the sediments which can be transported by the other river...[84]

Not only the nutrients but also the soil itself is lost. The humus layer is washed away, down the mountain sides into ravines and valleys. The mountains are gradually denuded. Long scars are soon opened, and big chunks of lime fall down into the valleys:

> The furious action of the runoff and the materials carried by it manifests itself clearly on its way down the steep mountainsides. The Port-au-Prince region, among others, offers many examples of this. During a period of a few years it has been witnessed how the mountainsides are being stripped of their flesh, how long scars open on the hillsides, how large patches of limestone tumble down as a result of cleavage of very erect layers or as a result of landslides of massive limestone, how piles of rocks congest the bottoms of the ravines.[85]

Every year erosion eats away a deeper layer of the soil until finally the bare rock comes into the daylight, eventually to be destroyed itself.

Once the soil has been washed away from the mountain sides down into ravines and river beds, the rivers, torrential during the rainy season, carry it away. The soil is deposited here and there along the course towards the sea. The river banks rise. Sometimes the deposits of eroded material left in the rivers force these to abandon their beds and dig new ones, frequently through arable land, thereby sterilizing new areas by depositing sand and gravel.

Figures for the annual loss of soil are scarce, but a few estimates are available. Schiller Nicolas in 1938 calculated that a total of 7 million metric tons of soil containing 8,000 metric tons of soil nutrients was carried away every year by the rivers,[86] and Joseph Wainwright in 1974 estimated that the Artibonite river every year transports 3.6 million cubic meters of arable soil.[87] These figures are hard to interpret, however. A better idea may perhaps be gained from Table 5.10, which shows three different estimates of the reserves of good, arable soil in Haiti.* In 1938, Nicolas estimated the area that had been abandoned due to erosion, at 210,000 hectares, while Burns in 1954 gave a figure of 500,000 hectares of 'sterile, abandoned soils'.[88] Figure 5.4, finally, shows a recent estimate by Wolf Donner of the area which has been wholly or partially rendered worthless by erosion.**

---

* However, the table should also be interpreted with care.
** The map is a result of a rough estimate which has to be verified by aerial photography or field surveys. (Wolf Donner, personal communication, dated 29 April 1978.)

212 Erosion

Table 5.10: Estimates of Good Arable Soil 1938-70 (hectares)

	1938		1954		1970
Cultivable plains	500,000				Cultivable soils proper for irrigation; plain or slightly rugged topography, limiting factors not severe and may be compensated for by more or less intensive management. High productivity with good management, require some moderate conservation measures:
eroded	110,000				
	390,000		Productive fertile soils with good humidity conditions		
submarginal	50,000	340,000			
Cultivable, mountains	500,000				
eroded	100,000			300,000	
	400,000				
soils with insignificant yields			Irrigated plains and valleys		
	200,000	200,000		70,000	
Total: good soils		540,000		370,000	225,750

Sources: 1938: Nicolas (1938), pp. 42-4; 1954: FAO (1955), p. 85; 1970: Giles (1973), p. 9.

Figure 5.4

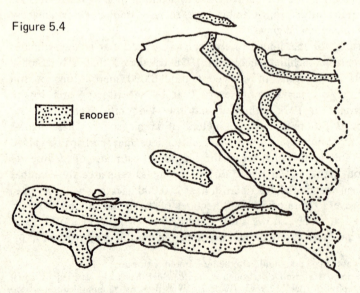

Source: Donner (1975), p. 34.

Erosion

The result of the erosion process in terms of output may be seen if we apply the Rybczynski theorem 'in reverse'. The destruction of the soil takes place mainly in subsistence production. When land is destroyed, labor intensity in the subsistence sector increases. Then, if relative commodity prices are to remain unchanged, land must be taken out of export production and be transferred into the production of subsistence goods, and in order to maintain the original factor proportions in export production some labor will also have to be transferred. Let us assume that only this labor (and none of the land) is put into the subsistence line. This makes the labor intensity of the subsistence line increase even further. There will be more labor than originally in this line, and less land. The only way to also re-establish the original factor proportions in subsistence cultivation is by adding the land taken out of the export line. This will (1) replace what has been lost in the erosion process, and (2) compensate for the increased input of labor. Once more, the output of export goods will decrease while that of subsistence crops will rise.

The tendency for population and labor force growth to gear the cropping pattern towards a higher percentage of labor-intensive crops and its concomitant, an increased rate of soil destruction, is *cumulative* at given relative commodity prices. This process is summarized in Figure 5.5. The growth of the population in rural Haiti makes the agricultural labor force increase in the absence of a sufficient number of employment opportunities in urban areas. This labor force growth changes the composition of peasant production at given relative commodity prices. A larger volume of the relatively labor-intensive crops (subsistence crops) and a smaller volume of the relatively land-intensive crops (export crops) is produced. This shift increases the probability of erosion. The supply of arable land contracts, and the process enters its cumulative phase. The falling supply of agricultural land gives an additional impulse to the shift into a more labor-intensive composition of output, which in turn causes more land to be destroyed, etc. Throughout the process, the population continues to grow. The size of the labor force continues to rise, etc. The net outcome of this combination of population growth, labor force growth and a shrinking natural base for agricultural production on the aggregate level, i.e. on the level of the peasant sector as a whole, is that diminishing returns to labor when added to a constant supply of land are reinforced by the tendency for the supply of available land to be reduced, and that as a result total income in the peasant sector has to be shared by a larger number of people than before. Rural per capita incomes slowly decrease

214   *Erosion*

towards the subsistence level.

Figure 5.5

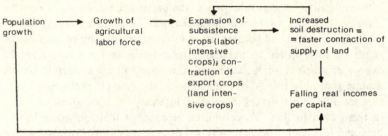

The Influence of Price Changes

Our conclusions so far are based on the assumption of constant relative commodity prices. If the only changes taking place had been supply changes within the peasant sector, as the analysis in Appendix 1 shows,* an excess supply of subsistence goods and an excess demand for export goods would have arisen which would have increased the relative price of the latter goods. The supply shift into increased subsistence production caused by labor force growth and shrinking land resources would automatically have been partly or wholly counteracted by this price change. A new shift in production would have taken place — a return to export production and a shift away from subsistence production. Coffee trees would once more be planted on the mountain slopes and the risk of erosion would decrease. Unfortunately, the relative price of export and subsistence goods is not only governed by supply shifts in the Haitian peasant sector. Demand changes as well must be taken into account, and even more important, the peasant sector is not a closed economy. The relative prices facing the peasants are heavily influenced by developments in the world market and by government policy with respect to taxation. During the 1950-70 period the price of export goods fell in terms of subsistence goods as a result of the interplay of these factors. The price changes probably did reinforce, not counteract, the shift into increased subsistence production. By the same token the erosion process presumably gained further strength.

In Appendix 1 the determinants of the relative price of export and subsistence goods (as received by the peasants) are analyzed in a three-commodity general equilibrium framework, the basic assumption being that Haiti exchanges export goods for manufactured goods in the world

* Cf. expressions (5:55) and (5:63).

Erosion

market and that Haiti is too 'small' to be able to influence its terms of trade. The subsistence goods do not enter into international trade but are consumed entirely within Haiti itself. The price of export goods received by the Haitian peasant equals the difference between the f.o.b. price and the export tax levied by the Haitian government:

$$P_X = P_{fob} - T$$

Both the f.o.b. price and the tax are known to have changed during the 1950-70 period. During these two decades the export prices received by the peasants fell (or at least remained constant).

If we go back to Table 4.6 in Chapter 4 we see very clearly that the price of coffee paid to the Haitian producers was severely reduced during the 1950-70 period. In Chapter 4 we analyzed the increase in the gross shares of the intermediaries, and it was found that this increase was probably due mostly to increased transport costs. Table 4.6 also shows that the f.o.b. (world market) price of coffee fell during the period, and that there was simultaneously a slight increase in the taxes on coffee. The decisive influence appears to have come from developments in the world market. From the early 1950s to the late 1960s this market was constantly threatened by over-production. During the 1953-63 period coffee surpluses steadily accumulated as world supply expanded faster than demand. After the 1954 peak, caused by frost damage in Brazil, the world market price of coffee began to decline as supply gradually outran demand. The International Coffee Agreement to stabilize the market, which began to function in 1963-64, was a direct outcome of this trend.

The agreement received some unexpected aid from a curtailment of Brazilian output due to frost and drought damage in 1964-65, and Brazilian production was on average 50 percent lower during the 1964/65–1973/74 period than during the preceding decade. Still, this reduction could not eliminate 'the tendency of prices to seek their long-term equilibrium'[89] until the end of the 1960s. World stocks of coffee increased from 70,700 bags in 1964 to 87,500 bags in 1967.[90] It was not until 1968 that prices began to rise,[91] and due to the long gestation lag for coffee – it takes four or five years before a coffee plant begins to produce – no supply response other than more careful picking of coffee cherries had time to make itself felt in Haiti until the beginning of the 1970s.[92]

In turn, the overall coffee tax increased markedly in the mid-1950s and after a fall until the mid-1960s, another rise took place with the result that the average coffee tax was higher at the beginning of the 1970s than 20 years earlier. (The taxation system for coffee is complicated. We will not go into any details here.[93] It is sufficient to say that during the period under consideration the coffee tax basically was a specific tax, which we have also assumed in the model in Appendix 1.)

Government policy seems to have hampered the development of sugar cane production. The price to those producers who sold to the three large, commercial mills was fixed at US $4.10 per ton — a figure that did not change between 1948 and 1973.[94] With the exception of HASCO, the large mills also required the producers to pay transport costs, which frequently amounted to between $1 to $1.50 per ton.[95] This left a producer price of $2.60 to $3.10, from which input costs had to be deducted. However, independent sugar producers were in no way compelled to sell their product to the large mills. The small rural refineries (*guildives*) were free to purchase at any price, which led to a diversion of deliveries from large to small mills. Still, at the margin, the unfavorable price obtained from the large refineries must have been of importance for production, since the entire production could not be swallowed by the smaller units, and in a situation where production was plentiful enough to permit deliveries to both kinds of mills* there could not have been strong incentives for the *guildives* to overbid the large mills by any substantial amount.

Table 5.11 shows the fall of f.o.b. price of sisal after the end of the Korean War until the early 1970s, when the oil crisis increased the production costs of competing synthetic fibers so as also to give an upward impetus to the price of raw sisal. The table also shows that the price received by the producers follows the f.o.b. price closely. We will deal more with sisal in Chapter 6, and the reader is referred to that chapter for more details.[96]

The price trends in the international cocoa market are shown in Table 5.12. The price at the beginning of the 1950s was somewhat higher than that prevailing in the late 1960s and the early 1970s, the latter years constituting a recovery in comparison with the downward trend from the mid-1950s to the mid-1960s.

When we come to bananas and cotton, finally, price arguments are less relevant: the banana boom of the 1930s and 1940s described in Chapter 2 was to a very large extent the result of the organization of

---

* It has been calculated that some 25-40 percent of the sugar cane is refined in the large sugar mills (IBRD (1972), p. 9).

Table 5.11: F.o.b. Prices and Prices to Producer of Haitian Raw Sisal 1951/52-1972/73 (US dollars per kilo)

Year	Price	Year	Price	Year	Price to producer
1951/52	0.40	1962/63	0.21		
1952/53	0.24	1963/64	0.22	1964	0.14
1953/54	0.21	1964/65	0.17	1965	0.09
1954/55	0.17	1965/66	0.16	1966	0.08
1955/56	0.18	1966/67	0.12	1967	0.07
1956/57	0.16	1967/68	0.11	1968	0.07
1957/58	0.15	1968/69	0.12	1969	0.08
1958/59	0.16	1969/70	0.11	1970	0.08
1959/60	0.18	1970/71	0.09	1971	0.10
1960/61	0.18	1971/72	0.13	1972	0.12
1961/62	0.17	1972/73	0.19	1973	0.18

Source: f.o.b. prices Fatton (1975), p. 45; prices to producer: JWK (1976 : 3), p. 25.

Table 5.12: International Cocoa Prices 1950/51-71/72 (US cents per pound)[a]

Year	Price	Year	Price
1950/51	35.5	1961/62	21.0
1951/52	35.4	1962/63	25.3
1952/53	37.1	1963/64	23.4
1953/54	57.8	1964/65	17.3
1954/55	37.5	1965/66	24.4
1955/56	27.3	1966/67	29.1
1956/57	30.6	1967/68	34.4
1957/58	44.3	1968/69	45.7
1958/59	36.6	1969/70	34.2
1959/60	28.4	1970/71	26.8
1960/61	22.6	1971/72	32.3

a. Cocoa beans, fair fermented main crop Ghana, New York quotation for immediate delivery.
Source: Singh *et al.* (1977), pp. 82-3.

the Haitian market by a US owned monopoly: the Standard Fruit Company. When this monopoly was lost, the company simply withdrew from the Haitian market, which led to unbelievable chaos. Small, irresponsible companies engaged themselves in a scandalous concession hunting, and soon ruined the reputation of Haitian bananas abroad due to bad methods of handling the fruit. The peasants were frequently cheated and responded by ceasing to grow bananas.[97] Efforts to resuscitate the banana exports by government financing failed, largely due to financial mismanagement, and in 1955 the Institut Haitien de Promotion du Café et des Denreés d'Exportation (IHPCADE) took over and tried a program of extension of banana plantations, but ran out of funds during the political and financial crisis of 1957.[98] Thus, the fall in banana production appears to be a product of insufficient organization of the market in combination with lack of confidence by the peasants, rather than of any other set of factors.

In the same way as bananas, cotton growing was an industry in decline at the beginning of the 1950s. This, in turn, was due to the appearance of the Mexican boll-weevil in 1935. The boll-weevil struck cotton production with devastating results. The average crop fell from a peak of approximately 19,000 tons per year in 1931-32 to some 5,500 tons during the early 1950s.[99] The boll-weevil continued to be a problem during the 1950s. Earlier, various efforts had been made to substitute annual varieties for the perennial one traditionally cultivated in Haiti, since that would solve the boll-weevil problem, but these efforts met with very little success until the introduction of the Stoneville 7-A variety in 1962. Cultivation of annual cotton quickly rose to the point where in 1970, the latter accounted for almost 40 percent of the production.[100] The substitution also managed to increase total production; however, due to the increasing demand from the domestic textile and vegetable oil industries, this is not yet large enough to cover domestic needs. From being an export product in the 1930s cotton has turned into a net import.

Looking back we thus find that (excepting the special cases of bananas and cotton) for all major export crops there has been either a deterioration or a stagnation in the price paid to the producer, and that this typically has been the result of a fall in the f.o.b. price and (in the case of the most important product) a rise in the export tax levied by the Haitian government. However, when it comes to analyzing the change in the composition of output, the changes in export prices *per se* are not interesting. What matters is the development of the *relative* price of export goods and subsistence crops. Therefore we also need some statistics regarding the prices of the latter type of goods. These are found in Table 5.13, where it is seen that (excluding a general decline in the early 1960s) there has been an upward trend between the mid-1950s and the late 1960s. Given the strongly competitive nature of the marketing system for these goods, the figures should also be a good approximation of the development of the prices received by the peasant producers.*

Table 5.13: Price Indices for Port-au-Prince for Some Important Subsistence Crops 1953-71 (1948 = 100)

	Rice	Corn	Red beans	Plantains	Sweet Potatoes	Sorghum	Manioc
1953	110	59	78	71	242	58	143
1954	131	60	90	82	300	72	143
1955	118	67	93	88	287	68	142
1956	126	64	86	92	333	67	134
1957	116	83	94	88	337	83	143
1958	110	71	98	90	283	73	143
1959	90	57	83	84	311	66	143
1960	81	41	89	54	179	52	143
1961	88	55	88	72	212	69	143
1962	84	62	83	76	216	72	143
1963	85	60	93	86	220	70	143
1964	107	67	101	95	200	66	143
1965	114	86	95	91	225	75	196
1966	117	82	108	101	281	80	214
1967	123	62	89	105	254	68	214
1968	130	91	93	110	266	74	90
1969	125	70	94	137	350	63	100
1970	143	71	93	119	300	61	143
1971	149	81	102	131	350	78	207

Source: IHS (1971), pp. 409-18.

* An analysis of the main determinants of the development of the price of subsistence goods (in terms of *manufactured* goods) is made in Appendix 1. Basically, changes in demand generated by changes in national income as the factor endowment and the price of export crops (in terms of manufactures) change tend to make the price of subsistence goods fall, while demand changes generated by the tendency to consume more food (subsistence goods) and less manufactured goods as the population increases (and incomes are kept constant) act so as to raise this price. (The reader is referred to the appendix for details.)

The prices of export goods reviewed above are current prices expressed in US dollars, and the prices of subsistence goods are also current prices, with indices based on quotations in Haitian gourdes. The gourde/dollar rate of exchange has remained fixed by law (as 5 to 1) since 1919. Hence, with the information just obtained, we have a rough idea about the development of relative prices of export and subsistence goods as well. We may conclude that for the two product groups as a whole, the price of export crops has fallen in terms of subsistence goods. Hence, provided that the supplies of export and subsistence goods are not unresponsive to changes in relative prices, the fall of the relative price of export crops should have reinforced the tendency for the peasants to shift out of production of these goods and to go into production of subsistence goods instead. By the same token, the rate of erosion should have increased further due to the increased exposure of the soil to wind and rains resulting from this shift.

We now sum up our argument. The growth of the population increases the supply of labor in Haiti and as long as the urban sector of the economy fails to expand fast enough to absorb this increase, there is only one place for the labor to go (unless it manages to leave the country) and that is into the traditional sector. Peasant agriculture cannot absorb the additional labor without serious difficulties, however. Given the relative prices of peasant export products and subsistence goods, the increasing labor force must go into production of the latter goods and must there be combined with some land taken out of export production. The output of subsistence goods must rise and the output of export goods must fall.

When land is transferred from export to subsistence production, soil destruction increases. The available supply of agricultural land falls. If we continue to assume that the relative price of the two types of goods is kept constant, the peasant sector thereby receives an additional stimulus in the direction of a higher proportion of subsistence goods in its output structure.* Once again the production of subsistence goods increases and the production of export goods falls.

---

* It should be observed that even with zero population growth some land would be eroded. The rate of erosion depends among other things on the absolute amount of land in subsistence cultivation. Consequently, as soon as subsistence crops are grown at all, there will be erosion. The influence of population growth is to *increase* the land area employed for growing subsistence crops and thereby also the rate of erosion.

Erosion

The erosion process receives a new impetus. The cumulative process is working, and if no counteracting forces enter the scene per capita real incomes in rural areas will slowly fall towards some kind of Malthusian stable equilibrium.

The above reasoning builds on the assumption of unchanged relative commodity prices. Quite obviously this is an unrealistic assumption, and it was made only to highlight the interaction between population growth and erosion. The relative price of export and subsistence goods must change, or the peasant sector would quickly become entirely specialized in the production of subsistence goods. Were the supply changes occurring within the peasant sector itself the only changes would be that the relative price of export goods would go up and act as a brake on the cumulative process, or bring the process to a complete halt, or reverse it.

Unfortunately, other types of changes emanating from the world market for peasant export goods, from the tax policy of the Haitian government and from population growth, may disturb the picture. We have taken a long-term view in the present chapter and have examined the development of relative prices from the early 1950s to the early 1970s — the only period for which reasonably reliable data are available. During this period, the effect of excess supply in the world markets for export goods, increased export taxes in Haiti, and demand shifts caused by population growth in Haiti probably was to reinforce the cumulative tendencies instead of counteracting them. The price of export goods fell in terms of subsistence goods. A further shift from export to subsistence production may have taken place and the rate of erosion may have increased as a consequence.

A convenient way to summarize our argument is by using the Edgeworth-Bowley box diagram[101] shown in Figure 5.6. At the outset, the peasant sector has a factor endowment which is given by the box OPQR. Land is measured on the vertical axis and labor on the horizontal axis. The production of subsistence goods is measured by means of a series of isoquants extending from O, and export production by an isoquant family extending from Q. (The isoquants are not shown in the diagram.) At the outset, the sector produces the output mix given by point A in the diagram with factor intensities given by the straight lines OA and QA respectively.

As the labor force grows, the shape of the box changes to OPQ'R', and the production point moves to B at given relative commodity and factor prices. The factor intensities, as seen by the diagram, remain unchanged, since OB is an extension of OA and Q'B is parallel to QA. However, at the same time, the available land resources shrink due to erosion. The new

Figure 5.6

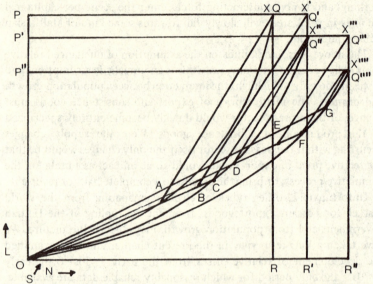

box becomes QP'Q"R', and at given prices the sector produces at point C. Constant relative prices are not compatible with equilibrium, however, as we have seen, but the relative price of export goods will fall, and the sector decreases its production of these goods and increases that of subsistence goods. We arrive at point D in the diagram. Here, the factor intensities have changed to OD and Q"D, respectively. When the relative price of export goods falls, so does the price of land in terms of labor, and the production methods in both lines of production become more land intensive as the peasants substitute land for labor.

As long as the population and the labor force continue to grow and as long as the supply of land continues to shrink, the process outlined above will continue as well. Labor force growth gives us the new box QP'Q' 'R' with production at (the new) constant prices in F, and continued erosion shrinks the box to OP"Q"'R" with production at F at given prices and at G if the relative price of export goods continues to fall. If the process continues, sooner or later the sector will become totally specialized, and thereafter remain so unless the relative price of exportables rises enough. Labor will be added to shrinking land resources in the peasant sector and will be subject to strongly diminishing returns which make per capita incomes fall off towards subsistence level. In practice, however, as we saw in Chapter 3, even though the peasant sector is not entirely specialized, we appear already to have reached the point where diminishing returns to labor in combination with the accelerating soil destruction are strong enough to depress per capita incomes in rural areas. The increased production of subsistence goods does not compensate for the fall in the value of export production.

The exposure of the peasant sector to the whims of an erratic government and to the fluctuations of world market prices makes it difficult to check the pace of erosion, given that the peasants continue to employ the same methods of cultivation as they do now. The growth of the population automatically accelerates the erosion process unless the relative price of export goods rises sufficiently, but there is no mechanism which automatically ensures that this takes place.

Erosion control presumably cannot be successful unless something is done to change the methods of cultivation. We will come back to the general problem of innovations in Chapter 12, but before that, in the concluding part of the present chapter, we will make an attempt to explain why the Haitian peasant himself shows no interest in undertaking measures which may put an end to or at least arrest the pace of soil destruction as well as to examine the efforts made by the government to control and prevent erosion and explain why in spite of a well-developed legislation the practical results have been virtually nil.

Absence of Erosion Control

Every year 'the rocks grow bigger' in the peasants' fields and soon 'the land does not want to produce anymore.'[102] Deforestation and erosion take a heavy toll in terms of the standard of living of future generations. While it takes only a handful of years to destroy the humus layer of the soil, to increase the same layer by 3 centimeters, nature requires between 250 and 1,000 years.[103] There are several things that the peasants could do to prevent erosion:

> . . .by planting along the contour and constructing countour drains, diversion channels, graded drains, stone walls, and earth embankments by planting tree crops instead of the usual ground crops, by strip-cropping, and by the establishment of vegetative barriers — the appropriate practices varying with soil quality and the slope of the land.[104]

Still, very few peasants do this in Haiti. Let us take a look at the rationale behind such a decision. An example is furnished by tree-felling:

> The reactions of peasants and woodcutters constitute an excellent example of external diseconomy which occurs when the actions of an individual inflict direct losses on others, i.e., those persons who cause the erosion do not necessarily suffer the unfortunate consequences...[105]

The peasants seldom own the forests where the trees are cut down. These as a rule are government property. Hence, the only cost of cutting a tree is frequently that of the labor expended on the operation. Denuding the mountain slopes in turn leads to increased run-off which affects not only those peasants that have cut down the trees but others as well. This makes it expensive for the individual peasant to protect himself from the influences of water erosion on his land. As long as other peasants are cutting down trees, he will also suffer the consequences, and hence there will be no incentive for him to refrain from cutting himself, for example.

The problem of erosion control may be analyzed with the aid of some simple game theory. Figure 5.7 shows a 'pay-off' matrix for two peasants, A and B. Let us assume that these two peasants are faced with the same two alternatives: to undertake measures of erosion control or not. The matrix shows the costs for each peasant associated with each of the two alternatives. If neither peasant does anything about erosion, both incur the cost of erosion resulting from A's inaction plus the cost resulting from B's inaction. (It is assumed that both costs affect the two peasants to the same degree.) If both peasants undertake measures to control erosion, A bears a cost of C_A and B a cost of C_B. Let us assume that each of these costs is lower than the sum of the costs of erosion, $E_A + E_B$, but higher than either of the individual components E_A or E_B. In this situation, it pays for the two peasants to control erosion, but only if *both* of them do so. If A undertakes to control 'his part' of the erosion process, but not B, A incurs a cost of $E_B + C_A$, i.e. he has to pay the cost of erosion control, which is lower than $E_A + E_B$, but in addition he still has to pay the cost of B refraining from control, E_B. Since $C_A > E_A$, $E_B + C_A > E_A + E_B$. Hence, A is worse off by controlling erosion as long as B does nothing. B, on the other hand, is better off, since $E_B < E_A + E_B$ (and also less than C_B). The same, *mutatis mutandis*, applies in the situation where B controls erosion while A does nothing. This means that there are no incentives for either of the two peasants to control erosion as long as they cannot rely on the other peasant to do the same. In this situation, both peasants will remain inactive, and both of them will be worse off than

Erosion

if both undertook the necessary measures to check erosion.[106]

Figure 5.7

	Peasant B: No control	Control
Peasant A: No control	$E_A + E_B$, $E_A + E_B$	E_A, $E_A + C_B$
Control	$E_B + C_A$, E_B	C_A, C_B

Figure 5.7 illustrates the simple case with only two peasants. The problems, i.e. the disincentives, are multiplied as the number of peasants increases. It is possible that a small group of peasants could agree to start a scheme of erosion control, but as long as there are others in the neighborhood who do not join the scheme, they cannot be certain of its success.

Other factors may provide further disincentives. This is illustrated in Figure 5.8. In this matrix we introduce the gross revenues of the two peasants, R_A and R_B. We also take into account that the costs of controlling erosion may have to be incurred during the present period while the benefits (and the effects of erosion) arise only in the future, after a longer or shorter gestation lag. Thus, in the situation where neither peasant attempts to control erosion, their present revenues are R_A and R_B, and their future revenues are $R_A - E_A - E_B$ and $R_B - E_A - E_B$, respectively. If A attempts control without B doing the same, he incurs the cost C_A during the present period which lowers his present net revenue, while his future net revenue increases by E_A. If we assume, as we did in Figure 5.7, that $C_A > E_A$, we find that, even without discounting future incomes, A is worse off than in the situation where he lets erosion take its course. B, as in the simpler case, is better off. His present net revenue is unchanged, and his future revenue is increased by E_A. The opposite case arises if B undertakes erosion control but not A.

So far, the conclusions are analogous to those reached from the matrix of Figure 5.7. If we look at the situation where both A and B control erosion, however, we see that this situation is not necessarily preferred by either A or B in comparison to the situation where they both do nothing. Their present net revenues fall by C_A and C_B respectively, and their future net revenues both increase by $E_A + E_B$ which is more than either C_A or C_B — *as long as we do not discount*

Figure 5.8

	Peasant B: No control	Control
Peasant A: No control	R_A, R_B $R_A - E_A - E_B$, $R_B - E_A - E_B$	R_A, $R_B - C_B$ $R_A - E_A$, $R_B - E_A$
Control	$R_A - C_A$, R_B $R_A - E_B$, $R_B - E_B$	$R_A - C_A$, $R_B - C_B$ R_A, R_B

$E_A + E_B$ *too heavily*. But this is precisely what the peasants are likely to do. Their incomes are insufficient already in the present. We saw in Chapter 3 that malnutrition is widespread in Haiti, and further evidence will be presented in the disucssion of the human factor in Chapter 9. With incomes being so close to the subsistence level, an element of shortsightedness is likely to dominate the actions of the peasants. In his classic work on the theory of interest rate determination, Irving Fisher wrote:

> Poverty bears down heavily on all portions of a man's expected life. But it increases the want for immediate income *even more* than it increases the want for future income.
>
> This influence of poverty is partly rational, because of the importance, by supplying present needs, of keeping up the continuity of life and thus maintaining the ability to cope with the future; and partly irrational because the pressure of present needs blinds a person to the needs of the future.
>
> As to the rational aspect, present income is absolutely indispensable, not only for present needs, but even as a pre-condition to the attainment of future income. *A man must live*. Any one who values his life would, under ordinary circumstances, prefer to rob the future for the benefit of the present — so far, at least, as to keep life going. If a person has only one loaf of bread he would not set it aside for next year even if the rate of interest were 1000 per cent; for if he did so, he would starve in the meantime. A single break in the thread of life suffices to cut off all the future. We stress the importance of the present because the present is the gateway to the future. Not only is a certain minimum of present income necessary

to prevent starvation, but the nearer this minimum is approached the more precious does present income appear relative to future income.

As to the irrational aspect of the matter, the effect of poverty is often to relax foresight and self-control and to tempt us to 'trust to luck' for the future, if only the all-engrossing need of present necessities can be satisfied.[107]

The case of the Haitian peasant fits the Fisher theory well. Balancing on the edge of starvation, what matters is today, not tomorrow. Incurring costs of erosion control today to receive the benefits only in the future is not an appealing prospect to the peasants. It is quite possible that they 'discount future benefits at a particularly high rate,'[108] to the point where the 'no control' alternative dominates the alternative where all peasants attempt to check erosion. If in addition the benefits of erosion control are perceived as uncertain, this effect will be reinforced. Thus, in addition to the temptation to 'cheat' their fellow peasants by not doing their share of erosion control in a situation where co-operation is possible, the inhabitants of rural Haiti may also have their own time preferences to overcome, if erosion is to be efficiently dealt with.

The final reason why it does not necessarily pay for the individual peasant to invest in erosion control is that somebody else may be reaping all the benefits. If the peasant is a sharecropper or a tenant farmer he will have very little interest in protecting the land. Planting trees would just make the land more valuable, and the landowner might then raise the rent to be paid, or evict the tenant to get somebody else instead.[109] Even if the peasant owns the land himself, this is no guarantee that he will be the ultimate person to benefit from anti-erosion measures. In Chapter 12 we will discuss the case where an innovation is made that increases the value of a particular piece of land. Then, the peasant who owns the land may often become involved in a lawsuit regarding the title to the property and may easily lose the latter.

Thus, erosion control must be regarded as an innovation in rural Haiti. In Chapter 12 we will discuss the factors that make innovation a difficult process. A special difficulty is the lack of formal education, which is dealt with in Chapter 10, and the lack of an extension service (and hence of informal training) which is discussed in Chapter 12. The peasants are not necessarily aware of the proper techniques to maintain soil fertility and prevent erosion,[110] but these techniques may have to be taught by outsiders.

In a situation where the peasants themselves cannot be trusted to undertake the necessary measures to stop erosion and restore the fertility of exhausted lands, the government has to step in and provide the necessary incentives. This could in principle be done by introduction of some type of legal sanctions or taxes. Going back to the example of Figure 5.8, the discounted net revenue for a peasant who does not control erosion (assuming that no peasants do) in the two-period case is

$$R_{net} = R + (R - E_A - E_B)e^{-it}$$

where i is the discount rate and t is the time it takes before future revenues and costs materialize. With erosion control by all peasants the discounted net revenue changes to

$$R_{net}^{control} = R - C + Re^{-it}$$

which we assume to be smaller than the revenue in absence of erosion control. To make the peasants undertake anti-erosion measures the government must make the net revenue of the no-control alternative decrease with

$$S > C - (E_A + E_B)e^{-it}$$

which, as stated above, can be done either with taxation or by other legal sanction. Let us see how the Haitian governments have tackled this problem in practice. This has been done mainly by introduction of a number of legal sanctions other than taxation.

Legal Measures to Combat Deforestation and Erosion

The problems of deforestation and erosion have received the attention of the Haitian legislators ever since the 1820s. The *Code Rural* of 1825 explicitly prohibits the felling of trees on steep slopes and on mountain summits as well as near springs and rivers.[111] This article was repeated in the 1864 Code, where it was also stated that all unauthorized wood-cutting would lead to immediate arrest.[112]

The Code, which was in effect until 1962, was later supplemented by other laws and decrees. In 1926, the Department of Agriculture received the authority to create forest reserves whenever it judged this necessary, and the same year a reserve was created in St-Raphaël, in the *Département du Nord*.[113] In 1933, cutting of trees (especially pines) in state forests or on private property without previous authorization from the Department of Agriculture was forbidden. The same prohibition was repeated in a 1936 decree which also outlined in greater detail where woodcutting was not allowed. That year another reserve was created in Plaisance and Cerisier. In 1937 a national forest was established in Fonds-Verrettes and Bodarie. During the same year a law preventing tree-felling and planting of anything but trees on steep hillsides was also promulgated.[114] Exports of precious woods were prohibited in 1944,[115] and the following year saw a decree regulating cutting, transport and selling of wood within Haiti.[116]

After promulgation of two more laws in the 1950s, in December 1959, a commission on the conservation of renewable natural resources presented a law project revising the old *Code Rural* and laying greater stress than ever before on combating erosion and tree-felling.[117] This project finally resulted in the *Code Rural François Duvalier*, promulgated in 1962. The new rural code regulates in detail where and how cultivation may take place, what measures must be taken to conserve the soil, where trees may and may not be felled and how reforestation is to proceed. The law divides the country into three types of zones: dry (with a rainfall of less than 750 mm per year), semi-dry (with a precipitation between 750 and 1,350 mm), and humid (with a precipitation of 1,350 mm or more per year). The law explicitly prohibits land clearing on slopes exceeding 30 degrees in dry zones, 40 in semi-dry zones, and 50 in humid areas. Land that has already been cleared of its natural vegetation in such zones must be reforested or planted with fodder crops. Only permanent cultures (coffee, cocoa, fruit, trees, etc.) are permitted on these slopes. Other cultivation is prohibited (unless special authorization is obtained) on slopes exceeding 25 degrees, 35 degrees and 40 degrees, respectively, and on lands with a slope less than the above but exceeding 10 degrees, soil protection measures must be undertaken unless the land is used for grazing. Bare fallows are prohibited on hillsides. A vegetative cover is required.

Direct burning of fields is not allowed, but whatever is to be burned must be gathered before fire is put to it. It is also prohibited to burn such material that may serve as compost, except in some special cases. The code also decrees that a forest shall be declared a reserve if it protects watersheds or mountain crests or slopes exceeding 60 degrees. Such forests cannot be exploited without special permission if owned privately. The same restriction applies to forests on slopes exceeding 30, 40 and 50 degrees in the three zones. In principle, all woodcutting without previous authorization is prohibited, and it is not allowed to use fruit trees or trees whose wood can be employed for other purposes to make firewood.[118]

Haiti has enough laws to protect its forests and soils. What is lacking is not legislation as such but enforcement of the existing laws. In spite of the letter of the law there are no actual sanctions which force the peasants to undertake erosion control.* To understand why, we have to examine how the Haitian government views the peasant sector of the economy. This will not be done in the present chapter, but the reader is referred instead to Chapters 6-8. One of the most important conclusions of these chapters is that few Haitian governments have shown any interest in the peasant sector and especially not in peasant welfare. This conclusion is highly relevant for the discussion in the present chapter. To implement the laws regarding forest conservation and erosion control, supervision of peasant activities is needed and supervision requires a control apparatus of fairly large dimensions. Such a control apparatus is of course not without its costs, and when a government is to decide whether it actually wants to incur the costs, the latter have to be weighed against the benefits. As the discussion in Chapters 6-8 will reveal, the only benefits that would enter this decision would be those of the government circle and of the other political 'ins'. Against the political and administrative history of Haiti it is not reasonable to expect that many of the governments should have adopted a perspective which focuses on the interests of the nation instead of on the interests of a small group of individuals. The benefits of erosion control to this group have always been virtually zero. The resources actually spent on supervision are ridiculously small. In 1976, there were only 175 untrained forest guards to handle the control of a rural population exceeding 4 million people,[119] and should these guards ever try to enforce the laws, bribing them to shut their eyes would presumably not require any excessive sums.

Conclusions

Soil exhaustion and erosion constitute the most serious problem facing Haitian agriculture. The rural population is growing at a natural rate of approximately 2 percent per year, and population growth has serious detrimental effects in that it leads to tree-felling and higher labor intensity of cultivations. The mountain sides are denuded of their natural vegetation, and cultivation takes their place. The soil is dried

---

* A problem in this context is what should be done to prevent peasant incomes from falling to an unacceptable level as a result of the enforcement of the laws.

out when there are no trees whose roots can help to store the water and whose branches and leaves can shade the soil from the blazing sunlight. As intense cultivation spreads, good soils gradually become worthless.

The erosion in Haiti is fundamentally a human erosion. The gradual turning of fertile land into worthless rocks is the outcome of the peasant system of farming. Erosion is entirely within the logic of the system. As the rural population grows, the mountain sides are stripped of their forests, either because more firewood and charcoal is needed in the absence of any economical substitutes, or because, given the relative price of labor- and land-intensive crops, there is a tendency for the former to expand and for the latter to contract, in both cases with erosion as an inevitable result.

In principle, the tendency for the economy gradually to lapse into production of subsistence crops should be counteracted by a tendency for the relative price of export crops to rise — were it not for the influence of above all the demand and supply conditions prevailing in the world market for Haitian export products. When these conditions are unfavorable in the sense that the world market is glutted, as it was in the 1950s and the 1960s, the erosion process will not be counteracted but may be reinforced by the development of the relative price of export and subsistence goods. Thus, the Haitian peasant is at the mercy of the world market in this respect. Given the prevailing technology, only a very favorable movement of the relative price of export products may preclude erosion from taking its toll.

Erosion is within the logic of the system, but this logic is very myopic. The present generations' struggle to make their meager living can only be at the expense of future generations. Since important external economies presumably are involved in woodcutting and erosion, and hence also in erosion control, there is always a temptation for the individual peasant not to attempt to control and prevent erosion. The peasant is probably caught in a 'prisoner's dilemma' which may also be aggravated by the natural tendency for people living on the brink of starvation to pay more attention to present than to future incomes. The costs of erosion control are incurred today, but the benefits arise mainly tomorrow and may hence be heavily discounted. Only the government can change this situation, but given the high cost of supervising and enforcing the existing laws, no Haitian government has ever attempted anything of the kind — especially since erosion control does not yield any direct benefit to the group of politicians who happen to be in power.

Notes

1. For a discussion of the concepts of static and dynamic efficiency, see Lindbeck (1971). Cf. also e.g. Balassa (1961).
2. Dorfman, Samuelson & Solow (1958), Chapter 12.
3. Cf. also the discussion in Schumpeter (1950), Chapter 7.
4. For an outline of such an intensification process see Boserup (1965).
5. Moreau de Saint-Méry (1958), p.29.
6. Logan (1968), p.10.
7. Parry (1969), p.213.
8. Victor (1944), p.24. Cf. Rotberg & Clague (1971), p.34.
9. Ibid., pp.24-5.
10. Leyburn (1966), p.33.
11. Victor (1944), p.28.
12. Rotberg & Clague (1971), p.395.
13. BTS, no. 10, September 1953, p.22.
14. Ibid.
15. See Victor (1944), pp.32-40.
16. Ibid., p.44. The low quality of the census was officially admitted (Cf. Bazile (1969), p.44).
17. Millspaugh (1931), p.13.
18. Rotberg & Clague (1971), p.395.
19. Ibid.
20. Brand (1965), p.18.
21. Saint Surin (1962), p.11. Before Saint Surin another age adjustment effort was made by Jacques Vilgrain (Cf. BTS, nos. 19-21, December 1955-June 1956). Saint Surin's calculations appear to be an improvement in comparison to the earlier study (Brand (1965), pp.18-19).
22. Rotberg & Clague (1971), pp. 263-4.
23. Segal & Earnhardt (1967), p. 77.
24. Rotberg & Clague (1971), p. 395.
25. Ibid., p.264.
26. IHS (1975 : 1).
27. Ibid., p.3.
28. IHS (1973), p.1.
29. IHS (1975 : 2), p.2.
30. Ibid.
31. République d'Haïti (1975), p.25.
32. Stycos (1964).
33. Rotberg & Clague (1971), p.267.
34. See CHISS (1975) and Lamothe & Haverberg (1976). Cf. also Segal & Earnhardt (1969), pp.81-2.
35. UNCTAD (1976), pp.333-4.
36. See Chapter 12.
37. Cf. Woodring, Brown & Burbank (1924), p.57.
38. Street (1960), pp.135-6.
39. Woodring, Brown & Burbank (1924), p.61.
40. Street (1960), p.137.
41. Moreau de Saint-Méry (1958), p.27, and quoted by Moral (1961), p.120.
42. OEA (1972), p.610.
43. Moral (1961), p.120.
44. Moral (1961), p.120, gives other figures for mahogany and logwood exports but does not state his sources.
45. This is discussed in Chapter 6.
46. Cf. Rotberg & Clague (1971), p.292. We will come back to this below.
47. DARNDR (1960 : 1), p.37.
48. Quoted by FAO (1955), p.37.

49. Woodring, Brown & Burbank (1924), p.57.
50. FAO (1955), p.85.
51. Moral (1961), p.116.
52. Rotberg & Clague (1971), p.294.
53. Woodring, Brown & Burbank (1924), pp. 488-94.
54. OEA (1972), p.421; Satcunanathan (1977), pp.3.4-3.5.
55. Moore (1972), p.180.
56. DARNDR (1960 : 1), pp.51-71.
57. Woodring, Brown & Burbank (1924), p.480.
58. Moore (1972), p.181.
59. Satcunanathan (1976), pp.7-8.
60. Pierre-Louis (1976), pp.14-15.
61. Satcunanathan (1977), p.4.8.
62. Ibid., p.4.11.
63. IBRD (1974), p.30; CIAP (1974), p.63.
64. IBRD (1974), p.30.
65. Sacunanathan (1976), p.7.
66. Woodring, Brown & Burbank (1924), pp.557-66.
67. Satcunanathan (1976), p.8.
68. Pierre-Louis (1976), p.18.
69. Golding (1956), p.16.
70. For some points regarding the use of nuclear power in developing countries see Satcunanathan (1976), p.3.
71. Cf. ibid., pp.4-6 and Satcunanathan (1977), pp.4.1-4.3.
72. See Table 3.11.
73. CONADEP (1976), Tables A-4 and A-6.
74. Ibid., Table A-5. The table has been corrected for a misprint regarding the 1950 male labor force in agriculture.
75. Cf. e.g. Bairoch (1975), pp.22, 24.
76. See e.g. Mintz (1966 : 1), p.xxxii; IBRD (1972), p.8; Estimé (1972), p.40; JWK (1976 : 1), pp.65, 67.
77. Cf. Rybczynski (1955). For a generalization of the theorem in algebraic terms see Södersten (1964), Chapter 3. For geometric expositions of the same result see Guha (1963) and Amano (1963).
78. Finck (1973), p.11.
79. Ibid., p.12.
80. Ibid.
81. Nicolas (1938), pp.36-7.
82. Ibid., p.35.
83. Ibid., p.36.
84. Ibid.
85. Moral (1961), p.114.
86. Nicolas (1938), p.42.
87. Quoted by Honorat (1974), p.24.
88. FAO (1955), p.85.
89. UN (1975), p.59.
90. JWK (1976 : 1), p.95.
91. For details regarding the world coffee market from the early 1950s to the late 1960s see e.g. Kravis (1968); UN (1975), pp.59-61; and Singh et al. (1977), Chapter 2.
92. Some statistics are given in JWK (1976 : 1), p.30.
93. Such details may be found in e.g. Gates (1959 : 2), pp.23-5; OEA (1974), pp.70-76; Tanzi (1976); JWK (1976 : 1), pp.71-86.
94. Lebeau (1974), p.24.
95. IBRD (1972), p.9.
96. Cf. also Fatton (1975).

97. See Chapter 7, below. Cf. also e.g. Rotberg & Clague (1971), pp.286-7.
98. Moore (1972), p.150.
99. Gates (1959 : 3), p.7.
100. OEA (1972), p.625.
101. Cf. e.g. Södersten (1970), Chapter 3, for a description of the technique.
102. Nicolas (1938), p.34.
103. Ibid., p.40.
104. Rotberg & Clague (1971), p.293. For an outline of an anti-erosion project see IICA (1974 : 1).
105. Rotberg & Clague (1971), p.292.
106. The above of course is nothing but the situation known as 'the prisoner's dilemma'. (See e.g. Luce & Raiffa (1957), pp.95-7.)
107. Fisher (1930), pp.72-3.
108. Rotberg & Clague (1971), p.293.
109. Métraux *et al.* (1951), p.15.
110. Nicolas (1938), p.47; Callear (1977), p.18.
111. Robart (1976), pp.31-2.
112. Code Rural (1929), Articles 14 and 7, respectively.
113. FAO (1955), pp.43-4.
114. Ibid., pp.45-6.
115. DARNDR (1960 : 1), p.11.
116. FAO (1955), p.47.
117. See DARNDR (1960 : 1) and DARNDR (1960 : 2).
118. Département de la Justice (1963), Articles 63-79, 184-207.
119. Callear (1977), p.18.

APPENDIX 1: The Composition of Peasant Output

In the main text of Chapter 5 we discussed how rural population growth caused soil exhaustion and erosion, and how this process during the 1950-70 period may have been reinforced by a fall in the relative price of Haitian export goods. In this appendix we will present the algebraic model behind that discussion.

The following notations will be used:

S_S = supply (production) of subsistence goods
S_X = supply (production) of export goods
D_S = demand for (consumption of) subsistence goods
D_M = demand for (consumption of) manufactured goods
L = total supply of agricultural land
N = total supply of labor
L_S = land use in the production of subsistence goods
L_X = land use in the production of export goods
N_S = labor use in the production of subsistence goods
N_X = labor use in the production of export goods
s = production function for subsistence goods
x = production function for export goods
Y = national income
P_S = price of subsistence goods
P_X = price of export goods to Haitian producers
P_{fob} = world market price of export goods
T = tax on export goods
1 = price of manufactured goods (*numéraire*)
r = rent of agricultural land
w = wage
t = time

The Development of Output at Constant Prices (The Rybczynski Effect[1]

Let us assume that the Haitian peasants produce two types of goods: subsistence goods (S) and export goods (X). We found in Chapter 2 that the use of capital in peasant agriculture is negligible. We will therefore not include capital at all in the model, but production of the two goods is a function of the use of land and labor only:[2]

$$S_S = s(L_S, N_S) \qquad (5:1)$$

$$S_X = x(L_X, N_X) \qquad (5:2)$$

235

It is assumed that $N_S/L_S > N_X/L_X$ at all factor and commodity prices. In Table A 5.1:1 we find two estimates of labor requirements per hectare of a given crop. The estimates leave the definite impression that for the two commodity groups as a whole the labor intensity is higher for subsistence products, especially when it is taken into account that the export crops are in the ground the entire year, while most of the subsistence crops are there only for a part of that period.

Table A 5.1:1: Labor Requirements per Hectare for Selected Crops with Traditional Techniques

Crop	IDB Man-days per hectare	Dorville Man-days per carreau	Time in the ground
Corn	120	154	4-5 months
Sorghum	120	–	–
Beans and peas	120	178	2½ months
Rice	200	258	4-5 months
Sweet potatoes	110	142	7-12 months
Manioc	150	193	8-12 months
Malanga	–	142	entire year
Pigeon peas	–	130	entire year
Coffee	60	77	entire year
Sugar cane	100	100	entire year
Cotton	120	–	–
Cocoa	–	77	entire year

Sources: IDB: BID (1974), pp. 144-6. Dorville: Dorville (1975:2), Annexe No. 7.

This evidence is further confirmed by simple observation. It is a well-known fact that in the case of coffee almost the entire cultivation is left to nature:

> The 'plantations' — the term is rather misleading in this context — are renewed by themselves: new sprouts come from the cherries which fall on the ground or which are transported by the rats who eat the pulp; therefore young, high-yielding coffee trees are standing next to venerable relics with moss-covered trunks. Pruning is practically unknown. The public authorities have attempted for a long time, without much success, to introduce this practice in the production sectors. They have always run into indifference or even die-hard opposition from the peasants. The nursing of the coffee trees as a

rule is limited to a summary weeding once a year, just before the harvest. The cherries, more or less ripe when picked, are dried on the tiny family glacis* or directly on the ground. Thereafter they are depulped, pounded by hand in mortars or wooden bowls. After the cleaning, which takes place in small palm leaf baskets, the 'café pilé', 'café naturel' or 'café habitant' is sold in small lots to the smalltown speculators. The product obtained this way still constitutes more than 9/10 of the total production of the country.[3]

Let us begin by analyzing what happens to the output of the two goods when the labor force increases. Differentiating the production functions gives us

$$dS_S = \frac{\partial s}{\partial L_S} dL_S + \frac{\partial s}{\partial N_S} dN_S \qquad (5:3)$$

$$dS_X = \frac{\partial x}{\partial L_X} dL_X + \frac{\partial x}{\partial N_X} dN_X. \qquad (5:4)$$

We also need the equilibrium conditions for the rural land and labor markets:

$$L_S + L_X = \bar{L} \qquad (5:5)$$

$$N_S + N_X = N(t). \qquad (5:6)$$

For the time being, we assume that the supply of land is given while the supply of labor changes (increases) with time. Differentiating the equilibrium conditions gives

$$dL_S + dL_X = 0 \qquad (5:7)$$

$$dN_S + dN_X = \frac{dN}{dt} dt. \qquad (5:8)$$

Furthermore, assuming that factor rewards equal marginal value products we have

$$r = P_s \frac{\partial s}{\partial L_S} = P_X \frac{\partial x}{\partial L_X} \qquad (5:9)$$

$$w = P_s \frac{\partial s}{\partial N_S} = P_X \frac{\partial x}{\partial N_X}, \qquad (5:10)$$

* Concrete slab.

Appendix 1

or,

$$\frac{P_X}{P_S} = \frac{\partial s/\partial L_S}{\partial x/\partial L_X} \qquad (5:11)$$

$$\frac{P_X}{P_S} = \frac{\partial s/\partial N_S}{\partial x/\partial N_X} \qquad (5:12)$$

Differentiating (5:11) and (5:12), keeping the relative price $\frac{P_X}{P_S}$ constant, yields

$$0 = \frac{\partial^2 s}{\partial L_S^2} dL_S + \frac{\partial^2 s}{\partial N_S \partial L_S} dN_S - \frac{P_X}{P_S}\left(\frac{\partial^2 x}{\partial L_X^2} dL_X + \frac{\partial^2 x}{\partial N_X \partial L_X} dN_X\right) \qquad (5:13)$$

$$0 = \frac{\partial^2 s}{\partial N_S^2} dN_S + \frac{\partial^2 s}{\partial L_S \partial N_S} dL_S - \frac{P_X}{P_S}\left(\frac{\partial^2 x}{\partial N_X^2} dN_X + \frac{\partial^2 x}{\partial L_X \partial N_X} dL_X\right) \qquad (5:14)$$

Equations (5:7), (5:8), (5:13) and (5:14) form a system of four equations and four unknowns (dL_S, dL_X, dN_S, and dN_X) which we may now proceed to solve. The solutions may thereafter be substituted into (5:3) and (5:4) to give us the desired expressions for the changes in output.

We may begin with a few substitutions in Equations (5:13) and (5:14). Assuming the two production functions to be linearly homogeneous,[4] Euler's theorem applies so that the production functions may be written as

$$s(L_S, N_S) = \frac{\partial s}{\partial L_S} L_S + \frac{\partial s}{\partial N_S} N_S \qquad (5:15)$$

$$x(L_X, N_X) = \frac{\partial x}{\partial L_X} L_X + \frac{\partial x}{\partial N_X} N_X. \qquad (5:16)$$

Taking the partial derivatives of (5:15) with respect to L_S and N_S and of (5:16) with respect to L_X and N_X gives us

$$\frac{\partial^2 s}{\partial L_S^2} L_S + \frac{\partial^2 s}{\partial L_S \partial N_S} N_S = 0 \qquad (5:17)$$

Appendix 1

$$\frac{\partial^2 s}{\partial N_S \partial L_S} L_S + \frac{\partial^2 s}{\partial N_S^2} N_S = 0 \tag{5:18}$$

$$\frac{\partial^2 x}{\partial L_X^2} L_X + \frac{\partial^2 x}{\partial L_X \partial N_X} N_X = 0 \tag{5:19}$$

$$\frac{\partial^2 x}{\partial N_X \partial L_X} L_X + \frac{\partial^2 x}{\partial N_X^2} N_X = 0 \tag{5:20}$$

$$\frac{\partial^2 s}{\partial L_S^2} \frac{L_S}{N_S} = -\frac{\partial^2 s}{\partial N_S \partial L_S} = -\frac{\partial^2 s}{\partial L_S \partial N_S} = \frac{\partial^2 s}{\partial N_S^2} \frac{N_S}{L_S} = \alpha \tag{5:21}$$

$$\frac{\partial^2 x}{\partial L_X^2} \frac{L_X}{N_X} = -\frac{\partial^2 x}{\partial N_X \partial L_X} = -\frac{\partial^2 x}{\partial L_X \partial N_X} = \frac{\partial^2 x}{\partial N_X^2} \frac{N_X}{L_X} = \beta. \tag{5:22}$$

Substituting (5:21) and (5:22) into (5:13) and (5:14) gives

$$0 = \frac{N_S}{L_S} \alpha dL_S - \alpha dN_S - \frac{P_X}{P_S}\left(\frac{N_X}{L_X} \beta dL_X - \beta dN_X\right) \tag{5:23}$$

$$0 = \frac{L_S}{N_S} \alpha dN_S - \alpha dL_S - \frac{P_X}{P_S}\left(\frac{L_X}{N_X} \beta dN_X - \beta dL_X\right). \tag{5:24}$$

Solving (5:7), (5:8), (5:23) and (5:24) for dL_S/dt, dL_X/dt, dN_S/dt, and dN_X/dt after some manipulations, since $N_S/L_S > N_X/L_X$, yields

$$\frac{dL_S}{dt} = \frac{dN/dt}{N_S/L_S - N_X/L_X} > 0 \tag{5:25}$$

$$\frac{dL_X}{dt} = \frac{-dN/dt}{N_S/L_S - N_X/L_X} = -\frac{dL_S}{dt} < 0 \tag{5:26}$$

$$\frac{dN_S}{dt} = \frac{N_S/L_S \cdot dN/dt}{N_S/L_S - N_X/L_X} > 0 \tag{5:27}$$

and

$$\frac{dN_X}{dt} = \frac{-N_X/L_X \cdot dN/dt}{N_S/L_S - N_X/L_X} < 0 \tag{5:28}$$

which, when substituted into (5:3) and (5:4) provides us with the expressions for the changes in peasant output when the rural labor force grows and relative prices are held constant:

$$\frac{dS_S}{dt} = \frac{\left(\frac{\partial s}{\partial L_S} + \frac{N_S}{L_S}\frac{\partial s}{\partial N_S}\right)\frac{dN}{dt}}{\frac{N_S}{L_S} - \frac{N_X}{L_X}} > 0 \qquad (5:29)$$

$$\frac{dS_X}{dt} = \frac{-\left(\frac{\partial x}{\partial L_X} + \frac{N_X}{L_X}\frac{\partial x}{\partial N_X}\right)\frac{dN}{dt}}{\frac{N_S}{L_S} - \frac{N_X}{L_X}} < 0. \qquad (5:30)$$

The growth of the labor force causes the supply of subsistence goods to increase at given relative prices, while the supply of export goods contracts.

Continuing to keep relative prices constant, we may go one step further and include erosion in our model. To do so, we express the supply of land as a function of time:*

$$L = L(t) \qquad (5:31)$$

We may now substitute (5:31) into (5:5) and repeat the analysis. Differentiating the resulting expression yields

$$dL_S + dL_X = \frac{dL}{dt}dt. \qquad (5:32)$$

Solving the equation system (5:8), (5:23), and (5:32) gives us new expressions for $\frac{dL_S}{dt}, \frac{dL_X}{dt}, \frac{dN_S}{dt}$, and $\frac{dN_X}{dt}$:

---

* Actually, with the technology employed in Haiti, the land also undergoes a gradual qualitative deterioration when the overall labor intensity in cultivation increases, but since here we are taking a long-run perspective, we have chosen to interpret the process as one of outright destruction of the soil. Assuming that as the population grows, the eventual fate of any given plot is to become eroded, we only regard two states of the plot: one where it is perfectly arable and one, where after a certain time it has become completely worthless for agricultural purposes.

Appendix 1

$$\frac{dL_S}{dt} = \frac{\dfrac{dN}{dt} - \dfrac{N_X}{L_X}\dfrac{dL}{dt}}{\dfrac{N_S}{L_S} - \dfrac{N_X}{L_X}} > 0 \qquad (5:33)$$

$$\frac{dL_X}{dt} = \frac{\dfrac{N_S}{L_S}\dfrac{dL}{dt} - \dfrac{dN}{dt}}{\dfrac{N_S}{L_S} - \dfrac{N_X}{L_X}} < 0 \qquad (5:34)$$

$$\frac{dN_S}{dt} = \frac{\dfrac{N_S}{L_S}\left(\dfrac{dN}{dt} - \dfrac{N_X}{L_X}\dfrac{dL}{dt}\right)}{\dfrac{N_S}{L_S} - \dfrac{N_X}{L_X}} > 0 \qquad (5:35)$$

$$\frac{dN_X}{dt} = \frac{\dfrac{N_X}{L_X}\left(\dfrac{N_S}{L_S}\dfrac{dL}{dt} - \dfrac{dN}{dt}\right)}{\dfrac{N_S}{L_S} - \dfrac{N_X}{L_X}} < 0. \qquad (5:36)$$

The expressions for the changes in output (5:29) and (5:30) now change to

$$\frac{dS_S}{dt} = \frac{\left(\dfrac{\partial s}{\partial L_S} + \dfrac{N_S}{L_S}\dfrac{\partial s}{\partial N_S}\right)\left(\dfrac{dN}{dt} - \dfrac{N_X}{L_X}\dfrac{dL}{dt}\right)}{\dfrac{N_S}{L_S} - \dfrac{N_X}{L_X}} > 0 \qquad (5:37)$$

and

$$\frac{dS_X}{dt} = \frac{\left(\dfrac{\partial x}{\partial L_X} + \dfrac{N_X}{L_X}\dfrac{\partial x}{\partial N_X}\right)\left(\dfrac{N_S}{L_S}\dfrac{dL}{dt} - \dfrac{dN}{dt}\right)}{\dfrac{N_S}{L_S} - \dfrac{N_X}{L_X}} < 0. \qquad (5:38)$$

We see that adding a constant rate of erosion to the model reinforces the tendencies of population and labor force growth to change the composition of output so as to make the production of subsistence goods rise and that of export goods fall.

So far the algebraic model. This model assumes the rate of erosion to be constant and shows how erosion influences the composition of peasant output. What the model does *not* show, however, is that the composition of output also exerts an influence on the rate of erosion. At given relative commodity prices, the amount of land used for cultivation of subsistence goods increases when the population and the labor force grow. In the main text it was explained how subsistence production increased the risk for soil destruction as compared to export production. In subsistence production, harvesting and planting generally take place several times a year, i.e. the soil is exposed to rain and winds more often than is the case in export production where for example coffee is a perennial crop which, once planted, yields crops for several years before replanting is necessary, and which in addition provides a better vegetative cover to the soil than do the subsistence crops. Hence, we should expect the rate of erosion to increase when more subsistence goods and less export goods are produced. This in turn, has a feedback effect on the composition of output. As the supply of agricultural land shrinks, land is again taken out of export production and put into subsistence production, etc. This adds a *cumulative* feature to the erosion process. Labor force growth, changing composition of output and erosion itself continue to destroy the arable soil at an increasing rate until the cumulative process runs into some counteracting force which is strong enough to stop the process.

Changes in Relative Commodity Prices

So far the analysis has been conducted on the premises that relative commodity prices remained unchanged. This assumption was nothing but an analytical device that was employed to make it possible to analyze the direct effects of the changing factor endowment. In the present section the assumption of constant prices will be removed and we will instead investigate how the composition of output (and hence also the rate of erosion) has been affected by changes in the prices of export and subsistence goods.

Beginning with the price of export goods, this may be split into two components, the world market price for exports (P_{fob}) and the Haitian export tax, mainly on coffee (T). Thus,

$$P_X = P_{fob} - T. \tag{5:39}$$

Appendix 1

From the peasant point of view both P_{fob} and T must be regarded as exogenously given. When it comes to international trade, Haiti is a 'small' country. It cannot influence the price of its exports or imports. In the case of coffee, for example, which is the most important export product, Haiti accounts for less than 1 percent of total world exports.[5] The tax rate, in turn, is determined by the Haitian government. In the main text we saw that the world market price of the most important Haitian agricultural exports fell during the period under consideration and that the tax on coffee exports increased. Hence, the price which the peasants received for their export products fell.

The main text has also revealed that the price of subsistence goods increased from the early 1950s to the beginning of the 1970s. Since this price cannot be regarded as exogenously given, we must, however, take a look at what may have caused this price rise. To do so, we employ the following general equilibrium system to describe the Haitian economy:

$$S_S = S_S(P_X, P_S, t) \qquad (5:40)$$
$$S_X = S_X(P_X, P_S, t) \qquad (5:41)$$
$$D_S = D_S(P_S, Y, t) \qquad (5:42)$$
$$D_M = D_M(P_S, Y, t) \qquad (5:43)$$
$$P_X = P_{fob} - T \qquad (5:44)$$
$$P_{fob} = P_{fob}(t) \qquad (5:45)$$
$$T = T(t) \qquad (5:46)$$
$$Y = P_S S_S + P_X S_X + TS_X \qquad (5:47)$$
$$S_S = D_S \qquad (5:48)$$
$$P_{fob}S_X = D_M \qquad (5:49)$$

Let us assume that two types of goods — subsistence goods and export goods — are produced in Haiti, and that by selling export goods at given terms of trade the Haitians may acquire manufactured goods in the world market. We also assume that no export goods are consumed in Haiti, but that the entire production is exported.* Equations (5:40) and (5:41) describe the choice of production point on the transformation curve of the Haitian economy as governed by the relative price of export and subsistence goods. The time parameter t allows the curve to shift e.g. as a result of changes in the factor endowment of the type

---

* This represents a simplification of reality. It is, for example, estimated that between 30 and 40 percent of the Haitian coffee production is consumed within the country (Tanzi (1976), p. 74).

described in the foregoing section. Equations (5:42) and (5:43) express the demand for subsistence goods and manufactured goods as functions of the relative price of these two goods (the price of M is used as *numéraire*), of incomes and of time. We will come back to the interpretation of the time parameter below. Let it suffice here to say that it shows the shift in demand structure at given relative prices and incomes.

The three equations (5:44)-(5-46) show that the terms of trade are exogenously given, that the export tax is determined by the government, and that the price of export goods received by the producers equals the f.o.b. price minus the tax.* Expression (5:47) shows that Haitian incomes equal the sum of the value of subsistence production, export production and tax incomes. It is assumed that the tax proceeds are spent in the same way as all other incomes. The last two equations, finally, are equilibrium conditions. The supply of subsistence goods must equal its demand in equilibrium (5:48), and the value of exports must equal that of imports (5:49).

The system (5:40)-(5:49) contains ten equations but only nine unknowns (S_S, S_X, D_S, D_M, P_X, P_{fob}, T, Y, and P_S). Using Walras' law, we find, however, that we may discard one of the equations. Assuming that all incomes are consumed, Walras' law may be written as

$$P_S S_S + P_X S_X + T S_X \equiv P_S D_S + D_M \qquad (5:50)$$

or

$$P_S(S_S - D_S) + \left[(P_X + T)S_X - D_M\right] \equiv 0. \qquad (5:51)$$

When the market for subsistence goods is in equilibrium, so is the balance of trade. Hence, we may discard e.g. (5:49) from our system to make the number of equations equal to that of unknowns. Since D_M only appears in (5:43) when (5:49) is omitted, we see that the former equation may also be discarded.

---

* During the period under study, the coffee tax was basically a specific tax. Subsistence goods and manufactures have also been taxed during the 1950-72 period (the main period analyzed in the present chapter), but since there appears to have been no definite changes in the taxation of these two commodity groups during the period, we may as well leave these taxes out of the present analysis.

Appendix 1

Differentiating the remaining equations yields

$$dS_X = \frac{\partial S_X}{\partial P_X} dP_X + \frac{\partial S_X}{\partial P_S} dP_S + \frac{\partial S_X}{\partial t} dt \tag{5:52}$$

$$dS_S = \frac{\partial S_S}{\partial P_X} dP_X + \frac{\partial S_S}{\partial P_S} dP_S + \frac{\partial S_S}{\partial t} dt \tag{5:53}$$

$$dD_S = \frac{dD_S}{\partial P_S} dP_S + \frac{\partial D_S}{\partial Y} dY + \frac{\partial D_S}{\partial t} dt \tag{5:54}$$

$$dP_X = dP_{fob} - dT \tag{5:55}$$

$$dP_{fob} = \frac{dP_{fob}}{dt} dt \tag{5:56}$$

$$dT = \frac{dT}{dt} dt \tag{5:57}$$

$$dY = S_S dP_S + P_S dS_S + S_X dP_X + P_X dS_X + S_X dT + T dS_X \tag{5:58}$$

$$dS_S = dD_S \tag{5:59}$$

or, after simplification,

$$dS_S = \frac{\partial S_S}{\partial P_X} \left(\frac{dP_{fob}}{dt} - \frac{dT}{dt} \right) dt + \frac{\partial S_S}{\partial P_S} dP_S + \frac{\partial S_S}{\partial t} dt \tag{5:60}$$

$$dS_X = \frac{\partial S_X}{\partial P_X} \left(\frac{dP_{fob}}{dt} - \frac{dT}{dt} \right) dt + \frac{\partial S_X}{\partial P_S} dP_S + \frac{\partial S_X}{\partial t} dt \tag{5:61}$$

$$dS_S = \frac{\partial D_S}{\partial P_S} dP_S + \frac{\partial D_S}{\partial Y} \left[S_S dP_S + P_S dS_S + S_X \frac{dP_{fob}}{dt} + (P_X + T) dS_X \right.$$
$$\left. + \frac{\partial D_S}{\partial t} dt. \tag{5:62}$$

Solving the simplified system (5:60) – (5:62) for $\frac{dP_S}{dt}$ yields:

$$\frac{dP_S}{dt} = \frac{1}{\Delta} \left\{ \frac{\partial D_S}{\partial Y} S_X \frac{dP_{fob}}{dt} + \frac{\partial D_S}{\partial t} - \left(1 - \frac{\partial D_S}{\partial Y} P_S \right) \cdot \right.$$
$$\left[\frac{\partial S_S}{\partial P_X} \left(\frac{dP_{fob}}{dt} - \frac{dT}{dt} \right) + \frac{\partial S_S}{\partial t} \right] +$$
$$\left. + \frac{\partial D_S}{\partial Y} (P_X + T) \left[\frac{\partial S_X}{\partial P_X} \left(\frac{dP_{fob}}{dt} - \frac{dT}{dt} \right) + \frac{\partial S_X}{\partial t} \right] \right\} \tag{5:63}$$

Appendix 1

where

$$\Delta = \left(1 - \frac{\partial D_S}{\partial Y} P_S\right) \frac{\partial S_S}{\partial P_S} - \frac{\partial D_S}{\partial Y}(P_X + T) \frac{\partial S_X}{\partial P_S} - \left(\frac{\partial D_S}{\partial P_S} + \frac{\partial D_S}{\partial Y} S_S\right). \quad (5:64)$$

The denominator of the expression for dP_S/dt is positive provided that subsistence goods are not inferior and provided that the supply of export and subsistence goods reacts 'normally' to changes in the relative price of the two goods. ($\frac{\partial D_S}{\partial Y} P_S$ is the marginal propensity to consume subsistence goods and must hence be less than or equal to one. From the Slutsky equation it follows that $\frac{\partial D_S}{\partial P_S} + \frac{\partial D_S}{\partial Y} S_S$ is negative.)[6] Excepting $\frac{\partial D_S}{\partial t}$ for the moment, under the same circumstances the remaining terms of the numerator are all negative. ($\frac{\partial S_S}{\partial t}$ and $\frac{\partial S_X}{\partial t}$ are our expressions (5:37) and (5:38), respectively, and we know that the world market price of export goods has fallen and that the tax rate has increased.) The first term of the expression shows how the demand for subsistence goods changes as a result of the fall in national income which would be the result of a *ceteris paribus* fall in the export price received by the peasants. The more this fall is translated into a decrease in the demand for subsistence goods, the stronger will be the tendency for the price of subsistence goods to fall. The third term shows what happens to the demand for manufactured goods when the national income increases due to a rise in the production of subsistence goods provoked by (1) the autonomous shift produced by labor force growth and soil erosion ($\frac{\partial S_S}{\partial t}$), and (2) the increase due to the fall in the price of export goods. The greater the proportion of this rise in national income that is dedicated to the consumption of manufactured goods, the stronger will be the tendency for the relative price of these goods to increase in terms of subsistence goods (the stronger the tendency for the relative price of subsistence goods to fall). Finally, to the increased income caused by the increase in subsistence production corresponds a fall in national income as a result of the decrease of export production caused by the same factors. The greater the share of this decrease that takes on the form of a reduction in the demand for subsistence goods the greater the fall in the relative price of these goods.

Then how are we to interpret $\frac{\partial D_S}{\partial t}$? We mentioned when commenting upon our general equilibrium system that $\frac{\partial D_S}{\partial t}$ expresses how the demand for subsistence goods changes when both relative prices and incomes are kept constant. The major change that causes a shift in demand away from manufactured goods towards subsistence goods (i.e. mainly food) when both incomes and prices remain constant is population growth. When the population grows, a shift in the demand structure of the households takes place. When a new family member arrives, he must be fed, and with prices and incomes given, the only way to increase the demand for food is by demanding fewer manufactured goods. This creates a tendency for the price of subsistence goods to rise in relation to that of manufactured goods. Hence, the direction of the change in the price of subsistence goods may be either positive or negative, depending on whether the most important effects are those emanating from income changes or those coming from demand shifts at given incomes.

This concludes our formal analysis of the erosion problem. From (5:60) and (5:61) we have that

$$\frac{dS_S}{dt} = \frac{\partial S_S}{\partial P_X}\left(\frac{dP_{fob}}{dt} - \frac{dT}{dt}\right) + \frac{\partial S_S}{\partial P_S}\frac{dP_S}{dt} + \frac{\partial S_S}{\partial t} \qquad (5:65)$$

and

$$\frac{dS_X}{dt} = \frac{\partial S_X}{\partial P_X}\left(\frac{dP_{fob}}{dt} - \frac{dT}{dt}\right) + \frac{\partial S_X}{\partial P_S}\frac{dP_S}{dt} + \frac{\partial S_X}{\partial t} \qquad (5:66)$$

The changes in output depend on three factors:

1. Changes in the factor endowment of the peasant sector as demonstrated in the first half of the appendix. These changes tend to increase the production of subsistence goods and decrease that of export goods.

2. Changes in f.o.b. export prices (terms of trade) and tax rates. Here, we have assumed that export prices have fallen in terms of manufactured goods and that tax rates have increased. Both these changes also tend to increase the production of subsistence goods and to decrease that of export goods.

3. Changes in the price of subsistence goods (in terms of manufactured goods). The model yields no clear-cut solution as to the direction of these changes. Hence, it is possible that the changes have been positive and also that they have been large enough to swamp the effects of changes in factor endowment, export prices and taxes. Our next step will be to reformulate the model to find out whether this actually has taken place.

P_S and P_X (i.e. $P_{fob} - T$) in (5:65) and (5:66) are both expressed in terms of manufactured goods. However, no suitable statistics are available which could give us an idea regarding the development of these two prices in the Haitian case. The general equilibrium model, as used hitherto, can be employed to illustrate the mechanisms behind the changes in relative prices, but does not yield any definite solutions. We have assumed P_X to fall in terms of manufactures to illustrate how this generates repercussions in the economy among other things on P_S, but we do not know much about the real development of these two prices during the period under consideration. This is a minor problem, however, for with a slight reformulation of the model we can find out how the output of export and subsistence goods depends directly on the relative price P_X/P_S, and, as the main text reveals, we have enough data to get an indication of the development of this ratio.

Going back to (5:52) we have for the change in the supply of subsistence goods

$$dS_S = \frac{\partial S_S}{\partial P_X} dP_X + \frac{\partial S_S}{\partial P_S} dP_S + \frac{\partial S_S}{\partial t} dt, \quad (5:52)$$

(and a corresponding equation for the supply of export goods).

Expression (5:52) may also be written as

$$dS_S = \frac{\partial S_S}{\partial \left(\frac{P_X}{P_S}\right)} \frac{\partial \left(\frac{P_X}{P_S}\right)}{\partial P_X} dP_X + \frac{\partial S_S}{\partial \left(\frac{P_X}{P_S}\right)} \frac{\partial \left(\frac{P_X}{P_S}\right)}{\partial P_S} dP_S + \frac{\partial S_S}{\partial t} dt \quad (5:67)$$

or

$$dS_S = \frac{\partial S_S}{\partial \left(\frac{P_X}{P_S}\right)} \frac{1}{P_S} dP_X \frac{-P_X}{P_S^2} dP_S + \frac{\partial S_S}{\partial t} dt =$$

$$= \frac{\partial S_S}{\partial \left(\frac{P_X}{P_S}\right)} \frac{P_S dP_X - P_X dP_S}{P_S^2} + \frac{\partial S_S}{\partial t} dt =$$

$$= \frac{\partial S_S}{\partial \left(\frac{P_X}{P_S}\right)} d\left(\frac{P_X}{P_S}\right) + \frac{\partial S_S}{\partial t} dt. \quad (5:68)$$

Appendix 1

Hence, instead of using expressions (5:65) and (5:66) we may use

$$\frac{dS_S}{dt} = \frac{\partial S_S}{\partial \left(\frac{P_X}{P_S}\right)} \frac{d\left(\frac{P_X}{P_S}\right)}{dt} + \frac{\partial S_S}{\partial t} \tag{5:69}$$

and

$$\frac{dS_X}{dt} = \frac{\partial S_X}{\partial \left(\frac{P_X}{P_S}\right)} \frac{d\left(\frac{P_X}{P_S}\right)}{dt} + \frac{\partial S_X}{\partial t} \tag{5:70}$$

where $P_X = P_{fob} - T$.

The changes in the output of subsistence goods and export goods are results of two sets of factors: a change at given relative commodity prices and a change in these prices themselves.

Notes

1. This section draws on Södersten (1964), Chapter 3.
2. This is common in less developed countries. Cf. e.g. Reynolds (1975), p. 4.
3. Moral (1955), p. 247. Cf. also above, Chapter 2.
4. This is a commonly applied assumption in agricultural economics (Cf. Georgescu-Roegen (1971), note, p. 251). For an application to developing economies see Clark & Haswell (1967), Chapter VI. See, however, also Georgescu-Roegen (1971) Chapter IX, especially pp. 250-53, for a critique of the traditional production function approach to agricultural problems. If the assumption of linear homogeneity is dropped, the results of the present section no longer necessarily hold (see Södersten (1964), pp. 64-8).
5. JWK (1976:1), p. 82.
6. See e.g. Green (1971), Chapter 5 and technical appendix 5 or Henderson & Quandt (1958), pp. 25-30.

APPENDIX 2: Agricultural Involution in Java and Haiti

In *Haiti, The Politics of Squalor*, Robert I. Rotberg suggests that

> The Haitian experience with respect to agriculture in several important respects parallels that sketched by Geertz (*Agricultural Involution*), and it may prove fruitful to view the 'shared poverty' of Haiti as a case of what he has called 'involution' (after Alexander Goldenweisser). There is the 'flaccid indeterminateness [which is so] highly functional to a society which is allowed to evade, adjust, absorb but not really allowed to change. . .the diversity, variability, fragility, fluidity, shallowness, and unreliability of interpersonal ties'. . .Haiti, like Indonesia, can be called an 'anthology of missed opportunities, a conservatory of squandered possibilities'. . .But until studies have been made of the ecological basis of Haitian society (her ecosystem), Geertz's work must remain, for Haiti, more suggestive than conclusive.[1]

The discussion of social or political involution falls outside the scope of the present study, but since it is obvious that Rotberg conceives of the possibility that the social patterns typical for today's Haiti have been engendered by the development of the country's economy, as they were in nineteenth-century Java (as indicated by the explicit reference to the ecological basis), a comparison of the economic and ecological characteristics Java and Haiti may be of a certain interest.

Between 1830 and 1900 the population of Java increased from about 7 million to more than 28 million people, which represents an annual population increase of around 2 percent per year.[2] This increased the demographic pressure on the existing land resources, since due to restrictions imposed by the Dutch colonial power the Javanese could not expand the area under cultivation. Neither was there any budding industry that could absorb the increasing population, so the only remaining alternative was to employ the growing labor force on land which was already under cultivation. The degree of labor intensity increased in Javanese agriculture.

From the productivity point of view, the absorption of the excess population took place without difficulties in Java. Per capita incomes declined very little, if at all, over the entire period,[3] and the land was not exhausted but kept its production potential intact. Clifford Geertz summarizes this process in *Agricultural Involution:*

> The process resembles nothing else so much as treading water. Higher-level densities are offset by greater labor inputs into the same productive system, but output per head (or per month) remains more or less constant from region to region. . .Slowly, steadily, relentlessly, [the Javanese] were forced into a more and more labor-stuffed sawah pattern of the sort the 1920 figures show: tremendous populations absorbed on minuscule rice farms. . .consequent rises in per-hectare productivity. . .[4]

Borrowing an expression from cultural anthropology, Geertz termed this process agricultural *involution*:

> Wet-rice cultivation, with its extraordinary ability to maintain levels of marginal labor productivity by always managing to work one more man in without a serious fall in per-capita income, soaked up almost the whole of the additional population that Western intrusion created, at least indirectly. It is this ultimately self-defeating process that I have proposed to call 'agricultural involution.'[5]

According to Geertz, the involutionary process operated not only on the ecological and economic plane, but the peculiar development of agricultural production also provoked a parallel response in the field of social relations in rural Javanese society. Agricultural production did not undergo any fundamental changes, at least not of the kind that could lead to any transformation of the social structure in a deeper sense. As the complexity of cultivation practices increased within the traditional framework with the refinement of planting and transplanting procedures, irrigation systems, etc. there was a corresponding increase in the complexity of rural social life. However, this increasing complexity was nothing but a superficial change. Since the process developed entirely within the limits of the traditional society it went hand in hand with stagnation. The Javanese society, like its economy, was not allowed really to change — only to continue a stationary process where the basic ingredients remained the same and where essentially the same relations were maintained, albeit with ever increasing variations.

Observing a similar pattern in contemporary Haiti, Rotberg raises the question whether this pattern is also an effect of agricultural involution as it was in nineteenth-century Java. This, however, is not likely to be the case. The natural rate of growth of the Haitian population today is approximately the same as that in nineteenth-century Java: 2 percent per year, but with that the similarities between the two countries also end. The fundamental difference between Java and Haiti is that Java during the 1830-1900 period was an agricultural society which basically was in a stable ecological equilibrium, while twentieth-century Haiti presents nothing of the kind.

The Javanese equilibrium was due to the unique properties of the ecosystem of the *sawah* — the wet-rice terraces. The latter were extremely stable in the sense that they could go on producing rice year after year, with several harvests annually, without any diminishing returns to labor. After an initial fall in yields during the first ten or twenty years of cultivating rice on virgin soils, yields were usually stabilized at given techniques for a long period to come. This, in turn appears to have been due to

> the permanent role played by water in the dynamics of the rice terrace. Here, the characteristic thinness of tropical soils is circumvented through the bringing of nutrients onto the terrace by the irrigation water to replace those drawn from the soil; through the fixation of nitrogen by the blue-green algae which proliferate in the warm water; through the chemical and bacterial decomposition of organic material, including the remains of harvested crops in that water; through the aeration of the soil by the gentle movement of the water in the terrace; and, no doubt, through other ecological functions performed by irrigation which are as yet unknown. Thus, although, contrary to appearances, the paddy plant actually requires no more water than dry-land crops for simple transpirational purposes, 'the supply and control of water. . .is the most important aspect of irrigated paddy cultivation; given an adequate and well-controlled water supply the crop will grow in a wide range of soils and in many climates. It is therefore more important than the type of soil.'[6]

Moreover, the dependence of wet-rice cultivation on elaborate irrigation systems made wet-rice cultivation particularly suitable for absorption of large quantities of labor:

> The supply and control of water is the key factor in wet-rice growing — a seemingly self-evident proposition which conceals some complexities because the regulation of water in a terrace is a matter of some delicacy. Excessive flooding is often as great a threat as insufficient inundation; drainage is frequently a more intractable problem than irrigation. Not merely the gross quantity of water,

Appendix 2 253

but its quality, in terms of the fertilizing substances it contains (and thus the source from which it comes) is a crucial variable in determining productivity. Timing is also important: paddy should be planted in a well-soaked field with little standing water and then the depth of water increased gradually up to six or twelve inches as the plant grows and flowers, after which it should be gradually drawn off until at harvest the field is dry. Further, the water should not be allowed to stagnate but, as much as possible, kept gently flowing, and periodic drainings are generally advisable for purposes of weeding and fertilizing. . . .the mobility of water makes it 'the natural variable par excellence' in those landscapes where its manipulation is agriculturally profitable, its bulkiness makes such manipulation difficult, and manageable only with significant inputs of 'preparatory' labor and at least a certain amount of engineering skill. The construction and maintenance of even the simplest water-control system, as in rainfall farms, requires such ancillary efforts: ditches must be dug and kept clean, sluices constructed and repaired, terraces leveled and dyked; and in more developed true irrigation systems dams, reservoirs, aqueducts, tunnels, wells and the like become necessary. Even such larger works can be built up slowly, piece by piece, over extended periods and kept in repair by continuous, routine care.[7]

The complementarity between increased care in irrigation and labor absorption made the ecosystem of the wet-rice terrace stable. There was always some scope for increased labor intensity without falling production per capita, and during the nineteenth century such intensification yielded a higher marginal return than the other feasible alternatives:

Because productivity is so dependent on the quality of water regulation, labor applied to the improvement of such regulation can often have a greater marginal productivity than the same labor applied to constructing new, but less adequately managed, terraces and new works to support them. Under premodern conditions, gradual perfection of irrigation techniques is perhaps the major way to raise productivity not only per hectare but per man.[8]

It seems fairly obvious that agricultural involution in nineteenth-century Java was the result of what probably must be regarded as a unique combination of ecological circumstances. The case of Haiti is entirely different. Far from being in a stable equilibrium of the Javanese type, the Haitian peasant sector exhibits a profound antagonism between man and his environment. The kind of dry farming practiced in Haiti does not have the same potential to absorb labor as did the irrigation-based Javanese rice fields. In Haiti, the point where diminishing returns to labor begin to set in was reached a long time ago. As we have seen in the main text of the present chapter, given the traditional technology, labor can now only be absorbed in the peasant sector at the expense of rapidly increasing soil exhaustion, deforestation and erosion, and hence also of falling per capita production. Whatever similarities there may exist between the Javanese and the Haitian social systems are likely either to be caused by other factors than agricultural involution, or — probably — to be entirely coincidental.

Notes

1. Rotberg & Clague (1971), note. p. 14.
2. Geertz (1970), p. 69.
3. Ibid., p. 79.
4. Ibid., pp. 78, 80.
5. Ibid., p. 80.
6. Ibid., pp. 29-30.
7. Ibid., pp. 31-2.
8. Ibid., p. 34.

6 LAND REFORM

In Chapter 5 the basic cumulative process operating in the agricultural sector was analyzed. We demonstrated how population and labor force growth leads to an increasing amount of land being transferred into labor-intensive activities at given relative prices, how this leads to destruction of the soil, and how erosion itself adds momentum to this process. The result is that little by little the foundations of agricultural production are destroyed and that whatever incomes are generated by the peasants have to be shared by an increasing number of people. Unless this process is arrested by counteracting forces, the peasant economy will eventually move towards some type of Malthusian equilibrium where death rates have risen and checked the expansion of the population and the fall in per capita incomes.

Chapter 5 also contained a discussion of two possible counteracting forces. The first was a possible rise in the price of land-intensive products relative to that of labor-intensive ones, i.e. a rise in the price of export goods in terms of subsistence goods. The second force was erosion control. If the peasants somehow could ensure that increasing production of subsistence goods did not cause the erosion process to accelerate, the growth of the population would not necessarily call forth the Malthusian spectre. However, at present, there is nothing to guarantee that the peasants would attempt to check erosion. Anticipating the analysis of Chapters 6-8 we also demonstrated that in spite of a host of regulations with respect to woodcutting and erosion control, Haitian governments have not shown any real interest in putting an end to soil destruction.

In the present chapter we will continue the analysis exactly at this point, where Chapter 5 ended, by beginning our dissection of government passivity. In a situation where the individual peasants cannot or do not want to attempt to break the downward cumulative process, a heavy responsibility falls on the government. Government action is probably the only way to counteract and reverse the vicious spiral, but in Haiti, ever since the early nineteenth century when the large colonial plantations were broken up and the land was redistributed, no government seems to have taken a positive interest in developing the most important sector of the economy.

This and the following two chapters will be devoted to an analysis of the causes of government passivity with respect to agriculture (in matters other than taxation). The present chapter will discuss the causes behind one of the decisive events of Haitian economic history: the land reform initiated by Alexandre Pétion in 1809 (and why subsequent attempts at re-introducing the plantation system in Haiti have failed). An understanding of the land redistribution process is of fundamental importance, since it was precisely the land reform which to a very large extent was responsible for creating what appears to be an unbridgeable gap between government and peasantry, a gap which has resulted in a more or less complete lack of government initiated action in the agricultural sector.

In an appendix we will deal with the choice of capital inputs. As we saw in Chapter 2, capital is very scarce in the Haitian peasant sector, so scarce that as a rule it is limited to seeds, plants and simple hand tools. The appendix contains a model originated by Amartya K. Sen which sheds some light on the reasons for this. The findings from the appendix will be used in the discussion of farm size in the main text.

Farm Size

In Chapter 2 we found that on the average a Haitian farm does not consist of more than 1.5 hectares. Haiti is a typical minifundia country. Plantations and other large estates are conspicuously absent in sharp contrast to the situation in most other Latin American countries. In the following we will trace the development of farm size throughout Haitian history and sketch a few hypotheses regarding the forces that have contributed to keep farm size at a low level.

The Sugar Economy

Throughout the Spanish period, western Hispaniola received little attention. The number of Spaniards was never large and no official interest was shown in developing that section of the island. This left the way open for settlers from other European nations, notably the French, who after the evacuation of the small Spanish settlement in the island of Tortuga, north of Haiti, at the beginning of the seventeenth century, gradually established a buccaneer stronghold in that island and later penetrated into western Hispaniola.

For almost a century the territorial status of Saint-Domingue, as the western part of Hispaniola was known among the French, was very uncertain. This uncertainty made the French settlers reluctant to undertake large investments. They concentrated their efforts on small-scale growing of cotton, indigo and cocoa. It was only when

Spain ceded Saint-Domingue to France by the Treaty of Ryswick in 1697 that a huge expansion of the cultivation of a crop requiring large amounts of capital took place. The sugar cane was extended across the colony.

Sugar had been a rare commodity in medieval Europe, and was long considered a luxury, but with the conquest of the Atlantic islands by Spain and Portugal and the introduction of sugar cane there during the fifteenth century, larger quantities of sugar were made available on the European market, and the use of sugar spread through society. A taste for the new commodity was soon acquired, and the European demand increased rapidly.[1]

At the beginning of the sixteenth century the first sugar cane was brought to Hispaniola. The West Indian climate proved to be excellently suited for its cultivation, and around 1515 the first exports to Spain took place.[2] Hispaniola was the first West Indian island to produce an exportable surplus during the sixteenth century.[3] Exports were never very large, however, and not until sugar plantations began to be extended to the French part of the island is it appropriate to speak of a 'sugar economy' in Hispaniola.

The expansion of sugar in Saint-Domingue was demand-led. In spite of occasional periods of falling prices due to expansion of the world supply, demand in Europe during the greater part of the eighteenth century was large enough to make sugar plantations an attractive investment in Saint-Domingue.[4] The small French colony drove English sugar out of the continental European market during the 1720-40 period, and in 1783 Saint-Domingue produced nearly as much sugar as all the British colonies in the Caribbean region.[5]

The domination of sugar cane had very definite consequences for farm size and factor combinations in Saint-Domingue. First of all it was of little use to cultivate sugar if the machinery required to process the cane into sugar was lacking, and the installation of crushing mills on the plantation clearly determined the optimum size of the estate:

> Once sugar cane had been cut, the first stages of processing had to be carried out very quickly, preferably within a few hours. Every plantation had to have ready access to a crushing mill that could handle quantities of cane cut and brought in at a rate appropriate to the size of the plantations. Moreover, up to a certain point, this large and costly equipment became proportionally less costly as its size increased. The optimum size of mill determined the size of the plantation. The minimum size of plantation that could keep a fully

> efficient mill fully occupied during the cutting season varied in different islands according to yield of sugar per acre, and ease of transport; it might be as small as a hundred acres (with forty to fifty acres producing cane each year), while it was nowhere likely to exceed three hundred acres for a single mill. These were the limits of the size of the operating unit, though ownership of two or three of these units by a single family was common in the eighteenth century.[6]

The quotation states that a sugar plantation was nowhere likely to exceed three hundred acres (120 hectares),* which is not, however, entirely true. In Cuba, the average sugar plantation in 1762 was almost 130 hectares (320 acres) and in 1790 almost 280 hectares (700 acres).[7] Not quite the same size was reached in Saint-Domingue, but the actual range was high enough: 150-300 hectares, while in for example Guadeloupe, a *sucrerie* of 50-60 hectares was considered large.[8]

Crushing capacity also regulated the size of the labor force. The heavy investments in the crushing mill made it necessary to take great care to keep the mill constantly and evenly supplied with cane during the cutting season:

> The crushing mill's capacity also determined the size of the labour force needed to keep it supplied at full stretch — which might well mean for twenty hours a day — during a large part of the cane-cutting season from January to March, as well as the number of draught animals, cars and hogsheads needed. The mills were often worked by cattle in those days, but it was more economical to use other forms of energy — as well as saving the grazing land that animals needed. . .and St Domingue was using many water mills in the eighteenth century.[9]

Labor at first was a problem in Saint-Domingue. As everywhere else in the New World the advent of the Spanish in Hispaniola had triggered off a demographic catastrophe. A combination of forced labor, hitherto unknown diseases, notably smallpox, and successive destruction of the primitive native agriculture by the herds of pigs and cattle introduced by the Spaniards wiped out the native population within a century.[10]

Instead Negro slaves were imported from Africa to supply the necessary labor for the plantations. The first slaves had been shipped

---

* 1 acre = 0.4 hectares.

as early as 1502, and in 1517 large-scale importation was begun by the Spaniards. The French followed the same pattern. The demand for slaves rose during the eighteenth century, and around 1750 it was not uncommon to have as much as nine-tenths of the total investment of a sugar plantation (excluding land) in slaves,[11] but so profitable was sugar production that apparently it was possible to drive the slaves quite relentlessly, renewing the stock by one-twentieth to one-fifteenth each year[12] rather than sparing them in order to ensure a longer economic life and a higher rate of reproduction.

It should be mentioned that sugar was a rich man's crop. Most of the French immigrants in Saint-Domingue did not have the financial means to incur the investment in the crushing mill and in the large number of slaves needed to work in the fields but went into other crops instead. Saint-Domingue never became a monoculture economy. The decline of sugar prices in the 1720s established coffee as an important crop, and on the eve of the French Revolution the value of coffee exports was almost as high as that of sugar exports.[13] Indigo, cotton and cocoa had been export crops even before sugar rose to domination. For none of these crops were the fixed capital and labor requirements as high as for sugar, which in turn meant that plantation sizes were smaller too. Most coffee and indigo plantations never exceeded 100 hectares; cotton plantations required a couple of decades of hectares and cocoa cultivation, finally, could be undertaken with as little as 10 to 20 hectares of land.[14] Still, all of these plantations were substantially larger than today's minifundia, and taken as a whole, Saint-Domingue must be considered as a latifundia-dominated colony.

Restoration of the Plantation System

During the three decades following the 1791 uprising against the French, the Haitian rulers maintained a strong interest in agricultural production and very actively intervened in its organization. Seen against the background of the revolutionary wars this interest is understandable. In several ways the wars had damaged the economy. Many plantations lay entirely in ruins. By the turn of the century it was calculated that one-third of the ex-slave population was no longer alive. Others had been enrolled in the revolutionary armies or had run off to the mountains to live a maroon life. Virtually the whole administrative cadre had disappeared with the French.[15] Foreign trade – the basis of the opulence of the French colony – was virtually dead. The figures in Table 6.1 show the development of the exports of the four most important commercial crops between 1789 and 1795. Five years of warfare had produced a catastrophic decline in trade. The colonial economy had more or less collapsed. Food production to meet subsistence requirements was the rule, and production of export crops was probably retained only in those remote areas of the country which had been least damaged by the wars.

Table 6.1: Saint-Domingue Exports of Four Agricultural Products 1789 and 1795

Product	1789 (pounds)	1795 (pounds)	Index (1789 = 100)
Sugar	140,000,000	1,750,000	1.2
Coffee	77,000,000	2,228,000	2.8
Cotton	7,000,000	48,000	0.7
Indigo	1,000,000	5,000	0.5

Source: Lepkowski (1968:1), p.75. Cf. Franklin (1828), p.322 for 1791 figures.

Toussaint L'Ouverture, the revolutionary leader, saw the reorganization of export production as a matter of vital importance for the country. Agriculture was the basis of national wealth, and foreign trade was the backbone of agriculture. In a letter dating from 1797 Toussaint wrote

> Feeling the necessity of favoring agriculture, the only thing that may give Saint-Domingue back its old splendor and its old products, I do not cease...preaching the love of work to my brethren, making them dedicate themselves entirely to cultivating the soil. My troubles have not been in vain and I rejoice when seeing how this essential part of administration flowers once again. May peace come to consolidate such fortunate beginnings. I have no doubts that this part of France will recover by means of its riches preeminent rank above all other colonies in America.[16]

As soon as Toussaint had gained the necessary military foothold to re-establish order he undertook again to build up the productive apparatus along these lines. The basic policy was to rebuild and maintain the colonial estates intact.* No lands with an extension inferior to 50 carreaux were to change hands. While some of the former landowners

---
* Toussaint here followed a formula which had been originated by the French civil commissaries Sonthonax and Polvérel following the abolition of slavery in 1793.

were allowed to keep their estates, the government moved in and seized other plantations which were leased to important army officers and other members of the emerging elite. Slavery had been abolished once and for all, but the problem of procuring a sufficient number of agricultural laborers for *la grande culture* to be efficient was solved by introducing the *fermage* system whereby every person who did not enlist in the army or who possessed an urban trade was attached to a plantation as a cultivator and was only allowed to leave this plantation with explicit permission from the authorities. *Marronage* and formation of small, independent farm units was combated. On the plantations the work was organized according to strict military principles. The laborers toiled under stern supervision with severe punishments ensuring that vagrancy was kept to a minimum.[17]

Dessalines, who had been one of the two inspectors-general of agriculture under Toussaint, and who became the first head of state of independent Haiti, continued Toussaint's agricultural policy after 1804. The laborers continued to be legally tied to the estates where they worked, and discipline, if anything, became even stronger than before. Dessalines also went one step further than Toussaint in his centralization efforts, by confiscating all land owned by whites before 1803, much of which was claimed by the mulatto group. Hereby he created a vast public domain, estimated to consist of two-thirds to nine-tenths of all productive plantations in the country, which were thereupon leased to the highest bidders, i.e. mainly to generals and other high army officers.[18]

Following the murder of Dessalines in 1806, Haiti was divided into two parts, as we will see in Chapter 7. The two parts followed different agricultural principles. Henry Christophe in the north adhered to the Toussaint-Dessalines pattern and tried to conserve the large estates. In the beginning, government lands were leased under five-year contracts, since the 1806 constitution had declared all land to be the property of the Haitian nation. Dessalines had stubbornly refused to create a nobility of any kind, but Christophe, on the other hand, after turning his part of the country into a monarchy, proceeded to hand out titles and instead of leasing government land he began to sell or grant land to his aristocrats. In all other important respects, however, his agricultural policy was a direct continuation of that of Toussaint and Dessalines.[19]

The restoration of *la grande culture* apparently met with some success during the period up to 1802 when the French invasion army landed and Toussaint once more had to dedicate his energy to military tasks. Table 6.2 shows that exports of sugar, coffee and cotton were exceeding or approaching one-half of their old levels (while indigo had been practically wiped out as an export product). It should be noted that the cultivated area had diminished. In 1802, only two-thirds of the pre-revolutionary acreage is believed to have been brought back into cultivation.[20] Naturally, the renewal of war activities in 1802 and 1803 caused new damages. More human lives were lost, and more plantations were burned.

Table 6.2: Exports of Four Agricultural Products in 1802 and 1804

Product	1802		1804	
	Pounds	Index (1789=100)	Pounds	Index (1789=100)
Sugar	53,400,000	38	47,600,000	34
Coffee	34,370,000[a]	45	31,000,000	40
Cotton	4,050,000	58	3,000,000	43
Indigo	37,600	4	35,400	4

a. This figure is probably an understatement of the true value. In 1801 the exported quantity was 43,420,000 pounds (Lepkowski (1968:1), p. 83). The 1802 figure comprises also the months of French administration under Leclerc which is likely to introduce a downward bias, since much of the coffee was produced in the mountains not subjugated by the French and this coffee was not exported. Note, however, that Haitian coffee has a natural two-year rhythm with good and bad years regularly alternating.
Source: Leyburn (1966), p. 320. Cf. Lepkowski (1968:1), p. 83 for 1801 figures.

Nevertheless, it appears as if most of the impetus generated by Toussaint's efforts was carried over into 1804. As Table 6.2 reveals, exports of the main commercial crops did not fall off markedly in comparison with 1802 in spite of eyewitness reports of severe damage to plantations and fields. Coffee, which was a mountain crop, suffered less than sugar and cotton which were cultivated in the plains where the destruction was more extensive, and due to the favorable climatic conditions of the country, regeneration of the latter two crops was presumably restarted quickly enough to mitigate the detrimental effects of the war.[21] As regards Christophe's administration, quantitative information for making an evaluation is lacking.[22] However, the general impression, at least in comparison with Pétion's republic where a radically different agricultural policy was pursued, is that Christophe appears to have been successful. Export crops were flowing from the northern plantations to the harbors of Europe and the United States, and obviously agriculture was efficient enough to give the state a substantial tax income believed

Land Reform

to be around 3.5 million dollars per year so that when Christophe died in 1820 his treasury contained more than 6 million dollars,[23] and to give the agricultural laborers an adequate standard of living:

> The quarter part of the total crop of any plantation was to go to the workers as wages, and since production increased and prices rose, this quarter which they were free to spend as they pleased provided a powerful incentive to further industry. As compared with anything they had known before, the workers were now recipients of an ample income. On the plantations they cultivated the money crops of sugar and coffee. In addition, each family had its own garden plot on which to raise the food crops — yams, plantains, beans, and bananas — for personal use.[24]

The *fermage* system was an efficient way of organizing agricultural production. By attaching the laborers to the soil, part of the ancient prosperity of Saint-Domingue could be retained in independent Haiti. Still, two decades after Christophe's death, Haiti was no longer a latifundia country but a nation where independent peasants were tilling their own small plots.

Transition to Small Farms

Alexandre Pétion, who was president in southern Haiti when Christophe ruled the north, followed a radically different agricultural policy, which was also to be followed by most later heads of state: he abandoned the forced labor system and decided to parcel the land. While the Toussaint law from 1801 did not allow the sales of any plots smaller than 50 carreaux,[25] Pétion lowered the minimum acreage to 10 carreaux and in 1809 started to give away land to his officers and soldiers.[26] Redistribution of property through grants or sales continued throughout Pétion's entire term at the presidency, and it is believed that more than 100,000 hectares of government land were thus redistributed from 1809 to 1818.[27]*

By abandoning the forced labor system and by initiating a redistribution of government land Pétion put an avalanche into motion. It is believed that some 10,000 persons benefited directly from the land reform,[28] but its indirect effects were much more far-reaching. For

---

* In the north, the large properties were preserved throughout most of Christophe's reign. It was not until in 1819 that he started to redistribute the land by grants to his officers and soldiers (Lepkowski (1968:1), p. 105; Cole (1970), p. 253).

reasons that we will soon deal with, redistribution of government land was soon followed by the break-up of many large private estates which were leased to the peasants, mainly under crop-sharing arrangements,* while their owners concentrated in the cities, removed from rural life.

Jean-Pierre Boyer, successor to Pétion and Christophe, at first followed Pétion's distribution policy, but in 1826 made an effort to go back to the *corvée* system with the issue of a new *Code Rural*. Basically there was nothing novel in the Code. It was a mere return to the old formula with some minor amendments. The effort failed in its purpose, however. Too much land had already been distributed, and the law was not to be enforced for small units. Even the administration of the few large estates still in existence proved impossible. Strict military supervision in order to secure the necessary labor force did not prevent the peasants from deserting the plantations to make a living in the mountains,[29] and as soon as the 1826 Code was forgotten, squatting gained new momentum. Peasants lacking financial resources to buy land could then easily claim a plot without risking eviction.

The average acreage declined. Altogether Pétion and Boyer distributed close to 150,000 carreaux.[30] By 1842, the year before Boyer's fall, probably none of the large colonial estates were left undistributed. Approximately one-third of the population consisted of peasant-owners with holdings from 3 to 10 carreaux. Another third were squatters, and the rest, with the exception of the urban population, were hirelings or more often sharecroppers.[31] **

The positive value of the redistribution of land begun by Pétion lay mainly in the fact that this measure spared Haiti the kind of latifundia-based development which has been a salient characteristic of most Latin American countries, with a class of landless agricultural laborers or tenant farmers being dependent on a class of dominant landowners for work, land and incomes. The Haitian peasants were free — working for their own benefit on their own land. This was an important social achievement. From the point of view of production efficiency the

---

* According to one source this practice was originated by Pétion himself on his own plantation. Following the Sonthonax-Polvérel formula the plantation laborers received one quarter of the value of their produce. This share was raised by Pétion to one-half (Lepkowski (1968:1), pp. 109-10. Cf. Lacerte (1975), p. 80). Cf., however, Moral (1961), pp. 36-7 regarding the obscurity of the origin of the *de moitié*-system.

** When the Boyer code failed most landowners embarked on a crop-sharing policy (Leyburn (1966), p. 79).

family minifundia were inferior to the large-scale plantations, however. Both Pétion's and Boyer's administrations witnessed a period of economic decline where the GNP appears to have been falling slowly. There was a drastic reduction in the production of the traditional export crops. Sugar and cotton disappeared from the list of Haitian exports, and the peasants instead turned to production of subsistence crops that could be consumed directly by their families or sold in the local market-places. This shift, taken *per se*, would of course not necessarily have caused production to decline, but it was accompanied by two other important changes. First, the family farm operations involved considerably less division of labor than did plantation agriculture, and second, the rigorous labor discipline which had been one of the cornerstones of the slave- or serf-based plantations was quickly relaxed when there were no longer any sanctions against shirking. As long as the soil yielded their immediate necessities without excessive efforts, the peasants did not need to increase their labor input. The result of these two mechanisms was that the GNP slowly but steadily declined.[32]

The decline in farm size continued after the fall of Boyer. President Philippe Guerrier (1844-5) sold at a low price such lands in the northern part of the republic that had not been reserved for public use. In 1862, President Fabre Geffrard passed a legislation bill stating that land was henceforth not to be sold in parcels exceeding 5 carreaux.[33] He also proclaimed that government land would be alienated only by means of sales and grants. Nobody was to squat on government property without legal rights. In order to give existing squatters such rights Geffrard tried to induce them to register their land claims. The suspiciousness of the peasantry against legal documents and government officials, however, turned this effort into a complete failure. The peasants continued to squat on government lands and abandoned estates, and no further organized measures were taken to prevent them. *

Towards the end of the nineteenth century the redistribution process gradually lost its momentum. Property grants and sales were still made, but on a lesser scale than before. The redistribution process also changed character. As Haitian domestic politics grew increasingly chaotic and the political scene became dominated by *coups* and uprisings,[34] few small property grants were made anymore. Instead, each new ruling clique did its best to deprive the previous one of

---

* During the American occupation of Haiti (1915-34) an effort was made to make a cadastral survey, but this had to be given up.

property. Thus, ownership of the larger estates often changed hands after each *coup d'état*. The peasants did not participate in this process but continued to squat on abandoned land when they wanted to extend their cultivations.

In 1883, President Lysius Salomon made the last, half-hearted effort to encourage peasant ownership of land. He decreed that anybody who signed an agreement to grow export crops would receive five to eight carreaux of government land for a period of two to five years. If three-fourths of this area were then cultivated, a permanent title could be obtained. Otherwise the grant would be void. The decree met with a very modest success. 1,700 applications were recorded in two years, but thereafter they ceased altogether.[35] The peasants lacked the complementary resources to grow the prescribed crops, and no steps were taken by the government to provide them with any financial support. The decree was a document devoid of practical content and changed virtually nothing in rural areas.

The 1883 decree represented the last serious plan to interfere with land tenure conditions in Haiti.[36] No further interference was necessary, however. By the end of the nineteenth century *la petite culture* dominated the rural scene completely. The plantation economy reminiscent of Saint-Domingue was nowhere to be seen. Haiti had in the course of less than one century become a peasant country where small family farms were the basic unit of production.

Attempts to Reintroduce Large Estates during the Twentieth Century

During and after the American occupation of Haiti (1915-34) attempts were made to reintroduce large-scale plantations in Haiti. In 1927, Emily Green Balch gave the list reproduced in Table 6.3 of American companies operating within the agricultural sector.[37] All Haitian constitutions before 1918 had explicitly prohibited foreign ownership of Haitian land. In the American-drafted 1918 constitution this clause was abolished, and in 1922, a law authorizing leasing of unoccupied lands for periods between nine and thirty years with an option of renewal was passed.[38] Still, when the Americans withdrew in 1934 only two significant plantation ventures remained in Haiti: HASCO and Plantation Dauphin. Low wages did not provide enough advantages to attract American investors in large numbers. The United Fruit could not be persuaded to enter Haiti on concession terms deemed appropriate by the State Department,[39] and during a 1922 Senate inquiry American businessmen voiced complaints regarding, among other things, the failure of the occupation to create conditions

Table 6.3: The Establishment of American-Owned Plantations in Haiti 1915-27

Company	Year of establishment	Area (hectares)
Haitian American Sugar Company	1915 [a]	9,600
Haitian Products Company	1915	4,000
United West Indies Corporation	1918	6,400
Société Commerciale d'Haiti	1918	1,200
North Haitian Sugar Company	1922	160
Haitian Pineapple Company	1923	240
Haitian American Development Corporation (Plantation Dauphin)	1926	5,600
Haitian Agricultural Corporation	1927	880
Total		28,080

a. Before the occupation.
Source: Moral (1961), note, p. 63. Quoted from Emily Green Balch, *Occupied Haiti* (New York, 1927).

favorable to capital investment.[40]

Later efforts did not fare much better. In 1941 a *Société Haitiano-Américaine de Développement Agricole* (SHADA) was created to exploit and develop the agricultural resources of Haiti, and large land concessions were given to the company, to the detriment of the peasants cultivating some of the company area.[41] The sisal boom of the 1940s led to the creation of some more large estates, but the boom had collapsed by the end of the Korean War. The plantation economy never again succeeded in penetrating the country efficiently, and today, not more than a small fraction of the agricultural land consists of holdings exceeding 20 carreaux.[42]

So much for the facts. To sum up: during the course of the seventeenth and eighteenth centuries French Saint-Domingue was turned into a plantation economy, the opulence of which was to a large extent based on exports of sugar, and to a lesser extent coffee, cotton, indigo and cocoa. The wars of liberation between 1791 and 1804 destroyed the colonial economy, but during the war years Toussaint made strong efforts to rebuild the colonial economy based on sugar, and his policy, which was based upon attaching the laborers to the soil in a *fermage* system, was continued by Dessalines and Christophe.

Beginning with Alexandre Pétion in 1809 a radically different agricultural policy was adopted — a policy which was to dominate the rest of the nineteenth century. Pétion began a redistribution of government lands and in the process broke up the colonial estates. In spite of a few attempts to stop the process, the average acreage gradually diminished until Haiti was a country whose economy was dominated by peasant minifundia holdings. During and after the American occupation of Haiti (1915-34) a number of efforts were made to reintroduce the plantation economy. These efforts failed, however. To this day Haiti continues to be a peasant country with average holdings equaling only 1.5 hectares.

The Haitian pattern of land distribution constitutes a radical departure from the typical Latin American case. The Haitian experience appears unique. It is therefore important to advance the question as to why exactly the land was redistributed during the nineteenth century and why the present century has not seen any re-emergence of large-scale farms or plantations. These questions appear so much more interesting since, as we have seen, the colonial plantation system and its sequel, the *fermage* system, both appear to have been efficient from the production point of view, while during the administrations of Pétion and Boyer the GNP appears to have fallen. In other words, why was a less efficient system substituted for a more efficient one?

The Causes of Redistribution

Seen against the personal background of Alexandre Pétion, his land reform comes as a surprise. It is true that Pétion is known to have been a firm believer in economic liberalism as advocated by Adam Smith and his contemporaries, and the president may have thought that ownership of the land would give a man a much better incentive to work with it than would a system based on forced labor and military supervision.[43] Still, nothing in his behavior during the first three years in office made a far-reaching land reform very likely. Pétion undoubtedly was a strong champion of mulatto aristocrat interests, and during the first two or three years a number of measures were taken to restore to large mulatto landowners the property that had been seized by Dessalines and to compensate them for the loss of crops. The tax structure was also changed for the benefit of the landowners, by abolishing the former tax of one quarter of the crop while simultaneously levying a sales tax on coffee, the cash crop of the small farms. This step was taken explicitly to encourage sugar production.[44] In 1809, however, Pétion gave up his support of the large estates and instead put the country on the road towards smallholdings.

The reasons given by Pétion himself for this change in policy are rather superficial and can probably not be taken too seriously. In various messages to the Senate the president declared that the people of Haiti deserved a reward for having defended their country,[45] and in a letter to a friend he stated that he wanted to 'root in everybody the love of the soil.'[46] This is not very convincing. As a matter of fact, it sounds more like an *ex post* rationalization than anything else, and as soon as we go beyond the façade we find more important mechanisms at work, that made it hard for Pétion and his followers to act differently and that turned all subsequent efforts to re-establish *la grande culture* into vain efforts.

These mechanisms may be grouped under four headings: (1) the use of land reform as a political instrument; (2) the relative scarcity of production factors; (3) the state of the export markets; (4) the lack of property rights enforcement.

Land Reform as a Political Instrument

After the assassination of Dessalines in 1806, Haiti was divided into two parts: the north – ruled by Henry Christophe – and the south – ruled by Alexandre Pétion. This separation did not end until after Christophe's suicide in 1820, when the country was united again under Boyer. The division of Haiti into two rival states was not a peaceful one but meant constant skirmishes and clashes between the north and the south, which in turn created a number of problems for Pétion.

Southern Haiti was something of an internally divided state – much more so than the north. In comparison to Christophe's north it was a mulatto stronghold, although the black population still constituted the large majority. Since the south was ruled by the mulattoes this created a potentially explosive situation that had to be avoided if the south was not going to succumb to Christophe. In consequence, the use of forced labor on the plantations was excluded so as not to risk an internal war along color lines.[47] It also meant that Pétion was bound to show a more lenient attitude towards the claims for land among the black masses.[48] The security of the state and hence of the mulatto aristocracy was intimately connected with obtaining freedom and access to land for the black masses. Conversely, a policy of freedom from forced labor combined with a redistribution of land proved to be an effective weapon for provoking desertions from the north.[49]

Internal peace was not enough to avert the external threat, since the south also needed a large standing army as a protection against the militarized north, and this army somehow had to be paid. As economic conditions declined in the south (largely because of the redistribution of land itself)[50] cash became increasingly scarce, and land grants were substituted for money. Land grants also contributed to the solution of the war veteran problem. Unemployed war veterans constituted a potential source of danger, and sometimes an actual one when pillage of stores took place, and in some way had to be resettled.[51]

Political reasons also governed the action of some later presidents. As Haitian domestic politics grew increasingly chaotic during the last half of the nineteenth century, land grants and sales began to play yet another role; that of political rewards. Thus, the year after the fall of Haiti's second emperor, Faustin Soulouque (1860), property that had been seized by Soulouque was distributed 'among militaries with twenty years of service or more', i.e. among those officers who had actively participated in the *coup*.[52] Similarly, those who had supported Nissage Saget in the 1870 *coup* against President Salnave were rewarded with land grants — five carreaux to each common soldier,[53] and in 1883, when President Salomon successfully had put an end to an insurrection in Miragoâne, the debt of gratitude was acknowledged by a law authorizing the 'sales' of state land to generals, senators, ministers, etc.[54]

The Relative Scarcity of Production Factors

It is unlikely that the large plantations would have continued in existence, even in the absence of political reasons to redistribute government land. It is true that the use of land reform as a political instrument precipitated the disappearance of the plantation economy, but economic forces alone would sooner or later have brought about the same result even without the aid of political ones. At the heart of this process was the change in factor endowments.

When Pétion took office in the south the Haitian economy was about to specialize in the 'wrong' product from the production point of view. Toussaint, Dessalines and Christophe all wanted to bring the destroyed sugar plantations into action again, and so did Pétion, at least at the beginning of his presidency. As we have seen, sugar is a product which requires large concentrations of fixed capital and labor. Such concentrations were, however, no longer available after the French had been ousted from Haiti.

The revolutionary wars had destroyed much of the capital equipment which was necessary to run the sugar plantations. Irrigation works and sugar mills were in ruins,[55] and very little new capital was forthcoming to replace what had been lost during the turbulent war years.

Foreign investors viewed Haiti with utmost suspicion. Naturally enough, the French were not interested. The English saw the existence of a nation of black ex-slaves in the Caribbean as a threat to the stability of their own colonies there,[56] and neither the United States nor Spain took any steps to help Haiti solve its capital problems.[57] In fact, Haiti was ostracized by most other nations for a long period following its independence. Not even Simón Bolívar, who had received considerable aid from Pétion during the struggle for independence in South America, wanted to recognize the black republic.[58] The Haitians themselves presented another formidable obstacle to foreign capital investment. Every single constitution from 1805 to 1918 emphatically prohibited foreign ownership of Haitian land.[59]

Domestic capital formation was hampered in various ways. Following the revolutionary wars the country was poor, and its productive apparatus was partly laid in ruins. Capital markets were non-existent or at best extremely undeveloped.[60] Government potential for capital formation was low, and revenues were diverted to other uses. As we will see in Chapter 8, Haiti was an overmilitarized country during the nineteenth century. The first rulers feared a renewed French invasion and as a safeguard kept a large standing army. Pétion and Christophe in addition fought an intermittent civil war. Overmilitarization continued after the settlement with France in 1825. Army expenditure absorbed more than 50 percent of the budget around 1850, and during the reign of Soulouque (1847-59) large amounts were spent on the army, the secret police and a paramilitary force known as the *zinglins*. Soulouque also involved the country in two fruitless campaigns to conquer the Dominican Republic.

Subsequently, insecurity of investment in the face of political instability added to the problems caused by excessive militarization. After the fall of President Geffrard in 1867, political chaos became the order of the day.[61] A repetitive pattern of events was established. *Coups*, uprisings and dictatorships came and went in a seemingly endless row. All presidents except one between 1867 and 1915 were army officers. With the aid of hired guerilla units (*cacos*) one president after another was overthrown. More or less professional financers of the revolutions – mainly German merchants resident in Haiti – provided the necessary funds against high interest. Finally, Haiti experienced no less than twenty *coups* or abortive uprisings in eight years (1908-15), before the United States intervened in 1915 and occupied the country.

Haiti also had to face the problem of a large external debt.[62] In exchange for French recognition of the country in 1825, Haiti was forced to pay an indemnity of 150 million francs in five years, which proved to be impossible. A loan of 30 million francs was immediately floated in Paris to raise money for the first instalment, which was also made. Subsequently Haiti defaulted, however, and in 1838 the terms were renegotiated to 60 million francs payable in 30 years. Even these proved to be harsh terms, and between 1839 and 1843 almost 60 percent of the customs receipts had to be sacrificed to amortization and interest payments of the foreign debt. Not until the middle of the 1870s was the indemnity practically paid off.

In 1875, 1896 and 1910 new loans of 36, 50 and 65 million francs respectively were taken in France. Very few of these resources were used for productive purposes; most of them were wasted on commission payments to the banks that had conveyed the loans, to bribes and to other political ends. Nevertheless, the loans still had to be repaid. Haiti, in sharp contrast to other Latin American nations, never defaulted on its foreign loans between 1875 and 1915, and this in turn meant that the country was drained of valuable foreign exchange which could have been used for capital formation e.g. in the agricultural sector.

So much for the lack of capital. Labor, at both supervisory and lower levels, also became scarce after the revolution. With the expulsion of the French an administrative and technical vacuum was created. Most of the educated people had been killed or had emigrated.[63] Thus, there was a lack of competent people to organize and lead the work on sugar plantations and crushing mills. The substitution of military discipline for the colonial organization met with only limited success and had severe repercussions on the supply of ordinary labor. The long period of slavery in combination with the *corvée* system employed by Toussaint, Dessalines and Christophe had placed a high premium on freedom so that the wage required by the peasants to recruit them for plantation work became prohibitive. The peasants preferred to work on land owned by themselves. This tendency had been clearly discernible for many years. Many had fled to the mountains during the colonial period and established themselves there as squatters, and this movement continued and increased throughout the period of forced labor. The effects of this drain were reinforced by the general decline in population by approximately 150,000 from 1790 to 1805.[64]

We may now summarize the results of the preceding account. During the first half of the nineteenth century both capital and labor were scarce factors in Haiti (in comparison to land). Foreign investors viewed Haiti with scepticism. Successive constitutions prohibited foreign ownership of land. The country was overmilitarized, and had to suffer the repayment of a large foreign debt. Thus, neither foreign nor domestic investment was forthcoming. Labor for plantation work was extremely scarce. Slavery and forced labor had created a prohibitive premium on freedom, and few people were willing to work for masters other than themselves. To go back to the sugar-based plantation system under such circumstances was not feasible. The plantation economy simply collapsed under the pressure of the gap between actual and desirable factor endowments. Even if the necessary capital could have been brought forward, the labor constraint alone would have precluded the re-establishment of the plantation economy. As is shown in the appendix to the present chapter, in a situation where labor is scarce relative to land, capital investment presumably takes the form of laboresque capital, i.e. of devices designed to substitute for human energy. Mechanization of the cultivation process could thus in theory have solved the labor supply problem, but given the technological knowledge of the time this was a sheer impossibility. Mechanization of the harvesting process has continued to be especially difficult, and it is only very recently that this problem has been tackled with reasonable efficiency. A good account of the issues facing the Cubans during their efforts to raise the sugar harvest figures during the 1960s has been given by Leo Huberman and Paul M. Sweezy in their book on Cuban socialism:

> If all cane were planted on flat land and, like corn, grew straight up to a more or less uniform height, the task of designing a mechanical harvester would be simple. One set of knives would lop off the tops and another cut the stalks just above the ground level; a blower would remove the chaff; and a loader would deposit the cleaned stalks in tractor-drawn wagons, ready for transportation to the mill. But in reality cane is often planted on hilly or uneven land and much of it (particularly the heavy and hence high-yield varieties) grows every which way, forming what appear to be impenetrable tangles. The problem is therefore anything but simple.[65]

What was true for Cuba in the 1960s was even more true for Haiti in the nineteenth century. Either a large labor force had to be used or sugar cane cultivation had to be abandoned. There was no other alternative.

The State of the Export Markets

In the discussion of relative factor scarcity it was stated that Haiti was about to specialize in the 'wrong' product when Pétion took office. In a situation where labor and capital are scarce in relation to land there are strong tendencies at work on the production side to specialize the economy on such commodities that do not require large amounts of labor or capital. However, this statement is subject to an important qualification.[66] If the structure of demand offsets the tendencies emanating from production so that the price of labor- and capital-intensive products become sufficiently high in relation to the price of land-intensive products, the economy will become a net exporter of the former. This was more or less the case with eighteenth-century Saint-Domingue. Following independence, however, the demand for Haitian sugar was weakened and this allowed the tendencies emanating from the factor endowment to dominate. Increased competition from Cuba and, to a lesser extent, the Dutch and British Antilles as well as from European beet-sugar made its effects felt by a downward pressure on sugar prices which continued throughout the first half of the nineteenth century.[67]

Disruptions caused by the Napoleonic Wars are likely to have played a certain role as well. First and foremost, the wars cut off important parts of the main export markets. Trade with France was out of question as long as the problems of recognition and indemnity had not been solved. The American market had gradually grown in importance during the decade preceding the French Revolution,[68] and American merchants wished to continue their trade with the island during the wars of liberation and also during their aftermath. Such trade actually took place.[69] This trade, however, was a constant source of friction between France and the United States and in 1806 (needing French diplomatic support in the dispute with Spain regarding the details of the Louisiana purchase) President Jefferson and the American Congress yielded to the pressure exerted upon them by Napoleon and prohibited trade between Haiti and the United States. The prohibition lasted until 1809.[70] This give ample opportunity to Britain to seize the Haitian trade, which to some extent ought to have compensated the Haitians for the loss of the French and American markets. Soon, however, another disturbance to Haitian exports arose: the war of 1812 between the United States and Great Britain (1812-15).

Unfortunately, since virtually no export statistics are available for the period between 1805 and 1818,[71] there is no way of obtaining quantitative evidence as to the magnitude of the influence of the wars,

Land Reform

but it is likely that peaceful conditions would have proved more beneficial to export trade.

The Lack of Property Rights Enforcement

When the sugar economy broke down family farm-based production of coffee and subsistence goods was substituted for the plantation system. Of course this was partly the outcome of the active redistribution of land by the government, but in a more fundamental sense it may be said to have been the result of something else: the lack of property rights enforcement, which in turn was a consequence of the absence of administrative control of the country by the government.

A comparison with the rest of Latin America is instructive on this point. In many Latin American countries cattle ranching is the predominant activity in the primary sector. Cattle ranching is a very land-intensive activity which requires much less labor than sugar cultivation, and land was plentiful in Haiti. At the same time it would have required a certain monopolization of the land and eviction of peasants from potential grazing lands. The latter, however, could not be achieved in Haiti. After the fall of Christophe in 1820 no Haitian administration was strong enough to oppose the squatting movement.[72]

The attempts to enforce Boyer's *Code Rural* of 1826 provide an excellent illustration of administrative weakness. The peasants were forced back to plantation work on only a few estates near the principal cities. Many plantation owners had left the countryside during Pétion's presidency when they found that it was impossible to obtain field hands, and when the Boyer administration tried to reverse this trend it was already too late. In spite of intensive government propaganda few large landowners proved willing to forsake the comparative pleasures of urban life to settle once more on their estates and take active part in management. Crop-sharing arrangements were a much easier way out, and the government could not mobilize the necessary political strength to prevent it.

With the landowners preferring urban life the responsibility for the administration of actively cultivated large estates fell heavily upon hired *gérants*, who as a rule had no education in economic or agrarian matters. Finally, military force and supervision was resorted to, but this solution, as we know, did not achieve any patent results. The peasants deserted from the plantations and instead squatted in other areas, where no attempts were made to enforce property rights.

During the rest of the nineteenth century the peasants were left in peace. The *Code Rural* was soon forgotten and henceforth a policy of complete *laissez-faire* was adopted by all presidents. This became increasingly necessary as the century advanced due to the growing political instability. In comparison to the problem of staying in power, illegal squatting was a very minor issue.

Christopher K. Clague has pointed out that the success of the peasant squatting movement was partly due to the fact that land was relatively abundant in nineteenth-century Haiti.[73] The landowners could not secure the labor force for their estates because there was always somewhere else for the peasants to go. No violent clashes ever arose between the two groups. This in turn may, however, largely be a consequence of the fact that a good deal of the land was government property when the redistribution process began. It has been estimated that in 1806 from two-thirds to nine-tenths of all productive plantations were in government hands.[74] Thus, in the beginning few peasants had to bother those landowners who opposed illegal squatting, but could instead use government lands and as the redistribution process gained momentum, the private landowners gradually lost their interest in the soil, which also opened the way for squatting on private property.

Summing Up: The Nineteenth Century

Summing up the foregoing arguments it is easy to understand why the large estates were subdivided in nineteenth-century Haiti. In one sense, Pétion's land reform was a political act. Southern Haiti was predominantly black, but the mulattoes constituted the elite. This situation was one of inherent tensions between black, subjugated masses (serfs in their majority) and elites, and redistribution of plantation lands was obviously an efficient way to pacify the masses. (This point will be elaborated upon in Chapter 7.) At the same time, land redistribution served as a means of paying the army. With an intermittent civil war going on against Christophe's north a standing army was needed, and this army somehow had to be paid. When the economic conditions deteriorated and when unemployed war veterans had to be resettled, land grants were a way out when cash was lacking.

However, the 'political' explanation of the land reform is neither a sufficient nor a necessary one. It is improbable that political considerations alone would have made Pétion, who was a champion of mulatto interests, depart so radically from the established system of land tenure. To arrive at a more tenable explanation we have to consider the economic realities. Political factors only added to the strength of the economic ones. The wars of independence had rendered the Haitian factor endowment entirely unsuitable for sugar production. Large parts of the capital stock needed for sugar cultivation and processing were destroyed, and there was no new investment forthcoming which could replace what had been lost. As a black independent nation surrounded by slave colonies, Haiti was ostracized by all the major powers of the time, and the Haitians for their part explicitly prohibited white ownership of land in the country. The domestic capital market was more or less non-existent, and government resources were squandered on military expenditures and repayment of foreign debts. Increasing political instability, finally, made capital investment a highly uncertain venture. The labor supply had decreased as well. The wars had taken a heavy toll. The Haitian population had decreased by approximately 150,000. The entire administrative cadre was gone, while the labor force for their part wished only to work for themselves. The wages needed to attract hands to work in the plantation fields became prohibitively high.

The sugar plantations badly needed both capital and labor. The technology of the time was such as to make an intensive use of both these factors an absolute necessity. With a lack of both capital and labor, the breakdown of the plantation system was only a matter of time. It was the fall in sugar prices during the first half of the nineteenth century as well as possibly the market disruptions caused by the Napoleonic wars, together with the above mentioned political factors, which acted as a trigger mechanism.

A possible way of saving *la grande culture* would have been to shift production into alternative lines, e.g. cattle-raising. This would, however, have required a much higher degree of administrative control than was feasible. In Chapter 7, the administrative weakness of the Haitian governments after Christophe will be discussed at some length. In the present context, this means that they could not prevent illegal squatting from taking place, either on government lands or on privately owned plantations. Once the redistribution mechanism had been set in motion, it was impossible to stop. The process of disintegration created its own momentum. Active redistribution in combination with illegal squatting quickly reduced the size of the Haitian farms.

The Twentieth Century: Obstacles to Large-scale Farming

Towards the end of the nineteenth century, the government redistribution of land had almost come to an end. Likewise, the pace of the squatting movement had slowed down. Most of the attractive land areas had been settled by that time. Nevertheless, the size of Haitian farms has continued to decline during the twentieth century, and we must now focus on the reasons for this phenomenon.

Subdivision through Inheritance

The most important mechanism that has actively promoted subdivision is one which was already present during the previous century: the system of inheritance. As active redistribution and squatting have ceased to have any practical importance, inheritance has become the prime vehicle of subdivision.

The Haitian laws governing succession have always been based on the principles of the *Code Napoléon*. All children have equal rights to the property of their parents when the latter die. This fundamental principle is valid not only for legitimate children but also for such natural children that have been acknowledged: *Tout piti sé piti*. Two categories are legally excluded – natural children born after marriage (who cannot be acknowledged) and adopted children, but custom and practice (at least as far as natural children are concerned) have deprived this limitation of its practical value. There are many ways to circumvent the laws:

> ...custom, which sanctions polygamy, impels a father to care for his adulterine children, even though the law does not compel him to do so. He can provide for them in various ways. He can give their mother some land, which they will sooner or later inherit. He can also transfer them property through a 'feigned sale' to them...Finally, he can ask his legal wife to acknowledge, as her own, the child of the concubine. The civil registrars, who are quite used to the peasants' irregular acts of commission or omission, show no surprise if a married couple 'declare' a child to them several years after its birth; and there is no lack of witnesses who are ready to come forward for this purpose.[75]

For adopted children the situation is more precarious. Neither law nor custom give them any right of inheritance, but even if there are other heirs, adopted children generally receive some kind of present or deed.[76]*

Thus, the inheritance system works so as to divide landed property into equal shares to be distributed among the heirs, and hence a small farm of perhaps not more than one carreau may be split into as many

---

* As a rule the surviving spouse administers the property of the deceased, so that the final division of the inheritance takes place only after both spouses are dead.

as seven or eight small plots in the course of a single generation.[77]

Relative Abundance of Labor

It is obvious that given the lack of a land market, an inheritance system where all heirs inherit equal shares of the property leads to smaller farms than for example, a system where the oldest son takes the entire landed property of his father. However, once we allow for the opportunity to buy and sell land in the market, the former system can no longer guarantee that farms are kept small. We must look for other reasons as well — factors of a more fundamental character which will operate regardless of the particular system of inheritance.

The population expanded during the nineteenth and twentieth centuries. Factor proportions changed once more as the demographic gap left by the revolution was filled. At the same time land became increasingly scarce. Labor, not land, became the relatively abundant factor in the economy, and this has acted to keep farm size down in at least two ways.

As we can deduce from the model in the appendix, growth of the stock of laboresque capital is likely to take place when labor becomes increasingly scarce in relation to land. This is the situation typical for the United States, for example, where there has been a drain of farm people into other occupations. Competition for labor from the non-agricultural sectors has exerted an upward pressure on agricultural wages. Thus, the exodus of farm people has led to increasing mechanization of farms, and since mechanized agriculture displays important economies of scale, farm size has had to be increased to take full advantage of this potential. The average farm size doubled in 25 years.[78] In Haiti exactly the opposite situation has prevailed. Labor has become increasingly plentiful in relation to land, and hence the incentives to mechanize agriculture have been lacking.*

On the other hand, according to the Sen model in the appendix, relative abundance of labor (relative scarcity of land) ought to stimulate the growth of the landesque capital stock — such capital that acts as a substitute for land. However, the possible economies of scale inherent in landesque capital are not likely to be nearly as strong as those stemming

---

* The increasing scarcity of labor in developed countries has typically been caused by the growth of the non-agricultural sector of the economy. As long as this growth is not significant enough to cause an upward trend in agricultural wages, the relative price of labor is likely to remain stagnant or fall (if population growth is fast enough). This mechanism may be analyzed either in a model of the Lewis type (Lewis (1954) or in a more conventional model of the Rybczynski type, where capital grows more slowly than labor (Cf. e.g. Johnson (1971), pp. 35-40). Thus this argument really is an argument based upon the slow overall growth of the economy.

from mechanization. Fertilizer, pesticides, insecticides, superior strains of plants and seeds, etc. (with the possible exception of irrigation) may be applied equally to large and small farms.

What is more, possible economies of scale connected with landesque capital have had very few opportunities to materialize and hence to affect farm size in Haiti. Returning once more to the appendix, we find that if total investment in the farm sector is too low, very little can be spent on landesque capital. Only acquisition of simple hand tools and necessary plants and seeds is possible. Such has been the fate of the peasants in twentieth-century Haiti. Poverty has by and large precluded those savings that take the form of productive investment, and the assistance from government credit sources has been negligible.[79]

Market Conditions

The disappearance of the colonial plantations in Haiti was intimately related to the development of the market conditions for sugar. During the present century the connection between the state of the markets for export crops and large-scale agriculture has continued to play an important role for farm size. Recalling that the only important large plantations in Haiti after the American occupation have been those of HASCO (sugar) and Plantation Dauphin (sisal) we will now proceed to examine the international sugar and sisal markets in the post-1915 period.

Sugar The general picture of the twentieth-century world sugar market is one of actual or potential overproduction, protection and regulation. This is nothing but a continuation of the trend from the nineteenth century. In 1927, Ramiro Guerra y Sánchez wrote in his famous book on sugar in the Caribbean:

> Over the last century, sugar prices have declined every year in value, in absolute or relative terms, compared with the steady rise in the cost of living for almost all civilized peoples. Prices have gone up when wars or other such events have disturbed the normal balance of production; but they have soon resumed their downward trend.[80]

If we compare the quotation to Figure 6.1, we find that this is a very accurate pricture indeed, at least up to the end of the Second World War. The nineteenth-century development of beet-sugar production in Europe and also the development after 1890 in the United States had raised the share of beet-sugar in world sugar production from 15 percent in 1850 to two-thirds in 1900.[81] This expansion had taken place largely with the aid of import prohibitions, quota systems, prohibitive tariffs, export subsidies, etc. The Brussels Sugar Convention of 1902 by and large put an end to the use of artificial measures for keeping the tropical cane-sugar out of European markets. Once more cane-sugar could compete with beet-sugar. It was not until the beginning of the First World War, however, that cane-sugar production finally outgrew its competitor, a position which it has maintained since that period.[82]

Throughout the first fifteen years of the twentieth century competition was keen. Not only had beet-sugar become a powerful competitor, but improved factory equipment, application of steam to milling in Hawaii, Java, Louisiana and Cuba had expanded production of cane-sugar, which in turn was further stimulated by heavy American capital exports to the sugar-producing areas of Cuba, Puerto Rico and the Philippines following the Spanish-American War.

Figure 6.1

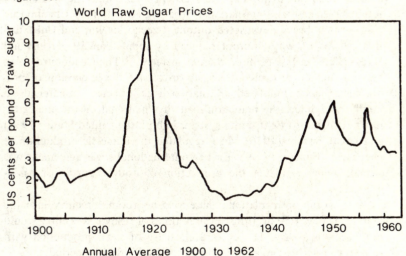

Annual Average 1900 to 1962

Source: Thomas (1971), p. 1565.

The First World War destroyed the European beet-sugar economy. There was a weakening of competition in the world market and prices went up, as can be seen in Figure 6.1 High prices in turn acted as a stimulus to the establishment of sugar plantations in Haiti. HASCO as a matter of fact was established in the country *before* the advent of American Marines.[83] However, in spite of the high sugar prices during the war the HASCO operations were not financially viable. Production was not started until 1918 and in 1921 the company was forced into receivership.[84] By that time world market prices had fallen once again. With time HASCO became a profitable venture. In 1928, the company had tripled its 1918 production and HASCO, as we have seen, was one of the two remaining American agricultural investments in Haiti when the occupation ended in 1934.

However, no further large sugar plantations were established in Haiti. In 1929-30 after a period of voluntary restriction of output Cuba put the hitherto largest *zafra* in its history on the market.[85] In the words of Guerra y Sánchez, '...the effect on world price was instantaneous and calamitous.'[86] The sugar price dropped to the lowest level yet during the twentieth century. The fall of the sugar price (which continued until June 1933)[87] immediately led to protective measures and efforts to restrict world production. In 1930, the United States raised its tariffs on sugar (the Smoot-Hawley tariff) and in 1931 all major exporters except Brazil and the Dominican Republic signed an international sugar agreement (the Chadbourne plan) which heavily restricted output. Czechoslovakia and Cuba had their shares of world output reduced by more than 50 percent and Java suffered a loss of more than 80 percent.[88] The Chadbourne plan did not include protected areas, however, and the expansion of production there, stimulated by nationalistic policies, threatened to nullify completely the reduction made by the signatories to the agreement. This led to tight quota systems in both the United States (1934) and Great Britain (1936) which regulated the domestic production of beet-sugar. Finally, in 1937, a new international sugar agreement was signed, which regulated the production of both exporters and non-exporters.

In a world of regulations there was no room for entry into the market of new Haitian firms. Even in times of rising prices entry would not have been easy. The upward elasticity of sugar production with respect to price was amazing in the post-First World War period:

> Java increased her output one million tons, or 50 percent, between 1923-24 and 1927-28. Cuban production increased more than a million tons, or 25 percent, in the single crop year 1924-25, as well as 30 percent between 1916-17 and 1918-19. In the first three years of the Smoot-Hawley tariff (1930-33), Philippine output almost

doubled. United States beet production, exceeded only by Germany and Czechoslovakia in 1923-24, doubled in the next decade behind a tariff wall. India, second in cane-sugar production only to Cuba when sugar protection was introduced, almost doubled its output within five years.[89]

Thus, the international sugar market during the inter-war period provided very strong disincentives to entry.

During the Second World War sugar prices rose anew. The beet-sugar provinces in the Ukraine were totally devastated by the German scorched-earth tactics. Java and the Philippines were lost to the Japanese, who almost wiped out sugar production in both places. This was potentially beneficial to Haitian production, and the country's sugar exports increased during the 1943-47 period.[90] Still, this was only temporary. After the war there was a rapid recovery of competing beet- and cane-sugar producers. International trade in sugar was once more regulated. The United States return to its pre-war quota system, allowing only a minimal quota for Haiti, averaging 2,500 tons in the mid-1950s, was of particular importance.[91] The rest of the exportable surplus had to be disposed of on the free world market, which was further reduced by the regulations imposed by the British Commonwealth Sugar Agreement of 1951 (amended in 1962), which established preferential quotas for Commonwealth countries, and the new international sugar agreement of 1953 (renewed in 1958). The change in political conditions in Cuba brought an end to the international sugar agreement and cut off the trade between the former country and the United States at the beginning of the 1960s. The latter circumstances were favorable to Haitian sugar production. Haiti's quota on the American market was raised gradually to around 30,000 tons in the late 1960s.[92]

This increase has not been sufficient to establish new large sugar plantations. Even the largest sugar producer, HASCO, largely relies on what it can buy from peasant producers. In the late 1960s it was calculated that around two-thirds of the total output was coming from holdings that were smaller than 3 hectares.[93] There have been no price incentives to introduce large-scale plantations. First of all, the price of sugar cane to the producer remained stationary between 1948 and 1974 at a level which even after the rise in 1974 was approximately one-half of what producers in other Caribbean areas received.[94] Second, incentives to invest in refining capacity have also been lacking, especially for the leading producer. In 1948 a government monopoly on the internal marketing of sugar was imposed, and HASCO was forced to satisfy the domestic demand for sugar before any exports could take place. The policy followed by the Haitian government has been to keep sugar prices low with the result that HASCO and its large competitors have not felt it profitable enough to expand their refining capacity. While HASCO's larger competitors have not had to face the domestic demand requirement, but have been able to export as much as they could, the policy of government intervention with regard to producer prices has also hampered the activities of these companies.

Sisal Sisal production began in Haiti after the establishment of the Haitian American Development Corporation (Plantation Dauphin) in 1926. A contract between the company and the Haitian government gave the former the right to lease up to 8,000 hectares of government lands for 30 years with an option to renew the contract for another 30 years, and the company was also authorized to purchase land from private owners. In 1929, the first sisal was exported.[95]

From 1929 to 1940 Plantation Dauphin (which became the official name of the company in 1936) dominated sisal production in Haiti. Production was concentrated to the dry Fort-Liberté area in the northern part of the country. No serious competitors appeared on the scene. This was mostly due to the unfavorable trend in export prices, as may be seen in Table 6.4.

Table 6.4: Average f.o.b. Price of Raw Sisal 1929/30-1951/52 (US dollars per kilo)

Year	f.o.b. Price	Year	f.o.b. Price
1929-30	0.12	1941-42	0.15
1930-31	0.09	1942-43	0.18
1931-32	0.06	1943-44	0.18
1932-33	0.06	1944-45	0.18
1933-34	0.08	1945-46	0.18
1934-35	0.08	1946-47	0.27
1935-36	0.11	1947-48	0.31
1936-37	0.12	1948-49	0.31
1937-38	0.09	1949-50	0.28
1938-39	0.07	1950-51	0.39
1939-40	0.09	1951-52	0.40
1940-41	0.08		

Source: Fatton (1975), p.6.

During the Second World War a new impetus was given to sisal production. The attack on Pearl Harbor and the Japanese conquest of the Philippines cut off the traditional US sources of supply, and the intensification of the submarine war in the Atlantic made it hard to import fibers from Africa. Sisal prices rose and this trend continued until the end of the Korean War, as is shown in Table 6.4.

Sisal is a product which is excellently suited for the drier areas of Haiti, and the rise in export prices during the 1940s quickly led to the establishment of new large and medium-size sisal plantations in the Port-au-Prince, Cap-Haïtien and St Marc regions (as well as to peasant cultivations in the southern peninsula). The development was so rapid that a law of 1951 prohibited further extensions of sisal cultivations without authorization from the Department of Agriculture.[96] It was felt that unchecked sisal monoculture was a severe threat to the cultivation of food crops.

The sisal boom was over with the end of the Korean War. As we have discussed in the preceding chapter, the 1950s witnessed a large fall in the sisal price, from $0.40 per kilo in 1951/52 (index 100) to $0.15 per kilo in 1957/58 (index 38).[97] During the early 1960s, the export price stagnated around $0.17-0.18 per kilo, thereafter rose moderately, only to fall to $0.09 in 1970/71.[98] The sisal plantations were abandoned, and in 1971 Plantation Dauphin closed its operations. By the early 1970s sisal cultivation had become part of the peasant *grappillage* which in 1968-69 accounted for 60 percent of total output.[99] Significant price rises in 1973 and 1974 subsequently led to a reopening of Plantation Dauphin, although another price fall forced it to close again in 1976.

The future of Port Dauphin, as the plantation is now called, after a change of management, is uncertain. Whether the plantation will continue its operations or whether it will instead diversify into other crops and livestock raising (projects which have been discussed) depends entirely on the world price for sisal. All the major Haitian sisal producers (not only Port Dauphin) can very easily expand their production if prices go up. As of 1976 there was considerable excess capacity in the industry.[100]

To understand the sisal market it is important to keep in mind that sisal is a product which has to face very keen competition from other natural or synthetic fibers, which is well borne out by the history of its price. Only during periods of weakened competition have prices been high, due to the Second World War and the Korean War and latterly to the oil crisis which increased the production costs of artificial fibers. As in the case of sugar, there was always a tendency to overproduction in the market for hard fibers, which goes a long way towards explaining the reluctance to establish new large sisal plantations, except under very special circumstances.

Unavailability of Large Land Tracts

The continuous subdivision of plots for more than a century (and the absence of clear land titles) created special problems for any investors wanting to purchase or lease large domains. Giles A. Hubert gives a good description of the obstacles confronting the Standard Fruit and Steamship Company in its efforts to obtain land for banana plantations in the 1930s:

> A dramatic case. . . .is that of the Standard Fruit Company's banana plantations of some 2,000 acres in the Artibonite Valley. In order to secure enough land in fairly contiguous territory for efficient operations, the company has had to sign lease and share contracts with hundreds of little land owners. A record of production has to be kept for each land plot and a record of payments to each peasant must be maintained. Even then there are small plots here and there within the contiguous area where the owners refused to lease their land and with whom arise interminable disputes with regard to whose bananas are whose, and whose land shall receive irrigation water and when, whose stock got into whose crops etc. Much land in Haiti is simply not available for large scale operations.[101] *

During the occupation the Americans did all that they could to remove the barriers to plantation development. In the first place there was a need to gain clear titles to holdings. The Marines made aerial surveys of large parts of the country in 1925 and 1926, as a preparation to a cadastral survey, and in 1929 an American lawyer was appointed to draft a land title legislation bill. Neither act was successful. The building in which the aerial photos were stored burned down under unexplained circumstances,[102] and the Haitian government opposed both the cadastral survey and the land title legislation.[103] This inevitably led to clashes between plantation interests and peasants. Not even in the northern part of the country where land was owned in comparatively large units could the Plantation Dauphin do without evictions of peasant squatters to secure the necessary areas for its sisal

---

* Paul Moral (1961), p. 64, considers this the most important obstacle to the establishment of large estates in Haiti.

cultivations, a situation which was duplicated when SHADA was established in 1941.[104]

It is difficult to gain an exact idea as to the importance of the unavailability of large land tracts as an obstacle to large-scale agriculture in Haiti. No doubt it is difficult to obtain vast land areas, but as the experience of Plantation Dauphin, HASCO and SHADA shows, it is not impossible. Quite likely, the available factor endowment and the conditions prevailing in the markets for sugar and sisal are much more important than the alleged unavailability of large land tracts when it comes to explaining why so few new plantations have been created in Haiti during the present century.

Summing Up: The Twentieth Century

The obstacles to a resurrection of the plantation economy in present-day Haiti differ somewhat from the causes underlying the fall of the colonial estates 150 years ago. Yet there is a certain similarity to be found in the pattern of explanations.

The Haitian system of inheritance, which is based upon the *Code Napoléon*, is often advanced as the primary reason for small farm size. The system (which operated during the nineteenth century as well) confers equal rights on all heirs to the property in question. Under *ceteris paribus* conditions, this means that in the course of a single generation, a given plot may be divided between many hands. Viewed in this light, the inheritance laws create a tendency for farm size to decline as time elapses.

Subdivision through inheritance is not a sufficient condition for farm size to remain small, however, unless market transactions are excluded from the picture. If a land market is introduced, the possibility of a reconcentration of plots arises. Therefore, to explain farm size, additional variables have to be introduced. As in the case of the nineteenth century, supply and demand factors have interacted to create a powerful barrier to further establishment of large estates. During the present century, labor has been abundant in relation to land. This fact has precluded mechanization of the agricultural sector and thereby also the reaping of possible economies of scale inherent in mechanization. Relative scarcity of land, on the other hand, should stimulate the accumulation of landesque capital to compensate for the lack of land itself, but due to the poverty of the Haitian peasantry the level of savings has been too low. The scale economies to be obtained from the use of landesque capital are also considerably smaller than those of laboresque capital. In short, there was a lack of the incentives to production which could have led to the renewed establishment of large-scale agriculture in Haiti.

Obstacles to production have interacted with the market situation prevailing for the most important Haitian plantation crops, sugar and sisal. The world market price of both these crops has been unfavorable throughout most of the present century, and both industries have shown clear signs of overproduction. The world market for sugar has been characterized by regulations, import quotas and tariffs, and during the periods of comparatively free trade in sugar, the elasticity of supply has proved to be high among Haiti's major competitors. A small rise in the price of sugar has triggered off strong supply responses. Both regulations and high supply elasticities have hence acted as barriers to the establishment of new large-scale ventures in the sugar industry.

For sisal, the situation has been similar. The 1930s were characterized by low sisal prices, and it was not until the Second World War and the Korean War that sisal production received some stimulation in the form of higher world market prices. After the Korean boom sisal prices fell again, and thereafter the most important Haitian large-scale producer of sisal has had to close its operations several times due to insufficient profitability. Sisal has become a peasant product instead of a typical exponent of *la grande culture*. The market has worked against the large sisal plantations as much as it has worked against large-scale sugar production. Both industries have been hampered by severe problems of overproduction in relation to world market demand.

A final reason often advanced to explain the reluctance of large-scale agriculture to return to Haiti is that land tracts large enough for plantation development have not been available in the country. Undoubtedly, some large-scale ventures have experienced problems when attempting to acquire land, but the historical experience also shows that these obstacles have not proved to be insurmountable. What is to be regarded as unavailable depends very much on what is considered to be permissible. From the administrative and legal point of view it has not been impossible to create new plantations. Market and production considerations are much more likely to have been the decisive factors behind the absence of new plantations than the alleged unavailability of land.

Conclusions

As the two following chapters will show, the redistribution of land in the nineteenth century is a decisive event in Haitian economic history, not only because the land reform turned a system which was based on large estates on the one hand and slavery or serfdom on the other into one based on production by free peasants on family farms, but also because the redistribution of land had important consequences in the political sphere — consequences which in turn had repercussions on the peasant economy.

The land reform shifted the interest of the Haitian elite away from agriculture and into government instead. When the traditional base of wealth and incomes in the form of landed estates disappeared, the elite cliques became involved in a rat-race for political power. The latter, in turn was used almost exclusively as a means of generating incomes and creating fortunes. The political process became totally distorted as a result of the land reform. The latter half of the nineteenth century and the first decade of the present was masked by a seemingly endless series of *coups*, revolutions, counter-*coups* and counter-revolutions with the single aim of dipping one's hands as deeply and as quickly as possible into the national treasure before the next clique took over.

The land reform also contributed to an almost hermetic separation of the masses from the elite. By setting the agricultural laborers free and by supplying them with land, Pétion satisfied the two most ardent desires of the ex-slaves. Having achieved these two objectives, the latter withdrew into subsistence cultivation (gradually supplemented by production for the market) and expressed no desire to take part in national politics. The peasants came to constitute a group without political articulation. The upper classes, for their part, lost all interest in agriculture, except as a source of taxes. Only when a *coup* or a revolution was brewing did the peasants participate in the affairs of the nation — and then only as hired mercenaries necessary to overthrow the sitting government. Peasant welfare was not a variable which entered the calculations of the cliques contending for power, and as the two following chapters will demonstrate, positive government action with respect to the agricultural sector has been conspicuously absent in Haiti after the land reform.

Notes

1. Parry (1966), p. 40; Davis (1973), p. 251.
2. Parry & Sherlock (1968), p. 16.
3. Ibid., p. 15.
4. See Davis (1973), pp. 255-6.
5. Rotberg & Clague (1971), p.31.

6. Davis (1973), pp. 257-8. Cf. Street (1960), pp. 111-12. Cf. also Thomas (1971), pp. 40-41 for a similar description from Cuba.
7. Thomas (1971), pp. 62-3.
8. Lepkowski (1968:1), p. 48. Cf. Street (1960), p. 125.
9. Davis (1973), p. 258.
10. Logan (1968), p. 11.
11. Davis (1973), p. 258. Cf. Street (1960), p. 117.
12. Cf. Rotberg & Clague (1971), note, p. 39.
13. Ibid., p. 28.
14. Lepkowski (1968:1), p. 49.
15. Rotberg & Clague (1971), p. 48.
16. Quoted by Lepkowski (1968:1), note, p. 77.
17. Franklin (1828), pp. 118-22; Mackenzie (1830:2), pp. 138-42; Lepkowski (1968:1), pp. 73-9; Rotberg & Clague (1971), pp. 49-50.
18. For details regarding Dessalines' system see e.g. Franklin (1828), pp. 189-90, 323-5; Mackenzie (1830:2), pp. 144-5; Brown (1837:2), pp. 148-9; Leyburn (1966), pp. 33-9; Lepkowski (1968:1), pp. 93-101; Rotberg & Clague (1971), pp. 54-5.
19. For details see e.g. Harvey (1827), pp. 247-53; Mackenzie (1830:2), pp. 146-52; Brown (1837:2), pp. 203-5; Leyburn (1966), pp. 44-51; Griggs & Prator (1968), pp. 45-7; Lepkowski (1968:1), pp. 103-6; Cole (1970), pp. 209-10; Rotberg & Clague (1971), pp. 58-9. (Another important aspect of Christophe's agricultural policy, the conscious introduction of innovations, is dealt with in Chapter 12.)
20. Rotberg & Clague (1971), p. 50.
21. Lepkowski (1968:1), pp. 89-93.
22. Cf., however, Mackenzie (1830:2), pp. 298-302. The figures presented there give an impression which runs contrary to the conclusions presented here. The Mackenzie figures are likely to contain a significant bias, however, since they were provided by adversaries to Christophe (Lepkowski (1968:1), p. 107).
23. Leyburn (1966), p. 51.
24. Ibid., p. 46. Similar opinions can be found in Franklin (1828), pp. 327-8; Brown (1837:2), pp. 240-41; Leyburn (1966), p. 64; Griggs & Prator (1968), pp. 46-7; Lepkowski (1968:1), p. 106; Cole (1970), p. 210; Rotberg & Clague (1971), pp. 58-62.
25. Moral (1961), p. 21.
26. Leyburn (1966), p. 56.
27. Lepkowski (1968:1), p. 112. Cf. Moral (1961), p. 31.
28. Moral (1961), p. 31.
29. Lepkowski (1968:1), pp. 120-21.
30. Leyburn (1966), p. 75.
31. Ibid., p. 76.
32. Ibid., pp. 51-87; Rotberg & Clague (1971), pp. 60-78.
33. Leyburn (1966), p. 94.
34. See Chapter 7 for details.
35. Leyburn (1966), p. 95. Other sources maintain that only 800 applications were made altogether (Ibid., note, p. 95).
36. Ibid., p. 96. Cf. however below, concerning Vincent.
37. The figures are uncertain. Millspaugh (1931), p. 153 gives a figure of seven companies and less than 20,000 hectares up to 1930.
38. Millspaugh (1931), p. 152.
39. Schmidt (1971), pp. 175-6.
40. Ibid., p. 171.
41. For details, see Chapter 7.

42. Cf. Chapter 2.
43. Lacerte (1975), p. 81. Cf. Leyburn (1966), p. 55.
44. Leyburn (1966), pp. 54-5.
45. Saint-Louis (1960), p. 92-3. Cf. Leyburn (1966), note, p. 53. See also Nicholls (1974), pp. 7-8.
46. Leyburn (1966), note, p. 53.
47. Lacerte (1975), p. 79.
48. Ibid., p. 81.
49. Leyburn (1966), pp. 53-4.
50. Cf. Rotberg & Clague (1971), pp. 60-61 and Leyburn (1966), pp. 59-60.
51. Lacerte (1975), p. 81.
52. Moral (1961), p. 50.
53. Leyburn (1966), p. 95.
54. Moral (1961), p. 50.
55. Lepkowski (1968:1), pp. 81-2, 91; Rotberg & Clague (1971), p. 47; Lacerte (1975), pp. 79-80.
56. Lacerte (1975), p. 79.
57. For a detailed account of Haitian-American diplomatic relations until the recognition of Haiti by the US in 1862 see Logan (1941), pp. 112-314 ('a record for non-recognition by any nation except a former colonial power' (Logan (1968), p. 101)).
58. Cf. Logan (1968), p. 100.
59. Leyburn (1966), pp. 258-9.
60. See Clague (1970), p. 19.
61. See Chapter 7 for details.
62. Haiti's foreign debt is discussed in Chapter 8.
63. Lacerte (1975), pp. 78-9; Rotberg & Clague (1971), p. 48.
64. Leyburn (1966), pp. 33-4.
65. Huberman & Sweezy (1969), p. 184. Cf. also Timoshenko and Swerling (1957), Chapter 6.
66. Cf. the discussion of the Heckscher-Ohlin theorem in e.g. Södersten (1970), Chapter 4.
67. Rotberg & Clague (1971), p. 38; Guerra y Sánchez (1964), pp. 52-3.
68. For an account of this trade see Logan (1941), Chapter 1 and Turnier (1955), Chapter 1.
69. See Logan (1941), Chapters 4 and 5.
70. Cf. ibid., pp. 176-83.
71. Cf. Moral (1961), note, p. 27.
72. See Chapter 7.
73. Clague (1970), pp. 20-21.
74. Leyburn (1966), note, p. 39.
75. Métraux *et al.* (1951), p. 23.
76. Ibid., p. 25.
77. Legal aspects of inheritance are discussed in Salgado (1967).
78. Bachman & Christensen (1967), p. 259.
79. Cf. Chapter 11, for details.
80. Guerra y Sánchez (1964), pp. 117-18.
81. Timoshenko & Swerling (1957), pp. 17-18.
82. See Thomas (1971), pp. 1563-4.
83. Millspaugh (1931), p. 153.
84. Schmidt (1971), p. 171.
85. Guerra y Sánchez (1964), p. 164.
86. Ibid.
87. Ibid., p. 167.

88. Timoshenko & Swerling (1957), p. 23.
89. Swerling (1949), p. 16.
90. Benoit (1954:2), p. 128.
91. Moore (1972), p. 147.
92. Rotberg & Clague (1971), note, p. 296.
93. OEA (1972), p. 296.
94. IBRD (1972), p. 9; IBRD (1974), p. 20.
95. Fatton (1975), p. 3.
96. Ibid., p. 11.
97. Ibid., p. 14.
98. Ibid., p. 45.
99. OEA (1972), p. 622.
100. JWK (1976:3), pp. 10-12.
101. Hubert (1950), pp. 25-6. Cf. also Millspaugh (1931) and Schmidt (1971), p. 179 for the situation during the occupation.
102. Schmidt (1971), p. 179.
103. Millspaugh (1931), pp. 157-8.
104. Cf. Chapter 7.

APPENDIX: The Choice of Capital

In his well-known book *Choice of Techniques* Amartya K. Sen presents a model which shows how farmers in less developed countries choose between different forms of capital inputs.[1] The point of departure for the Sen argument is the importance of land in agricultural production (as opposed to industrial production) and the low substitutability between land and labor in agriculture:

> The two serve very different purposes in agricultural production: land provides food and water for the plants (in addition to providing the necessary space for cultivation) and labour takes care of all the necessary movements that plants do not perform themselves. Some capital goods co-operate in these movements, thereby saving labour, while others raise the yield of land by supplying food and water, or by controlling floods, pests and other such free gifts of nature, or indeed, by improving the quality of the seed itself. Very few capital goods contribute substantially to both groups, though heavy machines for 'deep ploughing' might be an exception.[2]

Thus, Sen makes a distinction between what he calls 'laboresque' and 'landesque' capital. The former (exemplified by tractors) replaces labor (without raising yield per acre) and the latter (exemplified by fertilizer) replaces land (without replacing labor). In his model Sen assumes that the division between the two types is watertight. Both types are assumed to depreciate totally in one year.

Now let us look at Figure A6.1. On the vertical axis we represent the level of agricultural output and the investment in laboresque capital, respectively, and on the horizontal axis we have total investment (i.e. laboresque plus landesque capital) and labor. Sen assumes that the requirements of labor plus laboresque capital are constant per unit of land (and do not vary with output).[3] This assumption makes it possible to trace out the curve II' given the amount of land in the economy.

The curve shows the possible combinations of labor and laboresque capital that are required to farm all the agricultural land. The amount of cultivated land is assumed constant.* The total investment that it is possible to make in one year is represented by OA.

---

* The assumption that the requirements of labor and laboresque capital depend only on the amount of land to be cultivated and not on output is not an altogether realistic one. Strictly speaking, it implies e.g. that if we move north of the II' curve

293

Figure A6.1

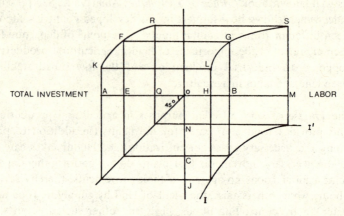

Source: Sen (1962), p. 92.

If the total labor supply is given by OB, full utilization of the available land area requires an investment in laboresque capital of OC, leaving AE of landesque capital, and a production volume of EF (measured as a function of the investment in landesque capital) or BG (measured as a function of the labor input). For a lower supply of labor (OH) the required investment in laboresque capital increases (to OJ) which (as the figure is drawn) leaves no room for any landesque capital. The production volume falls (to AK as a function of landesque capital,** or to HL as a function of labor). If we go to the extreme cases where the labor supply is large enough to depress the marginal productivity of labor to zero (OM) the required investment in laboresque capital

---

(by reducing the amount of laboresque capital) output would fall to zero (given the input of labor). Since the model is intended to focus upon the choice of capital, however, we are not interested in any points north of II' but only in the movement along the curve itself. To solve this, as Sen points out (p. 93), it is sufficient to assume that the marginal reduction in output resulting from a *ceteris paribus* reduction of one unit of laboresque capital exceeds the marginal increase in output when the amount of landesque capital is increased by an equivalent amount. In that case no points north of II' will ever be considered.
** Production in point K must be positive, since even though landesque capital is altogether lacking, still there is land.

Appendix

falls (to ON) and the landesque capital increases (to AQ), and production reaches a peak (at QR or MS).

Thus, we find that in a situation where labor is plentiful, as it is in Haiti, the output maximizing strategy in the Sen model is to use the relatively larger share of investment for landesque capital and relatively less for laboresque capital. Consequently, we would expect to find the use of irrigation, fertilizers, insecticides and pesticides, improved seed varieties, etc. to be commonly adopted in Haiti. But this is not the case. Why? Is the model wrong? Are its assumptions so heroic as to render it worthless?

The answer is that they probably are not. Instead there is another, logical solution of the paradox which is fully compatible both with the model and with the facts of the Haitian case, and this solution we find if we look at point N in Figure A6.1. ON may be interpreted as the minimum requirement of laboresque capital, or as Sen puts it: 'Strictly speaking ON is not *labouresque* capital at all, as it is something that labour cannot replace.'[4] In all agriculture labor must make use of a few simple implements, like the hoe and/or the machete, to use the Haitian example. Lack of these instruments would simply mean that no production at all could take place. The land cannot be cultivated only with the use of bare hands.

With this interpretation the only possible explanation of the capital structure in the Haitian peasant sector must run in terms of poverty. The production outcome in the sector is too low to allow any savings that will result in capital formation more than on a very rudimentary scale. If total investment is limted to e.g. OQ in Figure A6.1 all of this will go to formation of laboresque capital and nothing at all to landesque capital. This excludes any other capital use than employment of a few all-purpose hand tools and results in an agricultural output that is far smaller than QR or MS in the figure.

Notes

1. Sen (1962), pp. 90-97.
2. Ibid., note, p. 91.
3. The realism of this assumption is discussed in ibid., note, p. 91.
4. Ibid., p. 93.

7 THE PASSIVE GOVERNMENT

The redistribution of government land which converted Haiti from a plantation economy to a peasant country was the outstanding exception to a pattern which was to crystallize during the nineteenth century. The dominant attitude of the Haitian governments towards the agricultural sector was to become one of non-intervention or, rather, passivity (except in matters of taxation). In the present chapter we will examine the historical evidence behind this contention, and begin an attempt (to be continued in Chapter 8) to trace the reasons behind the reluctance to initiate agricultural change.

The first part of the chapter provides the appropriate factual evidence. It shows that the period up to the American occupation in 1915 was characterized by an almost total lack of government action in the agricultural sector, that half-hearted attempts to initiate change were made during the occupation years, that neglect, lack of interest and at best, *ad hoc* measures took over after 1934, and finally, that this tradition of passivity has continued to dominate Haitian governments up to the present time.

To understand why the most important sector of the economy has received nothing but neglect from the authorities we subsequently go on to sketch four different trends in Haitian social and political history which together have acted as formidable obstacles to positive government intervention in agriculture: (1) the formation of the social class structure; (2) the lack of peasant interest in politics; (3) the lack of government and upper-class identification with the peasantry; (4) the development of the economic goals of the Haitian governments.

We will begin with a description of the characteristics which traditionally have separated elite and peasants in Haiti. This description is followed by an analysis of how these differences developed out of the colonial social structure leaving, in the early 1840s, a fairly rigid class structure. The analysis then goes on to discuss the consequences of the land reforms by Pétion and Boyer, where the peasants lost all interest in national politics, and the ex-landowners simultaneously turned their back on agriculture to engage wholeheartedly in politics instead.

The latter half of the chapter traces the consequences of the separation of the governing classes from the masses. We demonstrate how government came to serve the single purpose of providing those in power with a substitute for the incomes and wealth that were lost with the landed estates and how politics in consequence was made synonymous with a race for the contents of the treasury, devoid of all meaningful purpose. The development and maintenance of a spoils system where graft and corruption became the main ingredients, the attempts made by the occupation forces to end this pattern, the reversal to the old pattern after the occupation and the new heights of corruption in the 1950s and 1960s are discussed in order to provide insight into the structure of objectives of the groups that held power in the field of economic affairs, and the lack of peasant participation in politics which is followed up to the present period. The chapter ends with an analysis of two other determinants of peasant passivity as far as politics is concerned: the form of rural government and the peasant *Weltanschauung*.

Government Neglect of Agriculture

The Nineteenth Century

Pétion's land reform created a class of free, independent peasants in Haiti. Nobody had to work for the benefit of others anymore, but whatever the soil produced accrued to the tillers themselves. In terms of productivity the land reform represented a step backwards, however. When the plantations disappeared, the GNP began to fall in Pétion's republic.

Boyer's attempt at recreating the plantation system in 1826 was clearly a reaction to the deteriorating conditions. When Boyer took over the northern part of the country from Christophe in 1820 he inherited a full treasury, while from Pétion two years earlier he had received nothing. In 1823, Boyer's treasury was empty, partly as a result of a corrupt administration, but even more due to declining agricultural productivity. The 1826 *Code Rural* proved to be a failure. It was simply ignored by the peasants, and there was nothing the administration could do to change this. A new agricultural policy was badly needed. Mere redistribution of land to the cultivators did not generate economic development but stagnation and retrogression, at least in terms of per capita production and incomes. New impulses were required to get agriculture going. Nevertheless, after the failure of the 1826 legislation, Boyer chose pure *laissez-faire* instead of active intervention.

Boyer's reluctance to intervene in agriculture set a precedent for virtually all his successors. Before 1826, the Haitian peasants did not receive any financial or technical assistance whatsoever from the government (other than continued land redistribution), and thereafter government undertakings with respect to agriculture were at best half-hearted. The main achievements are quickly accounted for. In 1862, President Geffrard attempted to take advantage of the strong upward trend in cotton prices caused by the US Civil War and the blockade of the southern US ports by northern naval forces, and started to make plans for an extension of cotton cultivation in Haiti, including a program of leasing certain machinery to cotton cultivators, but the practical impact of the program turned out to be negligible.[1] The next measure to encourage agriculture came in 1883 when President Salomon made an unsuccessful attempt to revitalize cultivation of certain export crops by means of giving land grants to those peasants who agreed to grow the prescribed crops.[2] In the 1890s, Presidents Hyppolite and Simon Sam finally undertook some repair work and new construction of roads and railroads linking various parts of the country which, if it had continued, might have proved beneficial to agriculture.[3]

Apart from these unsystematic efforts, agriculture received practically no assistance at all from 1843 to the beginning of the American occupation in 1915. Its share of the 1885-86 budget was a mere 6 percent,[4] a figure which by the turn of the century had been reduced to 3 percent,[5] most of which presumably went to salaries for the employees of the Department of Agriculture, which was diverted for other purposes, or which was not paid out at all. The main interest shown by the nineteenth-century governments in agriculture was as a source of taxes.[6] The peasants were left to solve their own problems.

The Occupation: First Efforts at Economic Development

During its first seven years, from 1915 to 1922, the American occupation of Haiti had only a negligible impact on agriculture. The period was one of pacification and adjustment, not one of constructive efforts. The emphasis lay on the military aspects of administration while the civilian side was lagging behind. The main achievement was the establishment of peace and order, so sadly lacking before 1915. Some road construction and repair was carried out, but the trails on which a majority of the agricultural population depended for communication with market-places were left almost untouched. Repair of irrigation works, which had been deteriorating after the French had left the island was begun.

In 1922, the occupation entered a more constructive phase which lasted until the 1929 student strikes and subsequent riots that led to the American withdrawal in 1934. Within the narrow confines drawn by the priority given to debt management (to be dealt with in Chapter 8) the Americans began a development program which, however limited, was the most ambitious that Haiti had ever experienced. 'It was fully realized that Haiti's future prosperity depends upon the development of her soil,' wrote the American High Commissioner in his yearly report for 1924. 'It therefore appeared essential that a well-drawn plan of agricultural development, comprising not only research and experiment but also theoretical and practical instruction in agriculture, be drafted. Vocational and manual training were also included in the plan.'[7]

The most important step towards agricultural development was taken with the creation of the *Service Technique* of the Department of Agriculture which launched a program of vocationally-oriented agricultural education at all levels from the primary to the tertiary including a normal agricultural school.[8] Extension agents and demonstration farms were used to establish direct contacts with the peasants in order to change their archaic methods.[9] A number of measures of indirect benefit to agriculture were also undertaken. The occupation created a strong public works department which put the sadly neglected road network (including trails and paths) into working order. Bridges were built across the rivers, etc.[10] Strong efforts were made to remedy the dismal health situation. The entire public health service was reorganized by the occupation forces. In particular, a number of rural clinics were opened, and a campaign against yaws, one of the most prevalent and crippling diseases of Haiti, was begun.[11]

The support given to agriculture by the Americans was mainly indirect. If we look at the actual expenditures of the Department of Agriculture the picture presented in Table 7.1 emerges. Agriculture (including rural education) received only small (albeit increasing) sums each year, on the average less than 7 percent for the years 1922/23-1929/30. The direct initiative was left to private US investment. Introduction of modern methods in agriculture was viewed as dependent on the introduction of large-scale plantation agriculture, and High Commissioner Russell strongly advocated the substitution of plantations for the peasant minifundia. The private investment failed to materialize, however, and only two large-scale American-owned plantations survived the occupation.

Nevertheless, to a certain extent the Haitian peasants felt the impact

Table 7.1: Expenditures of the Department of Agriculture 1922/23-1929/30

Fiscal year	Expenditures of the Department of Agriculture (million gourdes)	Agricultural expenditures in percent of total government expenditures
1922-23	0.01	–
1923-24	0.4	1
1924-25	2.0	5
1925-26	3.0	7
1926-27	3.6	8
1927-28	3.6	8
1928-29	4.6	10
1929-30	4.5	11

Source: Service Technique (1930), p. 16.

of the establishment of American-owned plantations in the country — especially in northern Haiti. While the exact extent of land concessions going to American companies during the occupation period is uncertain, an important part of these lands probably came from government lands which for several decades had been cultivated by peasants with or without the explicit consent of the authorities. The *Union Nationaliste* in 1930 denounced the expulsion of 'thousands of peasants' from their lands faced with the option of migrating or becoming landless serfs,[12] because of the land concession policy directed towards the substitution of plantations for peasant minifundia,[13] as it appears, with concomitant losses in land productivity in some parts. Harold A. Wood in his investigation of land use in the *Département du Nord* concludes:

> It is important to note. . .that plantations have brought local economic advantages only where sisal has been introduced in areas which are too dry to produce significant quantities of food. In more humid parts of the Département plantations have brought no overall benefits, at least from the point of view of the worker on the land. Plantation hands are no more prosperous than peasant farmers, and a square mile of plantations supports fewer people than a square mile of compatible productivity used for peasant farms. Of the two systems of land tenure, peasant agriculture is the stronger competitor for the land. . .[14]

In spite of the fact that management of the public debt absorbed a disproportionate share of the Haitian budget, the American occupation constituted the first (limited) effort towards economic development that the country had seen since the days of the early rulers. The immediate impact was not large. The annual report of the High Commissioner for 1929, the last constructive year of the occupation, stressed that in practically all fields the task was unfinished and that completion would require a time period which was assumed to lie way beyond the expiration of the occupation treaty in 1936. The High Commissioner believed that it would take at least twenty years before any 'pronounced success' could be achieved in agriculture. Public health, however immediately successful, was only in its initial stage. Repair and improvement of trails had been systematically carried out for only one year. The entire program begun by the occupation forces had to be conceived of as long-term in nature.[15]

The occupation was to show few lasting achievements. The infrastructural works undertaken by the Americans soon decayed for lack of maintenance.[16] The anti-yaws campaign died out and the rural clinics were slowly left to their own fate.[17] The vocationally-oriented school system built up by the Service Technique was discontinued or continued in theory only.[18] The government of Sténio Vincent refused to co-operate with the suggested American policy of gradual haitianization of the administration, and rapid withdrawal then became the most important objective of the American State Department with respect to Haiti. In this process the remainder of the development program was sacrificed.

Twenty Years of Ad Hockery

The American development efforts were followed by twenty years of what may be labeled *ad hoc* responses to the most pronounced economic and agricultural problems and opportunities on the part of the Haitian governments. While the complete lethargy which characterized the pre-occupation period had disappeared, there were still no pronounced long-term efforts of a more systematic kind to promote agricultural development. The problems were tackled when they arose and the opportunities were grasped when they presented themselves.

The agricultural policy of the Vincent government was intimately linked to finding solutions to immediate problems. Throughout the 1930s, the main agricultural concern of the government was how to avoid the unfortunate consequences of the Depression. The (nominal) value of Haitian exports between 1929 and 1934 was only one-half of that between 1924 and 1929,[19] and the value of coffee exports, which in 1923-29 accounted for almost 80 percent of the total export value,[20] had declined until in 1934-35 its value was only 20 percent of what it had been seven years before.[21] In 1936 another setback caused by the Depression occurred. France decided not to renew the commercial treaty existing between the two countries which had given Haiti considerable tariff favors but to apply its 'general' tariff rates to imports from Haiti instead. One year later, Brazil abandoned its price control scheme and began exporting large quantities of coffee at low prices. The value of Haitian coffee exports fell again, this time — in 1939-40 — to one-ninth of the 1928-29 figure.[22] Low prices of cotton, sisal, sugar and cocoa added to the problem throughout the decade.

Most of the measures undertaken by the Vincent government in the agricultural sector were directly designed to cope with the declining value of exports. The main strategy was to improve the quality of the Haitian coffee in order to make it more competitive in the world market and to diversify exports to reduce the dependence on one single crop. To this end the Vincent government began promoting the extension of a washing process by means of legislation and propaganda among the peasants.[23] The attempts to substitute high-yielding cotton varieties begun by the Service Technique in 1927 were continued until in 1935, the Mexican boll-weevil struck with terrible force, and during the latter half of the 1930s efforts were made to persuade the peasants to adopt annual varieties of cotton (to solve the boll-weevil problem).[24] In 1934 a law regarding so-called rural family property (*bien rural de famille*) was promulgated, according to which up to 5 hectares of land could be obtained by peasants who agreed to plant 50 percent of such acreage with export crops. The most successful venture of the Vincent government was the signing of the monopoly contract with the Standard Fruit Company in 1935 which launched a veritable banana boom in the country.[25]

Another widely-publicized measure — of an even more pronounced *ad hoc* character — to promote agricultural production was the creation of the 'agricultural colonies' in 1938. In 1937, on Trujillo's orders, up to 25,000 Haitian sugar-cane cutters were butchered to death in the Dominican Republic.[26] Many thousands of other Haitians returned to their country. The issue turned into an international scandal, and the *Benefactor* eventually agreed to pay an indemnity of US $750,000. With the first instalment, $250,000, five agricultural colonies were created in different regions of Haiti and land (totalling 4,400 hectares) was distributed to a total of 1,425 families.[27] The entire project turned out to be a failure, however. Once the colonies with their facilities had been established, nobody knew what to do next. No long-term plan for their functioning had been made. Nobody cared about continuity.[28]

In financial terms the support lent to agriculture by the Vincent government was unimpressive. Agriculture continued in the doldrums, and as shown in Table 7.2, its relative importance in the government expenditures fell in relation to the latter half of the 1920s.

Table 7.2: Expenditures of the Department of Agriculture 1930/31-1940/41

Fiscal year	Expenditures of the Department of Agriculture (million gourdes)	Agricultural expenditures in percent of total government expenditures
1930-31	1.9	5
1931-32	1.5	5
1932-33	1.5	5
1933-34	1.7	5
1934-35	1.7	4
1935-36	2.0	5
1936-37	2.1	6
1937-38	1.9	7
1938-39	1.8	6
1939-40	1.8	6
1940-41	1.4	5

Sources: Agricultural expenditures: 1930/31-1932/33: Benoit (1954:2), p. 86; 1933/34-1940/41: Wood (1955), p. 165. Total government expenditures: Benoit (1954:2), p. 76.

Agriculture continued to be relatively unimportant in the eyes of the Lescot government. Table 7.3 shows the percentage of government expenditures going to the Department of Agriculture during the war years. No significant changes took place in comparison with the 1930s. The Lescot government also followed that of Vincent in that it did not hold any comprehensive view of economic and agricultural development. Attention was paid only to the most immediate problems and outright opportunism characterized Lescot's actions in the agricultural sector.

The coffee export market had continued in a state of uncertainty,

Table 7.3: Expenditures of the Department of Agriculture 1941/42-1945/46

Fiscal year	Expenditures of the Department of Agriculture (million gourdes)	Agricultural expenditures in percent of total government expenditures
1941-42	2.0	7
1942-43	1.9	7
1943-44	2.4	6
1944-45	2.4	6
1945-46	2.0	5

Sources: Agricultural expenditures: Wood (1955), p. 165. Total expenditures: Benoit (1954:2), p. 76.

as the Second World War drew closer, and the actual outbreak of the war put new stress on the Haitian coffee producers. A new commercial treaty guaranteeing certain sales in the French market had been signed in 1938, but before this had any substantial effect on the Haitian coffee industry the Germans invaded France, and the market was lost again. Before the end of 1940, so was the rest of the Western European market. Haiti was not the only coffee producing country to suffer from the war. Other Latin American countries began dumping on the US market. Finally, a quota agreement was reached between the Latin American coffee producers and the United States in November 1940. This solved the worst problems, but as it became increasingly clear that the European markets would continue to be shut off during the war, the efforts of upgrading the quality of Haitian coffee by washing and other means was continued to secure a firm foothold in the US market, and a *Code du Café* regulating the preparation, transportation, marketing, etc. of coffee was issued in 1942.[29]

The best known agricultural project sponsored by the Lescot government developed into a major scandal. When the Japanese occupation of southeast Asia cut the United States off from the latter's traditional rubber supply in 1941, a Haitian-American joint venture, SHADA, began cultivation of an indigenous vine rubber — the *cryptostegia* — financed by a $5 million Export-Import Bank loan with a view to eventually substituting for some of the lost supply in the American market. 'The program...looked like madness to those who knew agricultural conditions in Haiti,' writes O. Ernest Moore,[30] and the balance left by SHADA was entirely negative. Lescot had avidly welcomed the American requests for creation of the society. The company had obtained jurisdiction over more than 100,000 hectares from which a large number of peasants had been evicted, their houses, fields and fruit trees being destroyed in the process. The productive results were zero. In spite of heavy spending on the project ($6.7 million by 1945), no rubber was ever exported. The Haitian government had guaranteed the repayment of the Export-Import Bank loan by 1956, but in view of the negligible results of the project this term had to be prolonged until 1961 and actual payment continued even beyond this date.[31]

The government of Dumarsais Estimé possessed more of a popular orientation than any other Haitian government before it. Estimé began a program of social and legislative reforms. Increasing amounts were spent on agriculture. (As Table 7.4 reveals, calculated in percent of total government expenditures agricultural expenditures fell in comparison with the Lescot administration, but this is mainly due to the fact that in 1946 rural education was transferred from the Department of Agriculture to the Department of National Education.)[32]

Table 7.4: Expenditures of the Department of Agriculture 1946/47-1949/50

Fiscal year	Expenditures of the Department of Agriculture (million gourdes)	Agricultural expenditures in percent of total government expenditures
1946-47	2.6	4
1947-48	4.3	5
1948-49	3.6	4
1949-50	3.7	3

Sources: Agricultural expenditures: Wood (1955), p. 165; Total expenditures: Benoit (1954:2), p. 76.

Two potentially important projects in the agricultural sector were inaugurated by Estimé. In 1947, UNESCO was invited to undertake — in co-operation with the Haitian government — a pilot project of rural education and development in the Marbial valley, and two years later, Estimé obtained a $5 million loan from the Export-Import Bank to irrigate 40,000 hectares in the Artibonite valley. For reasons dealt with elsewhere in the present work, both projects failed under the Magloire administration.[33] Still, the Estimé government emphasized urban sector activities and continued the *ad hoc* tradition in agricultural policy. With one possible exception, the encouragement of the co-operative movement in rural areas,[34] it is hard to trace any ideologically or otherwise founded strategy of economic development translated into practical agricultural policy. The UNESCO project was an opportunity coming from outside. The irrigation project was located in Estimé's home area, while other regions received much less attention. A third venture, full of opportunities, backfired. The monopoly of the banana trade given by President Vincent to the Standard Fruit and Steamship Company was broken up by Estimé in 1945 and 1947 with the purpose of awarding lucrative regional monopoly concessions to the president's political followers instead, a measure which ended by totally destroying Haitian banana exports.[35]

Planning without Content

Under Magloire the scope of government activities designed to further economic development increased to an extent hitherto unheard of in Haiti. The president was a pragmatic and energetic modernizer who with the aid of financial and technical assistance from the United States and the United Nations with its specialized agencies undertook to carry out an ambitiously conceived development program.

Comparatively little of the newly awakened enthusiasm for economic development touched the agricultural sector, however. In his inaugural address Magloire promised to give first priority to irrigation projects, soil conservation measures, and financial aid to co-operatives and individual peasant farmers.[36] The five-year plan of 1951/52-55/56 envisaged expenditures of 42.5 million gourdes in the agricultural sector.[37] In practice, the policy pursued was very different. Most of the development programs of the Magloire government affected peasant welfare and production only marginally. (A notable exception was the spectacular success experienced in the public health field in eradicating yaws by pencillin injections.)[38] The support for the co-operative movement and the efforts to extend agricultural credit via the creation in 1951 of the *Institut Haïtien de Crédit Agricole et Industriel* (IHCAI) were hardly successful,[39] and the overall amount spent on agriculture remained low. Table 7.5 shows the regular budget expenditures by the Department of Agriculture (i.e. excluding the projects covered by the five-year plan) during the Magloire presidency.* Only between 2 and 3 percent of the total budget was allocated to agriculture in this form.

---

* Expenditures for rural education continued to be assigned to the Department of National Education.

Table 7.5: Regular Budgetary Expenditure of the Department of Agriculture 1950/51-1956/57

Fiscal year	Expenditures of the Department of Agriculture (million gourdes)	Regular agricultural expenditure in percent of total budgetary expenditures
1950-51	4.0	3
1951-52	3.5	2
1952-53	3.0	2
1953-54	3.9	2
1954-55	3.6	2
1955-56	3.0	2
1956-57	3.1	2

Source: Moral (1959), pp. 147-8.

However, the expenditure of the five-year plan must also be taken into account. Far from reaching the planned 42.5 million gourdes (21 percent of the total plan expenditures) during the first four years of execution, the latter amounted to a mere 4 percent of a total expenditure of 170 million gourdes.[40] Adding these figures to the regular budget expenditure increases agricultural expenditures to an average of 3 percent of total budgetary expenditure.

The government had to admit that the five-year plan was not successful, at least not in the agricultural sector.[41] No public account for the final cost of the plan was made,[42] but it is perfectly clear that actual realizations fell very much short of planned achievements. Basically, only some irrigation and drainage works were executed. Spending was held back by unfortunate outside circumstances. The sisal price (and later also the coffee price) declined. The 1953 coffee harvest was smaller than expected and the following year, around 40 percent of the coffee crop and 50 percent of the cocoa crop were destroyed by hurricane Hazel.[43] It is also probable that some of the funds were squandered by corrupt government officials.[44] Corruption also destroyed the ill-conceived Artibonite valley scheme. Only the artificial lake and the dam at Péligre were constructed and 10 irrigation channels were dug, which sufficed to irrigate only one-half of the calculated area — 20,000 hectares — at a cost of 200 million gourdes.[45]

François Duvalier assumed power with explicit promises to improve the lot of the peasant — 'the great unacknowledged of the Haitian community.'[46] On the first anniversary of his inauguration he stated that

It is my responsibility to encourage and promote the economy by putting the country back to work on a practical and productive basis; to provide our hungry with food, to educate our peasants, to confer positive health upon them; to build the roads they so sorely need, and, lastly, to ensure for them an acceptable standard of living to which they are entitled. My responsibility is to rebuild, upon the shattered ruins, a truly beautiful and prosperous country.[47]

The prosperity was to be achieved through planned development. A two-year development plan for 1958-59 and 1959-60 was presented, totaling no less than 264.5 million gourdes emphasizing agricultural and social development (especially in the Artibonite valley), road improvement and construction of sugar mills. The plan 'remained a study document,'[48] however, and was never implemented.

Many of Duvalier's agricultural projects during his first five years as a president rested heavily on foreign aid. The Export-Import Bank continued to finance the Artibonite valley project in spite of the gross mismanagement of funds which had taken place during the previous regime. The rural and industrial credit institute IHCAI was converted to the Institut de Développement Agricole et Industriel (IDAI) with the aid of another Export-Import Bank loan in 1961. The International Cooperation Administration (ICA) of the United States financed irrigation projects in the northern and southern parts of the country, and in addition in 1959 started the *Opération Poté-Colé*, which was a joint Haitian-American program for integrated development in the *Département du Nord*. The goal was to increase production through improved practices by agricultural extension, demonstration farms, co-operatives, rural credit, education, public health service, road improvement, irrigation, drainage, etc. Poté-Colé was the most ambitious and coherent program hitherto launched in the agricultural sector and touched no less than 500,000 inhabitants.[49]

However, Duvalier soon showed that he had no real interest in improving the standard of living of the peasant masses. He shared the unwillingness of most of his predecessors to transform rural Haiti. The political climate rapidly deteriorated, and in 1962 the Kennedy administration began to reduce the size of its undertakings in the country. By that time it was perfectly clear that most of the American aid given to Duvalier had been wasted:

Agency for International Development inspectors had long been worried about the return on funds granted and lent to Haiti; by

1962 it was realized that the $18.5 million which had been spent in Haiti since Duvalier's accession had largely found its way into the hands of the regime. Of $3.4 million supplied for roads, the only visible result was a repaved main boulevard in downtown Port-au-Prince. There had been corruption on a grand scale, the government of Haiti had almost always defaulted on its obligations to pay its small share of projects, and Haiti refused haughtily to allow the United States to oversee the payment, employment, and discharging of all Haitians associated with American-aided projects. . . After the suspension was made permanent in late 1963 (a situation theoretically in effect as late as 1969) only the antimalaria program, surplus food distribution and small grants to Haiti made through international organizations, remained.[50]

The suspension of the American aid dealt a severe blow to such projects as Poté-Colé and the Artibonite valley scheme. The former was virtually killed,[51] and the latter slowly began to decay. In the Artibonite only the main canals had been completed, and when they began to silt up for lack of maintenance, flood water began inundating the alluvial plains for long periods creating an acute problem of waterlogging and salinization, and the production of rice started to decline after the initial upsurge.[52] In this situation, the *Conseil National de Développement et de Planification* (CONADEP) was created and in 1963 produced a two-year plan, *Le Démarrage* (The Take-Off) — envisaging a total investment of 490 million gourdes, 87.4 million of which fell within the agricultural sector.[53] The execution of projects which did not fall within the plan was prohibited, but in spite of this no take-off took place. The CONADEP figure for actual investments in the agricultural sector in 1963-64 and 1964-65 was only 1.5 million gourdes.[54] Without American aid the plan figures bore little resemblance to actual economic conditions, and in 1965-66 even the funds of CONADEP itself were exhausted.[55]

When Duvalier in 1967 summarized the achievements of his first ten years in power he stated that since 1957, 40 million gourdes had been invested in the agricultural sector.[56] To this he could add an expenditure of 90.5 million from the operation budget, while total government expenditures during the period (excluding those of the autonomous agencies)[57] amounted to 1,761.8 million.[58] Agriculture (including rural education) had received only 8 percent of the expenditure publicly accounted for (i.e. excluding those going to the *tonton macoutes*, etc.).

At the same time Haitian agriculture was hit by a series of natural disasters. Hurricanes Flora (1963), Cleo (1964) and Inez (1966) plus the drought of 1966-69 and the floods of 1963 and 1968 all called for emergency measures, which, however, due to the almost total neglect of the Duvalier government had to be supplied from abroad.[59] The yearly report of the CIAP in 1968 rightly stated that no government policy conducive to the necessary changes in the agricultural sector could be perceived but that the government instead presented an attitude of parasitism towards the peasants.[60] No agricultural investments were envisaged for the fiscal year 1967-68.[61]

However, a few improvements soon took place. In 1967, CONADEP was reorganized and proceeded to prepare three one-year development plans for 1968/69-1970/71.[62] Two years later US Governor Nelson A Rockefeller visited Haiti on his Latin American fact-finding tour and recommended that US aid to Haiti be resumed. This had immediate effects on the inflow of foreign capital to the country. The development plans also relied very heavily on foreign assistance: 41 and 42 percent during the first two years and no less than 57 percent during 1970-71 was assumed to be forthcoming from foreign sources.[63]

Table 7.6 shows the planned and realized expenditure of the three development plans in the agricultural sector. During the last three years of Papa Doc's administration, agriculture received increasing attention among the planners. The objectives were mainly to increase and diversify exports, to accelerate rural education, to increase the productivity of the sector and to reduce the dependence on imported cotton as an input to the textile industry. Realizations fell short of plan figures, however, especially in 1970-71, and seen in a wider perspective, the share of government expenditures continued to remain low in the late 1960s. Only 7 percent approximately of total government expenditure (including the expenditures of the autonomous agencies) went to agriculture in 1968-69 and 1969-70).[64]

After the death of Duvalier *père*, the level of aspirations of development planning in Haiti has increased. A five-year development plan for 1971/72-1975/76 was prepared by CONADEP and the Department of Agriculture.[65] The total investment volume of this plan was 729.6 million gourdes, 52 percent of which was calculated to be financed by foreign sources, and the share of agriculture was 196.2 million gourdes or 27 percent.[66] For the agricultural sector the plan envisaged increased food production, increased output of export goods, increased production of raw materials for the industrial sector, strengthened the agricultural infrastructure (especially irrigation), and planned a rational

Table 7.6: Planned and Realized Expenditure in the Agricultural Sector Development Plans (1968/69-1970/71) (million gourdes)

Fiscal year	Agricultural expenditure			Total plan expenditure			Agricultural expenditure in percent of total expenditure	
	a planned	b realized	b in % of a	c planned	d realized	d in % of c	planned	realized
1968-69	8.7	8.4	97	72.7	67.1	92	12	13
1969-70	10.2	8.4	92	62.2	61.7	99	16	15
1970-71	21.5	9.9	46	103.8	74.0	71	21	13

Sources: Planned expenditure: 1968-69: CONADEP (1968-69), table following p.50; 1969-70: P & D, No. 3, 1969, p. 21; 1970-71: CONADEP (1970-71), tables following p. 136. Realized expenditure: BID (1974), p. 160.

exploitation of forest resources to put an end to erosion.[67] A 'substantial take-off' was predicted for the agricultural sector between 1971 and 1976.[68]

However, the expected take-off never occurred. Table 7.7 shows that during the first three years of implementation of the plan, realized investments fell short of the plan figures — during the first two years with more than two-thirds, while during the third year* it was possible to reach 85 percent of the (substantially lower) target. The execution of the plan had run into 'serious obstacles'.[69] During the first two years covered by the plan, only 6 percent of total government expenditure went to the agricultural sector.[70] The reasons for the failure of the plan to reach its goals have not yet been analyzed in detail, but it is at least possible to point to one important factor: the failure to attract funds from the international lending organizations. More than one-half of total planned investment was to be financed by international donors. There were good prospects that this would be achieved. The death of Papa Doc had restored much of the confidence of the international organizations. The government of Duvalier *fils* was seen to contain many more 'technocrats' than that of his father and fewer 'politicians'. The technical competence of CONADEP was gradually strengthened, but obviously not enough. The planning commission also lacked effective guidance and communication with the ministries. The result was that the agricultural sector lacked projects that were sufficiently prepared to be candidates for international financing. The plan became a 'skeleton plan' without enough specific content. The international organizations have had to 'hunt' projects themselves. In 1974, for example, a joint FAO-IDB mission presented a report

---

* 1973-74 is the last year for which figures are available, at the time of writing.

identifying nine agricultural projects, none of which however, was sufficiently well prepared to be financed and implemented immediately within the five-year plan without further studies.[71]

Table 7.7: Planned and Realized Public Investments in the Agricultural Sector 1971/72-1973/74 (million gourdes)

Fiscal year	Planned investments in agriculture	Realized investments in agriculture	Realized investments in percent of planned investments
1971-72	32.5	8.1	25
1972-73	26.2	12.1	37
1973-74	15.9	13.6	85

Sources: Planned investments: 1971/72: P & D, no. 6, 1972, Table 22; 1972/73: BID (1974), p. 169; 1973/74: P & D, no. 7, 1973, p. 41; Realized investments: DARNDR (1976), pp. 16-17.

At a more fundamental level it appears that the official claims that agriculture should be a priority sector is an exaggeration. For example, only 8 percent of total operating expenses (*budget de fonctionnement*) during the period covered by the five-year plan were allocated to the Department of Agriculture.[72]

A second five-year plan, for 1976/77-80/81, was completed in 1976. The new plan aims at an annual growth rate in the agricultural sector of 2-5 percent[73] and emphasizes the relationship between economic and social aspects in the sector. The projects are to concentrate on small investments in rural areas to create employment opportunities, on improved educational and nutritional facilities, on the creation of regional growth centers which can absorb the agricultural labor surplus, and on the establishment of agro-based industries in rural districts.[74] The total public investment envisaged is 430 million gourdes. The presentation of the new five-year plan stresses that the plan is 'designed to be executed.'[75] One hundred and seventy years of governmental impasse makes the statement sound hollow. A successful implementation of the plan would imply a radical break with the entire history of the country. The probability that sufficient political willingness exists to ensure that this actually takes place is not unduly high.

Summing Up: Lack of Government Action

The overall picture emerging from a review of the efforts of the Haitian governments to promote agriculture is one of neglect, passivity and at best *ad hoc* solutions. Discounting the redistribution of government lands initiated by Pétion, the peasants received nothing in the way of support before 1862, and all governmental measures undertaken from that year until the beginning of the American occupation in 1915 had only indirect effects on the rural sector.

The occupation brought some ephemeral changes. Nothing really happened until 1922, but between that year and 1929 a development program with emphasis on vocational education, road construction and public health measures was launched. The direct initiative was left to private foreign investments, however, but these were few in the agricultural sector. Besides, the interests of the American-owned plantations clashed at times with that of the Haitian peasants.

Beginning in 1929, American policy was reversed. Passivity once more became the rule, and all initiatives were left to the Haitian government. Twenty years of opportunism and *ad hoc* measures followed. Less attention was now paid to agriculture than during the occupation. Only problems pressing for immediate solution provoked any response from the government. Not even the so-called social revolution of 1946 produced any changes for the rural masses. The emphasis was placed upon urban developments while both objectives and plans were lacking in the agricultural sector.

Planning was finally begun in the 1950s and has since continued to be a feature of the Haitian economy. However, its practical importance has been limited. The plans have lacked substantial content. Inadequate financing and insufficiently prepared projects have meant that the plans have borne very little relationship to actual economic conditions. Only a fraction of the programs envisaged has been executed.

An overwhelming majority of all Haitians have always been peasants, and virtually everything in the Haitian economy has always revolved around agriculture. Nevertheless, the agricultural sector has received on average less than 10 percent of total government expenditures in Haiti. To understand this apparent contradiction we will in the following sections analyze the reasons behind this lack of government interest in the rural economy. The first matter that we will investigate is the development of the Haitian class system and the characteristics of Haitian political life from the early nineteenth century to our own time, for without a proper comprehension of these two matters it is not possible to understand government action in the economic sector.

Economics and Politics

Contemporary theorizing on economic development has by and large avoided discussing the influence of political factors on the standard of living. As Gunnar Myrdal has persistently pointed out in his works, the tendency has been to isolate the 'economic' aspects of development or underdevelopment and forget that economic decisions are made within a political framework which exerts a heavy influence on how decisions are made and on the outcome of the decision-making process.[76] This neglect may introduce a serious bias into the research since it may contribute to focusing the attention on the wrong areas and also to incorrect policy conclusions which in turn may be acted upon with the concomitant risk of reinforcing the interaction of the factors which led the economy into underdevelopment.

The lack of political analysis in development economics has partly been due to a difficulty in arriving at quantitative observations:

> In shifting. . .to the differential aspects of political structure, we enter a field for which, with rare exceptions like the date of formal political independence, quantitative observations based on well-established data cannot be made easily. Unlike analysis of demographic movements in which we can count numbers and measure such clearly defined magnitudes as births, deaths, age, etc., and of economic processes in which the market provides an invaluable yardstick, the study of political processes and structure must rely upon the qualitative judgments of experts in the field; and only by means of such judgments can we group countries into different categories. Evaluation of such judgments is beyond the competence of an economist. . .Although the findings for such groups are based on a consensus of judgments and not on clearly testable quantitative data, their associations with economic performance and growth must still be viewed as significant, for they do suggest the interdependence between economic and political aspects of society that renders the process of economic growth so complex.[77]

Furthermore, when development economics began to emerge as a separate branch of economic science, it fell back upon the type of models which had yielded good results in explaining economic phenomena in the industrialized countries, models which abstracted from the influence of political factors.[78] Finally, interest groups at both ends of the political spectrum may have had important reasons for endorsing a wholesale 'economic' approach to development questions. Conservatives and traditional elites had vested interests in keeping things – including political power structures – unchanged, and radicals were attracted by the possibility of changing economic conditions by extensive planning, and planning, in turn, in capitalist and socialist countries alike, was based on the 'economic' type of models.[79] Consequently, the efforts of incorporating political structures into models of economic development have been few and have not always yielded satisfactory results. The study of political influence on development and underdevelopment remains underdeveloped, or perhaps undeveloped, itself.

The most ambitious studies of the influence of politics that have so far been undertaken are those of Irma Adelman and Cynthia Taft Morris, who, using a sample of 74 underdeveloped countries, have attempted to quantify some social and political variables in order to make generalizations about, for example, what non-economic aspects exert most influence on the per capita incomes at different levels of economic development.[80] Their results generally indicate only weak influences of differences in political conditions on the level of GNP per capita. In particular, politics appear not to act as a constraint to development at the lowest levels of GNP.

However, the results of the Adelman-Morris studies cannot be accepted at face value. Critics have pointed out, among other things, that some of the variables used in the studies are based on the same indicators, so that an element of spurious correlation is likely to bias the results, and that some of the measurement techniques used are not consistent with the further treatment that Adelman and Morris give the data. In addition, the limits between the variables are arbitrarily defined, the results are highly sensitive to these definitions, and there is frequently considerable confusion between hypothesis testing and formulation, especially in the sense that statistical association of variables often is interpreted as causality.[81]

Judged from the point of view of the present work, the Adelman-Morris studies present a special difficulty. Their approach is designed to obtain *general* results and yields much less insight into the situation of particular countries. One of the main conclusions that Myrdal drew from his study of the political conditions in South Asia was that 'in regard to political developments the differences were greater than in other respects.'[82] Myrdal stresses that general models offer little predictive value, basically because history is man-made, not a product of destiny. The political development of any country in a certain sense is unique which makes it difficult to bring generalized conclusions to bear on the particular case. There is no one-to-one correspondence between, say, the extent of centralization of political decision-making and the strategy of economic development pursued. Such relationships have to be established *de novo* in each case. The methodology that will be followed in the present study is that of an historical analysis of some dominant characteristics of Haitian political life and their determinants and of the implications for agricultural development. To do so we must, however, begin by looking at the social structure of the country.

Elite and Peasants

Throughout the history of Haiti, politics has been a matter of direct concern for very few people. The ruling parties have always been oligarchies or dictators without much popular support. The political arena has been dominated by elite or army factions while the masses have remained outside as mere spectators except under special circumstances. The peasants have been living their own lives without much chance of influencing the course of political events.

Ever since the early nineteenth century the Haitian population has been divided into two distinct social classes — the elite (and the near-elite)* and the peasants — with very little in common.[83] The two groups differ in most important respects: wealth, occupation, location, education, language, religion, family organization, culture and to a certain extent phenotype. The elite, who comprise less than 5 percent of the total population, traditionally constitute the wealthiest group in Haiti. Their incomes derive from government jobs, commerce, intellectual professions, etc., but never from manual work. The peasants, presently about 80 percent of the population, are poor and derive their incomes from manual labor on the land. The domicile of the elite is predominantly urban, with a high concentration to the capital itself, while the peasantry lives in rural areas.

Elite members have attended good Haitian schools and sometimes continued higher education abroad. The peasants are as a rule illiterate, never having been to school or having spent a few years only with irregular attendance in low-quality public schools.

In the cultural field the elite group has an outspoken Western orientation, drawing on the French tradition. In addition to the vernacular Creole language, French is completely mastered. The peasants only speak Creole and have developed a culture which derives mainly from the African heritage. This polarization of European and African elements is visible also in the religions practiced by the two groups. While the

---

* Here, the near-elite are defined as the social groups contesting the position of the elite and attempting to acquire elite status themselves. During the nineteenth century the near-elite group mainly consisted of army officers.

elite are Roman Catholics* the peasants generally practice voodoo. The elite marry formally. The peasants mainly form common law unions, some of which are polygynous (although much less so now than a few generations ago). Ethnically, finally, the elite at least until recently have been predominantly light-skinned while the peasants are black.

Haiti never possessed a numerous middle class. Until 1946, the country was mainly a two-class society without much of a buffer between the upper class (elite and near-elite) and the peasants. Whatever social aspirants had emerged after the occupation were still too few to constitute more than a disparate, embryonic group without well-defined characteristics. Following the 1946 revolution which brought Dumarsais Estimé into power and even more so under Duvalier, a black bourgeoisie has emerged: well educated, fluent in French, having non-manual, largely government occupations, and with incomes that allow a standard of living which is well above that of the masses. However, this group is still very small. Estimates from the late 1950s and the mid-1960s generally range as low as 2 to 4 percent[84]**

The extent of upward social mobility is low in Haiti. To arrive at elite status is a very slow process which may take generations. It is not enough to meet one or two of the criteria that define the elite group in order to be admitted into it. Wealth and education can typically be acquired but are of no significance unless accompanied by other charac-

---

* However, the importance of Catholicism among the upper classes should not be exaggerated:

> It is considered proper to attend Mass and otherwise to pay respect to religious forms; actually one loses nothing in prestige if he is not a practicing Christian. Society seems to exert no pressure in this matter. Only if a member of the upper class fears for the security of his social position, or knows that rumors are afloat of his addiction to Vodun, does he feel impelled to become assiduous in his open attentions to the Church (Leyburn (1966), p. 129).

It is sometimes, jokingly, stated that ninety percent of all Haitians are Catholics and that one hundred percent believe in voodoo. Francis Huxley states that 'Many of the elite (say some of the elite) have their own houmfors, tucked away in a corner of their country estates, with a resident houngan. That way they can attend to their supernatural affairs when everybody thinks they're merely holidaying; then they can resume their own life as good anti-superstitious Catholics.' (Huxley (1966), p. 43).

** It should be observed that the majority of the non-peasant population is not elite, the differences between urban groups are wide. However, in the present context it is the peasants on the one hand, and the governing classes on the other who are of interest, and the latter during most of Haiti's history have been elite groups or army groups aspiring to an élite position.

teristics. A rich peasant is a peasant with money. He is a *gros nèg* who is better off than his fellow peasants, but he does not belong to the elite. Life-style and manners, for example can only be superficially simulated by a rich peasant or by a member of the black middle class. Although presumably easier now than 30 years ago, it is still hard to marry into the elite. To a large extent (yet not strictly) the elite have maintained their superior social position by endogamous marriages.[85]

Accompanying the cleavage of the Haitian society into two separate classes has been a division of the nation into a small governing group and a large governed majority. The establishment of an elite (and near-elite) was simultaneously a crystallization of a ruling class. For reasons intimately connected with the historical development of Haiti and with the land reform in particular, the peasantry remained outside the political process and especially outside the government. Until the rise of the small black middle class after the Second World War Haiti was governed exclusively by the elite or by small black army factions challenging the elite, and even the recent political prominence of the black bourgeoisie means little from the point of view of the peasants. The peasantry continues to live without contact with the stream of political events. Neither the traditional elite nor the new black middle class identify themselves with the peasants. The ambitions of the middle class are rather directed towards reaching elite status, and both elite and army, for reasons that we will soon come to, had already lost their interest in agriculture by the mid-nineteenth century. This separation, in turn, has had very definite consequences for how the peasants have been ruled, for how they have viewed the authorities, for the economic philosophy of the government, and hence also for the view taken of the peasantry in the process of economic development.

To understand how the class structure of Haiti emerged, how the peasantry came to constitute a politically marginal group, how politics has been limited to an affair between the elite and the army, and recently of the small black bourgeoisie, we must sketch some of the more important historical events leading to this state of affairs. Without the historical background it is not possible to grasp the basis of the agricultural policy pursued.

Masters and Slaves

The embryo of the class division of contemporary Haiti was created during the colonial period. Saint-Domingue was a society which in most respects maintained a strict separation of the classes. At the outbreak of the French Revolution in 1789, the population consisted of four different groups: 40,000 whites, divided into *grands blancs* (high government officials, large plantation owners, wealthy merchants, etc.) and *petits blancs* (shopkeepers, artisans, smaller planters, etc.), 28,000 *affranchis* or *gens de couleur* (freed slaves or descendants of freed slaves), and 452,000 slaves.[86] Between whites, *affranchis* and slaves a rigid distinction was upheld.

The first and most important distinction was of course that between a free man and slave. From the very beginning the Creole slaves were inculcated into a role of absolute servility and submission to their white masters, and the great majority of the slaves chose submission rather than rebellion. There were slave uprisings in 1679, 1691, 1703 and 1758,[87] but these were deviations from normal behavior. Oppression, strenuous field work, low-quality food and physical violence took its physical and mental toll among the blacks. The general impression conveyed by the slaves to outside spectators appears to have been one of fatalism, indifference and docility. One contemporary observer found that on holidays, when the slaves were not working on their own plots or dancing, they were simply sitting for hours in front of their huts, giving few signs of life, and that many of them could not be induced to move at all unless they were whipped.[88] This was clearly a result of the conditions of slavery. Moreau de Saint-Méry reports that the Negroes who were brought in from the other side of the Atlantic rapidly lost their vigor and became 'indolent and lazy' in their new environment,[89] and Creole slaves who had spent their entire lives in slavery were known to be more docile than those imported from Africa.[90]

The indifference of the slave population was, however, probably more apparent than real. The slaves aspired for their personal liberty, and the main expression of these aspirations was *marronage* – the desertion of slaves from the plantations.[91] The *marronage* began at the end of the seventeenth century and continued throughout the rest of the colonial period.[92] It was not a phenomenon limited to a handful of runaway slaves. In 1720 alone more than 1,000 slaves escaped, and in 1751 at least 3,500 ran off to the mountains, where they hid in remote regions.[93] On the other hand, it was not a mass movement either, considering that there were more than 450,000 slaves in Saint-Domingue at the end of the colonial period.

Marronage was a solution for a minority. Those slaves who escaped and voluntarily subjected themselves to the hardships of runaway life were on the one hand among the most determined elements of the slave community, and on the other hand among those who considered the lot of slavery to be so unbearable that any substitute was better. Typically, the maroon was a field slave, not a household slave — who generally received much better treatment — that had either been mistreated or been given too little food.[94] The majority of the slaves suffered quietly under the whips of the overseers. 'The Negroes, as they are in the colony, generally show the courage of resignation rather than of bravery,' concludes Moreau.[95]

The slaves were not the only group to be discriminated against during the colonial period. The position of the *affranchis*, the free mulattoes, in some respects resembled that of the German Jews under Hitler. According to the 1685 *Code Noir* the *affranchis* were to be regarded as full French citizens but gradually the rights of the mulattoes were infringed upon during the eighteenth century, so that by 1790 few of the articles of the Code were anything but dead letters.[96] The mulattoes were forbidden to wear European dresses, to wear side arms (traditionally the distinction of a gentleman), to use the titles of 'monsieur' and 'madame', to purchase ammunition, to eat with whites, to sit with whites in the same sections in churches and theaters, to remain in France, to meet together, to play European games, to enter the goldsmith trade (which supposedly brought wealth), to practice medicine or pharmacy (for white fears of being poisoned), to hold public positions in teaching, religion or law (which were deemed as honorary), etc.[97]

In spite of all the discriminatory practices employed by the *colons* against the mulattoes the ways and customs of the planter society turned out to set the pattern for the behavior of the *affranchis* as well. The social position of the free mulattoes was not a well-defined one. While slaves and slave owners shared no common characteristics but were antagonistic classes, the mulattoes had certain things in common with both groups. With the slaves they shared the darker skin, and with the whites they shared the status of being free men. To define and improve their relative social position the *affranchis* strove to minimize the identification of the colored group with the black mass and to maximize the identification with the planters. The white colonial society became a blueprint to which the mulattoes could adhere.

The attempts of the mulattoes to approach the status of the whites had two important consequences for the later development of the class structure in Haiti. In the first place skin color became a line of division between slaves and *affranchis*:

The advantages of being white were so obvious that race prejudice against the Negroes permeated the minds of the Mulattoes who so bitterly resented the same thing from the whites. Black slaves and Mulattoes hated each other. Even while in words and, by their success in life, in many of their actions, Mulattoes demonstrated the falseness of the white claim to inherent superiority, yet the man of colour who was nearly white despised the man of colour who was only half-white, who in turn despised the man of colour who was only quarter white, and so on through all the shades.[98]

The second consequence was that the mulattoes became very intent upon improving their material and cultural position. Materially, they were quite successful and could frequently compete efficiently with the *grands blancs*. In 1791, the free mulattoes owned from one-fifth to one-fourth of all land and all slaves of the colony.[99] In the educational field they were successful as well. Many sent their children to France to be educated in the best schools available. Some chose to remain there, however, since many of the careers for which they had studied were closed to them in Saint-Domingue. For those never going abroad the situation with regard to education presumably left a lot to be desired since the entire colony is known to have possessed only two schools,[100] but on the whole, the educational standard achieved by the mulattoes was vastly superior to that of the slaves, who were given no opportunities at all of formal schooling and very few of informal learning.[101]

At the outbreak of the 1791 revolution, the stage was already set for the subsequent development of the Haitian class structure. Discounting the whites, who either left the country or were killed during the wars of liberation, there were two social classes in the country: the *affranchis* and the black slaves, and these two classes differed in at least three important respects. The mulattoes were lighter in skin color, had a better education and possessed more wealth than the slaves. Of equal importance was that among the *affranchis* a tradition of social climbing had developed, while the slaves mainly cherished a strongly subdued desire for personal freedom. Together these characteristics of an emerging class structure were to be given more or less free play during the nineteenth century, thereby reinforcing the cleavage of the population into two social classes with very strongly diverging appearances.

Completing the Class Structure. Political Marginalization of the Peasants
The wars of liberation put an end to French supremacy over Haiti, but not to inequality. Instead, during the nineteenth century the polarization of the masses and the upper classes was continued and completed. When Boyer was ousted from the presidency in 1843, the population was already separated into two strongly different groups, and with some changes this division has remained effective up to the present.

Democracy was not the first political concern of the early Haitian rulers. The masses did not press for popular participation. The slaves had revolted not to make their voice heard in political affairs but to escape the horrors of slavery, and the new leaders perceived that the most ardent and pressing task was to build a strong and unified nation upon the ruins left by the French. Until the 1825 treaty whereby France recognized Haiti as a sovereign nation, the Haitian leaders, and especially Dessalines, constantly felt the threat of a new French invasion, and consequently proceeded to prepare the defense.

A central feature in their program was discipline. A standing army had to be maintained, and the economy which had suffered heavy damages from the devastations of the wars had to be put back in working condition. This was no easy task, since all the experienced administrators left with the French. The only authority present in the country after the revolution was the military, and the new nation was built upon the foundations of military rule. Toussaint resorted to centralized government, concentrating the power in his own hands and organizing agriculture according to military principles. Dessalines and Christophe followed the same route.

The ex-slaves, on their part, were not prepared to submit themselves to the requirements of building the nation. Rather, they were intent on making use of their new-won freedom. During the cataclysmic years following the 1791 uprising, many of the freed slaves instead of joining the revolutionary forces preferred to escape to the mountains and remain there. In some parts of northern Haiti there were more maroons in 1800 than at any time during the colonial period.[102] Finally, the white masters were gone, and no one was eager to be commanded anymore.

The interests of rulers and ex-slaves clashed. The creation of the *fermage* system divided the population into two classes widely separated from each other occupationally. The masses were put back at the bottom of the social pyramid with absolutely no chance of upward mobility. The son of an agricultural laborer under the *fermage* system would always be an agricultural laborer himself. The great majority of Haitians were performing manual fieldwork under conditions which very closely resembled those of slavery, deprived of any opportunity to determine their own fate.

The ruling class held two different types of positions. One was that of higher state officials who were 'twice removed' from manual work,[103] since they issued the orders to those who directed the peasants. They handled public funds, and some of them even came into contact with the head of state himself. The majority of this group were mulattoes, for the simple reason that these positions required literacy, and the mulattoes were the only ones who had acquired some education during the colonial period. The second source of the upper class was the army, where the higher officers clearly were in 'the promised land of distinction'.[104] The composition of the leading military group differed from that of the civil elite in that promotion in the army did not require literacy and hence lay open to black Haitians as well as to mulattoes. Throughout the nineteenth century the army was the main vehicle for social promotion of blacks, who also strongly challenged the political position of the mulatto elite (while the mulattoes mainly chose the civil branch of the administration). The elite and near-elite groups were concentrated in non-manual occupations within the civil or military administration while the masses were fieldworkers.

The importance of education was also strengthened, for education was the key that opened the door to civil government positions. For natural reasons nothing was done to broaden education before the French were finally defeated, but no changes took place after the declaration of independence either. Dessalines, who was illiterate himself, cared nothing for the education of any social class, and Christophe, in spite of his dedication to schooling, excepted the masses from his zeal.[105] This neglect strengthened the position of the mulatto group.

During the first decade of the nineteenth century, two different views of government developed in Haiti. This division closely corresponded to the division of the administration into one military and one civil branch. The first view supported autocratic, centralized rule as practiced by Toussaint, Dessalines and Christophe, a tradition maintained mainly by the army officers: black, illiterate or semi-literate ex-slaves. The second tradition derived its roots from the efforts of the *affranchis* of securing the civil and political rights granted to them by the 1685 *Code Noir* during the last two years before the 1791 uprising. After 1804, the mulatto group continued to press for their share of government but this was bluntly denied by Dessalines, a refusal which provoked his assassination in 1806. Alexandre Pétion and his followers were no longer prepared to endure the rule of a black tyrant but wanted a presidency which shared the power with a legislature, i.e. mulatto rule.

Henry Christophe, who was elected president after the death of Dessalines refused to be bound by the mulatto-penned constitution of 1806 which limited the power of the president by creating a Senate and which did not grant life-time presidency. This clash with the mulatto elite divided the nation. Pétion was elected president instead, and Christophe created his kingdom in the north. Haiti remained politically divided until the death of Christophe in 1820, but more importantly, the clash between the autocratic and the 'liberal' traditions set the precedent for the political chaos which was to ensue during the latter half of the nineteenth century and which culminated in the American occupation of Haiti in 1915. To a certain extent the constant *coups* and contra-*coups* were a matter of mulatto clique rule or black strong man rule.

The Haitian masses belonged to neither tradition. Their attention was instead focused on far more fundamental issues. The long period of slavery and the serfdom inflicted upon them by the black autocrats had strengthened their desire for physical freedom. The *marronage* continued and was accelerated, particularly during the civil war between Christophe and Pétion. When the latter decided not to rely on *la grande culture* but to set the agricultural laborers free and to parcel out the state domains, the rumors of this new policy spread to the north, and laborers and soldiers alike began deserting to the south. Christophe maintained outposts near the border for supervision purposes but there was very little that he could do to prevent his citizens from escaping. Defections took place virtually every day.[106] The majority, however, had to abide their time, but as soon as the plantation system collapsed in the north as well, the desire for freedom and its concomitant, land, knew no limits. The laborers no longer wanted to work on the remaining large estates but leased land for themselves or squatted on vacant land instead. In the vacuum left by the French there was enough land available in Haiti for anybody to establish himself as a smallholder without being troubled. Haiti quickly became a nation of free peasants, intent on cultivating the soil, showing no articulate interest in the political life of the country.

The ruling classes, on their part, made no attempt to draw the peasants into politics. The differences between the peasants and the upper classes were too formidable for the latter to identify with the former. No patent advantages could thereby be gained after the land reforms. Up to 1809 (1819 in Christophe's territory) landed property was the most important source of income for the mulatto elite and the high black army officers. These were the people who owned plantations or leased government estates. Since the plantation operations built on the existence of a compliant labor force, the landlordism of the upper classes was given a mortal blow when Pétion in 1809 began his redistribution of government lands to officers and soldiers and at the same time abandoned the forced labor system. In a few decades the plantation system collapsed completely and with the disintegration of the plantation system, the elite and the army lost their interest in agriculture. The latter was no longer a source from which important incomes could be derived. The upper classes turned their backs on the countryside. The peasants were increasingly isolated from outside events and from contacts with urban areas and hence also from politics. This state of affairs, it seems, suited their needs well. They were left in peace to cultivate their plots and recognized the eminence and sovereignty of elite or military governments in exchange. By the time of Pétion's death in 1818, politics was the direct concern of no more than 600-700 people, although the elite population as a whole numbered a few thousand.[107] Political events were decided by the face-to-face relations of a small clique.

Following the overthrow of Boyer in 1843, the social structure of the country was more or less frozen. The elite, led by Boyer himself, pursued a cultural orientation which was entirely different from that of the masses. Once it was clear that there would be no renewed French invasion, France was no longer considered as an enemy but instead as a linguistic, cultural and educational ideal. The imitation of French habits and life-style became an indispensable feature of elite life. The lighter skin color and the close family ties were preserved by an extensive intermarriage between elite families. Education took place in private Catholic schools, while public rural education received little or no attention at all. The gap between elite and masses was maintained and widened. Only ambitious black army officers, never the peasants, applied for elite status and contested the power held by the elite.

The Development of the Soft State

The term 'soft state' has been coined by Gunnar Myrdal. A 'soft state'

. . .is understood to comprise all the various types of social

The Passive Government

indiscipline which manifest themselves by: deficiencies in legislation and in particular law observance and enforcement, a widespread disobedience by public officials on various levels to rules and directives handed down to them, and often their collusion with powerful persons and groups of persons whose conduct they should regulate. Within the concept of the soft state belongs also corruption. . . .The laxity and arbitrariness in a national community that can be characterized as a soft state can be, and are, exploited for personal gains by people who have economic, social and political power.[108]

According to Myrdal, all underdeveloped countries in varying degrees are soft states lacking the social discipline needed for successful economic and social development. A particular manifestation of the soft state is corruption:

. . .all forms of 'improper or selfish exercise of power and influence attached to a public office or to the special position one occupies in public life' and also the activity of the bribers.[109]

Corruption is made possible by the existence of a soft state and does itself, in turn, contribute to keeping the state soft.

During the nineteenth century, and especially after the fall of Boyer, Haiti developed into a soft state with ubiquitous corruption as one of its most distinctive characteristics. Politics degenerated into a simple fight for power and personal gain between 'ins' and 'outs'. These aspects have dominated the Haitian administration ever since.

Graft and corruption were not new to Haiti. Corrupt practices appear to have been widespread during the colonial period,[110] and in spite of the efforts by Toussaint and Christophe to introduce a measure of honesty in public administration[111] they were not wiped out in independent Haiti.[112] The land reforms of Pétion and Boyer added a new momentum to corruption by making government the most lucrative source of incomes in the country. As the plantation system collapsed and the upper classes moved into the cities, new ways of acquiring income and wealth had to be created. With a free peasant class that could not be tied to the estates it was no longer possible to squeeze the masses directly. The only way of getting an income out of agriculture without being a peasant was by taxing the goods produced or consumed in rural areas (as we will see in Chapter 8) and this source could be tapped only by the government. Accordingly, the former landowning classes went into politics instead, and politics became their prime concern. Only by sharing the spoils of office was it possible to compensate for the agricultural incomes foregone by the land reform. The administration was turned into a generator of legal and illegal incomes accruing to the followers of the politicians who happened to be in command at the moment, and the supremacy of this group was always contested by others fighting for their turn. All other functions of the administration were relegated to a secondary position. The pronounced concentration of the upper classes on politics and civil administration was further reinforced by the fact that after 1825, advancement to higher ranks within the army became increasingly difficult as promotion was submitted to rigorous rules.[113] It was only the possession of a high rank which allowed a really good life. For the majority of the upper class this left civil administration as the one remaining possible road to wealth.

For those in power, the spoils were plentiful. After the death of Christophe 'the presidency was equated with license to plunder and all energies, military and civil, were consciously devoted to the acquisition or retention of that license,' writes Robert I. Rotberg.[114] Boyer himself was known to possess an 'honest and upright' character,[115] but his administration was entirely different:

> Amidst the abject poverty of the treasury, and the total non-existence of any public credit, the hirelings and petty subalterns of the government swarm among the population of every commune, like so many vampyres exhausting the life blood of the country; as with responsibility to the chief of the government, which is merely nominal, these public agents make little pretensions to the vulgar qualities of honesty and conscientiousness, and immense sums are annually lost to the treasury by means which are perfectly inexplicable to the treasurer general.[116]

The practice of seeking office for personal gain only was firmly established under Boyer. Lesser government offices, especially, were used as stepping stones for obtaining other goals. The administration was intimately intertwined with business interests. To secure a government position was a good way of getting access to foreign trade in coffee or mahogany, pursuits which were inherently much more rewarding than the government position *per se*. The system also worked the other way around: the relatives of the businessmen got government jobs simply because the president needed the support of important families.[117]

In 1843, Boyer was overthrown by force. After this date, with few exceptions, *coups* and revolutions followed each other in rapid succession. The very essence of politics became to acquire and retain power and with that the spoils of office. At the same time, the struggles were struggles along color lines. The mulatto elite fought against a series of black strongmen with army background for control over the presidency. The lack of other sufficiently remunerating alternatives for the upper classes to focus their interests upon, converted government and politics into a veritable powder keg which frequently exploded. Of the 22 presidents between 1843 and 1915 11 held office for less than a year each. None of the 22 was anything but a representative of a faction or clique whose main, and in many cases only, interest lay in the pecuniary rewards accruing to the victors. Each new president came to power thanks to the aid of a clique. Consequently, each had accumulated a heavy political debt which had to be repaid in cash or by an office giving sufficient opportunities for remunerative exploitation. Both ways constituted a heavy drain on the treasury.

Boyer was followed by four ephemeral presidents who left little impact on Haitian history. Their main success lay in the spoils. 'During the time of Guerrier and Pierrot there was a perfect mania for public employment, and every officer appeared to wish to live in luxury at the expense of the state...'[118] comments Sir Spenser St John. The Riché administration may have been more honestly disposed, but Riché died within a year of entering office, to be followed by Faustin Soulouque, who during his twelve years as president and emperor again made 'graft...the order of the day.'[119] Large sums were wasted on his coronation in 1852,[120] and he allowed himself a yearly apanage of 150,000 gourdes as well as one of 50,000 for the empress.[121] Graft was quite open, and the financial manipulations employed by the Soulouque administration to cover missing funds were so obvious that they 'would not have deceived a schoolboy.'[122] The mainstay of government revenues, the customs houses, were converted in what amounted to be a sieve, with their contents steadily tapped by the administrative officials.[123]

Worse was to come. Fabre Geffrard, who succeeded Soulouque, pledged to reduce government expenditures, but began by raising his own salary to US $50,000 a year, by allowing himself another $20,000 for his secret service and as much for the 'encouragement of arts and sciences.' His meat bill was paid for out of the budget of his bodyguard. His champagne bill was paid by a hospital. Two large estates had their expenses covered by government funds, while the proceedings were appropriated by Geffrard.[124] No wonder that St John, otherwise a Geffrard supporter, reported that 'Every Haitian appears fully persuaded that his countrymen never seek office except for the purpose of improving their private fortunes...'[125]

Geffrard's behavior was the signal for completely unchecked robbery by subsequent administrations. The administrative history of Haiti between 1867 and 1915 has been eloquently summarized by Leyburn in an often quoted sentence: 'After Geffrard, the presidency was openly regarded as the juiciest financial plum in Haiti which if one could pluck it, would justify the necessary expenditures for a revolution.'[126] Salnave and Nissage Saget and their respective governments were worthy representatives of the degradation of the late nineteenth-century administrations. The ministers were as corrupt as ever, and plunder was officially sanctioned.

During the entire decade following the fall of Geffrard in 1867 the administrative disorder and corruption continued. Official reports stress the superabundance of employees in most government offices, many of whom were absent most of the time. The control was deficient and slow. The extent and distribution of public expenditures were never known in any detail until it was too late to change anything and sanctions could no longer be applied. Customs revenues, the most important part of government revenues, varied not only according to the volume of imports and exports, but also depending on the honesty of the customs officers and on the degree of independence of regional authorities. Most public employees were sadly underpaid which opened the door for graft and fraudulent practices.[127]

A new trick for filling the pockets of presidents and ministers was invented by Michel Domingue and his omnipotent nephew and minister, Septimus Rameau, who in 1874 and 1875 floated two foreign loans, nominally of 15 million and 50 million francs, but netting only 10 million and 7 million respectively (the latter after liquidation of the 1874 loan), most of which is believed to have ended up in the pockets of Rameau and his closest collaborators.[128] Rameau, 'the most grasping and unpopular jobber that the country had ever seen',[129] was finally killed by a Port-au-Prince mob when attempting to sail for Cayes with the contents of the vaults of the government bank.[130]

The peasants in principle were outside the peculiar political merry-go-round. The violent phases of the revolutions were concentrated in the major towns, especially Port-au-Prince, which lay outside the orbit of peasant life.

One generation after the wars which led to independence, the greater number of Haitians had practically forgotten that there was an outside world. Haiti was all they knew. With no standard of comparison for their lot in life the peasants ate, slept, raised their families, fell ill, and died without bothering their heads about such academic abstractions as equality. This uncomplaining acceptance of life, routine and fate seems to be the essence of peasant existence. The Haitian peasant has been bound to the soil by mental inertia and by the tradition much more effectively than by law.[131]

The peasants lacked the right to vote, and were 'on the whole, uninterested in politics except as they were inveigled, stampeded, or dragooned into the support of this or that aspirant for political honors.'[132] Politics for the peasants was more of a profitable part-time profession into which they entered half-heartedly without deeper involvement, than a genuinely felt need or desire for popular participation in government affairs.

The occasions for half-hearted participation presented themselves frequently during the last 25 years before the occupation. Most of the presidents of that period were black generals who waged a constant civil war or guerilla war upon each other, those 'in' to stay in power, and those 'out' to topple the government. In this whirlpool there was a steady employment of *cacos*, peasant mercenaries recruited in northern Haiti to march on the capital and dispose of the sitting government and who after having been paid off by the victor went back home to wait for the next solicitor of their armed services.

The climax was reached between 1883 and 1915, when 'revolution succeeded revolution' and 'the country sank deep into graft and scandal...'[133] A *Banque Nationale* was created in 1880. Three years after its foundation the bank was involved in a national scandal. A fire in 1883 destroyed the Finance Ministry and with it some of its records. This was used to put a number of *mandats* (bank drafts, payable on demand) which had already been redeemed back into commercial circulation and present them for payment a second time. The fraud was discovered, and a commission was appointed which established that the *mandats*, which had not been properly destroyed after the first redemption, had been stolen from the vaults of the *Banque Nationale*. The chief comptroller of the bank was convicted by a criminal court for being responsible of the affair. He in turn, accused the bank directors of deliberately having recycled the *mandats*, thus falsifying the accounts of the bank. A new commission appointed to investigate the case found that the books actually showed such deficiencies as indicated by the comptroller, but it was concluded that the case was one of 'involuntary errors', and the directors of the bank were acquitted.[134]

Justice, at any rate, was of doubtful quality. 'I may at once say that few have any faith in the decisions of the courts; the judges, with some bright exceptions, are too often influenced by pecuniary or political considerations,' wrote Sir Spenser St John.[135] Judges were not selected from among lawyers, but were instead given their positions as rewards for political services, which had the consequence that 'those selected considered that the appointments were given to enable them to make their fortunes as rapidly as possible.'[136]

The first half of the 1890s, under the administration of president Hyppolite, promised greater regularity in public administration and finances. The external circumstances were favorable. Coffee prices were high, and export of logwood had developed into a veritable boom. Hyppolite began a series of public works: iron markets in the two largest cities, bridges, canals, roads and telegraph lines. This, however, gave a new impetus to corruption. Insufficient care was taken in the selection of contractors. Contracts were given on the basis of nepotism rather than on professional competence and price competition.[137] Financial disorder reached such proportions that Hyppolite's successor, Simon Sam, had to make a 20 percent cut in the salaries of the lesser government employees. In 1896, a new foreign loan yielding 40 million francs was taken in France, and in 1897 a law was voted to consolidate the public debt.[138] The operations in connection with the alleged consolidation were scandalous. A commission appointed by Sam's successor Nord Alexis in 1903 concluded that between 1901 and 1903 around $2 million had been embezzled from the treasury by illicit means under the pretext of consolidating the floating debt. During the same period total annual government revenues were in the order of 4 million to 5 million.[139]

After the fall of Nord Alexis in 1908, Haitian pre-occupation politics reached its final tumultuous phase:

> A revolution was bought and paid for at an agreed upon price...It would seem that in the years immediately preceding 1915, any Haitian could be president who could raise sufficient funds. In some cases the cost was as low as $30,000, in others as high as $50,000. Except for the politicians engaged and the troops hired to depose and the other troops hired to defend, no other Haitians were

concerned in the revolution.[140]

Seven presidents came and went in as many years. Only the first of them, Simon, was capable of holding office for more than one year. Between 1908 and 1915 a recurrent pattern was established. A revolution was financed by resorting to a loan from one or more merchants, most of the time of German origin. With this money a *cacos* army was contracted which marched on the capital and ousted the government, and a new president was sworn in. Hereupon the merchants had to be paid off and the final instalment had to be made to the *cacos*. Both Leconte and Tancrède Auguste distributed considerable sums to the *caco* leaders as well as giving them important military commands to ensure their loyalty.[141] Generally, payment of political debts was accomplished by securing the rights to important customs duties and other valuable privileges, at the cost of the legitimate creditors of the state. New loans were also resorted to when the contents of the public treasury had sunk too low. Presidents Zamor and Oreste both floated interior loans for the purpose of meeting 'current' or 'extraordinary' government needs, i.e. for paying off revolutionary armies, financial backers and political friends, and for meeting more or less private expenditures. The latter was true of other presidents as well. Both Leconte and Auguste were preceded by a doubtful reputation having been convicted in connection with the consolidation scandal under Simon Sam.[142] At the time of the American intervention in Haiti, the degree of political and administrative honesty had fallen to zero.

None of the presidents holding their office between 1908 and 1915 were able to complete their term peacefully. Antoine Simon (1908-11) was ousted by a *cacos* uprising led by his successor Cincinnatus Leconte (1911-12) who in turn was blown up with his palace. Leconte was succeded by Tancrède Auguste (1912-13) who was probably poisoned. The victor emerging from the fights for the presidential office that ensued after Auguste's death was Michel Oreste (1913-14) who after a series of manoeuvers designed to paralyze his political opponents (including the establishment of a paramilitary body) fled to Jamaica in the face of a new *cacos* uprising. *Cacos* general Oreste Zamor (1914) became the new president, but in spite of intensive efforts to keep the *cacos* under financial control he lasted only eight months in office under constant fights with Davilmar Théodore (1914-15), who finally, aided by a new *cacos* army, defeated Zamor. Théodore held office a mere four months before he was overthrown by the *cacos*, this time headed by Guillaume Sam (1915), who in turn, after a massacre of political prisoners fell victim to the Port-au-Prince mob who literally tore him to pieces.

The redistribution of plantation lands under Pétion and later nineteenth-century presidents turned out to have very unfortunate consequences for the contents of politics and the quality of government up to the American occupation in 1915. Independent Haiti had inherited a tradition of corruption from the Saint-Domingue colony, and the land reform brought this tradition into full fruition. Both the colonial economy and the *fermage* system had conferred landed incomes upon the upper classes. However, these incomes derived from the use of slave or serf labor, and Pétion's decision to set the laborers free meant that this source of incomes was destroyed.

Since agriculture was virtually the only productive industry in nineteenth-century Haiti, it was not possible for the ex-landlords to compensate for their losses except by employing methods which permitted agricultural incomes to be transferred to them in some other way, i.e. by taxing the goods produced and consumed by the peasants. Only the government could do that, however, and as a direct consequence, politics and administration degenerated into a mechanism solely for generating personal incomes. Gradually, the interest of the upper classes was focused almost exclusively on political domination for the sake of plundering the treasury. Clique stood against clique. The second half of the nineteenth century became one of repeated quests and struggles for power. Ubiquitous corruption and recurrent revolutions characterized the period. The only important goal of virtually all Haitian administrations between 1843 and 1915 was self-enrichment. In this state of political and administrative degeneration there was no room for the peasants, except (as we will see in Chapter 8) in their capacity of taxpayers without representation and occasionally as *caco* mercenaries to help out during the revolutions. Few Haitian governments of the period considered them a group worthy of positive action. The peasants remained isolated in the countryside while the urban cliques fought over the government. Haiti had become a soft state.

The Failure of the Occupation

The occupation totally failed to prepare the Haitian masses for political participation after the withdrawal of the American forces. American rule itself was entirely from above.[143] Various elections and plebiscites were held from the beginning of the occupation to 1929, but all of them were rigged or controlled by the Marine Corps.[144] Some of the leading American officials appear to have regarded democracy and popular elections in Haiti as a lost cause from the beginning. In 1923, the American High Commissioner declared that 95 percent of the Haitians were illiterate and that a high percentage of them were in addition immoral. Democracy, he suggested, had a very empty sound under these circumstances. Two years later he stated that the peasants 'had the mentality of a child of not more than seven years of age reared under advantageous conditions.'[145] The educational system set up by the *Service Technique*[146] was concentrated on teaching the peasants manual skills, while literacy and understanding of democratic principles were put in the background.

In 1929, President Hoover appointed a commission under the chairmanship of W. Cameron Forbes to assess the occupation and to make recommendations as to the future policy of the United States towards Haiti. The Forbes commission visited Haiti in 1930 and reported that 'the commission was disappointed to find that the preparation for the political and administrative training of Haitians in the responsibilities of government had been inadequate,'[147] that the commission was 'under no delusions as to what might happen in Haiti after the convocation of the elected legislative Assembly and, to a greater extent, after the complete withdrawal of the United States forces,' and that its members were 'not convinced that the foundations for democratic and representative government were...broad enough in Haiti...Until the basis of political structure was broadened by education — a matter of years — the Government must necessarily be more or less unstable and in constant danger of political upheavals.'[148] A separate commission that evaluated the educational efforts of the occupation concluded

> that the number of schools in Haiti is insufficient to provide school facilities for all the children of Haiti at any level, primary, secondary or superior; that the children in the towns are far better supplied with opportunities to attend school than the children in the country; and that not enough types of schools are provided, especially at the secondary and superior levels, to serve the needs of the Republic.[149]

The occupation had failed to prepare the Haitian masses for participation in politics. 'After fifteen years the Occupation remained an authoritarian monolith; there had been no officially sponsored or even sanctioned movement toward democracy or self-determination'.[150]

The Haitian presidents between 1843 and 1915 had mostly been generals who were able to control the army (and the *cacos*). The Americans dissolved the old army and instead created a new unit: the *Gendarmerie d'Haïti* (later *Garde d'Haïti*) which was trained by the Marine Corps where Marines (mainly enlisted men) served as officers. This reorganization finished the old army. The *cacos* also suffered a total defeat. According to the 1864 *Code Rural* the peasants had the obligation to perform labor when local roads were to be repaired. This law had not been enforced before the occupation, however, but now the Americans revived the *corvée*.* The road gangs were kept under Gendarmerie supervision, and the peasants were roped together during the work and were brought outside their home areas in contradiction to the law. Practices like these of course recalled the old French slave gangs, and the peasants resisted the *corvée* with all means. In 1918 the practice was officially abolished because of the increasing hostility of the peasants, but in spite of two official orders it was continued illegally and fairly brutally in northern and central Haiti. The illegal *corvées* and their concomitant atrocities triggered off the 1918 *cacos* uprising led by Charlemagne Péralte who may have commanded up to 40,000 men (out of whom only a few thousand were armed, however). The uprising was brutally crushed by the Marines and Péralte was shot in the disturbance.

By dissolving the old army and by crushing the *cacos* uprising, the Americans had destroyed the two forces behind the revolutions preceding the occupation and had thereby also put an end to the clique fights. As we will see, however, by creating the Gendarmerie, they had simultaneously created a new platform for corrupt practices at the highest level. After the occupation, the road to the presidency and to a large extent the spoils went via the *Garde d'Haïti*.

A series of administrative reforms was carried out by the occupation forces. The government pay-rolls were scrutinized, and a number of non-working persons were deleted from the lists. By the same token all items that were deemed unnecessary were eliminated from the expenditures account. A modern accounting and auditing system was

---

* The selection of people to work in the *corvée* gangs was arbitrary. Very often the burden fell upon the poorest within the local area. In addition, the selection was clumsy. Once, Jean Price-Mars, Haiti's most well-known and prestigious intellectual, diplomat, deputy to the legislature, inspector of public education, in 1930 one of the candidates to the presidency of the republic etc., was arrested by a gendarme to be put into a road gang (Bellegarde (1929), p. 62).

created and implemented. The customs houses were purged and the internal revenue system was placed under the control of the General Receiver and some new laws in connection with the administration of this system were passed. The result was amazing: in ten years — between 1916 and 1926 — internal revenue increased from $100,000 to $813,000, i.e. by 700 percent, an increase that was above all due to improved honesty and efficiency in collection.[151]

The elimination of graft in reality was nothing but a temporary suppression of the phenomenon which was possible only thanks to the tight control taken by the occupation force over finances and government employment. This was anticipated by the Americans when the time came to hand the administration back to the Haitian authorities:

> Fitness to fill responsible posts involved something more than technical training. In many positions, particularly those concerned with the handling of money, character was...essential; and this quality could not easily be created by the administrative training of adults,

wrote Financial Advisor Arthur C. Millspaugh,[152] who clearly understood what would happen when the financial pie would once more become subject to sharing by the 'ins':

> No legislation, even the most rudimentary, had been enacted for the purpose of protecting meritorious employees. American offices endeavored to reward merit; but outside of their administrations the spoils system reigned unchecked, and it appeared that when American control should be removed the entire administrative personnel of the Government, with the possible exception of the judiciary, would be exposed to the worst set of political demoralization.[153]

The American occupation brought only superficial changes to Haitian politics. The peasants remained as distant as ever from political discussions and decisions. The Americans ran the country in a tightly centralized fashion and in no way attempted to prepare the way for a broader popular participation in government when the occupation ended. The administrative purge carried out was effective only due to tight American supervision, and as the future would prove, once the occupation had come to an end the old tendencies of corruption would once more dominate the administrations.

From the Occupation to Papa Doc

With Sténio Vincent (1930-41), clique rule was back, and 'ins' and 'outs' once more began their perennial fights. Nothing had changed with regard to the basic views on the contents and prerogatives of politics and power.[154] The old problems of corruption, nepotism and favoritism reappeared as soon as the Americans left. It has been argued that Vincent was able to remain in power only because he let enough people share the spoils of government not to provoke too much discontent while at the same time he managed to invest his closest political friends and backers with the special privileges traditionally considered as the perquisites of office.[155]

The heritage left by Vincent did not differ noticeably from what any nineteenth-century president would have left behind. The occupation had changed the outer circumstances somewhat. The *cacos* had suffered a final defeat and were not to intervene in Haitian politics again. The same was true with regard to the army. The old army was crushed and dissolved, and in its place the Americans had put a modern, Marine-trained, well-equipped Garde, drilled not to interfere in the political process, and which due to the determination of its leader, Colonel Démosthènes Pétrus Calixte, actually remained loyal to the president without stepping outside its proper sphere of action until Calixte was ousted. In 1939, the Garde was still loyal and efficient, but in addition it had been converted to the same type of political force that had been left in the hands of Batista in Cuba, Somoza in Nicaragua and Trujillo in the Dominican Republic by the Americans, and which were used for the sole purpose of perpetuating one man's rule in those countries.

The class structure had been left almost untouched by the Vincent presidency. The occupation had brought the old mulatto elite back in power. Dartiguenave, Borno, Roy, Vincent and Lescot were all light-skinned presidents. In their desire for an efficient, smooth administration the Americans had picked well-educated mulatto collaborators. For the first time since the mid-nineteenth century the mulattoes regained their domination of important government positions. The old demarcation lines continued to function. The elite still remained light-skinned, French-oriented, well-educated and still professed a manifest disdain for all kinds of manual labor. Politics remained their main occupation. Less than 2,000 persons and perhaps only a few hundred ran Haiti. The base for recruiting politicians was extremely narrow. The entire elite group consisted of no more than 150,000 people — around 5 percent of the population.[156] The gap between this group and the peasants remained as wide as ever. The peasants continued to be isolated in their rural districts, and with isolation followed illiteracy and lack of interest in urban affairs. A small middle class had begun to emerge following the occupation. The *Garde d'Haïti* became a social ladder for ambitious blacks. A mercantile class that had benefited from the purchasing power of some 2,000 Marines for twenty years had established itself. On the whole, however, the middle class remained numerically small as well as socially and politically inarticulate, mostly consisting of less successful social climbers.

The 1935 constitution explicitly forbade the extension of the presidency into a third term. In spite of this Vincent tried and failed to obtain United States support for his move, and therefore (1941) proceeded to have the legislature elect Elie Lescot instead. The record of Lescot, who ruled with the tacit consent of the Garde, was worse than that of Vincent as far as graft and corruption were concerned. Before becoming president in Haiti in 1941, Lescot had been Haitian ambassador to the US, and then embezzled considerable sums from the embassy budget, funds that were covered by money received from the Dominican dictator Trujillo. The latter also provided the funds which made it possible for Lescot to buy enough votes in the Haitian assembly to secure the presidency for him. Once in the saddle, Lescot regarded the office as a 'sanction for unbridled personal and presidential license' more than anything else.[157] A social security fund for the alleged benefit of the Haitian workers was established by law. Money was raised by a 6 percent deduction on the workers' salaries, but no records of the use of this money were ever kept, most of it going directly into the pockets of the president.[158]

The Lescot government also discovered that concessions to foreign companies could be a profitable venture. In 1935, the Standard Fruit and Steamship Company from New Orleans had been given a monopoly of all banana exports from Haiti. A banana export boom followed which generated a certain prosperity in the Haitian countryside. However, this boom came to an abrupt end in the space of a few years in the 1940s due to political machinations. With an eye on extracting as much as possible out of the concession business the Lescot administration in 1943 began extending concessions to other companies as well. This business was, as we will see, continued by Lescot's successor, Estimé.

In 1946, Lescot was overthrown and his place was taken by a military junta for a period of seven months before elections were held in relative order. These elections put Dumarsais Estimé (1946-50) into the presidency. Estimé's platform differed from that of Lescot. He was backed by the Garde but an important part of the background to his rise to power lay back in the 1920s when a movement of young intellectuals stressing new values and traditions began to take shape. This was the *négritude* movement. *Négritude* was not an exclusively Haitian phenomenon but rather the result of cross-influences between the francophone West Indies and French-speaking Africa. In Haiti it represented the reaction of young Haitian intellectuals to the American occupation of the country. The Americans had made little distinction between Haitians of different social classes. All Haitians were regarded as black peasants, and often the attitude was overtly racist.[159] This treatment was deeply resented by the Haitian intellectuals and called forth a cultural response which was very different from traditional elite ways. The young generation began to stress the African heritage and the amalgam of this heritage with the French influence.[160]

Although *négritude* exerted very little influence on the masses it still played a significant role in the political debate of the time with its insistent emphasis on the black masses as opposed to the mulatto elite. It was precisely this type of ideology that triumphed in the 1946 elections. It would be an exaggeration to claim that Dumarsais Estimé was a genuinely popular president. His main backing was that of black middle-class intellectuals and the *Garde d'Haïti*, but he definitely made an attempt to break up the rigid class structure which characterized Haiti. The ranks of the bureaucracy were opened to black people of humbler origins. Social reform legislation was begun. Creation of labor unions and rural co-operatives was actively encouraged by the government. Measures to improve the public health situation and to expand the public school system were undertaken. The criticism of the government by political parties and the press was also permitted.

It is possible that with time the seeds of reform sown by Estimé could have developed into something that would have broken with the dismal record of his predecessors in office. Estimé, however, was as bound as any other Haitian president by the political and social structure which had developed during more than two centuries, the accumulated weight of which severely circumscribed his efforts. The 1946 social revolution never managed to become anything but a revolution of the black bourgeoisie — of the *négritude* theoreticians and of the urban middle class that was beginning to take shape.[161] The reforms responded to the demands of these groups rather than to those of the real masses. Social climbing, rather than a desire for advancing the interest of the poorer segments of the population decided the course of political action. 'One does not achieve a popular movement like the one promised by 1946 only to obtain some more pseudo-bourgeois. It is illusive social shifting, because in Haiti more than anywhere else one cannot shift class despite a new financial and political standing. The newly rich, rocketed up by the revolution, have forgotten too quickly the old song of the humble-hearted,' said one of Estimé's cabinet members.[162] The rural masses, especially, received little attention in comparison to the urban groups.

The Estimé government continued the Lescot policy with respect to banana concessions. In 1946, the monopoly of the Standard Fruit Company was abolished, and a wholesale traffic in new concessions began. Export rights were extended to a large number of totally irresponsible companies connected with the political supporters of Estimé, with the eventual result that the entire banana export business collapsed.[163] The exhibition which in 1949 was arranged to celebrate the bicentennial of the foundation of Port-au-Prince was another graft-ridden enterprise of the Estimé government. The total cost of the exposition amounted to $12 million which was almost three times as much as the original cost estimates had indicated, a considerable portion of which could not be accounted for.[164] The new black bourgeoisie proved to be no better than the mulatto elite when it came to handling public funds, but proceeded to enrich themselves in exactly the same manner as the latter had done during the preceding administrations.[165]

Estimé's record as a reformist president was badly blotted by his last year in office when he became the victim of what Rotberg has called 'the national disease which afflicted most occupants of the presidential office,'[166] and began manoeuvering to retain his post in spite of the regulations of the constitution. Political foes outside and inside the country were silenced. A number of persons were denounced as conspirators and shot. One-third of the officers of the Garde were put in prison along with members of the opposition, until finally, the junta that had ousted Lescot four years earlier decided that time had run out on Estimé as well.

In the elections, Paul Magloire (1950-56) won a sweeping victory with 99 percent of the votes, backed by the *Garde d'Haïti* (Magloire had been a member of the junta overthrowing both Lescot and Estimé), the *Mouvement des Ouvriers et Paysans* (MOP) — the party of Daniel Fignolé, idol of the Port-au-Prince masses, and by the Haitian business community.

Magloire's victory was a victory for the old mulatto elite. The balance between the classes was superficial. Magloire neglected the interests of the lower classes and ruled in collaboration with his clique of military and commercial backers, while representatives of the lower middle class accused him of 'having so far forgotten. . .the prestige of the office as to act *vert* or *beaux gallant*, and to affect a snobbish attitude toward the humble people whom he had promised, under oath, to act in their interests. . .and reproached him for his excessive tolerance toward his relations and his haughty intolerance toward others.'[167]

With Magloire corruption reached new heights. 'The outstanding characteristic of the regime was its seizing of every advantage of the life of power, while ignoring problems of holding foreign enterprises responsible, since these enjoyed full power so long as they shared their profits,' summarizes Leslie Manigat,[168] and indeed, Magloire and his police chief, Marcaisse Prosper, shared a strong inclination towards treating the public treasury as their private purse, living on a grand scale, building exquisite and exclusive residences, etc.[169] Magloire personally is believed to have accumulated some $12 million to $28 million in personal wealth during his presidency.[170] Charges of graft and embezzlement were frequent, and at least once violence appears to have been used to cover up the events. Magloire's brother, Arsène, was minister of public works and as such spent an unusual amount of money.

The major corruption scandal under Magloire undoubtedly was the Artibonite valley project. In 1949, a loan of $4 million was obtained by the Estimé government from the Export-Import Bank for the irrigation of 40,000 hectares in the Artibonite valley. An American firm was contracted which after a study concluded that it would be necessary to build a dam and a reservoir to prevent floods in the valley. The project cost was recalculated at a figure of $22 million. In 1951, the Export-Import Bank consented to increasing the loan to $14 million, a sum which four years later was deemed insufficient, and the loan was increased anew, this time to $21 million. The following year, another $6 million had to be borrowed before at least part of the project could be completed. The results were disastrous. Only 80 percent of what was judged necessary to complete the first phase of the project, i.e. construction of the reservoir and ten irrigation channels, had been finished, and construction of the hydro-electric plant, calculated to cost $25 million, had not even begun. A total of

$40 million had been spent, $27 million of which were loans.[171] In addition, the Magloire government was responsible for some scandalous road projects, most prominent among them the 10 kilometer Pétionville-Delmas road which cost $3.8 million,[172] and a gross misappropriation of hurricane relief funds after Hazel struck the southern peninsula and the north west in 1954, when the money went into plantations and suburban residences owned by government officials and military.[173]

The Duvaliers: Family Rule

In 1956, Magloire, attempting to extend his term beyond its constitutional limits, was forced to step down after a general strike. The fall of Magloire put an end to traditional Haitian politics, i.e. to the manipulation of state affairs by tightly interwoven elite cliques or army factions. Time-honored practices of nepotism and politics of 'ins' and 'outs' were to be exchanged for complete one-man rule.

Magloire's removal from power was followed by ten months of political chaos of a kind that the country had not witnessed since before the American occupation. Five different military and civilian governments vainly tried to provide a minimum of order, but failed. Finally, backed by the army and with some support in rural areas, François Duvalier was elected president. He assumed power in October 1957, and immediately began the repressive politics designed to equate government, politics and power with his own person alone.[174]

It had been generally hoped that Duvalier would become a modernizer of Haitian politics. He possessed a comparatively clean record: for having taken part in the cultural renaissance connected with the *négritude* movement, for having been a reform minister under Estimé, and for presenting what was interpreted as an enlightened attitude towards the peasants. Immediately after assuming power, however, he began a violent eradication of every group that could possibly have constituted a future threat to his position. He did put an end to traditional Haitian politics, but in a quite unexpected way. Within a few years Haiti was converted into a repressive and tyrannical state, concentrated on the exaltation and perpetuation of one man and his absolute rule. Haiti became a predatory state: 'one in which brigandage is the predominant form of power, where effective power is exercised by praetorian specialists in violence who insure the safety of and respect for the formal center of power'[175] — a state where only Duvalier's own opinion counted.

Without the support of the army Duvalier would probably not have reached the summits of power, but once in the saddle Papa Doc proceeded to neutralize the army. Throughout his presidency he employed a policy built on constant reshuffles. No army officer was allowed to build anything resembling an independent position, but after a short time anybody who was perceived as a potential threat was removed and a younger officer owing allegiance only to Duvalier was substituted for him. The normal, hierarchical chain of command was abandoned and the officers were made to report in principle directly to Duvalier. The president was careful to supervise everything down to the lowest levels.

In addition to the reshuffling of officers in high command and disavowal of the normal chain of command, Duvalier created a paramilitary corps — the dreaded *tonton macoutes* — on the one hand to serve as an instrument of terror against his opponents but also to neutralize the army. All *tonton macoutes* were sworn in by the president himself, and all of them, except for 'the lowest ranking and most rural'[176] reported directly to him.

In the same way, Duvalier's cabinet was never allowed to play any real role. Within six months of Duvalier's installation, the cabinet was reshuffled for the first time, a device employed constantly during the years to come. No minister served continually from the beginning of the Duvalier regime until its end. Even the most trusted collaborators were periodically in disgrace with the president — a deliberate measure to prevent anybody from building up a private empire within the government, and from attempting to run his department independently.[177]

In the administration 'duvalierization' was almost total. All Haitian governments have made use of the spoils system, but in the case of Papa Doc the system was carried to its extreme. Experienced personnel in 'non-political' positions that had served under more than one of the previous regimes were forced out and replaced by inexperienced duvalierists of only obscure political merits.[178] Most government employees had to join the *tonton macoutes* or were recruited from their ranks,[179] while no attention was paid to positive merits.

Duvalier promoted a large number of middle-class blacks into government positions, built his *tonton macoutes* around the urban proletariat, and promoted younger black army officers in his periodic shake-ups of the army. Promotion of lower-class blacks certainly took place on a much larger scale than ever before in Haitian history, but this was not the result of any conscious social policy. It only served the personal political goals of the president. Neither did his upgrading of middle-class and lower-class black elements encompass the peasants. During his electoral campaign Duvalier had traveled extensively across the entire country and had promised to pay attention to the needs of the peasantry. The reality was very different. Duvalier shared with his predecessors the policy of leaving the peasants outside politics. In the late 1960s, Robert I. Rotberg had a series of interviews conducted with a sample of 50 people from rural districts, 21 of whom were peasant farmers. The results of these interviews, in so far as they can be interpreted, by and large confirm that politics was something of little concern to country people. Duvalier appears to have been a rather unknown entity to the respondents, neither especially liked nor disliked.[180] For the peasants the political changes had not made themselves felt:

> For the vast majority of the Haitian masses, the notion of the state is an abstraction beyond their comprehension. They generally know the name of the current president who represents for them a distant final authority. They are completely unaware of political events which occur only in the 'Republic of Port-au-Prince' and have no far-reaching effects on them. As the peasant sees it, the government is made up of the chief of the rural police and the local court of justice to whom he brings his endless land quarrels. He fears and respects these *autorités*, as he calls them, for he senses their overwhelming power and knows that sanctions can be brutal, and, of course, there is no appeal.[181]

The extent of corruption under Duvalier clearly exceeded that under Magloire.[182] The International Commission of Jurists in 1963 estimated that the Duvalier clique milked the Haitian treasury of about $10 million per year,[183] and concluded that the only objective of the Duvalier administration was 'to place the country under tribute in order to ensure the future affluence of those now in power.'[184] Much of this went into the personal accounts of the presidential family. Out of a $20,000 salary the president in 1968 was said to have bought two mansions for $575,000, one of which was resold to the Haitian state for $600,000.[185] Clément Barbot, the first *macoute* leader, who had an intimate knowledge of Duvalier's methods, after falling into disgrace told an American journalist that during the first few years in office Duvalier amassed some $400,000 and that he kept more than $1.5 million in a Swiss bank account.[186] These figures multiplied in later years, although it is impossible to determine the exact amounts. The lesser potentates shared the spoils. Officials with monthly salaries of less than $400-$500 and savings accounts of less than $50 in 1957 were soon building villas ranging from $40,000 to $50,000, equipped with the latest in European or American furniture,[187] and a minister of tourism in 1960 spent $350,000 on developing some of his beach property into a tourist resort.[188]

The money which was distributed among the faithful was raised in a number of more or less ingenious ways. As soon as he had assumed power, Duvalier declared that he would be an eager promoter of foreign investment in Haiti, but most of the ventures that showed up must be classified as dubious, being designed to take advantage of or resell a monopoly for the US market or to make fast money in some other way.[189] As a rule, the objective was not to carry out the project, but to share the money paid out by the government between the contracting firm and the government officials. The jet airport which was completed in 1964 provides a good example of this type of manipulation. Three expensive preliminary studies were carried out by different companies, and at least four different contracts were signed with foreign construction firms, but venture after venture collapsed because of the unabashed pushing by government officials for 'their' companies. Taxes that were earmarked for the airport were collected for five years, with the total amounting to several times the final cost.[190]

On occasion, the Duvalier government assumed a more direct control of business instead of relying on foreign interests. Thus, in 1963, representatives of the American AFL-CIO labor federation conducted an inquiry in collaboration with the Dominican sugar workers' federation which showed that between 1957 and 1963 Duvalier's labor contractors had supplied approximately 30,000 Haitian cane-cutters per year for the Dominican sugar harvest. The Dominican sugar mills paid the contractors $15 per worker. The latter in turn was paid one-half of his wage in Dominican pesos while the other half was sent back to Haiti, officially to guarantee the return of the worker, to be paid out there. Interviews made in nearly 200 cane-cutting communities in the Dominican Republic, however, showed that not a single worker had ever received anything upon his return to Haiti. The inquiry concluded that by this device the Duvalier government each year was able to pocket from 6 million to 8 million dollars.[191]

A second method of raising money frequently used was to ask for 'voluntary' contributions to 'worthy causes'. This device was employed for the first time in 1959 after the first abortive guerilla landing. Wealthy businessmen were compelled to make donations for the defense of the country, deputies had to do without one month's salary, and $17,000 was collected from army officers.[192] Similar tricks were to be used many times during the years that followed. In 1960, Osvald G. Brandt, believed to be Haiti's wealthiest person, purchased an entire issue of government bonds — supposedly secured by an earmarked increase of the gasoline tax — worth $1 million.[193] Beginning in 1961, the extortion activities on behalf of the government were organized and co-ordinated by the *Mouvement de Rénovation Nationale*. The originator of the MRN was Luckner Cambronne, a young deputy from the little town of Cabaret northwest of the capital, and the alleged objective was to convert Cabaret into a model town called Duvalierville. The Haitian legislature voted to contribute $10 per person out of the monthly salaries, and government employees, businessmen, army officers, etc. were asked for contributions — the amounts of which had often been determined in advance by the MRN. None of these funds were put into the budgeted accounts of the government. Accordingly, very little ever became of Duvalierville. Only a few buildings were begun, and they were never completed. The rest of the money was diverted for other purposes.

Extortions by the *tonton macoutes* on behalf of the Duvalierville project continued through 1961. Later other excuses were invented.[194] The activities of the MRN never amounted to anything but window-dressing. Its 'programs of work are pure fiction, it is not hard to guess where the funds of the MNR go. . .' concluded the report of the International Commission of Jurists in 1963.[195]

In addition to the organized, large-scale blackmail activities of the MRN *carte blanche* was given the *tonton macoutes* against most Haitian citizens, and that license was used. The *macoutes* could easily walk into a store and ask for goods without paying for them or could exact a 'private' contribution from anybody. Not all *tonton macoutes* received any regular pay. Those who did as a rule gained from 30 to 50 dollars per month, but more frequently the licence to steal and plunder. and if the circumstances made it necessary, get away with murder, was a more frequent means of paying for their services.[196]

Parallel to the 'voluntary' contribution business the duvalierist government operated a series of compulsory payments of various kinds: literacy funds, lotteries, 'economic liberation' bonds, road tolls, vehicle inspection, faked telephone bills, payments to pension funds, etc.[197] One of the most direct methods for raising money was simply to take over desirable property, businesses or jobs. Political exiles were systematically deprived of their property which instead went to duvalierists.[198]

People were exiled not primarily for political reasons but rather as a means of seizing a profitable trade or business establishment. Boycotts, threats, nightly raids and other forms of intimidation made the owners comply.[199]

Other traditional devices for raising and squandering money were also part of the duvalierist repertoire. Shortly after Duvalier assumed office, a $4 million loan was obtained from a Cuban bank, supposedly based on $7 million worth of deposits of Haitian sugar workers in Cuba. This loan never figured in the books of the Haitian government and no account was ever made of its use, but supposedly one million was distributed as a kickback to the Batista clique in Cuba, while the remaining three went to Duvalier, without repayment.[200]

Fund diversions did not only take place secretly. Since Duvalier ruled by decree during most of his presidency, budgeted items could easily be switched from one purpose to another. Such switches took place frequently. Once the official gazette listed no less than seventeen such switches at one time, all in favor of the *tonton macoutes*.[201] Not only state budget funds were reallocated, but as early as 1958 a law was passed which put certain municipal funds at the disposal of the central government. Such funds were to be put into a non-fiscal account and the law authorized their use by the *tonton macoutes*.[202] The most important source of funds never accounted for — the unbudgeted funds of the government — will be dealt with in Chapter 8.

The Duvalier family continued to hold Haiti in a firm grip even after the death of Papa Doc in April 1971. In January 1971 his son Jean-Claude had been elected as his successor for life in a popular referendum.[203] No political vacuum was allowed, but the power was to be retained within the family. The Duvaliers have been successful. For the first time since the late 1950s an attempt was made by somebody not belonging to the family to create an independent position, but this attempt failed. Luckner Cambronne at the beginning of Jean-Claude's reign emerged as the most powerful minister but apparently went too far in his zeal. In 1972, he was ousted and his supporters were arrested.[204]

The political struggles in Haiti after the death of Papa Doc (with the exception of Cambronne) have mainly involved the Duvalier family itself. The struggles appear to have taken place basically between the old supporters of Papa Doc and those owing allegiance directly to the younger generation.

In a way, the political situation has undergone an improvement since 1971, but a limited one. Some of the worst excesses have been done away with, and the government (especially after pressure from the Carter administration in the US) has tried to present as democratic a façade as possible, but these efforts have been more token in character than real. Power resides firmly with the Duvalier family and their supporters. The policy employed by Papa Doc whereby cabinet and army were subjected to periodic reshuffles has been continued by his successors. The fact that Jean-Claude's governments have presented larger numbers of technocratically oriented ministers than those of his father has meant little in practice. Their influence has been limited. Besides, in the periodic purges there have been several shifts from 'technocrats' to 'politicians' of the old duvalierist school and back again. Democracy is far from imminent in Haiti. The masses of peasants, as always, continue their lives without contact with the political decisions which concern only the small minority around the Duvalier family.

Jean-Claude Duvalier has promised to carry out an economic revolution in Haiti. After seven years in office little of this revolution is to be seen, at least in the agricultural sector. It is extremely doubtful whether the government has any real desire for change. Corruption, graft and brigandage presumably loom as large today as in the past. Although no precise estimates are available, it is rumored that the fortune of the Duvalier family, concealed in Swiss banks, amounts to some $180-$200 million (to be compared to a presidential salary of $24,000 per year).[205]

It has not been possible to hide a few fat corruption scandals involving some of the ministers. Luckner Cambronne, when minister of defense and the interior, managed to build up a private business empire of a highly dubious nature, involving the tapping of poor, underfed Haitians for blood to be exported to the United States and the delivery of Haitian corpses to US anatomical institutions, with alleged involvement in smuggling of heroin from Europe to the US via Haiti as the crowning achievement.[206] In 1975, the minister of trade and industry was dismissed after a post stamp fraud involving $2 million,[207] while the minister of public works is rumored to have had to leave his post in 1976 because of his refusal to open the vaults of his ministry to political plunder.[208] *

---

* In connection with the discussion of corruption in the present chapter it should be pointed out that corruption *per se* does not necessarily hamper development. A country may have a high corruption percentage (measured e.g. as a percentage of government revenues) and still develop rapidly if the government manages to provide e.g. the public goods and services needed for development.

From the peasant point of view, the political changes under the two Duvaliers did not amount to anything. The peasants continued to be removed from political life, living in comparative isolation in rural districts without contact with other politicians than the purely local bosses. Neither did the fact that a larger number of blacks than ever before were recruited into the administration mean anything. These blacks did not come from the masses, and especially not from the peasantry, but rather from the budding black bourgeoisie intent on social climbing towards an eventual elite status. This group naturally did not identify its fate with that of the peasants. In spite of the administrative changes the gulf between the governing clique and the peasants remained as wide as ever. It was only the composition of the governing clique that had changed, not its position and philosophy with regard to the masses.

Further Restrictions on Peasant Participation in Politics

The main part of the present chapter has been devoted to a historical analysis of the development of certain trends in Haitian economic policy and politics in order to explain the lack of government interest in the peasants and the separation of the peasants from the political process in general and political decision-making in particular. To complete this analysis we must finally add two more dimensions of peasant life to the picture, both of which act as strong obstacles to the political articulation of peasant interests: the mode of rural government and the peasant *Weltanschauung*.

Rural Government: The 'Chef de Section'[209]

The Haitian system of local rural government goes back to the *Code Rural* of 1826 and has, with minor modifications in the 1864 and 1957 rural codes, continued to be employed up to the present time. According to the system spelled out in these laws Haiti is divided into a number of rural *sections* (presently 555).[210] These sections exist for police purposes only, and have nothing to do with economic realities or communications. Each of the sections is presided by a *chef de section* — an officer of the rural police with a military rank. The *chef de section* is

---

This is, however, not the case with Haiti.

Also, it may be noted that even if the mentality of the Haitian government should change as far as the attitudes towards economic development are concerned, the country will probably have a long way to go to achieve the necessary changes. Corruption is deeply rooted at all levels of the administration. Haiti is a genuinely soft state, and this can presumably not be changed easily.

responsible for maintaining law and order in his district, for protecting property, for supervising cultures, labor, waterways, ditches, canals etc., and has at his disposal for these tasks policemen of lesser rank and forest guards. If the circumstances so require, he can also summon the aid of the armed forces.

Traditionally, the *chef de section* was a rural *gros habitant* appointed by the army chief of staff. This practice was changed by François Duvalier, however, who insisted on personally appointing the *chefs de section*. In addition, the requirements changed. Instead of primarily being somebody already important in the rural community, the first and foremost characteristic became absolute allegiance to the head of state. At any rate, for all practical purposes, the *chef de section* represents the government in the countryside, or rather: he *is* the government.* According to a well-known anecdote, once when a new Haitian president visited a peasant village, the local headman in the community was so impressed with him that he expressed the wish that some day the president would rise to become a *chef de section*.[211] The latter has the decision in all important matters concerning the peasants. He is the sheriff, he carries the registers of births and deaths, he collects taxes. His authority is vaguely defined, and he is inadequately controlled from above. This leaves ample room for extending his influence into all matters of importance and interest. Not knowing where his authority ends, the peasants dare not oppose him. Hence, he is the indisputable leader of the section and his word is law, particularly in the interminable squabbles over land ownership among the peasants. He can claim harvest offerings, rebates at local stores, unpaid help in the cultivation of his land, bribes or tributes to settle disputes advantageously. He literally has the power over life and death in the countryside, a power which is not to be contested and which he uses for any purpose he himself finds suitable. A simple threat of imprisonment is usually sufficient to make the peasants acquiesce. His word is final, since the peasants have virtually no other contact with the authorities. The *chef de section* is their only link with the government and urban politics, and this link is imposed entirely from above without building effective peasant representation into the process. Rural Haiti has always been autocratically and arbitrarily

---

* The 1957 *Code Rural* also makes provisions for an administrative council consisting of three members, the leader of which should be a rural notable (Département de la Justice (1963), articles 3-16) but in practice it is the *chef de section* who runs the local community.

governed without any outlets for peasant opinion.*

The Peasant 'Weltanschauung'[212]

Complementing the formal and officially sanctioned authority of the *chef de section* we find the informal influence of the voodoo clergy: the *houngans* (priests) and *mambos* (priestesses). Since the peasants lack any scientific, formal or informal education, the view they take of the world is intimately intertwined with the supernatural:

> Crop failure, pests, droughts, and floods are not interpreted as natural phenomena but as manifestations of the anger of neglected spirits or the envy of some neighbor. Equally, success is attributed to the protection of the gods or the magical power of an individual. In the valley of Marbial in 1948, most peasants were convinced that with enough money one could 'buy' rain and have it fall on one's plot. Sickness and its sequel, death, are seldom thought to be due to natural causes. Souls are stolen and kept in bottles; illnesses are 'sent'; magic turns the most healthy men sexually impotent; the blood of babies is sucked at a distance; tuberculosis can be cured by transferring it to a rooster. Proper offerings can secure success in economic, political, and amorous ventures. Since 'an ounce of prevention is worth a pound of cure,' preventive and counter-magic are available in the form of amulets, 'points,' special garments and the like.[213]

Central in this *Weltanschauung* is the voodoo religion. Voodoo provides a well-organized system of cause-effect relationships between known and unknown forces. It offers nothing less than a total picture of life, and one which is intelligible to the peasants.

Voodoo has adopted the Christian god — *Bon Dieu* — as a supreme being, who, however, is a very distant entity. The immediate contact takes place with the *loas* (the voodoo spirits or gods). These must be served by the faithful. They are very exacting and demand seemingly

---

* In some instances the rural codes actually invited the abuse of authority. Hence, the 1864 code which, with some modifications, was applicable until 1957 explicitly stated that it was the task of the *chef de section* to suppress *vagabondage*. A *vagabond* was defined as anybody who (except for on market days) was found in a *section* without having his domicile there, without being employed there, or without having a permission to be there. Such a person was subject to arrest. No peasant could leave his district for more than twenty-four hours without a permission from the authorities. (Code Rural (1929), articles 108-121. Cf. also Franklin (1828), pp. 337-42, for similar dispositions in the 1826 code.)

endless and accordingly costly ceremonies which must be performed over and over again if the *loas* are not to be offended. In exchange for the interpretation of the environment, the peasant has to accept the sovereignty of the *loas*. Nothing can be done against the will of the spirits. In addition, the peasants need help in their efforts to preserve good relations with the supernatural world. Such assistance necessarily comes from the voodoo clergy, and from *bocors* (sorcerers), who supposedly can manipulate the other worldly forces. The *houngan* is 'a teacher, a repository of cult knowledge, and a catalyst. He can give practical meaning to symbols and initiate resolutions to religious or workaday dilemmas.'[214] Voodoo has more to offer the peasant:

> ...a pattern of family relations, direct communication with original forces, emotional release, dance, music, meaningful socializing, drama, theater, legend and folklore, motivation, alternatives to threatening dangers, individual initiatives through placation and invocation, treatment of aliments by means of herb lotions and rituals, protection of fields, fertility, and a continuous familiar relationship with the ancestors...[215]

whereas Catholicism (or Protestantism) offers little more than a doctrine and a code of conduct.

The usefulness of voodoo to the peasant introduces a strong measure of social control and conformity exercised over him by the *houngan*. While voodoo once was a strong revolutionary force,[216] today it has been converted into one of the most conservative elements of rural Haiti.* *Houngans, mambos* and *bocors* all have a strong vested interest in fostering and maintaining the supernatural interpretation of the environment, since it is upon this interpretation of the occult that their very livelihood depends. Therefore, the voodoo clergy constitutes a force that under no circumstances can allow itself to teach the peasants that they can improve their situation by taking conscious political action conducive to economic and social change, but instead envisage soliciting their own services as the proper way out of misery and hardships.

With few exceptions voodoo has always been left in peace by the Haitian governments. Paradoxically enough the first three rulers, Toussaint, Dessalines and Christophe, who all had participated in the

---

* It should be stressed, however, that voodoo presumably is no more conservative than e.g. Catholicism.

revolution and hence had benefited from the capacity of voodoo to set the masses on fire, took action against it. Rather, it was precisely because of their awareness that they took action, fearing that dissident *houngans* would be able to gather groups of followers who could plot against their own grip of power. After 1815, however, voodoo was left to itself and could secretly proliferate. Haiti almost entirely lacked a Catholic clergy so that no natural countervailing power was available, and during the reign of Soulouque (1847-59) a very benevolent view was taken of voodoo. Soulouque openly patronized and practiced the mass religion, and almost turned it into a semi-official creed.

After the fall of Soulouque, the official importance of voodoo declined, but the religion could still develop without being molested by government intervention, in spite of a concordat with the Holy See in 1860. It was not until 1941 that the Catholic Church was given a free hand and state support as well in its efforts to eradicate voodoo. *Houmfors* (temples) were sacked, and the religious paraphernalia burned, etc. The effort failed, however, partly due to the very unfortunate timing of the campaign. The effort happened to coincide with the SHADA eviction of peasants[217] which turned into a national scandal. General discontent spread among the peasants, and fearing more serious consequences the Lescot government decided to end the anti-voodoo campaign.

This was the last time voodoo was tampered with, except for some onerous taxation under Duvalier. On the other hand, the latter also displayed a benevolent attitude towards voodoo. He had been an eager student of the subject during his early years before reaching the presidency and had realized its potential as a means of control. Those *houngans* who did not co-operate shared the fate of his other opponents, real or imagined, but those who proved loyal to him were protected and amply supported. This gave Duvalier two advantages. It mobilized a kind of mass support in his fight against the Catholic Church and also assured him of enhanced control over the peasant masses via a cadre of locally important loyal supporters. Not infrequently a single person combined the roles of *houngan, chef de section* and *tonton macoute*.[218]

Conclusions

In the present chapter we have dealt with some of the reasons for government passivity in the agricultural sector, i.e. with some of the reasons why the Haitian government has not proved capable of taking any initiatives to check the movement of the agricultural sector towards a Malthusian equilibrium.

After the land reform begun by Pétion and continued by later presidents, the common policy of practically all Haitian governments with respect to improvements in the agricultural sector has essentially been one of *laissez-faire*. At best, *ad hoc* measures have been undertaken in response to exceptional (favorable or unfavorable) changes in the external environment within which agricultural policy has to be decided. Beginning in the 1950s, a number of plans both for the economy as a whole and for agriculture in particular, have seen the light of day, but regularly the contents of these plans have borne little or no relation to facts, and it has not been possible to reach their goals. Basically, however, the attitude of the Haitian governments towards agriculture after the collapse of the plantation system has been one where the only interest shown has been that of exacting taxes from the peasants. (This will be discussed in Chapter 8.) When it comes to furthering peasant welfare, those holding power have not identified their own fate with that of the peasantry at all.

To understand why this passive view of agriculture has developed in Haiti, we have had to venture outside the scope of traditional economics. It is not possible to understand economic policy-making in Haiti without analyzing the political history of the country. The contents of politics to a large extent were determined by the land reform, and the turn taken by the political process has exerted a decisive influence on the structure of goals in the economic field and consequently also for government philosophy with respect to agriculture.

The social structure is intimately connected with the political process. Haiti has never been a country where the masses have participated in politics and government. From the earliest days of independence to our own time, politics have remained in the hands of the upper classes. The leading social characteristic of the country has been the cleavage between on the one hand the elite and the near-elite and on the other hand the peasants – with little of a middle class in between. The two classes have differed in most important respects: wealth, occupation, location, education, language, religion, family organization, culture and to a certain extent skin color. Very little has been done to bridge these gaps which on the political level have been translated into a difference between governors and governed.

The origin of the class division is to be found in the colonial social structure which, after the departure of the French, left the mass of ex-slaves, the ex-*affranchis* (free mulattoes) and those ex-slaves who had made a military career during the wars of liberation. This separation was reinforced by the employment of the *fermage* system in the attempt to save the plantation system whereby the ex-slaves were once more bound to the soil.

The redistribution of land which began in 1809 shaped the subsequent contents of Haitian politics. For the agricultural laborers it meant that the desire for freedom and land which had been built up during the periods of slavery and *fermage* could finally be satisfied. The laborers became peasants who refused to work on the plantations — which consequently collapsed — and then withdrew to dedicate themselves to the culture of the soil without professing any interest in politics. For the upper classes, the division of the large estates into smallholdings meant that they could no longer fall back on landed incomes for a 'proper' life. Instead, government positions became the prime source of their revenues. The mulatto elite began its struggle with the black army officers over power and over the spoils of the presidential office. These fights between 'ins' and 'outs' constituted the dominating feature of Haitian politics during the latter half of the nineteenth century up to the American occupation in 1915. The spoils system reigned supreme over the administration, and public finances became increasingly intertwined with private ones. As long as their private goals could be satisfied, few politicians bothered to contemplate any other purposes of government. The factional struggles for power culminated between 1883 and 1915, and especially after 1908, when revolutionary activities turned into a regular business venture for financial backers and *caco* mercenary armies and few presidents could think of the public treasury in terms other than those of plunder.

The American occupation made a strong attempt to break the corrupt tradition. Payrolls were purged. Modern auditing and controls were introduced in government offices. However, success was limited. Only the sector under the direct control of the Americans appears to have been relatively free from graft, and as soon as the occupation forces left, Haiti reverted to the old pattern of embezzlement, kickbacks and factional politics at all levels. The extent of corruption increased again and, as it appears, reached new, unprecedented heights under Magloire and, especially under the older Duvalier, i.e. during the main period under study in the present work.

Thus, the supreme goal of the Haitian politicians has been to ransack the national treasury and grab as much as possible. Haitian politics has been converted into a machine for grinding out wealth and incomes for those who happen to be in power, and all other aspects of administration and government have been pushed far into the background.

In Haiti corruption stems mainly from the top of the administrative hierarchy. After the fall of Boyer in 1843 most Haitian heads of state have been more or less corrupt, and their practices have set the precedent for the lower echelons of the administration. The essence of Haitian politics has been to reach the spoils of government. Most of the country's administrations can quite safely be termed 'kleptocracies' in the sense that other facets of government – apart from using public funds for private purposes – have been of a subordinate nature. Only rarely in the history of Haiti do we discern any initiatives coming from the head of state or other top government officials to stop or prevent the plundering and squandering of the public treasury, and too frequently do we find that the president has taken an active lead in the robbery, presumably to lay his own hands on the fattest share. This 'personal' view of public office and funds held by most heads of state makes for a corresponding pattern on lower levels of the hierarchy. Administrative positions are given to people with no expectations of getting the job done but as a payment for political support and help by the faithful. The man at the top does not expect his subordinates to accomplish anything positive but hands out offices merely as a license entitling the office-holder to cut a slice of the financial pie of a size which corresponds to his particular position.

Of course, corruption has not only come from the top. Other factors have contributed as well. Most Haitian governments, especially those of the nineteenth century, have been administratively weak – partly as a result of corruption itself – and have lacked control over local events, as demonstrated by their inability to prevent the destruction of the plantation system. Transportation and communication facilities have decayed due to the general lack of interest in rural affairs. This, in turn, has left ample scope for local initiatives, and the central government has not been able to do very much to prevent this state of affairs, even during the short and infrequent periods when control has actually been attempted. Nevertheless, the general pattern of Haitian corruption is not mainly one of underpaid petty officials making up for excessively low salaries (although this certainly exists) but rather, the right to use one's office as a source of kickbacks, bribes and other illicit incomes has been conferred from the top. The spoils system has been extended to encompass the right of plundering too.

Graft and the 'extended' spoils system are the direct outcome of the view of politics. We have shown how politics in Haiti has never been the concern of the masses, and especially how the combination of slavery during the colonial period, serfdom during the first Haitian rulers, and the redistribution of land beginning under Pétion on the one hand made the peasants lose their interest in politics, and how on the other hand, it made the landed aristocracy lose its interest in the peasants and turn towards clique politics instead, clique politics which seldom had more than one purpose: enrichment. In *The Challenge of World Poverty*, Gunnar Myrdal points out that the existence of a soft state does not appear to be a result of any particular form of government. Graft and corruption are as widespread in democracies as in authoritarian states.[219] In the case of Haiti, however, a definite link can be established between the form of government and the existence of a dishonest administration, and this link is the result of the distorted views of the purpose of government held by most Haitian politicians. Where power has been sought mainly as a means of enrichment, the appropriate form of government has been dictatorship. The political parties as a rule have not been dominated by a political ideology in the Western sense, but have rather been created as a means of legitimizing the vested interests in government and spoils and, when in power, few of these parties have shown any interest in maintaining working democratic institutions. In a situation where the authority and power of the president are uncontested, the scope for financial manipulations by the 'ins' becomes wider.

During the entire period from 1843 up to the present time the peasants have remained outside the fight for power and spoils. The soft state which developed during the nineteenth century had no need for them other than in times of *coups* and revolutions, and the peasants made no attempt to be heard at the national level. Rural Haiti has always been subject to purely military rule, with the *chef de section* having the decisive word in all important questions. There has not been any formal scope for political activities as regards the peasants. Formal authority has also been supported by the informal authority represented by the voodoo clergy. One of the central social aspects of the voodoo cult is that it provides a strong means for controlling those who adhere to it. Events and timings are interpreted and reacted upon with explicit reference to the spiritual world. The proper way to solve an immediate problem for a peasant is not to take action by himself or to resort to co-operation with other peasants (except the *coumbite*) but to approach a *houngan* or a sorcerer for help. Naturally enough, both the military and the religious authorities show little or no interest in changing peasant passivity into political activity.

Now that we have gained some insight into the mechanisms which have created peasant passivity in political matters on the one hand and

The Passive Government

clique rule (or one-man rule) and a distorted view of the goals for politics on the other, we may go on to examine the consequences in terms of the composition of government expenditures and revenues in the next chapter. This will complete our discussion of government passivity with respect to agriculture.

Notes

1. Benoit (1954:2), p. 83.
2. Cf. Chapter 6.
3. Rotberg & Clague (1971), p. 99. Educational efforts are dealt with in Chapter 10.
4. St John (1889), p. 387.
5. Benoit (1954:2), p. 85.
6. See Chapter 8 for details.
7. US Department of State (1925), p. 1.
8. These activities are discussed in detail in Chapter 10.
9. This is discussed in Chapter 12.
10. See the appendix to Chapter 4.
11. Cf. Chapter 9 on disease and malnutrition.
12. Union Nationaliste (1930), p. 17.
13. Moral (1961), p. 65; Nicholls (1974), pp. 29-30.
14. Wood (1963), p. 146.
15. Millspaugh (1931), pp. 181-2.
16. See appendix to Chapter 4.
17. See Chapter 9.
18. See Chapter 10.
19. Folsom (1954), p. 297.
20. UN (1949), p. 214.
21. Wood (1955), p. 257.
22. Ibid.
23. See Chapter 12.
24. See ibid.
25. See below.
26. For details see e.g. Galíndez (1962), pp. 196-201 and Hicks (1946), pp. 98-124.
27. Vincent (1938), pp. 219-225; Pierre-Charles (1965), p. 111-12.
28. Pierre-Charles (1965), p. 112.
29. Folsom (1954), pp. 200-4, 268-70.
30. Moore (1972), pp. 64-5.
31. Ibid.; Turnier (1955), pp. 300-3; Rotberg & Clague (1971), p. 169.
32. Cf. Chapter 10.
33. See Chapter 10, for the Marbial project, and the present chapter for the Artibonite valley project.
34. See Chapter 12.
35. See below.
36. Logan (1968), p. 151.
37. For details see Wood (1955), pp. 340-41.
38. See Chapter 9.
39. Co-operatives are dealt with in Chapter 12 and rural credit in Chapter 11.
40. Moral (1959), p. 149.
41. Cf. Blaise (n.d.), pp. 133-4.

42. Moore (1972), p. 251.
43. Rotberg & Clague (1971), p. 182.
44. Moore (1972), p. 75. Cf. Moral (1959), p. 149.
45. More details are given below.
46. Duvalier (1967:1), p. 62.
47. Ibid., p. 110.
48. Moore (1972), p. 255.
49. Rotberg & Clague (1971), pp. 209-10; Moore (1972), pp. 92-3; Pierre-Charles (1965), pp. 114-17; ICA (1961), pp. 22-4, 26-32. IDAI is dealt with further in Chapter 11, and *Poté-Colé* is discussed below in the present chapter.
50. Rotberg & Clague (1971), p. 238.
51. Pierre-Charles (1965), p. 117.
52. CIAP (1966), pp. 23, 89.
53. CONADEP (1963), pp. 30-31. A condensed version of the plan is given in COPALE (1963).
54. Duvalier (1967:2), pp. 38-40.
55. CIAP (1966), p. 50.
56. Duvalier (1967:2), pp. 53, 62.
57. IIIS (1971), pp. 335-47. Regarding the autonomous agencies, see Chapter 8.
58. 1957/58-1958/59: OEA-CEPAL-BID, p. 68, 1959/60-1964/65: CIAP (1966), p. 42; 1965/66-1966/67: CIAP (1972), pp. 72, 74.
59. See Wingfield (1966), note, p. 226; Rotberg & Clague (1971), pp. 241-2; Diederich & Burt (1969), p. 323-4, for details.
60. CIAP (1968:2), p. 93-4.
61. Ibid., p. 94.
62. The detailed plans are found in CONADEP (1968-69), P & D No. 3, 1969, and CONADEP (1970-71).
63. CONADEP (1968-69), table following p. 58; P & D No. 3, 1969, p. 21, CONADEP (1970-71), tables following p. 136.
64. Agricultural investments from BID (1974), p. 160, current expenditures from IHS (1971), p. 347, total government expenditure (excluding autonomous agencies) from CIAP (1972), pp. 72, 74. The expenditures of the autonomous agencies were assumed to be 15 percent of official total expenditure. (Cf. Chapter 8, Table 8.6).
65. The relevant documents are République d'Haïti (n.d.), CONADEP (1971-76), and Plan quinquennal (1971-76).
66. République d'Haïti (n.d.), table preceding p. 27.
67. Plan quinquennal (1971-76), pp. 6-7.
68. CONADEP (1971-76), p. 75.
69. DARNDR (1976), p. 16.
70. Agricultural investments, see Table 7.7, agricultural current expenditures in BID (1974), p. 173; total government expenditure (excluding autonomous agencies) in CIAP (1974), pp. 95-6; expenditures of autonomous agencies: 15 percent of the CIAP figures. (Cf. Chapter 8, Table 8.6).
71. BID (1974).
72. Ibid., p. 173; Le Moniteur, (1974), p. 82, (1975), p. 79.
73. DARNDR (1976), p. 3. Cf., however, ibid., p. 102 which envisages a yearly growth rate of 8 percent in food consumption per capita.
74. Ibid., pp. 3-4.
75. Ibid., p. iv.
76. Cf. e.g. Myrdal (1957), Chapters 2 and 8, (1968), passim, but especially prologue, Chapter 20, and Appendix 2 (1971), Chapters 1,7, 14. Cf. also e.g. Nafziger (1976), pp. 19-21.
77. Kuznets (1966), pp. 445-6. Cf. Adelman & Morris (1967), pp. ix-xxvi.

78. Cf. e.g. Myrdal (1971), pp. 32, 35.
79. Ibid., pp. 32-3.
80. Adelman & Morris (1965), (1967), (1968:1), (1968:2), (1973).
81. Brookins (1970), Rayner (1970), Yotopoulos & Nugent (1976), pp. 36-8. Cf. also the reply to Brookins and Rayner in Adelman & Morris (1970).
82. Myrdal (1971), p. 393.
83. The literature on the class structure of Haiti is abundant. The classic book is that of Leyburn (1966), where the evolution of the system up to the late 1930s is traced. The latter period is also discussed by Lobb (1940) and Simpson (1941). Further references to the historical development are those of Price-Mars (1942), Denis & Duvalier (1948), De Young (1959), Hoetink (1961), Saint-Louis (1970), Rotberg & Clague (1971) and Fleischmann (1971). These works also contain analyses of the development up to the late 1960s. For the 1950s and 1960s also see Bourguignon (1952), Schaedel (1962), Casimir (1965), Wingfield & Parenton (1965), Wingfield (1966), de Ronceray (1968), Brisson (1968).
84. De Young (1959), p. 457; Wingfield & Parenton (1965), p. 339.
85. Wingfield & Parenton (1965), p. 340.
86. Moreau de Saint-Méry (1958), p. 28.
87. Lepkowski (1968:2), p. 141. Cf. Herskovits (1971), pp. 59-60.
88. Baron De Wimpffen, quoted by James (1963), p. 15. Cf. also e.g. Lepkowski (1968:2), p. 140; Rotberg & Clague (1971), p. 38, and Dorsainvil (n.d.), p. 65.
89. Moreau de Saint-Méry (1958), p. 55.
90. James (1963), p. 17.
91. For extensive descriptions and analyses of this phenomenon see e.g. Debbasch (1961), (1962), Debien (1966), and Fouchard (1972).
92. Lepkowski (1968:1), p. 58.
93. Herskovits (1971), p. 60.
94. Debien (1966), pp. 34-5.
95. Moreau de Saint-Méry (1958), p. 77.
96. James (1963), p. 56.
97. Leyburn (1966), pp. 19-20; Rotberg & Clague (1971), p. 33, James (1963), p. 41.
98. James (1963), pp. 42-3.
99. Leyburn (1966), p. 18.
100. Brutus (1948), p. 16.
101. Logan (1930), pp. 407-9.
102. Lepkowski (1968:1), note p. 80.
103. Leyburn (1966), p. 36.
104. Ibid., p. 37.
105. The educational history of Haiti is sketched in Chapter 10.
106. Leyburn (1966), p. 50.
107. Lepkowski (1968:2), p. 139.
108. Myrdal (1971), p. 211.
109. Myrdal (1968), p. 937.
110. See e.g. Barskett (1818), pp. 107-8; Brown (1837:1), p. 109; James (1963), p. 34; Trouillot (1965), pp. 46, 48.
111. Cf. James (1963), p. 245; Korngold (1945), p. 172; St John (1889), pp. 71, 73; Lepkowski (1968:1), p. 79; Barskett (1818), p. 197; Griggs & Prator (1968), p. 254; Harvey (1827), p. 164.
112. See Lepkowski (1968:1), p. 79; Lepkowski (1968:2), pp. 92, 102; Leyburn (1966), pp. 39, 63; Gingras (1967), p. 31; Davis (1929), p. 98; St John (1889), pp. 77-9, Dorsainvil (n.d.), pp. 146, 149-50. Blaise (n.d.), pp. 38-9; Magloire (1909), p. 260; Trouillot (1960), pp. 39, 43, 53, 56-7.

113. Leyburn (1966), p. 217.
114. Rotberg & Clague (1971), pp. 63-4.
115. Brown (1837:2), p. 265.
116. Ibid., p. 263.
117. Leyburn (1966), p. 81.
118. St John (1889), p. 91.
119. Leyburn (1966), p. 93.
120. St John (1889), p. 97; Davis (1929), p. 121.
121. Bellegarde (1938), p. 118.
122. Leyburn (1966), p. 92.
123. Rotberg & Clague (1971), p. 81.
124. St John (1889), pp. 182-3.
125. Ibid., p. 185.
126. Leyburn (1966), p. 224.
127. Chatelain (1954), p. 16.
128. For details regarding these two loans, see Chapter 8.
129. St John (1889), p. 121.
130. Bellegarde (1938), p. 132.
131. Leyburn (1966), p. 108.
132. Quoted by Leyburn (1937), p. 393.
133. Leyburn (1966), pp. 222-3.
134. Chatelain (1954), pp. 65-6.
135. St John (1889), p. 301.
136. Ibid., p. 305.
137. Bellegarde (1938), p. 140; Dorsainvil (n.d.), p. 273.
138. Bellegarde (1938), p. 141.
139. Chatelain (1954), pp. 69-70.
140. Captain Edward Latimer Beach, quoted by Rotberg & Clague (1971), note, p. 104.
141. Bellegarde (1938), p. 151.
142. Ibid., pp. 149-50.
143. The Haitian view of the American methods of administration is eloquently stated by Bellegarde (1929).
144. See e.g. Schmidt (1971), pp. 99, 193, and Douglas (1927), p. 251.
145. Quoted by Millspaugh (1931), p. 137.
146. See Chapter 10.
147. Quoted by Schmidt (1971), p. 212.
148. Quoted by Millspaugh (1931), p. 185.
149. Quoted by Spector (1961), p. 241.
150. Schmidt (1971), p. 194.
151. Davis (1929), p. 274.
152. Millspaugh (1931), p. 173.
153. Ibid., pp. 173-4.
154. Rotberg & Clague (1971), p. 148; Montague (1940), p. 276.
155. Rotberg & Clague (1971), p. 153; Montague (1940), pp. 282-3.
156. Rotberg & Clague (1971), p. 148.
157. Ibid., p. 168.
158. Ibid., p. 169; Gingras (1967), p. 76.
159. See Chapter 10.
160. For an analysis of the *négritude* movement see Rotberg & Clague (1971), pp. 158-67. The influence of *négritude* on Haitian literature is dealt with by Efron (1955) and MacLeod (1962). Two of the most influential works are those of Price-Mars (1973) and Roumain (1947).
161. For an analysis of the latter see Sylvain-Boucherau (1951), Comhaire-

Sylvain (1959).
162. M. Laraque, quoted by Gingras (1967), pp. 83-4.
163. Moral (1961), pp. 309-12; Rotberg & Clague (1971), p. 173.
164. Rotberg & Clague (1971), p. 174.
165. Diederich & Burt (1969), p. 56; Manigat (1964), p. 37.
166. Rotberg & Clague (1971), p. 174.
167. Gingras (1967), pp. 88-9.
168. Manigat (1964), p. 41.
169. Rotberg & Clague (1971), p. 183.
170. Ibid., p. 186.
171. Turnier (1955), pp. 303-4; Pierre-Charles (1965), pp. 190-91.
172. Duvalier (1967:1), p. 108.
173. Manigat (1964), p. 41.
174. The literature on this aspect of Duvalier's presidency is abundant. Rotberg & Clague (1971), pp. 196-257, 342-78; Manigat (1964), passim; Wingfield (1966), pp. 221-66; Diederich & Burt (1969), passim, and (1972), epilogue; Pierre-Charles (1969:1), passim; Moore (1972), pp. 87-107; Gingras (1967), pp. 97-129; Mintz (1966:1). Cf. also Crassweller (1971) and (1972); Hardouin (1963); Latortue (1966:1); (1966:2), (1967), (n.d.), and OAS (1963).
175. Rotberg & Clague (1971), p. 342.
176. Ibid., p. 216.
177. See ibid., p. 360.
178. Manigat (1964), p. 54.
179. Diederich & Burt (1969), p. 172.
180. Rotberg & Clague (1971), pp. 362-5.
181. Wingfield (1966), p. 221.
182. Ibid., p. 250; Moore (1972), pp. 93, 104; Latortue (n.d.), p. 6.
183. Wingfield (1966), p. 252.
184. Quoted by Diederich & Burt (1969), p. 257.
185. Moore (1972), p. 104.
186. Quoted by Gingras (1967), p. 120.
187. Manigat (1964), p. 75.
188. Rotberg & Clague (1971), p. 241.
189. Typical examples are given in Moore (1972), pp. 90-91.
190. Diederich & Burt (1969), p. 319.
191. Gingras (1967), pp. 115-16.
192. Rotberg & Clague (1971), p. 207.
193. Ibid., p. 239.
194. See e.g. ibid., p. 240; Diederich & Burt (1969), p. 276.
195. Quoted by Diederich & Burt (1969), p. 257.
196. Ibid., p. 172. Cf. Rotberg & Clague (1971), pp. 227-8.
197. Examples are found in Rotberg & Clague (1971), pp. 211, 240, 255; Diederich & Burt (1969), pp. 173, 182, 184, 383.
198. Gingras (1967), p. 109.
199. Manigat (1964), p. 75.
200. Moore (1972), p. 91.
201. Velie (1962), p. 125.
202. García Zamor (1966), p. 82-3.
203. For details see Diederich & Burt (1972), pp. 395-8.
204. See e.g. KCA, 2-9 Dec. 1972, p. 25612.
205. Le Moniteur (1975), p. 293.
206. KCA, 2-9 Dec. 1972, p. 25612.
207. KCA, 7-13 April 1975, p. 27054; 1-7 Dec. 1975, p. 27472; QER, No. 2, 1975, p. 9.

208. Cf. QER, No. 1, 1975, p. 10; No. 2, 1976, p. 8.

209. Surprisingly enough, very little has been written about this central personage of rural Haiti. See, however, Comhaire (1955), (1956); García Zamor (1966), pp. 75-8; Fleischmann (1971), pp. 28-9; Code Rural (1929), articles 76-121; Département de la Justice (1963), articles 330-347.

210. IHS (1971), p. 11.

211. Diederich & Burt (1969), p. 25.

212. Probably no other subject has attracted the attention of as many students of Haitian life as voodoo, and in no other area has a comparable amount of garbage been produced. (Cf. the bibliographies in Bastien (1966).) For serious studies see e.g. Price-Mars (1973); Herskovits (1971), pp. 139-250; Leyburn (1966), pp. 131-74; Métraux (1958), which also contains a comprehensive bibliography; Courlander (1960), (1966); Bastien (1966). Interesting new light on the early history of voodoo is shed by Laguerre (1973:1), (1973:2), (1974:1), (1974:2).

213. Bastien (1966), p. 46.

214. Courlander (1966), p. 12.

215. Ibid., p. 21.

216. See Laguerre (1974:2) for details.

217. See above.

218. See Diederich & Burt (1969), pp. 354-67 for a detailed account of Papa Doc's use of voodoo in politics.

219. Myrdal (1971), p. 212.

8 HAITIAN PUBLIC FINANCE

The preceding chapters have established two important reasons for government indifference to peasant welfare, and hence also two explanations for the low proportion of government expenditure going to the agricultural sector. With the abolition of slavery and *fermage* and the simultaneous break-up of the large estates and the redistribution of these lands to the peasants, the rural masses became a marginal political group showing no interest of its own in political affairs as well as being of no interest as a target for government spending, since the main political groups lacked a direct pecuniary interest in peasant agriculture. Simultaneously, and somewhat ironically, the land redistribution and the accompanying decline of the plantation system gave rise to a perverted view of politics where the most important objective became the exploitation of government revenues for private purposes by the governing cliques, and where the only real issue involved in the political infighting was who was to have the privilege of this exploitation. The public good was subordinated to private vested interests of a very obscure nature.

Keeping the 'private' nature of political objectives in mind, and taking for granted that a substantial proportion of government revenues has been squandered in the process of ubiquitous corruption, we will now turn our attention to the composition of government expenditures. This will provide us with a more complete understanding of the economic policy pursued by the Haitian governments and will also reinforce some of the conclusions reached in the preceding chapter. After this examination we will go on to see how the political goals in turn also determine the revenue policy of the government and finally how this revenue policy affects the peasants.

The Structure of Government Expenditure

Let us begin our analysis by showing how a large proportion of government funds have been employed for purposes intimately (but not solely) connected with the course taken by Haitian politics. It is not necessary to make a detailed analysis of the composition of public expenditures in Haiti and their development over time. The aim of the analysis is to continue the examination of why only small amounts have been spent on agriculture and this can be done without going into any exhaustive scrutiny of expenditures. For the purpose of this analysis we will therefore limit our attention to the most significant items: (1) debt service; (2) expenditures on army and police; (3) wages and salaries.

Creating a Foreign Debt

After the independence from French sovereignty in 1804, the Haitian rulers feared a French invasion. France had not recognized the new nation and was not willing to do so until all claims that French citizens might have regarding loss of lives and property had been settled. This state of insecurity continued until 1825 when President Boyer finally agreed to pay an indemnity of 150 million francs in exchange for a formal French recognition of the independence of Haiti. 150 million was an extraordinarily high sum which had been negotiated at gunpoint with 14 French men-of-war outside the Haitian capital, and this indemnity was to be repaid within only five years.

The economic conditions in the country were hardly favorable for the payment of the indemnity. Sugar had virtually disappeared from the list of Haitian exports, cotton was exported only in small quantities, and indigo cultures hardly existed anymore in the country. To make the first instalment, a loan of 30 million francs had to be floated in France, a loan which, however, netted only 24 million, while the other 6 million had to be paid in specie out of the public treasury. Together with the indemnity the French loan became known as 'the double debt'.[1]

The double debt posed a heavy burden on the treasury. The first instalment on the indemnity virtually drained the country of specie, and Haiti defaulted on the following instalments. Eventually, the French government recognized the impossibility of the terms, and in 1838, the remaining 120 million outstanding were reduced to 60 million, to be paid in 30 years. Haiti also received an unconditional recognition by France. Even so, the country faced a serious problem of repayment. Between 1830 and 1843 interest and amortization on the double debt absorbed an average of almost 30 percent of total budget revenues.*
Debt service was maintained more or less in full during these years,[2] while during the 1843-48 period payment was suspended to be resumed

---

* Clague (Rotberg & Clague (1971), p. 397) gives an average of 58 percent between 1839 and 1843, but this figure builds on the tacit assumption that government receipts approximately equal customs receipts (Clague (1970), p. 12) which is not correct for the years before 1870. In 1837, customs receipts accounted for only 52.3 percent of total government revenues, the remainder mainly being made up for by proceeds from a land tax (Benoit (1954:2), pp. 22-3, Cf. also Leyburn (1966), p. 318).

again under Souloque in 1849. Around 1875, an estimated 20 percent of government revenues were pledged to the service of the 1825 debt.* It should also be noted that both the indemnity and the 1825 loan could be repaid only in specie, which meant that during the 1838-42 period almost 60 percent of total customs receipts were absorbed by the debt service each year.[3]

With the exception of the 1840s, the successive Haitian governments maintained an extremely good record of debt repayment up to 1875. In this year the outstanding foreign debt was approximately 13.7 million francs,[4] a reduction by almost 80 million since the end of the 1830s.** The price for this reduction had been high. The balance of the customs receipts and other government surpluses of foreign exchange had been absorbed by the double debt. Recognition of national sovereignty had been obtained by forswearing a large part of the possibilities of economic development.

Had the repayment of the 1825 debt and indemnity continued without further complications, Haiti would soon have been a country free from foreign debt, but in 1874, to satisfy 'current needs of different departments of the public service' and to collect the first funds for a national bank, a combined domestic and foreign loan operation was launched. The domestic interest was negligible, but the government managed to place a 15 million francs loan in Paris at a 33 percent discount, netting 10 million for the treasury. This sum, however, was deemed insufficient for the projects planned, and the following year a 50 million francs loan to consolidate the foreign debt and to finance public works was floated in France. The outcome was nothing short of a disaster. Bonds of a nominal value of 36 million francs were bought for 31 million. The commission of the French *Crédit Général* amounted to 9.5 million. The liquidation of the 1874 loan absorbed 14.5 million, etc., leaving only 7 million for the treasury. Both financing of public works and consolidation of the national debt had to be abandoned,[5] but Haiti had once again contracted a heavy debt, amounting to 43 million francs (including what was left of the 'double' debt) after a first instalment on the 1875 loan the year of its issue.[6] The conditions under which the 1875 loan had been negotiated were so scandalous that President Boisrond-Canal ordered a special

---

* Rotberg & Clague (1971), p. 397. The figure given there is for 1859-75, i.e. mostly for the period before the abolition of the land tax in 1870, and therefore presumably contains an upward bias.

** In 1839 the amount outstanding on the 1825 loan was approximately 33 million francs, and in 1838, 60 million were left to pay on the indemnity (Rotberg & Clague (1971), p. 397).

investigation which culminated in the French bankers' acceptance of lowering the amount to be repaid from 35 to 26 million francs.[7] Even so, debt payments absorbed an average of 14 percent of total customs receipts between 1876 and 1885,[8] money which was in reality paid to finance the corrupt practices of the Geffrard/Rameau administration which had floated the 1875 loan.[9]

The total debt burden was increased by another factor: the issue of paper money and coins without backing. The practice had been begun by Pétion and was continued by Boyer when the treasury had been emptied by the first instalment on the indemnity, as well as by several other presidents following Boyer. Table 8.1 shows the estimated annual increase in the money supply between 1843 and 1869. Nissage Saget who took office in 1870 successfully remonetized much of Haiti's depreciated currency.[10] Nevertheless, in 1889 more than one-fifth of the total public debt consisted of paper gourdes.[11] Tight monetary management and heavy emphasis on debt repayment reduced the total debt by almost 20 percent between 1889 and 1891.[12] By that time, the 'double' 1825 debt was also finally liquidated.[13]

Table 8.1: Estimated Annual Rate of Increase in Money Supply 1843-69

Year	Annual increase in money supply (percent)
1843	9.2
1847	7.0
1855	12.8
1859	14.8
1867	6.4
1869	116.9

Source: Clague (1970), Table 8.

A third foreign loan was negotiated and floated in 1896. Twenty-two million francs were still outstanding from the 1875 loan, and a further 50 million were added, nominally to refund the public debt. The operation yielded 40 million to the Haitian treasury, part of which went into the pockets of corrupt government officials.[14] This new loan caused further strain on the treasury. Between 1896 and 1910 an increasing share (from 15 percent in 1896 to 25 percent between 1902 and 1910) of customs receipts had to be dedicated to servicing the foreign debt.[15] During the same period, various short-term internal loans were floated — the principal backers of which were banks and commercial houses — on terms that often amounted to those of more or less forced loans. The bonds for these loans were usually sold at heavy discounts and carried high interest. (One of the purposes of the 1896 French loan had been to withdraw such short-term loans.)[16]

In 1910, the last foreign loan before the occupation was floated. With more than 60 million francs from the 1875 and 1896 loans still to be amortized an additional debt of 65 million francs was contracted, mainly to pay outstanding claims on the government (e.g. to liquidate short-term internal debts) and to withdraw some of the paper currency from circulation. The loan could only be floated at a large discount and yielded a little less than 47 million, or 40 million when commissions, etc. had been subtracted.[17] Debt payments increased again, to an average of almost 30 percent of customs receipts between 1911 and 1914.[18]

In spite of the decision to use some of the 1910 loan for paying off the internal debts outstanding, new internal loans were floated in 1912, 1913 and 1914 (four loans) mostly to pay the costs of revolutions or to meet 'extraordinary' or 'current' expenses.[19] In addition, the government had agreed to pay the deficit on the operations of the National Railroad if the profits of the latter fell below a certain percentage and to guarantee the interest on the funds invested by the railroad. By the time of the American intervention 'the credit of Haiti was exhausted and no further loans could be sold on any terms.'[20] Total foreign indebtedness amounted to almost 121 million francs — the highest since the original indemnity agreement — including arrears of 12 million francs on amortization payments.[21] There is no precise statement of total internal indebtedness for the period, but an approximate idea of the magnitude can be gathered from the fact that in 1919 the Haitian government owed a total of US$8.4 million (more than 83 million gourdes at an exchange rate of 9.90 gourdes to the dollar) on the loans of 1912, 1913 and 1914, on salaries and pensions overdue, and on account of issues of paper currency, not counting loans from private individuals and defaults on interest and amortization on the bonds of the National Railroad.[22]

The first debt contracted by Haiti was forced upon the country by France, but during the last quarter of the past century, up to the American occupation, a recurrent, self-generating pattern of loans and indebtedness, operating in circular cumulative causation developed. Corruption, revolutions and repayment of past debts caused a heavy drain on the treasury which periodically, with bankruptcy approaching, had to be replenished. This was accomplished by floating a loan, foreign or domestic, which due to the lack of confidence in the Haitian governments could usually only be issued at a heavy discount, thereby increasing the public debt by an amount that far exceeded the proceeds from the loan, which in turn were largely dissipated among corrupt government officials. The impact of this pattern was heavily felt in the treasury, especially since Haiti refrained from using a common device which might have mitigated the debt burden. Other Latin American governments often defaulted on their foreign loans during this period,[23] but Haiti, in spite of certain irregularities in repayment timing, maintained what must be a unique record of debt service until the final few years before the occupation.

Maintaining a good repayment record in face of a rising public debt, when the proceeds from the loans seldom were put to productive uses amounted to a severe mortgage of the development possibilities of the country. Instead of employing scarce foreign exchange for investment directly in the agricultural sector or in infrastructure, a large proportion of these resources had to be devoted to servicing a foreign debt which to a large extent had been caused by corruption and political machinations.

The Debt Management Policy of the Occupation

All the constructive efforts of the occupation took place during the 1922-29 period. Few of them touched the peasantry, however, and none proved to have a lasting effect. The main reason for this lack of impact was to be found in the financial management of the occupation. The Americans never made any funds available for Haitian economic development which had to be financed entirely out of domestic resources. In addition, the Haitians had to spend more than 10 percent of the government salary bill on salaries to American officials (although these to the largest part were paid by American money).[24] However, the management of the external debt posed far more significant restrictions on the sums available for development spending.

Beginning in 1922, the Haitian public debt was consolidated into American hands. Three loans were floated between 1922 and 1925. Six million dollars of the $16 million Series A loan to refund the external debt went to paying off French bondholders whose claims in terms of dollars had depreciated from $21.5 million in 1915 due to the devaluation of the franc during and after the First World War. A further $4.1 million went to the American controlled *Banque Nationale* as repayment for advances to the Haitian government, and

$2.2 million was used to pay the arrears of interest and amortizations on the National Railroad bonds. A Series B loan of $5 million was used to refund the internal debt and to pay the awards made by an International Claims Commission which had scrutinized all foreign claims made against Haiti except those settled by the Series A loan. The $3.5 million Series C loan, finally, was used for refunding the National Railway bonds at 75 percent of their par value.[25]

Repayment of the external debt was given absolute priority over all other expenditures during the occupation. The loan agreements and the 1915 Haitian-American treaty established that external debt service and payment of customs receivership expenses were to constitute a first lien on all Haitian revenues, but in practice American policy went even further. The occupation official responsible for debt service management and Haitian budgetary policy in general was the American Financial Advisor, and all advisors serving between 1923 and 1929 followed a policy whereby the debt was amortized in advance of the schedule established by the loan agreements and whereby large cash reserves were built up in anticipation of the leaner years that would eventually come. Financial Advisor W.W. Cumberland (1924-27) agreed that total Haitian government revenues were not large enough to cover the necessary programs for economic development but in spite of this formulated a plan according to which two-thirds of any budgetary surpluses went to retiring the debt ahead of schedule whereas only one-third was to be reserved for public works. The interest of the American bondholders had first priority.[26] This exaggerated debt management policy quickly reduced Haiti's external debt from $24.2 million in 1924 to $16.5 million in 1930.[27] During the same period substantial cash reserves were built up, as seen in Table 8.2.

Table 8.2: Amount of Cash Balance at the End of Fiscal Years 1924-30

Fiscal year	Cash balance (million US$)
1923-24	1.4
1924-25	1.3
1925-26	2.3
1926-27	2.5
1927-28	3.9
1928-29	4.1
1929-30	4.0

Source: Millspaugh (1931), note, p. 124.

Deducting the available cash balance in 1930 reduces the effective debt to $12.5 million. In six years Haiti's external debt was almost halved.

In 'normal' times the debt retirement policy would have given Haiti an improved credit standing in the international loan market, but after the onset of the Depression in 1929 any thoughts of externally financed economic development would have been entirely illusory. Nor could the accumulated cash reserves be used, since the latter were employed to service the debt during the 1930s (when all other Latin American states defaulted).[28] The Forbes commission which was sent to Haiti by President Hoover to investigate the activities of the occupation forces in 1930 concluded that debt retirement had proceeded too fast and that the surplus funds could instead have been used to reduce taxation (especially on exports) while the debt could have been left to work itself out during its normal term.[29] The kind of debt management pursued by the Americans left Haiti starved of development funds. In 1927, for example, no less than 40 percent of the Haitian budget was absorbed by the debt service while only some 20 percent was dedicated to the public works department and public health, agriculture, education, etc. shared another 20 percent.[30]

Liquidating the Debt

After 1929, rapid withdrawal became the most important objective of the US State Department with respect to Haiti. The only field where the principle of continuity was adhered to was in the management of the external debt. The US refused the Vincent government permission to float a development loan arguing that an agreement first had to be reached regarding the financial arrangements after the expiration of the treaty in 1936. Ten years of debt payment in excess of requirements proved of no help when it came to obtaining new funds.[31] Instead, the United States government continued to exercise financial control over Haiti also after the withdrawal of the occupation forces in 1934 right up until the bonds were finally redeemed in 1947. The executive accord of 1933 provided for an American fiscal representative to remain in Haiti and control customs, inspect the Internal Revenue Service, set limitations on the budget and if necessary, to set up and control reserve funds. Without the consent of the fiscal representative, the Haitian government could not increase its indebtedness, change taxes or tariffs or dispose of investments.[32]*

---

* In 1941 the functions of the fiscal representative were transferred to the *Banque Nationale de la République d'Haiti* which remained under American supervision until the 1922 loan was finally paid off in 1947.

The administrations of Sténio Vincent and Elie Lescot inherited the public debt policy of the occupation. In the mid-1930s, debt service absorbed some 25 percent of budget revenue.[33] Amortizations were paid at an increasing rate up to 1937, when continued payments were rendered impossible by a sharp decline in the coffee price due to the abandonment by Brazil of its coffee valorization plan which had maintained the level of coffee prices. Low prices of cotton, sisal, sugar and cocoa added to the problem, as did the sudden repatriation of Haitian sugar-cane cutters from Cuba and the Dominican Republic in 1937.[34] Continued amortization of the 1922 loan was impossible in spite of the fact that debt payment still had first priority among all budget expenditures. The Haitian debt repayment record until 1937 had been excellent, however, during a period when other Latin American countries regularly defaulted, and it was therefore possible to secure an accord with the American bondholders whereby only interest charges and mere token amortizations were paid.[35]

The return of the emigrants from Cuba and the Dominican Republic and the fall in export prices also contributed to increasing the Haitian public debt. In 1938, a $5 million loan was obtained from the Export-Import Bank (in 1941, increased to $5.5 million). The immediate purpose of the loan was to execute a number of public works: irrigation, drainage, flood control, road and rail construction, etc. with smaller sums destined to go directly to agricultural projects. A contract was signed with the American J.G. White Engineering Corporation to carry out the works. The company in all probability squandered most of the money leaving an increased public debt behind.[36] Postponement of amortizations of the 1922 loan together with the contracting of the J.G. White loan between 1938 and 1942 increased the debt by 26.5 million gourdes, as Table 8.3 shows. With the recovery in exports at the beginning of the 1940s, amortization of the public debt could, however, be resumed again. More than 21 million gourdes were paid off between 1942 and 1946 with a peak expenditure in the fiscal year 1943-44 amounting to more than 31 percent of total budget revenues.[37] Once again the development possibilities were forfeited in favor of rapid debt repayment.

In 1947, the Estimé government decided to liquidate what was left of the 1922 loan. After deducting the amortizations scheduled for the fiscal year 1946-47, 24.3 million gourdes' worth of Series A and C bonds remained to be redeemed. Liquidation of these bonds was accomplished by the issue of an internal dollar loan amounting to 35 million gourdes, the service of which constituted a first lien on internal and customs revenues for some years to come.[38] Even so, the percentage of budget expenditures that had to be devoted to debt management was quickly reduced. In spite of a national defense loan of 15 million gourdes floated in 1949 and a loan of $4 million from the Export-Import Bank taken the same year (subsequently raised to 14 million gourdes in 1951)[39] for irrigation works in the Artibonite valley, this figure was decreased from 23 percent in the fiscal year 1947-48 to 6 percent in 1953-54.[40]

Table 8.3: The Haitian Public Debt 1938-46

Year	Amount outstanding on 30 Sept. (million gourdes)
1938	44.0
1939	52.1
1940	60.9
1941	68.1
1942	70.5
1943	70.4
1944	60.5
1945	52.9
1946	49.4

Source: UN (1949), p. 298.

In later years, debt service has not been a heavy obligation for the Haitian government. Some new loans have been taken, but at no time during the 1954-75 period has debt service absorbed more than 10 percent of the budget resources.[41]

The consolidation of the Haitian public debt into American hands during the occupation and the policy established by the American Financial Advisors of repaying the debt in advance of the scheduled requirements and building up cash reserves in excess of repayments made it possible for Haiti to continue interest and amortization payments even during the depression years of the 1930s with the exception of the 1937-41 period. American financial control of debt repayment continued after the occupation until the last payment had been made in 1947 and debt redemption continued to absorb significant amounts of the public expenditures until the end of the 1940s, with a consequent reduction of funds that would otherwise have been available for investment purposes. It should be kept in mind that very little came out of these debt repayments which had originated with the French indemnity of 1825, and subsequently had been converted several times by means of new loans, the balances of which were rarely allocated to productive purposes.

With the French indemnity, there was no choice. Acknowledgement of the indemnity and the subsequent floating of the 1825 loan was necessary to prevent foreign intervention in Haitian affairs. The same is true with respect to the debt consolidation in the 1920s and the tight debt management policy up to 1947. On the other hand, the debt conversion policy of the last quarter of the nineteenth century was a more or less direct outcome of the corrupt politics of the period. Instead of being allocated to productive purposes, the balances of these conversions were squandered in ways which were only rarely accounted for. For a period of no less than 75 years corruption had thus continued to place a heavy hand on the public budget, disguised as interest and amortization payments on loans secured by a first lien on government revenues.

Overmilitarized Haiti

In the nineteenth century, Haiti was an overmilitarized country. Until the conclusion of the 1825 treaty where France in return for the 150 million francs indemnity had recognized the sovereignty of Haiti, the threat of a French return was imminent. Dessalines' main concern was to protect the country from a French invasion, and for that purpose he created a large standing army ranging somewhere between 15,000 and 37,000 soldiers, i.e. between one-tenth of the male population and one-tenth of the total population.[42] Large standing armies were also kept by Christophe and Pétion, partly as a defense against a possible invasion, but also for the purpose of fighting each other.

In spite of the conclusion of the 1825 treaty with France, overmilitarization continued to burden the economy. The size of the Haitian army between 1825 and 1830 is reported to have been somewhere between 25,000 and 30,000 men.[43] 'The existing government of Haiti is a sort of republican monarchy, sustained by the bayonet,' wrote the American physician Jonathan Brown in 1837,[44] and, in fact, five years later one in fifteen Haitians was a soldier without the country being involved in any war.* The size of the army was double that of Great Britain and most other European nations calculated on a per capita basis.[45] Although no figures are available it should go without

---

* Cf., however, below. Haiti occupied the Dominican Republic from 1821 to 1844.

saying that maintaining a soldiery that size must have absorbed a significant portion of the Haitian budget. From the economic point of view, most of these military expenses could be regarded as a subsidy to officers and soldiers. Before 1825 the threat of a French return had been real indeed, but after that year most of the reasons for a large standing army disappeared, and with them went authority, discipline and efficiency. Leyburn quotes a contemporary French observer:

> [The Haitians] who had never had more than a borrowed energy — that inspired by fear of French invasion — when they saw themselves freed, by a solemn treaty, from all attack on their coasts, seemed to allow their arms to drop relaxed at their sides, saying, Let's take a rest. The soldier who up till now had squeezed his body into a uniform and had subjected himself to European discipline, shouldering his arms, staring straight ahead as if seeing nothing, now began to leave unbuttoned the uniform which choked him, dragged a mattress into his sentry-box so that he might sleep through his watch, and let his cross slip to the earth never to pick it up again.[46]

Doctor Brown was equally harsh in his judgement: 'the troops of Boyer are but mere hireling cut-throats, without character or habits of industry and ever ready to employ themselves in scenes of disorder and depredation.'[47]

Not only did the army absorb budget resources, but it also dragged a portion of the available manpower away from the soil, which was left without cultivation, into an idle life in the garrisons:

> The soldiers of the army are, from the nature of their employment, which prevents them from becoming fixed residents upon the soil, schooled in idleness, vice and disorder, and the policy of the government tends to perpetuate and increase the evil, by conferring a conventional superiority of rank upon the class of militaires over that of cultivators.[48]

Still, Haiti continued to maintain its standing army. 'There was never any money for development...nearly all the available resources of the country being consumed, decade after decade, by the still enormous standing army, renewed wars against the Dominicans, and frequent *coups d'état*,' write Rotberg and Clague.[49] The 1848 budget indicates that almost 65 percent of total government expenditures went to the army (almost ten times as much as to justice, education and public worship together), to which had to be added the funds for the police. The following year, the figure lay around 55 percent.[50] Although these figures may be exaggerated (presumably they do not cover debt service, for example), and in spite of the fact that budget funds were frequently diverted for uses other than those indicated, the comparative importance of war expenditures in the budget is clear. Haiti had occupied the Dominican Republic from 1821 to 1844, and in 1849 and 1855 Soulouque, who besides having built his dictatorship on the armed forces and created a paramilitary terror group (the *zinglins*), made two abortive efforts to reconquer the eastern two-thirds of the island. Obviously, these wars were very costly. The second attempt ended in an armistice secured by French and British intervention, backed by the United States, which, it seems, was much due to European and American fears that Haiti would be unable to meet its debt obligations because of exaggerated military spending. The American Secretary of State, Daniel Webster, wrote to the US representative in the Haitian capital:

> The material interests of these three countries [Great Britain, France, and the United States] are largely involved in the restoration and preservation of peace between the contending parties in Santo Domingo. France is a creditor of the government of Soulouque to a large amount. She cannot hope for a discharge of her debt when the resources of his country, instead of being developed by pacific pursuits and a part, at least, applied to the purpose, are checked in their growth and wasted in a war which countermines the state...If the Emperor Soulouque shall insist upon maintaining a belligerent attitude...you will unite with your colleagues in remonstrating against this course on his part. If remonstrations shall prove to be unavailing you will signify to the Emperor that you shall give immediate notice to your government, that the President [of the United States], with the concurrence of Congress, may adopt such measures, in cooperation with the governments of England and France, as may cause the three powers to be respected.[51]

Soulouque's successor, Geffrard, spent at least $20,000 per year on a well-organized network of spies reporting on his political adversaries,[52] and according to Sir Spenser St John this practice was followed by several later presidents as well:

> Under Salnave and Domingue the spy system was much employed, and it appears likely that under the Government of General Salomon it was rampant, if we may judge by the series of military executions which marked that Presidency. Society was completely broken up, as if three met together one was sure to be a spy. Servants were often engaged to repeat the conversations of their employers, and I have often been reminded by a look of the presence of a listener.[53]

Geffrard in addition maintained a standing army believed to number around 20,000 in 1867, 6,500 of whom were general officers and staff, 7,000 regimental officers, leaving only 6,500 soldiers. At the beginning of the 1880s the total size of the army was 16,000, with no less than 1,500 generals of division.[54] The figures cited are very approximate, since no official statistics appear to have been published on the matter, but they still give a fair impression of what the Haitian army during the latter half of the nineteenth century was like. Even though it is possible that the absolute size of the troops had gone down since Boyer's days, the number of senior officers was ridiculously exaggerated in proportion to the number of common soldiers. The latter, as a matter of fact, were in reality civilians without any military training who had been recruited by forced conscription in a random fashion. The pay was generally quite inadequate and the discipline was low. Soulouque's two attempts at reconquering the Dominican Republic amply demonstrated that the Haitian soldiers would not fight except under very special circumstances. Many of the soldiers throughout the period never bothered to show up at their regiments except to collect their pay, with the risk of actually having to serve a few months, since the practice was for the officers to divide the pay of absent soldiers among themselves. Such an army could of course never be trusted to serve the government, but was always ready to overthrow the sitting president given sufficient financial inducements, as the tumultuous history around and after the turn of the century proved. Budget allowances amounting to some 25 percent of the total national budget did not suffice to keep a loyal army.*

Direct and indirect spending on the military presumably reached a climax under the ephemeral governments between 1908 and 1915. The

---

* St John (1889), pp. 384-8 gives the following percentages (army only, budget net of debt service): 1863-64: 22% 1876-77: 20% 1881: 26% 1885-86: 27% and Benoit (1954:2), p. 72, estimates that in 1894-95 27.2 percent of the budget went to the army and to the police and that in 1914-15 the corresponding figure was 26.4 percent.

candidates for the presidency quickly engaged in competitive bidding, and there was always somebody willing to pay the *cacos* more than the sitting president could offer. Finally, the Haitian treasury began defaulting on the amortizations of the public debt since it was unable to meet the competing demands of revolutionary expenditures and embezzlement of public funds by successive short-lived governments. Military spending (regular army plus *cacos*) had totally disrupted the public finances.

Before 1825, maintaining a strong army was a necessity for the Haitians. As long as no settlement had been made with France the new nation was in real danger of again being reduced to the state of a colony. Once the Franco-Haitian treaty had been signed, demilitarization should have been possible, but expenditure on army and police continued to absorb a disproportionately large share of the budget during the remainder of the nineteenth century — without much benefit for the country. The quality of the Haitian soldiery in terms of fighting ability was low, as shown by the rare occasions when the Haitian army actually had to go into battle. The soldiers were taken away from production on the land, and the idle life in the barracks fostered negative attitudes towards work among them. Organizations for espionage on political foes and secret police groups were founded, and in the final stage of nineteenth-century political development the army and the more or less professional mercenaries known as *cacos* produced a seemingly unending series of successful or abortive revolutions and *coups d'état*. Undoubtedly, the money spent in activities of this sort could have been better used.

The Twentieth Century

For obvious reasons spending on military and police forces remained high during the occupation. The United States taxpayers paid the salaries of the Marines, including those who served as officers in the *Gendarmerie d'Haiti* after (1927) the *Garde d'Haiti*), but the latter received additional payment as well which came out of Haitian funds. Also, all salaries of the Haitian *gendarmes* were disbursed out of the Haitian budget. (President Wilson had vetoed a suggestion that the Haitian government be required to pay the salaries of the Marines serving in Haiti.)[55]

Gendarmerie disbursements averaged a fairly stable $995,000 per year between 1916-17 and 1922-23. During the same period total government expenditures rose from $3 million to more than $6 million, making the percentage spent on the *Gendarmerie* fall from 30 to approximately 15 percent.[56] Five years later, in 1927, *Gendarmerie* expenses accounted for 18 percent of the total budget.[57]

When the Americans left Haiti, the *Garde d'Haiti* was the only important military force in the country and with time, the support of the Garde became necessary for anyone attempting to capture or retain the presidency. Haiti under presidents Vincent and Lescot fell into this pattern. Large sums were spent on 'national defence' as Table 8.4 reveals. Also Estimé and Magloire were backed by the Garde during their respective presidencies and both maintained a policy of generous military spending as Tables 8.4 and 8.5 indicate.

Table 8.4: Percentage of Public Expenditure Going to the Armed Forces 1933/34-1949/50

Fiscal year	Percentage of budget going to the army
1933-34	16.0
1934-35	15.8
1935-36	18.9
1936-37	19.4
1937-38	26.0
1938-39	26.4
1939-40	26.3
1940-41	25.0
1941-42	24.9
1942-43	23.6
1943-44	18.3
1944-45	20.9
1945-46	24.0
1946-47	19.0
1947-48	16.4
1948-49	16.2
1949-50	16.1

Sources: Wood (1955), p. 165; Benoit (1954:1), p. 103.

With Duvalier, the character of military and police expenditures changed. Since the beginning of the 1960s it is no longer possible to follow the development of the total expenditures on army and police in official Haitian statistics. Figures regarding budget allocations and realised expenditures on account of the Department of the Interior

Table 8.5: Percentage of Budget Expenditures Going to the Armed Forces and to the Department of the Interior 1950/51-1956/57

Fiscal year	Percentage of budget going to army and interior
1950-51	20.8
1951-52	17.6
1952-53	21.0
1953-54	20.5
1954-55	19.0
1955-56	17.3
1956-57	23.0

Source: Moral (1959), p. 148.

(including the armed forces) are published, but these figures are known to be gross underestimates of the real outlays. In addition to the regular armed forces the *tonton macoutes* had to be maintained. The exact numbers of the *macoutes* are not known. The first leader of the corps, Clément Barbot, in 1959 claimed that he had 25,000 men under him, but these claims were probably exaggerated. The *tonton macoutes* are not likely to have numbered more than 10,000 at any time, with a capital-based hard core of 2,000, and during the early years of Duvalier's regime the number probably did not exceed 5,000.[58]

However, the maintenance of a repressive machine on this scale was costly. In addition to the budget allowances, a substantial portion of the revenue of a number of the so-called autonomous agencies is known to have been spent on purposes connected with 'internal security'. The most important of these agencies is the *Régie du Tabac* – the government tobacco monopoly – which collects taxes not only on tobacco and matches, but which has also gradually been entrusted with the collection of taxes on sugar, cement, flour, soap, textiles, alcoholic beverages, edible oils, dairy products, candies, chocolates, etc. No official information has ever been published regarding the revenues and expenditures of the funds received by the *Régie* and the other autonomous agencies, and their accounts have never been open to public inspection in spite of repeated requests from international aid agencies. During the 1960s the funds of the *Régie* were not kept in the *Banque Nationale* but in the *Banque Commerciale d'Haïti*, a supposedly private commercial bank established in 1960. The *Banque Commerciale* was later closed on account of allegedly fraudulent practices, however, and the

Régie accounts were transferred to the *Banque Nationale*.

Since the accounts of the *Régie* and the other autonomous agencies have never been subject to open inspection and since no official figures have been published regarding revenues or expenditures, all we have to rely upon when it comes to quantifying the sums allocated to the *tonton macoutes* are unofficial guesses and estimates. Table 8.6 is based upon estimates made by the Inter American Committee on the Alliance for Progress (CIAP) in the mid-1960s. The table furnishes us with a maximum estimate of the spending of the Duvalier regime on army and police. The CIAP estimated that the revenues of the autonomous agencies during the period under consideration amounted on average to approximately 15 percent of budgetary revenue.

Table 8.6: Government Spending on Army and Police 1960-7

1	2	3	4	5	6
Fiscal year	Official expenditures on interior and defense (million gourdes)	Official government expenditure (million gourdes)	Estimated revenues of autonomous agencies (million gourdes) 15% of (3)	Total government expenditures (million gourdes) (3) + (4)	Total maximum expenditure on army and police in percent of total government expenditures (2)+(4) in % of (5)
1960-61	38.4	173.9	26.1	200.0	32
1961-62	37.8	196.8	29.5	226.3	30
1962-63	37.6	173.7	26.1	199.8	32
1963-64	39.1	174.5	26.2	200.7	33
1964-65	36.7	172.3	25.8	198.1	32
1965-66	35.1	155.2	23.3	178.5	32
1966-67	35.0	178.2	26.7	204.9	30

Sources: (2): IHS (1971), pp. 338-44 (realized expenditures), (3): 1960/61-1964/65: CIAP (1966), p. 42, 1965/66-1966/67: CIAP (1972), pp. 72, 74, (4): CIAP (1966), p. 39.

* This figure is believed to correspond reasonably well with detailed estimates of *Régie* revenues made by the World Bank for later years. The latest World Bank report for the period up to 1975 is IBRD (1974). The *Mission d'Assistance Technique Integrée* of the OAS, on the other hand, at the beginning of the 1970s estimated that the revenues of the autonomous agencies for the fiscal years 1964/65-1967/68 amounted to 35, 40 and 50 million gourdes respectively (OEA (1972), p. 63). These estimates are, however, probably too high.

If it is assumed that the expenditures of the autonomous agencies equal their revenues and that all expenditures go to security purposes we arrive at a figure for total spending on army and police of approximately 30 percent of total government expenditures. This is a maximum estimate, but it should be kept in mind that even if less than the entire revenues of the autonomous agencies were spent on 'security' the remainder is still likely to have been diverted to unproductive purposes, with the same detrimental effects for economic development.

The diversion of funds to unproductive purposes via the autonomous agencies is also likely to have continued after the death of Papa Doc in 1971. The World Bank is known to possess detailed estimates of the revenues of the *Régie*, which have remained at a high level.

The large sums spent on army and police can only partly be explained by national security purposes. During the early nineteenth century, before the settlement with France had been negotiated in 1825, a large standing army was obviously a necessary evil, but also after the settlement, disproportionate amounts continued to be spent on 'defense'. Another obvious reason for heavy expenditure on the army was that a majority of the nineteenth-century presidents were army generals, but a more important reason was probably the fact that army backing was needed to achieve or retain the presidency. For the same reasons spy organizations and secret police forces were maintained. Not only was the official army paid out of the government treasury, but when the practice of employing *caco* mercenaries for revolutionary activities became widespread towards the end of the nineteenth century, these troops were financed with public funds as well. With some variations, the same pattern continued after the turn of the century. The old army and the *cacos* were permanently destroyed during the occupation, but instead a constabulary was created which soon became a political instrument exercising a strong influence on politics. The importance of the Garde diminished in the late 1950s and the 1960s, but those years instead witnessed the build-up of a system of purely political repression that is still in existence. The conclusion is evident. Expenditures on army and police forces have been nothing but political expenditures in disguise, all subordinate to the vested interests of the politicians inside or outside the government.

Wages and Salaries

As a consequence of the extreme use of the spoils system described in the preceding chapter — a system which essentially has served as a way of rewarding political friends — a large proportion of government expenditure has been absorbed by the payment of salaries and wages. A host of political followers with varying claims on the government purse have been kept on the payrolls of the ministries thus limiting the resources which may be used for investment and operation purposes.

Before the American occupation of Haiti, government expenditures were not properly recorded,[59] and it is therefore not possible to get even an approximate idea of how much of the budget was dedicated to wages and salaries. There seems to be no doubt that the proportion was exaggerated, however, because one of the first measures taken by the occupation officials was to eliminate from the government payrolls 'employees who were deceased, not working, or grossly incompetent.'[60]

Nevertheless, wages and salaries, even during the constructive years of the occupation was probably the most important budget item of the ministries. An illustration is given in Table 8.7 which shows that out of the total expenditures of the *Service Technique du Département de l'Agriculture et de l'Enseignement Professionnel* (the main vehicle for agriculture development) almost one-half went to salaries and wages. The dominance of wages and salaries in the budget continued and was reinforced after the American withdrawal. Table 8.8 gives some figures for the *Service National de la Production Agricole et de l'Enseignement Rural*, the successor of the *Service Technique*. The salaries and wages share of the SNPA&ER by far exceeds that of the *Service Technique*, with an average around 75 percent of total expenditures.

Table 8.7: Wages and Salaries Expenditures of the Service Technique 1925/26-1929/30

Fiscal year	Total expenditures of the Service Technique (million gourdes)	Expenditures on wages and salaries (million gourdes)	Wages and salaries in percent of total expenditures
1925-26	3.0	1.3	43
1926-27	3.6	1.7	47
1927-28	3.6	1.7	47
1928-29	4.6	2.1	46
1929-30	4.5	2.4	53

Sources: Total expenditures: Service Technique (1930), p. 16, wages and salaries: Service Technique (n.d.), p. 17; (1928), p. 19; (1929:1), pp. 25-6; (1929:2), pp. 17-18; (1930), p. 15.

Between 1949 and 1951 a little more than 40 percent of total government expenditures was absorbed by the salary budget,[61] and almost as much, as Table 8.9 indicates (excluding the expenditures of the autonomous government agencies) was spent during the 1960s. In the agricultural sector 50 to 55 percent of the total resources were absorbed by wages and salaries between 1968 and 1972.[62]

Table 8.8: Wages and Salaries Expenditures of the Service National de la Production Agricole et de l'Enseignement Rural 1933/34-1939-40

Fiscal year	Total expenditures of the SNPA & ER[a] (million gourdes)	Expenditures on wages and salaries (million gourdes)	Wages and salaries in percent of total expenditures
1933-34	1.8	1.3	72
...	...	...	...
1936-37	2.3	1.7	74
1937-38	2.0	1.5	75
...	...	...	...
1939-40	2.1	1.5	71

a. The figures of this column differ slightly from those of Table 7.2, as the sources differ.
Sources: SNPA & ER (1935), Table 2; (1939), tables following p. 10; (n.d.), p. 15.

Much of the expenditure on salaries and wages has not served any constructive purpose. The 1948 United Nations mission to Haiti pointed out that the salaries of the government employees absorbed such a large share of the budget that other essential spending was held back,[63] and the so-called Tripartite mission from the OAS, ECLA and the IDB in 1962 labeled the high manpower expenditures a 'deformation of the structure of public expenditure. . .which corresponds to a traditional practice of disguised absorption of the unemployment by the intervention of political bodies.'[64] In the opinion of another eminent authority on Haitian life, Sidney W. Mintz, 'the ministries do little more than perpetuate themselves unchanged' for lack of funds for other purposes than salaries.[65] The absorption of budget funds for personnel expenditures is largely unwarranted. The quantity and quality of the work performed by most of the Haitian public administration in no way corresponds to the sums spent on the salaries of the civil servants. A large proportion of these salaries are paid out for political services, past or present, and nothing in the way of work is expected. The employees frequently do not even bother to come to the office except on payday. The administration has been distorted by politics and serves mainly political ends.

Table 8.9: Wages and Salaries Expenditures of the Haitian Government 1959/60-1971/72

Fiscal year	Total government expenditures excluding autonomous agencies (million gourdes)	Expenditures on wages and salaries excluding army and police (million gourdes)	Wages and salaries in percent of total expenditures
1959-60	163.2	63.8	39
1960-61	173.9	63.0	36
1961-62	196.8	63.8	32
1962-63	173.7	63.5	37
1963-64	174.5	63.8	37
1964-65	172.3	65.4	38
1965-66	155.2	69.6	45
1966-67	178.2	74.2	42
1967-68	184.8	70.4	38
1968-69	209.9	76.8	37
1969-70	228.6	81.0	35
1970-71	273.2	95.4	35
1971-72	276.4	98.4	36

Sources: 1959/60-1964/65: CIAP (1966), p. 42; 1965/66-1969/70: CIAP (1972) pp. 72-4; 1970/71-1971/72: CIAP (1974), pp. 99, 104.

The Structure of Government Revenues

The analysis of politics and corruption in Chapter 7 and the discussion of expenditures in the present chapter should leave little doubt as to the aim of Haitian public finance. The very essence of Haitian politics, at least after the fall of Boyer in 1843, and possibly seventeen years earlier, after the death of Christophe, has been to seek power in order to enjoy the spoils and prerogatives of office. During the course of the nineteenth century, politics increasingly assumed the role of a mere source of personal enrichment for the clique in power, and this tradition has persisted ever since. If this is not correctly understood it is not possible to understand Haitian public finance either. All the main categories of expenditure have been subordinated to motives of personal wealth. A large public debt was created originally to avoid Foreign intervention, but subsequently mainly to raise money which could be distributed among the politically faithful. Large sums have been spent on a police and army apparatus either to obtain or to retain power, and the public administration has constantly been packed with the political supporters of the governing groups. Political expediency, rather than concern with economic development or general welfare, has been the most important determinant of public expenditure policy.

The dominance of selfish motives in politics not only determines the structure of public expenditures but exerts an important influence on revenues as well. Maximization of public revenues has always been the objective of Haitian tax policy.[66] In order to make the spoils as large as possible maximum revenues have had to be extracted. This maximization process has not been unconstrained, however, but has had to take place within certain fairly rigid limits, some of which are direct consequences of the state of politics itself. The first constraint (which is only indirectly connected with politics) is so obvious that it needs no discussion, namely the general poverty of the country. Keeping this in mind, we will instead concentrate on the two politically determined constraints: the inefficiency of the administrative apparatus and the reluctance to distribute the tax burden equitably.

Inefficiency in Administration

The administrative machinery has always been weak in Haiti. In the first place it has suffered from excessive centralization. All important decisions as well as many routine ones have been concentrated at the highest levels. Real power has always been vested only in the hands of the president, and from the point of view of administrative efficiency this has too often had unfortunate effects. Delegation of authority has been very rare. It has seldom extended beyond the level of ministers and directors general of the various government agencies, while little or no initiative at all is left to the middle and lower echelons in the hierarchy. The inevitable consequence is that too much time is spent on purely routine matters at the higher levels with the result that the administrative process has little continuity.[67] This centralization of the decision-making process was carried to its extreme during the presidency of Duvalier *père*. The only loyalties expected and accepted were those towards the chief executive, and even people in relatively insignificant positions were made to report events directly to the top. The intermediary ranks lost whatever importance they had held, and a wait-and-see or do-nothing attitude developed even at the ministerial level. In 1971, Robert I. Rotberg wrote:

> In...[Haiti]...it is [Duvalier] who makes all of the vital (and many of the non-vital) decisions affecting the state and its citizenry, operates as the state, and personifies all of the functions usually exercised by an ongoing government of a modern nation-state. He makes and enforces the rules – the laws and the tacit understandings which accompany them - and provides machinery for the maintenance of civil order, the adjudication of disputes, the punishment of transgressors, and the secular operation of the bureaucracy without which even the most illusory state would cease to have meaning. He ordains social change and stagnation and provides direction for the process of political development and decay.[68]

After the death of Papa Doc in 1971, the concentration of power appears to have become somewhat less absolute. A little more scope for independent action by the ministers seems to have been created. This should not be taken as a sign of a trend towards increased decentralization, however. Rather, it must be interpreted as a step back to pre-1957 conditions. The administration as a whole still remains too centralized to be efficient.

Centralization is not to be regarded as evil *per se*. If coupled with a genuine commitment to economic development on behalf of the leaders of the nation, centralization may be a very efficient way of promoting egalitarian reforms which otherwise may be opposed.[69] In Haiti there are no signs of this potentially fruitful union. The heavy centralization of administrative decisions has instead been accompanied by an almost total lack of commitment to development. The political history of the country clearly demonstrates that the goals of the ruling classes and of a vast majority of the presidents have not at all been geared to public welfare. At the level of public administration this has been translated into a general lack of purpose and efficient guidance. Precision and clarity with respect to objectives have been sadly lacking which in turn has created a situation where administrative work has been improvised rather than deliberately planned.[70]

The quality of administrative performance is also lowered by a general lack of appropriate administrative techniques and routines. Hierarchical levels and order chains are only insufficiently defined except at the highest levels in the system. Job descriptions are lacking. Responsibilities are vaguely stated and shared by too many hands for the same task. Organization manuals and charts have not been developed.[71]

Furthermore, many public agencies, and not least the tax administration, have had too little information on which to base their operations. Thus, it is not known with any degree of accuracy how many companies and individuals should rightly be subject to taxes on profits and incomes, let alone who these subjects are and what bases should be used to compute their contributions.[72]

Finally, the administrative problem is compounded by the relatively low quality of public employees. For at least two reasons the administration in general is characterized by an excessive number of 'general administrators' lacking specific competence in relation to the number of qualified technicians. The first reason stems from the way all public servants are appointed. Article 93 of the Haitian constitution of 1964 states that 'the president of the republic shall appoint and dismiss secretaries of state, undersecretaries of state and government employees and officials.'[73] This article is nothing other than the constitutional sanction of a spoils system carried to its extreme. It is customary in most countries that high government officials are appointed by the head of state to whom they are attached by political bonds. However, the lower echelons of the administrative hierarchy remain more or less intact when one government is substituted for another. This is not the case in Haiti, where only the political followers of the president are eligible for government jobs and promotion even at a fairly modest level. Conversely, a civil servant does not know when he is going to lose his job. Everything depends on political judgements, even in the middle hierarchy, and especially with the type of government represented by Duvalier *père* where the relative political standing of almost anybody could change considerably overnight. 'The abuse of dismissals sometimes assuming scandalous dimensions' led to a 'nomadism' of public employees.[74] Papa Doc used his power to dismiss civil servants to a much larger degree than any other modern Haitian president[75] — with very unfortunate consequences. When Magloire left the country there was at least some level of competence in the public office with a fair number of experienced civil servants and/or university graduates in the ministries. Under Duvalier many of these people lost their jobs and were driven out of the country to be replaced by less able people lacking the necessary training. As a direct political strategy Duvalier frequently employed the practice of appointing people with a professional training to posts where their background was of no use, while others — with equally deficient qualifications — were assigned jobs suitable for the former category — a deliberate and systematic misallocation of scarce manpower resources.[76]

An extreme spoils system also inevitably leads to discontinuity in public administration. The top and middle cadres are changed with relative frequency. New functionaries constantly have to take over jobs without the proper knowledge and without anybody to instruct them – with a concomitant loss of efficiency.

The second factor to be taken into account is one which is intimately connected with the foregoing. Given the fact that the overall budget is small and that too many politically justified appointments of personnel have been made, the general salary level of public employees has remained too low to attract competent people. However, it has not just been a consequence of low salaries but also of the fact that payments have been highly irregular, with frequent arrears ranging from one to three months.[77]

When these facts are put together: that appointment to government jobs even at the middle level has been mostly political, that nobody has been able to feel safe with respect to his or her political standing and that government salaries (excepting the highest offices) have been quantitatively inadequate and irregularly paid out, it comes as no surprise that a majority of the properly trained technicians have turned away from the government sector and have moved to the private sector or emigrated. The Haitian public administration has been left with a body of public servants, most of whom possessed no merits other than political ones when appointed, and an excessive number of whom were put into 'general administration' positions to and beyond the point of overstaffing.[78]

Government employees work comparatively short hours – officially six hours, five days a week. This reinforces the tendency to pad staffs excessively. A given amount of work is divided between more hands than necessary had the work day been longer. Operations become more costly and the adequacy of their performance is reduced. The combination of short hours, low salaries (themselves partly as a result of the short hours), frequent arrears in payments, and politically determined opportunities for promotion has led to a slow, disinterested governmental service, and to a situation that is even more serious: it has added another dimension to the pattern of graft and corruption discussed in Chapter 7. Irregularly and inadequately paid civil servants without a chance of promotion and lacking interest in their work have developed a host of practices which are not at all compatible with administrative moral integrity.[79]

The overall effect of exaggerated centralization, lack of commitment to economic development, deficient administrative routines, insufficient basic information and awkward manpower policies has

Haitian Public Finance

been to reinforce the patterns of the soft state. An administrative apparatus has been created and perpetuated, which given its task — in the present case tax collection — contains too many dysfunctional elements to be able to operate with any degree of satisfactory efficiency. The spoils system has been extended beyond all reasonable limits. Government jobs have been held mainly as a reward for political support, and political backing could not be sacrificed just to increase revenues.

Unequal Taxation

A second constraint has been imposed by the marked reluctance of virtually all Haitian governments to distribute the tax burden in an equitable fashion. The ability-to-pay approach to taxation has had no application in Haiti.[80] The upper classes successfully resisted taxation for the whole of the nineteenth century. Haiti's first income tax did not become law until 1903 and never had any practical importance.[81] It was not until 1942 that Haiti got an income tax that was actually collected, and this tax conspicuously excepted personal income and discriminated against such incomes that were derived from business. This was not remedied until 1948 when a bill taxing all income, personal as well as business, was passed.[82] The governing elements have not been interested in placing the burden of taxation upon the wealthier elements of the population. Even the 1948 tax legislation was very modest. Incomes of less than 15,000 gourdes were to be taxed at a rate of only 5 percent, and the marginal income tax in the top bracket was no more than 30 percent (on incomes exceeding 200,000 gourdes).[83] Today, the degree of progression of the tax system has increased somewhat. The 5 percent rate applies up to 5,000 gourdes only, and thereafter the marginal rate increases up to 35 percent above 35,000 gourdes and 50 percent above 500,000.[84] However, the practical importance of taxes on income is very slight. In 1970-71 and 1971-72, only some 3,500 taxpayers filed personal income declarations, and only a little more than 1,100 actually paid taxes. Slightly more than 1 percent of GNP was declared as liable for personal income taxes, while it has been calculated that the 'true' figure should lie in the neighbourhood of 20 percent.[85] The registration of taxpayers is defective, and the scope for evasion is virtually unlimited, it seems, since no efforts are being made to prosecute evaders. Most professionals, for example, are known to have comparatively substantial incomes, but in 1971-72, 24 percent of those filing paid nothing whatsoever, and the rest only paid a tiny average of 589 gourdes. The average paid by physicians was 323 gourdes and that by lawyers 277 gourdes.[86] The collection of urban property taxes has likewise been hampered by a lack of realistic assessment of property values. Assessment is to take place every five years, but in practice this period tends to be extended.[87]

The concentration of wealth and political power in the same hands has precluded almost any efforts to place a reasonable share of the tax burden on those who can best afford to pay. The very wealth of the governing cliques, however, has been heavily dependent on the ability of the government to extract taxes and other revenues. To resolve this apparent contradiction in a situation where the tax administration is in addition very inefficient, strong emphasis has been placed upon taxes on foreign trade. Collection of import and export duties is much easier than collection of taxes on domestic goods (or on income) since fewer commodities are involved in foreign trade than in the domestic economy. The need for trained personnel is smaller and the potential for effective tax enforcement is greater than in the latter cases. Taxes on foreign trade presumably allow a government in an economy where development has not yet begun to obtain more revenue than can be obtained from other sources, and this is definitely the case when almost by definition the possibility of levying high taxes on incomes and wealth has been forsworn.[88] From the administrative point of view there may be a particular preference for export taxes, because they usually cover fewer commodities than is the case with import duties, since both the complexity and variety of the commodities and the number of firms are likely to be lower than on the import side.[89] In addition, imports on low per capita income levels are to a large extent likely to consist of luxury goods, consumed mainly by the richer classes, who in Haiti also happen to correspond fairly well to those groups who impose the taxes.

Table 8.10 gives an overview of the importance of import and export duties in Haitian government revenues up to the late 1950s. During the nineteenth century, the importance of duties on foreign trade was gradually built up, until virtually the entire income of the treasury consisted of revenues from imports and exports. This trend began at an early date. Although Toussaint, Dessalines and Christophe all employed a crop-share tax amounting to one-fourth of the total agricultural production, they also (except for Christophe) depended on taxes on foreign trade.[90] Pétion abolished the crop-share tax, but (in addition to a land tax) kept the duties on imports and exports and, with a few changes, this system has continued to exist ever since.[91] At the beginning of the 1880s, export taxes were slightly more important than import tariffs, while forty years later the roles had been reversed. The preponderance of import duties has continued during the present century. Table 8.10 shows the situation until the late 1950s. For later years, detailed classification of taxes is available only for the so-called fiscal revenues.* The shares of import and export duties of these revenues are presented in Table 8.11. The taxes on foreign trade account for between 55 and 60 percent of fiscal revenues. Due to the complexity and opacity of the Haitian tax system it is not possible to establish the percentage of total government revenues that has been covered by import and export taxes, but the proportion is probably significant. Import duties are known to cover almost 40 percent of the revenues of the *Régie du Tabac*, the most important autonomous agency,[92] and out of the duties on coffee exports (the largest single source of export taxes) the amounts going to non-fiscal revenue are of the same magnitude as those classified as 'fiscal'.[93] **

Table 8.10: The Shares of Import and Export Duties in Public Revenues 1837-1957 (percent of total revenues)

Years	Import duties	Export duties	Import + export duties
1837	33.3	19.0	52.3
1880-81	46.6	51.6	98.2
1917-22	49.9	44.4	94.3
1922-27	59.1	30.1	89.2
1927-32	56.0	27.5	83.5
1932-37	54.0	28.9	82.9
1937-42	65.5	14.0	79.5
1942-47	57.1	18.4	75.5
1947-52	53.4	19.8	73.2
1952-57	49.5	18.1	67.6

Sources: 1837, 1880-81: Benoit (1954:2), p. 22, rest of table: Moral (1959), p. 143.

To sum up: The concentration of Haitian politics on the conquest and retention of power mainly for the sake of plundering the public treasury has had important consequences for the composition of public expenditures. Even excepting the outright squandering of public funds that does not appear in any statistics, it can be said that the expenditure pattern to a large extent has been determined by the personal

---

* These, during the latter half of the 1960s accounted for approximately 60 percent of domestic government revenues, excluding those of the autonomous agencies (CIAP (1972), pp. 72, 74).

** The appendix to this chapter gives an idea of the overall efficiency of the fiscal system in Haiti by presenting time series of total public expenditures.

Table 8.11: The Shares of Import and Export Duties in Fiscal Revenues 1959/60-1970/71 (percent of fiscal revenues)

Fiscal year	Import duties	Export duties	Import + export duties
1959-60	42.0	19.2	61.2
1960-61	41.5	15.2	56.7
1961-62	38.4	19.9	58.9
1962-63	33.2	19.2	52.4
1963-64	36.5	16.0	52.5
1964-65	34.5	16.8	51.3
1965-66	39.3	19.4	58.7
1966-67	42.2	16.6	59.8
1967-68	43.0	16.2	59.2
1968-69	47.4	14.5	61.9
1969-70	42.8	12.5	55.3
1970-71	41.7	14.2	55.9

Sources: 1959/60-1964-65: CIAP (1966), p. 41, rest of table: CIAP (1972). p. 71.

ambitions of the politicians. Haiti's history of recurrent indebtedness, overmilitarization and excessive spoils payments may be interpreted as a direct outcome of the view that holds government and public administration as a pie to be shared by those in power.

Hence, it is easy to understand why so little has been spent on agriculture in spite of the importance of this sector for the economy. It is similarly quite evident that the contents of politics have also determined the revenue policy of the government. The goal of most Haitian presidents with respect to public finance has been one of simple revenue maximization in order to make the pie to be shared as large as possible. However, this maximization process has operated within certain constraints which are also, at least partly, the results of the political process. These constraints, apart from the general poverty of the country, have been on the one hand the general inefficiency of the tax administration and on the other hand the unwillingness of those in power to tax the upper classes, i.e. themselves. Administrative inefficiency and discontinuity have been bred by excessive political interference. Functionaries have not been appointed upon their merits but instead the criterion has been that of political allegiance. The decision-making process has been too centralized to be efficient, and lack of appropriate administrative routines has added to the general confusion. The combination of political appointments and low salaries has fostered corruption at all levels. The unwillingness of the politicians to tax their own social class, in turn, is well borne out by the history of income taxation in Haiti. Together, the two constraints in combination with the political goal structure have led to a tax pattern which has been concentrated on the taxation of foreign trade. These taxes have been easy to collect, even with an inefficient tax system, and have in addition provided an opportunity to avoid taxation of the upper classes and to shift most of the tax burden to other groups, notably the peasants, instead.

Effects on Peasant Welfare

Several studies have advanced the argument that the incidence of both import and export duties rests very heavily on the peasants. During the American occupation of Haiti the occupation officials viewed a revision of the Haitian tax system as an absolute necessity. The prevalent system of import and export duties was viewed as 'one of the worst tariffs in existence,'[94] and it was felt that it rested too much on the shoulders of the rural population. The Financial Advisor believed that internal revenues should at least equal or even exceed that from customs duties to shift the incidence away from the peasants, and in 1924 a Bureau of Internal Revenue was created to that end. As Tables 8.10 and 8.11 demonstrate, however, this objective was not achieved.

On the import side, the peasants have been hit by taxes on necessities such as cotton cloth, soap, flour, fish and rice, all of which were imported by the time of the occupation and all of which were articles of prime interest to the peasants. Luxury goods, such as fine liquors, on the other hand, which were consumed primarily by the urban elite, received a much more favorable customs treatment and came in at practically no duty.[95] The situation had not changed much in the 1930s, the 1940s or the 1950s. Items like cotton textiles, kerosene and soap which are consumed to a large extent by the peasants bore the main burden of the import taxes, while with a few exceptions luxury items continued to be absent from the lists of commodities subject to duty.[96] Subsequently, domestic production of some of the import goods purchased by the peasants has been taken up, but that has changed little from the point of view of taxation, since these commodities have instead been subject to excise duties — to a much larger extent than luxury foodstuffs for example. In the late 1960s, three mass consumption products — flour, cigarettes and oil — contributed 80 percent of the government revenues from excise taxes, and flour alone yielded fifteen times as much as luxury foods. A revision of the system of excise duties in 1971 did not include any changes in the duties on these necessities.[97]

The argument above does not take into account that the imposition of an import duty could lead to substitution effects in consumption among the peasants or that the duty would affect peasant incomes and thereby consumption. Without empirical studies, for which data are presently lacking, it is not possible to determine the net effect of import taxes on peasant welfare when the possibilities of substitution in consumption due to changes in relative prices and peasant incomes are taken into account.

The incidence of export taxes as well is believed to be mainly shouldered by the peasants. The most important export product, and consequently also the one which accounts for the bulk of government revenue that comes from export taxes, is coffee. Viewed in a world perspective, Haiti is only a small producer with a share in total world exports which amounted to less than 1 percent in the 1960s.[98] This means that Haitian exports cannot influence the world market price of coffee. Instead Haiti must be considered a price taker. A tax on Haitian exports cannot be shifted forward to foreign consumers but has to be borne by the domestic economy.[99] The interesting question then becomes which group within Haiti will have to bear the taxes.

One way of looking at this problem is to examine the relative bargaining power of producers and intermediaries in the marketing of coffee. The conventional wisdom here is that the peasants are facing an oligopsonistic market with a high degree of concentration and collusion among the exporters, and that the *spéculateurs* who act as middlemen between the exporters and the peasants as a rule are mere agents of the export houses. In our discussion of the marketing of peasant products in Chapter 4, we found, however, that this argument is highly questionable. It is quite obvious that the degree of power that the exporters hold over the peasants has been exaggerated. The very fact that the gross share of the intermediaries increased between the early 1950s and the beginning of the 1970s does not prove that the degree of concentration has increased on the buyer side. Increasing freight and marketing costs must also be taken into account.

On the other hand, it is also obvious that there is no concentration on the producer side, i.e. among the peasants. In this situation, it is probable that the peasants bear the entire burden of the tax. Foreign demand for Haitian coffee should be almost perfectly elastic due to the competition on the world market. The demand of the Haitian intermediaries is derived from the world market demand and should

Haitian Public Finances

hence also be very elastic. In this situation, regardless of what the elasticity of supply may be, the incidence of the tax should fall on the producers, i.e. on the peasants. Table 8.12 provides an estimate of the burden borne by the coffee-producing peasants. The table assumes that the entire tax is shifted backward to the peasants and points to an average burden of more than 40 percent of potential incomes from coffee production.

Table 8.12: Coffee Export Taxes in Percent of Peasants' Potential Coffee Incomes 1964-71

Year	Average annual f.o.b. price (1)	Taxes (2)	Producer price (3)	Producer price plus taxes (4) = (2) + (3)	Effective tax (%) (2) : (4) x 100
1964	48.0	15.5	24.0	39.5	39.2
1965	50.4	16.1	20.4	36.5	44.1
1966	51.0	16.1	21.0	37.1	43.4
1967	47.4	16.1	19.2	35.3	45.6
1968	44.3	16.1	18.5	34.6	46.5
1969	43.5	15.9	17.0	32.9	48.3
1970	56.4	16.3	29.3	43.6	37.4
1971	52.2	16.3	24.4	40.7	40.0

Source: JWK (1976:1), p. 84.

When discussing the effects of coffee taxation on peasant welfare, we must also take into account whether there are any substitution possibilities on the production side or not, i.e. whether the peasants after the imposition of the tax will continue to produce the same amounts of coffee as without any tax or whether they will shift into e.g. subsistence production instead. Vito Tanzi has claimed the following to be an accurate description of the Haitian case:

> If producers are many (while the exporters are few), if they own and work the land themselves, *if the particular output requires the use of very specialized resources which cannot easily be shifted to other lines of activities, or other crops, as is the case with trees,* and if the yield of the next best use is relatively low, *then it can safely be concluded that the producers will bear the burden of the tax*...*this is the situation which most likely has prevailed in the coffee sector in Haiti.*[100]

The truth of this statement depends on the time perspective that is taken. It is quite probable that in the short run the peasants will continue to grow coffee even if a tax is imposed or if the existing tax is increased, but if a longer time perspective is taken, the peasants will probably shift from coffee production to production of subsistence goods instead, as was seen in Chapter 5 where a twenty-year perspective was taken (as Tanzi also agrees).[101] Hence the export tax will have effects on relative prices and peasant incomes which in turn will influence peasant consumption, and these have to be taken into account when the effects on peasant welfare are to be analyzed. Unfortunately, as in the case of import duties, the relevant date for such an analysis are lacking.

Conclusions

We have now arrived at a fairly good understanding of why for more than a century the Haitian governments have shown a pronounced reluctance to intervene in the agricultural sector. The background to this *laissez-faire* policy was given in Chapter 6 where we analyzed the reasons behind the Haitian land reform which began in 1809. One possible consequence of the reform was that the GNP started to fall. In Chapter 7, it was shown that in spite of the declining GNP, no serious efforts were made by nineteenth-century governments to inject new life into the agricultural sector. We also showed how this reluctance to intervene (with the exception of the American occupation) has continued up to the present time. On average, the agricultural sector has received less than 10 percent of total government expenditures.

We continued by analyzing the goal structure of Haitian politics as it developed following the collapse of the plantation system. By 1843, when Boyer was ousted from the presidency, the peasantry already constituted a politically marginal group. Three centuries of slavery followed by a few years of forced labor under conditions closely reminiscent of slavery had created a strong desire for freedom and land among the majority of the Haitian population (i.e. among the latter-day peasants), and when the land reform began, it proved impossible to stop it until Haiti had been converted into a peasant minifundia country. The peasants had then reached their most important goals and showed no further interest in national affairs.

This passivity has in turn been reinforced by the fact that the rural environment has been dominated by military rule on the one hand and a supernatural interpretation of the world on the other.

During the same period politics developed into a game for the few — a game where the spoils of presidential office constituted the price. Landed incomes were a thing of the past. The only way of tapping agriculture to yield incomes for the elite and near-elite groups was by means of taxation, and to tax the peasantry, control over the administration was necessary. Mulatto elite and black army generals fought each other for the spoils. Haitian nineteenth-century politics developed into a succession of *coups* and revolutions until the country was finally occupied by the United States in 1915.

The occupation turned out to become a mere parenthesis. With the Haitians back in power again after 1934, the treasury could be milked anew, the only difference from pre-occupation times being that after 1946 a tiny black bourgeoisie, currently in power, began to participate in the political process. Otherwise, the political goals remained basically the same as before the occupation. The treasury has continued to be legitimate prey for the cliques in power, and power is viewed as a means to reach the prey.

In the present chapter we have examined how the Haitian view of politics has determined the composition of both the expenditures and the revenues of government. Instead of spending on the most important sector of the economy, successive governments have created an expenditure pattern which by and large is an outcome of the infighting between political cliques and of the corruption resulting from the course taken by politics. A foreign debt was contracted in 1825 when Haiti was forced to pay an indemnity to France in return for an official recognition of national independence. On several occasions up to 1915, new foreign (and domestic) loans were taken under the pretext of consolidating the 1825 debt which, however, due to the scandalous manipulations by the politicians, left next to nothing to the treasury, while the pockets of the members of the 'in' cliques were filled. The foreign debt was increased without yielding any benefits to the average Haitian, and foreign debt service continued to be a heavy burden on the budget, until in 1947 the debt was finally liquidated.

Two other important expenditure items bear an even more direct relation to politics than does debt service. Haiti has always been an overmilitarized country. Before 1825, this was natural enough. The new-won independence had not yet been formally recognized. The

Haitians had to guard against the possible return of the French and were therefore forced to keep a large standing army. Army and police expenditures remained large after 1825, however. During the revolutionary fights of the past century, control of a large and loyal army was necessary for the incumbent president if he were to remain in office. The contenders for the presidency, in turn, kept recruiting *caco* mercenary armies which were regularly paid off with the contents of the government treasury when the incumbent president had been overthrown. When the vaults were empty, loans were flotated to ensure payment.

The American occupation destroyed the old army and pacified the *cacos* but instead created a constabulary – the *Garde d'Haïti* – whose support was necessary for all post-occupation presidents up to 1957. The older Duvalier reduced the importance of the Garde virtually to zero but simultaneously built up his own private army – the *tonton macoutes*. Army and police expenditures continued to absorb large amounts.

The final expenditure category dealt with in the present chapter is that of personnel. As a consequence of the 'kleptocracy' view of government, the Haitian administration has become packed with the supporters of whatever government that happens to be in power, and when a government is overthrown, the administration is always purged. A new group of people with mainly political merits is substituted for the old one. Administrative positions are regularly given as a reward for political favors, and a high percentage of the budget funds are spent on manpower, leaving little for actual operations.

Politics also dictate the revenue patterns pursued by the Haitian governments. The goal of the Haitian kleptocracies with respect to public finance has been to extract as much money as possible. Hence, maximization of public revenues has become a most important goal in itself. However, Haitian politics has also created its own limitations or constraints within which the maximization process has had to proceed. There are two main constraints. First, the tax administration is utterly inefficient. Since the administration is recruited not on merit but on political grounds, its competence and efficiency is low. Excessive centralization of decisions has created a wait-and-see attitude which dominates the administration. Salaries are low and corruption goes unchecked. The second constraint is that of a limited political willingness to act in matters of taxation. We should not expect a kleptocracy to tax itself or the groups from which it is recruited, as is clearly illustrated by the practice of income taxation in Haiti. In order to

Haitian Public Finance 401

maximize revenues within an inefficient system of tax administration and where the taxation of income and wealth is precluded for political reasons, resort has been made to taxation of foreign trade. The bulk of public revenues have derived from export and import taxes.

Notes

1. Rotberg & Clague (1971), pp. 66-7; Benoit (1954:2), p. 95; Pierre-Charles (1965), pp. 172-3, Folsom (1954), p. 391.
2. Folsom (1954), p. 392.
3. Rotberg & Clague (1971), pp. 392, 397.
4. Benoit (1954:2), p. 97.
5. Chatelain (1954), p. 16.
6. Rotberg & Clague (1971), pp. 397-8.
7. Folsom (1954), p. 394.
8. Rotberg & Clague (1971), p. 397.
9. See Chapter 7.
10. Rotberg & Clague (1971), p. 91.
11. Benoit (1954:2), p. 98.
12. Ibid., pp. 98-9.
13. According to Folsom (1954), p. 392 in 1888, but according to Benoit (1954:2), p. 99 in 1893.
14. See Chapter 7.
15. Rotberg & Clague (1971), p. 399.
16. Folsom (1954), p. 396.
17. Chatelain (1954), pp. 79-80.
18. Rotberg & Clague (1971), p. 399.
19. For details regarding these loans see Folsom (1954), pp. 396-8.
20. Ibid., p. 398.
21. Ibid.
22. Ibid., pp. 398-9.
23. Schmidt (1971), p. 43.
24. Rotberg & Clague (1971), p. 131.
25. Millspaugh (1931), pp. 118-22; Chatelain (1954), pp. 146-50.
26. Millspaugh (1931), pp. 123-5; Schmidt (1971), pp. 165-6.
27. Millspaugh (1931), p. 125.
28. Schmidt (1971), p. 167.
29. Spector (1961), p. 208.
30. Rotberg & Clague (1971), p. 130.
31. Schmidt (1971), pp. 223-4.
32. Ibid., pp. 225-6.
33. Folsom (1954), p. 414.
34. Emigration will be dealt with in the epilogue.
35. Folsom (1954), p. 404.
36. See Turnier (1955), pp. 298-300; Pierre-Charles (1965), pp. 187-8.
37. Folsom (1954), p. 414.
38. UN (1949), pp. 297-301.
39. For details, see Chapter 7.
40. BTS no. 10, September 1953, pp. 72-3.
41. Figures are given in IHS (1971), pp. 332-46 for 1954/5-1969/70, in BID (1974), p. 177 for 1970/71-1973/74, in Le Moniteur (1974), p. 82 for 1974/75 and in Le Moniteur (1975), p. 79 for 1975/76.
42. Leyburn (1966), note, p. 36.

43. Mackenzie (1830:2), pp. 201-2; St John (1889), p. 310.
44. Brown (1837:2), p. 259.
45. Rotberg & Clague (1971), p. 77.
46. Leyburn (1966), p. 71.
47. Brown (1837:2), p. 267.
48. Ibid., pp. 267-8.
49. Rotberg & Clague (1971), pp. 86-7.
50. St John (1889), pp. 382-3.
51. Davis (1929), pp. 123-4.
52. Rotberg & Clague (1971), p. 87.
53. St John (1889), pp. 327-8.
54. Ibid., p. 310.
55. Schmidt (1971), p. 88.
56. Folsom (1954), pp. 386-7.
57. Schmidt (1971), p. 168.
58. Rotberg & Clague (1971), p. 215.
59. Folsom (1954), p. 386.
60. Schmidt (1971), p. 160.
61. Folsom (1954), p. 389.
62. BID (1974), pp. 171, 183.
63. UN (1949), p. 296.
64. OEA-CEPAL-BID (1962), p. 68.
65. Mintz (1966:1), p. xxxiv.
66. Cf. Folsom (1954), pp. 336, 381, 383; IBRD (1972), p. 24; CIAP (1974), p. 125.
67. See e.g. García Zamor (1966), p. 64; CIAP (1968:2), p. 120; CIAP (1974), p. 79; OEA (1972), pp. 13, 19, 29.
68. Rotberg & Clague (1971), p. 343.
69. Cf. e.g. Adelman & Morris (1973), pp. 44-5, 61-3.
70. Cf. CIAP (1968:1), p. 17; OEA (1972), pp. 19, 33.
71. OEA (1972), pp. 19, 31-4; CIAP (1974), p. 79.
72. For details, see OEA (1974), pp. 86-98.
73. Constitution (1968), p. 16.
74. Vieux (1969), p. 559.
75. Ibid., p. 558, Latortue (n.d.), p. 3. Insecurity of tenure due to political factors did not begin with Duvalier, however. See e.g. UN (1949), pp. 9-10.
76. Latortue (n.d.), p. 2; OEA (1972), p. 33.
77. CIAP (1971), p. 36; OEA (1972), p. 20; OEA (1974), p. 101.
78. See e.g. CIAP (1971), p. 60; CIAP (1972), p. 63.
79. CIAP (1974), p. 80.
80. Cf. Musgrave (1959), Chapter 5, for a statement of this principle.
81. Folsom (1954), p. 356.
82. Ibid., pp. 356-8.
83. Ibid., p. 358.
84. OEA (1974), p. 64.
85. IBRD (1974), technical note 4, p. 16.
86. OEA (1974), pp. 94-5.
87. IBRD (1974), p. 62.
88. Cf. Due (1970), pp. 28, 30; Tanzi (1976), p. 66.
89. Prest (1972), p. 67. Cf. also Ayal (1965), p. 331.
90. Leyburn (1966), pp. 317-18, Benoit (1954:2), Chapter 2; Turnier (1955), p. 98.
91. For details, see Benoit (1954:2), Chapter 2; Bellegarde (1934), pp. 144-5; Folsom (1954), Chapter 9; OEA (1972), pp. 61-100.

92. IBRD (1974), p. 51.
93. Ibid., pp. 47-8; JWK (1976:1), p. 79.
94. Millspaugh (1931), p. 127.
95. Folsom (1954), pp. 318-19.
96. Ibid., pp. 330-32.
97. IBRD (1974), pp. 57, 59.
98. JWK (1976:1), pp. 82, 97.
99. For a discussion of the incidence of export taxes see e.g. Ayal (1965), pp. 335-44; Goode, Lent & Ojha (1966), pp. 461-6; Shoup (1969) pp. 416-17, and Tanzi (1976), pp. 67-73.
100. Tanzi (1976), p. 68 (italics mine). Cf also Goode, Lent & Ojha (1966), p. 465.
101. Tanzi (1976), p. 73. Cf. also JWK (1976:1), pp. 91-3.

APPENDIX: Total Government Expenditure

In order to gain an idea of the overall scope of the Haitian public finances we can examine the level of total government expenditure. Table A8.1 shows the development of government spending from the 1920s to the 1950s in nominal and real terms. The table shows that while the nominal value of government expenditures increased more than five

Table A8.1: Total Government Expenditure 1922/23-1951/52 (million gourdes)

Fiscal year	Nominal government expenditure	Import price index[a] (c.i.f.) 1946/47-1948/49 = 100	Real government expenditure
1922-23	30.6	61.0	50.2
1923-24	34.2	61.7	55.4
1924-25	39.2	72.0	54.4
1925-26	40.9	65.1	62.8
1926-27	39.7	59.8	66.4
1927-28	41.0	61.0	67.2
1928-29	44.1	60.2	73.3
1929-30	40.6	53.0	76.6
1930-31	36.2	44.4	81.5
1931-32	32.9	38.4	85.7
1932-33	33.2	34.8	95.4
1933-34	36.8	37.3	98.7
1934-35	42.3	37.9	111.6
1935-36	36.6	39.1	93.6
1936-37	35.0	42.8	81.8
1937-38	28.9	42.7	67.7
1938-39	29.6	36.8	80.4
1939-40	28.5	38.9	73.3
1940-41	25.6	39.1	65.5
1941-42	27.7	56.3	49.2
1942-43	28.0	64.0	43.8
1943-44	42.0	73.3	57.3
1944-45	42.5	75.3	56.4
1945-46	40.4	76.2	53.0
1946-47	60.4	108.4	57.6
1947-48	83.6	106.2	78.7
1948-49	93.3	85.2	109.5
1949-50	106.9	82.0	130.4
1950-51	121.8	94.0	129.6
1951-52	159.9	94.3	169.6

a. The use of the import price series as a deflator stems from the lack of better price data. No general index is available for the period covered by the table. Still, the degree of accuracy in the estimates may not be too bad. Benoit (1954:1), p. 102, states that the coefficient of correlation between c.i.f. prices and prices of indigenous products in Haitian market-places is as high as 0.9. The table should be interpreted with caution, however.

Source: Benoit (1954:1), pp. 77, 103.

times between 1922-23 and 1951-52, real expenditures only increased by rather more than three times during the same period. It is also noteworthy that real expenditures fluctuated widely, and that their value in the mid-1940s was no higher than in the 1920s. Table A8.2 gives series of nominal and real government expenditure for a more recent period. In nominal terms expenditures doubled from the early 1950s to the early 1970s, while in real terms the increase amounted to about one-and-a-half times. Calculated on a per capita basis, however, real expenditures increased very little from the beginning of the 1950s, as Table A8.3 shows.

Table A8.2: Total Government Expenditure 1952/53-1971/72 (million gourdes)

Fiscal year	Nominal government expenditure	Price index[a] 1948 = 100	Real government expenditure
1952-53	152.1	101.3	150.1
1953-54	175.0	105.7	165.6
1954-55	189.4	107.4	176.4
1955-56	190.4	111.3	171.1
1956-57	163.3	113.8	143.5
1957-58	191.0	113.6	168.1
1958-59	183.0	108.2	169.1
1959-60	187.7	102.8	182.6
1960-61	200.0	106.6	187.6
1961-62	226.3	106.0	213.5
1962-63	199.8	110.5	180.8
1963-64	200.7	120.8	166.1
1964-65	198.1	123.5	160.4
1965-66	178.5	133.6	133.6
1966-67	204.9	129.8	157.9
1967-68	212.5	131.5	161.6
1968-69	241.4	133.3	181.1
1969-70	262.9	134.2	195.9
1970-71	314.2	148.1	212.2
1971-72	317.9	152.8	208.0

a. The price index is the cost of living index for Port-au-Prince.
Sources: Nominal government expenditure: 1952/53-1956/57: Moral (1959), p. 147, 1957/58-1958/59: OEA-CEPAL-BID (1962), p. 68, 1959/60-1964/65: CIAP (1966), p. 42, 1965/66-1969/70: CIAP (1972), pp. 72, 74, 1970/71-1971/72: CIAP (1974), pp. 99, 104. For the years 1959/60-1971/72, 15 percent have been added to official expenditure figures to arrive at the totals presented in Table A8.2. A justification of this procedure was given above. Price index: 1952/53-1970/71: IHS (1971), p. 421; 1971/72: BTS, No. 92, 1973, p. 100.

Table A8.3: Real Government Expenditure Per Capita

Fiscal year	Total real government expenditure (million gourdes)	Population (million)	Real government expenditure per capita (gourdes)
1952-53	150.1	3.6	42
1953-54	165.6	3.7	45
1954-55	176.4	3.7	48
...	...	...	...
1969-70	195.9	4.2	47
1970-71	212.2	4.3	49
1971-72	208.0	4.4	47

Sources: Total expenditure: Table A8.2. Population: 1952/53-1954-55: Saint Surin (1962), p. 24, 1969/70-1971-72: IHS (n.d.), p. 1.

Seen in an international perspective Haitian government expenditures are small. Table A8.4 compares the total expenditures of the central government as a percentage of the gross domestic product for a number of countries in the Caribbean and Central America in the early 1970s.

Table A8.4: Total Government Expenditure in Percent of GDP in Central America and the Caribbean 1970-4

Country	1970	1971	1972	1973	1974
Barbados	28.7	30.1	29.7	33.5	33.7
Jamaica	23.1	24.4	25.4	27.1	30.5
Trinidad and Tobago	21.8	23.2	24.1	20.3	28.0
Panama	20.2	18.6	20.4	20.1	19.6
Nicaragua	11.2	12.8	13.2	13.3	19.2
Costa Rica	13.7	16.2	16.2	17.1	16.4
Dominican Republic	17.2	17.7	16.3	16.1	15.5
Honduras	17.0	15.2	14.8	13.2	14.7
El Salvador	11.7	12.0	13.1	12.9	13.8
Mexico	9.9	9.8	12.5	13.5	13.4
Haiti[a]	11.0	11.8	12.0	11.0	11.3
Guatemala	10.0	9.7	11.4	9.9	10.4

a. The table presumably does not include the expenditures of the autonomous agencies.
Source: BID (1975), p. 442.

As we can see, Haiti ranked second from the bottom during the entire period. The capacity of the Haitian government to raise funds for development and for other purposes was smaller than that of almost all other Caribbean and Central American governments.

A small government budget is in itself an insufficient reason for starving agriculture of government funds. It would have been perfectly possible to dedicate a large share of a comparatively small budget to the most important economic sector, but this has not been the case in Haiti. As we have seen, funds have been devoted to other purposes than increasing the productivity and welfare of the peasantry. However, given the low priority assigned to agriculture, the absolute size of the budget affects the amount allocated to that sector. If the budget is very small, the non-priority sectors are likely to receive very little, while with a larger budget the possibility that at least some attention is also paid to these sectors increases. Hence, it is possible to argue that one of the reasons for the comparatively small amounts going to agriculture is the limited capacity of the government to extract sufficient revenues.

9 MALNUTRITION AND DISEASE

Chapters 5-8 have presented the basic problems of Haitian peasant agriculture. At the center is the erosion process. The growth of the population creates an accelerating process of soil destruction which goes unchecked. Neither the peasants themselves nor the Haitian government have proved willing to make any attempts to control erosion. We have also gained some insight into the philosophy of the Haitian governments with respect to agriculture. The peasant sector is seen as a source of taxes, while the reluctance to spend the tax proceeds to improve the production capacity of that sector has been notorious. Against this general background, the remaining chapters of the book will be devoted to a more detailed investigation of four important specific areas: nutrition and health, education, rural capital formation, and technological change in the agricultural sector. We will make an attempt to sketch the development in each of these fields in the past 25 years (or longer when possible) in order to identify the possible changes (or lack of changes) resulting from government action or otherwise.

This discussion will also enable us to compare the contribution (or lack of contribution) of land, labor, capital and technological change to the development (or lack of development) of Haitian peasant agriculture. In Chapter 5 we found that land resources are slowly contracting. In Chapter 11 we will discuss some of the factors which have hampered capital formation, and in Chapter 12 we will examine the lack of technological dynamism. Before that, however, we will in the next two chapters concentrate on the human factor. Chapter 10 will deal with the development of rural education, while the present chapter will examine the nutrition and disease characteristics of the rural population. Beginning with nutrition we will first evaluate the state of child and adult nutrition in rural areas and its development over time. The middle section of the chapter will be devoted to a similar analysis of disease conditions, and in the final part we will trace the implications of changes in malnutrition and disease for the peasant economy.

When the contemporary interest of economists in human capital formation began to take shape in the early 1960s, the attention was almost exclusively focused on the possible influence of education on economic growth,[1] while disease and nutrition were treated more *en passant*, if they were dealt with at all.[2] In the 1970s, this bias is beginning to be corrected, and development economists increasingly realize that an improved health status should not be regarded only as a direct measure designed to increase the welfare of the individuals but that it may have an instrumental value too when it comes to increasing output and productivity and hence also indirectly the standard of living.

This is the strand of thought which we will pursue in the present chapter. However, the reader should be warned at once that the conclusions which will emerge are not particularly substantial — for several reasons. First of all, the analysis of malnutrition and disease is a comparatively new branch of development economics, and so far mainly very general results which are difficult to apply to specific cases have been established. A second difficulty lies in the fact that many of the connections between health factors and economic performance in less developed countries have been postulated rather than established empirically in a methodologically satisfactory manner. A related problem is the difficulty of developing operational measures for a number of the theoretical notions. Furthermore, concepts which are easy to deal with in theoretical analysis are sometimes extremely difficult to separate empirically. Finally, at least in the case of Haiti, comparatively little attention has been paid to the possible connections between health and economic performance which in turn means that the type of data needed for a satisfactory empirical analysis are sadly lacking.

There is very little that can be done about these difficulties. The scope of the present work does for example not permit us to gather 'new' primary data in the field, but we must remain content with what is already available and base our discussion on that, which means that during the course of the presentation we will run into all the difficulties enumerated above. Nevertheless, a discussion of malnutrition and disease is definitely desirable. Both undoubtedly play an important role for agricultural production, and plenty of research is needed in this area — research which we cannot aspire to carry out here. We must limit ourselves to identifying some of the most important health problems, to tracing their development over time and to pointing to some of the most probable consequences in terms of agricultural production — thereby setting the stage for more penetrating research in the future.

It is not easy to find a definition of health which would meet with universal acceptance. As Victor R. Fuchs has observed, definitions of health abound and range from the WHO 'state of complete physical and mental and social well-being' to the simple stress of 'the absence of, or the ability to resist, disease and death.'[3] Here, we will choose the latter approach and define health as the absence of disease and malnutrition. We will be concerned with identifying the presence of what are commonly considered as diseases. The practical difficulties connected with operationalizing health definitions of the 'positive' WHO type force us to take this 'negative' approach. Basically, the same approach will be followed in the discussion of nutritional status — one of the most important aspects of the health complex. Our procedure will be to look for symptoms which are commonly recognized as indications of deviations from the 'normal' state. Hence, to the extent that we can establish the incidence of the more important diseases and of malnutrition we also get an idea of what the health situation in Haiti is like. Let us begin with the nutrition factor.

Malnutrition

We will define malnutrition as a state of inadequate intake of food and/or malabsorption of the nutrients that are eaten.[4] Malnutrition may be a consequence either of too low an intake of energy (calories) or protein (protein-calorie malnutrition — PCM) or of specific deficiencies in the vitamin or mineral intake. The quantitatively most important of these deficiencies — most severe and most widespread — in less developed countries, is PCM.[5] In the following we will attempt an evaluation of the nutritional status in rural Haiti with respect to each of the three types of deficiencies. In this analysis we will single out one specific age group that is known to be in an especially precarious nutritional situation in most less developed countries — pre-school children[6] — and discuss this group specifically. Before we go into the Haitian case, however, we need a background consisting of a discussion of some possible physiological consequences of child malnutrition.

Some Physiological Consequences of Inadequate Nutrition in Children

Inadequate nutrition affects the human body whenever it occurs, but the character of the influence varies considerably over the life cycle of the individual. The most critical period presumably is the fetal stage and the first months after birth, since it is during this period that the brain is developed, so that exposure to malnutrition during this sensitive stage may have consequences for the later development of the mental faculties of the child.

It is, however, only incompletely understood how pre-natal

malnutrition is related to the process of cerebral development. The main problem is that it is not possible to perform controlled experiments with human beings, but experiments with animals, examination of living children and post-mortem examination of fetuses and children are the main sources upon which one has to fall back. The evidence accumulated so far lends some support to the hypothesis that malnutrition *in utero* may damage the brain but since the evidence is limited it would be too much to state that this support is conclusive.[7]

The problems may continue after birth. A number of investigations have been made of the effects of malnutrition during early childhood on mental abilities. Generally these studies indicate a positive relationship between nutritional conditions and scores on intelligence tests of various types.[8] Whether nutritionally caused brain damage, if it exists, is irreparable or not is not known yet with certainty, but as Héctor Correa has remarked, the question may lack practical relevance, at least in our case. It is not likely that in a country like Haiti nutritional deficiencies can be improved unless special programs for doing so are available. Therefore, malnutrition during the early childhood is usually followed by nutritional deficiencies during later stages of life, and the mental deficiencies, irreparable or not, easily become permanent.[9]

Malnutrition is usually also connected with disease. The malnourished individual will fall ill more easily than a person whose diet is satisfactory. If malnutrition continues, recuperation will either be very slow or not take place at all. This is the case especially with severe malnutrition (third degree malnutrition).* It is believed that most children suffering from that die either as a result of malnutrition itself or as a result of infections before they reach their sixth year of life.[10] Those who survive are likely to be physically weakened.

The combination of malnutrition and illness may have disastrous consequences for school performance.[11] Many children lack both energy and motivation to attend school at all, and are not in any way urged by their parents to do so. Of those who actually go to school, many do so only irregularly because of lack of the necessary stamina. They repeatedly have to stay home out of pure weakness or because of diseases. They have trouble following what is taught in class, which in

---

* According to the Gómez criteria, a body weight of 90 percent or more of the standard weight of the age group in question is considered as an indication of normal nutrition, a percentage of 75 to 89 as first degree malnutrition, and percentages of 60 to 74 and below 60 as second and third degree malnutrition, respectively. Usually all cases of edema, irrespectively of body weight, are classified as third degree malnutrition.

turn increases the rate of absenteeism. They have to repeat grades and finally drop out altogether. What is left in the way of informal education as a rule is reduced to what is offered by the generally very poor stimuli coming from an environment characterized by the existence of a deprivation syndrome.

Body size and muscle development are also known to be affected by malnutrition during childhood. In countries like Japan and Taiwan, where the nutritional situation has improved considerably in recent years, the improvement has been accompanied by increases in average stature, whereas in countries with widespread malnutrition the average generally falls short of the norm. The same is true with respect to muscular development. Lack of protein (and calories) during childhood and adolescence means that the muscle tissue becomes only inadequately developed. Malnourished nine-year-old children look like (healthy) six- or seven-year-olds.[12] Both body size and muscle development are important for the latter performance in strenuous occupations, like agricultural field work.

Besides protein-calorie malnutrition, the most common nutritional deficiencies among children in less developed countries appear to be Vitamin A and (to a lesser extent) Vitamin B deprivation and nutritional anemia.[13] The former in severe cases leads to total blindness, and is believed to be the major cause of this defect in underdeveloped areas. Under less serious circumstances, apart from causing ocular defects (e.g. night blindness), Vitamin A deprivation will affect the skin condition and growth of the child who is subjected to it. Lack of Vitamin B causes fatigue and lack of appetite, and in severe cases symptoms connected with the gastro-intestinal tube, the nervous system or the skin may develop which in certain cases may be deadly. Anemia, finally, is common among older children. One effect of anemia is the reduction of the level of physical performance. It causes fatigue and increases the vulnerability to diseases.

Malnutrition among Haitian Preschool Children

There is little to indicate that malnutrition *in utero* or infant malnutrition might be a problem in Haiti. If we look at the figures of Table 9.1 we find that during the first few months the weight of Haitian infants does not appear to differ significantly from that of American (Iowa) children the same age.

This presumably is due to the fact that during this period most Haitian children are breast-fed (and it is also an indication that undernourishment probably is not a problem among either pregnant or lactating women).* Correa mentions that for all groups of children from less developed countries for which data exist, the average growth rates of wholly breast-fed babies are very satisfactory and that the rates may even exceed the figures regarded as normal in the United States or Great Britain.[14] After four to six months, however, rural Haitian children begin to lag behind their American counterparts in the way shown in the table. At ten months, retardation of height begins as well.[15] A comparison of height (which was made only for children above five years) showed a 10 percent inferiority in stature.[16] ** Haitian children from wealthy urban families are known to have both normal stature and normal weight,[17] and the fact that in rural areas weight lags more than stature behind the norm is an indication that malnutrition is the cause of the retarded physical development.

Table 9.1: Weight of Preschool Children in Fond-Parisien, June 1964

Age	Average weight in percent of average weight of American children the same age
0-5 months	102.1%
6-11 months	89.8%
12-17 months	81.1%
18-23 months	81.0%
2-3 years	81.0%
3-4 years	77.2%
4-5 years	79.8%
5-6 years	75.0%

Source: Beghin, Fougère & King (1965), p. 296.

The precarious nutrition situation among rural children of preschool age is well documented. Beghin, Fougère and King, in their exhaustive survey or the nutritional situation of Haiti, which covers about all the literature up to 1968 conclude that around two-thirds of all preschool children in (rural) Haiti are subject to protein-calorie malnutrition, and that 7 percent suffer from third degree malnutrition — which is believed

* A 1958 survey of 707 mothers in 14 villages showed that no less than 99 percent of all children included were breast-fed during the 0-5 month period (Jelliffe & Jelliffe (1961), p. 26).
** The retardation of both weight and height appears to conform well to average figures for less developed countries. At the age of four, children from these countries regularly show a deficiency of up to 20 percent in height and 40 percent in weight as compared to children from developed countries (Correa (1975), pp. 22-3).

to be fatal in most cases.*

Clinical observations confirm the results obtained by application of the Gómez criteria. The most widespread nutritional diseases in underdeveloped countries (especially among children) are kwashiorkor ('bloated bellies and glassy stares') which is principally a result of protein shortage, and marasmus, total starvation ('shrunken, wizened features and gross physical retardation'), which is caused by a gross deficiency of both proteins and calories.[18] A study made in 1958 of more than 2,300 children in the entire country indicated an incidence of 'complete' kwashiorkor (with all the clinical signs present) of 7 percent and one of 'incomplete' kwashiorkor (with some signs lacking) of 10 percent, while the incidence of marasmus was around 2 percent.[19] **

Besides protein-calorie malnutrition Haitian rural children present vitamin deficiencies and anemia. While comparatively few cases of Vitamin A deficiencies have been detected,[20] Vitamin B is a much bigger problem. Very frequently, riboflavin (Vitamin B_2) deficiencies appear among children and adolescents. The incidence on the south coast in 1960 was almost 40 percent. In some localities the frequency almost reached 80 percent.[21] Similar findings are reported in other surveys.[22]

Anemia due to iron deficiencies caused by too low consumption of meat is probably frequent among children. The Jelliffes in 1958 observed an incidence of 5 to 10 percent in the 0-1 year group, 20 percent between 1 and 3 years, 18 percent between 3 and 6, and 12 percent between 6 and 12 years of age, and in a 1962 survey of children in the 5-16 year group, the incidence was higher than 60 percent, with a significantly higher figure for the 5-10 year children than for the 11-16 year group.[23]

We may now attempt to sum up the nutritional history of the rural child. Probably the child is 'normal' at birth. At any rate, during the first few months, he has an adequate supply of calories, proteins and vitamins. The reason is that virtually all rural children (99 percent

---

* It should be observed that Beghin, Fougère & King (1970), p. 155 contains an important misprint. It is stated there that two-thirds suffer from second and third degree malnutrition. Cf., however, Beghin (1965), p. 51.
** A 1975 survey reports significantly lower figures — around 1 percent for kwashiorkor and 0.6 percent for marasmus (Gédéon, Lamothe & Haverberg (1976) Table III), but differences in selection procedures plus the fact that the 1958 survey was conducted during the 'dead season' in agriculture in June-July, while the 1975 survey was carried out during the coffee harvest, when cash is relatively plentiful, render the two surveys not strictly comparable.

according to the Jelliffe survey) are breast-fed for the first six months of their lives. Thereafter, weaning begins. During this process the nutritional situation of the child gradually worsens. The lactation of the mother becomes increasingly inadequate, and only insufficient substitutes take the place of human milk. (Often milk consumption is left out of the picture altogether.) White starchy soups, corn starch, manioc, vegetable broths, etc. 'from which protein [is] conspicuously absent'[24] is what the infants are weaned on. Eggs and meat are customarily not given to children below the age of one year,[25] since it is believed that eggs will cause caries and that meat will infest the children with worms. Older children should not eat sour fruits like oranges, pineapple, or *quénèpes*, because they cause constipation.[26] The results of the gradually increasing malnutrition are eloquently summarized by Ivan Beghin:

> These malnourished children do not die of starvation. They die of the consequences of a prolonged disequilibrium in their diet, where the quantity of nutrients is insufficient and where the quantity of proteins is even more insufficient. The proportions of proteins and calories which an adult consumes cannot suffice for a child who must develop bones, muscles and tissues. Thus, the malnourished infant reacts by reducing his rate of growth. Thereafter, his appetite decreases, thereby aggravating the situation. He becomes apathetic, indifferent, and thereafter hostile. His limbs swell, his hair loses its color, light or dark spots appear on his skin which sometimes is shed in flakes or cracks and waters. This is followed by diarrhea and a rapid death unless another diesase from which he is already suffering deprives the child of the life from which he is already detached. This illness is characteristic of the weaning period and often begins as the mother becomes pregnant again. All her care and milk then go to the new-born. The child of 1 1/2 or 2 years receives an unbalanced supply of food from the family table and the illness begins. It is common to see families where the child of 2 years and his younger brother, aged 6 to 9 months, have the same weight. The latter is chubby, gay and happy, while the former is miserable and sullen — already presenting the symptoms of the redoubtable disease.[27]

The combination of poverty, food taboos and insufficient knowledge give the children a deficient diet which leads to malnutrition. Haiti probably has one of the highest incidences of malnutrition among preschool children in the world.*

To complete the picture we add the generally very poor level of sanitation that is found in rural districts, which exposes the children to all kinds of infectious diseases (to be dealt with later) and to which they have weak or no resistance due to their undernourished state. Malnutrition continues through childhood and adolescence, however, with the 1-3 and 3-6 year groups in the most precarious situation,[28] and is successively accompanied by riboflavin deficiencies and anemia among the somewhat older children.

Malnutrition among Adults

What constitutes an adequate nutritional standard for an adult person? In the early 1950s, the statement that two-thirds of humanity were suffering from hunger was often heard, and during FAO's Freedom from Hunger campaign it was claimed that half the world was suffering from malnutrition. Both figures proved to be entirely wrong.[29] Gradually, the claims were lowered, and it was soon discovered that more sophisticated and disaggregated computations had to be made that took into account that what the human organism needs to function depends on several factors. The most important determinants are: (1) body size and composition; (2) sex; (3) age; (4) climate; (5) the extent of physical activities.[30] The first four factors do not need much comment. It goes without saying for example that big and tall persons need more calories than small people, that men eat more than women, that small children need less than adults, and that more calories need to be consumed in a cold climate than the tropics. More interesting from the point of view of the present study is the last item on the list: the extent of physical activities.

The relation between calorie intake and physical activity runs both ways. A person with a physically strenuous occupation needs more calories than one having a desk job. Conversely, if the calorie intake of the former is lowered, he will have to adjust his physical activity accordingly. This relation is well documented in the literature on nutrition. Thus, during the Second World War a reduction in the calorie intake of German coal miners of the Ruhr district from 4,500 to 3,500 calories per day made the output per worker fall 15 percent and the miners simultaneously lost weight.[31] Similar experience is reported with German steelworkers and railway track workers during

---

* Beghin, Fougère & King (1970), p. 58. These authors quote the study of Bengoa (1966) which revealed that at least up to 1966 Haiti had the highest rate of protein-calorie malnutrition among preschool children ever reported.

the same period.[32] Costa Rican construction workers gradually increased their work four-fold after receiving a better diet.[33] The examples could easily be multiplied.[34]

The malnourished individual will avoid physical (and presumably also mental) efforts and increase the period of rest. Experiments with semi-starvation diets in Minnesota report loss of energy, general weakness and a state of apathy.[35] Muscle strength and precision of movements are both lost.[36] To preserve the basic, internal processes of the body the individual adjusts by slowing the extent and pace of physical activities.[37]

The Haitian peasant in general spends only 0.45 gourde per day on food for each member of his family, including the value of what he produces in his own fields.[38] This is clearly insufficient. The average calorie and protein needs for Haiti, according to the most reliable estimates, those by Beghin, Fougère and King, are 2,200 calories and 55 grams, respectively.[39] In Table 9.2 we find a number of survey estimates of calorie and protein intakes for rural areas. All of them, except the one for Guérin, fall short of the calculated norms both with respect to calories and with respect to protein. Results obtained by calculating the overall availability of calories and proteins and dividing the resulting figures by the population figure seem to confirm the results of these surveys. Thus, the latest available estimate of the calorie intake at the time of writing gave a figure of 1,450 calories per day and

Table 9.2: Surveys of Average Daily Calorie and Protein Intakes in Rural Areas 1951-65

Locality	Year	Calories	Proteins (grams)
St-Marc	1951	1491	—[a]
Whole country[b]	1958	1580	37.4
Port-Margot	1962	1105	26.8
Fond-Parisien	1964	1360	31.7
Ganthier	1964	1524	36.1
Fond-Parisien	1964	1580	40.4
Guérin	1965	2203	55.8

a. The protein figure for St.Marc (70 grams) is known to be too high. (Cf. Beghin, Fougère & King (1970), p. 68.)
b. Includes both urban and rural areas.

Sources: 1951 BTS, no. 2, Oct., 1951, p. 61; 1958-65: Dominique (1965), p. 69.

person in rural areas for 1975 — a deficit of almost 35 percent in comparison to the recommended quantity.[40] For proteins, the latest available calculation is for 1966 (undertaken by Beghin, Fougère and King): 41 grams. However, as pointed out in Chapter 3, the 1966 estimates are based on too high a population figure. If a more accurate population estimate is used the protein intake increases to 48 grams per day and person, which still represents a deficit of 12 percent.[41]

The insufficient intake of calories and proteins is shown by the fact that most adult Haitians are underweight for their height. The Sebrell team, covering both rural and urban areas, found that 51 percent of all the persons examined were 10 percent or more underweight (while only 4 percent or more overweight) in relation to their height.[42]

In order to complete the picture as far as adults are concerned, vitamin and mineral deficiencies have to be added. With regard to Vitamin A it is probable that a slight deficiency exists among wide groups of the population. Beghin, Fougère and King propose an average 22 percent deficiency for the whole year.[43] The intake varies considerably during the year, however, as seen in Figure 9.1 (for the Cayes region). During the summer months, when the supply of mangoes and avocados is plentiful, the need is more than well covered, and some of this vitamin is also stored in the body and can be used as a reserve. Between September and April the intake falls. The average deficiency when mango consumption is not included lies around 65

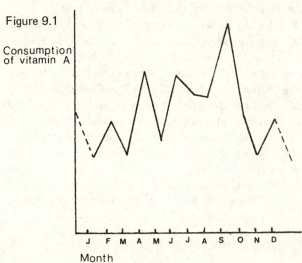

Figure 9.1

Consumption of vitamin A

Month

Source: Beghin, Fougère & King (1970), p. 75.

percent.[44] *

Riboflavin deficiencies are probably even more widespread than Vitamin A deficiencies. The average deficit has been estimated to lie around 30 percent of the daily need.[45] It is quite probable that the riboflavin deficit is also seasonal in nature, since one investigation found that almost one-half of the intake in the month of June came from mangoes and avocados, but no time series from one locality exists, so that the evidence remains more suggestive than conclusive.[46] Recently, some evidence pointing to a possible Vitamin B_{12} deficiency among Haitians has also been presented.[47] Anemia, finally, is also prevalent among adults. The Sebrell team, which covered the entire country in 1958, found that an average of 13 percent of the examined persons had an abnormally low hemoglobin content in the blood.[48]

Quite probably, the nutritional situation in rural Haiti is undergoing a deterioration as we saw in Chapter 3. How long this deterioration has been going on is, however, not known. Nutrition research during the 1930s and 1940s left little quantitative evidence. It was not until the 1950s that budget studies and nutritional surveys began to be carried out in a systematic fashion. These studies were summarized in Chapter 3, and the reader is referred to that chapter for details. Although the evidence is somewhat contradictory, it appears as if at least during the 1962-75 period the average nutritional standard has been falling in Haiti. Estimated daily calorie intake in 1962 was 2,140 calories per person while in 1975 the figure had fallen to 1,450.

To sum up: Rural Haiti presents a gloomy nutritional perspective. It appears that the worst conditions are to be found among the children of preschool age. During the first six months of life, the development of rural children appears fairly normal in terms of weight and height, presumably because virtually all children in Haiti are breast-fed during this period and because lactating mothers probably are not undernourished. Gradually, however, the rural children begin to fall behind the norm both with respect to weight and with respect to height, and in the 1-4 year group as many as two-thirds may suffer from slight or severe malnutrition. Moreover, protein-calorie malnutrition is not the only problem for the children in the preschool age group, but both Vitamin B deficiency and nutritionally related anemia are frequently encountered.

---

* Note, however, that both the 22 percent and the 65 percent figures are over-estimates, since they build on too high a population estimate. Cf. note 41.

Malnutrition and Disease

While the preschool children obviously constitute the nutritionally most vulnerable group in rural Haiti, nutritional deficiencies continue to plague adolescents and adults as well. The average intake of both calories and proteins very definitely falls short of the prescribed norms, and Vitamin A and B deficiencies occur during certain periods of the year (while they do not seem to be chronic).

The nutritional picture of rural Haiti is not a static one. In order to recognize fully the magnitude of the malnutrition problem we must examine the trends. As we saw in Chapter 3, only scanty and incomplete time series data are available, but in so far as these can be interpreted, they point towards a very high probability that the average nutritional standard is falling in the countryside (as a result of falling per capita incomes). We will come back to the economic significance of this towards the end of the present chapter, but before that we will attempt to sketch the disease situation in rural Haiti and its development since the American occupation.

The Disease Situation

While the nutritional state of rural Haiti is known with a fair degree of accuracy, the same cannot be said about the disease situation. Only limited surveys have been undertaken, and most of the available data are hospital statistics only. No attempts have been made to cover a larger share of the population via cross-sectional sample studies, and few time series that allow meaningful comparisons can be found.[49]

The American Occupation

During the American occupation, the first quantitative research on diseases was carried out. Four illnesses were found to be especially serious threats: yaws, malaria, intestinal parasites and tuberculosis. In 1924-25, it was found that in the neighborhood of the capital, yaws incidence was 78 percent.[50] Yaws is a terrible affliction,

> a non-venereal contagious disease that maims patients and causes open infectious lesions. It does not kill but attacks the vital organs and dooms its victims to living torment. It can shrink and twist limbs to uselessness, eat away facial features, or cripple by ulcerating the soles of the feet. It is caused by a spirochete similar to that of syphilis (ironically each disease immunizes the victim against the other). It is transmitted by contact and flourishes particularly in tropical areas where people go barefoot and do not bathe often.[51]

Since most of the peasants go barefoot the initial lesion (*maman pian*) as a rule appears a few days of weeks after the infection on the lower extremities, where scratches are common. The ulcerous mother yaw usually leaves a scar which persists throughout life. Around three months after the primary lesion the secondary stage begins. The skin starts to peel, and where this has occurred red papulas resembling raspberries appear. At the end of this stage the soles of the feet and the palms of the hands become calloused. Fingers swell, and nails are deformed. The secondary stage lasts 6 to 12 months. During the tertiary stage, which follows thereafter, ulcerous lesions replace the papulas. Rheumatic pain (*douleur pian*) in knees, ankles, wrists or shoulders appears. These symptoms may last for the rest of life.

At the same time, it was also found that near Port-au-Prince 67 percent of the population had malarial parasites in the blood,[52] and another survey in 1928 gave incidences for adult workers and children under 14 years of age of 24 and 51 percent, respectively.[53] The high frequency of intestinal parasites in Haiti was detected for the first time during the American occupation. The Americans found that they had trouble with the physical resistance of the soldiers of the *Gendarmerie d'Haïti*. An examination undertaken in 1918 showed that 70 percent of the soldiers of the Gendarmerie (which was posted all over the country under approximately equivalent sanitary conditions to those of the local population) had one or more intestinal parasite,[54] and out of a sample of more than 3,750 persons examined in 1924-25, 38 percent had hookworm (*Ancylostoma*), 43 percent had roundworm (*Ascaris*), and 56 percent had whipworm (*Trichuris*)[55] in the neighborhood of the capital.

These three worms are all intestinal nematodes. *Ascaris* and *Trichuris* often appear together in the same host, and both of them are dependent on fecal contamination of the environment for their origin. *Trichuris* is especially harmful for children, and *Ascaris* is one of the most common parasites of man, with incidences of 90 percent or more reported in parts of the Far East. Hookworm, again, is a parasite with an estimated 460 million infections throughout the Third World.[56] The parasite enters through the soles of the bare human feet when the victim treads on feces-contaminated soil. In one way or another the three helminthic diseases mentioned are strongly dependent on a state of poor sanitation, and all of them are believed to cause great fatigue and discomfort in the human body.

Hospital data, finally, revealed that tuberculosis was the single most important cause of death (around 25 percent of all cases)[57] Even higher figures were reported for the *Gendarmerie d'Haiti* — 45 percent.[58]

The sanitary facilities were sadly deficient when the Americans entered the country. In 1915 there were 10 hospitals (each with a dispensary) with a scanty total of 880 hospital beds and in addition four provincial dispensaries, in the whole country.[59] The Americans reorganized the public health service in Haiti. By 1929, the country had 15 modern hospitals, however, still with a limited capacity — 1,413 hospital beds altogether, less than one per 1,000 inhabitants. Only 159 physicians and 53 dentists were practicing in the country.[60] The Americans also proceeded to open rural clinics (146 in 1930) to treat the common diseases of Haiti.[61]

Yaws proved to be a special problem. A campaign where injections of arsenicals and bismuth were given, was begun, and up to 1931, almost 2.7 million injections had been given.[62] The results were not satisfactory. Many saw the initial relief and thought they were cured, but never fulfilled the whole three-month treatment that was necessary for complete cure. Traveling clinics were tried, but still yaws continued to be a problem long after the American occupation. Higher regularity of treatment would have been necessary.

Steps to reduce the incidence of other illnesses were also taken. Swamps were drained and filled, quinine was distributed, the water supply in the capital was chlorinated, markets and slaughterhouses were improved, public and private latrines were constructed, garbage and trash was collected, etc.

Stagnation 1931-50

Little progress took place during the 1930s and 1940s. The health situation around 1950 as a whole showed very few changes in comparison to the situation 20 years earlier. Statistical reports from 1944-49 still indicate TB as the main cause of death in the hospitals.[63] Hookworm was common, although figures to establish the incidence were lacking.[64]

A malaria recognition survey in 1947 found that few areas in Haiti were not infected with the parasite, with rates in Haiti reported to be higher than anywhere else in the Western Hemisphere.[65] Yaws incidence continued to be high, in spite of renewed campaigns. In 1948, it was estimated that in certain rural areas as much as 85 percent of the population was affected.[66] The intramuscular and intravenous injections of bismuth and arsenicals required too many treatments, and this fact also hampered the efficiency of the new campaign. It had been discovered that penicillin was a much more efficient treatment,[67] but due to its high cost, large-scale injection campaigns were not feasible.

Around 1950, most of the medical resources were concentrated in Port-au-Prince. In purely rural districts there were only 26 physicians for a population of approximately 2.5 million.[68] The United Nations mission report quotes an interview with one of these doctors, one of the ten employed by the Public Health Department:

> He stated that he had been unable to visit most of the dispensaries in that area because of lack of transport and allocation of travel expenses. Nevertheless, he did sometimes travel, but was obliged to make good his travel expenses by private practice. The poor will get very little help, indeed, from rural doctors in his position.
>
> It must be feared that travel practices are the same everywhere, for a civil service which does not provide means of transport or compensation for travelling expenses cannot reasonably order its officials to travel on duty. Yet it must have been the intention of the department that the hospital physicians should attend the clinics and dispensaries; in fact, in the annual report for 1944 it is stated that they must visit these institutions by turns. It cannot be readily ascertained whether this instruction has ever been generally and efficiently lived up to; that this is not so at present seems evident.[69]

The UN report concluded regarding the health situation around 1950:

> In examining the over-all situation it was found that the fundamental difficulty in the field of health, and the one having the most immediate bearing on and raising the gravest obstacle to the economic development of Haiti, is the unsatisfactory state (not to say the virtual absence) of public health service in the rural areas, whose more than 2,500,000 people are sadly lacking in medical care...the system of rural clinics and dispensaries, inadequately equipped and lacking in medical attendance and supervision, needs vigorous strengthening and vitalization. Indeed, the institution of a well-conceived, comprehensive and dynamic rural public health programme is an urgent necessity.[70]

Progress and Failures 1950-75

The UN mission pointed to yaws as the major obstacle to the improvement of the working capacity of the rural population and hence to economic development. In 1950, the government signed a contract with WHO and UNICEF and a large-scale penicillin treatment program was begun. With medical officers going from house to house, by 1954 almost 90 percent of the population had received long-acting single pencillin shots.[71] The campaign ended in 1955. The results were spectacular. Incidence figures fell to less than 1 percent of the population in 1953,[72] and by the end of the campaign it was believed that yaws was eradicated in Haiti. This was not entirely true. In 1961, it was found that transmission was still going on,* but from the practical point of view the disease appears to be under control. Only 26 cases were reported in 1974.[73]

Malaria became the subject of another nationwide large-scale campaign. In 1961, an eradication program was begun by the *Service National d'Eradication de Malaria* (SNEM), financed by the US government. The initial strategy was to spray all residences below 500 meters of altitude with DDT or Dieldrin. This procedure proved inefficient. In 1963, following hurricane Flora, a serious malaria epidemic with 50,000 cases flared up in the southern part of the country.[74] An experiment was then undertaken in Petit-Goâve, with chemotherapy in the form of tablets which were distributed every three weeks. The behavior of the malaria vector was also investigated, and it was found that activity reached its maximum around two hours after sunset and that the vector rested outside the huts instead of inside. This was an unfortunate coincidence, since most Haitians in rural areas eat outside, and the evening meal is generally served around sunset, or a little later, which rendered spraying inefficient. On the basis of this experience it was decided that anti-malaria tablets should be distributed to the population in malarial areas every three weeks. Acceptance rates were high, around 90 percent, and the incidence fell from 10,000 cases in 1965 to 2,600 in 1968.[75]

It was hoped by that date that malaria would be absent from Haiti within five years.[76] but this expectation has not been fulfilled. In 1974, more than 7,000 cases of malaria were reported,[77] and out of 333,770 blood samples examined by the SNEM the same year more than 25,000 were malaria positive.[78] The incidence has risen once more. The main difficulty with malaria eradication is that no single operation seems capable of achieving the goal:

---

* Noël (1969), p. 338. Noël points to two possible hypotheses that may explain the persistence of transmission: either new cases could have been introduced from abroad, or venereal syphilis by non-venereal transmission through several generations might have developed into yaws.

The type of malarial parasite may change and/or become resistant to insecticides, and geographical configurations may be altered by public works, new crops, floods, and hurricanes, each of which will ordain new spraying or drainage tactics. Even a *fête*, which inspires people to repaint their houses (neutralizing the insecticides) or cluster in the streets (during evening hours), may provide new opportunities for the transmission of parasites and undo months of careful control work.[79]

As has been witnessed in other parts of the world, notably Sri Lanka, malaria has a strong tendency to break out violently with epidemic force even after a prolonged absence, and therefore requires further attention even after the termination of an anti-malaria campaign. Given the present state of knowledge it does not seem possible to combat malaria in Haiti efficiently.[80] While the anti-yaws campaign must be classified as a success the eventual results of the anti-malaria program thus remain uncertain.

Tuberculosis continues to be one of the chief hazards for the adult Haitians. The incidence of active TB has been estimated to lie around 3 percent at any time, and most adults are tuberculin positive in tests which indicates that they have had the disease in the past.[81] Intestinal parasites finally, remain a problem in all age groups. Incidence diverges widely between different surveys,[82] but it is perfectly clear that the rate of intestinal parasites is high. For Ganthier and Fond-Parisien in the mid-1960s King reports a parasite infestation rate 'of essentially 100% incidence',[83] and a similar figure is given by Roland Wingfield for the country as a whole during the same period.[84]

For preschool children, other diseases than those just discussed appear to be more important. Hospital data from the 1960s clearly indicate that tetanus neonatorum due to the deficient sanitary conditions under which birth generally takes place in the countryside is the most frequent case of death before the age of one month. Between one month and one year for the country as a whole, gastro-intestinal disorders take the place of tetanus as the leading cause of both hospitalization and death in the hospitals, both with rates of around 70 percent of all cases.[85] In rural districts proper, however, malnutrition appears to be more important as a cause of both mortality and morbidity.[86] The two diseases are of course interrelated. Diarrheas are frequently caused by malnutrition which, as we have found, gradually increases as the infant is weaned to an insufficient diet. Many of the cases attributed to diarrheas could equally well be classified as malnutrition cases. It makes more sense to speak of a malnutrition-diarrhea complex than to treat the two separately.

Between tetanus neonatorum, diarrheas and malnutrition, infant mortality reaches high figures in Haiti. The exact percentage of children that die before they reach the age of one has not been determined with any satisfactory degree of accuracy, but the minimum estimates lie around 160 per mille, while the maximum estimates exceed 200 per mille.[87]

As we move to the 1 to 4 year group malnutrition takes over the leading position in hospital statistics as the cause of morbidity and reported deaths. Mortality in this age group is believed to exceed 25 per mille.[88] Here, as well as in the under one year age group, malnutrition is often coupled with intestinal disorders.[89] As soon as malnutrition is present, the resistance to other diseases is lowered, and the development of the illness in question is likely to differ from those cases which are not troubled by any complications. Otherwise harmless diseases may easily become fatal.

It is not easy to summarize the development of the public health situation between 1950 and 1975 using only the sparse information which is available regarding the relative incidence of diseases. The only thing which is known with any degree of accuracy is that the incidence of yaws has fallen considerably. Yaws has ceased to be one of the most serious illnesses affecting the peasant. Its incidence is now down to less than 100 cases per year in the whole country. The development of the malaria situation is much more difficult to evaluate. A number of steps have been taken to reduce its incidence, and it is probable that some success has been achieved. Still, the number of reported malaria cases remains rather high, and it is doubtful whether the disease is really under control, especially given the tendency of malaria to flare up with unexpected force after several years of comparative absence. For diseases other than yaws and malaria all evaluation of incidence trends is impossible. What is really needed is a nationwide cross-section survey of the same type as those undertaken in the nutritional field in the late 1950s. Until then our knowledge of the health panorama will remain utterly incomplete.

An alternative way of evaluating the development of the health situation is to look at the statistics regarding the availability of medical facilities in the 1950s and the 1970s.* This is done in Table 9.3. A

---

* Ideally, the comparison should include data on drug consumption as well, but no such data are available.

comparison between columns 3 and 6 (rest of country) shows that, except in the case of dentists, the availability of medical facilities outside the capital, at least quantitatively, has increased slightly. This points towards an improvement in the public health situation over the past 25 years. The table must be interpreted carefully, though, since most of the facilities even outside the capital are concentrated in the cities, so that the medical situation in rural areas proper was less favorable than the table shows both in 1952 and in 1973. It is impossible to determine the influence that may have been exerted by the inclusions of provincial towns on figures designed to show the situation in rural districts.*

The availability of medical personnel has always been a problem in Haiti. The Faculty of Medicine at the University of Haiti has around 50 medical graduates a year,[90] but most of them emigrate. Table 9.4 shows the percentage of medical graduates in Haiti that leave the country after graduation.[91] Higher wages in combination with political disagreements has caused the exodus. The situation is similar for nurses. In 1960 *all* of that year's graduates, without exception, left the country,[92] and it was estimated that only some 30 percent of all nurses who have graduated in Haiti since 1921 worked in the country at the beginning of the 1970s.[93] The vacuum for both doctors and nurses has been only partly filled by foreign personnel. In 1969, a government decree was issued which explicitly prohibited doctors, dentists, nurses and laboratory technicians from leaving the country without authorization by the Department of Public Health. In addition graduate medical doctors (with the exception of those specializing) are by law required to spend one year in rural districts or in a program of preventive medicine, and two years in hospital internship. However, out of some 80 physicians from the 1965-67 graduates subject to this service, it was estimated that only 12 ever served in rural areas.[94] Earnings and life conditions in general are not sufficiently attractive to make the medical personnel settle outside the capital.

Popular knowledge of herbal concoctions and consultations with *doktè-fèy* (herbalists) has always been the basic mode of curing illnesses in the countryside and still remains so today.[95] Secret recipes are passed down through the generations, some of considerable value,

---

* Subsequently the number of physicians and nurses fell, to 346 and 407, respectively for the country as a whole in 1975. The number of dentists had increased to 96 and the number of hospital beds to 4,003 (CONADEP (1976), p. 42).

Table 9.3: Public Health Facilities in 1952 and 1973

	1952			1973		
	Whole country	Port-au-Prince district[a]	Rest of country	Whole country	Port-au-Prince district[a]	Rest of country
Number of						
Physicians	241	153	88	522	340	182
Dentists	94	69	25	64	25	39
Nurses	223	163	60	484	240	244
Hospital beds[c]	2,168[b]	1,001[b]	1,167[b]	3,868	1,781	2,087
Population[c]	3,380,000	498,000	2,882,000	4,315,000	656,000[d]	3,659,000
Per 100,000 inhabitants						
Physicians	7	31	3	12	52	5
Dentists	3	14	1	1	4	1
Nurses	7	33	2	11	37	7
Hospital beds	64	201	40	90	271	57

a. This refers to the sanitary district of Port-au-Prince.
b. 1954.
c. The population figures are for 1950 and 1971 respectively.
d. This figure is based on a projection of the 1950 census figures, and is hence not strictly comparable to the other 1971 population figures, which come from that year's census.

Sources: Medical statistics, 1952: BTS, no. 10, September 1953, p. 32, 1973: BTS, Supplément Annuel — VII, Année 1973, pp. 7-8, 11-12. Population statistics, whole country: 1952: Saint Surin (1962), p. 11; 1973: Table 3.3; Port-au-Prince district, 1952: BTS, no. 10, September 1953, p. 32; 1973: Département de la Santé Publique (1972), p. 11.

Table 9.4: Percentage of Physicians Graduated in Haiti 1928-68 Practicing Abroad

Year	Percent abroad	Year	Percent abroad
1928-29	92	1950-54	72
1930-34	92	1955-59	69
1935-39	85	1960-64	66
1940-44	68	1965-68	68
1945-49	63		

Source: UNESCO (n.d.), p. 90.

others worthless or even harmful. Healers are well established in market-places, and the practitioners of voodoo and black magic — *houngans* and *bocors* — usually enjoy a high prestige as popular doctors as well.[96] Often, the predilection of the peasants for popular medicine is so strong that they will choose the *houngan* even if free treatment with Western methods is available:

> It is. . .true that the Haitian peasant is reluctant to get professional medical attention. . .The resistance of the Haitian peasant is less against the medicines which he accepts readily from the houngan as from known friends, than it is against the doctor, as a total stranger. The Haitians prefer their houngan because they trust him. And they trust him not only for religious reasons, but as a human being whom they have known all their lives, whom they have observed under all sorts of conditions, whose personality and character is hence familiar and predictable. They know the percentage of success and failure in his cures. Above all, he lives in their community and is subject to their control: to their approving patronage or the censure of their withdrawal.
>
> But the professional doctor in the city (and their experiences with the city have not always been pleasant) is a man whom the peasants do not know very well. His dress, his speech, his every gesture emphasizes the distance between their world and his. His professional objectivity contributes to their impression of his human detachment, and they see in this a potential irresponsibility towards them. Small wonder that they are reluctant to surrender themselves to his ministrations.[97]

Economic Effects of Malnutrition and Disease

In the first two sections of the present chapter we have furnished the available evidence regarding the development of the health and nutrition situation in rural Haiti. As far as nutrition is concerned, we know that the group which is most exposed to the danger of undernourishment is the children of preschool age.

Malnutrition continues to be a problem for adolescents and adults, albeit to a lesser degree than is the case with preschool children. On average it appears as if the nutrition situation in the countryside has undergone a process of deterioration at least during the past ten to fifteen years.

Health records go further back than does the evidence on the state of nutrition, but the available data are not easy to interpret. During the American occupation it was found that yaws, malaria, intestinal parasites and tuberculosis were the main threats, and the occupation officials took a number of steps to organize an efficient public health service. In practice, it appears as if few patent results came out of these efforts. At any rate, the situation in the early 1950s did not present any major positive changes in comparison to that of two decades earlier. The same diseases continued to plague the Haitians, and the availability of health care to the average rural inhabitant had probably not increased.

In the early 1950s, yaws was brought under control thanks to the employment of penicillin treatment, and a serious effort was made to eradicate malaria which, however, met only with limited success. Apart from these changes the health panorama of rural Haiti continues to present the same problems as 20 or 30 years ago. For young children tetanus and later malnutrition coupled with gastro-enteritic disorders are the most important causes of morbidity and mortality, and for the older age groups we still encounter malaria, intestinal parasites and tuberculosis. The main treatment of these diseases is what the the peasants are able to obtain from popular healers, herbalists and *houngans*. Popular medicine dominates the scene, and progress with respect to availability of modern preventive and clinical treatment has been only marginal, judging from available statistics.

If somewhat boldly we attempt to sum up the development with respect to health and nutrition during the past 15 years (which is the period for which we have the best documentation), we unfortunately have to conclude that the only major breakthrough that has occurred in the medical field in Haiti is the virtual eradication of yaws which had been widespread during the 1930s and the 1940s in rural areas and, possibly but not certainly, a reduction of the incidence of malaria. Against this, however, we must set the fact that the average state of nutrition seems to have deteriorated during the same period. Hence it is not possible to reach any definite conclusions with regard to the overall development of the health panorama.

The issue is further complicated by the fact that changes in health due to diseases and changes due to malnutrition cannot be analyzed separately, but malnutrition and disease, as we have pointed out, interact and reinforce each other. Resistance to diseases is lowered by malnutrition, while parasites and gastro-intestinal diseases, for example, increase the incidence of malnutrition in preventing the body from absorbing the nutrients properly.

The conclusion to be drawn from the evidence of the first two sections of the present chapter is thus that while we have some knowledge regarding the development of the nutritional situation on the one hand and the disease situation on the other, we cannot be sure of whether the net change is for better or for worse, especially not since nutrition and disease interact, so that a declining calorie intake should lead to a higher sensitivity to infections. However, it may be worthwhile to identify some of the main possible economic effects of the changes in disease and nutrition to make our understanding of the problems of the peasant economy more complete. Our interest will be focused on the instrumental aspects of malnutrition and ill health, i.e. we are not interested in the direct welfare effects but rather in how the change in incidence of diseases and malnutrition affect per capita production and incomes. This analysis will be performed in two steps. First we will look at the impact of changes in malnutrition and disease on the size of the rural population and thereafter we will investigate the effects on agricultural production.

Before we proceed with the dicussion we will, however, simplify the analysis in one respect, and that is that we will assume that the effects of the anti-malaria campaign have been negligible. We have already seen that the results in terms of health are likely to have been small, which in turn means that the effects on per capita production ought to have been small as well, whatever their direction.[98] But now, for the analysis.

The principle is simple indeed: as long as improvements with regard to disease and nutrition have a heavier impact on production than on the rural population, rural per capita incomes will rise when such improvements take place and fall if the health standard deteriorates. Let us begin with the effects on population size.

Nutrition, Disease and Population Growth

The deteriorating nutritional standard should have a definite impact on the rate of population growth in rural districts. The age group which probably is worst off from the nutritional point of view is, as we know, the preschool children. Malnutrition and gastro-intestinal disorders, sometimes in combination with diseases as well, are the primary reasons behind a death rate in the 1 to 4 year group of 25 per mille, whereas, as we saw in Chapter 5, the overall death rate for all age groups is 15 per mille in rural areas. Hence, child malnutrition clearly has an impact on death rates. Assuming that no food redistribution in favor of preschool children has taken place during the past 25 years, and keeping the disease situation constant, the death rates in this age group should have risen slightly, while higher up in the ages, the calorie intake is more likely to be at least high enough not to affect the death rates (except during years of exceptionally bad harvests).

A deteriorating nutritional standard may affect birth rates as well:

> Better maternal nutrition could result in more births rather than less when contraception is not practiced. Improved nutrition reduces pregnancy wastage and lengthens the reproductive period, both because puberty occurs earlier in healthier young women and a healthier, longer life can mean more years to conceive,

writes Alan Berg.[99] Unfortunately, in the case of Haiti no data are available which would allow us to confirm or reject this hypothesis. Neither do we know anything with respect to the possible effects on birth rates of the nutritional status of Haitian males. All we can do is to point to the possibility that birth rates may fall as a result of inadequate nutrition among adult men and women.

It should finally be mentioned that changes in the nutritional standard in rural areas may also affect rural-urban migration. Presumably, as the nutritional standard falls, the rate of out-migration increases in the countryside. When the average standard of living is already inadequate and undergoes further deterioration, while urban living conditions remain unchanged, some people will leave the rural districts in search of a better life in town. It is of course also possible to argue that increased malnutrition will reduce out-migration from rural areas. Some people who, if they did not suffer from malnutrition, would emigrate may feel too weak or discouraged to do so if their nutritional standard falls and hence abstain from doing so. Unfortunately, there is a lack of empirical material against which to test these propositions, but perhaps one would after all guess that deteriorating nutrition leads primarily to the first type of changes. It appears unlikely that the persons who are probably most vulnerable to an overall deterioration in the nutritional standard are those who would otherwise have enough initiative to leave the countryside and attempt an urban life. The migrants are more likely to be found among the somewhat better nourished groups.

Thus, the most probable effect of increased malnutrition is to reduce the growth of the rural population. The case of yaws is different. As far as death rates are concerned, eradication of yaws is likely to have had only a negligible effect. Yaws is mainly a crippler, not a killer and death rates are hence not likely to be affected. Birth rates may, however, have risen as a result of yaws eradication, namely if yaws for some reason may have precluded mating or conception for those affected by the disease. It is also possible that the disappearance of yaws has led to increased out-migration from the countryside, i.e. by allowing some individuals who would otherwise have been too infected and debilitated to leave for the towns or for the capital, but neither in the case of birth rates nor in the case of migration are data available to test the hypotheses.

Summarizing the tentative results of the discussion of the impact of health changes on population growth, we find that the most likely overall effect is that the deteriorating standard of nutrition has decreased the rate at which the rural population is increasing, while the effects stemming from yaws eradication are uncertain.

Nutrition, Health and Agricultural Production

In *Asian Drama*, Gunmar Myrdal emphasizes that underutilization of labor in less developed countries when occupational distribution, natural resources, capital availability and technology are given may result from low values of either or all of the following three ratios:[100]

(1) participation $= \dfrac{\text{working members}}{\text{labor force}}$

(2) duration $= \dfrac{\text{man-hours}}{\text{working members}}$

(3) labor efficiency $= \dfrac{\text{output}}{\text{man-hours}}$

However, these three ratios do not give a complete picture of the labor utilization problem. Further disaggregation is possible, and some

Malnutrition and Disease

additions may be made. Then, for the peasant sector (not the entire economy) we have:[101]

(1) participation = $\dfrac{\text{rural labor force}}{\text{rural population}}$

(2) employment = $\dfrac{\text{working members}}{\text{rural labor force}}$

(3) duration = $\dfrac{\text{man-hours}}{\text{working members}}$

(4) intensity = $\dfrac{\text{work units}}{\text{man-hours}}$

(5) efficiency = $\dfrac{\text{output}}{\text{work units}}$

Total production in the peasant sector equals the product of five ratios and the size of the rural population:

$$Q = \frac{Q}{WU} \cdot \frac{WU}{MH} \cdot \frac{MH}{WM} \cdot \frac{WM}{LF} \cdot \frac{LF}{n} \cdot n \qquad (9:1)$$

To simplify the discussion, we use the fact that n/n = 1 and rewrite (9:2) as

$$Q = \frac{Q}{WU} \cdot \frac{WU}{MH} \cdot \frac{MH}{WM} \cdot \frac{WM}{LF} \cdot LF^* \qquad (9:2)$$

Changes in health and nutrition conditions lead to changes in agricultural production.** Then, what influences are deteriorating nutrition

---

* If we retain the formulation (9:1) we have to discuss the impact of yaws eradication and increasing malnutrition on the participation ratio:

$$\frac{d\left(\frac{LF}{n}\right)}{dH} = \left(\frac{\frac{d(LF)}{dH}}{LF} - \frac{\frac{dn}{dH}}{n}\right) \frac{LF}{n} \qquad (9:3)$$

We then have to compare the direction of labor force change to the change in rural population (growth). By using (9:2) instead, we avoid making this comparison and can instead compare all the changes in the components of this equation to the changes in population at the end of the present section.

** Assuming that a change in one of the variables does not affect the other four, we have that

$$\frac{dQ}{dH} = \frac{Q}{LF} \frac{d(LF)}{dH} + \frac{Q}{WM} LF \frac{d\left(\frac{WM}{LF}\right)}{dH} + \frac{Q}{MH} WM \frac{d\left(\frac{MH}{WM}\right)}{dH} +$$
$$+ \frac{Q}{WU} MH \frac{d\left(\frac{WU}{MH}\right)}{dH} + WU \frac{d\left(\frac{Q}{WU}\right)}{dH} \qquad (9:4)$$

nutrition and yaws eradication likely to have on the size of the rural labor force, and on employment, duration, intensity and efficiency within the peasant sector? As Myrdal has pointed out, we should generally expect a high value of one of these factors to be related to high values of the other factors as well.[102] Bad health and widespread malnutrition would thus keep the rural labor force at a low level. The number of people in the labor force who actually work would be limited. They would work short hours, and during these hours, little actual work would be performed, and the output resulting from this work would be small.

Hence, in a static perspective the effects appear to be fairly straightforward. The problems arise when we are to analyze the *changes* in the five variables, e.g. because the occupational distribution of the labor force is not given. In our case, the analysis is further complicated by the lack of hard data. Finally, although it is conceptually easy to make a distinction between the ratios, it is very difficult to separate some of them in an empirical analysis of the effects of nutrition and health changes. For these reasons we are compelled to limit the analysis to some fairly general remarks.

The Effects of Yaws Eradication When yaws was eradicated in the early 1950s, the rural labor force ought to have increased. Presumably, migration to the cities increased as well, as we found in the dicussion of the effects on population growth. Migration from rural areas is typically selective in that it involves a comparatively high percentage of young people who look for employment.[103] Hence, the entire addition to the labor force probably did not remain in the countryside, but neither did all of them emigrate to the cities. Without doubt, some remained in the countryside.

The employment ratio probably remained unaffected by the improvement in health status. Virtually everybody in rural areas is employed in agriculture, and the predominant production unit is the small family farm. Essentially, this means (1) that the employment ratio WM/LF should lie close to one and (2) that this ratio is more or less constant, so that virtually the whole increase in the rural labor force is absorbed into peasant agriculture.

The duration and intensity ratios are particularly difficult to separate in empirical analysis, the most severe problem being how to define a 'work unit', especially when the production process takes time as it does in agriculture and when several different crops are grown that require different types of operations. On the other hand, most of the

Malnutrition and Disease

speculations regarding the impact of health measures on production have centered precisely on these two ratios. Improved health is generally assumed to increase both the numbers of hours worked per working member of the labor force (duration) and the number of work units performed per hour worked.[104] It should increase the number of hours which the cured individual can work, but should also make him capable of raising his standards of performance in both physical and mental terms, by completing a given task in a shorter time and by undertaking more imaginative and ambitious activities than before. (Strictly speaking, the latter effect is one of technical progress which we will deal with in Chapter 12.)*

Another difficult problem when it comes to evaluating the impact of disease eradication on duration and intensity is that a whole series of relationships must be established before it is known that a given disease actually has any economic impact at all (i.e. in instrumental terms). This series is summarized in Figure 9.2. The first step is to establish the existence of an infection. Second, its intensity has to be measured. Thereafter, it has to be found out whether the intensity of the infection is high enough to cause a severe disease, whether the severity actually leads to physical or mental dysfunctions, and finally, whether these dysfunctions are important enough to result in a significant reduction of the duration and/or intensity of work.[105]

Figure 9.2

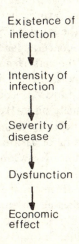

Source: Prescott (1978).

* It should be noted that the intensity and efficiency ratios are defined in terms of work units with given characteristics, i.e. of a given quality.

Most of the time, the entire series of relationships is postulated instead of being derived from available facts,[106] and when quantifications are attempted, these are often exceedingly crude.[107] Proper empirical investigations coupled with satisfactory quantitative tests are sparse indeed.[108]

In the case of Haiti, no systematic discussion of the relationships between disease and economic performance has so far been attempted, let alone any quantifications of the magnitude of the possible impact. In particular, no such investigations exist with respect to yaws. In the meantime, we must limit ourselves to postulating a probable connection between yaws eradication and higher duration and intensity ratios in peasant agriculture.

The final ratio to be discussed is efficiency. This ratio is less likely to be at all affected by yaws eradication. It is specified in terms of a relationship between work units and agricultural output. Changes in this ratio require that some type of change occurs in the production function for peasant agriculture, $Q = g(WU)$, where WU denotes the number of uniform work units. In principle, such a change could result from e.g. a change in investment and savings as a result of yaws eradication. Savings in the peasant sector will be discussed in Chapter 11. We may, however, anticipate one of the results of that chapter, namely that savings in the Haitian peasant sector are not likely to take the form of investment in agricultural production capital. Hence, whatever (marginal) changes in savings that may be produced by yaws eradication should not affect the efficiency ratio.

A second possible change concerns land reclamation. In principle, it is conceivable that some of the persons no longer suffering from yaws could put hitherto unused lands under cultivation.[109] In practice this has probably not happened, however, since the scope for expansion of the cultivated area is virtually nil in Haiti. The main way in which agricultural output can be increased is instead to increase the labor intensity on the given agricultural or pastoral area.

Summing up: the eradication of yaws in the early 1950s is likely to have had mainly two (possibly three) effects on total agricultural production — all of them positive. In the first place the size of the labor force should have increased in rural areas, and since almost everybody in rural Haiti works in agriculture, most of this increase ought to have been translated into an increase in the number of working members as well. The second effect, which properly speaking should be divided into two components, is that of a probable increase in duration and intensity. The larger number of working people should have been able to work longer and to undertake more actual work per hour.

The Effects of Increasing Malnutrition The declining standard of nutrition in rural areas is likely to have effects which are just the opposite to those of yaws eradication. When the nutritional level decreases, some people will presumably leave the labor force because they become too weak to participate. Others, who are stronger, will probably leave for the cities and try to find a job there. Given that the employment ratio lies close to one and remains constant, most of this decrease is a decrease in the number of people actually working in rural districts as well.

The most important effect of the increasingly deteriorating standard of nutrition is that it quite probably reduces the duration and intensity of work in agriculture. The shortfall in nutrition, especially of calories and proteins, affects working capacity visibly. The experience of Haitian firms demonstrates this conclusively. Provision of extra calories has given spectacular results:

> The shortage of calories is undoubtedly a major factor in the impression of laziness or lethargy that is often given by Haitian laborers. Of course, these men are not productive workers; they simply aren't getting enough food to be productive.
>
> As an illustration, when the Caribbean Mills wheat plant was opened, it was found that a labor force three times that estimated was needed to get the work done. After a company lunch program providing several thousand calories a day was initiated, it was possible to cut the labor force back to the original estimates. Roughly speaking, the same men put out three times as much work when their diets were supplemented as when they ate only at home. Other Haitian firms report similar experiences with their laborers.[110]

While no similar evidence exists for rural areas, there is no reason to expect that the results should differ, especially not since the nutritional situation in the countryside appears to be worse than the one in urban areas.[111] Nor should we always expect that malnutrition can be cured quickly. David Turnham and Ingelies Jaeger observe that

> even where generous incentive is offered for increased work input, the response may be disappointingly slow because improvement from low level diets takes time; the inheritance of a deprived childhood

440 Malnutrition and Disease

canot be shrugged off in a few weeks or months and indeed the scars may be permanent.[112]

Chronic malnutrition begun in early childhood poses a far more difficult problem than temporary malnutrition at a later age.

Turnham and Jaeger also suggest the existence of a low nutritional equilibrium trap:

> For adults in low income groups there is a substantial gap between food intake and the requirements for efficient living and working. The evidence therefore strongly suggests the existence of a vicious circle or trap whereby low productivity is part cause and part result of low income and low work input.[113]

A particularly interesting argument based on the existence of such a trap has been advanced by Carl S. Shoup.[114] This argument may be summarized with the aid of Figure 9.3. On the horizontal axis we have the intake of calories (c) by the peasant, and on the vertical axis we measure the resulting production, f(c), i.e. production is a function of the calorie intake. The slope of the curve measures the marginal productivity of nutrition (MPN).

Figure 9.3

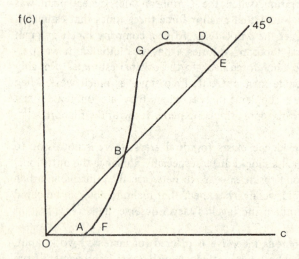

Source: Shoup (1965), p. 176.

Between points O and A, the peasant only consumes but produces nothing. The MPN is equal to zero, and the peasant has to live entirely on aid from other people. At point A, which is the resting metabolism, the MPN on the first occasion assumes a positive value which, however, is lower than one. By increasing his calorie intake marginally, the peasant can only produce a quantity of food which is lower than that which he has to consume to ensure this production. Between points F and G, however, the MPN is larger than one. Any added intake of calories will result in a more than proportional increase in output. At B, the peasant for the first time produces as much as he consumes. (B lies on the 45° straight line from the origin.) All points on the curve above the 45° line represent combinations where the peasant produces in excess of his consumption. When point G is reached, the MPN has once more fallen and become equal to one. The peasant can no longer make any gains in output by increasing his intake of calories. Beyond point C further increases in calorie intake no longer contribute to increased production at all, after point D, total production begins to fall due to excessive consumption, and after point E finally, the peasant once more consumes more than he produces.

The most interesting segment of the curve is that between points F and G which is where increased calorie consumption is gainful. By increasing his calorie intake the peasant can increase his production by an amount the value of which is higher than the cost of the additional calories. With access to a properly functioning credit market, a peasant who is at some point between F and G should be able to climb to the latter point by borrowing money to invest in his food consumption. If he is between B and G the loan will immediately yield a surplus over what the peasant has to consume which may be used for interest and amortization payments. If the peasant starts from a level below B, the situation is more difficult, because then his production falls short of his consumption. He has a deficit, not a surplus, and must postpone interest and amortization payments until he is past B.

Even though, as Shoup points out, 'observation suggests that even in an under-developed country, only a narrow range of consumption separates the resting-metabolism. . .and a level at which further increments of consumption again have no effect on production,'[115] the problem of reaching point G is not so simple in practice. The most serious difficulty is that of obtaining a consumption loan at an interest rate which does not absorb more than the surplus which is available and an amortization period which is sufficiently long. In

Chapter 11 we will analyze the rural credit market, and we will then find that the peasants have notorious difficulties when it comes to obtaining longer loans at reasonable interest rates. Hence, the practical possibilities for credit financing of gainful consumption must be regarded as small indeed.

An even greater difficulty presents itself in the situation with which we are presently dealing: when the nutritional standard is deteriorating. If this happens to a peasant who is in the FG interval, his production will fall more than proportionally, and this of course tends to depress per capita incomes in rural districts. In extreme cases the peasant may easily slide below point B, to a situation where his production no longer covers his consumption, and perhaps all the way down to the resting metabolism, where the individual is too enfeebled to be able to perform any kind of work.

However, in practice, we should not expect to be able to observe excessively violent downward movements. In societies where malnutrition is widespread, a large number of individuals may be locked in between points F and G (or, rather B and G) without experiencing more than temporary, small downward movements. The reason for this comparative inertia is that compensatory mechanisms may be called into action. The first buffer is the reserve of fat accumulated in the body which smooths out a fluctuating calorie intake and which hence may help the individual to maintain his producing capacity for a shorter time. A second compensatory mechanism could be the one indicated by Harry T. Oshima: an inadequate work effort *after* the peak seasons. Oshima noted that in Asia during the harvesting periods peasants work long hours and that during that time they eat four or five meals a day, which brings the calorie intake up to even 4,000 calories a day. After the harvest, the supply of calories slowly decreases as the harvest is consumed. This directly affects working activities. No weeding takes place, no outside jobs are sought to supplement incomes, energy is lacking to plant more crops etc.[116] This case may very well apply to Haiti. In Chapter 2 we saw that a great deal of the agricultural process is left to nature. Harvesting, clearing the land for new crops, planting and sowing together form the peak seasons, but once the seeds or plants are in the ground, very little is done until it is time to harvest. Thus, work efforts are concentrated to the periods when they are desperately needed, and when in the face of an inadequate food supply they can be dispensed with, the periods of rest become longer.

A third regulating device is to redistribute consumption within the family.[117] When the production capacity of the breadwinning member

Malnutrition and Disease

(usually the male) for some reason slides towards the point where production and consumption balance each other, other members of the family may have to sacrifice some of their consumption in order once more to bring the calorie intake of the breadwinner up to its former level. The wife relapses for a while to a point where her calorie intake falls towards the resting metabolism level; younger or older members are temporarily given less than usual to eat. In Haiti it does not appear likely that the women will suffer much from a temporary fall in their husband's calorie intake since the women are almost as important as the men as breadwinners. Instead, the burden appears to fall on the children, who as we know are nutritionally in an especially precarious situation:

> ...it is clear that the present national food resources preclude the possibility of a really well nourished nation. On the other hand, the resources that are presently available are enough that no one need to starve to death. In spite of this, thousands of Haitian infants do not get their fair share of calories and protein from the family pot.[118]

In terms of potential production lost, the cost to society of child malnutrition may be very high:

> The slack in the family that enables the breadwinning member to remain roughly in equilibrium may be obtained at a very heavy cost in production when the next generation has come of working age. Lack of protein intake in early childhood may lower the money value of working age output by many multiples of the cost of the protein increments. Calories can carry the individual to working age, but the amount of work he can do will depend in many occupations on the amount of muscle tissue he has laid down during his early years of growth, and this will be a function of protein intake.[119]

The only ratio left to discuss is efficiency, and here the same principles apply as in the case of yaws eradication. We should not expect the production function to be affected by the deteriorating nutritional standard as long as we define work input in terms of work units with given characteristics. The possibility that these characteristics themselves may change as a result of increasing malnutrition is dealt with in Chapter 12, which discusses technical progress.

If we sum up the probable effects of increasing malnutrition on total agricultural production, we find that these are likely to be negative. The deteriorating nutritional standard lessens the number of people who participate in the labor force, and both the duration and the intensity of the work performed will fall.

A Comparison of Yaws Eradication and Malnutrition

A comparison in per capita terms of the relative impact of yaws eradication and increased malnutrition is difficult. Yaws eradication has probably made a positive contribution to total agricultural output, but it is quite possible (although not necessarily) that it has also increased the rural population, while increasing malnutrition should have had a negative influence on both agricultural output and the size of the rural population. Without access to relevant empirical data there is no possibility of weighing these changes against each other, but one conclusion which can be drawn is that the analysis carried out in the present chapter and the results obtained do not *exclude* the possibility that the net effect of yaws eradication and increasing malnutrition has been to lower agricultural production per capita in the peasant sector.

The time perspective taken may be of some interest, since *if* the effect of increased malnutrition actually is to make agricultural production per capita fall, the possibility arises that in the long run, this negative effect increasingly outweighs the possible positive effects of yaws eradication as well. This may be illustrated in the following way.

Let us look at Figure 9.4. On the vertical axis we have agricultural

Figure 9.4

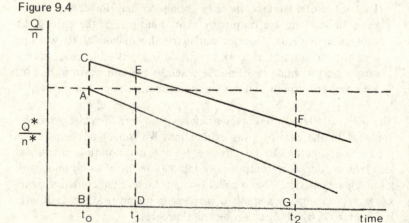

production per head of the rural population: Q/n. On the horizontal axis we have time. The lower curve in the diagram shows what would happen to per capita production in agriculture if the only change that took place was that of a deterioration of the nutritional status. (To keep the analysis simple we assume this curve to be a straight line.) The upper curve shows what happens to per capita production after an eradication of yaws at the beginning of the period. (This curve is assumed to be a straight line as well, with a slope inferior to that of the lower curve — to indicate that after the eradication of yaws per capita production may fall more slowly.)

If we start at time t_0 we find that with a given yaws incidence and a given nutritional standard, per capita production would have been equal to AB (i.e. Q^*/n^*). Assume now that yaws is eradicated. The effect of this is to raise per capita production to CB. (We assume that this change is instantaneous.) If we go on to time t_1 we find that per capita production is now ED. It has declined in comparison to CB but is still higher than Q^*/n^*, i.e. higher than what it would have been at t_0 in the absence of yaws eradication. Hence, evaluating the combined changes of yaws eradication and increased malnutrition at time t_1 gives a favorable net effect on per capita incomes.

Let us now go to t_2. Here, per capita production has decreased to FG, which is both less than CB and less than Q^*/n^*. In other words, if we choose to evaluate the change in per capita production at time t_2 instead of at time t_1, the result is negative. The combined effect of yaws eradication and increasing malnutrition has been to depress per capita incomes below the level at which they would otherwise have been if neither of these two changes had taken place.

This serves to illustrate an important point. As long as the slope of the upper curve in the diagram is negative, i.e. as long as increasing malnutrition exerts a depressing influence on per capita incomes, it is possible to find a point at which the negative effects emanating from this change outweigh the positive shift generated by yaws eradication (a point in time where per capita incomes fall below the Q^*/n^* level).

This in turn, means that if the time interval under consideration is long enough, the net effect of a positive health change (undertaken at the beginning of the period) and a negative change in nutritional status will be negative. In the present case we are considering a period of more than 20 years. The incidence of yaws had fallen to a negligible level by the end of 1953, and thereafter the only change operating has presumably been the deterioration in nutritional standards. Therefore, in the long run it is the effects emanating from the decline in nutritional standards which are of main interest. It must be stressed that during the period under consideration we do not know whether here these effects have been negative or positive. On the other hand, we cannot, given the present knowledge, exclude the possibility that increasing malnutrition does have a detrimental effect. If so, and unless something is done to improve the health and/or nutrition status of the peasants, this effect will sooner or later dominate the (possible but not certain) positive effect of yaws eradication, which, seen in this perspective, will appear only as a parenthetical episode.

Conclusions

A situation where public health care improves at the same time as nutrition remains constant or deteriorates may have very undesirable consequences in the long run. Improvements in medicine and health care may lead to lowered mortality and increased population. When the population increases, so does the labor force. If the non-agricultural sectors of the economy cannot absorb this increase, the addition to the labor force goes into agriculture, and the marginal productivity of labor falls in the absence of capital formation, increased land resources and technical progress. Agricultural production per capita falls and this leads to a fall in nutritional standards which may have already been inadequate and falling before that date. Malthusian checks may begin to present themselves. These may first go without much notice. Compensating mechanisms set in. The breadwinners may keep their consumption standards unchanged at the expense of other family members. Malnutrition among children increases. First degree cases become second degree cases and second degree cases turn into third degree cases. Child mortality due to malnutrition goes up.

It is quite possible that a process of this type is already working in Haiti. An indication may be that death rates appear to go up very fast during drought periods. Street quotes evidence of hundreds of deaths due to famine in Côtes de Fer following a drought in 1948,[120] and King reports that after an 18-month drought which came to an end in late 1959 in Boucan Patriot, where normally there should be some 150-200 children in preschool age he only found three living children, all severely undernourished.[121] This type of famine is at first hardly noticeable at all for the people outside the stricken area:

> At the outset, the effects of the drought are not obvious. They escape the attention of the authorities. The people begin to sell their harvest, then their goats, and finally their cattle. Some people

leave the region. Prices begin to rise. The general mortality increases but it is not really possible to state that people starve to death. Finally, the existence of the famine becomes known, and when aid arrives, the famine is relatively advanced.[122]

Unless extreme conditions are reached a lot of starvation inevitably goes unnoticed. The risk of a famine is always present in dry areas:

> No year passes without the appearance of the specter of famine in some region; without the people of the driest parts having to rely upon what is left of the natural vegetation for food, i.e. on gathering herbs and roots. The general scarcity of resources does not permit an organized exchange of food between cool and hot lands, especially not in February-March and June-July. One must be blinded by optimism not to see that the majority of the rural population niggardly lives on the margins of chronic starvation. In the Haitian countryside people still die from insufficient nutrition.[123]

Where acute famine is latent, medical care and public health measures may prove inefficient, especially if their main effect should be to raise the size of the population without at the same time increasing agricultural production. In this situation, the existence of widespread (and possibly increasing) malnutrition may render health assistance worthless, and health assistance itself may only contribute to a worsening of the nutritional situation. Application of public health measures or medical care without a simultaneous attack on the nutrition problem may quite conceivably have a negative impact on rural per capita incomes.

Possibly, the nutrition problem, and the problem of poverty will have to be solved before a public health revolution or a medical revolution can be achieved in rural Haiti. R.M. Hartwell, in an exposé of the economic history of medical care has argued persuasively that the advances in health and longevity that took place in Europe before the Industrial Revolution were caused by a breakthrough in the production of food while medical care had no effect at all.[124] Part of the reason for this was of course to be found in the fact that the medical knowledge of the time was limited. Contemporary Haiti is not quite in the same position. In principle the country has access to whatever modern medical techniques may be needed and, funds permitting, these techniques could be introduced. On the other hand, it is *still* possible that beginning with medical care or public health measures is an inefficient way of solving the health problem. Malnutrition may be the binding constraint.

Our knowledge of the impact of changing health conditions on agricultural production per capita in rural districts is limited — by lack of empirical data and an incomplete knowledge of the mechanisms relating health changes to economic variables. A lot more research is needed in both these fields. Still, it would not be an overstatement to say that rural nutrition has been overlooked in Haiti. With the exception of the establishment of a number of mothercraft centers beginning in the mid-1960s[125] and some assistance from international and bilateral aid organisations,[126] the Haitian governments have shown little interest in taking any steps to improve the nutritional standard in the countryside. Against the facts we found in Chapters 7 and 8, this is hardly surprising. On the other hand, it is only fair to say that to combat malnutrition efficiently is presumably much more difficult than to eradicate diseases* or to improve the system of rural education, for malnutrition is intimately interwined with rural poverty itself — both as a cause and as a consequence. It may not be possible to eradicate malnutrition without simultaneously solving most other problems discussed in the present work. Simple distribution of food is not enough to improve the nutrition standard of the rural masses, but the peasant sector must also be put in the position where it can produce enough to cover the needs of the rural population — an extremely difficult task.

Notes

1. Cf. the introduction to Chapter 10.
2. Notable exceptions here are Correa (1963) and Myrdal (1968).
3. Fuchs (1966), p. 144.
4. Berg (1973), p. 15. A short discussion of definition problems can be found in Reutlinger & Selowsky (1976), pp. 8-9.
5. Berg (1973), p. 15.
6. Ibid.
7. See e.g. Palmer (1972:1), pp. 21-7; Belli (1971), pp. 3-4; Berg (1973), p. 9; Correa (1975), pp. 15-16, for a summary of some of the most important studies.
8. See e.g. Belli (1971), pp. 4-10; Correa (1975), pp. 18-23.
9. Correa (1975), pp. 21-2. Cf. also Selowsky & Taylor (1973).
10. Palmer (1972:1), p. 32.
11. See e.g. the cases quoted by ibid., p. 28; Berg (1973), pp. 10-11, and Selowsky & Taylor (1973). Cf. also Correa (1975), pp. 28-31.
12. Berg (1973), p. 12.

---

* Significantly enough, however, both yaws eradication and the efforts to cope with malaria involved foreign technical and financial assistance.

13. Ibid., pp. 15-16.
14. Correa (1975), pp. 22-3.
15. King (1969), p. 351. Cf. also Street (1960), p. 441.
16. Beghin, Fougère & King (1965), p. 284.
17. King et al. (1963), pp. 106-9.
18. Berg (1973), p. 15.
19. Jelliffe & Jelliffe (1961), p. 13.
20. Beghin, Fougère & King (1970), pp. 169-70.
21. Ibid., p. 173.
22. Ibid., pp. 173-4.
23. Ibid., pp. 182-3.
24. Rotberg & Clague (1971), p. 261.
25. Bordes (1965:2), p. 278.
26. Bordes (1965:1), p. 79.
27. Beghin (1965), p. 52.
28. Beghin, Fougère & King (1970), p. 153.
29. Clark & Haswell (1967), Chapter 1 gives an account of these computations.
30. Oshima (1967), p. 386.
31. Leibenstein (1957), p. 65.
32. Oshima (1967), p. 391.
33. Ibid. Cf. also Correa (1963), pp. 30-38, where it is suggested that better nutrition in general could double and in some cases treble working capacity in less developed countries.
34. See e.g. the sources quoted by Leibenstein (1957), pp. 62-6.
35. Oshima (1967), p. 391.
36. Berg (1973), p. 13.
37. Ibid.
38. Beghin, Fougère & King (1970), p. 80.
39. Ibid., p. 107, where also the methodology employed in the calculations is explained.
40. CRN (1975), pp. 30, 35.
41. Cf. Chapter 3, and Beghin, Fougère & King (1970), pp. 51-2.
42. Sebrell et al. (1959), pp. 568-9, 572-3, 576-7.
43. Beghin, Fougère & King (1970), p. 167.
44. Ibid., p. 166.
45. Ibid., p. 177.
46. Ibid., p. 176.
47. Klipstein, Samloff & Schenk (1966), p. 591.
48. Sebrell et al. (1959), pp. 562-3.
49. Rotberg & Clague (1971), p. 264.
50. Leyburn (1966), p. 275.
51. Diederich & Burt (1969), p. 48.
52. Leyburn (1966), p. 274.
53. Léon (1953), p. 21.
54. Ibid., p. 127.
55. Ibid., p. 128.
56. Weisbrod et al. (1973), pp. 54-5.
57. Melhorn (1930), p. 14; Léon (1953), p. 184.
58. Léon (1953), p. 185.
59. Moore (1972), p. 182.
60. Melhorn (1930), pp. 18-19.
61. Stuart (1930), p. 47.
62. Leyburn (1966), p. 274.
63. See UN (1949), p. 70. Département de la Santé Publique (1953), p. 4,

Département de la Santé Publique (1954), p. 6.
64. UN (1949), p. 73.
65. Paul & Bellerive (1947).
66. UN (1949), p. 66.
67. See Dwinelle et al. (1947); Duvalier (1968:1), pp. 525-38.
68. UN (1949), p. 62.
69. Ibid., pp. 65-6.
70. Ibid., p. 76.
71. Rotberg & Clague (1971), p. 265.
72. Moore (1972), p. 189.
73. Département de la Santé Publique (1974), p. 7.
74. See Mason & Cavalié (1965).
75. Rotberg & Clague (1971), p. 266.
76. CONADEP (1970-71), p. 120.
77. Département de la Santé Publique (1974), p. 6.
78. Ibid., p. 22.
79. Rotberg & Clague (1971), pp. 265-6.
80. Noël (1969), p. 389.
81. Rotberg & Clague (1971), p. 265.
82. See Beghin, Fougère & King (1970), pp. 181-2.
83. King (1969), p. 352.
84. Wingfield (1966), p. 117.
85. Laroche (1965), pp. 86-7.
86. Beghin, Fougère & King (1970), pp. 27, 146.
87. Ibid., p. 26.
88. Ibid.
89. Cf. Laroche (1965), p. 87. Cf. Titus (1965), pp. 104-5.
90. Noël (1969), p. 378; Gómez (1974), p. 25.
91. Cf. also Rotberg & Clague (1971), p. 269.
92. OEA-CEPAL-BID (1962), note, p. 57.
93. Gómez (1974), p. 24.
94. US Department of Health (1972), p. 17.
95. Huxley (1969), passim, quotes a number of popular recipes.
96. Cf. Moral (1961), p. 218.
97. Deren (1975), p. 156.
98. For an analysis of the economic effects of malaria eradication, see Barlow (1967). Cf. also Kamarck (1976), pp. 66-9. For the impact on population growth see e.g. Newman (1970); Frederiksen (1960); Meegama (1967). Cf. also Titmuss & Abel-Smith (1961), p. 49; Petersen (1969), pp. 562-3.
99. Berg (1973), p. 38.
100. Myrdal (1968), p. 1016.
101. The definition of intensity presumably coincides with that by Reynolds (1975), p. 14. Note also the change in terminology as compared to Myrdal.
102. Myrdal (1968), p. 1017.
103. Cf. Ahlers (1977), p. 28.
104. Cf. e.g. Mushkin (1962), p. 105; Barlow (1970), p. 133.
105. See Prescott (1978) for a penetrating discussion of the case of schistosomiasis (bilharzia).
106. Cf. e.g. Myrdal (1968), Ch. 21, sections 15 and 16. See, however, also Ch. 30, pp. 1616-17 where this lack of factual knowledge is discussed. Cf. also Weisbrod et al. (1973), pp. 21-2.
107. Cf. e.g. Correa (1963), pp. 42-6, and Malenbaum (1970). See also the survey of the literature on diseases and economic development in Weisbrod et al. (1973), Chapter 2.

108. Cf. however, Weisbrod *et al.* (1973); Baldwin & Weisbrod (1974); Weisbrod & Helminiak (1977).
109. Cf. Prescott (1978), p. 135.
110. King (1969), pp. 353-4.
111. Ibid., p. 354.
112. Turnham & Jaeger (1971), pp. 91-2. Cf. also Berg (1966), pp. 191-2.
113. Turnham & Jaeger (1971), p. 91. Cf. also Reutlinger (1977), p. 717.
114. Shoup (1965).
115. Ibid., p. 183.
116. Oshima (1967), p. 390. Cf. also Herskovits (1952), pp. 290-4 and Turnham & Jaeger (1971), note, p. 83.
117. Shoup (1965), p. 187.
118. King (1969), p. 187. This is a common situation in less developed countries (Berg (1973), p. 46). Interestingly enough Shoup directly quotes the case of Haiti (Shoup (1965), p. 190).
119. Shoup (1965), pp. 190-1. Cf. Selowsky & Taylor (1973), p. 30.
120. Street (1960), p. 440.
121. King (1969), pp. 354-5.
122. Beghin, Fougère & King, (1970), p. 193.
123. Moral (1961), p. 217.
124. Hartwell (1974).
125. For an account, see Fougère & King (1975).
126. See e.g. CONADEP (1974).

10 THE ROLE OF EDUCATION

In Chapter 9 we made an attempt to establish whether the development of the health and nutrition status of the Haitian peasants may have acted as a positive influence on agricultural production per head of the rural population which may have served as a brake on the tendency for rural per capita incomes to fall. Health and nutrition are, however, not the only dimensions of interest in this context, but if it can be established that the quantity and quality of rural education have undergone substantial and manifest changes for the better, we may discover another brake mechanism which mitigates the declining trend in incomes.

Until 1960, much of the literature on economic development was heavily concentrated around the role of investment in physical capital as the propelling force in the growth and development process.[1] It was finally discovered, however, that physical capital formation alone could not explain why some countries were developed economically while others were not. Development economists had to search elsewhere for the explanation.

Following the presidential address delivered by Theodore W. Schultz to the annual meeting of the American Economic Association in December 1960,[2] extensive research on 'human capital' formation was begun. Education was now singled out as one of the most important components in the development process. Many of the differences in growth rates and incomes between countries and individuals were attributed to differences in schooling.[3] What Gunnar Myrdal in the late 1960s termed 'the newest approach' to economic development[4] by and large became another type of panacea, and improved education was advocated as the prime instrument for improving the standard of living in developing countries. The confidence in education was high. There 'are apparently [no cases] in which better schooling of farm people who continue farming is associated with a stagnant agriculture,' wrote Schultz in 1964.[5] Others were not as convinced. The same year Thomas Balogh wrote:

> There is, perhaps, no field of economic pseudo-scientism where more absurdity is being published — and, alas, acted upon — as that of education. One almost longs to be back in the 'bad old' days when classicist educational pundits and administrators established completely irrelevant types of university education happily ignorant of the need for any fresh analysis of social and economic requirement.[6]

Like all other explanations of economic development that concentrate upon a single variable, the identification of development with educational progress proved in due time to be exaggerated.[7] The economists' view of education was gradually modified and extended. An important article by Kenneth J. Arrow in 1973 formalized the concept of (higher) education as a filtering or screening device which only serves to sort out individuals of differing abilities, conveying information regarding their relative (given) productivity to potential employers without actually giving any real contributions to superior economic performance, i.e. in principle without changing the existing abilities at all.[8] Put bluntly, with this view, the contents of education become more or less irrelevant. To teach agronomy in a basically agrarian society would not necessarily yield better results in terms of screening than would Latin or Greek. Arrow, and after him Joseph E. Stiglitz, have also demonstrated that an educational system which works mainly as a screening device may give rise to negative social returns from education.[9]

The human capital view of education has also come under more radical attack. Thomas Balogh and Paul Streeten, for example, have pointed out that the benefit to the individual from investment in schooling need not take the form of an increase in his or her productivity. Unless there is free entry into the educational system, the main function of certain types of schooling may be to enable the individual to capture a monopoly rent accruing to the members of certain professions.[10]

Marxist criticism has gone even further. The works by Herbert Gintis and Samuel Bowles, for example, suggested that the principal function of formal education was to legitimize a reproduction of the existing and unequal class structure by creating some sort of façade of meritocracy, and that schooling served to elicit uniform responses from the students in a manner based upon rewarding of certain behavior patterns e.g. by stressing subordination and proper orientation to authority through hierarchical lines, docility, industry and ego-control. This type of education, Gintis suggests, could very well inhibit personal development. With this view, the school system mainly serves the interest of the employers and perpetuates a capitalist social hegemony.[11] Dealing specifically with the educational systems of less developed countries, Martin Carnoy contends that schooling may have a negative effect on the growth of output in these countries.* The educational system is nothing but an ideological arm of the state which contributes to

---

*Carnoy also discusses education in the United States.

maximizing – not output – but the incomes of certain groups in society by reinforcing and perpetuating the existing economic organization, which is dominated and created by these very groups.[12]

Towards the end of the 1970s, education in poor countries is no longer looked upon as necessarily conducive to rapid economic development. Economists have now realized that education is not a homogeneous input which can always be relied upon to speed up the growth and development process.[13] Its effects may vary very widely depending on the concrete circumstances under which it is attempted. Education is a blessing with certain qualifications.

The purpose of the present chapter is to investigate the effects of rural education in Haiti and the changes that this education has undergone up to the present time. (The discussion will mainly be limited to general education while such activities as agricultural extension will be dealt with in Chapter 12.) We will begin by sketching a human capital approach to rural education in less developed countries in order to find out how education may contribute to raising agricultural production per head in rural areas. Against this background we will subsequently follow the development of the Haitian system of rural education from the beginning of the nineteenth century until the present day to find out whether this system has managed to make any contributions to human capital formation or not. In the final part of the chapter we will leave the human capital approach and question the main function of rural education in Haiti.

Any attempt to analyze rural education in Haiti solely in terms of human capital formation would lead us completely astray. Haiti provides a very clear illustration of the fact that education is not a homogeneous commodity but that the contents of education and the construction and the characteristics of the educational system may be totally decisive for the economic and social effects of education. An analysis in terms of human capital formation therefore has to be complemented with an analysis of other aspects as well. In the Haitian case, exclusive concentration of human capital will obscure some of the most important issues and hence represents an inefficient approach to the study of rural education. What needs to be looked into and to be stressed besides human capital aspects are the strong discriminatory characteristics of an educational system based upon elite philosophy, formalism, linguistic dualism and filtering principles.

A Human Capital Approach to Rural Education in Low-income Countries

In spite of their criticisms of the human capital concept of education, authors like Arrow, Bowles and Gintis do not deny that education may enhance the productivity of the individual who is subject to schooling.[14] Obviously, the educational system *can* promote the creation of human capital which will enable the individuals to produce more and better goods in one sense or another, if the system is properly constructed. We will in the present section adhere to this view and discuss some of the effects which schooling (in so far as it leads to human capital formation) may have on agricultural producers as well as some of the most important features that a school system which is to be efficient from this point of view ought to possess.[15]

A dynamic viewpoint probably offers the best perspective of the positive role of education in agricultural development. Increased productivity in agriculture and a rising standard of living for the farming population is achieved by introduction of new crops, inputs and methods of cultivation within an appropriate institutional setting. These changes do not take place by themselves but are governed by human action. Hence, human behavior needs to be altered too, and this is where education enters the picture. If the human agent does not undergo the appropriate changes called for by the development process, bottlenecks will arise on the manpower side that will check and hamper development. In a somewhat general fashion we may say that here the role of education is to change what Clifton R. Wharton, Jr calls the 'economizing behavior' of the peasant and the economic setting within which the peasant makes his decisions.[16] One way of achieving this is to give such a content to the education as to motivate the peasant to change his ways,[17] i.e. to make him break with the traditions of the past and teach him to act upon his own initiative and exercize his own judgement. Instead of being caught in the web of time-honored ways the peasant must be induced to seek new directions.[18] His rationality must be increased. He must learn why change is desirable and how to judge correctly the results of change and innovations. His inquisitiveness must be increased. His attitudes, values and goals must be given a different content.[19] Economic incentives must be given more opportunity to exert their influence on his actions.[20] Presumably education has an important role to play in all these changes.

The second influence of education on peasant behavior lies in its contribution to better farm management.[21] The farmer combines at least two economic roles in his person: that of a producer and that of a seller. He must be a good technician as well as a good businessman, and both require skills to which education may make a positive contribution. To be successful he must master the very difficult task of economic decisions involving two comparisons: (a) a comparison of costs and returns for any enterprise or combination of enterprises; and (b) an economic comparison among possible enterprises or combinations of enterprises. The rational calculus involved in both comparisons is far more difficult than is usually appreciated. The farmer must know the expected physical return (production) from a variety of alternative choices of product and techniques of production. He must know expected costs of producing these various levels of output under these various technological conditions. He must be able to estimate with reasonable accuracy the future price which he is likely to obtain for each of the possibilities he is considering. Proficiency in manipulating these variables to arrive at a reasonably successful decision is no small accomplishment. It is one thing to raise a crop or an animal technically: it is another to do so economically.[22]

It is precisely within the area of farm management and decision-making that the dynamic viewpoint cited earlier assumes special importance. In the traditional setting decisions are often standardized and heavily molded by tradition, which of course is nothing but the result of long periods of trial and error which in the stationary setting end up being well adjusted to the requirements of the situation.[23] Standardized and ritualized decision-making of a repetitive type is comparatively simple, since it rarely involves the exercise of personal judgement. Most of the time there are precedents for the peasant to draw upon and the environment presents a reasonably stable aspect.

When the environment begins to change, due to technological progress or institutional reforms, the standardized decision rules break down. Optimal adjustment to changing conditions leaves plenty of room for unprogrammed decision-making. The skill requirements put on the peasant in his capacity as manager increase considerably. Each situation is new, and before the necessary adjustments have been made and a new equilibrium has been reached, a number of hitherto unfamiliar decisions must be made (and if the ability to make decisions is not up to the minimum standard the returns to other factors remain low, and it might not even be profitable to introduce innovations at all). The only thing for the peasant to fall back upon here is his general ability and education.

Additional strain is put on the peasant in a changing pattern of agriculture by the inherent heterogeneity of the physical environment (and perhaps also by the resources at the disposal of the peasant).[24] It may be difficult or even impossible to draw upon the knowledge of other farmers. The application of new methods may have to be tailored to suit the particular needs and resources of the peasant, and as a rule nobody except the peasant himself can assure that this individualization leads to the desired results.

The third and most obvious benefit which the peasant may draw from education is of course when the schooling takes the shape of conveying direct knowledge of crops, inputs and farming methods.[25]

We will deal only with the formal part of education in the present chapter, i.e. with the development of a basic, general knowledge and with that teaching of agricultural subjects which takes place within the formal education system and which is aimed directly at the peasants. Discussion of direct extension activities will be deferred until Chapter 12 which deals specifically with technological change.[26]

Practical farming skills can be taught either through formal vocationally oriented schools or through direct extension education on the spot. Vocational education with an agricultural content may be introduced already into the curriculum of rural primary schools but is in general postponed until the secondary stage. While the importance of vocational education in raising farming skills should be fairly obvious to most readers, a few words on the function of more general knowledge may be in order.

From the human capital point of view, the basic function of primary education in most countries of the world is to develop certain 'infrastructure skills'[27] like the three traditional Rs: reading, writing and arithmetic, whose functions are to facilitate the transmission of further knowledge, to serve as an extension of the human memory, and to make certain simple operations of everyday farm management easier to carry out.[28] In all three respects, the three Rs represent a roundabout way of production. While their direct impact on farming productivity perhaps is rather low, their indirect contribution may be important.

To reach illiterate peasants with extension education, for example, two requirements have to be met. Demonstration must be direct, and take place on the spot, and it must be timed so as not to interfere with important activities of peasant life. Agents and peasants have to meet in person

> and instructions on preparing the land for water, on methods of ploughing and seeding, on techniques of using fertilizers, on the purchase and maintenance of tools and implements, and on the packing

and shipping of produce have to be imparted orally, again and again, until the farmer remembers them. If it were possible to issue printed *aides-mémoires,* the work of agricultural extension could be considerably speeded up.[29]

A literate peasant can in principle be reached at any time with brochures, booklets, journals, etc. While the effects of direct on-the-spot demonstration are probably more impressive than those achieved with printed material only, the latter method is much less costly since it economizes on scarce trained manpower:

> Experience with agricultural extension in Africa and elsewhere suggests that the average extension officer can effectively service about five villages, each of which contains 100 farm households...If the officer could distribute simple instruction leaflets to the farmers, or specially prepared pamphlets reminding them of what they just had witnessed in their visit to the demonstration farm, he might be able to service as many as fifteen or twenty villages, or 1,500 or 2,000 farmers.[30]

Hence, while exclusive reliance on impersonal, printed material is not desirable, use of the printing press as an additional reinforcement to direct demonstrations is an efficient method, but this presupposes literacy among the peasants. Literacy opens up an entirely new channel of communication.

It is sometimes argued that literacy is of low relevance in rural areas of less developed countries on the grounds that the direct uses that the peasants may make of this skill are few, and that mass communication via radio or TV is at least as efficient as the printed word. This argument, plausible as it may sound, is probably not correct. Mass communication suffers from some of the same defects as does direct demonstration. The peasant must be present at a certain place at a certain time to listen or view, while reading can be done at his own convenience.[31] There may also be a correlation between e.g. radio listening and literacy due to such factors as superior knowledge of the availability of programs and greater interest in news etc. due to education.[32] Finally, it must not be forgotten that frequently the relevant question to ask is not whether one method of instruction is superior to another, but what *package* of educational methods will have the best effect in a given situation. Media education, for example, may not be efficient unless there is somebody to supervise the sessions, conduct discussions after the transmissions, etc.[33]

That infrastructure skills constitute a useful extension of memory, and that they enable the peasant to carry out certain operations with more ease is fairly obvious. The ability to make notes and records of demonstration activities makes it possible for the peasant to go back to these whenever they are needed.[34] Arithmetical skills permit the peasant to calculate yields and returns and to keep accounting records whereby a systematic element is introduced into peasant farming.[35] The usefulness of arithmetical knowledge is very strongly stressed by Gunnar Myrdal who argues that

> 'Arithmetical literacy' is a vital aspect of functional literacy: from the standpoint of economic development it is at least as important as 'verbal literacy'. Obviously, the ability not only to read and write figures with understanding but also to add, subtract, multiply, and divide is of importance in all industrial work, in rationally managed agriculture, in commercial and credit transactions, and of course, in such specific development efforts as planning on the local level and building up a network of cooperatives. *It is a serious deficiency in the discussion of literacy that the ability to use numbers meaningfully and effectively is ignored in the literature.*[36]

Infrastructure skills are taught not only in primary schools but also via adult education courses of various kinds. In principle there is no difference between what is learned in primary school education and what can be acquired later in life through evening courses, etc.,[37] but in one important respect basic adult education may differ from ordinary primary school classes: it may also lend an immediate and direct support to the education of children in rural areas. Experience from several underdeveloped countries shows that it is impossible to make even 70 or 80 percent of the children of school age attend first-year classes if their parents are not literate themselves, and it is even more difficult to put the children all the way through primary school. Hence, in order to make formal education in rural areas more efficient the level of adult literacy must presumably be raised.[38]

Provided that we are prepared to accept the view which contends that the important effect of formal education is that it leads to formation of human capital, the main contribution of rural education to farming appears to be that it may change the economizing behavior of the peasant so as to make him better prepared for agricultural production in a changing environment: (1) by making him understand why and how change is desirable; (2) by facilitating his economic and technical decision-making; and (3) by providing him with direct knowledge regarding crops, inputs and farming methods. The conveyance of this knowledge may proceed directly, via vocational education concentrating on farming skills, or it may take place indirectly, by concentrating on general, supportive knowledge like literacy (including arithmetical skills) which serves to prepare for the later acquisition of specific farming knowledge by agricultural extension.

We will next discuss the Haitian system of rural education and its development. During this discussion we will assume that the main effect of education is human capital formation by conveyance of general, basic knowledge and direct farming skills to the peasants. (Towards the end of the chapter we will drop this assumption and raise the question whether the human capital aspect is actually the most important one or whether the system may have other effects as well which may render human capital formation a minor issue only.) Given this assumption, the important question to answer then is whether the extent of human capital formation is increasing or decreasing in rural areas as a result of changes in education.

Rural Education in Haiti

Educational Beginnings

Educational beginnings were slow in Haiti. There is hardly any evidence of schools in the French colony.[39] The planters naturally showed no interest in developing schools for the slave population and many free mulattoes sent their children to France.[40] When independence finally came in 1804, few had a formal elementary education. Dessalines made no efforts to establish a school system, but both Christophe and Pétion showed considerable interest in the matter. The former brought British teachers to Haiti with the help of the English abolitionist William Wilberforce and founded eleven *grandes écoles nationales* as well as a secondary level royal college.[41] In the constitution of 1816, Pétion laid down the principle of free primary education which is still in force, and in addition founded the most well-known *lycée* of the country.[42] However, the practical results were meager. Apparently, when Pétion died, only one free primary school and a handful of private institutions existed,[43] and the British minister Charles Mackenzie reports that in 1828 there were primary schools only in six towns, and only one secondary school – the *Lycée Pétion*.[44]

Boyer was a passive president in educational matters. A nineteenth-century observer suggests that this mainly was due to his realization of the fact that ignorant subjects are far easier to deal with than those who have received a measure of education,[45] but equally likely is that the demand for education at the time was too weak to provoke any response from a *laissez-faire* inclined president.⁴⁶ At any rate, in 1842 it was reported that Haiti possessed only ten free schools with an enrolment not exceeding 1,000 pupils.⁴⁷ Six years later, Soulouque promulgated a law which made a seven-year (free) education compulsory and which contained provisions for both *lycées* and primary instruction (including rural schools)⁴⁸ but led to few practical results.* In 1860, President Geffrard sought to enforce the Soulouque legislation, and the number of rural schools increased from 90 in 1860 to 200 in 1875. However, less than 6,000 pupils were enrolled in rural schools eight years after the end of Geffrard's term, and attendance rates presumably were much lower still.⁴⁹

The political chaos leading to the eventual American occupation of the country in 1915 also had its effects on the school system. In 1887, it was stated that Haiti had 606 public primary schools, 400 of which were rural, but less than one-third of these schools were in working condition for lack of funds.⁵⁰ Four years later the official number of rural public schools was no less than 504, most of which existed, however, only in the minds of the politicians.⁵¹ The schools opened and closed according to the whims of the revolutionaries and their armies. The lack of suitable buildings was widespread and teachers were incompetent and underpaid. In 1906, the country had a total of 594 public primary schools, out of which only 184 were located in rural areas.⁵² In 1913, the figures were 465 and 250, respectively.⁵³ However, these figures were mere façades. The whole school system was in a deplorable state. Constant uprisings and revolutions drained the public funds and all good intentions with respect to education were thwarted. In 1915 the entire public school system had reached a state of 'total ruin'.⁵⁴

Not even the private school system appears to have escaped the general stagnation and retrogression. After the signing of the concordat between the Holy See and Haiti in 1860, a number of Catholic schools had opened in the country. In 1905, the total number was estimated to be 82 (with a total enrolment of 11,300 pupils) but ten years later only 53 of these schools remained.⁵⁵

Neither the public nor the private school system had much impact

---

*Logan (1968), p. 161. It is interesting to compare Logan's evaluation of Soulouque's contribution to Haitian education: 'His long rule proved that a black leader did not necessarily take more interest in educating the people than had Pétion and Boyer' — with that of Paul (1965), p. 24, who views Soulouque as the first head of state to show a real interest in educational matters.

on rural life before the American occupation. Rural schools existed officially, but the reality was often very different. Many so-called schools did not even have access to a building, much less to necessary books or other pedagogic equipment. Teachers were ill-paid and negligent themselves. When the Americans entered the country in 1915, the literacy rate in rural districts for all practical purposes must be regarded as being close to zero, informal estimates for the country as a whole ranging well below 10 percent.[56]

American-directed Vocational Education

Suggestions for improvements of the educational system had not been lacking during the years before the occupation. Dantès Bellegarde, who was Minister of Public Education in 1902-8 and 1913-14, made strong efforts to reform the schools and to build up sufficient funds to carry out the reform proposals, but in 1914, the Oreste government was overthrown before any practical results had been achieved, and the money was spent on the military instead.[57] In 1918, Bellegarde became Minister of Education again and once more began formulating reform proposals. He wanted to create a normal school for boys, raise teacher salaries, provide regular inspection of all schools, open rural schools and vocational schools, etc. However, almost every single one of Bellegarde's proposals were blocked by the Americans — the one on normal education no less than three times.[58] The occupation forces employed a policy of more or less systematic financial starvation of the Haitian school system.[59]

During the 1922-9 period, after the pacification of the *cacos* by the Marines, the American occupational force undertook to create a system of agricultural and vocational education—ironically enough along the lines that Bellegarde had proposed. The existing Haitian school system with its French-derived emphasis on literature and classical studies was regarded as completely unsuited to meet the needs of the agricultural population, since it was deemed to create nothing but disdain for manual labor. In his 1925 yearly report the American High Commissioner of Haiti wrote:

> [Traditional Haitian education has drawn the young Haitians] *from*, rather than toward productive industry. This is the primary cause of the low productivity of Haiti as contrasted with neighboring countries with soil no more fertile nor climate no more favorable than that of Haiti...It is therefore essential that the educational system of Haiti should, at the present time, be designed to furnish agricultural

education to the rural classes.⁶⁰

A similar view is given by the American Financial Advisor, Arthur C. Millspaugh: '...small farmers could be induced to adopt better production methods for the most part only by direct instruction of the adults, or more slowly, by the education of the children in the schools.'*

In 1924 the *Service Technique du Département de l'Agriculture et de l'Enseignement Professionel* was created to propagate these ideas. The kind of agricultural education that was chosen by the Service Technique very closely followed the outline of the system conceived at Booker T. Washington's Tuskegee Institute to teach chiefly manual skills to southern US blacks. At the lowest level this philosophy was translated into the creation of *fermes-écoles*. Along with teaching the basics of the general primary curriculum practical agricultural education was given on the primary level in rural areas. From 1924-25 to 1929-30, the number of farm schools increased from 10 to 78 and the number of pupils increased more than ten-fold (from 646 to 7,456).⁶¹

School and enrolment statistics however, do not give an entirely correct picture of the development of the farm schools. The average number of pupils per teacher was high throughout the period (63 in 1925-26 and 54 in 1928-29),⁶² which made efficient teaching difficult. It was also hard to recruit qualified teachers who were prepared to forsake the attractions of city life for a low salary,⁶³ ** and most important of all, attendance rates were low, ranging from 55 percent to 75 percent.⁶⁴ The latter fact was due to several reasons. First of all, the peasants were not particularly interested in agricultural education. They claimed to know agriculture already, and those who were at all interested in education preferred to have their children learn how to read and write in order to leave rural areas to go to the capital and get a job instead.⁶⁵ Often the peasants kept their children at home on market days and when they were needed in agriculture instead of letting them attend school. Other, more compelling reasons were also acting to lower the rates:

---

*Millspaugh (1931), pp. 149-50. Interestingly enough the Americans conceived of the educational process as being 'spiral in character: improved education leading to increased productivity; increased productivity assuring higher standards of living, and higher standards of living permitting added expenditures for the further development of education.' (Financial Advisor W.W. Cumberland, quoted by Millspaugh (1931), note, p. 142.)

**Subsequently, an effort was made to educate teachers within the educational program of the Service. (Cf. Chapter 12.)

> Here is a typical case: a farmer has six children, none of whom has ever been to school. However, he has got clothes only for one boy. Since he does not want his children to go to class without clothes he consequently sends only the one he can dress. Illness is another important factor. Malaria, syphilis, intestinal parasites, and other diseases are so common in rural areas that school attendance necessarily suffers from it even though parents desire that their children go to school.[66]

After five years of operation, the annual report of the Service Technique stated that the farm school system was still in its first phase, and that it was too early to evaluate the results.[67] The farm schools never got beyond the first stage. In 1930, the Americans had already begun to plan for the evacuation of Haiti and the farm school budget suffered a heavy cut.

Primary education in farm schools for children in 1927 was supplemented by evening classes for adults, but only 635 students were enrolled (1928-29) and most of these were ex-literates who wanted to relearn what years of lack of practice had undone.[68]

After the 1929 student strikes and riots and after the massacre of 24 peasants by the Marines in Cayes in December 1929, the Hoover Administration decided that it was time for the US to leave Haiti, and to that end sent two commissions to the country to investigate the activities of the occupational forces. The Moton commission, headed by Dr Robert R. Moton, president of Tuskegee Institute, which looked into the educational balance of the occupation concluded with regard to the Service Technique that:

> 'the setting up of a distinct and separate system of schools for primary children in city and country under a different state department, the Department of Agriculture, was a mistake'; that a limited program of demonstration of a desirable type of school for town and country is all that can be justified under temporary American occupation, and to attempt more was 'to incur the serious risk of having the whole superstructure collapse at the close of the occupation'...[69]

The efforts of the Service Technique were too thinly spread. Funds were adequate during the entire 1922-29 period, with the Service commanding a sum of about $600,000 per year in the late 1920s.[70] In 1929-30 it administered around 65 percent of the total educational budget.[71] Concentration was lacking, however, so very little came of the efforts. George F. Freeman, the American agricultural expert heading the Service was decidedly not an administrator, and failed to focus the activities to the desired extent.[72] Rotberg and Clague sarcastically remark that in the educational field the Service had accomplished 'little that was economically useful beyond reading and writing.'[73] and that a great deal more probably would have resulted from putting the money into the Haitian school system instead. In fact, the percentage of illiterates is believed to have been approximately the same before and after the occupation.* The Moton commission shared the above view and recommended that a unified educational program be restored under the sole direction of the Secretary of State for Public Education.

Lack of concentration was not the only reason for the failure of the Service Technique in the educational field. There were also other more profound causes. Even if the Service had been more efficient in its work, its educational program would never have become a success. Hans Schmidt, in his study of the occupation has advanced some explanations for this, and we will briefly summarize them here.[74]

The basic problem was that the Americans never managed to co-operate with the Haitian elite in educational matters during the constructive 1922-29 period. The Haitian elite was essentially light-skinned and had a strong tendency to emphasize the European elements of its life-style and to repudiate the African heritage. With the occupation the higher layers of Haitian society suddenly found themselves being regarded by the Americans as being no different from the black, illiterate peasantry, and what was more: found themselves subject to outright racial discrimination. All Americans in Haiti were white. The Marine Corps at the time had not yet begun to accept black recruits. A strong racial prejudice was brought to Haiti by the Marines, and elements of Jim Crow segregation soon appeared. Contacts between American women and Haitian men especially, were taboo.** The elite retaliated by excluding Americans and Haitian collaborators from social life (while cordial relations were still maintained with other white foreigners).

On top of the facial prejudices, the Americans clashed with the Haitian elite on the cultural plane. The elite strongly identified with the French culture and life-style, and looked down upon American

---

*In 1915 the estimated number of illeterates was 95-97 percent, and in 1930 the figure still was approximately 95 percent (Schmidt (1971), pp. 19, 182).
**At the same time, American men lived openly with Haitian mistresses.

The Role of Education

materialism, while the Americans denounced and resented the sophistication, refinement and pomposity associated with French-derived values. The occupation made no distinction between the elite and the masses, but persisted in regarding all Haitians as peasants who were thought ignorant and uncivilized.[75]

The entire educational program of the occupation was shaped in harmony with this type of preconceptions. As mentioned, the blueprint was Booker T. Washington's Uncle Tom philosophy of education for US blacks 'with its abnegation of intellectual, cultural, and social aspirations for blacks in favor of manual-technical education and material betterment through efficient performance at low-status trades.'[76] Naturally, the Haitian elite, representing a level of sophistication from their point of view not compatible with any type of degradation into second-class citizenship, remained hostile towards all such ideas. Manual training programs were associated with concepts of racial inferiority, and the idea of basing primary education, even rural education for peasant children, on vocationally-oriented conceptions was alien to them. By evoking racial undertones, the Americans failed to obtain the cooperation which would have been necessary for the farm school program to become a success. After the conclusion of the occupation the French-based school system once more took over. As in so many other areas, the American efforts in the educational field became but a parenthesis in Haitian history.

Haitianization and Stagnation

The Americans had paid no attention to that part of the school system which was administered by the Department of Public Education and which continued urban and rural education along traditional Haitian lines.

Table 10.1 compares on the one hand the number of pupils in the schools administered by the Service Technique and in the schools administered by the Haitian Department of Public Education and on the other hand the financial appropriations to the two types of schools. The table demonstrates that even towards the end of the 1920s, when the system managed by the Service had been built up, the financial appropriation per pupil in the Service schools was between fifteen and twenty times as high as that for the Haitian-run schools.

Hence, the Haitian-administered schools were in a deplorable state at the beginning of the 1930s. In 1931, a government commission visited a number of rural schools and reported the following abysmal statistics:[77] school houses in most cases were nothing but rudimentary shacks; some schools existed only nominally; out of 361 visited schools, 89 had no benches, and 157 had only from one to three benches for the pupils. One-third of the benches were ready to be scrapped. 122 schools had no blackboards, and 341 had no maps. Of the 26 maps actually found, 13 could hardly be read. Nevertheless, this was nothing in comparison to the teacher situation: 257 out of 335 teachers could not read, and 278 did not know the four simple arithmetical operations. Salaries were miserable: on average little more than 32 gourdes per month.* Attendance rates did not reach 25 percent.

Table 10.1: Financial Aspects of the Haitian School System 1924-9

Fiscal year	Schools managed by Service Technique			Schools managed by the Haitian Department of Public Education		
	Number of pupils	Appropriations (gourdes)	Gourdes per pupil	Number of pupils	Appropriations (gourdes)	Gourdes per pupil
1924-25	825	2,172,885	2,634	67,239	1,942,599	29
1925-26	1,659	3,226,500	1,945	82,119	1,965,167	24
1926-27	2,479	2,713,600	1,095	n.a.	1,996,720	n.a.
30 June 1927	4,496	n.a.	n.a.	85,359	2,059,020	24
30 June 1928	7,925	2,786,660	352	n.a.	n.a.	n.a.
November 1928	n.a.	n.a.	n.a.	95,696	n.a.	n.a.
1928-29	11,430	6,574,910	575	n.a.	2,443,008	n.a.

n.a. = statistics not available

Source: Logan (1930), p. 442.

The Vincent administration (1930-41) claimed to have remedied this situation and to have made steady progress in the educational sector thoroughout the 1930s. In 1931, the entire rural school system (rural schools and farm schools) was unified under the direction of the Division of Rural Education of the Department of Agriculture. In 1935, 123 schools of 63 small towns were added, since it was felt that the small towns belonged to the rural economy.[78] After an initial period of two years to achieve 'order and discipline'[79] in rural schools, an attempt to upgrade them was made. In 1934, it was stated that all teachers in rural schools knew how to read and write.[80] A few even held certificates of completed teacher's training. Salaries were raised to

*The salaries in the schools managed by the Service Technique started at 600 gourdes a month (Schmidt (1971), p. 183).

an average of 67 gourdes per month in 1934.[81]* Agricultural education was begun in a number of rural schools. Benches, blackboards and agricultural implements were distributed. The farm schools were enlarged and improved.

The above sounds impressive. If we go behind the official façade, we find that the reality was a little bit different. In Table 10.2 some statistics for rural primary education under presidents Vincent (1930-41) and Lescot (1941-46) are given. The following conclusions emerge from an examination of the contents of the table:

1. In 1935, 123 small-town schools were taken over by the Department of Agriculture, and subsequently more schools of this type were transferred from the Department of Education. In order to make a correct evaluation these schools should be subtracted, beginning in 1935-36. It has not been possible to find the exact number for each year,** but using the figure 123 we get an approximate picture of what has happened. A slight increase took place in the 1930s,† followed by a decrease during the Lescot administration. In terms of the number of schools the education given by Protestant missions in rural areas appears to have been more important than that furnished by the government.

2. The situation with respect to the number of pupils is more discouraging. In 1936-37, the number of pupils in small-town schools was 7,207.[82] Deducting this figure from the one in Table 10.2 leaves us with a decrease in rural enrolment rates during most of the 1930s, with an increase during the last two years of the Vincent administration. Again, under the Lescot government there was a fall in the number of pupils. The figures for the Protestant missions are not

---

*In 1939-40 the average salary in rural schools was 63 gourdes (SNPA & ER (n.d.), p. 174.)
**In 1938/39 the number was 98 (Holly (1955), p. 202). Using the number 123 takes the (gross) decrease in the number of schools into consideration but does not account for later transfers of small-town schools.
†We find a similar trend when enrolment figures for farm schools (which were not affected by the 1935 reform) are examined:

1931-32	6,714	1936-37	8,036
1932-33	7,621	1937-38	7,562
1933-34	7,194	1938-39	9,799
1934-35	7,542	1939-40	8,011
1935-36	7,755		

(Sources: 1931/32-1937/38: SNPA & ER (1939), p. 126; 1938/39: Holly (1955), p. 204; 1939/40: SNPA & ER (n.d.), p. 226.)

Table 10.2: Rural Primary Education 1933-46

Year	Number of schools[a] Public[b]	Number of schools[a] Presbyteral[c]	Number of schools[a] Protestant	Number of pupils Public schools	Number of pupils Presbyteral schools	Average attendance Public schools	Average attendance Presbyteral schools	Number of teachers in public schools	Number of pupils per teacher in public schools
1933-34	301	132	n.a.	23,584	n.a.	58%	n.a.	426	55
1934-35	299	n.a.	n.a.	22,269	n.a.	65%	n.a.	413	54
1935-36	400	n.a.	n.a.	29,416	n.a.	64%	n.a.	594	50
1936-37	n.a.	n.a.	n.a.	29,699	n.a.	64%	n.a.	585	51
1937-38	455	n.a.	n.a.	27,006	n.a.	67%	n.a.	585	46
1938-39	455	n.a.	n.a.	29,699	n.a.	68%	n.a.	639	46
1939-40	n.a.	n.a.	n.a.	33,346	n.a.	67%	n.a.	650	51
1940-41	458	n.a.	n.a.	32,204	n.a.	69%	n.a.	667	48
1941-42	456	n.a.	611	38,932	n.a.	69%	n.a.	692	56
1942-43	417	n.a.	566	38,093	n.a.	70%	n.a.	667	57
1943-44	420	n.a.	574	38,550	14,211	68%	80%	n.a.	n.a.
1944-45	410	n.a.	553	37,541	14,014	n.a.	n.a.	n.a.	n.a.
1945-46	n.a.	n.a.	n.a.	35,196	15,254	n.a.	n.a.	695	51

n.a. = statistics not available

a. In addition to the three categories in the table there was an insignificant number of private schools.

b. Includes all kinds of schools outside urban areas (i.e. both 'rural' and 'farm' schools).

c. These are schools managed by the Catholic clergy, held in or attached to the chapels in remote areas and supported financially by the government (Cf. Logan (1930), p. 428.) Statistics for these schools (and the Protestant schools) are only available on a very irregular basis.

Sources: Number of schools: BTS, no. 22 (1956), pp. 17-18. Enrolment, average attendance: BTS, no. 23 (1956), p. 11. Number of teachers: BTS, no. 22 (1956), p. 29.

known, but if the average number per school lay around 40 which is not an implausible figure, Catholic and Protestant schools altogether accounted for as many pupils as the public rural school system during the first half of the 1940s.*

3. With respect to the quality of education the progress appears to have been slow. Not counting the 1933-34 figure, attendance rates remained rather stagnant throughout the period under consideration, as did the number of pupils per teacher. The latter was virtually unchanged in comparison to the situation in the farm schools during the American occupation. In both farm schools and rural or small-town schools the pupils were heavily concentrated in the lower grades.[83] The farm schools appear to have been a little better off than their rural and small-town counterparts in some respects. The buildings were designed especially to serve as schools while rural and small-town schools very often had to rent unsuitable houses. The qualifications of the teachers on the average appear to have been better in the farm schools, and the equipment situation was more satisfactory. Many rural schools lacked garden plots that could be used for practical agricultural education.[84] Both types of schools suffered from the fact that there was not a single elementary illustrated textbook on tropical agriculture available for Haitian children.[85]

Obviously, the 1930-46 period was one of educational stagnation, at least in rural areas. In an evaluation of government policy in the educational field during those years, Marc A. Holly claims that the government lacked a 'true and sincere desire to help effectively the rural population.'[86] The peasants were regarded as little more than production factors, and their welfare was never given any consideration by the government. The efforts were concentrated on the towns instead of on the rural areas. Whatever measures that were taken to promote rural education were 'manifested principally in a rush to tackle new problems and undertake new activities, whereas the problems at hand remained unsolved.'[87] No steady programs were maintained, but new projects were added, modified and dropped constantly without any consistency or permanency. Transfers, promotions, salary increases, etc., in the educational administration all smelled strongly of

---

*It should be stressed that this figure is highly hypothetical. Judging from the figures for Catholic schools alone, however, the relative importance of religious education is obvious.

corruption. The budget alloted to rural education remained insufficient,[88] and due to unsatisfactory material conditions (salaries, housing, etc.) few teachers considered education a career, but stayed in duty only for a few years, while eagerly looking for other work opportunities.

Following the 1946 revolution that brought Dumarsais Estimé into power, the school system was again reorganized. Rural education was transferred to the Department of National Education. Many of the small-town schools incorporated into the system of rural education following 1935 were now brought back into the urban division of public instruction. Manual work and agricultural subjects virtually ceased to exist in rural schools and the old classic-oriented curriculum of urban schools was extended to cover the entire public primary sector.[89] In 1947, a *Direction Générale de l'Education des Adultes* was created, and an alphabetization campaign was begun.[90]

In spite of the transfer of some small-town schools, the number of pupils in the government-run rural primary schools increased by almost 45 percent. Attendance rates continued to be below the 75 percent level, and the number of pupils per teacher remained high.[91] Qualified teachers were scarce. In 1949 it was expected that only 40 elementary school teachers would graduate in the entire country, and out of that number only 30 would presumably apply for teaching positions.[92] The overwhelming majority of these were probably absorbed by the urban, private schools. The extent of the achievement in adult education remains rather uncertain. One source states that between 1943 and 1951 around 13,000 adults received their literacy diplomas as a result of alphabetization campaigns, but that more than 40,000 actually learned to read and write in Creole.[93] Whether these figures had any real meaning is doubtful. The orthography used in adult Creole reading was of the phonemic Laubach variety,[94] which was not of any help in reading French, which in turn means that those who had achieved literacy by means of the adult courses could only read Creole texts, which were few in number anyway.

The 1950 census revealed that Haiti had by far the highest illiteracy rate of any Latin American nation. The overall rate lay around 90 percent in the age groups over 15, with an average for rural areas of 93 percent.[95] In some districts official figures reached 96-98 percent.* Even

---

*Hence, in the *commune* of Côtes de Fer, not quite 4 percent of the 20-24 age group were literates (Street (1960), pp. 446-7) and in Marbial not more than 2 percent knew how to read and write (BTS, no. 2, Oct. 1951, p. 14).

these figures are presumably too low. The question asked in the census was 'Do you know how to read and write?'[96] and no effort was made to check what an affirmative answer really implied. The only possible interpretation of the census results is that in 1950 very few people knew how to read and write in rural areas.

Further Stagnation

The fall of Estimé and the rise of Magloire to power in 1950 did not change much in the field of rural education. The number of schools, pupils and teachers all continued to increase as they had done under the previous administrations. Attendance rates and pupil/teacher ratios, on the other hand did not show any signs of improvement.[97] Going below the surface we also find that the quality of the education given remained at a low level. In 1955, only 8 percent of the teachers had any formal teacher's training at all.[98] Salaries continued to be too low to attract young people into rural teaching. The average monthly salary in rural schools in 1954-55 was 245 gourdes in comparison with a figure of 180 gourdes (in real terms) in 1939-40.[99] In the mid-1950s around 90 percent of all trained teachers worked in urban areas.[100] Not more than 12 percent of all rural children in school age were enrolled in the public schools,[101] and these were concentrated in the lower grades. Nearly 70 percent of all the pupils in 1954-55 had gone less than three years to school,[102] and less than 1 percent of all pupils enrolled in the first grade completed the entire primary cycle.[103] The burden placed on the private schools finally, continued to be heavy, with the presbyteral schools accounting for approximately 30 percent of the number of pupils that the public schools could handle.[104]

A limited number of people, presumably less than under the previous administration, were made literate by adult education. Between 1947 and 1954 UNESCO ran a pilot project of rural education in the Marbial valley, near Jacmel, The teaching of basic skills to improve cultivation and soil conservation methods, to establish rural industries and improve sanitary conditions was to contribute to the improvement of living conditions in a small, isolated, poverty-stricken area.[105] The main ingredients of the program were primary and adult schooling in Creole (to be followed by French), health education and medical services, agricultural and veterinary education in combination with extension work, development of small-scale crafts and industries as well as producer and consumer co-operatives.[106] The aim was to train Haitian counterparts and to turn the project over to them as soon as possible (which took place in 1954).

The Marbial program failed. Paul Moral describes the general impression of the project *'à sa belle époque'* between 1950 and 1953 as:

> an. . .enterprise run by experts who certainly had good intentions but who persisted in employing an artificial pedagogy in which the peasants pretended to show an interest either because of amour-propre or because of their natural gentleness.[107]

As soon as the foreign experts had left Marbial, things reverted to their old state. Only faint traces of the new techniques, like soil conservation measures and alphabetization (mainly among younger people) were left. The choice of Marbial for the pilot project was a clear mistake. The area was underdeveloped. It also happened to be in a state of acute depression at the time.[108] Moreover, the government took only a feeble interest in the whole experiment.[109]

Other efforts in adult education were hampered by the lack of an agreed orthography for Creole. Up to 1953 the Laubach method had been the only one in use, but subsequently there arose a trend towards a spelling which would facilitate literacy in French, and no agreement on a unified orthography could be reached.[110] As a result, the literacy campaigns lacked perseverance and regularity, but some 7,000 new adult literates are believed to have been educated between 1951 and 1956.[111]

Under Duvalier, the educational administration was once more reorganized. Rural instruction again became the responsibility of the Ministry of Agriculture. In practice, however, the reorganization meant very little. Rural education remained stagnant during the 1960s. Virtually all the annual reports of the Inter-American Committee on the Alliance for Progress (CIAP) emphatically stress this fact. The following quotations are typical:

> Haiti has lost in recent years several thousand elementary and secondary school teachers. Hundreds of these are now in the employment of international agencies and are serving in several African countries, about 500 of them in the Congo. Since these persons have not been replaced either by a quickened out turn of the internal educational system or by the entry from abroad of any significant number of correspondingly educated persons, the irrefutable conclusion is that the grievous loss of this exodus has greatly lowered the already poor, general educational standards of Haiti, and has at the same time reduced the capacity of the school system to respond in the short

run to increases in purely financial resources.[112]

A study of available information on education in Haiti reveals no significant progress to suggest that the country is overcoming the limitation of its educational system with the necessary speed. Everything indicates that educational activities continue to be blocked by lack of schoolrooms, very scant supply of equipment and materials, shortage of teachers and professors, and limited budget resources. The sharp decline in the national economy is undoubtedly the main obstacle confronting educational authorities in their efforts to extend and improve education.[113]

The situation regarding education is particularly distressing in Haiti. It is estimated that the national literacy rate for persons over 15 years of age is 13 per cent. Overall budgetary appropriations for education (including those included in the Ministry of Agriculture and in adult literacy programs) amount to some gde 24 million in fiscal 1971...but this figure was about the same 10 years ago. This effort in any case is not sufficient to prevent a deterioration of the literacy situations as primary enrolment is increasing at an accumulative rate inferior to the rate of increase of the population between 5 and 14 years of age...rural education is completely neglected. There is still not enough recognition in the Government of the fundamental need to develop education in rural areas as a basis for strengthening the productivity of agriculture in a country where 85 percent of the population is rural.[114]

Financial starvation of rural education could only lead to stagnation in quantitative as well as in qualitative terms. The figures of Table 10.3 show that after an initial increase in the number of pupils in public schools up to 1963, enrolment rates then stagnated up to 1970. A comparison with the year 1950 shows that the percentage of rural children of school age that were actually enrolled was virtually unchanged. In 1950, the figure was estimated to be 10.4 percent,[115] and twenty years later the official estimate lay between 11 and 12 percent.[116] The quality of the education probably fell somewhat. While Table 10.3 indicates a slight fall in the number of pupils per teacher, it hides the fact that a substitution of untrained teachers for trained personnel seems to have taken place, as indicated by the quotation from the CIAP report above. For political reasons a number of qualified teachers left the country during the 1960s. The capacity of the normal schools remained insufficient to make up for this loss,[117] and rural school teacher salaries in all probability continued to be too low to attract the newly graduated teachers, starting at a level of Gde 225 per month in 1968-69 and averaging no more than Gde 262.[118] The concentration of children in the lower grades continued. In 1959, 60 percent of the rural children in school were registered in the two nursery school classes, and less than 1 percent was registered in the final grade *(Moyen II)*. In 1967 the proportions were almost identical with 59 percent in kindergarten and slightly more than 1 percent in the final grade.[119]

Table 10.3: Rural Primary Education 1959-71

| | Number of schools | | Number of pupils | |
	Public	Private[a]	Public	Private
1959-60	445	n.a.	85,893	n.a.
1960-61	452	668	91,670	n.a.
1961-62	464	n.a.	97,783	n.a.
1962-63	477	n.a.	100,769	n.a.
1963-64	480	n.a.	97,413	n.a.
1964-65	487	n.a.	99,589	n.a.
1965-66	492	n.a.	100,442	n.a.
1966-67	495	n.a.	98,200	n.a.
1967-68	508	n.a.	100,148	n.a.
1968-69	517	697	101,684	46,182
1969-70	521	n.a.	108,585	n.a.
1970-71	530	n.a.	108,582	n.a.

| | Number of teachers | | Pupils per teacher | |
	Public	Private[a]	Public	Private
1959-60	1,315	n.a.	65	n.a.
1960-61	1,332	n.a.	69	n.a.
1961-62	1,429	n.a.	65	n.a.
1962-63	1,543	n.a.	65	n.a.
1963-64	1,526	n.a.	64	n.a.
1964-65	1,543	n.a.	65	n.a.
1965-66	1,547	n.a.	65	n.a.
1966-67	1,632	n.a.	60	n.a.
1967-68	1,632	n.a.	61	n.a.
1968-69	1,656	1,115	61	41
1969-70	1,659	n.a.	61	n.a.
1970-71	1,659	n.a.	65	n.a.

n.a. = statistics not available.

a These include presbyteral schools and Protestant mission schools. Statistics for those schools are available only for few years.

Sources: Number of public schools 1964/65-1965/66: CIAP (1968:2), pp. 82-3. Rest of table: UNESCO (n.d.), pp. 45, 47.

Table 10.3 also shows that the role of private schools in rural education continued to be important during the 1960s. Around one-third of the enrolled pupils were registered in private schools towards the end of the decade. Presumably the overall situation in the private schools was better than in the public schools as indicated by the lower number of pupils per teacher.[120]

In 1958 the Duvalier administration promulgated a law launching a new alphabetization drive, and in 1961 the *Office Nationale d'Education Communautaire* (ONEC) was created.[121] The objectives were modest. In six months an illiterate person was to learn to read and write 600 words in Creole, to make use of the four fundamental arithmetical operations, and to receive some civic instruction. This was later to be followed by post-alphabetization campaigns.[122] After two years 11,800 persons had received their literacy diplomas, a figure that up to 1965 increased to 66,000 (for both rural and urban areas). Some statistics for the first half of the 1960s are shown in Table 10.4.

Table 10.4: Adult Alphabetization 1961-6

Year	Number of alphabetization groups	Number of post-alphabetization groups	Enrolment	Average attendance
1961-62	196	–	8,343	50%
1962-63	693	–	41,418	72%
1963-64	1,772	–	93,755	71%
1964-65	3,069	–	136,302	68%
1965-66	3,196	513	115,586	66%
Year	Number of literacy certificates	Number of teachers	Pupils per teacher	
1961-62	2,017	196	42	
1962-63	9,772	693	59	
1963-64	22,770	1,913	49	
1964-65	31,306	3,069	44	
1965-66	n.a.	3,135	36	

n.a. = statistics not available.
Sources: Number of alphabetization and post-alphabetization groups: OEA (1972), p. 191; rest of table: CIAP (1968:2), p. 86.

Post-alphabetization campaigns were begun in 1965-66, and the number of post-alphabetization groups rose from 513 in the first year to 1,820 in 1968-69. Simultaneously, however, the number of regular alphabetization groups declined by almost 50 percent to 1,650 in the latter year.[123] No figures for total enrolment and average attendance seem to be available for the second half of the 1960s but it appears as if the literacy drive lost most of its momentum by 1970.[124] The newest official statistics regarding illiteracy show an overall decline from 90 percent in 1950 to 80 percent in 1971, with changes within the age groups as shown by Table 10.5. For our purposes the most interesting figure is the average for rural areas (over five years of age). In 1950, as we have seen, this average was 93 percent. In 1971, the corresponding figure was 89 percent which means that only a very small step had been taken towards the eradication of illiteracy in rural areas.

Table 10.5: Official Illiteracy Estimates for 1950 and 1971[a]

Age group	1950 Whole country	1971 Whole country	1971 Rural areas
All age groups	89.5%	79.8%	89.2%
20-34	88.4%	74.9%	84.4%
35-49	91.4%	84.8%	92.1%
50-64	91.5%	87.2%	94.3%
65 and over	92.0%	90.7%	96.6%

a. Only those claiming to know *both* how to read and how to write have been classified as literate.

Sources: 1950: Calculations based upon Brand (1965), p. 26 and Mirville (1959), p. 10; 1971: Unpublished data from the Institut Haïtien de Statistique.

At the beginning of the 1970s it was evident that the preceding decade had not yielded the desired results in the educational field, and new efforts were made to increase the quantity and quality of rural education. Some results regarding primary education can be seen in Table 10.6. The main achievement is that the number of pupils enrolled in public rural schools has been increased by 25 percent since the end of the 1960s which has brought total enrolment (public plus private) to around 20 percent.[125] This, however, has created an acute shortage of teachers, raising the average number of pupils per teacher from a little more than 60 to around 70 and up to 150 in extreme cases.[126]

In the private schools, whose enrolment is more than three-fourths of that of the public schools, the ratio was far lower: around 40 per teacher. The quality of the curriculum and of the teachers also continued to cause problems. It was felt that the curriculum of the rural schools was not sufficiently adapted to the needs of the rural population, and the pedagogic quality of the teachers is low, in spite of

Table 10.6: Rural Primary Education 1971-5

	Number of schools		Number of pupils	
	Public	Private	Public	Private
1971-72	545	698	117,935	48,249
1972-73	557	n.a.	121,841	n.a.
1973-74	565	n.a.	125,166	n.a.
1974-75	571	1,157[a]	124,676[b]	98,762[a]
	Number of teachers		Number of pupils per teacher	
1971-72	1,693	1,115	70	43
1972-73	1,704	n.a.	72	n.a.
1973-74	1,720	n.a.	73	n.a.
1974-75	1,765	2,462[a]	71	40

n.a. = statistics not available.

a. The big difference in comparison to 1971-72 is probably due to differences in reporting.

b. The decline appears to be due to the drought in 1975.

Sources: 1971/72-1972/73: UNESCO (n.d.), pp. 45, 47; 1973/74-1974/75: DARNDR (1974-75), pp. 156-7.

It was also realized that ONEC was a failure, and in 1969 a new law created the *Office National d'Alphabétisation et d'Action Communautaire* (ONAAC) which has a more ambitious goal than its predecessor, since it aims at functional literacy for adults in urban and rural areas. The aim is to make the new literates correctly understand the problems related to their their own situation and to give them a means by which it could be improved.[128] In 1970, the number of new literates created by the ONAAC was almost 66,000[129] — virtually as much as was accomplished by the ONEC during its first five years. The ONAAC program seems to have performed reasonably efficiently within the limit given by its budget which in 1969-70 was not more than 1.2 million gourdes,[130] but at the same time the activities of the ONAAC are known to have beeen hampered by a bureaucratic and stiff organization at least during the first years of the 1970s.[131]

In 1977, the Inter-American Development Bank agreed to a loan of US $9.6 million for a new major program to improve formal and informal educational facilities in rural districts.[132] The new project aims at the creation of a number of integrated multi-purpose educational centers — *Centres d'Education Integrée pour le Développement Rural* (CEIDER).[133] The CEIDER approach represents an attempt to take a comprehensive view of the educational needs of the Haitian countryside. Each CEIDER will include basic community schools and farm schools to cover the children of school age as well as complementary education and technical assistance directed at the older age groups. The program is vocationally oriented and puts stress on farming skills. If carried out in its entirety, the CEIDER package will directly or indirectly affect some 350,000 people. The enrolment in rural schools is planned to increase by approximately 40,000 pupils during the first four-year period, and some 40,500 adults will achieve literacy each year. The project aims at covering the entire country in twelve years.

Summing Up: Rural Education in the Twentieth Century

The general picture of Haitian rural education during and after the American occupation of the country is one of stagnation and impasse. The occupation attempted a break with the existing primary school system which stressed humanities at the expense of practical skills and tried to lay the foundation for a vocationally oriented education in rural districts. The main effect of this reorientation, however, was to expose the already existing, Haitian-run school system to more or less systematic starvation of resources. The new system met with no success, mainly because the Americans failed to elicit the necessary cooperation from the Haitian elite, and when the occupation was over, the old system with its emphasis on classical and literary studies once more took over, and vocational education was relegated to a secondary position.

After the withdrawal of the American forces, up to 1950, in spite of government claims of progress, stagnation appears to have reigned in rural education. The 1950 census showed that rural illiteracy was around 95 percent, a figure of the same order as before the American occupation. Only 10 percent of the rural children of school age were actually enrolled in the public school system.

These trends continued for the next 20 years. Neither enrolment nor illiteracy rates appeared much different at the beginning of the 1970s than at the beginning of the 1950s. Some efforts with respect to adult literacy had been made, but it is doubtful whether the success of these efforts was very widespread. The 1971 census showed that illiteracy in rural areas remained somewhere in the region of 90 percent.

Possibly, some progress has been made in rural education during the 1970s. Enrolment figures have increased, and a new adult literacy drive

The Role of Education

has been undertaken. Recently the government has obtained a major loan from the Inter-American Development Bank to finance an integrated program of rural education, involving not only primary and secondary education for rural youths but adult literacy and direct technical assistance as well. It is thus possible that during the last five years there has been a slight improvement, but its impact so far is bound to be very small, and it still remains to be seen whether this is a real trend or, as in the past, a temporary recovery that will soon be halted or reversed.

The point of departure for our examination of the Haitian system of rural education in this section has been the assumption that education leads to human capital formation in the sense of conveying basic general knowledge, such as literacy and arithmetical skills, which facilitates the later acquisition of direct knowledge of farming methods as well as of economic and technical decision-making related to farm operations. Assuming that this is actually the case, quantitative and qualitative improvements in rural education should increase the stock of human capital in the Haitian countryside and hence may also act as a brake on the tendency for rural per capita incomes to fall. It must be stressed that basic, general education is presumably not in itself enough. Literacy, for example, must be complemented with direct teaching of those skills that the peasants can use in their farming operations. The most important role of education is presumably in the situation where the environment within which the peasants have to operate changes, and especially when the prevailing technology is undergoing a modernization process. The teaching of new methods to the peasants will probably be much easier if the percentage of literates is already high, for example. Thus, general education may be a necessary but not sufficient condition for human capital formation to have an impact on the production capacity of the rural economy.

We will return to the problem of technological change in Chapter 12. In the meantime we may, however, conclude that rural education in Haiti presents a fairly stationary picture during the period after the American occupation at least up to the early 1970s. Few rural children have been enrolled in the schools. Fewer still have actually attended classes to the extent where they have acquired any lasting knowledge. Adult education has been undertaken only in comparatively recent years and then fairly sporadically. The result appears to be that little human capital formation which may facilitate the modernization of the peasant economy has taken place. The average educational level of the rural labor force was probably not much higher at the beginning of the

1970s than at the beginning of the American occupation of Haiti, and it therefore appears unlikely that education has mitigated the tendency for per capita incomes in rural areas to deteriorate in the long run.

Domination by Education

Hitherto, the discussion of rural education in Haiti has been based on the explicit assumption that the main role of education is to contribute to human capital formation in the countryside. This assumption was made only to provide a background to the investigation of some quantitative and qualitative trends in the rural educational system. Our conclusion was that, given that rural education can contribute to human capital formation, the average quality of the rural labor force, in terms of education, is likely to have undergone only insignificant changes during the post-occupation period at least up to the early 1970s.

Thus, we know that the rural educational system has probably not changed or expanded in such a way as to make any notable positive contributions to the development of the peasant economy in Haiti. We could stop here, but it may be interesting to pursue the analysis one step further and raise the question as to what the main role of rural education in Haitian society is. To answer this question, let us try to find out why so few rural children go to school and why even fewer manage to complete the entire cycle of primary education. We can begin with a number of factors related to the pupils themselves.

The Pupils

Due to the poverty of rural Haiti, going to school is a very complicated affair for the children. The opportunity cost of sending a child to school is presumably high for the parents[134] and rises with the age of the children. There are a considerable number of tasks that the children can carry out in farming, especially during the peak seasons of the agricultural year. The boys can watch the cattle and help out in the gardens or fields, while the girls help in the household and look after the younger children. Both boys and girls have to carry water to the household, sometimes from wells that may be several kilometers away.

Those who attend school during the greater part of the day are often put to strenuous physical work when they come home, thereby foregoing any opportunities to do homework, both because of fatigue and because of the fact that there is no electrification in rural areas. On market days one or both parents may be a long way from home, sometimes for more than a day, leaving all household and nursing duties to the older children in their absence.[135]

Besides, the high opportunity cost of schooling poverty creates other effects which make school attendance difficult. A survey conducted by the *Institut Haïtien de Statistique* among school teachers at the beginning of the 1950s reported that more than 40 percent of the teachers (in some areas more than 75 percent) had observed symptoms of malnutrition among their pupils, and that more than 80 percent indicated signs of poor health among the children.[136]

Inadequate clothing is another result of poverty. In the countryside, children frequently go around naked, sometimes until puberty. In order to go to school, however, the children have to wear a uniform, and this cost will have to be borne by the parents.

The predominant settlement pattern of rural Haiti is one of extreme dispersion. The peasant families do not live in villages but are scattered all over the countryside, in clusters of a few huts. The dispersion of the population makes the choice of a convenient location for the school extremely difficult. No matter where the building is erected, the majority of the pupils may still have to walk many kilometers to get to school, on steep mountain roads or paths, without protection from the torrential rains or from the blazing sun. On many occasions, this trip will have to be undertaken with nothing but a cup of coffee in the stomach and the children will have to go on all day without any other food than what they may bring with them from home, i.e. generally nothing.

In the first part of the present chapter we mentioned that as a rule it appears to be virtually impossible to enroll more than 70 percent of the children of school age in societies where the parents are not literate. This mechanism presumably operates in Haiti as well, where enrolment rates are far lower still, Unless the children in question are being trained explicitly to leave agriculture for the town, where some basic education may yield tangible benefits, the parents will not agree to enrolment of their children unless they have received some education themselves.* This trend, in turn, is reinforced by the low quality of the education that the children are likely to receive in rural schools (cf. below). If education is perceived as a meaningless waste of time it is not surprising

---

*Myrdal (1968), p. 1801, remarks with respect to South Asia: 'Since lower class parents usually have little or no education and are illiterate they tend to have less interest in seeking an education for their children or in keeping them in school after they are enrolled. The talk of the "hunger for education" in the village is largely a romantic illusion...'

that few children are sent to school.

High opportunity costs, malnutrition, illness, fatigue, lack of clothes, dispersion of the population and indifference on part of the parents interact so as to depress enrolment and attendance rates and to keep drop-out rates at a high level. Only 20 percent of the population of school age is enrolled, and attendance rates vary across the agricultural year with peaks during the dead seasons and troughs during harvest periods. There is also a tendency for attendance to increase during years with good harvests or favorable prices for agricultural products.[137]

Malnutrition, illness and fatigue make those who actually go to school unreceptive to what is taught there, which in turn lowers attendance even further. Many pupils are forced to repeat grades, and reach the end of the compulsory school age without having advanced very far through the primary cycle. Others drop out altogether. It should be stressed that some of these factors are mutually and cumulatively reinforcing. Low attendance leads to repetition of grades. Repetition becomes boring, and attendance goes down. Low attendance also makes it difficult for the pupils to understand what is going on in school. They prefer to stay home or drop out instead.

French as a Filter

The low enrolment and the high drop-out rates in rural primary schools are not caused exclusively by problems related to the pupils and their environment. Of equal importance is that the Haitian rural school system works in at least three ways as a discriminatory filter which makes it extremely difficult for the rural children to complete the primary cycle. It uses a foreign language as the medium of instruction. The quality of teachers and schools is low -- lower than in urban areas. Finally, the system is formalistic and is strongly concentrated on examinations.

Haiti presents a case of what we may term *linguistic dualism*. The language that every Haitian, regardless of which social class he or she belongs to, can understand and speak is Creole. The latter is also the only language generally understood by the peasants, while the elite in addition display a complete mastery of French. Among the elite

> Creole is used exclusively in private informal situations, such as between peer groups of children and adolescents and between parents in the home; French is used exclusively in formal public situations, such as in administrative proceedings, or in official speeches. Both Creole and French are used interchangeably in private formal

situations (receptions, conversation with mere acquaintances) and public informal situations (in shops, in conversation with friends).[138]

The mastery of French not only means the acquisition of an additional means of communication for the elite. To speak French is also a way of associating with French culture and civilization which are very highly regarded in Haiti. Conversely, Creole is often spoken of, not as a language (which by any reasonable definition of the term it is) but as a *patois*, nothing but a corrupted or debased French.* The explanation of the glorification of French and of the disdain for Creole can be cast in terms of a social distinction:

> When the French yoke was thrown off, the free mulattoes suddenly found that the slaves were legally now their equals. Being a free man was no longer a distinction. Attachment to the French language and French ways suddenly became much more important as a means of maintaining a status of superiority over the ex-slaves...Since the liberation, the élite...not only have had their children educated in Catholic and private schools conducted by teachers whose native language was French, but have whenever possible sent their offspring to France for the higher levels of instruction. As a result most of the élite have an impressive command of the French language and of French culture in general.[139]

This social distinction must not be regarded as pure snobbery. Actually, from the point of view of the upper classes, linguistic dualism is very functional. French is the medium of instruction in all schools instead of the vernacular Creole, including those in rural districts, but few rural children have had any contact at all with French before going to school and must therefore master two difficulties simultaneously in their literacy education: that of learning how to read and write as well as that of having to learn it in a language which most of the time is completely new to them.** Creole is used only in adult literacy

---

*Moore (1972), p. 112, maintains that 'the easiest way to get into a heated argument with some members of the Haitian elite would be to say something about the Creole "language".' For an extremely interesting discussion of the differences between French and Creole and of the origins of Creole see Valdman (1969).
**Berry (1969), p. 222, estimates that 90 percent of the work involved in learning how to read and write in Haiti is learning the language.

courses.* From the point of view of social stratification this division has important effects. The rural children begin their formal education at a tremendous disadvantage in comparison to urban children who are more familiar with French and especially in comparison to elite children who speak French with the same *finesse* as they speak Creole already when they begin school. Thus, the use of French as the medium of instruction provides a tremendously efficient filtering or screening device whereby urban elite children are allowed to pass through the elementary school system while the rural peasant children are hindered. The French language erects a formidable barrier to learning for those not sufficiently proficient in it.

It may be possible to build a partial defense for French on the grounds that printed material in Creole is exceedingly scarce, so that literacy in that language would be forgotten at least as soon as literacy in French. This is a dubious argument, however. In the first place it hardly harmonizes with the teaching of adult literacy courses in Creole, and second, elite thinking is very much to blame for the lack of printed material. Since French has always been the means of written communication and expression for the elite group, no serious attempts have been made by the government to arrive at a standardized orthography for Creole. Typically, the first efforts were made by foreigners. The result was the phonemic McConnell-Laubach orthography that while obviously serving the needs of foreign students of Creole adequately was less suited to Haitian needs. The main drawback of the McConnell-Laubach method is that it does not qualify as a means to facilitate the subsequent teaching of French. For this a 'gallic', not a 'phonemic', orthography is needed. Steps to develop such an orthography have been taken, but still no agreement on standardization has been reached. Given a genuine willingness on part of the government to really do something about this matter, standardization along French lines should be a fairly simple affair.[140] Another way in which the elite view of Creole has precluded the emergence of reading material in the vernacular is that since Creole is held in contempt, few efforts have been made to write works of fiction and non-fiction in Creole — by elite members as well as by others.[141]

Whatever the merits of learning French appear to be to the elite,

---

*An inquiry among Haitian students abroad is particularly interesting on this point. While only 16 percent advocated French for rural adult literacy courses, no less than 45 percent thought it to be the proper medium for rural primary education (Morose (1970), pp. 116, 121).

they are not likely to be very substantial for most peasants. The occasions when French is needed are few in rural areas, and the probability that it will soon be forgotten — and with it literacy — is high. It would make much more sense to build the entire primary cycle on Creole and within that teach French as what it is: a foreign language. An experiment along these lines has been made with beginners in three schools in the plain of Léogâne by the *Centre Haïtien d'Investigation en Sciences Sociales* (CHISS).[142] In one school (the experimental group) the entire instruction was carried out in Creole, including reading and writing, and French was taught as a foreign language. In the second school (control group I) French was used throughout and advanced pedagogy was employed to facilitate the learning process. The third school (control group II) also used French as the sole medium of instruction but without pedagogic refinements, adhering to the traditional Haitian methodology. Strong efforts were made to control the experiment, but at the outset control group I turned out to be significantly more advanced than the other two groups (which showed no significant differences between them). During the course of the first year attitude tests (towards school, teachers, parents, etc.), sociometric tests and tests regarding verbal attitude were administered to the pupils, and at the end of the year tests of reading, arithmetic and French were undertaken. The results were perfectly clear. On all tests, except the one of French, the experimental group showed a significantly better performance than any of the control groups.

From time to time clear-sighted Haitians have criticized the use of French. Arguing from the point of view of social justice Jean Price-Mars, the dean of all modern Haitian intellectuals, had the following to say in 1959 in defense of Creole:

> . . .if the right-minded in their inveterate [romanticism] would raise new objections I would like to ask them whether we must continue to apply the system which actually prevails, i.e. whether we must continue to teach French as the only compulsory language which all citizens must know since it is the official language prescribed and ordered by the constitution.
>
> We know that this is the situation which exists right now, but we also know that it hides the most evident and hypocritical lie, that statistics and demographic trends denounce it as a violent class antagonism since only a tiny minority benefits from it at the expense of the masses. And in this country ostentatiously labeled democratic and where the magic words *liberté, égalité, fraternité* are considered

the symbols of public life, nine-tenths work the soil, sowing and harvesting, nine-tenths work with their hands, toiling strenuously to permit the remaining one-tenth to [rule the country] as if they were the only Haitians, in the same way as our ancestors worked to ensure the luxury of a privileged minority.

Well, I find that such a system is simply odious and that it constitutes the most flagrant and dangerous injustice in the mid-twentieth century. May those who want to conserve it at any cost sit down and probe into themselves, and may they ponder the scope of the evil and its predictable consequences.[143]

Teachers and Schools

The use of French instead of Creole in primary education is a direct outcome of the lack of identification of the upper classes with the peasants, which we analyzed at length in Chapter 7; at the same time it constitutes a way of maintaining the social distance between the two groups. It is, however, not the only way in which filters have been built into the educational system. A second filter, also an outcome of the lack of identification between elite and masses, is the reluctance of the Haitian governments to provide the majority of the population with anything but low-quality schools and teaching staff. We have touched upon these aspects several times in the foregoing, but it may be worthwhile to provide a comprehensive summary here.

The material standard of primary rural schools is low. Very often the buildings are intended for other uses and are not at all adapted to educational needs. Inadequate appropriation of funds has precluded the erection of a sufficient number of proper school buildings, and renting other types of premises has had to serve as an imperfect substitute. The schools frequently lack garden plots where agricultural subjects can be taught and practiced, and sports and recreation grounds are non-existent. No special provision is made for the teachers, but they have instead to rent a house or board with a local family. The supply of fresh drinking water leaves a lot to be desired, as do other sanitary facilities. Often only polluted water from streams or ponds is available, if at all. Toilets as a rule are completely lacking. Classrooms are too small for the number of pupils they have to cope with; benches are lacking and the existing stock has often been used for so many years that it should have been discarded long ago. Blackboards are either too small or non-existent. One outdated book has to serve many pupils simultaneously. Writing materials — pens, paper, crayons, etc. — are deficient in number as well as in quality. Picture files, maps, globes, encyclopedias, charts, etc. are hardly ever seen.

The situation with respect to teachers is exactly analogous. Haiti had no more than three rural normal schools working in the mid-1970s with a total capacity of less than 250 students.[144] The emphasis of the normal school curriculum is heavily biased towards theoretical studies, whereas no practical stage has been inserted that could make the future teachers used to the classroom situation. No special account is taken of the fact that the rural normal school graduates are going to work in rural areas, not in towns. Even those who have completed the rural normal schools will not necessarily end up teaching there anyway. The salaries are low, isolation is a problem in the countryside, housing is also a problem, there is nowhere to send the teachers' own children after primary school, etc.

All these factors make many normal school graduates go into the urban school system or into jobs that have no relation to their normal school training instead. The turnover of teachers becomes high in rural schools, since many teachers take teaching only as a temporary occupation while looking from something more remunerative. The inevitable result of this is that the absolute number of teachers is too low.* Frequently teachers serving in the first grades have to handle as many as 100 children alone. In addition most of the rural teachers will not have any formal qualifications at all. In the late 1960s only slightly more than 20 percent of all rural elementary school teachers held a diploma from a normal school.[145]

Untrained teachers with an inadequate supply of books and other elementary pedagogic aids, teaching in a foreign language (sometimes Creole has to be resorted to in spite of the instructions) has fatal consequences for the standard of the education which is offered to rural children. Rote, recitation and simple memorization take the place of comprehension and understanding of the studied matters. The teacher frequently has to lecture and make do only with the aid of the blackboard, while the pupils, if they have writing material, take notes. If no such material is available, unison mechanical memorization is used instead.

---

*Schaedel (1962), p. 95, notes, that '...the peasants themselves in many areas hired their own self-taught teachers from the community and sent their children to the teacher's house or rented one specially for the purpose. In other communities with a lack of staff, the communities supplied the additional teacher's salary. Both of these measures are illegal.'

Emphasis on Examination

The low standard of teachers and schools is seen in a correct perspective only if it is known that the Haitian school system puts considerable emphasis on examinations. The following extract from an official publication gives a good summary of how this works on the primary school level:

> *Examinations.* The examinations organized at the end of the school year determine the promotion of pupils from one class to the next higher one. They are left to the judgment of directors who generally choose the subjects for such examinations.
>
> *The written examinations.* The most important are added to the oral for obtaining the average for promotion.
>
> In principle, the averages for the two first trimesters are added to the third and constitute the decisive note for promotion.
>
> At the end of elementary cycle, the pupils are sent to an offical examination organized by the general Administration of National Education for obtaining their *Certificat d'Etudes Primaires.* Superior primary studies which last 3 years after the *Certificat d'Etudes Primaires* are confirmed by *Brevet Elémentaire.*
>
> These examinations cover the subjects prescribed by the official program. The subjects for written examinations are: orthography, arithmetic, French composition, Haiti's history and geography, general information, natural and social sciences, and oral reading. Marks 0 and 1 are eliminatory for each subject. The average of marks obtained (30 over 50) gives the right to *Certificat d'Etudes Primaires* and *Brevet Elémentaire.*
>
> To be admitted to Sixième or first year of secondary studies, one must in principle have [the] *Certificat d'Etudes Primaires* and participate in a selective examination because of so many applications for admission.[146]

The chances that most rural children enrolled in the schools will be able to meet these requirements are small indeed.

Rural Education: A Discriminatory Filter

The peasant children face a number of obstacles to education which are posed by the circumstances under which they live. Sending a child to school for a few years means that the peasant family loses labor which is needed especially during the peak season. Hence, the opportunity cost of going to school may be high. The general poverty of rural areas also means that children are often excluded from education because they are undernourished, ill or lack clothes, and a high percentage of those who actually attend classes do so on an empty stomach after a fatiguing trip of several kilometers on foot. Under these circumstances naturally enough many have to repeat classes or drop out altogether before they complete their primary education.

At the same time, however, three factors make rural primary education act as a filtering or screening mechanism rather than as a mechanism for building up a stock of human capital in rural areas. French, a foreign language, is used as the medium of instruction instead of Creole. The lack of government interest in the peasant community precludes the provision of anything other than low-quality school buildings, materials and teachers. Finally, great emphasis is placed on examinations. This type of screening device is primarily discriminatory, i.e. it does not aim at sorting out pupils with certain skills which will be utilized at a later date. Rather, it makes a very high percentage of the children fall by the wayside during the course of their education. In short, the rural school system prevents, rather than facilitates, the education of the peasant children.

The discriminatory aspect of the filter is amply borne out by the statistics showing the distribution of children in various grades. As Table 10.7 shows, in the mid-1970s only 2 percent of all children in the public rural schools[148] were in the highest grade, while more than 50 percent were concentrated in kindergarten. Thus very few children manage to complete the entire primary cycle, at least in the public schools, those run by the Haitian government. In the mid-1970s it was estimated that the rural population of primary-school age amounted to approximately 1.4 million.[147] Out of this population, some 125,000, or less than 10 percent, were enrolled in the public rural schools. Assuming that all those enrolled in *Moyen II* also completed that grade, we find that less than 2 percent of all rural children of primary school age manage to get a complete primary education in the public school system.*

It is unlikely that those who actually manage to pass the entire primary cycle will remain in rural areas. Even formal vocational agricultural education is known to pose a particular problem in low-income

---

*Assuming the number of rural children in school age to grow at the constant rate of 3 percent per annum and assuming a constant enrolment rate, we would expect the percentage of children in each grade to be constant as well, provided that all children pass their grades. With eight grades, the expected percentage of pupils in the highest grade is 11.2. Now, we find in this grade only 2 percent, or 18 percent of the expected figure. Only 1.8 percent of all rural children hence finish the primary cycle.

Table 10.7: Enrolment by Grade in Public Rural Primary Schools 1974-5

Grade	Percentage of total enrolment
Enfantin I + II	52.5
Préparatoire	17.5
Préparatoire II	12.5
Elémentaire I	7.5
Elémentaire II	5
Moyen I	3
Moyen II	2
Total	100

Source: IICA (n.d.), p. 65.

countries like Haiti. While formal vocational training is undoubtedly very useful to a person who remains in farming, there is a very real danger that the vocational element of that education is wasted in countries where there is a strong demand outside the agricultural sector for people with the kind of general competence which is usually generated by a vocationally-centred education in additon to the purely vocational skills. In such a situation there is a strong probability that vocational education leads to a 'brain drain' from rural areas.[149] On the one hand there is a demand for general skills and on the other, persons with a secondary education stand a much better chance than those without it to find a good job in urban areas.

Thus, it is extremely doubtful whether rural education contributes at all to any formation of human capital which may increase agricultural production per head of the rural population. We have seen how during the American occupation of Haiti the peasants considered education not as a way of enhancing their productivity in farming but as a way of leaving rural districts for a better job in the cities. Although no data appear to exist for later periods, one would expect the same type of attitudes towards schooling to prevail today, especially since rural per capita incomes seem to be falling slowly which in turn may increase the pressure to leave the countryside on those receiving some type of education and who are consequently best suited to a life in the urban environment.

It is also possible that education in rural areas may have directly detrimental effects. Education in the form which it takes in the Haitian setting, with emphasis on theory, always entails the risk of creating disdain for manual labor. An inquiry designed to evaluate the Haitian school system given to a number of Haitian students abroad a few years ago was very conclusive on this point. 97 percent of the respondents stated that the Haitian in general thinks that intellectual work is nobler than manual work, and 83 percent stated that their parents would like them to have an intellectual job and not a manual one. It was also believed that these attitudes prevailed among a majority of the Haitian intellectuals.[150] The inquiry dealt with university students and is therefore of course not representative of the attitudes prevailing among those who have completed the primary cycle only, but it is quite possible and even probable that to a certain extent the same type of attitudes may also be fostered at lower levels of the educational system. In this context it must be recalled that one of the great dividing lines in Haitian life is that between people with a manual occupation and people performing non-manual tasks, as we found in Chapter 7. Education is the means of transfer from the former to the latter group and is consequently often sought for this purpose. By the same token, the members of the group that view education mainly as a ladder for social climbing would also tend to look down upon manual work and the peasant way of life.[151] This view is likely to become increasingly prevalent in relation to the number of grades passed.

An educational system which works as a filter in a discriminatory sense and which at the same time increases the social distance between educated and uneducated (especially when it makes the newly educated distance themselves from their own origins — the masses — and instead become intent upon acquiring elite status by accepting elite values) as the case may well be in Haiti, effectively precludes the rise of what Paulo Freire has called *conscientização* among the masses.[152] Education as conceived in Haiti does not allow the peasants to arrive at an understanding of the reality within which they live, to grasp the social and political antagonism between themselves and the governing groups, nor to act to improve their lot on the basis of such consciousness.

The educational system in Haiti clearly helps to maintain the existing social order. Mass education is ruled out, and the system works as a filter to legitimize 'economic inequality by providing an open, objective, and ostensibly meritocratic mechanism for assigning individuals to unequal occupational positions.'[153] The construction of the educational system works to the net disadvantage of the peasant masses. In *Education as Cultural Imperialism,* Martin Carnoy states that 'even if children spent all their time away from their families and in school after the age of six, and there were no home influence after that age, we would find that schools in most countries and locales are geared to reinforce the cultural and verbal skills of those who have spent their first years with higher-income and higher-schooled parents.'[154] Carnoy's statement is eminently true with respect to Haiti. The most important factor to keep in mind in an analysis of the Haitian educational system is the basic cleavage of Haitian society into two distinct social groups with very little in common. This cleavage is intimately related to the educational system both as a cause and as a consequence of the latter. Both in Chapter 7 and in the present chapter we have seen how the educational system during the entire nineteenth century remained undeveloped and how existing educational facilities were concentrated in urban areas. The lack of peasant participation in politics and administration was to a very large extent a function of the lack of a sufficient education in the countryside which would have prepared the rural population for taking part in political affairs.

This pattern was reinforced during the American occupation. The Americans never attempted to use education to prepare the way for a broad popular participation in politics based on democratic principles. We have seen that the effort of the Service Technique departed from a philosophy according to which the Haitians in their capacity of blacks were to be prepared for manual jobs through vocational education, while little emphasis was put on enhancing mass influence on government.

Hence, the Americans lost a unique opportunity to prepare the way for bridging the gap between elite and masses. The social structure of Haiti was frozen by the mid-nineteenth century, largely due to the failure or unwillingness to provide education for the masses. Thereafter, upward social mobility became a cumbersome and difficult affair finally leading to a state where one of the leading authorities of Haitian life found it proper to speak of a caste and not a class system.[155]

While the term caste is too strong,[156] the division into an educated governing group and an illiterate mass of governed peasants remains effective to this very day, and the educational system continues to uphold the distinction:

> Since poor children generally do badly in school, they are branded as 'failures' early in life, destined for jobs which require little skill and originality, simply because they were unable to succeed at these school tests and exercises. Worse, perhaps, is the self-concept of these drop-outs. The society reinforces, through schooling and other institutions, the self-image of incompetence and ignorance for those who do not succeed in school. As a result, society invests more

schooling (earning capability) and gives a higher self-image to those who already have high-status parents when they enter school, and invests little schooling and may reduce the self-image of those who have low-status and poor parents...

If schooling is very efficient in this model of development, it helps preserve stability in the system by indirectly acting to make this group believe that they have no right to the fruits of development because they are not sufficiently prepared to participate in the development process. This is Illich's point again: people without schooling in a society where schooling is revered come to believe that they are not worthy of participating as fully in the development process as those with schooling. Those who have attended school for a few years may have direct indicators that they deserve to be 'failures'. Not making it to higher grades is proof that they don't have what it takes to get a piece of the 'good life'...

Schools...help convince or reinforce children in believing that the system is basically sound and the role they are allocated is the proper one for them to play. Through such 'colonization', the society avoids having to redistribute the increases in national product and reduces the necessity for direct repression of the populace.[157]

It is not very likely that the dominating elite is very interested in extending education to the masses. Boyer is not the only president who may have realized that from the political point of view it is far easier to deal with illiterates than with educated subjects:

...a great many decisions are made in Haitian life because of their political consequences. Haiti has always been characterized by the centralization of political power. Broadening the base of education, literacy and status is highly likely to undermine the centralization of power, so that even governments dedicated to the 'arrière pays' may be expected to approach it with some hesitancy.[158]

This non-identification does not operate only passively. Ignorant peasants are to remain ignorant peasants. What is good for the peasant is not necessarily, nor even probably, good for the elite.

Conclusions

We began the present chapter by sketching a model of rural education conceived as a process of human capital formation. According to this view, schooling may contribute to increased agricultural production by making the peasants better prepared for production and economic and technical decision-making in a changing environment. In this setting, the main function of general, basic knowledge would be to prepare the peasants for the subsequent acquisition of specific knowledge directly related to the problems of farming. Assuming the human capital perspective to be correct, we then proceeded to examine the development of Haitian rural (primary and adult) education from the beginning of the nineteenth century until the present period.

Before the American occupation of Haiti, education had little impact on rural life, for the simple reason that little schooling was available in the countryside. In 1915, for all practical purposes, the Haitian peasantry must be considered as nearly 100 percent illiterate. The Americans attempted to change the rural educational system along lines previously tried out on southern US blacks, according to which concentration on vocational education and manual training would be the schooling that would suit Haiti best. The program failed, largely due to the failure to obtain the necessary co-operation from the Haitian elite who would later take over the responsibility for its continued existence.

At the same time, the traditional Haitian school system with its emphasis on literary studies was starved, but when the occupation had come to an end, the American-directed system was gradually pushed into the background and was unified with the Haitian school system. Little was achieved up to 1950, when the census demonstrated that illiteracy was still well above 90 percent in rural areas. Stagnation continued to reign during the next two decades. The rural illiteracy rate according to the 1971 census was almost 90 percent in spite of some efforts at adult education. It is only very recently that some progress may have taken place, although it still remains to be seen whether this progress is real and sustained or only apparent and temporary.

Thus, if we use the human capital approach, the conclusion must be that rural education in Haiti has been largely stagnant during most of the present century, and that consequently the contribution of schooling to human capital formation has remained stagnant as well. However, human capital formation is not likely to be the most important function of Haitian rural education. To conceive of rural education only in these terms would clearly be a mistake. Few rural children ever go to school, and fewer still manage to get a complete primary education. The reason for this is that the rural school system mainly works as a discriminatory filter which prevents an extremely high percentage of children from passing their grades.

It is true that rural children face a number of obstacles to an efficient education which emanate from peasant life and poverty itself, but it is equally true that the construction of the school system is such as to make it virtually impossible for a rural child to complete the primary cycle. The medium of instruction is not Creole but French, which is a foreign language to the peasant children. For reasons largely connected with the lack of identification of the elite with the peasantry, the rural schools are in poor condition both in terms of buildings and materials and in terms of teachers. Finally, the school system places a considerable stress on examinations.

The net effect of this system is that less than 2 percent of all rural children manage to pass all grades in primary school. Few of those who pass will presumably remain in agriculture but will instead migrate to the cities. The system is also likely to produce detrimental effects in that it may very well create attitudes among those educated within the system that increase the social distance between themselves and the illiterates. In this way education serves mainly to maintain the existing social order. Few peasant children get enough education to escape from agriculture or (if they migrate) from low-paid manual work in the cities. Reserving the privilege of schooling for urban elite groups (or at least upper class groups) and creating a system which breeds educational failure among the peasant children is presumably an efficient way of dominating the peasants. Ignorant peasants are less likely to question the existing order than educated farmers.

Notes

1. Some of the most influential works were those by Rosenstein-Rodan (1943); Nurkse (1953); Lewis (1954), (1955); Rostow (1960).
2. Schultz (1961).
3. See. e.g. Schultz (1963); Becker (1964); Denison (1962) and (1967), and Harbison & Myers (1964).
4. Myrdal (1968), pp. 1542-3.
5. Schultz (1964), p. 181.
6. Balogh (1966), p. 101.
7. See e.g. Blaug (1970), Chapters 2 and 3 for an evaluation. Cf. also Carnoy (1977).
8. Arrow (1973). Cf. also e.g. Stiglitz (1975).
9. Ibid.
10. Balogh & Streeten (1963).
11. See Gintis (1971); Bowles (1975); Bowles & Gintis (1975).
12. Carnoy (1974).
13. Cf. e.g. the discussion of misplaced aggregation in Balogh & Streeten (1963).
14. Arrow (1973), p. 194; Bowles & Gintis (1975), p. 75.

15. The following discussion is concentrated on the investment aspects of education. For discussions of consumption aspects, see e.g. Schultz (1963), pp. 8-10 and Blaug (1970), pp. 16-22.
16. Wharton (1965), p. 205.
17. Mellor (1966), pp. 347, 352; Myrdal (1968), p. 1621; Vaizey (1962), p. 127; Blaug (1970), p. 248; Wharton (1965), p. 206; Schuman, Inkeles & Smith (1968), pp. 4-5, 11. Cf. also Welch (1970).
18. Montgomery (1967), p. 149.
19. Wharton (1965), pp. 206-7.
20. Blaug (1970), p. 248.
21. Mellor (1966), p. 347; Myrdal (1968), p. 1621; Vaizey (1962), p. 127; Blaug (1970), p. 248; Wharton (1965), pp. 212-14.
22. Wharton (1965), pp. 213-14.
23. Cf. Schultz (1964) passim and Mellor (1966), p. 347.
24. Wharton (1965), p. 214.
25. Montgomery (1967), p. 149; Mellor (1966), p. 348; Wharton (1967), p. 212.
26. Cf. also Wharton (1965), p. 204 and Mellor (1966), p. 346 for a discussion of agricultural education to groups who serve the peasants directly or indirectly.
27. Wharton (1965), p. 208.
28. Ibid., pp. 208-9; Schultz (1964), p. 200; Myrdal (1968), p. 1668; Mellor (1966), p. 352.
29. Blaug (1970), p. 255.
30. Ibid.
31. Wharton (1965), pp. 208-9.
32. Such a correlation was found among peasants and factory workers in East Pakistan by Schuman, Inkeles & Smith (1968), p. 8.
33. The complementarity of different teaching methods forms one of the principal conclusions of a UNESCO evaluation of the 'new' media., i.e. radio and TV (Schramm *et al.* (1967), pp. 63-4).
34. Mellor (1965), p. 352.
35. Blaug (1970), p. 255.
36. Myrdal (1968), pp. 1681-2.
37. A comparison of the relative desirability of the two types of education is made by Blaug (1970), pp. 247 ff.
38. Ibid., p. 248.
39. Brutus (1948), pp. 15-16; Logan (1930), pp. 405-10.
40. Logan (1930), pp. 407-8.
41. Ibid., pp. 416-17.
42. Ibid., pp. 412-13.
43. Logan (1968), p. 161.
44. Mackenzie (1830:1), p. 121.
45. Bird (1869), p. 140.
46. Leyburn (1966), p. 281.
47. Logan (1930), pp. 418-19.
48. See Brutus (1948), pp. 157-77 for an extensive account.
49. Logan (1930), p. 423; St John (1889), p. 293.
50. Brutus (1948), p. 290.
51. Logan (1930), p. 423.
52. Brutus (1948), p. 335.
53. Ibid., p. 390.
54. Ibid., p. 434.
55. Logan (1930), p. 439.
56. Cf. ibid., pp. 423-34.

57. Leyburn (1966), p. 282.
58. A very interesting account of these efforts is given by Bellegarde himself (Bellegarde (1929), pp. 173-451). Cf. also Bellegarde (1934), pp. 34-69; Logan (1930), pp. 450-59, and Brutus (1948), pp. 462-90.
59. Cf. Bellegarde (1929), p. 178.
60. Quoted by Millspaugh (1931), p. 162. Cf. also US, Department of State (1925), p. 32.
61. Service Technique (1931), p. 48.
62. Service Technique (n.d.), p. 44; Service Technique (1929:2), p. 103.
63. Service Technique (1928), p. 36.
64. Service Technique (1931), p. 48.
65. Service Technique (1929:1), pp. 58-60; Schmidt (1971), p. 183.
66. Service Technique (n.d.), p. 49.
67. Service Technique (1929:2), pp. 97-8.
68. Ibid., p. 105.
69. Quoted by Millspaugh (1931), p. 189. Cf. also Spector (1961), p. 249; Schmidt (1971), p. 195.
70. Rotberg & Clague (1971), pp. 135-6.
71. Logan (1968), p. 137.
72. Schmidt (1971), pp. 177-84.
73. Rotberg & Clague (1971), p. 135.
74. Schmidt (1971), especially Chapters 7 and 9.
75. Cf. e.g. the quotations in ibid., pp. 48, 79, 146.
76. Ibid., pp. 13-14.
77. Dartigue (1936), p. 167.
78. Ibid., p. 189; Boisgris (1944), p. 45.
79. SNPA & ER (1935), p. 75.
80. Ibid., p. 78.
81. Ibid., p. 81.
82. SNPA & ER (1939), p. 115. The figure for 1936-37 was 6,613 (ibid.), and that for 1939-40 6,252 (SNPA & ER (n.d.), p. 126).
83. SNPA & ER (n.d.), pp. 135, 154.
84. Holly (1955), p. 203.
85. Ibid., p. 224.
86. Ibid., p. 217.
87. Ibid., p. 220.
88. Indeed, even government reports complain about this. (See e.g. SNPA & ER (1935), p. 71, (1939), pp. 111-112, (n.d.), p. 123.)
89. Viélot (1969), p. 327.
90. Paul (1965), p. 25.
91. Cf. BTS, no. 22, September 1956, pp. 17, 29; BTS, no. 23, December 1956, p. 11.
92. UN (1949), pp. 57-8.
93. Quoted by Dale (1959), p. 101.
94. See below.
95. Moral (1959), p. 45.
96. Département de l'Economie Nationale (1950), p. 13.
97. Cf. BTS, no. 22, September 1956, pp. 17-18, 29; BTS, no. 23, December 1956, p. 11; Mirville (1959), p. 30.
98. Mirville (1959), p. 38.
99. BTS, no. 22, September 1956, p. 37.
100. Dale (1959), p. 26.
101. OEA-CEPAL-BID (1962), p. 54.
102. BTS, no. 23, December 1956, p. 54.

103. Mirville (1959), p. 41.
104. BTS, no. 23, December 1956, p. 11; Mirville (1959), p. 30.
105. UNESCO (1951), p. 12.
106. Moore (1972), p. 68. For an extensive description see UNESCO (1951), passim.
107. Moral (1961), p. 332.
108. Ibid., pp. 332-3.
109. Brand (1965), pp. 51-2.
110. For an interesting description of the history of Creole orthography through the 1950s see Paul (1965), pp. 43-51.
111. Ibid., p. 51. Cf. L'effort du gouvernement (n.d.), p. 138.
112. CIAP (1966), p. 60.
113. CIAP (1969), p. 84.
114. CIAP (1971), pp. 64-5.
115. Brand (1965), p. 48.
116. P & D, no. 2, 1969, p. 21; CONADEP (1971-76), p. 95; CIAP (1969), p. 89.
117. Cf. OEA (1972), p. 183, and CIAP (1969), p. 89. The emigration of diploma-holding teachers, however, ought to have had more repercussions in urban than in rural areas.
118. DARNDR (1968-69), p. 6.
119. CIAP (1969), p. 87.
120. CIAP (1971), p. 65.
121. Paul (1965), p. 26.
122. OEA-CEPAL-BID (1962), p. 52. Cf. also the guidelines in ONEC (1962).
123. OEA (1972), p. 191.
124. Rotberg & Clague (1971), p. 316; CIAP (1968:2), pp. 85-6.
125. IICA (n.d.), p. 63.
126. UNESCO (n.d.), p. 38.
127. Duvalier (1973), p. 19.
128. Paul (1970), p. 129. For a more extensive description see ONAAC (1969).
129. OEA (1972), p. 191.
130. Ibid., p. 176.
131. UNESCO (n.d.), p. 60.
132. QER, 3rd Quarter 1977, p. 12.
133. The project is described in IICA (n.d.).
134. Cf. Schultz (1963), pp. 6, 30-31.
135. Cf. Courlander (1960), pp. 113-14; Schaedel (1962), p. 95; OEA (1972), p. 180; CIAP (1974), note, p. 73; Holly (1955), p. 226.
136. Quoted by Moore (1972), pp. 134-5.
137. Cf. BTS, no. 23, December 1956, pp. 25, 28-9 and DARNDR (1968-69), pp. 8-9.
138. Valdman (1969), p. 164.
139. Moore (1972), p. 114.
140. Proposals already exist. See e.g. Berry (1964).
141. See Berry (1969), pp. 229-30, for an example.
142. The experiment is reported in De Ronceray & Petit-Frère (1975).
143. Price-Mars (1959), pp. 113-14. Cf. Berry (1969), p. 217, for a similar view.
144. DARNDR (1974-75), p. 154; IICA (n.d.), p. 62.
145. OEA (1972), p. 183. Cf. PNUD (1971), p. 9.
146. Quoted by Dale (1959), p. 56.
147. IICA (n.d.), p. 63.
148. Ibid., p. 65.

149. The best example here is that given by Foster for Ghana (Foster (1965)). Foster's findings are confirmed by similar studies for the Ivory Coast and Tanzania (Blaug (1970), pp. 245-6). See also Wharton (1965), pp. 216-17. A very interesting comparison is that of Gisser's findings regarding the outmigration of educated farm people in the US (Gisser (1965)).
150. Morose (1970), pp. 83-7.
151. Cf. Griffin & Enos (1970), pp. 159, 162.
152. See Freire (1970).
153. Bowles & Gintis (1975), p. 78.
154. Carnoy (1974), pp. 11-12.
155. Leyburn (1966), passim.
156. Cf. the criticism of Leyburn in Lobb (1940) and Price-Mars (1942).
157. Carnoy (1974), pp. 12-13.
158. Berry (1969), p. 217.

11 PROBLEMS OF RURAL CREDIT

The two preceding chapters discussed whether changes in the quality of the 'human capital' employed in agricultural production in the peasant sector could have exerted any significant counteracting influence on the tendency for rural per capita incomes to fall. We found that this was unlikely to have been the case other than to a limited extent. It proved difficult to analyze the effects stemming from changes in disease and nutrition, especially since it is quite plausible that changes in the incidence of disease have had a beneficial effect whilst at the same time the deteriorating nutritional situation may have counteracted, and even swamped, these positive influences. In the case of education the effects were more clear-cut. The system of rural education appears to have scarcely contributed to the formation of human capital. Its main function seems to have taken a different form, namely to ensure the domination of the many by the few – of the peasants by the governing cliques. Hence, it appears unlikely that changes in the quality of the human factor have been very active in counteracting the decrease in per capita incomes. The most likely positive effects stem from improvements in health, although their impact remains highly uncertain.

In the next two chapters we will consider the role of capital formation and technological change. The latter is often regarded as one of the most important and efficient ways of breaking the bonds which keep incomes low in traditional economies.[1] Chapter 12 discusses the difficulties that technological change has encountered in rural Haiti. However, in order to deal effectively with these difficulties we require an analysis of savings and credit in the rural economy, since technological change usually requires capital formation. It is with this analysis that we will be concerned in the present chapter.

The discussion of rural credit is also important from another point of view. In Chapter 2 we showed that the agrarian structure of Haiti does not give rise to exploitation of the peasants by a landlord class. In Chapter 4 we analyzed the rural marketing system in order to find out whether or not the middlemen of this system are exploiting the peasants and found this not to be the case. The analysis of Chapter 4 was, however, limited in one respect. We did not take into account the possibility of exploitation of the peasants by intermediaries when the latter act in their capacity of lenders in the rural credit markets. To complete our discussion of exploitation we therefore have to investigate the conditions prevailing in these markets as well. This will be done in the present chapter.

We will begin with a discussion of the extent and the forms of peasant savings in Haiti. Thereafter we will briefly examine purposes for which the peasants may be expected to borrow. The third section deals with the informal credit markets – the most common source of loans in rural Haiti. We will attempt to determine the reasons behind the comparatively high interest rates prevailing in these markets and see if these rates may be interpreted as a sign of exploitation of the peasants by the lenders. The final section examines the formal credit sources available to the peasants and discusses why these sources have failed to reach more than a tiny fraction of the rural population.

Rural Savings

In Chapter 2 we discussed how the Haitian peasant has an extremely small amount of productive capital at his disposal; as a rule only seeds, plants and one or two hand tools. Capital formation obviously poses one of the biggest problems that he encounters. Capital formation in agriculture may be financed either out of the peasants' own savings or out of credit obtained from formal or informal sources of credit. In Haiti, the funds available to the peasants for investment purposes often originate in the informal credit markets while savings are either non-existent or low. In the latter case they usually appear to take on forms which are not likely to result in an increase of the stock of farm capital.

This is a pattern which is common in less developed countries. In *The Theory of Economic Growth,* W. Arthur Lewis observes that peasants, proverbially thrifty, often have a strong tendency to be in heavy debt and at the same time points out some of the most commonly held assets in peasant societies:

> The peasants are a class who paradoxically combine a thrifty temperament with a high propensity to be burdened by debt. Peasants learn to be thrifty because they know how near they live to the brink of disaster. In some communities hardly a year passes without flood, or drought, or locusts, or cattle plague or some other Act of God which reduces to destitution all the peasants except those who have some savings to fall back on...those peasants who save tend to invest either in lending to less fortunate peasants, or else in buying land, and in neither case is the result an increase in capital formation. Buying land raises the price and alters the distribution of land, but

it does not make land more productive...Peasants also like to invest in cattle...Considering the precarious life of the peasant, and his... attitude towards his land and his cattle, it is not surprising that net capital formation by peasants is only a very small part of the national income.[2]

No systematic investigations of peasant savings behavior have been made in Haiti, but the general pattern is known. As we found in Chapter 1, rural per capita income in 1971 amounted to 318 gourdes (US $63.50), while in Chapter 9 we discovered that at roughly the same time the average daily per capita outlay on food was 0.45 gourdes in rural districts. On a yearly basis, the latter corresponds to a figure of 164.25 gourdes, i.e. more than one-half of the income goes on food alone. Deducting other necessary expenditure on clothes, shelter, etc. (cf. below in the section on informal credit), we conclude that little is left which can be used for the purpose of savings even in a 'normal' year when no extraordinary expenditures occur.[3]*

The Haitian peasants rarely convert whatever savings they may have accumulated into farm capital. We know from Chapter 2 that the only capital inputs used in peasant farming most of the time are seed and hand tools. The peasants store their own seed when possible and sometimes attempt to accumulate enough money to buy a new hoe or machete. Savings in excess of these 'minimum' requirements tend to take on other forms. The two most important assets held are livestock and land,[4] and the most common pattern seems to be that the peasant begins by buying a small animal like a calf or a pig. These animals are then fattened and sold at a profit. When this operation has been repeated a sufficient number of times and enough has been saved, the peasant usually proceeds to buy land. There are several reasons for this behavior.

The Haitian peasant is often described as being strongly emotionally attached to his soil:

---

*Cf., however, the figure in Zuvekas (1978), pp. 36-43 (based on Schaedel (1962), pp. 82-7) from five different areas. These indicate savings rates running from 10-45 percent (except for one community with a rate of 1 percent) of *cash* incomes only. These rates are probably too high to be representative of the average rural district. Schaedel stresses that the incomes and expenditures were 'a little higher than a true country average.' (Schaedel (1962), p. 73.) Furthermore, it is possible that cash expenditures were incompletely accounted for, and finally, the year of the study may have been an exceptionally favorable one (Zuvekas (1978), p. 41).

The land is invested with considerable effect: gods live in it; it is the ultimate security against privation; family members are buried in it; food and wealth come from it; and it is good in itself, even if not cultivated. While such attitudes are common in yeoman societies, Haiti's history of slavery, and of access to land through revolution, has given a special symbolic significance to landowning. Land is valued above all else and is sometimes held 'uneconomically' — that is even when the capital and labor power to work it are lacking.[5]

In a geographical investigation of northern Haiti Harold A. Wood found that in the Cap-Haïtien area more than 90 percent of the population lived in the *commune* where they had been born. One of the reasons stated was that the *loas* that the peasants worship were closely associated with the soil.[6]

This view, however, is challenged by Alfred Métraux and his associates:

> The Haitian peasant's clinging devotion to his land is not due to any belief, on his part, that he has some mystic affinity with it. His feeling in regard to it is quite elementary, and is due to the particularly hard conditions of his economic and social life. It is a feeling that is practically never unmixed with anxiety, for this land, upon which not merely his existence and security but his standing and influence depend, is a delicate asset that is under constant menace. If he loses it he will become a vagabond, a poor, wandering being.[7]

The Métraux argument should perhaps be given more weight in relation to the lowest income groups, but once we leave this subsistence level, emotional and social factors may rapidly gain in importance:

> among the peasants the worth of an individual is roughly the number of carreaux he 'holds'. . .Holding land is a value highly esteemed by all Haitians and serves as one of the most decisive indicators of the person's status. The tendency of most peasants who accumulate savings is to reinvest in land even though the investment means dead capital for a long time to come. . .The value of the land is mostly in prestige accruing to the holder. . .If [a peasant] acquires more land, he does not invest in ploughs or machinery to increase production but enters into sharecropping or *plaçage* which give him power over several more people.[8]

This was especially true a few decades ago when the standard of living was higher than it is today:

> The more ambitious peasant aspired to two farms, or even three, with a homestead and a family on each.
>
> If a man worked hard and made a success of one plot, he could put away money and eventually buy a second. The additional land might be separated by some miles from the original farm. On the new ground the man would build another house and take another wife to take care of it in his absence. Known as *plaçage* this arrangement had complete community sanction.[9]

Even now, however, the *gros habitants* of the Haitian countryside derive their superior social position mostly from their landownership, and the 'Haitian dream' is to become a man with considerable landed property:

> The displaced peasant, whether he is now a hotel 'houseboy', a taxi driver, or a cane cutter, dreams of returning to the land some day and growing bananas, coffee, and cotton that will make him independent. In far-off places such as Havana and New York, Haitians work and save money with the expectation that one day they will come home, buy fifteen or twenty acres of ground, build a new house, and live out their lives as decently prosperous *habitants*. The traditions of the agricultural society...continue to play a significant role in the life of the people.[10]

Another argument may be derived directly from the analytical findings of the present work. Our central theme is the tendency for peasant incomes to fall with time. This calls for protective measures. The peasants know that the 'rainy' day will eventually come and may therefore, whenever possible, i.e. whenever the size of incomes permits, wish to save some of their present incomes in a form that can help to increase their future incomes. Given the traditional low-yielding technology, possessing enough land is presumably the best guarantee against family incomes falling towards subsistence level. By acquiring land, the peasants add to their future incomes by increasing their future production potential.

Hence, there is a 'hierarchy' of assets in rural Haiti. The peasants buy animals to be resold with a profit in order to make an eventual land purchase possible. Land in this sense is the 'ultimate' goal of the peasant-saver. The difference between land and other assets, notably animals, is demonstrated by an example given by Sidney W. Mintz, who describes how during the slack season in agriculture, the female traders invest in small livestock such as pigs and goats which can easily be sold when the harvest comes and trading activities are resumed. Land on the other hand is regarded as an investment of a much more long-term nature. Female traders often do buy land for their trade profits but once invested in land, this money is rarely freed again to be reinvested in trade.[11] Livestock and comparable assets represent short-term investment, and when the peasants have enough to put aside during longer periods, land seems to be the predominant choice.*

The general poverty of the Haitian peasants plus the fact that those who are in the fortunate position to be able to save generally prefer to hold assets like land and livestock explains why little agricultural capital is generated out of peasant savings. There is a general scarcity of funds for capital formation in the Haitian countryside. This scarcity of course has an impact also on the availability of funds in the rural informal credit markets. Borrowing in these markets has had little impact on agricultural capital formation. Scarcity of funds is, however, not the only reason for this. Other factors intervene as well. To understand exactly how these markets function, let us begin by a look at why the peasants may need to borrow funds.

The Demand for Rural Credit

In a rural economy where incomes are close to subsistence level a need for credit arises for a wide variety of purposes. In principle it is possible to distinguish between two kinds of loans: (1) those taken to hedge the borrower against certain unforeseen events, which, employing Keynesian terminology, we may label precautionary loans;[12] (2) those taken to cover such expenses that will be incurred with certainty or that have already been incurred, henceforth called actual expense loans.

The relative extent of these two kinds of loans in rural Haiti is not

---

*The predominance of land among the assets held by the peasants points to the possibility of dissaving for example among poorer peasants. Individual saving can take the form of buying land, but national saving cannot. As soon as one individual buys land, the seller of that land either must put his money into some other form of saving or must consume it. Of course, livestock is an alternative here, since the stock of animals can always be increased, but since it appears that land is generally preferred to livestock, some dissaving is likely to take place as well. (On the national level, it appears as if some dissaving of livestock may have taken place from 1950 to 1970 (Zuvekas (1978), pp. 43-5).)

known. However, although peasants may hold a certain amount of cash as a protection against unknown contingencies, other popular assets, such as livestock, are relatively liquid. Besides, in a situation where incomes are close to the subsistence level it is simply not possible to hold enough cash to meet any foreseeable adverse event. This would probably require too extensive an interest payment to be financed out of current production, leaving too little for current consumption.[13] When it comes to precaution against unforeseen events, it is probably not *actual* borrowing which is important. Instead, credit may be used as a reserve by *not* using it for borrowing. The very *access* to credit may thus be considered an asset held by the peasant which he can fall back upon in times of need. A credit line may be regarded as a substitute for cash or other liquid assets.[14] It is preferable to go into debt once the event is a fact. Thus, the practical importance of precautionary loans is probably negligible as compared to the volume of actual expense loans.

Since incomes are low in rural areas, most large expenditures involve a loan. One of the most important categories of loans arises from the need to feed the family during the period elapsing between sowing or planting and harvesting. While consumption expenses are fairly evenly distributed across the year, incomes occur mainly when the harvest (particularly coffee) is sold, and since it is very difficult to store perishable agricultural commodities in a subtropical climate, peasants often have to sell immediately after the harvest when there is a glut in the market, which in turn causes them to be without money later on.[15] These difficulties tend to be compounded by the necessity to obtain seeds and plants for the next crop to be grown, which is a further drain on liquid resources. Purchase of tools and purchase or rent of land are other reasons for taking loans that are connected with the agricultural production process.

A second important category of loans is derived from the life cycle of the individual and includes consumption loans for ceremonies such as weddings and funerals, for lawsuits concerning inheritance, and for the repayment of debts contracted by parents after the death of the latter. Lastly, adverse fortune in the form of illness or harvest failure, for example, often makes it necessary to supplement insufficient incomes with loans. An illustration of some of the above categories is given in Table 11.1. Out of a sample of 103 Catholic and 44 Protestant families in the Marbial valley, more than 45 percent were indebted with an average of 153 and 174 gourdes respectively of acknowledged debt per family.*

Table 11.1: Some Reasons for Indebtedness in the Marbial Valley in the Late 1940s[a]

	Catholics	Protestants
In the Cochon Gras region:		
Total acknowledged debt:		
Funerals	993.00	—
Sickness	3.35	37.50
Clothing	110.00	—
Purchase of land, surveying	650.00	690.00
Marriage	—	300.00
Inherited debts	149.50	—
Unspecified reasons	1,527.00	1,469.00
Total	3,432.85	2,496.50
In the surrounding neighborhoods:		
Total acknowledged debt:		
Sickness	450.00	—
Clothing	15.00	105.00
Purchase of land, surveying	1,515.00	600.00
Marriage	—	37.50
Inherited debts	10.00	—
Unspecified reasons	1,619.70	75.00
Total	3,609.70	817.50
Grand total	7,042.55	3,314.00

a. The table does not give any particulars about loans extended to bring the peasants over the difficult period between planting and harvesting. This is probably included under 'unspecified reasons', however. (Cf. Métraux et al. (1951), pp. 130-31. Cf. also PNUD (1971), p. 10.)

Source: Métraux et al. (1951), p. 194.

*Métraux et al. (1951), p. 193. Cf also Pierre-Charles (1965), p. 101, who quotes a survey from the Départment du Nord, indicating an average debt of 50 gourdes per family.

Informal Sources of Credit*

The most common source of credit for a peasant is a loan in the informal credit markets. Such loans may come from various sources. Probably the most commonly utilized sources are the intermediaries in the marketing process of peasant goods, i.e. the *spéculateurs* and the *Madam Sara*. The usual procedure is that the loan is made against some of the future crop.[16] The peasant obtains the loan immediately, when he needs it, and pays it back at the beginning of the harvest. The loans are normally not secured by land or other real property as collateral. The only security is the growing crop and the relations built up in the course of the regular buying and selling between borrowers and lenders, perhaps in the form of *pratik*. The peasant could also ask a townsman or a wealthy colleague for a loan but would then probably have to offer some kind of collateral to secure the debt.[17] Alternatively, smaller loans may come from relatives or friends, generally without collateral and without interest.[18]

A less well-known or at least less well-documented form of credit is the rotating credit association which in Haiti is known as *sangue*.[19] The exact composition of a *sangue* may vary according to the particular circumstances, but the basic principles are the same. The *sangues* are associations formed by a number of voluntary participants, headed by a president (usually the founder), who make regular contributions to a fund *(main)* which is handed out to each contributor in rotation, the usual interval being once a week. No securities or collaterals are involved in the operations of a *sangue*. The members generally know each other very well, being from the same locality, so that the simple word of honor is enough to guarantee the regularity of the members' contributions.

Interest rates in the unorganized or informal credit markets of the underdeveloped countries are notoriously high. In an extensive survey U Tun Wai has estimated the worldwide average to be around 36 percent per year in real terms.** The Haitian experience confirms this finding. While the real rate of interest charged by the formal agricultural

---

*An unorganized or informal credit market usually 'consists of regionalized transactions of money, real goods, and services among family, friends, neighbors, relatives, shopkeepers, itinerant traders, landlords and moneylenders and their clients to facilitate consumption, production, and trade.' (*Spring Review* (1973:2), p. 3.)
**Tun Wai (1957), p. 102. Tun Wai gives two figures: 24 and 36 percent, but in the computations of the former figure he includes credits from governmental credit banks, development banks, co-operative credit unions, etc., which in reality constitute a part of the formal credit market.

finance institutions rarely exceeds 10 percent, rates are much higher in the unorganized rural credit markets. Even though in some instances credit may be given at extremely low rates or at no interest at all as a means to strengthen *pratik* relations,* lending transactions in the informal credit markets normally take place at what many students of Haitian life classify as 'exorbitant' rates. No uniform rates exist, but the following examples provide an illustration of the possible range:

> A peasant who really has his back on the wall prefers to turn to the 'spéculateur' to whom he is accustomed to sell his coffee. From this man he will receive a loan at 50 percent interest, which has to be paid back either in cash or in coffee, when harvest time comes round (January). Other 'spéculateurs' drive harder bargains. Here is an example of the kind of loan they make: the price of coffee being 0.75 gdes per lb, the 'spéculateur' makes his client an advance of 50 gdes, and demands 200 lbs. of coffee in turn. If prices are maintained, the lender makes a net profit of 100 gdes...In country districts, some peasants lend money at exorbitant rates. The sums are usually small, and lent for a short term – for instance 10 gdes, for which 15 gdes will be repayable in a fortnight or a month.[20]

The quotation indicates a range of 50 to 1,200 percent per year. Since no detailed surveys of the rural credit market have yet been undertaken in Haiti, we do not know how representative these figures are, but at least they serve as an indication that interest rates are high.**

Clearly, effective interest rates ranging from perhaps 50 to 100 percent per year preclude the peasants from borrowing large amounts for production purposes. However, the distribution of the loans according to the rate of interest is not known. Neither the loans from relatives and friends nor those coming from the *sangues* carry interest, while at least those taken from the *spéculateurs* do, as well as frequently those given by the *Madam Sara*. On the other hand, this is of less

---

*It is questionable, however, whether low interest rates really are the general rule in such transactions. At least as far as loans to producers are concerned, high interest rates are quite common (Mintz (1961:1), p. 58).

**Cf. also Moral (1961), p. 247 and OEA-CEPAL-BID (1962), p. 37, for a similar view. The latter source states: 'We do not have figures available which would permit us to know the exact conditions, such as the interest rate and the average duration of informal loans. But it is possible to establish, without fear of contradiction that the rate of interest is at least higher than 20 percent per year and in many cases it reaches 50 percent per year.'

importance. One of the most common patterns of rural borrowing in Haiti is to obtain a loan from a speculator against relatively high interest, and if a sufficient number of low-interest sources had been available, the peasants would presumably not have resorted to the speculators. (We will return below to the question of whether the speculators exercise any monopoly power in the credit markets.) Hence, it becomes important to investigate why interest rates in many cases are high in the informal credit markets. We will begin with a look at time preferences.

The Rate of Time Preference

To see how the general scarcity of funds influences the rate of interest in the informal credit markets, we may apply the Fisherian theory of interest.[21] A central concept of this theory is the rate of time preference. Irving Fisher defines time preference (or impatience) as 'the. . . excess of the present marginal want for one more unit of *present* goods over the *present* marginal want for one more unit of *future* goods.'[22] The rate of time preference is one of the most important determinants of the rate of interest. We must therefore attempt to find out the rate of time preference prevailing in the rural informal credit markets. In this discussion we will concentrate our attention on the peasants, i.e. mainly on the borrowers, for if we know something regarding their time preferences we also know whether they are prepared to pay a high rate of interest or not. A brief comparison with the lenders will be made at the end of the present section.

Let us assume that the peasants' endowments of production factors in the absence of borrowing and lending as well as their investment opportunities, i.e. their technological capacity to transform present goods into future goods, are given. This in turn means that the size and time distribution of peasant income* are also given as long as we do not allow any borrowing or lending to take place. Assume now that we open up the possibility of borrowing and lending in a credit market. Then, presumably the peasants will not leave the time distribution of their incomes unchanged, but will engage in borrowing and lending until their (marginal) rate of time preference equals the rate of interest prevailing in the market. In other words, when people with different

---

*In Fisher's work 'income' really means consumption, but this fact needs not bother us here, since what is intended is a measure of the standard of living, and at least in the present case, the ordinary income concept seems to be a reasonable approximation too. (Cf. Fisher (1930), Chapter 1, and the discussion of peasant savings above.)

time preferences engage in transactions in the credit market, an equilibrium rate of interest is gradually established which equals the marginal time preferences of the individuals after these transactions have been undertaken. Hence, the time preferences of borrowers and lenders in the credit markets constitute one of the most important determinants of the rate of interest.

We know that the average rate of interest in the informal credit markets of rural Haiti is probably high. One of the possible reasons for this is that the borrowers in these markets have strong preferences for present over future consumption when no borrowing or lending is possible. In the Fisherian theory what determine the rate of time preference are the characteristics of (peasant) incomes in the absence of a credit market with respect to size, time distribution and uncertainty.*
Thus if we know these characteristics for the peasants we also know something with respect to their time preferences which in turn exert an influence on the rate of interest.

As mentioned above, per capita incomes are low in rural Haiti – 318 gourdes in 1971. In Chapter 5, we quoted Fisher's views on the importance of low incomes for the rate of time preference and found that low incomes tend to generate strong preferences for additions to present incomes as compared to additions to future income. On the one hand, a peasant with only a slight margin between his present income and the starvation level is not likely to lend any of this income even at a very high rate of interest, simply because he needs that income desperately to feed himself and his family in the present. His rationally calculated rate of time preference is high. In addition, he may be myopic in the sense that his precarious present situation makes him blind to the needs of the future and makes him intent on satisfying present needs at all costs. This size argument assumes special force when incomes are close to the subsistence level as seems to be the case in rural Haiti. In such a situation almost the entire income is needed to keep the peasant and his family alive, which in turn is an absolute precondition for the enjoyment

---

*Fisher also, although 'only for completeness', includes the composition of income in his theory, by which he means 'to what extent it consists of nourishment, of shelter, of amusement, of education, and so on.' (Fisher (1930), p. 71.) The composition of income, or rather the composition of the budget, however, to a great extent is determined by the size of the income, at least on low income levels where most of the income is absorbed by expenditures for food and shelter. Fisher also admits that it is hard to see any definite patterns regarding the effects of this variable, and prefers to conduct the analysis in terms of a single commodity (p. 76). For these reasons, especially the first one, composition is not included in the present analysis.

of *any* future income whatsoever. It is simply not possible to defer consumption to future periods. Thus, a poor Haitian peasant should be prepared to pay a substantial sum as interest in order to obtain an addition to today's precarious income and consumption standard. This is true especially of the situation where the peasant is suddenly faced with a large unexpected expense, for example in the form of a funeral.

The second influence of incomes on the rate of time preference derives from their time distribution. This distribution is likely to assume special importance in one particular situation where very many loans are taken in rural Haiti. In the preceding section we found that many of the loans advanced to the peasants are made to carry them over the difficult period before the harvest comes. The peasants lack incomes when these loans are entered into but know that they will have a crop to sell later and need money for consumption immediately. This time distribution serves to increase the preferences for present income at certain times of the year. In this situation, additions to peasant incomes during the dead season when the peasants are waiting for the harvest period are likely to be particularly welcome in comparison to additions to income once the harvest is in full swing and cash is readily available.

The above is probably true mainly in the short-run perspective, i.e. over a few months. In the longer run — over a few years — the rate of time preference is probably considerably lower. We have already pointed out how declining per capita incomes may make the peasants want to add to future earnings by buying land. Thus, under *ceteris paribus* conditions (i.e. given for example the absolute size of present income) the average peasant probably has a comparatively high rate of time preference over a period of a few months, whereas when the time perspective is lengthened to a couple of years or more, the rate of time preference is lower. (It must be stressed that we are here discussing in comparative terms. Thus, the absolute long-term rate of time preference may still be high, as we hypothesized in Chapter 5, due for example to the influences emanating from the low absolute size of incomes.)

The low level of incomes and the short-run time shape of the income stream are not the only reasons why the peasants are prepared to borrow at interest rates ranging perhaps between 50 and 100 percent while waiting for the harvest. An alternative to borrowing would be to sell some assets and then buy them back at the time of the harvest. The rise in the price of animals or land which is likely to take place during this period should not exceed 50-100 percent, and therefore sale and repurchase of assets ought to constitute a cheaper way of financing a temporary need for cash than taking a loan at these rates.

This is not necessarily the case. In the first place, not all short-term consumption loans carry high interest rates. Presumably, those who are able to prefer instead to borrow from relatives and friends at little or no interest, and this is a cheaper alternative than either the sale of animals or land.[23] The argument probably holds for the group of peasants who possess some animals but are unable to borrow at low rates of interest. This group is likely to prefer trading these assets for cash. The group which is likely to prefer loans at high interest rates is the one which possesses land but no animals and which has no access to cheap credit. To sell land is a business transaction which does not take place without certain transaction costs. In the section on peasant savings we have already seen how the peasants are likely to be reluctant to part with land for emotional or social reasons. There is a 'psychic' cost connected with land sales. Secondly, the peasants may fear that they may be unable to get their land back or at least land of comparable quality or location, if they engage in these types of transactions. We saw in Chapter 2 that the quality of land is highly uneven in Haiti. This often leads to disagreements and disputes with regard to price and other conditions for sales and purchases.[24] To avoid disputes it is often necessary to resort to a surveyor, who, however, is entitled to a certain share of the land surveyed in exchange for his services.* Nor does surveying necessarily solve the problem: 'Surveying, which is designed to eliminate disputes, actually creates them, and to a serious degree, if...[any of the parties involved] suspects that the surveyor has been corrupted into favoring one of them.'[25] The likelihood that an agreement will be reached under such conditions is rather low. Finally, we must take into account that in Haiti there is no political and legal framework within which property rights in land are completely protected. In Chapter 2 we stated that the peasants generally own the land that they cultivate. On the other hand, as we will see in Chapter 12, when outside interests claim peasant landholdings, the peasants may end up losing their holdings. The best way for a peasant to have the title to his land generally recognized is probably to inherit the land from his father. If this type of land is traded and another piece is acquired, on the other hand, in the absence of documents that can be validated in court, the peasant may lose the rights to both plots if disputes arise.

An alternative to real land transactions would be to use land as

---

*According to Métraux *et al.* (1951), p. 25, no less than one-fifth of the land surveyed!

collateral to secure a loan at a lower rate of interest, but even this has proved to be difficult. Formerly, a common device for taking a loan was to make a *vente à réméré* (sale with privilege of repurchase) of land. Such a sale consisted in signing a deed stipulating that the land would become the property of the lender, once and for all, should the borrower be unable to meet his obligations on the date of repayment.[26] Since the *vente à réméré* system was frequently used to defraud the peasants of their land by unscrupulous lenders who stayed out of reach for the peasants only to appear after the repayment date had passed, a law regulating this kind of transaction was passed during the Vincent administration, which makes this fraudulent practice harder to get away with.* (Moral, however, maintains that the practice still occurs.)[27]

When transaction costs are introduced into the picture it no longer appears as a paradox that peasants with a comparatively low long-run rate of time preference under certain circumstances are prepared to borrow money at high interest in the short run. This is clearly seen from Table 11.2. Let us assume that the peasants have the following choice. Either they may sell an asset with a certain annual financial return and repurchase it later, or they may take an interest-bearing loan in the informal credit market. Let us furthermore assume that the transaction costs connected with asset transactions amount to 5 percent both on sale and purchase, i.e. to a total of 10 percent.

The table shows the annual interest rates at which the peasants may be willing to take a loan instead of selling and repurchasing assets under different assumptions regarding the financial yield of the assets in question and the duration of the loan. It is clearly seen that for short periods (the most common case in Haiti) even with very modest assumptions regarding yields peasants are likely to prefer loans at high interest rates (while for longer periods asset sale becomes relatively more attractive). Thus a three-month loan at a yearly interest rate of more than 40 percent is superior to asset transactions with transaction costs amounting to 10 percent during the same period.

The third important determinant of time preferences in the Fisherian theory of interest is the probability or uncertainty of incomes:

the risk of losing the income in a particular period of time operates,

---

*Métraux and his colleagues mention that this was a serious problem in the Marbial valley. Many peasants had been dispossessed of their lands by Jacmel townspeople, some of whom in this way had obtained no less than 150 carreaux of landed property in the valley. (Métraux *et al.* (1951), p. 20.)

in the eyes of most people, as a virtual impoverishment of the income in that period, and hence increases the estimation in which a unit of certain income in that particular period is held. If that period is a remote one, the risk to which it is subject makes for a high regard for remote income; if it is the present (immediate future), the risk makes for a high regard of immediate income; if the risk applies to all periods of time alike, it acts as a virtual decrease all along the line.[28]

Table 11.2: Maximum Interest Rates that Borrowers May Be Willing to Pay (Percent per annum)[a]

Yield of assets (percent per annum)	Duration of loan (months)				
	1	2	3	6	12
1%	121	61	41	21	11
2%	122	62	42	22	12
5%	125	65	45	25	15
10%	130	70	50	30	20
15%	135	75	55	35	25
20%	140	80	60	40	30

a. Some of the figures of the table have been rounded.

In Haiti, the peasants always have to calculate with the possibility e.g. of a crop failure or of a fall in the price of the commodities that they produce. (We will discuss this in Chapter 12.) Realized incomes may easily fall short of expected ones, and this of course tends to increase the relative preferences for *certain* additions to income in those periods where incomes are deemed uncertain. The problem, from our point of view, is that it is difficult to make generalizations as to whether present or future incomes are likely to be most uncertain. In some instances, like during a prolonged drought which is expected to continue in the immediate future, time preferences may temporarily shift heavily in favor of present incomes, but, as Fisher expresses it,

> If, as is very common, the possessor of income regards his immediately future income as fairly well assured, but fears for the safety or certainty of his income in a more remote period, he may be aroused to a high appreciation of the needs of that remote future and hence

may feel forced to save out of his present relatively *certain* abundance in order to supplement his relatively *uncertain* income later on. He is likely to have a low degree of impatience for a *certain* dollar of immediate income as compared with a *certain* dollar added to a remoter uncertain income.[29]

Hence, most realistically we should expect the peasants in general to view future incomes as more uncertain than incomes during the present period, unless under special circumstances. Thus, the tendency for the long-run rate of time preference to be low is reinforced while, when it is felt that present incomes are endangered, short-run preferences for the present are increased.*

Summing up: an analysis of the determinants of the rate of time preferences among the peasants in the short and in the long perspective (*à la* Fisher) yields some interesting insights into the structure of demand for informal credit in rural areas. First of all, peasant incomes are very low which in turn tends to keep interest rates at a high level. The peasants need present incomes simply to ensure their survival into the future and therefore *ceteris paribus* welcome additions to these incomes more than additions in the future. Their demand for credit as determined by the size of incomes is high.

When we proceed to examine the intertemporal distribution of peasant incomes we discover a difference in the rate of time preference depending on whether a short- or a long-term perspective is taken. Most borrowing in the informal credit markets is presumably short-term in nature. Frequently, the peasants need credit to carry them over the dead season before the coffee harvest brings in cash incomes. During the period preceding the harvest they are therefore likely to display a high rate of time preference which makes them borrow at high interest rates. In the long perspective, on the other hand, the rate is likely to be lowered considerably. The peasants may well be aware that there is a strong tendency for their real incomes to fall with the passage of time and hence save in the form of land which may help them to improve their future production potential.

---

*Fisher also discusses the influence of 'personal factors' like foresight, self-control, habit, expectation of life, concern for the life of other persons, and fashion, on time preferences. These factors are of subordinate interest in an aggregate analysis, though, unless any definite trends or characteristics that apply to a large segment of the population could be discerned. Therefore we have left them out of the present discussion. For an account of these factors the reader is invited to consult Fisher (1930), pp. 80 ff.

To explain this combination of short-run borrowing at high interest and long-term accumulation of landed assets (the size of income permitting) we need to look at the transaction costs connected with land sales which appear to be fairly high and which may make short-run borrowing and long-run land acquisition the optimal strategy.

Hence, we may conclude that viewed from the borrower's side, the short-term rate of time preference and the large short-term demand for credit (in the long-term perspective both are likely to be lower) is due to a combination of low incomes, uneven distribution of the income stream during the agricultural year, the secular tendency for per capita incomes to fall, and the high transaction costs in connection with land sales.

We have so far dealt exclusively with the borrowers. Looking at the lenders, by analogy we may make the following predictions:

1. The absolute size of their total incomes is likely to be larger than for the average borrower.

2. The time distribution of these incomes is probably somewhat less uneven than that of peasant incomes. For those engaged in rural commerce there is of course a tendency for income peaks to arise at harvest time, but, since these groups sell goods to the peasants and also to the urban population during the slack season (although to a lesser extent than at harvest time), these peaks are likely to be somewhat less pronounced. In addition, incomes from commerce may be supplemented with other types of incomes.

3. The uncertainty with respect to present incomes is lower than the uncertainty with respect to future incomes (as was the case with peasant incomes as well).

Hence, before we allow for the possibility of lending and borrowing in a credit market, the rate of time preference should be lower among those who choose to lend in the market than among those who borrow.

The Role of Investment Opportunities

We now know that under certain circumstances the peasants have a high rate of time preference and that they therefore may be willing to pay high rates of interest on loans obtained in the informal credit markets. We also know that the lenders are likely to have a lower rate of time preference in the absence of borrowing and lending opportunities. These conclusions are both based upon the assumption that the investment opportunities of borrowers and lenders, i.e. the technological capacity of these groups to transform present goods into future goods and vice versa, was given. This presumably is a realistic assumption as far as the borrowers are concerned. There is not much the peasants can do to alter the time shape of their incomes (excepting transactions in the credit markets). In the main they have to follow the agricultural calendar and sow, plant and harvest at given times of the year. (Cf. Chapter 12.) The lenders, however, may be in a different position, since they have more contact with urban areas than do the peasants. Therefore we must examine whether outside investment opportunities may play an important role when it comes to determining the rate of interest that lenders will ask, i.e. we must look at the opportunity cost of moneylending.

In a situation where competition prevails in all markets, in equilibrium, the marginal return to moneylending must equal the marginal return to holding other assets. Hence, in principle it should be possible to arrive at an approximation of what that return would be if we could identify one or more assets which are comparatively risk-free, have negligible transaction costs, and are supplied under approximately competitive conditions. Possible candidates for assets of this type are national and foreign government papers, savings deposits and real estate, land, cattle, jewelry, precious stones and precious metals.[30]

Nothing indicates that jewelry, gold, silver, etc. are popular financial assets in Haiti, so these will consequently be left out of the present discussion. Land and cattle, on the other hand, are among the most commonly held assets in the countryside. However, land (and probably also urban real estate) is as we know connected with what appears to be substantial transaction costs, and must therefore be ruled out as well. Cattle, finally, are subject to transaction costs in the sense that they must be fed and looked after.

The best way of estimating the opportunity cost of lending is probably by examining domestic and foreign government papers and savings deposits. In the main, neither government papers nor savings deposits appear to have been very attractive for the Haitian savers. O. Ernest Moore mentions that when he came to Haiti as a financial advisor in 1951

> There were frequent complaints by the Haitian authorities about the absence of a capital market in Haiti and the unwillingness of well-to-do citizens to buy government bonds or any type of local securities. This unwillingness did not appear to be due to any lack of confidence in the currency, which was freely convertible and (at the time)

strongly backed by dollars and gold. It reflected rather the existence of more profitable fields for local investment such as mortgages and real estate. Mortgages were attractive, in part, because of their high rates in the absence of a mortgage or savings bank. Real estate was attractive because of the very low property and inheritance taxes and the absence of capital-gains taxation.[31]

To remedy this, Moore suggested the issue of a small amount of very short-term, tax-exempt treasury notes, running from 6 to 9 months, carrying an interest rate of 5 percent (later to be followed by larger issues of longer maturity), which, according to Moore, was regarded as a very attractive investment.[32] The situation would probably have been different for long-term securities. The political history of Haiti has always been one of corruption, political turmoil and/or dictatorship and repression, and neither situation is conducive to the creation of financial stability and confidence in government securities.

There was no savings bank in Haiti when Moore arrived. The *Banque Nationale de la République d'Haiti* accepted savings deposits, but only at such low interest rates as ¼ to 1½ percent, while the Royal Bank of Canada paid no interest at all on its savings accounts.[33] When the BNRH raised the interest rate on savings accounts to 2 percent and combined this measure with active soliciting of such accounts this led to a substantial rise in the time and savings deposits of the bank (from 12.7 million gourdes in 1951 to 27.1 million in 1956). Following the political troubles of the election year 1957 and the general insecurity during the Duvalier regime, these deposits fell to 10.8 million gourdes in 1966, after which they recovered again, reaching 20.1 million in 1969.[34] Subsequently, interest rates on savings accounts have been higher. The *Banque Nationale* paid 3 percent in 1972 with the Royal Bank of Canada following a general policy of staying 1 percent below this rate.[35] Recently, a number of foreign and domestic banks have started to operate and their competition (in combination with the increased rate of inflation) gradually raised the interest rate to 6 percent during 1973 on deposits of over one year, which more than doubled the savings accounts between 1971 and 1973.[36]

Since the interest rates paid by the banks in Haiti have been low during the past two-and-a-half decades, well-to-do savers generally have frequently invested outside the country to earn a higher rate of interest (but also due to reasons connected with domestic political risks). However, during the period of consideration it has scarcely been possible to earn more than 10 percent (in nominal terms) on money deposited in the major financial centers abroad. Only after the worldwide rise in the rate of inflation in the early 1970s, especially after the oil crisis in 1973, have higher nominal interest rates been offered. In real terms, however, interest rates have remained below 10 percent during the entire period.[37] Besides, investing outside the country is not likely to be a realistic alternative for more than a small fraction of the lenders in the informal credit markets.

Thus, judging from the above, it seems as if the opportunity cost of moneylending (under competitive conditions) does not exceed 10 percent in real terms. Neither domestically or internationally has the Haitian saver been able to earn a higher *safe* return on his money during the past two decades. In addition we know that the rate of time preference prevailing among the lenders (in the absence of borrowing and lending possibilities) is likely to be lower than that of the peasant borrowers. However, the opportunity cost of lending is the equilibrium cost, but in equilibrium, the marginal time preferences for both groups must be equal and also equal to the opportunity cost of lending, unless risk, transaction costs or monopolistic practices disturb the picture. We must therefore examine to what extent these three inperfections are present.

Risk

Two separate categories of loans may be distinguished with respect to risk: secured and unsecured ones, where the first category is secured against default by some kind of collateral whereas the second category is not.[38] In Haiti, some loans are guaranteed by land, or in the case of minor transactions perhaps by smaller valuable items like gold rings.[39] As long as the collateral is easily saleable and its market value does not fluctuate too much, the risk premium of the loans remains low.[40] Most frequently, however, it appears as if loans are totally unsecured in the informal credit markets, and this probably is the case in Haiti as well,* usually, for example when the peasants borrow from the *Madam Sara*. In this case there is nothing to guarantee repayment but the oral promise of the peasant. These loans will often either carry a high risk premium or lead to high transaction costs.

---

*These loans generally constitute the majority of all loans taken in the informal rural credit markets in underdeveloped countries. Anthony Bottomley quotes evidence from India, Nigeria and Ecuador giving a figure of 80-85 percent of all loans as unsecured (Bottomley (1971), p. 110), and Charles Nisbet in a study from Chile found that 66 percent of all loans were unsecured (Nisbet (1969), p. 82).

The first hazard that the lender has to face when giving an unsecured loan is the risk that the borrower does not *want* to pay back the loan. Default due to unwillingness to pay is, however, not likely to be a real problem. Lenders may be expected to have a very good first-hand knowledge of the personal character of the borrowers, either because they come from the same community (peasant-to-peasant loans) or because they are already involved in other types of business transactions (loans by *Madam Sara* and *spéculateurs*).*

A more substantial risk is that the peasants simply cannot pay back their loans even though they want to. Harvest failure is a common occurrence in Haiti, and when nature is adverse there is not much that the lender can do if the means of repayment are lacking. In such a situation, naturally the basic needs of the peasant families themselves come first, and only if these are satisfied will outside payments be honored:[41]

> In the long run a farmer must provide for his family's subsistence regardless of whether he can repay his debts or not. Initially he may harvest less than he requires for this purpose, and he may still repay a loan in the expectation of being able to borrow again prior to the next harvest. But if his harvest should fail again and again there will come a time when he will feel that he has accumulated debts, together with interest owed, which cannot possibly be repaid. He will then defy the moneylender and retain his crop in order to ensure his family will be fed. When this happens, the best that a moneylender can hope for is that the farmer will try again in the future to pay off his debts, but in the meantime he will have to forgo the use of his principal as well as any compound interest on it, and this loss must be made up from the charges on his other loans.[42]

Basically, the lender has two different options in dealing with defaults. The first option is to try to recover his money by charging higher interest rates on all loans, so that the return from non-defaulters is sufficient to cover both the loss of the principal and the loss of interest on defaults. U Tun Wai has calculated how much a lender would have to increase his interest rate to cover his losses under different assumptions regarding the normal interest rate in absence of defaults and the

---

*One would also expect that the system of social sanctions works so as to enforce repayment of informal loans. A peasant refusing to pay his debts would soon lose his creditworthiness and have problems in making other business transactions.

percentage of defaults.[43] Tun Wai postulated that: (1) the lender does not recover any money from the defaulters; (2) the lender tries to recover both the principal and the interest; and (3) the rate of interest charged does not influence the volume or value of the defaults. His results are summarized in Table 11.3. For our purpose, the most interesting figures are those for a normal interest rate (including transaction costs) of 10 percent, which corresponds fairly well to the probable maximum opportunity cost of moneylending under competitive conditions. We find that for the default-adjusted rate of interest to exceed 20 percent a default percentage of 10 is required. When the default rate increases to 15 percent the adjusted interest rate almost reaches 30 percent, and at a default rate of somewhat more than 25 percent the rate of interest reaches 50 percent per year.

Table 11.3: Estimates of Interest Rates that Lenders Would Have to Charge to Compensate for Defaults (percent per annum)

Value of defaults as percentage of total loans	Normal interest rate in absence of defaults						
	1	2	5	10	15	25	50
1	2.02	3.03	6.06	11.11	16.16	26.26	51.52
2	3.06	4.08	7.14	12.24	17.35	27.55	53.06
5	6.32	7.37	10.53	15.79	21.05	31.58	57.89
10	12.22	13.33	16.67	22.22	27.78	38.89	66.67
15	18.82	20.00	23.52	29.41	35.29	47.06	76.47
25	34.67	36.00	40.00	46.67	53.33	66.67	100.00
50	102.00	104.00	110.00	120.00	130.00	150.00	200.00

Source: Tun Wai (1957), p. 110.

However, there are reasons to believe that lenders in Haiti do not generally follow the procedure described by Tun Wai. The normal way of dealing with the risk of default seems to be one of making a distinction between various types of loans. Larger loans require some kind of collateral,[44] and the treatment of risky loans probably differs from that of less risky ones. This must be true especially if there is competition among lenders, for then a lender that wishes to compensate for defaults à la Tun Wai would not be able to obtain any borrowers, since the latter could as well go to another lender, who had less or no defaults at all to cover. Thus, we should not be obsessed by any average rate of interest, but view the rural credit market as consisting of a set of transactions that vary, among other things, according to the degree of risk involved, leading to a series of different interest rates instead of a single one.[45]

However, it is unquestionable that very many lending transactions really involve a substantial risk premium. A very common way of lending money is to make an advance against some future crop. This is done by both *spéculateurs* and *Madam Sara*. In this case the lender runs a double risk, i.e. that of a harvest failure and that of a fall in the price of the crop. There is not very much that the lender can do to protect himself from a harvest failure, but to compensate for the price risk, repayment customarily takes place at the beginning of the harvest season when only small volumes of the product in question have yet been put on the market, and prices are still high. This guarantee is not waterproof, however:

> In the Saint Raphaël region of the north, loans are made to producers of onions, which are subject to rather rapid spoilage, and to producers of rice and tobacco, both relatively durable. These loans are paid off in kind rather than in cash. Creditors are entitled to claim their stock at the very start of the harvest, at which time market prices are high. It appears to be the usual practice to estimate the price-to-be of the product and to lend money on these terms. Though some intermediaries claim that they have lost money on crop loans, the opening market prices for rice in the fall and onions in the spring make this unlikely. In the case of tobacco, however, marketing difficulties and the complaints some informants made indicate that they did lose money — some said they would advance no more money for tobacco crops, and this will probably affect the next year's tobacco crop.[46]

Thus, it is likely that crop loans entail a risk premium to cover both the risk of harvest failure and the risk of market glut. A loan against the future crop will, *ceteris paribus,* carry a higher rate of interest than a loan to be repaid in cash.* The average size of this difference, i.e. the size of the risk premium is, however, for lack of data impossible to determine.

---

*From the viewpoint of the borrower a loan to be repaid in kind could be looked upon as an insurance against these two risks, and the additional interest as an insurance premium.

Transaction Costs

To a certain extent, the risks of moneylending can be reduced by careful administration of the loans by the lender, but tight supervision, on the other hand, will raise the transaction or administration costs.* Even though high administration costs are sometimes advanced as one of the most important determinants of the high rates of interest in the rural credit markets of less developed countries,[47] these costs are likely to be low in the Haitian case.

The transaction costs connected with moneylending mainly consist in the sacrifice of time by the lender. The amount to be lent, the duration of the loan, the terms of repayment, the rate of interest, the collateral, etc. will all have to be discussed with the prospective borrower. The lender may have to make some inquiries about the latter's creditworthiness through other people. He may want to find out what the loan is going to be used for, and in the case of production loans he may have to calculate the likely outcome of the crop and forecast the likely market price for it, etc. After the loan has been made he may have to supervise that it is used exactly for the purposes stated. He may have to spend some time urging interest payments and repayment of the principal if the borrower does not see to those matters himself.

At least, this is what one may expect. In practice, matters are generally much simpler. If the lender is experienced he already has some idea of the terms that he would require for a given loan of a given duration and for a given purpose. Frequently, he does not have to supervise how the loan is used, since if a loan is taken for consumption purposes, as is frequently the case, there ought to be few if any reasons to suspect that it is used for something else. Only when loans are to be used for productive purposes may the lenders feel that they ought to keep an eye on its use. On the other hand, it is only when a production loan finances a project that would *not* otherwise have been undertaken without the loan that the lender has any factual reasons to supervise the use of the loan. Thus, if a loan is taken to obtain seeds and plants for a crop that would have been planted in any case (i.e. with or without the loan) the borrowed money actually finances something else (production or consumption). It is more likely that the lender will try to get some insight into the *total* economic situation of the borrower instead of emphasizing any earmarking of the loan since the lender's sole considerations in principle are amortizations and interest payments. He is likely

---

*These two terms will be used as synonyms in the present work.

to already have this knowledge if he knows the borrower, which is highly probable both in the case of a loan given by an intermediary (*spéculateur* or *Madam Sara*) and a loan granted by one peasant to another. Hence, even though most loan transactions in the rural credit market involve only smaller amounts of money, there is no reason to believe that this will increase the administration costs per gourde loaned.

Another possible source of high transaction costs is the fact that most loans appear to be only of short duration. As a rule, the length of a loan appears to lie somewhere between a few weeks and a year, perhaps the most typical transaction being a loan taken some time during the dry season to be repaid on the arrival of the harvest period. If lenders engage mainly in short-term transactions they may have a problem with idle funds during certain periods of the year if their money cannot readily be invested in other assets during these periods, and may therefore seek to compensate themselves by charging a higher rate of interest on short-term loans.[48] While such a description may give a fair picture of some countries, it certainly does not fit Haiti, since in Haiti moneylending must be viewed as a subordinate activity that mainly takes place during the dry season when there are few other investment outlets. Sidney W. Mintz has shown how the *Madam Sara* use moneylending as a means to employ their funds during the period when their trading activities slacken.[49] The problem for these market women is that

> The variations in trade, particularly during the year, pose investment and saving problems for traders. When market conditions are poor, a central question for them is how to keep their capital available for future trading without consuming it, squandering it in nontrading activities, or investing it in ways that make it difficult to transform it again into trading capital, swiftly and easily. Women dislike holding capital in the form of cash, and avoid doing so if possible. The onset of summer usually means a slackening of trade for most marketers, however, when they must withdraw capital from trade and use it in ingenious ways until trade picks up once more.[50]

An often employed device is to lend money against a future crop, preferably to be harvested around the time when trading activities begin to gain new momentum. In this case short-term transactions do not lead to high transaction costs. If anything, there would be a tendency for this type of short-term moneylending during the slack season to lower interest rates. It is important for the *Madam Sara* not to have their funds tied up in too long-term transactions, since this would only limit the amount of working capital for subsequent trade, so that in this case they will probably be prepared to lower the rate of interest if this could help them to get their money back at the most appropriate moment. Moneylending during the slack season 'usually means that money must be lent for a long period – perhaps several months' use – which leaves Haitian market women feeling anxious' writes Mintz.[51]

Finally, transaction costs may be of relevance if lenders finance their activities by taking loans themselves in the formal credit market, since for each link in the chain of formal lending institutions that a gourde lent to a *spéculateur* has to pass through, an administration charge will be added. It is not known to what extent lenders in the informal credit markets actually resort to outside financing, and it is therefore not possible to get any idea of the relative importance of this kind of costs. It should be noted in this context, however, that such administration charges do not necessarily get passed on to the final borrower in their entirety. The problem of determining what fraction of the administration costs will be shifted to the final borrower is analogous to the well-known textbook problem of determining the incidence of an excise or sales tax.[52]

High transaction costs are a commonly adduced reason for high interest rates in the informal credit markets of less developed countries. However, the explanation does not seem to fit the Haitian case particularly well. The lenders are not likely to bother too much about the supervision of the use of the loans, nor do they have to spend much time finding out about the creditworthiness of the buyers, whom they probably already know.

Monopoly

It is frequently alleged in the literature on Haitian agriculture that the high interest rates in rural credit markets are a result of monopolistic practices by the lenders.[53] However, this is a mere assumption, and no attempts have been made so far to prove that the statement is actually true. What evidence is there to sustain such a statement?

If we can make an estimate of the total number of potential lenders in the rural credit markets and relate this estimate to an estimate of the total number of potential borrowers, we get an idea of the market situation. Discounting friends, relatives, *sangues*, etc. the main sources for loans in the formal credit markets are *spéculateurs*, market women *(Madam Sara)* and wealthy peasants.[54] Around 1960, there was an estimated 1,500 licenced speculators in Haiti. (Cf. Chapter 4.) The number of *Madam Sara* during the same period has been estimated at 36,600.[55] Together, this gives us a total figure of approximately 38,100 potential lenders in the commercial sector. To this we have to add the number of potential peasant lenders. Richard P. Schaedel, Roland Wingfield and Vernon J. Parenton all estimate that 5 percent of the rural population qualify as *gros habitants*, i.e. have some wealth (and power).[56] If we continue to use Brand's figures for 1960 we get a rural population for that year of 3,578,000,[57] leaving a total number of *gros habitants* of 178,900. A typical Haitian family today consists of five to six persons — man, woman and children.[58] Assuming that each family only contains one potential lender (a family = 6 persons) the number of potential peasant lenders becomes 29,800, giving a total of approximately 67,900 potential lenders.

To calculate the number of potential borrowers, we start once again from Brand's rural population figure: 3,578,000. From this, we deduct the potential lenders *and* their families (still assuming that a family consists of six people), i.e. 178,900 *gros habitants* and 228,600 *spéculateurs* and *Madam Sara* including their families. This leaves us with approximately 3,170,500 potential borrowers (including their family members). Retaining the assumption that a family consists of six individuals, and assuming that each family only contains one borrower, the approximate number of potential borrowers in the informal rural credit markets around 1960 becomes 528,400.

Comparing the figures for potential borrowers and lenders, a borrower/lender ratio of a little less than 8 emerges. This is a low figure indeed, and although it should not be taken too *ad notam* but rather as a rough indication of the magnitude, it enables us to advance the hypothesis that moneylending is a competitive activity in rural Haiti.

This hypothesis may be sustained in other ways as well. Two of the most important categories of lenders are the *spéculateurs* and the *Madam Sara*, both of whom we have met in the context of rural trade in Chapter 4. The main conclusion emerging from that chapter was that trading activities are strongly competitive in rural Haiti. Credit is used as a means of attracting customers and sellers among both groups of intermediairies, and this, in turn means that neither *spéculateurs* nor *Madam Sara* should be in the position where they can extract monopoly profits in moneylending.

For monopoly profits* to arise in a market, entry to this particular

---

*By monopoly profit we mean any return to moneylending in excess of opportunity cost, risk premium and transaction costs. Observe that when using this

Problems of Rural Credit

market must somehow be restricted, so that the number of sellers (in the present case lenders) can be kept low. In rural credit markets entry is usually restricted for either of two reasons: sanctions directed towards actual or potential entrants or lack of information.[59]

It is hard to think of any principal difficulties barring entry to the rural credit market:

> Only a modest capital is required to enter the moneylending business. It can easily be done on a part-time basis by prosperous peasants as well as by middlemen. Ease of entry serves to keep interest rates relatively well in line with the costs of administration and loss from bad loans. When the profit margin becomes large, we can expect more entries. In rural areas, with a prosperous peasant farmer class, relatively low returns to investment, traditional consumption patterns, and poor investment opportunities outside the local area, the local 'pure' interest rate may be quite low.[60]

In some countries socio-religious attitudes, sometimes formalized in written or unwritten laws, restrict the number of potential lenders to certain minority groups,[61] but that is not the case in Haiti.

Millard F. Long discusses a particular case of temporary monopoly which may be of some interest to us,[62] and this is when a harvest failure occurs. In that situation, the number of potential lenders may be drastically reduced, sometimes to the point where a monopoly may arise in the short run. On the other hand, when a harvest failure occurs, another important change takes place as well: the rate of time preference increases markedly in the economy, which may lead to a substantial rise in the rate of interest without any monopoly element being present. In practice it is hard to distinguish one of these interest-raising elements from the other.*

The situation where monopoly profits are most likely to arise in the rural credit market is probably when there are imperfections in other

definition a monopoly profit may arise even if there is more than one lender in the market.

*Another case which is sometimes pointed to as a potential monopoly situation is when there is a legislation establishing a ceiling on the interest rates allowed in the informal markets. (See e.g. Long (1968:1), p. 280.) However, in this case, a black market will probably arise, and risk considerations will increase interest rates. Only if the number of lenders is reduced and lenders act in collusion, will monopoly profits arise. In the case of Haiti, no usury legislation exists.

markets. If the land market or the market for those products that peasants buy is monopolized, or if the rural labor market or the market for peasant products is monopsonized, the peasants will in all probability be tied to a particular lender as a result of the monopsony or monopoly power that the latter exercise over the peasants. In Haiti, however, most markets appear fairly competitive. Landownership is widespread. In Haiti we do not find the latifundia-minifundia polarization which is so characteristic for most Latin American countries, and the absence of the strong landlord-tenant bonds is usually accompanied by the absence of a monopsonistic labor market.[63] Finally, we know that the product markets are characterized by intense competition.

It is sometimes maintained that lenders may exercise a strong hold over borrowers because the latter are already indebted to the former so that any attempt by borrowers to transfer their business to other lenders would lead to demands for immediate payment or raise other difficulties.[64] However, this argument is not very satisfactory. In the first place all borrowers are not already indebted and are hence free to go to any lender of whom they know. Secondly, a substantial share of all loans is taken only for a short period, and is repaid in cash or in kind at the time of the harvest. After that, the peasants should in principle be free from this kind of debts. It is only in the situations where peasants have borrowed larger sums which require a longer period for repayment, that the argument may be of relevance. On the other hand, such practices would give a lender a bad reputation and make it more difficult to attract new borrowers or suppliers (for a *spéculateur* or a market woman).

Monopoly profits may also arise out of a lack of information among borrowers and/or lenders regarding the availability of borrowing opportunities and with respect to borrower characteristics.[65] The peasants may not know that moneylenders other than the local ones are available. This, however, is not likely to be the case in Haiti. The network of market-places offers ample opportunity for contacts between peasants and *Madam Sara* throughout the year, and during the period preceding the coffee harvest, when most loans presumably are taken, there are intensive contacts between the peasants and the *spéculateurs* competing for purchases and sales.

If information regarding the creditworthiness of the borrowers is unequally distributed among the lenders, this may also lead to a certain type of monopoly profits. Lenders with a good knowledge of local conditions ('inside' lenders) should be able to distinguish between 'good' and 'bad' risks among the borrowers and hence should have to ask for collateral or for a higher rate of interest only in the cases where the likelihood of default is high enough to warrant such procedures, while 'outsiders' will not be able to distinguish low-risk borrowers from 'lemons'.* In this case, if the number of 'insiders' is low, by colluding they may convert their information advantage into a monopoly profit equal to the risk premium which the 'outsiders' would have to charge (without asking for collateral).

This type of monopoly profit may be temporary only. If the risk premium that an 'outside' lender would have to charge in the absence of enough information to distinguish between lender categories with respect to risk is high, it may pay the outsider to search for information which would make it possible to increase his competitiveness and which would hence also bring interest rates and the monopoly profits of the insiders down.

In Haiti, the lack of information among potential lenders is not likely to constitute any serious problem. The same process which disseminates information regarding the availability of lenders among the borrowers also works in the 'opposite' direction, in that it allows the lenders to gather knowledge regarding borrowers at a very low cost. Monopoly profits based on imperfect information are not likely to be more than a very temporary phenomenon in the informal credit markets of rural Haiti.

The conclusion that monopoly power is not likely to be present in the informal credit markets adds the last important piece of information to our discussion of the alleged exploitation of the peasants by landlords and intermediaries. In Chapter 2 we found that no important landlord class with power enough to monopolize the supply of land exists in Haiti and hence also that monopsonization of the rural labor market is not a problem. In Chapter 4 we discussed marketing of peasant produce and peasant consumption goods and found that no exploitation of the peasants takes place via the commodity markets. The investigation of the informal credit market completes this picture. The high interest rates prevailing are not likely to be a result of monopolistic practices among the lenders. Hence, the Haitian rural economy is essentially one of competition in all markets. It is not possible to blame the abject poverty of the peasants on an exploitative market system. The reasons, as we have attempted to demonstrate, are first and foremost to

---

*In the US bad cars are known as 'lemons'. Akerlof has used the term to designate bad-quality goods in general. (See Akerlof (1970), esp. pp. 498-9, which deals with informal credit markets.)

be sought elsewhere.

If we sum up the reasons for the comparatively high interest rates which sometimes prevail in the informal credit markets, as they appear when viewed from the lender side, we find that the most important determinant of these rates is probably risk. The rate of time preference among lenders in the absence of a credit market is likely to be lower than that prevailing among would-be borrowers. The opportunity cost of lending money under competitive conditions in the absence of risk and transaction costs is not likely to exceed 10 percent in real terms and is presumably lower than this in practice. It is also difficult to discover any substantial transaction costs for the lenders in these markets. These lenders usually feel no need to supervise the use of their loans. Rather, their main consideration is to obtain enough information to arrive at a comprehensive picture of the borrower's situation. To gather this information is presumably a fairly simple affair because the lenders already know the borrowers sufficiently well because of their residence in the area in question or because they already have engaged in business dealings with the borrowers in the commodity markets.

Largely for the same reasons, monopoly profits are unlikely to play an important role in the determination of interest rates. The number of potential lenders is not particularly low in comparison to the number of potential borrowers, and it is difficult to find any permanent obstacles to entry in the credit markets. In theory, a handful of 'inside' lenders with a superior knowledge of local conditions could extract a monopoly profit, but due to the relatively widespread information regarding the borrowers such monopolies are unlikely to arise, and if they should arise, will probably be difficult to maintain during longer periods.

This leaves us with the risk component. The most important lending transactions are those which take place during the dead season before the coffee harvest begins, and these loans are usually given against repayment in kind — i.e. against part of the future harvest. This in turn means that the lenders have to face both a price risk and a risk of harvest failure. Hence, they are likely to add a risk premium to the 'pure' rate of interest.

On the borrower side we have seen that this risk premium corresponds to an increased willingness to pay high interest rates while the peasants are waiting for the harvest to begin, due to the relatively high cost connected with sale and repurchase transactions with other assets.

The Absence of Long-term Loans

Most loans in the informal credit markets are short-term loans. With regard to long-term credit the situation differs considerably from the short-run one in one important aspect. The rate of time preference among the borrowers is high mainly in the short run. In the longer perspective, this rate is likely to be lower due to expectations of secularly falling per capita incomes. This lowers the demand for long-term credit. When it comes to the lenders, however, there is no reason to believe that they would be prepared to extend long-term credit at an interest rate low enough to be compatible with the rate which the prospective borrowers are prepared to pay. Risk considerations are important to the lenders even in the short-run perspective (say, over a couple of months). In the context of transactions which perhaps are to extend over several years, they are likely to assume an even more pronounced importance. In the eyes of the lenders in the informal credit markets, lengthening the time perspective in an economy of the Haitian type where uncertainty exists with respect to weather, prices and perhaps political factors as well, quite probably leads to a considerable increase in the risk premia which would have to be asked. In addition, the lenders are likely to perceive the declining trend in rural per capita incomes as well as the peasants themselves. Hence, they know that the ability of the peasants to pay back a long-term loan may be lower than the ability to handle a loan of a couple of months. This should increase the risk premium for long-term credit as well.

Comparing borrower and lender behavior we find that a situation where the demand and supply curves do not intersect is quite conceivable in the market for long-term credit. The borrowers are interested in accumulating landed resources by saving if possible and place a comparatively low value on long-term credit, while the lenders feel that long-term lending operations are so risky, because the economic standing of the borrowers may easily change in the longer run, that they demand substantial risk premia (or good collateral) to extend this type of credit. This, in turn, explains why no long-term borrowing for the purpose of capital formation in traditional peasant agriculture takes place.

Formal Sources of Credit*

The first two sections of the present chapter have been devoted to an

---

*The formal or institutional credit markets 'comprise the conventional suppliers of loanable funds, e.g. private and public commercial banks, private and public savings and loan institutions (cooperative, development banks, credit unions, etc.) and specialized agrarian reform institutions and their clients.' (*Spring Review* (1973 : 2), p. 3.)

investigation of why peasant savings are limited and why they rarely take the form of capital formation in agriculture. We have also analyzed the reasons behind the high rates of interest prevailing in the informal rural credit markets and which constitute the main obstacle to financing rural capital formation via loans in these markets. The third and final section deals with the formal credit market that is available to the peasants. We will determine to what extent the peasants have been touched by formal credit and discuss some of the problems inherent in the extension of formal credit in the Haitian setting.

The first efforts towards extending organized credit to the agricultural sector were made around the First World War when the existing banks attempted to create departments that were specialized on agricultural and industrial lending operations. However, these efforts failed — allegedly due to administrative difficulties and due to the general lack of trained technical personnel. In the 1930s a new attempt was made, this time by the Agricultural Extension Service of the Department of Agriculture. The peasants were to borrow for the purpose of buying seed and to repay in kind after the harvest. In 1948, a program to extend credit for the purchase of plows, for example, to be repaid in annual instalments, was initiated. Both these programs failed as well, due to the tendency of the peasants not to repay the loans but to consider them as gifts instead.[66]

In 1951, the *Institut Haitien de Crédit Agricole et Industriel* (IHCAI) was founded, with an authorized capital of 10 million gourdes (the following year increased to 25 million).[67] The maximum rate of interest was put at 7 percent per annum.[68] However, only an insignificant part of the credits accorded went to agriculture. During the first five years of the life of the institute, only 10 percent of the total amount (1.4 million gourdes) consisted of loans to agriculture,[69] and in 1957-58 the percentage was down to 5.2 or 19,375 gourdes.[70] Instead most of the loans were given for entirely different ventures outside the agricultural sector. Many hotel owners borrowed substantial amounts (1954-55: 410,000 gourdes; 1955-56: 946,000 gourdes; 1956-57: 250,000 gourdes)[71] which in many cases were never repaid.[72]

The relatively unfavorable position of agriculture in total lending operations was mainly due to the fact that the institute was conservatively run. The emphasis was on safety. Credits were accorded only after an inspection of the borrower's property had been undertaken, and the technicians of IHCAI were supposed to keep the projects for which loans were given under constant supervision as well as to keep an eye on the borrower's affairs.[73] Thus, the IHCAI loans were only granted

Problems of Rural Credit

to people or enterprises with enough securities to make lending a relatively risk-free venture.* Nevertheless, IHCAI ran into severe financial trouble. The tourist business suffered a severe decline in the late 1960s** due to the political conditions of the time, which meant that amortization payments were soon in arrear or ceased altogether. Neither were repayments collected in other sectors. The good-will of the institute was lost, which soon led to a general cessation of both repayments and loans, and IHCAI had to be liquidated:

> Without going into details one could say that when its liquidation was decided, the Institut was liquidated in practice, since it did not dispose of any resources which would have made it possible to extend new loans, excepting tiny sums in isolated cases. In addition, since its debtors were generally in arrear, it would soon have found itself without funds, even to pay salaries to its personnel.[74]

In 1961 the institute was reorganised. Its name was chaned to *Institut de Développement Agricole et Industriel* (IDAI) and its authorized capital was increased to 60 million gourdes. A loan of 17.5 million gourdes was obtained from the Inter-American Development Bank, to be amortized at 4 percent in fifteen years.[75]

Between 1961 and 1969, the agricultural lending activities of IDAI accounted for 36 percent of the total amount loaned by the institute or 5,980,000 gourdes, leaving a yearly average of 747,500 gourdes.[76] The most important of these activities is the supervised credit program which has been in operation since 1962. The program is mainly designed

---

*Dossous (1969), p. 103. Viewed from the traditional banker's standpoint it is understandable that such a policy was adopted:

> It is not principally the fact that the profit margin in agriculture is generally very small and that certain industrial enterprises only manage to develop very slowly that handicaps their financing by the Institut. On the contrary, the Institut is anxious to assist such enterprises and offer them a reasonable interest rate for a period of time related to their repayment capacity. However, its action is, unfortunately, frequently paralyzed by the lack of fundamental information: the non-existence of cadastral survey and of insurance policies for the crops, the lack of rural police, the disorganization of the exploitations and the inexperience of the entrepreneurs (BIHCAI, Exercise 55-6, p. 9).

**After a steady rise during the 1950s the number of tourists dropped from 145,000 in 1959 to 85,000 in 1961 and the number of tourist-days declined from 259,000 to 201,000 during the same period (IHS (1971), p. 57). The figures apply to Port-au-Prince only.

to finance the cultivation of cotton, corn, beans, peanuts and rice in five localities (Gonaïves, Mirebalais, Jacmel, Miragoâne and Cayes), but also allows for purchase of tools and cattle. The interest rate of this program is 8 percent and the duration of the loans extends from six months (in the case of crop financing) to twenty-four months (for tools) and somewhat longer (for cattle).[77] Amounts loaned up to the early 1970s under the supervised credit program are shown in Table 11.4. During the 1962-69 period, almost one-half of the supervised credits (in gourdes) were given for cotton growing, 30 percent for corn growing, and 10 percent for bean cultivation.[78]

Table 11.4: Amounts Loaned under the IDAI Supervised Credit Program 1962-73

Year	Amount loaned (current gourdes)
1962-69	1,785,675
1967-68	187,277
1968-69	398,461
1969-70	359,995
1970-71	419,376
1971-72	740,274
1972-73	886,757

Sources: OEA (1972), p. 347; Giles (1973), p. 37.

The impact of the IDAI supervised lending scheme has been very limited. It has been calculated that only 1.3 percent of the rural population was affected by these credits in 1972-73,[79] and in terms of the area cultivated the figure did not even reach 1 percent.[80] The number of new job opportunities created with the aid of the supervised credit system was as low as 1,465 during 1972-73, corresponding to 0.4 percent of the total employment in agriculture and animal husbandry.*

---

*Giles (1973), p. 25. A job is defined as 300 work-days. It is assumed that it costs 2 gourdes (in cash) to create one work-day. Total supervised cash credits in 1972-73 amounted to 343,166 gourdes (ibid., p. 38). This leads to a direct job creation of 569 to which Giles adds 896 'indirect' jobs, the calculation of which is not accounted for: 'work which the owner normally undertakes with family labor...' (ibid., p. 25). Total employment in agriculture and husbandry is given by Giles as 400,000 jobs (p. 25). These calculations cannot of course be taken to convey more than a very gross idea of the magnitudes involved.

IDAI has not been able to utilize its entire lending capacity. Table 11.5 furnishes a comparison between the volumes of authorized and actually advanced credit. It should be observed that the 1972-73 figure is largely spurious, since the volume of authorized credit had been cut to less than half the size of the authorized volume of the preceding year. Subsequently, the lending activities of IDAI have been intensified. In 1974-75, almost 15 million gourdes were lent to the agricultural sector (more than 90 percent as supervised credit).[81] Still the percentage of peasants reached is low: slightly more than 3 percent.[82]

Table 11.5: Authorized and Advanced Credits under the IDAI Supervised Lending Scheme, 1968-73

Year	Authorized credit (current gourdes)	Advanced credit[a] (current gourdes)	Advanced credit in percent of authorized credit
1968-69	2,191,005	379,240	17.3
1969-70	2,204,033	337,528	15.3
1970-71	2,953,515	635,282	21.5
1971-72	4,619,453	645,008	14.0
1972-73	1,755,386	1,180,827	67.3

a. These figures differ from those in Table 11.1. The magnitude of the unutilized capacity does not change very much, however, if the latter figures are used instead.

Source: Giles (1973), p. 44.

In 1956 a second credit institute, the *Bureau de Crédit Rural Supervisé* (BCRS) was established to give short- and medium-term credits (1-5 years) to the rural sector in order to increase the production per hectare and to improve cultivation techniques among the peasants. The bureau met with no success, however, and when it was closed in 1959, the total of its lending operations was found to have been no more than 178,000 gourdes, and only 113 borrowers had benefited from its lending operations.[83]

Following the closure of BCRS in 1959 the *Bureau de Crédit Agricole* (BCA) was created to promote especially coffee- and cocoa-growing. One of its principal aims is to grant supervised credit to those peasants who are too small and too lacking in creditworthiness to qualify for the IDAI scheme. The bureau received an initial capital of approximately 5 million gourdes.[84] In principle its activities are supposed to cover the entire country, but in practice operations have been concentrated to the Artibonite valley and the *Département du Nord,* where BCA has taken part in the financing of the ODVA program and the *Poté-Colé* project, respectively.*

In 1966, BCA had advanced short- and medium-term loans to some 1,500 peasants. The short-term loans averaged 655 gourdes apiece and were mostly used for the production of coffee (39 percent), and livestock (17 percent), while the medium-term loans reached an average of 1,400 gourdes and were used mainly for irrigation facilities (71 percent).[85] Low repayment rates have led to serious trouble, however, and the continuation of operation has frequently been jeopardized. In 1971, a United Nations evaluation concluded that:

> For reasons which are too complicated to be analyzed here, BCA is far from able to play its role to the full extent, due to a wide range of difficulties that it encounters particularly when it comes to recovering its outstanding debts. A paragraph from the report of the Agricultural Districts of Artibonite from the 1963-66 period may cast some light upon these difficulties: 'One is forced to wonder whether one really is dealing with a credit institution or with an institution charged with the distribution of money or insecticides to certain categories of people.'[86]

Between 1970 and 1975, a total of 742 loans were made, the total amount being 1,847,800 gourdes, one-third of which was outstanding at the end of 1975.[87] It is thus obvious that the impact of the BCA credits has been virtually nil. Fewer peasants have been affected by the BCA scheme than by the IDAI operations, which in turn affected around only one percent of the rural population.

In recent years the *Institute Haïtien de Promotion du Café et des Denrées d'Exportation* (IHPCADE) has extended credit in kind to peasants by providing fertilizers (at a subsidized rate — sold at half price). The program has been limited to approximately 600 tons a year.[88]

---

*ODVA *(Organisme de Développement de la Vallée de l'Artibonite),* a joint Haitian-American organization, was created in 1949 to stimulate agricultural production in the Artibonite valley. The aim was to modernize agriculture in the region via adoption of modern techniques and via infrastructural investments, mainly in irrigation. (For a description see Moral (1961), pp. 325 ff.) The *Poté-Colé* (Creole for 'pull together') started as another Haitian-American joint venture in 1959, and aimed to develop agriculture in the northern province. (For a description see ICA (1951), pp. 29 ff.) Cf. also Chapter 7, above.

Problems of Rural Credit

At the end of the 1940s the first rural co-operative credit unions were organized in Haiti by the *Pères Oblats*. This private effort was soon followed by the establishment of government-organized credit societies, rapidly increasing the number of rural credit societies to 47 in 1952 and 60 in 1956. After that year, the number of *Caisses Populaires*, as they are called in Haiti, declined so that in 1962 no less than 41 had been dissolved leaving only 28 remaining units.[89] (Often embezzlement of co-operative funds was the reason behind the dissolution.) The impact of the rural co-operative credit movement has been comparatively small. In December 1961 the number of borrowers fell short of 2,000, and the geographical dispersion of the *Caisses Populaires* was very uneven, with no less than 19 out of 28 units concentrated in the *Département de l'Ouest*.[90] In 1969, the number of credit unions had increased somewhat, to 36,[91] but it seems clear that the results have not been those originally desired. That same year the commission reporting on the Haitian co-operative movement during the Second National Labor Congress concluded that

> The difficulties presently encountered by the co-operative movement, at the head of which is the Conseil National de la Coopération, have their roots in the weakness of the co-operative education of the members. The savings and credit societies in particular have suffered from this deficiency, since these deal exclusively with money. The absence of a banking organization in provincial towns in most cases confers on the treasurers of the caisses to keep considerable sums at home, and this constitutes a very large danger.[92]

Thus, although it is possible to find examples of successful co-operative ventures,* it is clear that the co-operative savings and credit movement in Haiti has not yet been able to operate more than on a limited scale. Problems of administration and lack of confidence still stand in the way of an extensive development of the *Caisses Populaires*.

The Failure of Formal Credit

The preceding account shows that organized credit from the early

---

*Lebeau quotes the case of Milot in the northern province, where 11 credit unions have been established — organized as a federation. This federation is reported to have invested almost 500,000 gourdes in such commodity development projects as a small power plant, serving some 8,000 people in four different communities, irrigation works, drinking water systems and road improvement (Lebeau (1974), p. 48). Cf. IBRD (1972), pp. 18-19.

1950s up to the mid-1970s has on average reached less than 1 percent of the peasants. In other words, formal credit has foundered, and it is important to find out the reasons behind this failure. These reasons may be divided into two groups: those emanating mainly from the borrower side and those coming from the lender side. Let us begin with the former.

The Borrower Side

Formal rural credit as conceived in Haiti has concentrated on production loans which are to increase peasant output:

> In idealized form, the scenario for a public sector program of credit for small farmers goes as follows: the government or central bank loans money to an agricultural bank which in turn relends the funds either directly or through co-operatives to small farmers. The farmers use the funds to purchase productive inputs — fertilizer, seeds, pesticides, etc., which are combined with family labor to produce more output. The additional output is sold and the proceeds are sufficient to repay the loan yet leave the farmer better off. The payments received from the farmers by the agricultural bank are sufficient to regenerate lending capacity, to cover administrative costs and to pay the interest on the government loan.[93]

Dividing the assets of a peasant farm into equity (the peasant's own claim) and debts, the annual growth of equity may be written as[94]

$$g = (rA - iD)(1 - c) \qquad (11:1)$$

where g is the growth rate of equity, r is the rate earned on assets (net except for interest), A stands for total assets, D for total debt, i is the interest rate paid on debt, and c is the rate spent on consumption.

Dividing both sides of (11:1) by E (equity) yields

$$g' = \left[\frac{D}{E}(r - i) + r\right](1 - c) \qquad (11:2)$$

where g' is the growth rate expressed as a percentage of equity, and D/E is the debt/equity ratio. Expression (11:2) shows that, as long as the (given) rate r, earned on total assets exceeds the (given) rate i, at which the peasant may borrow, the growth in equity is maximized by maximizing the debt/equity ratio, i.e. by borrowing as much as possible.

Problems of Rural Credit

By borrowing the peasant may increase his equity, and thereby also his ability to generate future incomes.*

In practice, this type of borrowing does not, however, take place. If the peasant retains his traditional technology, borrowing is not likely to be a profitable venture for him. The borrowing rate, i, from formal credit sources has not exceeded 10 percent in real terms and as a rule has been lower. A peasant who retains the traditional Haitian technology however, is, not likely to be able to earn a rate of return on total farm assets which exceeds 10 percent, and probably the figure is even lower.[95]

Hence, for external finance to be a profitable venture for the peasant, a change in the technology at the disposal of the peasant must presumably take place.[96] New types of productive assets must be substituted for the old low-yielding ones. Furthermore, the new technology must not only be more productive in physical terms than the traditional mode of production, but it must also be profitable. In addition, if adoption of a new technology is to increase the rate of physical capital formation in agriculture, the new technology must also be more capital-intensive than the old one.[97]

The tying of formal credit to changes in farm technology is a common feature of organized credit programs in many parts of the developing world, and this recipe has been tried in Haiti as well. Thus, to qualify for the benefits of the IDAI supervised credit scheme the peasants must change their cultivation techniques. They are obliged to sow in straight lines, to combat plant diseases, to use chemical fertilizers and selected seeds, to use the plow, etc.[98] The IDAI experience demonstrates, however, that wholesale introduction of new technologies in agriculture is a difficult process which is also likely to meet with strong resistance when coupled with credit. Christopher K. Clague describes the situation in the Cayes area at the beginning of the 1970s:

> The bank's thirteen agents in the Cayes area carefully screen loan applicants, all of whom must agree to follow the bank's advice. The agents insist that soils must be prepared properly by plowing behind draft animals, chemical fertilizers used, and improved varieties of

---

*The expression also shows that high consumption out of farm production keeps the rate of growth in equity low. This is, however, not necessarily true. Recalling the analysis of Chapter 9, on the effects of nutrition, increased food intake in certain cases may increase the rate of return on assets, r, thereby offsetting the effects of a high c.

corn sown. Plots of the traditional millet and beans are also supposed to benefit from the good soil preparation and fertilization. In order to facilitate the learning of new techniques, the agents have not only operated demonstration farms but have even borrowed patches of their clients' land for similar purposes. But the change in techniques which the agents are asking the peasants to perform is great. Although the Cayes region is one of the few in Haiti where the plow is used at all, the total number in the region is minimal — perhaps 250 at most. Experience with this difficult technique is not widespread. Furthermore the use of fertilizer requires a long, sustained effort, and often produces uncertain results. Since small applications of fertilizer are unprofitable because the heavy rains quickly wash them away, the bank has begun a program of 'renewal fertilization': the application of large amounts of fertilizers over many years is designed to build up organic material in the soil and to increase its ability to retain new fertilizing elements. But the economic profitability of this scheme is still questionable. The bank scheme may or may not be economically sound but, even if it is, the program is highly *dirigiste* and depends upon continued governmental support (which is always problematical) over a number of years before the peasant borrowers will be sufficiently experienced and well endowed to continue without assistance.[99]

Thus the IDAI scheme entails compulsory technological change. This coercive feature may easily make the supervised credit scheme less attractive to the peasants, especially if the economic viability of the scheme, as viewed by the peasants, is doubtful. We will not pursue the matter of technological change further at present, but the reader is referred to Chapter 12 for a discussion. Suffice it here to say that the IDAI example very clearly illustrates a point on which we will elaborate further in that chapter, namely that while long-term credit on reasonable terms probably is a necessary condition for effective technological change in peasant agriculture, it may not be a sufficient one.

Resistance to technological change is not the only reason why the peasants may reject government-sponsored programs of formal credit. Against the findings of Chapters 7 and 8, dealing with government reluctance to promote the agricultural sector, we may also hypothesize that one of the fundamental reasons behind the comparative failure of formal credit has been that these schemes are viewed with a great deal of scepticism and suspicion by the peasants. Cynthia Gillette and Norman Uphoff stress that

> The distrust displayed toward government-sponsored credit programs may be rooted in a long history of antagonism between centralized power and the rural population...Center-periphery relations have generally in the past been characterized by taxation and military or labor conscriptions on the part of the center with a minimum of services going to the periphery...So long as the government is seen as distant and voracious, it is unlikely that farmers will view the programs as instrumental in meeting their needs.[100]

The tradition of strongly military-flavored rule in the countryside, the concentration of taxes on the peasants, both as producers and as consumers, and the marked reluctance of virtually all Haitian governments to further peasant welfare by stimulating agriculture has hardly been conducive to an atmosphere where people perceived as government representatives — be they extension or credit agents, or be they *chefs de section* or tax collectors — are viewed as helpful and benevolent by the peasants. Extension of formal credit under such circumstances is bound to meet with strong psychological resistance on the part of the peasants, and the time and effort required to break these psychological barriers is likely to be considerable.

A third reason why the peasants may not demand credit from formal sources has to do with the possibility of substitution between formal and informal credit. Borrowing from a formal credit source may under certain circumstances destroy or at least act as an obstacle to the possibilities of borrowing from informal sources. In the section on the demand for rural credit we mentioned that *access* to credit for the peasants is a close substitute to cash. In the rural economy, where serious risks of all kinds which threaten the precarious standard of living of the peasants are ubiquitous, and where most peasants are too poor to be able to save much, the possibility of getting a quick loan without questions or red tape if for example the harvest fails is too valuable to the peasant to be risked. Such a loan can only be obtained from the informal sources, since these easily adjust to the particular needs and conditions of an emergency situation, while formal lending, at least in the Haitian case, makes no provision at all for anything but production credit. Thus, if the peasants consider that using a formal credit source may jeopardize their customary credit lines in the informal markets they will not accept loans from formal sources.

Turning to a formal source of credit may cut off the credit line from the informal moneylender in the situation where the borrower is tied to the lender by some type of monopoly power, but in the Haitian case this is a less likely situation. As a rule we should expect competition to prevail in the markets, so that if one informal lender refuses credit all the peasant would have to do is to turn to another source. However, he may reject formal credit for fear of indebting himself to the extent that he will not be able to secure an emergency loan from his customary informal source of credit e.g. when the harvest fails. Alternatively, a peasant who is indebted to a formal source, having taken a long-term loan, may be considered a bad risk by informal lenders and may therefore only be able to secure emergency loans at a high rate of interest (comprising a risk premium which is higher than it would be had the peasant not been in formal debt).

The Lender Side

Resistance to technological changes imposed in connection with credit, reluctance to deal with government officials, and fear of losing the informal credit line desperately needed in time of emergency probably constitute the main 'borrower' reasons making organized credit a difficult venture in the countryside. If we turn our attention to the lender side, the most striking feature is the sheer physical impossibility of reaching more than half a million farms with formal credit. There is a lack of the necessary personnel. Lack of agents who are trained to act as credit agents and as extension workers at the same time is common in underdeveloped countries:

> Given the millions of small farmers living in the developing countries, it is essential to recognize the inherent limitations of centrally planned and administered programs. In almost all LDCs it is quite unrealistic to assume that centrally trained and controlled personnel will be able to reach more than a very small fraction of these farmers. In order to expand beyond this minuscule coverage, it will certainly be necessary to rely on the farmers' own motivations and leadership potential. To this end it is worth the time and energy required to gain detailed information concerning local conditions, especially the informal economic system, and to attempt to adapt government programs to these conditions. The incorporation of farmers into the planning process could easily introduce data on local conditions as well as develop local leadership. The cost of not adopting this approach is often virtual failure of government programs to penetrate the countryside in any significant way.[101]

Nothing of this kind has ever been contemplated in Haiti. Even the limited number of peasants reached by present credit schemes present a problem in terms of extension and credit agents. Again, the IDAI operations provide a good example. In 1972-73 the number of peasants per extension worker in the scheme was: Gonaïves: 148; Mirebalais: 59; Jacmel: 90; Miragoâne: 29; Cayes: 57.[102] Thus, without allowing for any holidays during the year, the maximum number of days that an agent could spend with a peasant per year ranged between 12.5 (Miragoâne) and 2.5 (Gonaïves). To increase lending operations under these circumstances is hardly a feasible proposition.

There are other reasons as well why formal credit has proved unable to reach more than a minuscule number of peasants. Most obvious, given the lack of positive government interest in agriculture, is of course that not enough funds have been allotted to rural credit. Moreover, as the experience of IHCAI during the 1950s (and partly also that of IDAI) demonstrates, when the credit institutes are intended to cover not only agriculture, but other sectors as well, there has been a strong tendency to concentrate on lending to the other sectors where it is comparatively easier to calculate the risks, to obtain collateral, and to lend larger sums at one time. Outright diversion and embezzlement of funds has also taken place, not least, as it appears, in connection with co-operative lending operations.

The above reasons cannot, however, explain why for example IDAI has not been able to utilize the entire volume of authorized credit but often has advanced far less to the peasants. (Cf. Table 11.5.) This must be explained in other ways. The first explanation is that the characteristics of the supply of formal credit do not match the requirements of the peasants. We saw in the sections on the demand for credit and on informal credit that the most important credit need among the peasants is that of *consumption*, not production, credit. When it comes to enhancing their production potential, the peasants prefer to invest in land, not in capital, and the usual mechanism for assembling enough funds for land purchases appears to be by 'trading up' via successive purchases of animals (although as Table 11.1 reveals, these purchases to a certain extent may be financed by loans in the informal credit markets as well). Credit is demanded mainly to satisfy consumption needs, especially during the dead season in agriculture.

The credit offered by the formal institutions, on the other hand, is concentrated on production, nothing else. Also, it is difficult for a formal lending institution to compete with the versatility and timeliness of delivery of the informal sources.[103] Formal credit is likely to be formal also in the sense that its use is strictly supervised and monitored by the credit agency to avoid diversion from its prescribed use. This may make it difficult for the peasants to use what is given as production credit for consumption instead even though the need for the latter, as perceived by the peasants, is much greater than the need for the former. Formal credit programs usually fail to cover *all* the needs of the peasants, and the latter therefore remain dependent on the informal sources for what they themselves consider the most essential forms of credit while the forms offered in the institutional market fail to meet with any demand, especially if the procedures required to obtain them are too bureaucratic.

Two other factors are of interest in this context. The first is that the bureaucrats within the lending institutions are likely to be risk minimizers in a certain sense. For example, they are likely to attempt to minimize the default rate by extending loans mainly to peasants whom they consider safe. Showing too high a default rate may affect their own possibilities of advancement inside or outside the organization, whereas underutilization of the lending capacity can always be defended on 'safety' grounds. Hence, as was the case with IHCAI, creditworthiness is stressed, and comparatively few peasants are reached.

In a way, emphasis on safety may be regarded as a 'sound' policy. The probability of a formal credit organization without intimate knowledge of the local scene to attracting the 'lemons', i.e. the bad credit risks, is much higher than the probability that the local, informal lenders will do the same thing. The latter possess a strong comparative advantage when it comes to sorting out good risks from bad ones.[104] This in turn means that the probability that the formal institution will make a loss on a given loan transaction is higher than the possibility that this will occur for the informal lender. Hence, the ruin probability of the formal credit institution may be relatively high. This of course can be compensated for by authorizing a higher level of capital for lending purposes, but unless the organization is able to 'learn' efficiently about the conditions prevailing on the local scene, the rate of defaults may continue to be high.[105] Naturally, in this type of situation, and especially if bureaucratic procedures impede efficient learning, there should be a strong tendency among credit agents to restrict lending to 'safe' borrowers. Alternatively, the administration costs per gourde loaned become unduly high.

High default rates are known to have been a problem for the government-sponsored lending organizations in Haiti. In 1972-73, for example, after 12 years of operation, 57 percent of the loans granted by IDAI had not been paid back. (Four years earlier, the figure was even higher: 85 percent.)[106] Repayment constitutes a severe problem especially during years of comparatively bad harvests:

> it will be necessary to consider the difficulties which the farmers may have during the years when the harvests are unsatisfactory. In this case one ought to design a system for amortization over several years. It may be the case that, fearing an inability to pay, the farmers solicit a loan which is smaller than necessary, and that thus they cannot employ the necessary amounts of insecticides and fertilizer. In addition, it may well be the case that due to this the areas benefiting from the credit also remain very small.[107]

However, the niggardliness of nature expressed in the form of a crop failure is probably not the only reason behind the high default rates, but — and this is the second factor referred to above — the likelihood that the peasants conceive of institutional credit as something ephemeral is high. Several of the most important agricultural lending institutions have been liquidated long before their programs had any real impact. This might easily have set a poor precedent among the peasants, for if the credit program in question is perceived as temporary and unreliable, the risk of default is high.[108] The loans taken may then be thought of, not as loans which are to be repaid at a future date, but as gifts, especially in the case where no real sanctions against default exist (frequently the only one being that no new credit can be obtained),[109] when there is a lack of identification between the peasants and their government so that no moral obligation to repay is felt by the former,[110] or when expectations that the program will not continue arise out of the fact that the peasants perceive the interest rates as subsidized and hence doubt the economic viability of the scheme.[111]

The final reason for the inability to utilize lending capacity fully is that, at least in the case of IDAI, lending costs, or rather the extension costs in connection with the program of technological change, have been too high. Since each loan under the supervised credit scheme is tied to technological change, technical assistance has to be given to the peasants covered by the scheme, and this is a very costly affair. Table 11.6 shows the cost of technical assistance in comparison to the production value per gourde loaned by each of the five local branches of IDAI. In three of the branches, Jacmel, Miragoâne and Cayes, the cost of the technical assistance exceeds the market value of the production made possible by the loans.*

Table 11.6: The Costs of Technical Assistance under the IDAI Supervised Credit Scheme 1972-3

Branch	Technical assistance cost per gourde loaned	Production value per gourde loaned
Gonaïves	4.16	7.1
Mirebalais	2.80	5.0
Jacmel	8.46	5.9
Miragoâne	17.47	4.77
Cayes	4.03	1.62

Source: Giles (1973), pp. 41, 48.

Actually, the figures presented in Table 11.6 probably represent an overstatement of the profitability of the IDAI scheme. To arrive at value-added figures for each of the five regions, we would have to deduct the value of inputs purchased, which would lower the values in the right-hand column considerably. To judge the social profitability of the lending scheme, of course a cost-benefit analysis ought to be undertaken, which, however, for lack of data cannot be done here, although judging from the magnitudes of Table 11.6, it does not *a priori* appear very likely that the indirect benefits of the scheme would be great enough to make up for the high administration costs. If so, it is also quite understandable if the local IDAI branches are somewhat reluctant to expand the scale of their operations.**

Summing up: formal credit has failed to reach more than a minuscule fraction of the Haitian peasants. This may be explained both from the borrower side and from the lender side. In the first place, the peasants have proved unwilling to take loans for productive purposes when obtaining a loan simultaneously requires that farm technology be changed. Secondly, they are likely to distrust people from public agencies, and finally, they may not want to jeopardize their traditional credit lines upon which they have to fall back in times of emergency.

---

*However, the figures for Cayes are largely due to climatic factors (Giles (1973), p. 56).
**It is of course always possible to let each extension agent handle a large number of peasants, but this is only likely to further decrease the efficiency of the lending scheme.

On the lender side, the most obvious constraint is the lack of trained credit and extension personnel. It is simply not possible to reach more than a small number of peasants with the existing cadres when credit is tied to technological change. The lack of positive government interest in agriculture explains why comparatively little money has been devoted to rural credit. To this we also have to add diversion and embezzlement of funds.

Some of the lending institutions have not been able to utilize their entire lending capacity. The formal credit organizations have concentrated on production loans whereas it is consumption credit that is mainly demanded by the peasants. Thus, demand and supply characteristics do not match. In addition, the lending institutions themselves may have been reluctant to expand the scope of their operations. The probability that formal credit institutions attract a high percentage of bad risks among their borrowers is high in a situation where knowledge regarding local conditions is required, which in turn may lead to a high default rate. The rate of default may also be high due to the fact that the peasants may perceive formal credit as temporary and unreliable, because they feel no moral obligation to pay back borrowed funds as there are no effective sanctions against default, etc. Finally, the lending costs of at least some of the organizations coupling credit with technological change have proved to be extremely high, to the point where they exceed the value of the output generated by the credit.

Conclusions

The basic problem discussed in the present chapter is why capital formation is deficient in Haitian agriculture. Capital formation in principle may be financed in three different ways: by saving, by borrowing in the informal credit markets, and by borrowing from formal lending institutions. Few peasants are able to save effectively in the Haitian economy, and those who can save generally prefer to accumulate landed assets instead of farm production capital. There is a general scarcity of funds for capital formation in the Haitian countryside.

Very little borrowing for capital formation purposes appears to take place in the informal credit markets. The peasants tend to borrow mainly for consumption purposes rather than for the purpose of enhancing their production potential. The most typical loans presumably are those which run only for a short time and which are designed to carry the peasants and their families over the dead season before the coffee harvest brings in cash.

The high interest rates prevailing in the informal markets constitute an important obstacle to borrowing for production purposes. The peasants typically have a high rate of time preference in the short run. Taking a short-term loan against a high rate of interest is probably a better way of ensuring short-run consumption needs than for example selling and repurchasing assets, due to what appears to be high transaction costs in connection with the latter type of operations. In the longer perspective, on the other hand, the rate of time preference is likely to be lower, since per capita incomes show a tendency towards secular stagnation and decrease. Hence, to protect themselves, the peasants who are able to, buy land which, given the low-yield traditional technology, may be the best way of adding to their production potential.

Their demand for long-term credit to finance capital formation, on the other hand, is likely to be low. Against this we have to set the behavior of the lenders. The main element behind the high interest rates in the informal credit markets seems to be risk, and the longer the duration of the loan, the more risky the latter is likely to be in the eyes of the lender, and hence, the higher will be the risk premium demanded. In this situation, it is quite possible that long-term demand and supply schedules never intersect. The lenders may demand a far higher rate of interest than what the borrowers are willing to pay.

No capital formation is financed out of informal borrowing. The formal credit institutions, on their part, have not been able to reach more than a tiny fraction of the peasants. Borrowing for production is not likely to be profitable for the peasants unless their technology is changed, but the attempts to couple credit and technological change have hardly produced any substantial results. For reasons to be dealt with in Chapter 12, the peasants have a strong tendency to resist innovations, and in the present context this also means that they resist formal credit. In addition, they are likely to lack confidence in the government in general and may also feel that they cut themselves off from traditional consumption credit sources by contracting formal debts. The lending institutions themselves are faced with a number of supply constraints, the most important of which are probably the tendency to attract a high percentage of bad risks among borrowers (which is conducive to a high rate of defaults) and the tendency to be faced with unduly high lending costs when credit is tied to technological change.

A second important conclusion which has emerged from the present chapter is that the high rates of interest prevailing in the informal credit markets are not likely to be the result of usury or monopolistic practices. The Haitian peasants do not seem to be exploited by moneylenders, but the rural credit markets appear to be fairly competitive in

Problems of Rural Credit

the same way as the markets for commodities, land and labor.

The Haitian peasants act rationally in the sense that they do their best to protect themselves against the secular tendency for per capita incomes to fall by accumulating land. This is probably the best they can do, given the traditional technology. At the same time they finance some of their current consumption needs by borrowing in the informal credit markets for shorter periods. Long-term borrowing for the purpose of capital formation in agriculture, on the other hand, has not proved to be a viable proposition. The informal credit markets have a tendency to break down when it comes to long-term loans. Supply and demand may not be equaled. Formal credit has foundered, largely due to the resistance of the peasants to technological change and due to the administrative problems of uniting such change with credit, but also due to the general reluctance of the Haitian governments to attack agricultural problems vigorously. Capital formation in Haitian peasant agriculture remains an urgent problem.

Notes

1. Cf. the introduction to Chapter 12.
2. Lewis (1955), p. 227.
3. Cf. Métraux et al. (1951), annex II; BTS, no. 24, March 1957, pp. 15-60; BID (1974), p. 152.
4. Herskovits (1971), pp. 131-6; Bastien (1951), p. 141; Courlander (1960), pp. 112, 116; Underwood (1964), passim; JWK (1976:4), pp. 1, 11, 33-4; Zuvekas (1978), p. 41.
5. Mintz, (1966), p. xxvii. Cf. Hubert (1950), p. 18.
6. Wood (1963), p. 21.
7. Métraux et. al. (1951), p. 30. Cf. Bastien (1951), p. 484.
8. Schaedel (1962), pp. 105, 107.
9. Courlander (1960), p. 112. Cf. also the argument in Underwood (1964), passim.
10. Ibid., p. 116. Cf. also Wingfield & Parenton (1965), p. 346; Casimir (1965), pp. 51-2; Schaedel (1962), p. 17; Herskovits (1971), pp. 135-6; Moral (1961), p. 209.
11. Mintz (1964), pp. 272-4.
12. Cf. Long (1968:2), note, p. 997.
13. Ibid., p. 1000.
14. Cf. Baker (1973), p. 47.
15. Cf. Métraux et al. (1951), p. 130; Holly (1955), p. 235; Rotberg & Clague (1971), p. 280.
16. See e.g. Moral (1961), p. 247; Mintz (1961:1), p. 58.
17. Mintz (1961:1), pp. 58-9.
18. See e.g. Domínguez (1976), p. 23.
19. Laguerre (1976:2). Rotating credit associations are common in less developed countries. For a sample of descriptions see the papers collected in Spring Review (1973:1).
20. Métraux et. al. (1951), pp. 130, 131.

21. Cf. Fisher (1930), especially Chapter IV. Expositions of the Fisherian theory can also be found in Hirshleifer (1970), passim; Lutz (1967), Chapter 7. Frisch (1964) makes an interesting comparison.
22. Fisher (1930), p. 62.
23. Cf. Métraux et. al. (1951), p. 130.
24. Cf. the situation when land is to be inherited (ibid., pp. 25-6).
25. Ibid., p. 26.
26. Ibid., p. 20.
27. Moral (1961), p. 179.
28. Fisher (1930), pp. 78-9.
29. Ibid., p. 77.
30. Cf. Bottomley (1971), pp. 81 ff.
31. Moore (1972), p. 243.
32. Ibid., pp. 243-4.
33. Ibid., p. 237.
34. Ibid., p. 239.
35. IBRD (1972), p. 27.
36. IBRD (1974), p. 40.
37. See e.g. IFS, March 1961, p. 29; March 1963, p. 29; March 1974, p. 26, and January 1977, p. 25. Cf. also IBRD (1974), p. 41.
38. Cf. Bottomley (1971), pp. 101 ff.
39. Métraux et al. (1951), pp. 130-31. Cf. Holly (1955), p. 235.
40. Bottomley (1971), p. 102.
41. Cf. Wolf (1966), Chapter 1.
42. Bottomley (1971), pp. 106-7.
43. Tun Wai (1957). pp. 109-10. Cf. Bhaduri (1977), p. 342.
44. Cf. Métraux et al. (1951), p. 130; Mintz (1961:1), p.58.
45. Cf. Holly (1955), p. 234.
46. Mintz (1961:1), p. 58.
47. Cf. Bottomley (1971), pp. 99-100. For a discussion and criticism of Bottomley's arguments, see Lundahl (1974), pp. 228-30.
48. Cf. Bottomley (1971), pp. 95-6.
49. Mintz (1964), pp. 271-4.
50. Ibid., p. 272.
51. Ibid., p. 274.
52. A discussion of this problem can be found in most standard textbooks. See e.g. Musgrave (1959), pp. 295 ff. or Shoup (1969), pp. 275 ff.
53. For example UN (1949), p. 92; Métraux et al. (1951), p. 131, and Rotberg & Clague (1971), p. 280. The latter are ambivalent, however, for at the same page it is stated that 'interest rates are so high that a substantial fraction if not all [sic!] of the interest represents a risk premium rather than a return on capital.'
54. Cf. Métraux et al. (1951), pp. 130-31.
55. Brand (1965), p. 40.
56. Schaedel (1962), p. 17; Wingfield & Parenton (1965), p. 346.
57. Brand (1965), p. 30.
58. Moral (1961), p. 176.
59. Cf. Bottomley (1971), pp. 113 ff.
60. Mellor (1966), pp. 318-19.
61. Long (1968:1), p. 280.
62. Ibid., p. 281.
63. Cf. e.g. Griffin (1974), pp. 30-34.
64. Cf. e.g. Bottomley (1971), p. 116.
65. Ibid., pp. 114-15.
66. CUNA (1976), p. 1.

Problems of Rural Credit

67. BIHCAI, Exercises 51-2 & 52-3, p. 13.
68. Ibid., p. 16.
69. BIHCAI, Exercise 55-6, p. 17. Cf. Pierre-Charles (1965), p. 107.
70. CIDA (n.d.), p. 53.
71. Ibid., p. 52; BIHCAI, Exercise 55-6, p. 18.
72. OEA-CEPAL-BID (1962), p. 36.
73. Moore (1972), p. 76.
74. OEA-CEPAL-BID (1962), p. 36.
75. Estimé (1972), p. 63.
76. Ibid., p. 66.
77. Ibid., p. 67.
78. Giles (1973), p. 34.
79. Ibid., pp. 23-4.
80. Ibid., pp. 27, 16.
81. DARNDR (1974-75), pp. 60-61.
82. Ibid., p. 63. The number of farms can be found in Table 2.4 above.
83. Pierre-Charles (1965), p. 108.
84. Moore (1972), p. 167.
85. Ibid.
86. PNUD (1971), p. 11.
87. CUNA (1976), pp. 10-12.
88. Lebeau (1974), p. 47.
89. Rotberg & Clague (1971), p. 289.
90. Vallès (1967), pp. 34-5.
91. Laroche (1969), p. 108.
92. Ibid., p. 110.
93. Long (1973), p. 75.
94. Baker (1973), p. 69.
95. Cf. e.g. Schultz (1964), Chapter 6, (1965), pp. 36-9; Mellor (1966), pp. 179, 193 (1967), p. 46; Long (1968:2), p. 1006; Tinnermeier (1973), pp. 95-6.
96. This point is emphatically stressed by a number of authors dealing with rural credit problems. Cf. e.g. Gayoso (1973), pp. 7-8; Long (1973), pp. 4-5; Tinnermeier (1973), passim.
97. Long (1973), p. 77.
98. Estimé (1972), p. 69. Cf. OEA (1972), p. 349.
99. Rotberg & Clague (1971), pp. 288-9.
100. Gillette & Uphoff (1973), p. 161.
101. Ibid., p. 151.
102. Giles (1973), p. 43.
103. On this point, cf. the examples from other countries provided by Nisbet (1971), pp. 73, 75-80 (1973), p. 6.
104. Cf. Akerlof (1970), pp. 498-9.
105. On this point, cf. the interesting article by Stein (1963).
106. Giles (1973), p. 46.
107. Ibid., p. 45.
108. Baker (1973), p. 53.
109. Long (1973), p. 83.
110. Gillette & Uphoff (1973), p. 161.
111. Baker (1973), p. 55.

12 RESISTANCE TO INNOVATION

'Stage' models of economic development often include technological progress as one of the decisive factors for breaking the vicious circle of low productivity and low per capita incomes. Thus, the celebrated and disputed five-stage model by W.W. Rostow makes the introduction of Newtonian natural science and scientifically-based techniques a major watershed in the transition from the traditional society to the take-off and maturity stages.[1] Likewise, John W. Mellor in a three-stage model of agricultural development envisages a gradual transformation of techniques from the impasse or deadlock in the first, low-productivity phase via growth-generating labor-intensive technologies to a final, technologically highly sophisticated capital-intensive phase, where high productivity is the rule.[2] The stress on technological change is also the main ingredient in the well-known book *Transforming Traditional Agriculture* by Theodore W. Schultz, where it is argued that there are no major inefficiencies in the resource allocation of traditional peasant societies so that consequently no significant changes in the standard of living can be brought about unless modern inputs are substituted for traditional ones.[3]

It is not necessary to state the argument in terms of economic stages to acknowledge that technological change is one of the strongest forces affecting the speed and course of economic growth and development. Few economists would challenge that position.* What is more, today economists are inclined to think that their science is of immediate relevance when it comes to investigating technological change itself:

> By the middle of the 1950s evidence had accumulated which strongly suggested two things: that technological change is a major — many economists would argue *the* major — determinant of the economic growth of rapidly growing economies, and that the forces shaping technological change are, at least to a very large extent, economic,

---

*It is important to keep in mind, however, that in practice the effects of technological change are hard to sort out from other sources of increased input. Discussions of the relative importance of technological change in the growth process tend to be blurred by inherent measurement difficulties and errors. (This problem is discussed in Gould (1972), pp. 295 ff.)

and therefore far from being an exogenous variable, it can be examined and understood directly in terms of economic analysis.[4]

There is no lack of economic models that in one way or another incorporate technical progress as one of the main ingredients of the growth process. However, most of these models take technological change as a given fact. In spite of the undeniable fact that the world abounds with technologically stagnant economies the emphasis among economists has been on the effects of technological change rather than on the sources or, what is even more important for our particular purposes, on the factors that inhibit technological advance. If we are to understand why certain economies develop and others do not, the presence or absence of technical progress cannot be taken for granted. Some kind of systematic treatment of the reasons behind either state must be provided as well, and this is what we will attempt to do in the present chapter, i.e. to examine why the Haitian peasant sector is technologically stagnant.

Before we proceed, we ought to define the subject of our study: innovations or technological change. (The two terms will be used synonymously.) Schematically, two types of innovations may be distinguished: process innovations and product innovations. The latter give rise to new products, while the former allow more of a given commodity to be produced with a given factor input — or equivalently: the same output as before may be produced with a smaller factor input. Both types of change will be discussed.

The first part of the present chapter will be dedicated to a presentation of the empirical picture, i.e. to a description of the technology and the products of Haitian peasant agriculture which with few exceptions have remained unchanged from the early nineteenth century up to the present time, and of how it appears as if even a technological retrogression took place during the course of the nineteenth century. The second part will attempt an analysis of the reasons behind this lack of change, building on some of the findings of earlier parts of this book, especially Chapters 9-11.

The Empirical Picture

Technological Stagnation in Nineteenth-century Haiti

Haiti has never been a technologically dynamic economy, and this is true especially of the agricultural sector. Yet from time to time efforts have been made to change this. As far back as the second decade of the nineteenth century, Henry Christophe, who was very conscious of the crucial role of agriculture for the future welfare of Haiti, tried to put his part of the country on the road to what was at the time a superior agricultural technology. In 1814 he began a correspondence with William Wilberforce, then the parliamentary leader of the British abolitionists. Christophe, who was an admirer of British society, was eager to establish European agricultural methods amongst his own peasantry, and therefore requested that Wilberforce send him British farmers who could act as teachers to the Haitians.[5] Two instructors were sent, and demonstration plots were started in the northern plains, where experimentation with new crops like Irish potatoes, wheat, barley and oats began. Fertilizers were introduced, and new irrigation works were built to substitute for those that had been ruined by the wars of liberation.[6] In addition to the British farming instructors Wilberforce sent plows, which were tried in the Haitian environment.*

Christophe's efforts never brought any success. The new staples did not thrive and the use of the plow failed to become widespread.[7] Christophe was unique in his experiments in planned change. His contemporary, Pétion, followed a radically different agricultural policy in the south, one of non-intervention in peasant life, and when Christophe committed suicide in 1820, the short experiment in innovation — it had lasted less than a full decade — came to an end. Thereafter, the level of technology deteriorated. The nineteenth-century literature on Haiti is rich in descriptions of the state of neglect that reigned in the Haitian countryside. In 1828, James Franklin observed the state of the plantations in the Cayes area:

> the soil has gone into great neglect, and exhibits on the face of it that relaxation in culture which is so general throughout the republic ...the cane plantations are little attended to; they are allowed to go on years in succession without cleaning, without manure, or any other requisite to render them productive...the whole country... exhibits nothing but neglect and waste, and their concomitants, poverty and wretchedness.[8]

He also noticed the depressing aspect of the coffee plantations:

---

*Harvey (1827), pp. 249-51. Haiti had seen the plow before Christophe's time, though. Its use is mentioned by authors from the colonial period (see De Young (1958), p. 51), and it is probable that the Spanish brought it to Haiti. Nevertheless, plowing was not the common practice. The hoe was more efficient at the going price of labor (Rotberg & Clague (1971), note, p. 30).

A person must be somewhat conversant with travelling in Haiti before he can discover on his road that a coffee plantation is near him. For my part I could see nothing that resembled one, nor should I have known the coffee tree, growing as it did in a pyramidal form, surrounded by numberless other shrubs, had it not been for the appearance of a few red berries on its lower branches. I alighted from my mule to examine some trees just around the spot: as nearly as I could ascertain, every tree must have exceeded twelve feet in height, and I am convinced that each of them at the time would not have produced two pounds of coffee in the husk.[9]

The situation was in no way better fourteen years later. In 1842, Victor Schoelcher wrote:

The fields of Haiti are dead. There where under slavery thousands of tons of sugar were made, now one sees only a few crops and a little syrup to turn into raw rum. Lively growths of cactus cover with thorns the acres of cane, of fields of pastures deserted by the hand of man...On the one hand, no one cultivates with regularity, because everyone is discouraged by the thefts of cane and fruit by people without any moral discipline, and in a country without police; while on the other hand, people complain of being poor, and of not being able to devote enough money to indispensable improvements.[10]

Part of the lazy appearance of rural Haiti during the nineteenth century may be explained by the changing factor endowment of the economy. After the revolutionary wars and the subsequent redistribution of plantation land under Pétion and his successors labor and capital became scarce factors while land suddenly was relatively abundant. In that situation it was perfectly natural that agriculture should become less labor- and capital-intensive than during the colonial period. This form of extensive land use may very well have been interpreted as laziness and decay by the foreign visitors to Haiti.

On the other hand, the transition from labor-intensive to land-intensive methods of production appears to have been accompanied by a genuine technological retrogression as well. Cultivation and preparation of agricultural products in both colonial Saint-Domingue and in the Haiti which emerged under Toussaint, Dessalines and Christophe was based on a very rigorous discipline. In the slave society of Saint-Domingue, managers and overseers saw to it that long work hours and a regular work pace was kept. The slaves were driven extremely hard.

Justine Girod-Chantrans, a Swiss traveler, described a slave gang at work in the early 1780s:

> They were about a hundred men and women of different ages, all occupied in digging ditches in a cane-field, the majority of them naked or covered with rags. The sun shone down with full force on their heads. Sweat rolled from all parts of their bodies. Their limbs, weighed down by the heat, fatigued with the weight of their picks and by the resistance of the clayey soil baked hard enough to break their implements, strained themselves to overcome every obstacle. A mournful silence reigned. Exhaustion was stamped on every face, but the hour of rest had not yet come. The pitiless eye of the Manager patrolled the gang and several foremen armed with long whips moved periodically between them, giving stinging blows to all who, worn out by fatigue, were compelled to take a rest — men or women, young or old.[11]

Sugar cultivation, in particular, required hard and steady labor:

> The tropical earth is baked hard by the sun. Round every 'carry' of land intended for cane it was necessary to dig a large ditch to ensure circulation of air. Young canes required attention for the first three or four months and grew to maturity in 14 or 18 months. Cane could be planted and would grow at any time of the year, and the reaping of one crop was the signal for the immediate digging of ditches and the planting of another. Once cut they had to be rushed to the mill lest the juice became acid by fermentation. The extraction of the juice and manufacture of the raw sugar went on for three weeks a month, 16 or 18 hours a day, for seven or eight months in the year.[12]

Forced labor did not end with the liberation from the colonial power. Toussaint, Dessalines and Christophe all made strong efforts to maintain the production potential of the plantation system, which once again necessitated a docile labor force. The ex-slaves were sent back to the fields and were once more attached to the soil with virtually no possibilities of movement from one plantation to another. Work hours were regulated by law, and military supervision in combination with severe punishments guaranteed that the necessary labor effort was forthcoming.

The subsequent disintegration of the plantation system relaxed work discipline. The free Haitians slowed the pace down. Labor became less efficient. There was also a second reason for this, apart from the relaxation of discipline. The plantations had been efficient economic units where the advantages of the division of labor had been employed fairly systematically. Each plantation had concentrated on a single crop which allowed a better development of specialized skills and operations. When the plantation system was superseded by the peasant-owned smallholdings these advantages were lost. The smaller scale of operations did not permit any sophisticated division of labor.

In addition to relaxed work discipline and decreasing specialization, nineteenth-century Haiti also had to face an increasing depreciation of the colonial capital stock without any corresponding replacement. Given that there is a connection between the level of technology and the size and composition of the capital stock, capital disinvestment or replacement of sophisticated capital by less sophisticated will lead to technological retrogression.

The declining productivity of labor and the loss of capital also appear to have affected the productivity of land. Not only did the land/labor ratio increase initially, following independence, but the productivity of agricultural land must have continued to fall for a few decades more in spite of the presence of a growing population. Leyburn gives the following account of land prices during the first half of the nineteenth century:

> In the eighteen-twenties the finest land in the republic did not sell for more than $60 an acre, even when contiguous to a port for shipping or extremely fertile. Such a price would have been ridiculous the days of the French colony. Farms in the plains and mountains, suitable for cocoa and cotton, could be had in Boyer's time for $20 or $30 an acre in any quantity from ten to five hundred acres. In the rich Artibonite Valley small plots for horticultural purposes sold for $40 an acre; indigo and cotton land rarely brought over $30; and a complete cotton plantation which had borne richly in colonial days sold for from $12 to $20 an acre. In the North, despite its fertility and more careful cultivation under Christophe, land seldom brought more than $40 or $45, while pasture lands could scarcely find purchasers at $40...Fifteen years later even these prices were fantastically high, for by then no one was wealthy enough to purchase an estate.[13]

This is hardly what one would expect given the fact that the Haitian population increased from 400,000 in 1805[14] to 600,000 in 1824 and 1.1 million in 1864.[15] With the low degree of urbanization of nineteenth-century Haiti this population growth also meant an increase in the rural labor force. One would expect land prices to rise, not to fall.[16] The figures make sense only if the productivity of land fell during the period.

The adoption of inferior methods of production in the light of the foregoing appears to have been due largely to the transition from forced to free labor, from large specialized plantations to diversified smallholdings, and from sophisticated to less sophisticated capital equipment. The labor force could no longer be driven relentlessly, no longer could certain economies of specialization be realized, and simple general-purpose hand tools became the only important capital input.

The Case of Coffee

An illustration of the technological retrogression during the nineteenth century is found in the case of coffee. During the colonial period the coffee trees of Saint-Domingue 'each...produced on an average a pound weight, equal sometimes to that of Mocha.'[17] So good was the reputation of this coffee that in 1789, Saint-Domingue produced no less than 60 percent of the world's coffee.[18] The French planters had, in fact, pioneered new techniques of coffee cultivation and preparation.[19] The most important operation was that of pruning:

> The entire secret of the Saint-Domingue coffee lies in the pruning technique...Pruning was frequently practiced on the plantations of the colonial period. Numerous advantages were attributed to it: it goes without saying that the picking becomes easier. The tree, we are told, is more wind-resistant. It acquires more vigor, and its inferior branches become those which yield most. Finally, the tree takes on a regular, harmonious form, very agreeable to the eye in the geometric outline of the plantation.[20]

The best drying techniques were very elaborate and comprised no less than seven different operations:

> The coffee first goes into the 'rasping mill', run and fed by a team of 11 Negroes, which depulps the cherries at a pace of 33 barrels per hour — an enormous task, carried out in the evening and recompensed for by the master with a small glass of rum. The washing, in turn, consists in softening the coffee for twenty-four hours by

constantly stirring it in a large decantation basin. The 'slags' that gather on the surface are conducted into a nearby reservoir. When dried and rinsed apart, these yield a coffee of inferior quality. The coffee is then drained again for 24 hours on a platform. Afterwards it is spread out on the cement slab, in the morning before the dew has evaporated. It is raked several times a day, and it is gathered for the night when the rain is threatening in the middle of the platform, in the *bassicot*.* When drying is completed, the coffee 'in pulp' goes to the mill proper. Virtually all the habitations possess one, regardless of the way their coffee is prepared.[21]

Great care was taken to clean the beans and to separate high quality beans from lower grades:

the winnowing of the coffee takes place in a *ventilateur,* reminiscent of those employed in Europe for the winnowing of wheat. Once the coffee is winnowed it is rinsed by hand on long tables. The task alloted to each sorter is 100 pounds per day. The defective and broken beans constitute the *café triage*. Finally, when the coffee is completely prepared, some planters make it pass the mill once more, 'for a dozen turns', in order to give it a shiny aspect, a better character.[22]

Of course, such elaborate methods as those just described were not universally used by the colonial coffee planters. Very often simpler techniques had to suffice.[23] Still, colonial cultivation and preparation practices appear, on the average, to have been superior to those of latter-day Haiti. There are strong indications that the quality of the Haitian coffee deteriorated during the nineteenth century. Table 12.1 shows how the unit values of US imports of Haitian coffee declined in comparison to the unit values of total American coffee imports between 1821 and 1914.[24]

One part of this relative decline may be attributed to improvements in cultivation and preparation methods in competing coffee-producing countries, but it is also likely that the decline was not only relative but absolute as well. The Haitian peasant quickly reached the point where everything except harvesting and drying was left to nature.[25] Obviously, the transition to less labor-intensive cultivation and preparation methods

---

*The *bassicot* was a small, circular masonry construction, where the coffee was covered with banana leaves or cloth.

also implied a technological retrogression: an adoption of inferior methods:

> Judging from the available evidence, the colonial mode of cultivation depended on the careful pruning and the attentive care given to the plantation: cleansing, weeding, elimination of sick bushes, fertilizing with the residuals of the preparation process. Left to itself, the coffee tree would be weakened. It would yield more or less abortive cherries, the *crocros*. It must be added that the coffee plantations were located in the most fertile areas and that a nursery ensured the rejuvenation of the plantation. Only the large plantation which possessed a numerous labor force could satisfy all these technical requirements. The independence and the ruin of the colonial system naturally led to the partial abandonment of the former techniques and modes of cultivation. The cultivators, who were in principle free but threatened with quasi-forced labor on a certain number of large habitations which had been conserved or restored, spread out among the mornes and settled preferably among the dense forests where they at the same time found nourishing fruits in the trees and safe hide-outs. Presumably it was this double compulsion which made the coffee move under the natural cover, where it prospered and where it has remained.[26]

Table 12.1: Unit Values of US Coffee Imports 1821-1914
(US cents per pound)

Year	Haitian unit values (1)	Total unit values (2)	(1):(2)
1821-25	17.00	16.20	1.05
1843-47	5.67	6.16	0.92
1883-87	8.46	8.80	0.96
1910-14	9.05	11.29	0.80

Source: Rotberg & Clague (1971), note, p. 92.

As in the general case, the adoption of inferior methods of coffee production in the light of the foregoing appears to have been due largely to the transition from forced to free labor and from large plantations to smallholdings. The labor force could no longer be driven relentlessly and no longer could certain economies of specialization be realized. When the transition from large specialized plantations to diversified smallholdings took place, the peasants would no longer devote as much time and effort to the cultivation and preparation of coffee as before. The quality of the output declined.*

The Non-transforming Economy

The nineteenth century witnessed the almost complete disintegration of the plantation system in Haiti and its concomitant — a retrogression to less productive cultivation techniques. A *laissez-faire* economy evolved where peasant development was left to take its own course. A static economy was created, one with a strong built-in resistance to change. Nineteenth-century Haiti was what Charles P. Kindleberger calls a 'non-transforming society' where 'consumption and production were carried on in the same way from generation to generation.'[27] Production techniques stagnated at a low technological level, and the structure of peasant output became more or less 'formalized' with food crops for local consumption as the most important item supplemented with coffee for exportation.

The long-term structure of exports provides an excellent illustration of the incapacity of the Haitian economy to develop new products. When the price of coffee declined (see Table 12.1) no new significant exports developed except for logwood (and mahogany).** Significantly, logwood to a very large extent resembled coffee in that it 'required no skill, no long-term investment, and no physical infrastructure to gather and ship abroad.'[28] Otherwise, the major export opportunity in the Caribbean area in the late nineteenth century was the banana. Haiti entirely missed this opportunity, while neighboring Jamaica eagerly seized it and received a strong economic momentum from it between 1890 and 1930.[29]

Only under special circumstances and for shorter periods could new export crops be introduced. During the presidential term of Fabre

---

*The case of coffee also illustrates the influence of the change in overall factor proportions following the expulsion of the French. On the supply side there was a strong tendency towards an increase in the production of land-intensive goods, e.g. low-quality coffee. On the demand side it is likely that there was a shift towards a larger consumption of foodstuffs, which are fairly labor-intensive. Simultaneously the demand for high-quality coffee declined due to the cut-off of important export markets following independence. Hence, most of the labor went into food production while coffee increasingly became a land-intensive product of inferior quality. (Cf. the discussion in Chapters 5 and 6.)

**Actually, both were exported during the colonial period, but only in insignificant volumes. (Cf. Chapter 5.).

Resistance to Innovation 567

Geffrard (1859-67) cotton* prices rose enormously due to the northern blockade of southern harbors during the American Civil War.[30] To take advantage of this increase Geffrard began a program of incentives for the cotton-growing industry. Irrigation facilities that had been in ruins since the expulsion of the French were repaired, certain machinery was made available to cotton planters, and around 2,000 colored immigrants were brought in from the United States to be given land for cotton cultivation.[31] Cotton exports (in quantity terms) increased fivefold between 1860 and 1864,[32] but it is probable that this expansion was more due to the astronomical price increase than to governmental stimulation devices, since once cotton prices dropped to 'normal' levels, cotton exports from Haiti once more became insignificant.**

Another, even less successful, attempt to introduce new export crops was made by President Salomon in 1883, when five to eight carreaux of government land were granted to anybody who undertook to cultivate sugar, coffee, cotton, cocoa or tobacco for a period of two to five years. In spite of 1,700 recorded applications during the first two years of the scheme, the program eventually failed. Incentives were simply not strong enough. In the absence of such spectacular price increases as in the case of cotton 25 years earlier, the peasants felt that they needed financial support in addition to the land grants, but no such support was ever given by the government.[33]

Such were the conditions on the eve of the American intervention in 1915. The technological transition to simple methods had been completed and no efforts to upgrade peasant techniques or to introduce new crops had been made for 30 years. Peasant Haiti had reached an almost stationary state where the variations in production and consumption patterns basically were geared to the growth of the population and to the development of the world market price of coffee.

Change without Success

The landing of the American Marine Corps in 1915 marked the end of the period of non-intervention in peasant life. During the 1922-29 period, after the *caco* uprisings had been crushed and a reorganization of Haitian finances and administration had taken place, and before the riots and strikes that eventually led to the American withdrawal from

---

*Cotton was really not a 'new' export product. It had been exported during the colonial period, but Pétion's land reform had put an end to cotton exports. (Cf. Chapters 2 and 6.)

**See Rotberg & Clague (1971), pp. 389-90. The settlement scheme also failed. Very few of the American immigrants remained in Haiti (Moore (1972), p. 265).

Haiti had commenced, a strong effort was made to modernize Haiti along American lines.

As we saw in Chapter 10, there was a strong tendency among American officials to identify all Haitians with the peasants, while no attention was paid to the Haitian elite. On the practical plane this was translated into a strong interest in agricultural development. The main emphasis lay on education. We have already discussed the changes in formal primary education. Measures to improve the teaching of agricultural methods in other ways were also taken. At Damien a Central Agricultural School was built to teach modern cultivation techniques to students of agriculture and to provide a suitable education for future teachers in rural (primary) schools. An estimated 400 agriculturalists and teachers received their training at Damien up to 1930.[34]

The main problem with the Central School was that all the students came from urban areas and had a background with an emphasis on classical studies and literature. Recruitment of students proved to be an outright headache. Since no peasant boys had a sufficient preparation for entering the school, only the city group remained, and this group was very reluctant to work with its hands. The curriculum particularly stressed manual activities and in order to overcome this reluctance, students had to be procured by means of attractive scholarships. Even so, the number of teachers in farm schools remained insufficient in relation to the number of pupils. The educational standard in these schools suffered, and the Service Technique deemed this to be an unsatisfactory situation. Besides, the Damien graduates were city boys, while it was felt that rural teachers should come from rural areas. On the other hand, the students coming from the farm schools were not sufficiently prepared to enter Damien. To bridge the gap a secondary agricultural school was opened in 1928 at Chatard. Ten boys from the oldest farm schools of the country were selected.* The school never had any impact, however, since by the time it was started only one year of effective efforts on the part of the Service Technique remained.

Formal education in agriculture was supplemented with methods designed to reach the peasants directly in their rural environment. In 1927, evening classes to teach adult Haitians better agricultural methods were begun, and two years later, 16 rural evening schools had reached an enrolment of 635 students, but most of these were ex-literates who wanted to relearn what years of lack of practice had undone.[35]

---

*Service Technique (1929:1), p. 87. The funds available did not permit a larger number of boys to be accommodated at the school.

However, the main instrument for reaching the peasants was the extension agent system. Thirteen agents made 4,000 visits to Haitian peasants in 1927.* In 1929, the number of agents had increased to 16 and in addition an agricultural extension department with 34 Haitian supervisors and demonstration agents had been created.[36]

Fairs and demonstration farms were also used. Experiments with new equipment and modern, sophisticated techniques were presented at five experiment stations where a variety of new crops like tobacco, pineapple, bananas and new strains of cotton[37] were also tested and introduced to the peasants.** Special care was also taken to improve the country's main export, coffee. Before 1926, ten coffee demonstration farms had been established and in 1927, a coffee experiment station was started. The principal aim of the coffee program was to ensure a steady and rising export income, and as an important part of this program an attempt to standardize the different grades of Haitian coffee was begun in 1928.[38]

Education and introduction of new techniques and products dominated the activities of the Service Technique in the agricultural sphere, but some other measures were taken as well. The Service sponsored the first geological and soil quality survey ever to be undertaken in Haiti,[39] and the Public Works Service rebuilt and extended some of the irrigation works mainly in the Cul-de-Sac plain.[40]

Taken at face value, the achievements of the American occupation force in raising the technological level in agriculture appear to be fairly good, if not overly impressive. In reality, the occupation changed virtually nothing in the peasant sector, and with the exception of the introduction of sisal and the establishment of the Central Agricultural School at Damien (which established the prestige of agronomy in Haiti) the rest of the agricultural sector was left virtually untouched. Haiti was as dependent on coffee for export incomes as before the occupation. The peasants continued to use the same primitive methods as ever before. Melville J. Herskovits after his 1934 visit to the Mirebalais

---

*This means that on the average each agent had to make almost 308 visits.
**Experimentation with new crops was not only a means for peasant development and diversification of export. Of more than equal importance was the fact that one of the cornerstones of American agricultural development policy in Haiti was to stimulate the inflow of American capital in order the create a plantation economy. Hence, the Service Technique took a very active part in the development of sisal production in the Fort-Liberté area and strong efforts were also made to promote the installation of American-owned rubber plantations in Haiti. (See Schmidt (1971), pp. 175, 177; Rotberg & Clague (1971), p. 136. An account of the development of Plantation Dauphin is given in Pettigrew (1958).)

district noted that the Haitian economy showed a lack of specialization 'that in the main [was] only relieved by the sex division of labor,'[41] and after a seven-month field trip three years later George Eaton Simpson concluded that

> not more than eight or ten of the four or five thousand families in the Commune of Plaisance were cultivating their fields in the manner recommended by the Agricultural Service. These persons were using spading forks instead of hoes to prepare the soil for planting, they were planting coffee and bananas properly, rotating their crops, and using some drainage.[42]

Most of the peasants, according to Simpson

> [needed] instruction in how to cultivate bananas and other crops. This is not a simple proposition because the habits of generations are well established, and the agricultural agent's task is not only to demonstrate new methods of cultivation, but to inveigle the peasant into trying them.[43]

In spite of some apparent success in coffee pruning demonstrations very little of lasting value had been accomplished, and the peasants 'in most cases...[continued] in their old ways.'[44]

Change and Resistance during the Post-occupation Period

Resistance to change has continued to prevail during the post-occupation period. In 1959 William B. Gates summarized the state of production technology in coffee cultivation:

> The long list of poor peasant practices in Haitian coffee culture has been well-known for at least eighty years, and, in fact, seems to have remained about the same. Dependence on natural seeding rather than selection in nurseries; poorly planned shade cover; plants too close together; little mulching and no use of fertilizer;...inadequate pruning and cleaning; poor use of available land and jumbling together of various crops with little attention to soil adaptation. So it goes...right on thru improper harvesting methods and careless preparation.[45]

These poor practices survive in spite of many government efforts to introduce better methods. In the mid-1930s, when an attempt was made by the Vincent government to penetrate the American coffee market (following a severe fall in coffee export prices between 1925 and 1933 and the suspension of the commercial treaty with France in 1936), washing, better drying processes and extended care in the preparation of coffee beans for export were introduced. Demonstration farms were set up to propagate the new techniques, and new varieties of coffee seeds were given away without charge.[46] This effort to upgrade the quality of the Haitian coffee was sustained and reinforced throughout the 1930s, and in 1942, President Lescot issued a *Code du Café* which in detail regulated cultivation, transportation, storage, processing and marketing.[47] New improvement programs were launched in 1946 and 1951 as parts of the Estimé revolution and the first five-year agricultural plan respectively.[48] All these attempts led to nothing but 'minor, fleeting victories' at best.[49] The peasants continued to use their old methods and resisted change. Christopher K. Clague checked the percentage of Haitian coffee that is washed to yield a superior quality and found that (including the few larger coffee plantations) this percentage grew from a feeble 3 percent in 1929 to an average of 9 percent in the 1950s and to 12 percent in 1967. These figures may be compared with a rapid spread of the washing practice in Jamaica after 1942 to a figure of about 95 percent in 1965. Neither does a long-term comparison of the prices of Haitian and Brazilian coffee indicate any other quality improvements.[50]

The same picture of technological stagnation emerges in virtually every study or report from the immediate post-occupation period up to our time. In 1949, the UN mission to Haiti gave the following description:

> The typical peasant cultivates his land with a hoe and a machete, almost his only farming tools. He plants his land with the same crop year after year – sometimes two or three crops a year. His seed is often poor, and his yields are low. He uses no fertilizer or animal manures, and usually burns the crop residue instead of adding it to the soil. As a consequence, much of the land of Haiti is worn out, and produces only inferior crops of probably reduced nutritive value.[51]

The prime vehicle of technological change and innovation during the 1950s was the American Point Four program. This had started in 1944[52] as a program intended to overcome the disruptions in agricultural production due to the Second World War, and was subsequently expanded to include an enlarged agricultural program as well. Basically, each technician of the Point Four program was to 'disseminate his technical knowledge and skills through his work in the field as an advisor and "counter-part" to Haitian technicians.'[53] The Point Four agricultural program was administered via a specialized agency in the Department of Agriculture – the *Service Coopératif Interaméricain de Production d'Aliments* (SCIPA).

The emphasis of SCIPA lay in what may be termed the purely technical aspects of agriculture: in irrigation works, improvement of storage and of conservation methods, introduction of better crops, improved livestock, better tools, soil and water conservation and extension work.[54] Only a modest success was achieved. A certain amount of change could be introduced at a high cost directly in the areas where SCIPA operated, while the spread effects emanating from the project areas proved to be very weak.[55]

Since the 1950s, most foreign assistance programs in the agricultural sector have contained technological change as one of their main ingredients. Efforts to improve the technological level of the Haitian peasant sector are constantly being made by indigenous, foreign and international organizations. Some are promising, while others are not.[56] However, the technological balance still weighs heavily on the archaic side. In comparison with for example their Dominican or Jamaican neighbors, the Haitians have shown an extremely high degree of resistance to change in their choice of techniques and inputs.[57] To an overwhelming extent the peasant sector must be characterized as a capital-starved hoe and machete economy, and except under special circumstances there is still not very much to distinguish it from the Haitian peasant mode of cultivation of a century or more ago. As Paul Moral has observed, some of the practices closely resemble those of the colonial period:

> The rice harvest in the lower Artibonite, for example, still takes place in the same way as that described by Descourtilz one-and-a-half centuries ago: 'With the nail the cultivator separates the ear from the stalk and then puts it into a basket which he carries on his other arm. The ears are left to dry, and then the chaff is separated from the rice by pounding in a mortar.'. . .The cutting of sugar cane into pieces of about one meter, the packing of the pieces, and their loading on the 'carbrouets'* constitute activities which have remained

---

*A *cabrouet* is a two-wheel chariot used to transport sugar cane, and is drawn by two or four oxen.

unchanged for a century.⁵⁸

Moral also observes that those techniques which have been preserved are by no means those that prevailed on the plantations during the 'golden age' of Saint-Domingue, but rather those that were used during the 'pioneering phase of the colonization'⁵⁹ and that were later to characterize the plots allotted to the slaves for their subsistence.

Harold Courlander makes the same observations:

> Technological developments were slow to reach Haiti; and having reached Haiti they were regarded as largely irrelevant to Haitian life. In fact, even some of the rudimentary technology of a century or more ago remains irrelevant.⁶⁰

Hence, it is clear that Haiti has got a long way to go towards an efficient agricultural technology. At the same time it is evident that there is a clash between superior techniques on the one hand and peasant society and behavior on the other. Given the abject poverty of the peasants this may strike the observer as surprising:

> Haitian peasants are desperately poor, and the output per man and acre of their tiny plots is low when compared with nearly all other Latin American and Asian countries. Yet there are techniques capable of yielding markedly higher outputs per unit of input than those obtained by most Haitian peasants.* But these techniques are

---

*Cf. e.g. the following list of possibilities, gathered by Ronald L. Tinnermeier:
  1. new water management techniques for storing and using water, including the economics of small-scale irrigation projects;
  2. water-nutrient interactions for crops presently grown on small farms as well as those with potential, i.e., horticultural crops, fruits and nuts, especially under less than ideal rainfall or irrigated conditions;
  3. new output-increasing techniques for the more traditional crops such as cassava, potatoes and legumes and for livestock activities;
  4. information on the sensitivity of yields to land preparation and timing;
  5. feeding rations utilizing the increased output from the traditional crops;
  6. seeds with high yields but with less variation under different climatic conditions;
  7. new animal powered farm implements;
  8. mechanical tillers and other small power implements, as needed;
  9. low-cost and effective on-farm storage and drying facilities;
  10. new techniques of multiple- and inter-cropping to increase incomes and reduce risk;
  11. techniques for improving managerial skills.
(Tinnermeier (1973), p. 100.)

not widely adopted, and it is important to ask why.[61]

We now turn to the analysis of this question.

The Causes[62]

Population Growth: An Inducement to Innovation in Agriculture

In any predominantly agrarian society it is possible to define an optimum population density. With a given technology and a given input of land, this density is where output per head of the agrarian population is maximized.[63] If the rural population grows, output per capita in agriculture will gradually fall, and sooner or later the fall will be perceived as severe enough to trigger off some type of response mechanism designed to reestablish the former optimum or to reach a new optimum position.

These responses may be of various kinds.[64] The most obvious one is perhaps that the overpopulated community attempts to reduce its numbers by lowering birth rates or by increasing the rate of migration. The latter appears to be the way chosen in Haiti, as we will see in the epilogue, while birth rates have not been visibly affected.* Another common response is to extend the area under cultivation. This response is simple to carry out since it requires no change of techniques. The increase in the labor force can simply be added to new land in the same proportions as before. In Chapter 5 we mentioned that this was probably the most frequent practice during the nineteenth century while uncultivated land was still available. Finally, new crops and technologies may be substituted for the old ones.

In an admirable little book on economic-demographic change in agrarian societies Ester Boserup has shown how in a long-run perspective population growth may act as an inducement to technological change.** She specifically sets out to explain the gradual shortening of the fallow period from a minimum of 20 or 25 years under conditions of shifting agriculture (forest-fallow) to only a few months in systems of annual cropping and its final disappearance in multicropping systems where two or more crops are grown annually. The process of shortening

---

*Mortality may also increase, but this is hardly a 'voluntary' response.
**Boserup (1965). A similar view is given by Julian L. Simon, who in a sample of 48 countries found that there was a tendency for increasing pressure of population on cultivated land to lead to a higher proportion of irrigated land out of the total cultivated area (Simon (1975)). A critique of Boserup is found in Diebold (1968).

the fallow period is also a process of technological change according to Boserup, so that the transition from forest-fallow to bush-fallow (a fallow period of six to ten years) and from there to short-fallow (one or two years), annual cropping and multi-cropping may be interpreted as a series of shifts in the production function.

The triggering mechanism in the Boserup schema is the growth of population, which is taken as an exogenous variable. As population grows and the man/land ratio increases in agrarian districts the system of land use changes in the direction of shorter fallow periods. When this happens the set of agricultural tools and methods changes as well. In shifting forest-fallow cultivation trees have to be cut down using axes or are burned together with the short vegetation. Sowing and planting is done in the ashes with a simple tool such as a digging stick. When the period of fallow is shortened to leave only bushes and grass before the fields are cleared a hoe must be used to turn the soil over before planting and sowing can take place. Mere burning would be inefficient in this system since when the natural grass content of the vegetation increases, the grass roots will have to be destroyed too before other plants can be put in the ground. This problem becomes more and more important as the period of fallow is shortened, and after a point the introduction of the plow becomes necessary. As cultivation is further intensified, methods to preserve or regain soil fertility have to be introduced, and fertilization and irrigation techniques as well as careful weeding practices are employed. Hence, there is an appropriate set of tools and methods according to each type of fallow, designed to cope with the particular problems of the fallow system in question.

The Boserup schema must not be conceived of as rigid. It is quite possible that a 'stage' in the process outlined is omitted. Frequently, population growth may become so rapid that the plow is never introduced. Instead the number of years when the soil is cultivated in the bush-fallow fashion is increased and when no further increase is possible a direct transition to annual or multicropping with retention of the hoe-based technology takes place. It is also possible, and even likely, that various stages may coexist at the same time, since when transition begins it first affects those lands that are best suited for the stage to come, while other lands are lagging behind.

Where does Haiti belong in the Boserup schema? The overall man/land ratio in rural areas is fairly high, one of the highest in the Caribbean area with a rural population per hectare of arable land around 2.5 persons at the beginning of the 1970s. The growth rate of the population (excluding migration) is 2 percent, which is a high figure given the quality of the land. The technological picture is a divided one. Multicropping is the rule, and the plow is seldom found, which indicates a jump from bush-fallow directly into annual cropping and multicropping. On the other hand, neither fertilizer nor irrigation is commonly employed. Instead, when soil exhaustion is deemed to have reached unacceptable proportions, fallow is resorted to, for periods up to five years. This is in turn more reminiscent of bush-fallow.*

It is obvious that Haitian agriculture is in some kind of incomplete transition into the multicropping stage. Such a transition is probably not an uncommon occurrence in the underdeveloped world. Ester Boserup states that

> If it is true, as suggested here, that certain types of technical change will occur only when a certain density of population has been reached, it does of course not follow, conversely, that this technical change will occur whenever the demographic prerequisite is present. It has no doubt happened in many cases that a population, faced with a critically increasing density was without knowledge of any types of fertilization techniques. They might then shorten the period of fallow without any other changes in methods. This constellation would typically lead to a decline of crop yields and sometimes to an exhaustion of land resources. The population would then have to face the choice between starvation and migration.[65]

For reasons that we will now examine, the forces emanating from the increasing pressure of the population on the land have not been strong enough to overcome the forces opposing the technological transformation in Haiti, and this has precluded any check to the slowly decreasing per capita incomes in the rural sector as population growth proceeds.

In the remainder of this chapter we will devote our energies to the investigation of those factors that have been acting as prohibitive obstacles to innovations. First we will make some observations on the inherent difficulties of agricultural technological change and then go on to consider some other binding constraints on the innovation process.

The Limited Scope for Innovations in Agriculture

In the first chapter of *The Wealth of Nations* Adam Smith makes the observation that technological progress in agriculture seems to proceed at a slower pace than innovation in manufacturing industry.[66] Partly,

---

*Boserup puts the lower limit for this system at six years.

of course, these differences may stem from such obstacles that we are to discuss later, but there are also some differences that are due to the inherent characteristics of the production process in each branch. These differences have been stressed most notably by Nicholas Georgescu-Roegen in various contexts, but also by others before him.[67]

Organic and Inorganic Matter. On the most fundamental level we have the fact that agriculture deals with the processing of organic or living matter, while industrial production in the main is concentrated to inorganic substances. There is a 'lasting obstacle to man's manipulating living matter as efficaciously as inert matter.'[68] Biology abounds in astronomically large numbers. The structure of living cells is infinitely more complex than that of inorganic matter.[69] Furthermore, man can handle matter only in bulk. It is impossible to construct living cells or molecules part by part as a car or a building is constructed.[70]

The general impossibility of gradually erecting the complex structures of the macromolecules of biology has led to a slower development in biological science than in physics or chemistry. In agricultural and animal husbandry man has to play the role of a passive observer and imitator of nature:

> it takes us just about the same time as in ancient Egypt to grow a rice plant from a rice seed. The gestation period of domestic animals also has not been shortened by an iota. And little, if anything, has been achieved in shortening the time necessary to bring such an animal to maturity. Whatever progress we have made in husbandry, it has been the result of simply waiting for mutations to happen and imitating thereafter the work of natural selection.[71]

The Time-consuming Nature of Agricultural Production. Agriculture is a time-consuming activity. Production is strongly governed by the seasonality of the year. The timing of production in manufacturing is much easier than in agriculture. This we see when looking at the production functions of the two industries in Roegenesque terms.[72]

Georgescu-Roegen departs from the notion of the *elementary process*, which is defined as a partial process whereby *one* unit of the product output can be produced. Every production system is a system of such processes. Each elementary process is in principle described by a production function which contains two different categories of productive elements: *flows*, which are used by the agents, and *funds*, which are the agents of the process and leave the process with their efficiency intact. The flow elements are natural resources (solar energy, rainfall, etc.), current input flows of materials (lumber, coke, etc.), and inputs needed for maintaining capital equipment intact (paint, lubricants, etc.). The fund elements in turn, are the traditional three: Ricardian land ('the original and indestructible powers of the soil'),[73] capital and labor.

All elementary processes involve a certain degree of idleness of fund factors:

> All elementary processes have one important feature in common. In relation to any given elementary process most of the fund factors involved in it must remain idle during a great part of the production time. This idleness, it should be emphasized, is not the result of our own fault or wish. It is an unavoidable consequence of the material conditions of the process itself. A superficial observation of a cabinet maker at work should suffice to convince us of the general validity of this truth. The saw, the plane, the sander, etc., are never used simultaneously in the production of a table considered by itself. Every tool is used by turns; in the meantime it lies idle. Should there be specialized workers — say, one specialized in operating the saw, another in applying varnish, etc. — they, too, would be idle by turns in relation to every elementary process. Moreover, all tools and all workers are idle (in the same sense) during the time when the varnished table is set out to dry. During this phase, nature is the silent partner of man, its forces operating through some flow elements included...A flow input of oxygen from the air oxidizes the varnish while the varnish solvent evaporates as an output flow.[74]

The scope for reducing the inherent idleness of fund factors differs widely between manufacturing industry and agriculture. When more than one unit of the product is demanded during the period of production so that more than one elementary process is needed, the choice is between arranging the processes *in parallel* or *in line*. When elementary processes are set in parallel to satisfy a demand for n units of the product per production period, n elementary processes have to be started simultaneously and are repeated only after they are completed. Hence, production in parallel does not in principle reduce the idleness of the fund factors, since most of them are now needed in an amount n times as large as when only one elementary process is run. Unemployment of fund factors is amplified by a factor of n.* With elementary processes

---

*Of course there are exceptions to this rule. Georgescu-Roegen himself mentions

arranged in line 'the time of production is divided into equal intervals and one elementary process is started at each division point.'[75] The fund factors used in production are periodically shifted from one elementary process to another, in the ideal case without ever being idle.

Production in line is a characteristic of manufacturing industry, while in agriculture the same principle may be applied only in very special cases.* In manufacturing, the production period may be regarded as a freely variable parameter, whereas in agriculture and animal husbandry it is largely determined by nature. Agricultural production is confined within the limits given by the parallel system of production. Most of the time variations in production techniques will have to take place within the framework given by seasonal variations.

While the limitations on inventive and innovative capacity due to the organic nature of agricultural production are universal, the influence of the time factor may vary considerably between countries and regions depending on their geographical location thereby causing differences in the scope for innovations.

In Haiti, as in most other tropical countries, the most important determinant of the starting points of the elementary processes is the rains. We found in Chapter 2 that rainfall in Haiti is very unevenly distributed during the year with peaks in spring and fall contrasting with relatively dry summers and winters. This also limits the extent to which it is possible to introduce artifical irrigation, since there is a tendency for the main water supplies to dry out during the dry seasons. With some variations this pattern occurs throughout the country, and this in turn affects the possibilities of introducing innovations negatively. First, the dependence on natural recipitation may create complementarities:

> It looks simple enough to persuade farmers to sow certain crops three weeks earlier than is their custom, because this may have

---

the case of the large bread oven, that may accommodate many elementary processes simultaneously (Georgescu-Roegen (1971), pp. 237-8).

*Examples of production in line are not altogether absent in agriculture and animal husbandry. The greenhouse and the broiler 'factory' are clear instances of line production (Georgescu-Roegen (1971), pp. 250, 253), and Georgescu-Roegen also points to the case of Bali, where due to the uniformity of the climate continuous rice-growing throughout the year can take place without any idleness of fund factors (ibid., p. 253). A further example from Singapore and Hong Kong is given by Gale Johnson. There, ten or twelve crops per year are realized by intensive seed-bed transplanting (Georgescu-Roegen (1969), p. 531).

disproportionate effects on yield. . . .But the ground may be so hard that the hoe or the ox-plough cannot break it until the first rains start, and this may be too late. A new plough, or a tractor, or irrigation is needed.[76]

The problem of complementarities will be discussed at length below. The second effect of the dependency on natural precipitation is to create a 'congestion' problem immediately before the rainy seasons. Since the Haitian peasant takes more than one crop per year there is not time for the soil to lie idle (unless totally exhausted). As soon as one crop is harvested another is sown or planted. Both harvesting and sowing or planting take place in direct association with the rainy periods, and the time margin between harvest and rains is often narrow. New, superior crops sometimes have very different timing requirements than the traditional ones and this difference may exclude the adoption of the former. When the harvest is over it may already be too late to sow or plant the new superior varieties, or their yield may fall drastically.*

To a degree the Haitian peasant has been able to cope with the peak-load problem. Reserve labor is mobilized when there is need for it, and special forms of labor organization — the *coumbites* — are put into use. Also, the peasant as a rule practices multicropping. Each field carries several crops at any given time which allows the peasant to make maximum use of scarce land. Multicropping is nothing but a step towards production in line, since to the extent that the fund requirements of different crops do not coincide in time it is possible to shift resources from one activity to another to reduce the seasonal unemployment of these resources.

Still, it must be concluded that timing remains a real problem for the peasant. It is not possible to increase the number of crops indefinitely without detrimental effects. The soil soon becomes exhausted and will have to be left in fallow (if other methods of regaining or conserving soil fertility are not feasible). Also, the sowing and planting of crops cannot take place indiscriminately during the year. For most crops the dependence on water at least during the early stages of the growth process remains and cannot easily be tampered with. Line production is an exception in Haitian agriculture.

---

*Hunter (1969), pp. 116-17. This is the case with e.g. hybrid rice which is very sensitive to the timing of water supplies (Palmer (1972:2), p. 23).

Limitations due to the Topography

The Georgescu-Roegen approach focuses on the importance of time in agricultural production as compared to industrial. Agriculture and industry differ with respect to another important characteristic of their production functions. In studies of manufacturing industry, land frequently remains of such limited interest that its existence in production can conveniently be assumed away without any danger of oversimplification. To a lesser degree, this may also be true for advanced agriculture[77] but once we discuss agricultural systems in less developed countries the land factor assumes supreme importance. If often becomes the most important single factor.

Hence, when land becomes an important factor one must also analyze what effects the characteristics of land may have. In Haiti the most striking feature of course is the topography. The country is enormously rugged. Less than 30 percent of the total area of the country consists of land with a slope of less than 10 percent. This ruggedness in at least three ways may act as an obstacle to innovation. First of all it may render certain practices inferior in mountainous areas. As soon as steep hillsides are being farmed, the use of the plow is excluded. It simply becomes impossible to use plows, draft animals or tractors in fields where the peasants can hardly sustain themselves without the aid of ropes or other devices.*

Secondly, the rugged topography may intereact with the limitations due to time. In his discussion of the division of labor Adam Smith remarked that

> time is commonly lost in passing from one sort of work to another ...It is impossible to pass very quickly from one kind of work to another that is carried on in a different place and with quite different tools. A country weaver, who cultivates a small farm, must lose a great deal of time in passing from his loom to the field, and from the field to his loom. When the two trades may be carried on in the same workhouse, the loss of time is no doubt less.[78]

Problems of transport and communication are multiplied in mountainous country. We have seen how the equality principles guiding the system of inheritance tend to scatter the fields of the peasants. Each peasant gets two or more plots (of unequal quality) at some distance

---
*This argument does not explain why so few plows are seen in the plains. The explanation of this will be postponed until later.

from one another. This distance may be considerable, and hence the peasant will lose a lot of time traveling on foot between the fields and between the fields and his home.* Time-consuming walking in turn limits the time which is available for effective work, and hence also the scope for innovations.**

Transport and communication problems stemming from the topography may finally 'limit the extent of the market' (to paraphrase the Adam Smith dictum) and hence reduce the scope for realization of economies of scale that may be necessary for specialization on some potentially interesting products to be adopted. Peasant women and intermediaries often have to travel long distances in mountainous terrain between farmsteads and markets and between markets in different regions, carrying heavy, bulky and perishable products. In the appendix to Chapter 4, we discussed how the deplorable state of the road network impedes the transportation of large volumes of goods by the *Madam Sara*. Perishable goods can be transported only over short distances.† This, in turn has consequences for the pattern of crops grown. Most Haitian peasants grow a wide variety of crops and do not specialize, and the crop patterns resemble each other fairly closely from region to region. Specialization is an exception, and one of the underlying explanations is the difficulty in obtaining a large enough market.††

The Influence of Relative Factor Prices

An important determinant of whether new technologies will be accepted or not is the prevailing relative prices of the production factors, and especially that of labor and capital. This aspect of technological change has been emphasized by Keith Griffin in his study of the Green Revolution.[79] Griffin's argument may be summarized with the aid of the production isoquants and the isocost lines (relative factor prices) of Figure 12.1. On the vertical axis we measure the employment of capital

---

*Harold A. Wood mentions that in the *Département du Nord* distances up to four miles between fields are common (Wood (1961), p. 10).
**Cf. Métraux *et al.* (1951), p. 31: 'This location of their fields in different places compels the farmers to be continually on the move, which causes both loss of time and physical exhaustion.' (Cf. also Bastien (1951), p. 144.)
†Washed coffee, for example, cannot be produced in large quantities among other things due to the lack of penetration roads. Unless the coffee cherries are washed within twenty-four hours of picking, they ferment (JWK (1976:1), p. 37).
††In the foregoing we have stressed the inherent difficulties of innovation in agriculture as compared to manufacturing industry. The opposite may also apply. See e.g. Kilby (1972) for an argument along the line that it is easier to acquire skills that are needed for innovation in agriculture than in manufacturing.

Resistance to Innovation

(C), and on the horizontal axis we have the employment of labor (N).

Figure 12.1

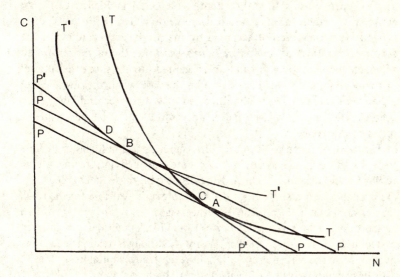

Let us assume that the relative price of labor and capital is the one indicated by the price line PP, and that the technology at the disposal of the peasants is the one indicated by the isoquant TT. In this situation, the peasants will choose the combination of labor and capital given by point A, the point of tangency between the price line and the isoquant. Assume next, that a new technology, indicated by the isoquant T'T' is introduced to the peasants (where T'T' indicates the same volume of output as TT). Will the peasants adopt this new technology?

The answer is no. Given the relative price PP, the peasants would have to choose the factor combination given by point B, if they wanted to adopt the new technology, but, recalling that the price lines are simultaneously isocost lines, we see that this can be done only by increasing the total cost of inputs. B lies on a PP-line which lies to the northeast of the PP-line which has a point of tangency with TT and hence represents a higher cost. The peasants will reject the new technology. For T'T' to be accepted, the relative price of capital must fall to a level which is lower than the one indicated by the price line P'P', which is tangent both to TT and to T'T'. (The peasants, given the relative factor price P'P', will be indifferent between point C – old technology – and point D – new technology.)

In Haiti, the relative price of capital is high in terms of labor, as we saw in Chapter 2. The peasants employ very labor-intensive techniques. This in turn, means that the situation depicted in Figure 12.1 may easily arise, where new technologies are not what Griffin calls *ultra-superior* (i.e. they are not accepted by the producers regardless of the factor price ratio) but *economically irrelevant* (i.e. the factor price ratio at which the technologies would be accepted are not those that prevail in the economy).[80] This is likely to be the case when the new technologies tend to be biased in the direction of a higher capital/labor ratio than the old ones at a given factor price ratio (i.e. when the isoquants intersect only once).

It cannot be taken as given that ultra-superior technologies or technologies with such a bias as to be accepted by peasants facing a high relative price of capital (what Griffin calls peasant-biased technologies)[81] are available. 'To assume that new technology is available for the small farmer and that it is profitable is the biggest error the proponents of agricultural credit have made,' writes Ronald L. Tinnermeier in a survey of technology and rural credit.[82] Many of the high-yielding seeds connected with the Green Revolution have a strong capital-using bias.[83] This has been observed by Clague in the Haitian context:

> New cash crop varieties may require different methods of cultivation which are vulnerable to pests and thus require the use of insecticides or fungicides. Fertilizer frequently does not raise the yields of traditional varieties because they have been selected by farmers in the absence of fertilizer. Hence the introduction of fertilizer often requires the simultaneous introduction of new crop varieties. In addition, single applications of fertilizer in poor soils may prove uneconomic; annual applications over a considerable period of time may be required in order to make the practice advantageous.[84]

The high-yielding seed varieties thus appear to exhibit strong complementarities between the seeds themselves, fertilizer and irrigation.[85] This raises the capital/labor ratio in comparison to the traditional, unselected varieties. The same appears to be true with regard to fertilizer, irrigation and a number of other capital inputs and farming practices:

> The important point is that fertilizers, like other agricultural aids, will yield maximum results *only if applied in the context of an over-*

all improvement in farming methods. To begin with, 'Moisture must be available if plants are to absorb the supplied nutrients. In regions with only 10-15 inches of rainfall per year, fertilizer is largely ineffective unless supplemented by irrigation.' By the same token, irrigation will not make a maximal contribution to raising yields unless there is a simultaneous input of fertilizer. Furthermore, 'Different varieties of grain often have widely varying degrees of responsiveness to fertilizers. Traditional, unselected varieties of many crops often show little or no response.' Thus, like water, improved seeds are an important complement to fertilizers and *vice versa*. The same is true in regard to most other technical improvements specified in the development plans: deeper plowing, soil conservation and improvement of soil structure, green manuring and the use of natural fertilizers, better weed control, plant protection, improved crop rotation, etc.[86]

Hence, we should expect that a number of potentially high-yielding technologies are not accepted in Haiti because they are economically irrelevant. Their use is not compatible with the current relative prices of capital and labor.

Indivisibilities

Related to the problem of complementarities is the problem of indivisibilities. The former often create the latter or reinforce them, and the existence of indivisibilities may in turn hamper the introduction of new crops or techniques. Three examples may illustrate this problem.

One obvious case is fertilizer. In 1973, an American team gathered information regarding fertilizer use in Haiti,[87] and then identified the Artibonite valley as the area that provided the best immediate opportunity for extension of fertilizer employment. However, it was found that in order to render fertilizer use efficient three other prerequisites had to be fulfilled. A functional irrigation system (i.e. an indivisibility) had to be created, complementary agricultural inputs had to be purchased (e.g. seed) which in turn required an efficient credit system, and a working delivery system to provide fertilizer and the other new inputs had to be created.[88]

Another case is quoted by René Dorville.[89] Attempts to introduce fast-growing and high-yielding varieties of sorghum to supplant the traditional *piti mi* have met with strong resistance, since the new varieties exhibit limited storability under Haitian climatic conditions. This is a severe problem, since the indigenous varieties of sorghum constitute one of the staples of the peasant diet. *Piti mi* is consumed throughout the year, and in times of abundant harvest the peasant attempts to store the grain for long periods (sometimes as much as a year) in order to ensure that the daily needs of the family are met. Hence, the call for heavy (indivisible) investments in refined storage facilities necessarily reduce the attractiveness of the new crop.

The third example derives from an OAS/Israeli-sponsored project of agricultural development in the Cul-de-Sac plain (the Bas-Boën project). In the main the project has been successful in changing peasant techniques and in substituting new crops and plant varieties for the traditional ones, but an attempt to introduce animal traction (bullocks or horses — indivisibilities) created problems. To be efficient as draft animals, bullocks and horses must be provided with regular grazing opportunities or with sufficient food in some alternative manner. Instead the Bas-Boën peasants left the animals to seek their own food in whatever way they could, as is customary in Haiti, which in turn lowered the efficiency of the scheme.[90]

One effect of indivisibilities is illustrated in Figure 12.2. We depart from the same situation as in Figure 12.1. Given the traditional technique TT and the relative factor price PP, the peasants produce at point A. Let us now introduce a new technology T'T' which also entails an indivisibility caused by complementarities or otherwise. The indivisibility is expressed in the diagram as EF, which is the minimum amount of capital the peasants must use if they want to adopt the technology T'T'. As the diagram indicates, to the right of point E, labor can no longer be substituted for capital. With technology T'T' it is not possible to reduce the employment of capital below the EF level. The T'T' isoquant becomes a straight line, parallel to the horizontal axis.

This in turn, may have consequences for the relative price of capital and labor at which the technology will be adopted by the peasants. Had T'T' been without indivisibilities, the isoquant would have been smooth, as indicated by the broken line, and the peasants would have adopted the new technology at any relative price of capital lower than P'P' in diagram 12.1 (not shown in Figure 12.2) — i.e. given any relative price line with a point of tangency with T'T' to the northwest of point B. (Cf. Figure 12.1.) Given an indivisibility of the magnitude EF, this is no longer possible. We must instead look for a price line going through point E which is at the same time tangent to TT. This price line is P''P''. Hence, the relative price of capital must fall in comparison to the situation where there are no indivisibilities. Only at a relative price of capital lower than that indicated by P''P'' will the peasants adopt the new technology. If the price is lower, the traditional technology will be retained, i.e. the new one becomes economically irrelevant.

Figure 12.2

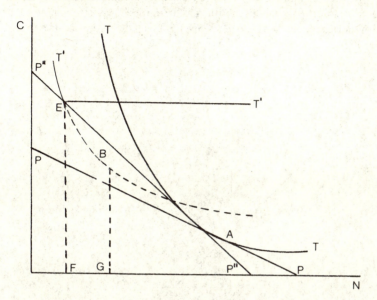

It should be observed that this result is not independent of the size of the indivisibility. Any indivisibility smaller than BG in Figure 12.2 will not constitute an effective constraint in the present case. For smaller indivisibilities, it is the relative factor price which provides the binding constraint. One does not have to postulate any indivisibilities to rule out all points to the right of B on the broken isoquant.

At this point we may also relate the analysis to the discussion of the informal credit markets in Chapter 11. One of the most important effects of indivisibilities is that financing technological change becomes more difficult for the individual peasant. Instead of borrowing (or saving) marginal amounts, large sums may now be required, and this creates a problem when the only available credit market is the informal one, with all its imperfections. This is illustrated in Figure 12.3 which is a diagram of the Fisherian type.[91]

Let us assume that the peasant depicted in the diagram has an income in period one of Y_1 if no investment is undertaken, and a corresponding income in period two of Y_2. Given the peasant's rate of time preference, as indicated by the set of indifference curves, the peasant

Resistance to Innovation

will alter the inter-temporal distribution of incomes, however. By investing $Y_1 - Y_3$ and by borrowing $Y_4 - Y_3$ in the credit market (to cover present consumption) at an interest rate of i_1, he maximizes his utility within the limits given by the traditional farming technology T.* The new intertemporal distribution of incomes is given by point B which corresponds to the utility level indicated by the indifference curve U.

Figure 12.3

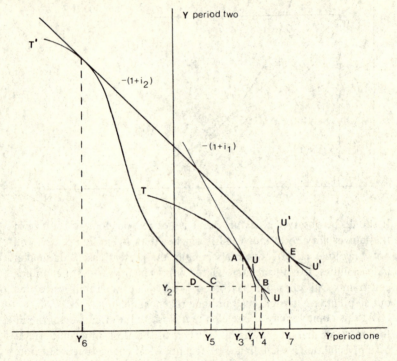

The T' curve shows a superior technology, which in period two (and subsequently) will give the peasant a higher income. This technology, however, shows a discontinuity in returns, caused by the requirement of an initial purchase of e.g. irrigation *cum* fertilizer and improved seeds or a plow in combination with animals or mechanical traction. An

---

*The transformation curve extends to the left of the axis representing incomes in period two since it is assumed that investment opportunities exceed initial endowments.

investment of $Y_1 - Y_5$ must be made before any output at all can be produced with the aid of the new technology, i.e. the latter is subject to an indivisibility. In contrast to the case of the traditional technology it is no longer possible to proceed marginally in the investment decision. The discrete step from Y_1 to Y_5 must be taken or the peasant cannot adopt the new technology.

This is a mere first step, though, since in point C both current and future incomes are lower than if the peasant had continued with the traditional technology. To reach a future level of consumption which is comparable to what the traditional technology offers the peasant would have to move at least to D, but in doing so he reduces his current income towards the zero level, and going further still will soon make his current consumption negative (which of course is impossible).

There is only one way out of this dilemma. The peasant must make an investment which is large enough to take him past the 'knee' of the T' technology. This step presupposes borrowing, since the original resource endowment is not large enough to cover a discrete investment of let us say $Y_1 - Y_6$. If the peasant could borrow enough to take him for example from Y_6 to Y_7 at an interest rate of e.g. $i_2 < i_1$, he would accept the new technology, since he would attain a higher level of utility, represented by the indifference curve U' in point E.

Unfortunately, the rural credit market in Haiti does not permit such a change to take place automatically. The diagram shows the prevailing rate of interest in the rural informal credit market, which is the only one generally available to the peasants, as i_1, which exceeds i_2. The peasants, as we know, generally only have access to small sums of short-term credit at high interest rates.* As long as the volume of credit in comparison to the value of output remains low, the peasants can pay their loans back without getting into financial trouble (unless anything unforeseen happens), but when large investments, caused by indivisibilities, must be undertaken, there is a limit to the rate of interest that the peasants can afford to pay.** Hence, indivisibilities may easily lead to a situation where the peasant is trapped within the narrow confines of the traditional mode of production and has to reject superior

---

*As we know from Chapter 11, the long-term rate that the lenders in these markets would ask, is presumably higher yet.
**The highest rate of interest that the peasant will pay if he is to accept the new technology is given by the slope of the common tangent to T' and U. This rate would leave him indifferent between the new and the old technology (provided that when retaining the latter, the peasant has to borrow at interest i_1).

technologies.*

*Indivisibilities and Farm Size: The Case of the Plow***

In the preceding chapter we saw how most attempts at persuading the peasant to adopt the plow have failed in Haiti. Part of the reason for this has already been given in the influence of the highly rugged topography of the country. However, the topography cannot explain the general absence of plowing practices in the plains. In the Cayes area, for example, which *per se* is excellently suited to a substitution of the plow for the hoe, in the late 1960s, no more than perhaps 250 plows were found.[92] The presence of indivisibilities appears to be a principal cause.

The plow is essentially a labor-saving device (a piece of 'laboresque capital' in Sen's terminology). Substitution of the plow for the hoe and machete saves a number of man-days per hectare plowed. Let us, for the sake of simplicity, assume that this number does not vary with the number of hectares and call it N_S. Denote the agricultural wage with w (assumed to be constant). The total wage bill saved by the introduction of the plow is $S_t \cdot N_S \cdot w$, where S_t is the number of hectares plowed.

Now, plows are hard to come by in Haiti. Erasmus states that 'the plow is a manufactured implement which must be purchased and its diffusion is dependent upon the rate of its numerical ingress into [a certain] area.'[93] It is generally not possible for a peasant to rent a plow if he needs one, but the plow has to be purchased, and this is a fact which has very important implications. It means that the relevant cost for the peasant of using the plow is the annual cost over the life of the equipment (assumed for the sake of simplicity to be constant). Let us call this cost c. Then, when

$$c = S_t \cdot N_S \cdot w \qquad (12:1)$$

i.e. when the cost of using the plow equals the labor cost saved by its introduction, the peasant will be indifferent between using the plow and the simpler hoe and machete technique. Equation (12:1) may be

---

*The existence of indivisibilities also precludes the farmer from gaining insight into the relative merits of new crops, factors or techniques via making experiments in a small scale.

**The argument in this section may also apply e.g. to certain kinds of irrigation devices like pumps or tubewells (Hunter (1969), p. 145) or storage facilities (ibid., p. 155).

Resistance to Innovation

rewritten as

$$S_t = \frac{c}{w} \cdot \frac{1}{N_s}. \qquad (12:2)$$

This formulation is very interesting since it shows that there is a direct relationship between the number of hectares that have to be plowed and the relative cost of capital (amortization and interest charges in relation to wages). Equation (12:2) defines what Paul A. David has termed a 'threshold farm size'[94] with respect to plowing. Unless the number of hectares at the disposal of the peasant is at least equal to S_t, the peasant will reject the plow and stick to the traditional technique. The indivisibility created by the impossibility of renting a plow precludes its use on small plots. It is seen that the higher the relative cost of capital, the higher will the threshold farm size be. In this way the lumpiness of the plow may be regarded as a direct function of relative factor prices.

The indivisibility of the plow looms larger yet when it is recognized that the plow cannot be introduced solely, but that there is a strong complementarity between the plow and animal or mechanical traction which is hard to get around. If mechanical traction is to be used the average annual cost of using the plow increases which in turn increases the threshold farm size. Simultaneously the need for borrowing increases and the dimension of the problem dealt with in Figure 12.3 increases.

If animal traction in the form of draft oxen or horses is used the same difficulty arises (although it may be easier to lease a horse or bullock than to lease a tractor), and in addition the problem of feeding the animals must be considered. To be useful, horses or oxen must be properly fed. They cannot be left to find their own food, but grazing facilities or fodder crops must be provided. As the Bas-Boën experience demonstrates, this is, however, not very easy in an economy of the Haitian type, where land is scarce. The peasants resist such practices and, as it seems, on good grounds:

> In most parts of the world, the area an animal can till with a primitive plough is much smaller than the area needed to feed it on natural grazing. Hence, under short fallow the need to provide fodder for the draught animals means that one of three conditions must be fulfilled: a considerable part of the land must be left as permanent grazing; or the cultivation period must be considerably shorter than the fallow period during which the fields are left to grow wild

grasses for the animals to feed on; or finally, a part of the harvest from the cultivated fields must be given to the animals.[95]

It is, according to Ester Boserup, precisely due to this complementarity that there often is a tendency in agricultural communities subject to strong population pressure to jump directly from bush-fallow cultivation to annual cropping and multicropping using hand tools instead of plows:

> intensive systems of bush fallow with up to eight years of uninterrupted cultivation, followed by a similar period of fallow, have a larger carrying capacity for human populations than short fallow with ploughing by animals. Where cultivation under long fallow has developed into this intensive type, it may be impossible to relieve population pressure by a change to short fallow with feeding of the draft animals on natural grazing. If population is increasing in communities of this type a change directly to annual cropping or multicropping imposes itself.[96]

While produced fodder requires less land per unit of output than does natural grass,[97] the former creates yet another complementarity, since it requires additional labor to be supplied:

> Owing to the seasonal character of agriculture a couple of hectares is often all that can be ploughed per animal. If a draft animal ploughing a few hectares must be fed on produced fodder all the year round, or most of it, the peasant must see his work load increase considerably. It is not surprising, therefore, to observe in communities living by the system of short fallow that cultivators hesitate to undertake change to produced fodder when fallow or other grazing areas are becoming scarce owing to an increase of population. Instead, cultivators are apt, by exposing their animals to half-starvation on overgrazed areas of stubble and natural grazing during the long periods of the year, when the animals are doing little or no work. Only in the short seasons of field work would the animals be given some of the cereals or other food crops cultivated in the fields in order to keep them in tolerable working condition.[98]

If the preferences for leisure are strong, as is sometimes indicated with respect to the Haitian peasant,[99] the relative attraction of leisure in combination with the prevailing land shortage may put the economy in a situation where plowing with animal traction will be rejected by the peasants, because it would either make too heavy claims on the available land resources or interfere too much with non-work activities. Even without strong preferences for leisure it is possible that the increased labor requirements when fodder has to be grown will increase the resistance to innovation. If we look at the right-hand side of expression (12:2) we find N_s — the labor-saving effect of the plow — which is reduced if additional efforts are needed to grow fodder crops. This in turn increases the threshold size of farms with respect to plowing. On the other hand, a reduction of the labor-saving impact of the plow should also reduce the relative cost of capital. Wages will be bid up, and the price of plows should fall. The falling efficiency of the plow will be counteracted by a simultaneous fall in the relative cost of the equipment. The net result with regard to threshold size is indeterminate, but there is always a possibility that this size will increase.*

In a rough way we know something about threshold farm size in relation to the size of existing Haitian farms. The cost of capital in terms of labor is high in the rural sector. There are also very strong reasons to believe that the labor-saving effects of plowing are small. It is generally not very efficient to turn the soil over with the use of the plow when farm size is very small and cultivations are highly differentiated so that the area covered by each crop is minute, and even less when multicropping with several plant varieties on the same plot simultaneously is the dominant pattern. Great care must be taken not to destroy growing crops when the soil is turned over, and this requires labor. A further complication lies in the discontinuity of plots. Since most peasants do not own a single piece of land but two or more at some (often considerable) distance from each other the plow will have to be transported between the plots. If, on top of this the peasant owns both flat and steep land, the area where the plow may be used is reduced. It is therefore very likely that the threshold size of farms with respect to the plow, given the relative factor cost and the efficiency of the plow, is larger in Haiti than the area which most Haitian peasants

---

*Here, very much depends on what is assumed about rural wages and plow costs. If the supply of labor in agriculture is infinitely elastic — 'unlimited' in the terminology of W. Arthur Lewis (see Lewis (1954)) — and if plows are imported (which has been the case until recently — see Duplan (1975:2), p. 34) or otherwise sold at a given price which is not affected by Haitian demand, relative factor prices will remain unaffected, and decreasing efficiency per hectare plowed will always increase the threshold size of farms.

have at their disposal.*

The results of our analysis are at least partly confirmed by empirical data. Charles John Erasmus relates two instances where the plow was introduced spontaneously in the districts of St Raphaël and St Michel.[100] There in various ways the farmers were able to circumvent the indivisibilities connected with plowing. First of all, draft oxen already existed in the area. The peasants were used to work with them in the powering of sugar mills, and when plowing began, the animals were simply trained to draw the plows too. Thus, during the introductory stage there was no need to finance more than the plow itself. As the plowing practice began to spread, other ways of reducing indivisibilities were introduced. Some peasants began contract plowing which later developed very fast:

> Contract plowing has become something of a specialization in the area. A few men at St Raphael, for example, who are considered to be superior plowers, are regularly contracted by others to plow their land at planting time. Plowing costs $12 to $20 a *carreau*...the lower figure being the price for loose, and the higher for harder soil. The daily rental price of a team of two oxen with plow has also become standardized at a figure of approximately $1.[101]

Contract plowing and leasing of plows and oxen was beneficial both for the peasants who own plows and oxen and for those who do not. The plowmen can care well for their animals so that the latter are well fed at least during the plowing season since they can include the cost of fodder** in the price they charge for plowing. Those who buy the different plowing services in turn avoid the threshold size problem.† Local agricultural extension agents have also been supplying plows to the peasants on a rental basis, and the fact that when Erasmus made his investigation the demand for plows from the agent by far exceeded what he could supply strongly points to the importance of indivisibilities as an obstacle to plowing.

---

*By 'area' is meant the area which is at all suitable for plowing, i.e. excluding steep mountain-sides, etc.
**The fodder mainly consisted of sugar cane which was presumably already grown in the area so that no separate land for growing fodder crops should have been required.
†It is also probable that some of those peasants who owned plows and oxen bought more land to benefit fully from the economies of scale that are inherent in plowing. (See Erasmus (1952), p. 25.)

Why Not a Co-operative Solution?

So far, we have seen that a high relative price of capital in relation to labor in various ways may act as an obstacle to innovation. Especially when indivisibilities are present, technological change may be precluded given the current relative price of capital in rural Haiti. The existence of indivisibilities may also make borrowing necessary if new technologies are to be adopted, but such borrowing cannot take place in the informal credit markets at a rate of interest which does not exceed the probable yield of the investment in the new technology, and formal credit, as we know, is almost non-existent. The plow, finally, presents a special type of indivisibility. If the acreage which is to be plowed is small, the probability is high that the plow represents an economically irrelevant innovation as long as it has to be purchased (and cannot be leased). This problem is compounded if in addition to the plow, a draft animal has to be bought.

However, the experience with the plow at St Raphaël and St Michel leads directly to an important question: Why are not co-operative efforts resorted to among the peasantry to overcome the indivisibility obstacle? Haiti possesses a long tradition of co-operative work in the *coumbite* system, and consequently there should be a very fertile ground upon which to sow the seeds of co-operation in somewhat more advanced forms. Creation of co-operatives in Haiti (for various purposes) has also been suggested by a number of authors,[102] and several practical efforts to found a viable co-operative movement have been made in the past. The first beginnings took place as early as in 1937,[103] and more systematic attempts began in the late 1940s.[104] Yet the co-operative history of Haiti can by no means be regarded as a success story. In 1952 Erasmus wrote:

> Many attempts have been made by agricultural extension agents to organize groups of Haitian farmers into work or production co-operatives. Nearly all such cooperatives have resulted in failure after about one year. They may fail when the agent is moved to a new locale, or when jealousies spring up among the members, or when members fail to fulfill their duties, etc. Attempts to persuade groups of farmers to buy animals and plows under a system of joint ownership also meet with resistance and failure.[105]

Probably the main weakness of the co-operative movement in Haiti is that the majority of the co-operatives have been formed from above.[106] They have been government institutions that have been more or less forced upon the peasants and have hence, as Clague remarks, been 'of little immediate use to most peasants.'[107] The dangers of the *dirigiste* approach are well-known. Guy Hunter eloquently summarizes some of the most important issues:

> In the circumstances of small-holding peasant agriculture, the principle of co-operant action is in many instances the only escape from the closed circle of poverty. The point is to use it for clearcut, understood and fairly narrow purposes; to use extreme caution in extending it beyond them; above all to refrain from erecting Co-operatives as an ideological cure-all for the inevitable difficulties of a distributive system operating on the narrowest of margins in a poor society and dealing with the gross fluctuations in output and demand which characterize agriculture, where production is at the mercy of the seasons and demand is fickle.
>
> It is this ideological use of Co-operatives which has probably done most damage. 'Founded by farmers in the interests of farmers' is a Co-operative motto which is common in England. Government-sponsored Co-operatives, used to exclude the growth of middlemen or capitalism, are usually not founded by farmers, nor do they always seem to be in the interests of farmers. The whole morale and dynamic of Co-operation is thereby lost; Co-operatives are treated as another branch of bureaucracy, the secretaryship is just another job with opportunity for gains on the side, the Executive Committee is the usual clique of village bosses. This is not a new way of living and working together.[108]

Apart from the *sociétés* and the *escouades*,[109] few instances of spontaneous formation of co-operatives from below in rural Haiti can be cited. It is possible that the development of more ambitious associations may have come to be identified with the government-sponsored co-operatives and their problems so as to be rejected on these grounds, but other factors are probably more instrumental yet in precluding the establishment of peasant co-operatives.

One such factor is the overwhelmingly high rate of illiteracy in rural districts. The 1971 census indicated that 89 percent of the rural population of Haiti could not read and write.[110] Forming a co-operative in turn means that books and accounts of various kinds have to be kept. That this is a formidable problem is shown by the experience of the government-organized credit co-operatives, where the responsibility for all records and accounts have had to be put on the extension agents and their supervisors.¹¹¹

Another interesting hypothesis departs from the fact that the Haitian population as a rule is not concentrated in villages. The most common pattern of rural settlement is that of an evenly dispersed population.¹¹² The peasants have seldom felt themselves to be members of any well-defined community, however small.¹¹³ The ties that exist are those between family members and relatives, and to lesser extent, between neighbors and friends who participate in the mutual *coumbites*.* When a well-defined social network and information structure (such as that of a village) is lacking, the tendencies to co-operation are correspondingly weakened at least in so far as they require a formal structure, handling of member money and contacts with the outside world. Natural local leaders with an eye to innovation are lacking:

> local leadership becomes exceedingly diffused. It comes to rest almost exclusively in the local *houngan* or voodoo priest, and in the representatives of Christian churches, whose influence depends, however, more upon their personal character and past achievement than upon their sacred office.¹¹⁴

Most important of the two is undoubtedly the *houngan,* but

> Vodoun lacks hierarchy capable of formulating and imposing a new policy for the benefit of the rural population. It can only thwart or at least remain indifferent to the efforts of the state to initiate changes which might menace the local control of the houngans over their flocks. To our knowledge, no houngan has ever sponsored the building of a school, promoted a program of community development,

---

*Sidney W. Mintz has pointed to an additional reason for the weakness of community organization, not only in Haiti, but also in the rest of the Caribbean area. He states that: 'Perhaps particularly important in this connection was the strength of the plantation system in maintaining the division of society into two substantially different segments, and the relative inability of the system to produce or to attract intermediate social groupings that could serve as links between the powerful and the powerless in local community life.' (Mintz (1966:3), p. 933.)

Also, 'the individualism of Haitian peasants can be employed within a creative framework, in those instances where the cash nexus has not penetrated so far as to destroy the economic coherence of kin groups. The difficulty is, in the nineteenth century Haiti was brought once again into the world economy, and the American Occupation intensified its incorporation. I believe that it has been the increasing absorption of the Haitian economy within the world economy that put an end...to all forms of cooperative endeavor...' (Sidney W. Mintz, personal communication, dated 21 June 1978.)

sought to introduce new crops, or innovated an agricultural technique. His overspecialization not only guarantees him relative power and wealth, but it also makes him unfit for the kind of true leadership which places the material and spiritual welfare of the community above personal advantages. The type of change needed today is beyond the comprehension of Vodoun and contrary to its interests.[115] *

To this it may be added that the style of government in rural Haiti never has been such as to encourage any initiatives taken by the peasant masses themselves. The countryside is governed in a strongly military fashion,[116] where the *chef de section* is the all-important person who generally rules autocratically.

Under these conditions it is not unnatural that no co-operative efforts of a more ambitious kind than the time-honored and socially well-sanctioned *coumbites* arise spontaneously. Locked in a world of ignorance and religious and political dominance where social bonds among equals are weak, the peasants cannot reasonably be expected to take their fate into their own hands unless outside assistance is forthcoming, and such assistance will have to be better geared to the needs and particularities of peasant society than have most government-directed co-operative ventures so far undertaken.

---

*Courlander surprisingly suggests the conscious use of voodoo cult centers as a possible road to modernization:

> One is tempted to speculate on what social and economic reforms might be accomplished through intelligent and benevolent use of the Vodoun cult centers by a progress-minded government. In the southland of the United States for many years the Negro church was the main contact point of the Negro community. The church was the center of social organization and co-operation. It was used not only for religious purposes but for educational projects. In the church there were meetings to discuss local problems (later on, national problems) or to listen to experts on agriculture or chicken raising or health matters. It was no accident that when the civil rights movement materialized in the southern states, ministers of the churches provided the main leadership. This phenomenon was also clearly observable in the northern urban centers. The typical Haitian cult is a community center headed by a houngan or a mambo whose words carry great weight. The transformation of this center into a place where fundamental educative processes, as well as religious rites, could be carried on could vitally affect the nation's welfare. Health rules and precautions, agricultural advice, elemental literacy, sound management of income and acreage, all these things could be taught or at least stimulated. The basic organization already exists. And so far it has never been used by the state except for political advantage. (Courlander (1966), pp. 20-21.)

Risk

Farmers in underdeveloped countries have typically to face four kinds of risks or uncertainties which are furthermore interrelated. The first is a *production* risk. Drought, floods, hurricanes, parasitic diseases, etc. are recurrent phenomena in tropical and subtropical areas, and their effect is to reduce production, sometimes very drastically.

The second risk is that the *price* of peasant *output* may fall. A bumper crop is not necessarily an unqualified blessing, but following a good harvest, markets are easily glutted so that product prices fall, and with them peasant incomes. If the peasants are involved in export production or otherwise in production where there are many competitors in a large area, the problem is compounded, since then it is not only local or regional production (and demand) conditions that matter. A local harvest failure may be combined with a supernormal crop in competing areas, and the effect of the latter may easily swamp the former. If the peasants concentrate on one or a few crops the effects become yet more severe, since a larger percentage of their incomes is affected.

Peasants that concentrate on other products than foodstuff may also suffer a third adversity, namely that of an increase in the *price of food*. When food has to be produced in the market a decline in peasant terms of trade can reduce the standard of living of non-food-producing rural households severely. (The same effect may be produced by a fall in the price of the products of these households.)

Finally, when inputs are purchased or rented, an increase in the *price of* any such *input* which is hard to substitute for may reduce output and incomes, or reduce consumption or increase indebtedness if production is to be kept at the planned level. A good illustration of this risk is the rise in the price of fertilizer caused by the combination of rising food and oil prices and shortage of capacity in the world's fertilizer industry during the early 1970s.[117]

The stochastic character of agricultural output is not a feature that is in any way unique to the underdeveloped areas of the world. To some extent it is present in all kinds of agriculture. What makes risk such an important issue in developing economies in comparison to industrialized ones is that the presence of risk is coupled with two other features which are absent in the industrialized countries: general poverty and absence of satisfactory insurance arrangements.

When discussing the quality of human capital in the rural sector we found a good indication of the severity of the poverty problem in Haiti. The calorie deficit around 1975 had almost reached a level of 35 percent, which is a very strong indication of the poverty of the average

Haitian. The peasant is not only poor. He also has few means to protect himself against the adverse effects of his income that result if any of the aforementioned risks materialize. Haiti does not possess any social security system which can deal with sudden falls in peasant incomes, but all risks in principle have to be borne individually by the peasants.* One of the most important traditional insurance devices of underdeveloped countries — the extended family system — to a large extent may have been put out of action with the decline of the *lakou*** and the emergence of the nuclear family as the central family unit.[118] Other compensating mechanisms are resorted to instead. We have in the foregoing seen how the peasants grow such crops as they can consume themselves to reduce the dependence on the market, how they diversify their cultivations,[119] among other things to avoid excessive concentration on one or a few crops, how savings to a certain extent take the form of such assets (animals) as can readily be sold in time of need, and how access to credit in the informal credit markets may serve as a substitute for a cash buffer.[120] A fifth mechanism for protection against risk is repayment of loans in kind instead of in cash. The common pattern is that when a loan is taken from a *spéculateur* or a *Madam Sara*, repayment takes the form of a part of the future coffee crop. The peasant is hereby protected against a fall in the price of the product as well as against some of the risk of harvest failure, and some of the risk is borne by the intermediary instead.†

The number of protective devices is limited, however, and their efficiency is probably low. Consequently the peasants are likely to display aversion against risk. Peasant incomes are low, and the risks that

---

*American aid has been resorted to several times in the past when hurricanes or droughts have struck, but of course, peasants cannot rely on such measures, which may take too long to reach them.
**The *lakou* (from the French — *la cour*, yard) denotes an extended family of three to four generations with 'a common physically demarcated residence.' (Schaedel (1962), p. 25.)
†See Chapter 11. A similar device is the *de moitié* (sharecropping) system, where the risks are pooled between the landlord and the tenant in proportion to the share received by each. Whether sharecropping actually is a device for protection against risk is debatable, however. Stephen N.S. Cheung has suggested that it is (Cheung (1969). Cf. also Griffin (1974), pp. 22-6) but this position has been criticized by other authors, notably Bardhan & Srinivasan (1971); Rao (1971); Stiglitz (1974) and Newbery (1973) and (1975:1). The latter two authors demonstrate that sharecropping as protection against risk is at best equal to a combination of fixed rent and pure wage contracts.

the peasants have to face are of a serious kind.* As the figures on the nutrition situation indicate, the margin between the income during a 'normal' year without harvest failures or price falls and that of a 'bad' year leading to outright starvation is often very slight. Relatively small changes in output or prices may have fatal consequences. The very existence of the peasant and his family is at stake.

The combination of risk, poverty and inadequate protection against risk is likely to make the peasant adopt some kind of 'survival algorithm',[121] where the available choices are evaluated first and foremost against their relative capability to maximize the probability of survival of the peasant and his family. The adoption of a survival strategy in turn, has very definite consequences for the pace at which innovations are accepted in rural areas.

Innovations in tropical or subtropical agriculture are always potentially connected with risk and uncertainty. Before a new technique or a new product has been tried and tested under local conditions, uncertainty with respect to the consequences of adopting the technique or the product is always present — objectively or subjectively. Laboratory tests or tests under demonstration farm conditions with expertise present cannot be substituted for actual trial within the peasant system of cultivation. Many new techniques or new products increase yields per hectare, sometimes drastically, but at the same time they also increase the variability of output and hence the probability of an unsatisfactory outcome.[122] Traditional varieties of seed, for example, may yield less than improved varieties but on the other hand be more resistant to drought, diseases, etc., and unless the peasants clearly perceive that the former confer such advantages on them that they are willing to forgo the benefits of the traditional varieties, innovation will be resisted.

There are clear cases where this kind of rationality dominates over profit maximization in the literature on Haiti. Erasmus, in the only article written so far dealing specifically with resistance and acceptance of innovation in Haitian agriculture writes:

> The Haitian farmer knows, for example, that a dependable source of water will materially increase his production, and will never oppose an irrigation project as such. In the case of a new plant or species

---

*Arrow convincingly argues that the propensity to hold risky assets is a function of the wealth of the individual. (See Arrow (1971), Chapter 3. Cf. also Lipton (1968:1).)

he is far more sceptical. While government experimental and demonstration farms are valuable tools for preliminary research in determining what plants and cultivation practices are best adapted to the locale, they are seldom effective as a means of introducing new traits to the farmer. Usually, some individual farmer must be persuaded to try out the new trait for himself. Often he will relinquish only a very small plot for the initial trial. But when he himself has witnessed the greater yield or the greater market price, he becomes convinced, and the word soon spreads to others.

Haitian farmers seem quick to follow another farmer's success. Suspicious of government-operated farms, they prefer to let someone else take the risk of following the agronomist's advice before trying it themselves...

Subject to innumerable vagaries of chance, multiplied by the primitiveness of his hoe technology, the very livelihood of the Haitian farmer is at the mercy of a great many unpredictable factors over which he has little or no control. He is not prone, therefore, to risk even greater insecurity by accepting new practices as long as he retains any doubt as to the certainty of their immediate profit to him. Traits of long-term benefit such as composting, crop rotation, and soil conservation are apparently more difficult to present in such a way as to bear immediate proof of their desirability. Even in the case of new plants or improved species, the margin of greater yield or profit at the Haitian level of agricultural technology may be only 10 to 20 percent higher than the customary yield or profit. Late rains or a pestilence may wipe out the margin with the result that the farmer fails to see any measurable advantage in the new practice.[123]

All innovative activity in tropical or subtropical agriculture is risky. It is never possible to tell *a priori* whether a new technique or product will be successful under local conditions. Many new techniques that increase yields also increase the variability of the volume of output. For a risk averter to accept new practices or products, the benefits of the latter must be established beyond doubt. A profit-maximizing peasant would base his judgement on whether the expected benefits from adopting the novelty exceed the expected costs, while a risk averter would be much more concerned e.g. with the possibility of a bad outcome in an individual year. The Haitian peasant cannot afford to have a satisfactory standard of living four years out of five, with a drastic fall in income during the fifth year, since his possibilities of saving are small, and hence he will not have any reserves to back him for the case that his income should fall short of subsistence requirements during the fifth year.

Risk aversion is probably an important explanation of why new seed varieties are rejected, for example, but risk aversion presumably also goes a long way towards explaining the behavior of the nineteenth-century 'non-transforming' Haitian economy, which we described earlier in the present chapter, where the attempts at introducing new export crops as the price of coffee declined, were almost universally resisted. It took no less than spectacular price increases, as in the case of cotton during the American Civil War, to induce the peasants to overcome their adherence to the safer subsistence crop pattern.

In Chapter 2, we described the situation with respect to land titles in Haiti, and found that the majority of the peasants are generally qualified as 'owners', but that very few of them can present any legally registered deeds to the land that they claim as theirs. Historical possession of a given piece of land for successive generations within the peasant community takes the place of written titles. 'The proof is in the reputation,' as Paul Moral expresses it.[124] Legally, 20 years of uninterrupted possession without titles establishes an undisputed right to the land in question.[125] Tenant farmers and sharecroppers are worse off. A landlord can always terminate whatever agreement he has with a peasant when the period of lease expires, and there is not very much that the tenant can do about that.[126]

The absence of written deeds and of tenants' rights creates a potentially precarious situation for most peasants in the longer run, and this situation very often becomes acute when some innovation takes place that increases the value of the land. Alfred Métraux relates a case from the Marbial valley:

> A peasant friend of ours had leased three-quarters of a 'carreau' from a townsman, at a rent of 40 gdes. Encouraged by the fact that for ten years he had been on excellent terms with the lessor, he started a small coffee plantation on the plot. The flourishing condition of this plot prompted a neighbour to ask the landlord to transfer the lease to him, in return for a rent of 60 gourdes. This suggestion was immediately accepted, and our friend was informed of the cancellation of his lease, in a note which offered no compensation whatever for the young coffee plantation he had started.[127]

In this case it was the introduction of a new crop that led to the unfortunate consequences. In other cases a change in methods e.g. by the introduction of new forms of capital may have similar effects. The realization of irrigation works in the lower Artibonite valley around 1950 attracted outside more or less 'legally' founded interests who soon began to evict the peasants. A commission of inquiry was later appointed and reported that

> It was of the opinion that the promise of prosperity created by the important works realized in the Artibonite had aroused an immediate desire to become owners of the lands close to the river among many citizens...
> Among the latter there are not only enlightened peasants, but also, and above all, townsmen who have discovered a sudden vocation to become agricultors, and even friends, favorites and members of the previous government acting directly or via intermediaries.[128]

Incidents such as these clearly point to how innovations may threaten peasant holdings. Insecurity hence acts as a strong obstacle to change. If a peasant or tenant cannot be sure of reaping the benefits of an innovation himself they may instead prefer to reject it and at least not jeopardize the right to their land, their ultimate security, however insufficient, against deprivation and starvation.*

---

*Anything that increases the value of peasant land is potentially threatening. The expansion of the Plantation Dauphin sisal cultivations in the Fort-Liberté area in the 1920s was accompanied by a massive forced dispossession of smallholders, and similar incidents took place when SHADA in 1941 obtained a monopoly of rubber production from the Haitian government. A large number of peasants were driven from their homes and their lands were turned into rubber plantations. (See République d'Haïti (1946-47), passim; Honorat (1974), pp. 90-91; Moral (1961), p. 295; Rotberg & Clague (1971), p. 169; Moore (1972), pp. 64-5.)

In some other Latin American states, viz. those with strong landlord domination, the kind of resistance to change discussed here is even stronger. Gerrit Huizer in his book on peasant rebellion in Latin America argues that strong landlord power over the peasantry is the *main* reason for the apparent apathy towards innovation. Opportunities for substantial change are often *purposely* blocked by the landowning class, and according to Huizer it is only when peasants can expect a change in the system which blocks effective improvements that they will respond. Within the existing structure their behavior is governed by a hierarchy of fears:

> fear of death by capital punishment, fear of the pain of corporal punishment, fear of incarceration, fear of the landlord's disapproval, fear of the loss of property, fear of hunger, and fear of the supernatural...the behavior of the serf peasants [is] often defined by the strongest of competing fears. A peasant whose animal [is] taken away by the estate owner [will] not complain, since

Finally, it should be mentioned that there is yet another way in which the absence of secured deeds may be detrimental to innovations, and that is when it comes to borrowing money for production and innovation purposes. If titles are not clear, the land cannot be used as security in the loan transactions which means that the rate of interest that the peasants will have to pay goes up correspondingly due to the addition of a risk premium.[129]

Summing up: risk is an important factor in an economy of the Haitian type. The existence of the peasants in a critical way depends on the outcome of the harvest and on the levels of the prices of outputs, inputs and peasant consumption goods. The Haitian peasants only have limited means at their disposal for protecting themselves against the whims of nature or the fluctuations of demand and supply in the market-place. Under these circumstances, aversion to risky enterprises is a natural reaction. Many innovations are risky. New seeds, for example, often increase not only expected yields but also the variability of yields. Given the low level of peasant incomes and the weakness of the protective devices at the disposal of the peasants, it is then quite understandable that the latter often may resist the introduction of new techniques as long as the safety of these techniques cannot be established unequivocally. Aversion to risk may also act as an obstacle to innovations in another way. It is not difficult to find examples of innovations which by increasing the value of peasant land attract outside interests who (often successfully) attempt to deprive the peasants of their farms. By sticking to the traditional technology, the peasants

> fear of patronal disapproval or even of incarceration [is] stronger than the fear of the loss of property, or of hunger (Huizer (1973), pp. 9-10).

Such fear and distrust, on the other hand may become instrumental when it comes to changing the peasants' lot:

> Experience...showed that peasant distrust can be one of the most important promoters of change and development if it is used as a force that brings peasants together in a common struggle in opposition to the traditional vested interests of landlords and other repressive forces. The growth of several strong peasant organizations that have been crucial in the promotion of radical change in some Latin American countries was one result of these forces... (ibid., pp. 3-4).

The implication of this for Haiti is that we should not expect any spontaneous creation of peasant organizations, for in addition to the obstacles mentioned in the discussion of co-operatives, the triggering cue in the form of landlord repression is absent, or at any rate is not strong enough.

may at least be comparatively certain that they will not be turned into landless laborers.

Malnutrition and Disease

In Chapter 9 we mentioned that changes in the health standard may influence the efficiency of agriculture in the sense that the output per work unit performed may change e.g. if the peasants when better nourished may be able to undertake more imaginative productive activities than before. By the same token, the low average calorie intake and the disease situation in the countryside may act as obstacles to the introduction and diffusion of innovations in rural districts.

Very little has been written regarding the connections between health and innovative activities, but a few points should be made. Ill health and malnutrition in the individual case probably have little influence on the rate of innovations. The problems arise when, as in the case of Haiti, large population groups are affected. The traditional technology probably takes the health standards of the workers into account. The activities have been designed to suit a labor force with a certain physical and mental capacity. Technological change in turn poses added physical and mental requirements. In addition to the customary daily range of activities, the farmers have to plan ahead, learn new techniques, evaluate the outcome of the new methods in the local setting, etc. They may also have to increase the amount of physical energy expended, e.g. when the new technology requires capital formation in which labor constitutes an important input.[130] In a situation where the mental and physical energy of the peasants is sapped by a deficient calorie intake and diseases of various kinds, the result may be that otherwise superior innovations may meet with resistance or at least indifference on part of the peasants.

Information and Education

So far, we have tacitly assumed that all the relevant information regarding the characteristics and effects of available techniques, crops, etc. has been available to the peasants (with the exception of the discussion of risk) so as not to constitute any barrier to their choice or to cause any bias in it. This assumption is of course not likely to be fulfilled in practice.

Lack of information reportedly leads to the emergence of what Richard M. Cyert and James G. March have termed problemistic search.[131] A problem is perceived, and to find a solution to it the person perceiving the problem begins to scan his environment for relevant information, and as long as the expected utility from continuing the search process exceeds the expected costs connected with further search, the person will presumably go on searching. In principle, this kind of search should take place in the Haitian peasant sector as well as in other sectors and economies, and one potentially fruitful field for search activities in a stagnant agriculture might be to look for new products, factors and production techniques. Typically, however, the amount of search for innovations in such societies is low. According to Theodore W. Schultz,

> It is highly improbable that any small farmer situated in a typical poor community would engage in such a search unless there were some experimental plots nearby or unless he were to act through some co-operative arrangement. Even if he were of a mind to search for such information, to do it on his own and to extend his search to other farming communities a considerable distance away would become prohibitively expensive for him. To go abroad for this purpose would be out of the question.[132]

We will soon come back to demonstration and extension activities, but first we must stress the role of education. Lack of formal instruction and literacy are factors that are likely to restrict and bias search. Although little is know with any degree of certainty regarding the relation between literacy, education and innovative behavior, the general presumption appears to be that the connection is strong. The more educated the farmer, the more innovative he becomes, *ceteris paribus*.[133] This hypothesis may be phrased in terms of the search process. In at least six different ways search and evaluation of its findings may be affected by education.

First, increased education may increase the amount of search done by the peasant himself. It is generally assumed that education increases the inquisitiveness of the farmer, his values and motivations, etc. so that he may become aware of hitherto unperceived problems in agricultural production and also of new, hitherto unknown opportunities,[134] which in turn may result in a more active search on his own part. The marginal utility of search activities may increase.

Second, literacy provides an additional means of communication and hence largely facilitates the problem of how to reach the peasants in their environment with relevant information regarding new techniques and products. Illiteracy is a formidable obstacle to all extension efforts since it drastically reduces the number of peasants that can be efficiently served by the extension agents. (On the other hand, while written communication is less costly, oral and visual demonstration may be more efficient in showing the benefits of a new technique or product, so that the most appropriate measure presumably is a combination of both techniques where pamphlets, books, etc. are used to support and reinforce the effects of direct demonstrations on the spot.)[135]

Third, the direction and extent of search is likely to change. According to Cyert and March problemistic search always tends to be simple-minded, since it relies basically on two simple rules. Search first takes place in the neighborhood of the problem symptoms, i.e. it is believed that the cause of a problem is 'near' its effect. The search procedure also relies heavily on past solutions to similar problems. It is only when these two rules prove unfruitful (when search is not immediately successful) that search becomes more 'distant'.[136]

In both these phases of the search process the educated and the uneducated peasant are likely to proceed differently. To take one example, the illiterate peasant is often likely to refer to the will of God or the *loas* (or that of a *bocor* – sorcerer) in times of misfortunes,[137] while the cause-effect reasoning of the educated peasant is likely to run in more rational terms (or at least to provide rational explanations in addition to the supernatural ones). When the illiterate peasant has to fall back on empirical procedures and oral tradition in the process of gathering information, the educated farmer has additional sources to draw upon as well. Similarly, when the simple-minded search procedure proves insufficient, the attitudes towards e.g. the 'outside' knowledge represented by people like the local extension agent are likely to differ considerably.[138] In sum: the chances are that the illiterate will cover a much smaller area in his search than the educated peasant with a smaller probability of success.

Fourth, the better educated peasant probably has a longer time horizon and a better developed ability to understand complex reasoning than his illiterate colleague. Erasmus states that one of the clearest patterns emerging from his survey of resistance to and acceptance of innovations was that it was much easier to persuade the peasants to adopt such techniques and crops that yielded an immediate benefit than those whose benefits were of a long-term nature. Thus,

> the introduction of a new plant or species which results in a greater market price, or results in a greater yield, can be effectively demonstrated in a single season and its success is often immediate. A refinement in cultivation practices such as spacing between plants, planting in rows, or planting fewer seeds to a hole is less spectacular

in its results and diffuses more slowly. Finally, attempts to introduce such refinements as composting, prevention of burning, rotation of crops, pruning, building of animal shelters, seed selection, and soil conservation may meet with little or no acceptance.[139]

An illiterate has either to take the word of the extension agent for granted (which is seldom done) or otherwise judge the results of new practices on the basis of casual observation, and in the case of long-term projects the probability is high that the peasants do not grasp the connection between the new traits and their results (unless something goes wrong and the innovation is blamed). Erasmus found that the long-term projects stood the best chance if they also included some short-term benefits:

> In [one] valley the local agronomist has had considerable success in a short period of time in persuading the farmers to make seedbeds for trees which will be transplanted on hillsides to check erosion. Since it is a traditional coffee area, the peasant is easily persuaded to cooperate with the agent in starting seed beds of coffee plants. From the standpoint of the farmers, the tree nurseries which adjoin their coffee nurseries are not being planted with the view of checking erosion, but to provide shade for the coffee. Thus a long-term benefit is being served by associating it with a short-term benefit of immediate interest to the farmer.[140]

Such indirect approaches are not always feasible. Better education presumably is the best alternative for lengthening the time horizons of the peasants and for improving their ability to judge the merits of an innovation correctly.

Fifth, better education for some peasants is likely to have some spillover effects in relation to other peasants.[141] If the uneducated see that the lot of the educated improves due to acceptance of innovations, it is possible that the former will begin to seek the advice of the latter in matters which they feel are too complicated to be handled on the basis of their own knowledge and experience only. As borne out by the experience related by Erasmus, the Haitian peasant is reluctant to undertake experiments himself, but once he has observed that an innovation really works out for somebody else he willingly follows in the steps of the latter, other conditions permitting.[142] In this way the distance between the extension agent and the peasant is shortened. Somebody who himself is a peasant (but with some education) can act as a 'broker' and by example bring others (uneducated) along with him in the process.

Finally, a better education is likely to reduce the amount of risk perceived by the peasant when judging a new crop or technique. Risk aversion to a large extent is a function of the ability to judge accurately the consequences of alternative action, and the better educated presumably have a better understanding of the implications of different courses of action or at least have got a better preparation to learn how to judge them. Thus, some of the subjectivity inherent in situations where decisions must be made in a risky environment may be reduced and with that the degree of risk perceived.

Against the background of our findings in Chapter 10, it is, however, easily seen that the Haitian system of rural education is not likely to provide the kind of support needed for rendering peasant search more intensive and efficient. Too few manage to complete primary education. The majority never attend school at all, and a large number of those who do drop out sooner or later. Those who pass in turn, are not very likely to remain in the countryside to do farm work but will presumably migrate to urban areas instead in search of a job where they can earn more than in agriculture. Possibly, the kind of education received also fosters negative attitudes towards peasant farming.

The Role of Government Efforts

Both from the point of view of the individual producer and from the point of view of most nations, it is true that the majority of innovations are borrowed from the outside.[143] Most innovations cannot, however, be transplanted from one environment to another without modifications to suit the local circumstances,[144] and obviously, this is a much greater problem in agriculture than in manufacturing, since the direct dependence on the natural environment is much more pronounced in the former sector than in the latter. This problem of transferring and reshaping products and technologies from one environment to another calls for creation of private or public agencies specialized in fostering technological development in agriculture. For reasons already discussed, spontaneous technological change in an economy of the Haitian type is only likely to proceed at an extremely slow pace. The time perspectives involved are likely to be those of centuries rather than of decades.*

---

*This long-term view has been stressed especially by Schultz (1964), who argues that the existing technologies in peasant societies are a result of centuries of accumulation of experience and trial-and-error within the local environment.

In a country like Haiti it is hard to envisage any agents of change and innovation in rural areas other than government-run or government-sponsored agencies,[145] and at the beginning of this chapter we have quoted a number of instances where Haitian governments have promoted technological change in the agricultural sector. Yet, 'in Haiti, no examples of the spread of consciously introduced technological progress can be cited.'[146] Most of the reasons for this failure have already been analyzed, but it still remains to make some specific comments on the role of the government itself in spreading innovations.

Government-sponsored technological change entails creation of domestic research capacity in several, interconnected fields. In a survey on problems of science and technology in less developed countries Graham Jones points to the following major roles of research in the development process:[147]

1. To help select and adapt existing scientific and technological knowledge to meet specific local needs.

2. To maintain contact with developments elsewhere of potential local importance.

3. To augment existing knowledge in fields of potential relevance, with particular emphasis on those areas which, for various reasons, are not or cannot be properly studied elsewhere, as in relation to specific biological or mineral resources, climatic and soil conditions, or social problems.

4. As far as possible within the limits of the foregoing, as a necessary activity in the training of scientific and technical personnel and their teachers.

Various efforts have been made in Haiti to meet these demands. These efforts go as far back as to the beginning of the present century. After repeated failures on part of the government, in 1907, the Catholic Brothers opened the first experimental farm in Turgeau — without success. (The following year the farm, which also included educational activities, had only three pupils.)[148] Serious attempts to start agricultural research in Haiti did not take place during the American occupation, when, as we have seen earlier in the present chapter, the Service Technique maintained five agricultural experiment stations and in addition one station specialized on coffee farming.

However, agricultural research has never managed to gain a firm foothold in Haiti. Gradually, the activities initiated by the Americans died out. By the end of the 1940s the UN mission reported that the experimental work had 'largely ceased.'[149] Twenty-five years later, the situation was no better. Some agricultural research had been carried out, mainly at Damien, but in 1974 the Inter-American Development Bank reported that agricultural research was deficient, and that the majority of the experimental stations run by the Department of Agriculture had been abandoned. Co-ordination between projects and agencies was lacking, and the experiments carried out often took place in fields where the results were already known with a high degree of certainty.[150] No substantial changes are in sight in this important field in the immediate future. The five-year plan for the agricultural sector 1976-81 provides an allocation of funds for research purposes of only 20 million gourdes or 4.6 percent of total plan expenditures[151] — a consequence of government lack of interest in the rural population.

The consequences of failure to develop an adequate domestic agricultural research capacity must not be under-rated. A high-yielding rice technology was developed in Japan as early as in the 1880s,[152] but as Vernon W. Ruttan has pointed out, this technology did not reach South and Southeast Asia until the late 1960s (with the exception of Korea and Taiwan, where introduction took place in the 1920s). It was not until public sector investment in local experimental station capacity to develop and adapt local varieties was initiated in the early 1960s in the Philippines and India, that transfer of the high-yielding technology to these areas could take place. The lag in developing research institutions caused a delay of several decades.[153]

Research cannot proceed in isolation. If its results are to be of any practical value it must be intimately connected with a dissemination or extension service. The role of this service is two-fold. On the one hand, it must ensure that the results of the scientific process are brought to bear on practical problems in the local environment, by bringing the new knowledge to peasants. The extension agents must be active in reaching out to individual farmers. They must be 'prime movers' of innovation.[154] On the other hand, extension agencies 'must remain guides and servants, not masters.'[155] This means that the extension service must also serve as an organization for 'market research', by which the needs and demands of peasants for improved methods and products can be traced.

From the point of view of the individual producer, the economic importance of an efficient public organization to transfer and reshape technologies and products is perhaps best understood in terms of information costs. All search processes that may be generated from a perceived need for technological improvements are bound to be limited and expensive in a society where there is no specialized and more or less centralized systematic gathering and processing of such information that may be relevant. Individual peasants, as we know, can cover only a very limited range in their search and may not know in which area search is likely to yield the best results. Furthermore, the relevant information may not be directly useful for the problem at hand. There may be considerable costs connected with restructuring and developing the information before it becomes applicable. Individually or taken together these costs may be so high as to preclude innovation altogether. An efficient system of transfer, reshaping and extension lowers information costs by providing a short-cut in the search process.

The educational component is of course the most important part of the extension process. A starting point in the process of diffusion of innovations is to bring the factual knowledge regarding the existence and features of the potentially beneficial innovations to those who are to benefit from them, i.e. to the peasants. All unfamiliar production factors, for example, require some learning process to take place before they can be used efficiently:

> Obviously some new factors are simple in this respect while others are exceedingly complex. Hybrid corn is comparatively simple in this score. Yet even here farmers must learn not to select next year's seed from a field produced by a hybrid variety, because it will not reproduce itself as closely as the open-pollinated variety to which they are accustomed — the hybrid soon loses its hybrid vigor where seed is selected in this way. The stalk may be shorter, it may lodge, the ear may be less firmly attached to the stalk after it has ripened, and the kernels may be softer and even different in color. To acquire the best yield, plants need to be planted closer together than is proper with the larger stalk of an open-pollinated variety, more fertilizer needs to be applied, and where there is irrigation the optimum water requirements are likely to differ from those of the open-pollinated variety. So even a simple factor like a corn hybrid entails some learning before the best farm practices can be followed.[156]

Typically, some kind of complementarities are involved in agricultural innovations and these increase information requirements. Directly or indirectly the peasant has to be educated about which new seeds, fertilizers, pesticides, insecticides, animals, animal feeds, tools, implements and or equipment that are available and about time and technique of planting (depth, elevation, watering; if irrigated, drainage and spacing); maturation and protection of crop or animal (weeding, spraying, fertilizing plus timing and rate of application); harvesting; culling, weaning, feeding and fattening, inoculation, general medication (spraying, dipping, vaccinating, pills); and crop rotation, cover, forage, soil conservation.[157]

Clearly, extension education has a central role to play in all this.

An extension service was created during the American occupation by the Service Technique. In 1930, this service employed 35 extension agents who managed to attend almost 6,000 farms.[158] In the 1930s, the number of government extension personnel gradually increased, to 60 in 1933-34,[159] 70 in 1937-38[160] and 100 in 1939-40.[161] In absolute terms, these numbers remained too low. Each agent had to cover far too large a territory to be able to assist the peasants efficiently.[162] This situation persisted throughout the 1940s as well. In 1949, the UN mission to Haiti concluded that

> the task has been too great. The bulk of production continues to be carried out by primitive means, and the volume and quality of valuable export crops have declined. Evidently the means available and the methods in use are inadequate to cope with factors of administrative discontinuity, political instability, and economic insecurity which act against the development of agricultural production...the training of agronomists tends to be overly academic, with insufficient emphasis on practical field experience...The effort to bring about an improvement in the quality of agricultural produce by inspection and the imposition of penalties has not only failed entirely, but among the peasants has brought into disrepute the efforts of true extension agents seeking to teach the use of better methods and means of production. The Technical Services, thus divorced from vital contact with the farm population, have also suffered in quality.[163]

Agricultural extension continues to face a number of serious problems today. In countries with a relatively simple agriculture of the Haitian type, it is probably quite sufficient that extension agents have completed a specially-designed secondary education.[164] However, agronomists with a university education must be used in supporting and supervising positions. It is indispensable that 'the University specialist should be at the elbow of the field Extension worker,'[165] when needed: to help out in difficult situations, and to disseminate new research findings that may be applied in the practical extension work. Employment of agronomists in extension work has proved difficult in Haiti. In 1967, only 2.6 percent of all university students chose agronomy,[166] and in absolute terms enrolment was ridiculously small. The number of students in 1945 and 1956 was 31, a figure that had only increased to 40 in 1967, i.e. by 9 students in 22 years.[167] An inventory of all Haitian agronomists graduating at home or abroad between 1924 and 1965 revealed that out of a total of 298, 32 worked abroad and 106 were occupied with activities not related to agriculture, which left only 138 agronomists actually practicing their profession within the country[168] (totally — not only in the extension service).

The number of regular extension workers has remained low as well. In the 1970s, DARNDR, IDAI and IHPCADE together disposed of a cadre of some 750 agents.[169] The number of rural families that each one of these had to cover was excessively high. Thus, in 1970 each DARNDR agent would have had to cope with on the average 6,300 rural families (ranging from 3,500 in the Port-au-Prince district to 14,500 in the St Marc region).[170] It was estimated that fewer than 20 percent of the agents had received the appropriate training for their task.[171]

Of course, the extension service has suffered from all of the common defects of the Haitian administration pointed out in Chapters 6-8. The reader is referred to these chapters for appropriate details. We will only point to three specific problems here. First, most of the budget of the extension agencies is absorbed by salaries and wages, and this creates a tremendous lack of equipment, buildings, vehicles and other material necessary for the actual operations. As an example it may be mentioned that in 1973, 82 percent of the cars used by DARNDR were more than 11 years old and that the average age was 10 years.[172] Secondly, it is difficult to persuade agents with an adequate education to move out of the capital. Average salaries are low, and this is often compensated for by holding two or more different jobs. The availability of suitable jobs in turn, is higher in the capital than in the provinces.[173] The third and last factor to be stressed is that co-ordination between different agencies appears to be lacking. Very often duplication or triplication of the same type of tasks takes place or conversely, often the extension agents from a particular agency work in isolation with 'their' peasants without contact with their colleagues in other agencies.[174]

Finally, it should be mentioned that the probability of a radical improvement in the quantity and quality of extension work sponsored by public agencies is low. The 1976-81 five-year plan for the agricultural sector only provides 20 million gourdes to extension, or less than 5 percent of the total expenditure in the sector.[175]

Conclusions

Haitian peasant agriculture has been technologically stagnant for more than a century. Early efforts by Henry Christophe to introduce the modern methods of the day failed, and instead the agricultural sector underwent a process of technological retrogression during the early nineteenth century. The efficient specialized operations of the French plantations could not be duplicated on the peasant smallholdings. Likewise, the severe work discipline upheld in colonial Saint-Domingue was relaxed in free Haiti. The productivity of a given labor force fell. Finally, during the wars of liberation the fairly sophisticated capital equipment of the plantations was destroyed and the simple hand tools still employed today were adopted instead. The situation with respect to product innovations presented the same stationary picture. Virtually all attempts to introduce new export crops when the price of coffee declined towards the mid-nineteenth century proved in vain.

During the American occupation a number of measures designed to enhance the productivity of the agricultural sector were initiated. The impact was virtually zero. The peasants stubbornly continued their old ways, and post-occupation attempts to change these ways have led nowhere. The technology of the Haitian peasant today remains essentially the same as that of a century or more ago — a technology which given the existing factor endowments of the peasant sector, is utterly incapable of ensuring a satisfactory standard of living for the peasant masses.

One of the most conspicuous features of the Haitian peasant sector is the combination of population growth and shrinking land resources which slowly depresses per capita incomes in rural districts as time elapses. A possible, and in the Haitian case probable, response of an agrarian society to population growth is to adopt new technologies or crops which will permit a rise in the standard of living to its former level. For a number of reasons, as the historical evidence demonstrates, this has not taken place.

Some obstacles to innovations stem directly from the nature of the agricultural production process. Cultivation is a question of handling organic matter, the structure of which is so complex as to reduce man to a simple imitator of nature. Besides imitating nature there is little man can do to change production conditions. This problem is in turn complicated by the fact that time has a paramount place in agricultural production. The most important periods of the agricultural year are the rainy seasons. The production process is so intimately connected with natural precipitation that most innovations will have to take place within the narrow scope drawn up by the timing of the rains.

Another natural factor rendering innovations difficult is the rugged terrain of the country. Certain innovations, like the plow, become inferior in steep terrain. The mountains create problems of transport and communication between the scattered plots of the peasants and possibly restrict the market for peasant produce as well as eliminating the opportunity for economies of specialization in production.

Turning our attention to economic factors, we first find that new technologies which require an intensive use of equipment or other material inputs may be irrelevant for the peasants because the price of these inputs is too high in relation to that of labor. This effect may be reinforced by the existence of indivisibilities in capital. Indivisibilities may lead to trouble in at least one more way: by necessitating external borrowing for the peasants to be able to finance the investments required if a new technology is to be adopted. Borrowing, in turn, as we know from Chapter 11, can usually only take place at high rates of interest for short periods of time in the informal credit markets. Long-term finance at reasonable interest rates is virtually impossible to obtain. Finally, a special case of indivisibilities arises in connection with such equipment which cannot be hired for shorter periods but which must be purchased by the peasants if it is to be used at all. The relatively small size of the Haitian farms may make this type of equipment (e.g. the plow) unprofitable – the more so the higher the price of capital in relation to that of labor.

Indivisibilities may in principle be overcome by means of co-operative solutions, but this has in most cases not worked in Haiti. The co-operative movement has failed, largely because the co-operatives have been introduced from 'above' without paying due attention to the needs and wishes of the peasants. Spontaneous creation of co-operatives has been rare due to the lack of natural leaders in the rural community who emphasize change and also due to a lack of education among the peasants. The existence of risks of various kinds is probably one of the most important reasons why the peasants reject innovations which *prima facie* appear to be profitable. Extreme poverty in combination with inadequate protection against risks has made risk averters out of the peasants. Since all innovations to a greater or lesser extent are connected with risks, there is a natural tendency for the peasants to continue with well-known, time-honored crops and practices, which are understood to be more predictable. An additional complication in connection with risks is the insecurity of peasant landholdings which may make the peasants reluctant to adopt innovations because they feel that someone else may attempt to evict them from their land, should the innovations increase the value of the latter.

Factors connected with 'human capital' may also be behind the problems of change. An unhealthy peasant is less likely to be innovative than a healthy one. More important still is that the general lack of education in the countryside restricts the amount and efficiency of search for information regarding new technologies and products. Here, the government could help by searching for new technologies, by evaluating them, by adapting them to local circumstances, by disseminating the knowledge regarding these innovations to the peasants and by educating the peasants with respect to the necessary change when refined technologies or new crops are to be introduced. This has, however, not been the case in Haiti. The peasants by and large have to rely only on their own limited capacity for change. The result is there for everybody to see: a lack of change for more than a century. The peasants are stuck with the traditional low-yielding methods of production, methods which cannot counteract the secular tendency for peasant incomes to fall.

Notes

1. Rostow (1960), Chapter 2.
2. Mellor (1962), (1966), Chapter 13 et seq. Cf. also e.g. Hunter (1969), esp. pp. 24-9.
3. Schultz (1964), passim.
4. Rosenberg (1971), pp. 9-10.
5. Griggs & Prator (1968), p. 62.
6. Leyburn (1966), pp. 46, 85; Lepkowski (1968:1), p. 105.
7. Leyburn (1966), p. 46.
8. Franklin (1828), pp. 302-4.
9. Ibid., pp. 352-3.
10. Schoelcher (1843), pp. 263 ff.
11. Girod-Chantrans (1785), p. 137. Cf. Rotberg & Clague (1971), pp. 35-6 for further documentation.
12. James (1963), p. 10.
13. Leyburn (1966), p. 74.
14. Victor (1944), p. 28.
15. BTS, no. 10, September 1953, p. 22.
16. Cf. Clark & Haswell (1967), Chapter VI.
17. James (1963), p. 45.
18. Rotberg & Clague (1971), p. 29.
19. Clague (1970), p. 7.
20. Moral (1955), p. 242.
21. Ibid., pp. 244-5.
22. Ibid., p. 245.

23. See ibid., pp. 244-6.
24. Cf., however, ibid., p. 251.
25. Clague (1970), p. 8.
26. Moral (1955), p. 249.
27. See Kindleberger (1962), Chapter 7. The quotation is from p. 100.
28. Rotberg & Clague (1971), p. 97.
29. Ibid., p. 98.
30. Ibid., pp. 89, 300.
31. Moore (1972), p. 31.
32. Rotberg & Clague (1971), p. 388.
33. Cf. Chapter 6.
34. Millspaugh (1931), p. 163.
35. Service Technique (1929:2), p. 105.
36. Millspaugh (1931), p. 150.
37. For account of the cotton experiment see Rotberg & Clague (1971), pp. 284-6 and Gates (1959:3), pp. 5-6.
38. Millspaugh (1931), p. 149.
39. Rotberg & Clague (1971), p. 136. The results of the survey are presented in Woodring, Brown & Burbank (1924).
40. Millspaugh (1931), p. 154; Schmidt (1971), p. 185.
41. Herskovits (1971), p. 67.
42. Simpson (1940), p. 519.
43. Ibid., p. 518.
44. Ibid., p. 519.
45. Gates (1959:2), p. 32.
46. Rotberg & Clague (1971), p. 282.
47. Street (1960), p. 259.
48. Gates (1959:2), p. 33.
49. Ibid.
50. Rotberg & Clague (1971), pp. 282-5.
51. UN (1949), p. 88. Cf. also Métraux *et al.* (1951), pp. 56-66 where a description from the Marbial valley during the same period is made.
52. ICA (1961), p. 1.
53. Ibid.
54. Moore (1972), p. 72; Moral (1961), p. 330. A detailed description is given in ICA (1961).
55. Moral (1961), p. 331.
56. Extensive descriptions of these programs are given in OEA (1972), pp. 343-79 and CONADEP (1974).
57. See Street (1960), pp. 219-22 and Rotberg & Clague (1971), pp. 282-3.
58. Moral (1961), p. 194. The quotation is from Michel-Etienne Descourtilz: *Voyage d'un naturaliste et ses observations faites sur les trois règnes de la nature, Vol II*, Paris 1809, p. 399.
59. Moral (1961), p. 395.
60. Courlander (1966), p. 5.
61. Rotberg & Clague (1971), p. 277.
62. A shorter and somewhat different earlier version of this section can be found in Lundahl (1977).
63. Grigg (1976), p. 138.
64. Cf. ibid., passim.
65. Boserup (1965), p. 41.
66. Smith (1970), p. 6.
67. See Georgescu-Roegen (1969) and (1971) and Brewster (1950).
68. Georgescu-Roegen (1971), p. 298.

69. See ibid., appendix G.
70. Ibid., p. 299.
71. Ibid., p. 300.
72. Ibid., pp. 211-53.
73. Ricardo (1971), p. 91.
74. Georgescu-Roegen (1971), p. 236.
75. Ibid., p. 238.
76. Hunter (1969), p. 116.
77. Cf. Schultz (1953), Chapter 8.
78. Smith (1970), p. 8. Cf. Lewis (1955), p. 126.
79. Griffin (1972), (1974).
80. Griffin (1974), p. 49.
81. Ibid.
82. Tinnermeier (1973), p. 5. For examples, see ibid., pp. 5-7. Cf. also Long (1974), pp. 26-7.
83. Griffin (1974), pp. 51-2. Cf. also Myrdal (1968), pp. 1290-1.
84. Rotberg & Clague (1971), p. 278.
85. Cf., however, Roumasset (1976), pp. 3-4.
86. Myrdal (1968), p. 1290.
87. The results are reported in Brummitt & Culp (n.d.).
88. Ibid., p. 34.
89. Dorville (1975:1), p. 22.
90. Becerra de la Flor & Abarbanel (1974), p. 23.
91. The analysis here follows McKinnon (1973), Chapter 2, with some modifications.
92. Rotberg & Clague (1971), p. 289.
93. Erasmus (1952), pp. 25-6.
94. David (1975), Chapter 5, esp. Addendum.
95. Boserup (1965), p. 35.
96. Ibid., p. 36.
97. Ibid.
98. Ibid., pp. 36-7.
99. See e.g. Rotberg & Clague (1971), p. 280.
100. Erasmus (1952).
101. Ibid., p. 25.
102. See e.g. Lamothe (1958); Vallès (1967), and most recently Laguerre (1975), who explicitly bases his recommendations on the *coumbite* system. Cf. also Griffin (1974), pp. 66-8 for similar observations on Asia.
103. Vallès (1967), p. 14.
104. Ibid., p. 73.
105. Erasmus (1952), p. 22.
106. Rotberg & Clague (1971), p. 320.
107. Ibid.
108. Hunter (1969), p. 157.
109. See Chapter 3.
110. See Chapter 10.
111. Erasmus (1952), p. 23. Cf. also Chapter 11, above.
112. See Moral (1959), pp. 30-31, 32-6 and (1961), pp. 232-7.
113. UNESCO (1951), p. 17; Domínguez (1976), p. 41.
114. Friedmann (1955), p. 48.
115. Bastien (1966), p. 48.
116. Cf. Rotberg & Clague (1971), p. 17.
117. See Allen (1977) pp. 526-7. Cf. also Brummitt & Culp (n.d.), p. 25, for the Haitian situation.

118. Moral (1961), pp. 169-72. Cf., however, Schaedel (1962), pp. 25 ff.; Honorat (1974), note p. 27; Domínguez (1976), pp. 6, 15, 16, 21, for evidence that the *lakou* system may still be strong in many places.
119. Cf. Chapter 2.
120. Cf. Chapter 11.
121. Lipton (1968:1). Cf. Roumasset (1976), for an application.
122. Cf. Lipton (1968:1), pp. 332-4, 348; Weeks (1970), p. 30 and note 6, p. 35; Myrdal (1968), pp. 1292 ff. Cf. also Griffin (1974), pp. 62-6.
123. Erasmus (1952), pp. 20-21. Cf. OEA (1972), p. 631.
124. Moral (1961), p. 181.
125. Ibid., pp. 181-2.
126. Métraux *et al.* (1951), p. 18.
127. Ibid.
128. Duvigneaud & Figaro (1958), p. 1. See also Moral (1961), p. 182. Some special problems of innovations in connection with shareholdings are discussed by Newbery (1975:2).
129. Cf. Chapter 11.
130. Kamarck (1976), pp. 61-2.
131. See Cyert & March (1963), pp. 120 ff. Cf. Schultz (1964), p. 169.
132. Schultz (1964), p. 169. Cf. Jones (1971), pp. 74-5.
133. Cf. Sansom (1970), p. 177; Schuman, Inkeles & Smith (1968), pp. 4-5; Mellor (1966), p. 347.
134. See e.g. Wharton (1965), pp. 206-7; Schuman, Inkeles & Smith (1968), p. 5; Montgomery (1967), pp. 148-9.
135. Blaug (1970), pp. 255-6.
136. Cyert & March (1963), pp. 121-2.
137 See e.g. Métraux *et al.* (1951), pp. 65-6; Herskovits (1971), pp. 78-81.
138. Cf. Hunter (1969), pp. 240-41.
139. Erasmus (1952), p. 20.
140. Ibid., p. 21.
141. Cf. Blaug (1970), p. 248; Schultz (1964), p. 172.
142. Erasmus (1952), pp. 20-21, 24.
143. March & Simon (1958), p. 188; Jones (1971), pp. 12-13.
144. Jones (1971), pp. 21 ff.; Solo (1966); Gould (1972), pp. 350 ff.; Mellor (1966), p. 269; McPherson & Johnston (1967), p. 222.
145. Cf. Hunter (1969), p. 175; Harbison (1965), p. 237.
146. Rotberg & Clague (1971), p. 331.
147. Jones (1971), p. 26.
148. Logan (1930), p. 429.
149. UN (1949), p. 102.
150. BID (1974), pp. 36-7.
151. DARNDR (1976), p. 71.
152. Hayami & Ruttan (1970), p. 1122.
153. Ruttan (1975), pp. 176-80.
154. Harbison (1965).
155. Jones (1971), pp. 74-5.
156. Schultz (1964), pp. 170-71.
157. Wharton (1965), pp. 212. Cf. Rotberg & Clague (1971), p. 327.
158. Service Technique (1930), p. 39.
159. SNPA & ER (1935), pp. 5-6.
160. SNPA & ER (1939), pp. 7-8.
161. SNPA & ER (n.d.), pp. 8-9.
162. Holly (1955), p. 301.
163. UN (1949), pp. 102-3.

164. Wharton (1965), p. 216; Hunter (1969), p. 181.
165. Hunter (1969), p. 84.
166. CIAP (1969), p. 91.
167. Rotberg & Clague (1971), p. 315.
168. CIAP (1966), p. 110.
169. BID (1974), pp. 36-7.
170. PNUD (1971), p. 40.
171. Ibid., p. 7.
172. BID (1974), p. 21.
173. Ibid., p. 20.
174. Ibid., p. 38. Cf. OEA (1972), pp. 346 ff.
175. DARNDR (1976), p. 71.

EPILOGUE

The chapters of the present book have covered a broad range of topics related to the Haitian peasant economy. The secular tendency for peasant incomes to fall has been analyzed. We have seen why the governments of Haiti have not identified their fate with that of the peasants and what this has led to in terms of economic policy. An attempt has been made to discover the relations between changes in health and economic performance. The discriminatory nature of the educational system has been emphasized. We have pointed to the difficulties connected with capital formation in agriculture. Finally, the reasons for technological stagnation in the peasant sector have been explored. Now we have reached the end of our analysis, and the time has come to sum up, to draw conclusions on the basis of our analytical findings and to attempt some predictions with respect to the future of Haitian peasant agriculture.

We will begin by reviewing some of the available evidence with respect to external and internal migration. One of the main results of the poverty prevailing in the Haitian countryside appears to have been that of creating an outflow of people from rural districts either to urban areas or out of the country. The second and last part of this epilogue will present some of the main conclusions to be drawn from our study.

Migration: A Result of Poverty

Internal population movements have always been an important part of Haitian history. After the eradication of the indigenous population during the sixteenth century, the coastal plains, the river plains and the mountain flanks surrounding these plains (i.e. the areas favorable to sugar and later also coffee cultivation) were colonized first by Spanish and later by French settlers who both also brought in large numbers of black African slaves. Some escaped slaves (maroons) from the end of the seventeenth century established themselves in some of the uninhabited mountain ranges. After independence in 1804, the colonization of mountain lands, especially in the Plateau Central, begun by the maroons, was continued by those ex-slaves who did not want to become wage-earners on the plantations, and as the latter gradually disintegrated,[1] migration to what Georges Anglade calls the 'new lands' (*pays nouveau*) increased.[2]

Towards the end of the nineteenth century the population pressure had increased enough to create new migratory currents. Haiti was in the situation described by Keith Griffin and John L. Enos:

> In the past there has always been ample land into which the growing population could expand. Whenever the number of families in a village grew too great to be employed by customary methods in the surrounding fields, the most adventuresome would migrate, establishing a new village and clearing new fields. This pattern, having grown up over a considerable length of time, is embodied in the customs of the people, so that their methods of cultivating any single plot of land are extremely slow to alter. When confronted with the pressure of population upon land, their first reaction is to move rather than change their methods of cultivation. To any existing stock of land, therefore, labour will tend to be added in fixed proportions; if there were more land, it would be unoccupied; if more labour, it would tend to be unemployed. Thus output is limited by the amount of the least abundant resource.[3]

Land was beginning to be a scarce resource, and therefore one part of the expanding population in the 'new lands' was forced to undertake cultivation of marginal dry areas and/or steep mountain lands, while a second group turned back to the 'colonial space' to seek wage employment in the towns, and a third group migrated out of Haiti, permanently or temporarily.[4]

After a Negro revolt in Cuba in 1912, the United Fruit Company obtained permission to bring in 1,400 Haitians to work on the plantations in the Oriente province,[5] and soon emigration to Cuba began on a large scale. Table E.1 shows an estimate of the legal emigration between 1915 and 1929.

To these figures has to be added the illegal immigration, estimated to be from one-third to one-half of the legal traffic.[6] The majority of the Haitian immigrants stayed in the Oriente province where they worked as sugar-cane cutters for the American *ingenios*. Most of the Haitian migration to Cuba was only temporary. Technically, the immigrants were supposed to stay only during the harvest and then return home, but many did not do so. Still, it has been estimated that some two-thirds of the Haitians in Cuba eventually returned to their own country.[7]

The same period also saw a large-scale migration of Haitians to the Dominican Republic. According to some sources, the extent of the

Haitian migration to the Dominican Republic exceeded that to Cuba.[8] It formed a 'veritable border "osmosis", anarchic and uncontrolled.'[9] As in the Cuban case the purpose was seasonal employment during the *zafra*. This migration had begun towards the end of the nineteenth century and increased as the American interests increased their sugar-cane plantations, in particular after the establishment of American financial receivership in 1905 and after the American occupation of the country in 1916.

Table E.1: Estimated Legal Migration from Haiti to Cuba 1915-29

Year	Number of immigrants	Year	Number of immigrants
1915	23,300	1922	10,250
1916	4,900	1923	20,100
1917	10,200	1924	21,500
1918	11,300	1925	23,000
1919	7,300	1926	21,600
1920	30,700	1927	14,000
1921	17,600	1928-29	5,500
		Total[a]	221,500

a. Castor's total, 200,500, does not correspond to the sum of the individual years.

Source: Castor (1971), p. 83.

The causes of the Haitian emigration to neighboring countries are not entirely clear, but it appears as if it could be viewed in terms of income differences. The expansion of American capitalism in the Dominican Republic and the opening of the Cuban labor market gave the Haitians an opportunity to escape domestic poverty. Neither Cuban nor Dominican wages were high,[10] and the conditions under which the Haitians had to work left a lot to be desired:

> They are subjected to exhausting work, subdued by the draconic conditions of the employer, exposed to the exactions of the rural police, without finding any protection extended to them by the Haitian consular representatives. They suffer the mean intrigues of the [plantation] agents and live miserably in the filthy barracks of the large 'fincas', losing their meager savings on gambling and drinking, often deserting the plantations to maroon for a while before they end up in the shanty-towns of Santiago. 'Haitiano' in Cuba has

become synonymous with 'poor devil'....[11]

Suzy Castor gives a similar account:

> A small fraction of these emigrants managed to command a better life. These are the so-called 'viejos' who have constituted a colorful theme in the Haitian literature. They came back with a few hundred dollars savings, good clothing, shoes, gold teeth and small mirrors. But the majority returned as poor as before, after suffering innumerable humiliations and being physically exhausted after working 10 to 15 hard hours a day in the cane fields. The work contract turns the immigrant into a serf, almost a slave.[12]

It is obvious that for a person to choose to work and live under these conditions, the alternatives before him in the home country must have been even worse. Paul Moral states that only 'destitute peasants' emigrated to Cuba.[13] In spite of the low level of real Cuban wages and the extremely onerous working conditions, a comparison with Haitian standards was enough to outweigh any of these considerations.[14]

After 1923, the Haitian government tried to limit emigration to Cuba by increasing passport fees and by controlling the operations of the Cuban hireling companies in the country. As Table E.1 shows, these efforts were in vain. Even a 1928 law prohibiting emigration to Cuba proved worthless and had to be revoked. It took the depression of the 1930s and the decision of the Cubans in 1937 to repatriate the Haitian cane-cutters, after pressure from the Cuban labor unions, to curb the migration to Cuba.[15]

The migration to the Dominican Republic was also temporarily checked in 1937 after a massacre of Haitians ordered by Trujillo. Closing the Haitian-Dominican border in 1930 had had no effect on migration streams, but in 1937, up to 25,000 Haitians were killed, and many thousands returned to Haiti.[16] In spite of this slaughter, migration was resumed the following year. Trujillo conceded to making a token payment in compensation for the lives lost, and soon after, an agreement was signed between the two countries to regulate the migratory flows. This agreement has been off and on since then, but its practical importance has been limited, because throughout the period clandestine migration has taken place. In 1950 it was estimated that 19,000 Haitians were living in the Dominican Republic; in 1964 their number was estimated to lie between 30,000 and 60,000,[17] and in the mid-1970s, 200,000-300,000 Haitians were believed to live there permanently.[18] In addition, there is considerable seasonal Haitian migration into the Dominican Republic (perhaps 20,000 persons each year)[19] which lasts three to four months, i.e. for the period of the *zafra* only.

The conditions under which the migrants work and live are as onerous as those encountered in Cuba:

> The life of a Haitian migrant worker in the Dominican Republic is reminiscent of slavery days. Their work consists of cutting or carting cane from dawn to dusk. The companies provide them with shacks and hamacs but they have to shift for themselves for food. It is incredible how they subsist on a meager diet of a little rice and beans which they cook themselves on open fires with occasionally some bread and very rarely some meat. They get their energy from the cane that they chew all day long while working...The return trip is at the expense of the worker and sometimes uses up half of his savings. Some actually walk all the way back. Since the majority are illiterate, they are occasionally short-changed when converting their Dominican pesos into Haitian gourdes...it is on the whole a shocking exploitation of people who are educationally and economically deprived and defenseless.[20]

In spite of this, the conditions appear to many to be better than those they find back in their own country.

With the tourist boom in the Bahamas in the 1950s, a new field for Haitian emigration was opened. The tourist industry needed cheap labor which the Haitians willingly supplied. (This new outlet was needed especially after Castro's takeover in Cuba, when the legal migration of Haitians there was cut off for good.) Migration to the Bahamas is almost entirely illegal, but due to the inherent difficulties of supervising the Bahamas territory the rate of infiltration of Haitians is high. It has been estimated that at any given time as much as one-fifth of the total population of the Bahamas consists of Haitian *emigrés*.[21] However, the turnover is high. Many are apprehended by the police to be repatriated.

The 'Nassaumen', as they are known in Haiti, soon flooded the Bahamian labor market, but despite this glut the Haitians persisted in coming — to take whatever job they could find in Nassau:

> This exodus to the Bahamas, in spite of miserable treatment by unscrupulous sea captains,[22] hardship suffered in Nassau and the

likelihood of deportation back to Haiti, reflects the conditions of the poor Haitian masses who notwithstanding persist in their intent to seek a better life outside Haiti.[23]

Recently, the emigration of Haitians has expanded to other areas. In spite of the difficulties of obtaining a visa for the United States an unknown number of Haitians each year manage to get into the country where they quickly disappear in the big cities, notably New York, where half of the illegal aliens are believed to come from either Haiti or the Dominican Republic.[24] The total number of Haitians residing in the United States was believed to be approximately 200,000 in 1975.[25] Canada and the Caribbean are affected as well. Haitian unorganized laborers are known to undercut the domestic labor unions in the sugar-cane fields of Guadeloupe, and migration to Martinique and Saint Martin is known to take place,[26] although nothing is known of the quantitative importance of this migration.

Emigration from Haiti seems to have increased in the 1950s and the 1960s. When Jacques Saint Surin in 1962 published a projection of the Haitian population from 1950 to 1980, he assumed that the Haitian population could be regarded as closed, i.e. that emigration (and immigration) was negligible. The 1950 Dominican census had revealed only 18,772 Haitians residing in the Dominican Republic, and the 1953 Cuban census yielded a corresponding figure of 27,543.[27] The subsequent emigration to the Bahamas was not foreseen, nor was the development of the 1960s and the 1970s. Today, the net emigration according to official statistics amounts to 0.4 percent of the population. The most recent estimates of population growth in Haiti give a natural growth rate of 2 percent per year, and when international migration is taken into account this figure falls to 1.6 percent.[28] These figures may underestimate the extent of emigration, however. According to detailed unofficial estimates, the real rate of emigration may be approximately twice as high as the official figure.[29]

Given the conditions which the temporary or permanent emigrants are likely to meet abroad, and which have been briefly described here, it is difficult not to interpret emigration very much as a result of the conditions in the countryside. The absolute unattractiveness of some of the countries of destination is turned into a relative attractiveness when it is compared to the situation within rural Haiti itself.

This conclusion receives further support when we go on to examine internal migration. The 1950 census indicated that only 12.2 percent of the total population lived in urban areas — the lowest proportion of any Latin American country.* The census data also revealed that in general the mobility of the Haitian population was low. Only 2.6 percent of the total population had moved from one *commune* to another within the same *arrondissement*. Another 4 percent had moved from one *arrondissement* to another within the same *département*, and 2.5 percent, finally, had moved from one *département* to another.** The main exception to this pattern was migration to the capital. Out of the 1950 Port-au-Prince population (146,000),[30] 48 percent were born outside the city itself, and it was calculated that 60,000 of the inhabitants represented net in-migration. The age distribution of the in-migration also showed that the in-migration to the capital must have been negligible before 1920.[31]

Table E.2: Increase in Urban Population 1950-61

Urban zones	1950 (1000s)	1961	Annual rate of increase (percent)
Port-au-Prince	146	251	5.0
Cities with more than 10,000 inh.	66	82	2.0
Cities between 5,000-10,000 inh.	49	66	2.8
Cities between 1,000-5,000 inh.	113	138	1.8
Cities with less than 1,000 inh.	37	42	1.1
Total	411	579	3.1

Source: Brand (1965), pp. 28-9.

In the 1950s, there was an increase in the in-migration to the cities, especially to Port-au-Prince. Willem Brand in 1965 presented the calculations shown in Table E.2. Brand estimated the urban proportion of the population to be 13.6 percent in 1960 and projected that in 1972 it would reach 15.8 percent. The 20 percent level, according to Brand,

---

*Brand (1965), p. 28. This figure appears to be an overstatement. No definition of the term 'urban' was made. All administrative centers in the *communes* were counted as 'urban' regardless of their size. Thus, places like Môle St Nicolas (477 inhabitants), Sainte-Suzanne (383), and St-Jean du Sud (272) were included in the urban category. If instead 'urban' is defined as a community with at least 2,500 inhabitants, the total urban population is reduced to 9 percent of the total (Moral (1959), p. 29).
**The administrative division of Haiti is: 5 *départements*, 27 *arrondissements*, 116 *communes* and 555 *sections rurales* (IHS (1971), pp. 10-11.)

would not be reached until 1982.* The 1971 census proved his projections to be underestimates. Table E.3 compares the 1950 and 1971 census figures. It is only during the 1950s that the growth rates for cities with a population over 10,000-12,000 exceeded those put forward by Brand. Assuming the latter's calculations to be fairly reliable we find that the rate of in-migration to the cities must have accelerated in the 1960s. The 20 percent level had already been reached in 1971, a whole decade in advance of Brand's projection.** Port-au-Prince in particular has been growing at a very rapid rate — around 6 percent per year — which is an internationally high figure as a comparison with Table E.4 shows.

Table E.3: Increase in Urban Population 1950-71

	Population 1950[a]	1971	Annual growth rate 1950-71 (percent)
Total population	3,092,140	4,314,628	1.6
Urban population	378,806	879,708	4.1
Rural population	2,713,334	3,434,920	1.1
Port-au-Prince	143,534	493,932	6.1
Regional towns with a population over 12,000	76,514	146,361	3.1
Cap-Haïtien	24,423	46,217	3.1
Gonaïves	13,634	29,261	3.7
Les Cayes	11,608	22,065	3.1
Jérémie	11,043	17,624	2.3
Saint-Marc	9,401	17,263	2.9
Port-de-Paix	6,405	13,931	3.8

a. 1950 figures differ from those of Brand, who used the Saint Surin estimates instead. (Cf. Saint Surin (1962).)

Source: Ahlers (1977), p. 2.

*'In passing, it may be mentioned that an expert on potable water...who was in Haiti during our stay, supposed in his calculations that even by 1970 the urban population would be around 20% of the total population. This forecast seemed to me highly unlikely.' (Brand (1965), p. 30.)
**IHS (1973), p. 1. However, as in 1950, no clearcut definition of the term 'urban' was made. For census purposes not only the capitals of the *communes* of the Republic are considered as 'urban zones' but also 'those agglomerations [of a certain importance which present] residential units resembling those usually encountered in the towns' (ibid., p. 1).

Table E.4: Population and Growth Rates for Selected Caribbean and South American Cities

	Population		Annual growth rates
Forte-de-France	60,648 (1954)	104,415 (1967)	4.3
Kingston	289,245 (1953)	475,548 (1970)	3.0
San Juan	465,741 (1950)	695,055 (1970)	2.0
Santo Domingo	181,553 (1950)	671,402 (1970)	6.8
Bogotá	648,324 (1951)	2,850,000 (1973)	7.0
Buenos Aires	7,000,000 (1960)	8,191,000 (1970)	1.6
Caracas	693,896 (1950)	2,175,400 (1971)	5.6
Lima	1,436,231 (1961)	3,158,417 (1972)	7.4
La Paz	321,073 (1950)	525,000 (1969)	2.6
Quito	209,932 (1950)	564,900 (1972)	4.6
Santiago	1,350,409 (1952)	3,068,652 (1971)	4.4
São Paulo	2,017,025 (1950)	5,869,966 (1970)	5.5

Source: Ahlers (1977), p. 3.

In sum, migration from rural areas to towns and cities, and especially to the capital, seems to have accelerated during the 1950s and the 1960s. No systematic studies of the determinants of this migration have ever been made,[32] but it is generally suspected that the conditions in rural areas constitute one of the most important factors leading to the decision to migrate. Paul Moral in 1959 emphasized that poor young peasants formed one of the most important migrant groups and concluded that although 'the statistics remain silent...one may guess that this [type of] out-migration has assumed larger and larger proportions during the last thirty years.'[33] A similar view is given by Roland Wingfield:

> Those who migrate to the towns are generally the extremes of the

rural social hierarchy: the landless peasant who has no alternative but to join the floating population of urban slum dwellers and the better off peasant farmers who if lucky might make the jump in three generations from a rural coffee buyer to provincial lawyer-teacher to the new middle-class dweller of the capital.[34]

Wingfield presents a case study of migration to Cap-Haïtien which points to the importance of poverty as a determinant of migration in Haiti. Interviews with La Fossette slum dwellers revealed that the reasons for migrating were primarily economic: land exhaustion, land expropriation because of incurment of heavy debts, etc. The migrants accepted whatever jobs they could find:

> Cap Haïtien has no industry to speak of and has difficulty in absorbing this excess population. The migrants accept whatever work they can find. Many of the girls fall into prostitution or part-time prostitution. Others work as servants for a few dollars a month often with the tacit understanding that they are to serve as a sexual outlet for the master and the sons of the family. If a pregnancy occurs they are sent back to the countryside with some money. The men work as laborers, stevedores, shoe shiners, or assistants to truck drivers. A much-sought job is that of street cleaner, which is a government job and has some kind of civil status and permanency. Some of the younger and more alert men become artisan's apprentices or mechanic-apprentices. Likewise some young girls become seamstress-apprentices. In general, it is years before an apprentice earns a salary beyond his expense money and during that time he is at the mercy of the whims of his boss. Other migrants are street peddlers, beggars or depend on the generosity of their relatives for a corner of a room to sleep in and a food handout. Most of the migrants live by expediency.
>
> There was a noticeable hostility between the native population of La Fossette and the migrants. The latter were generally dissatisfied with their present state and, while few wanted to return to rural life, many were awaiting an opportunity to move on to Port-au-Prince and even out of the country to Nassau. In the meantime, little if anything was being done by governmental authorities to alleviate the plight of thousands of people caught in a socially unhealthy milieu with little hope and chance to get away from it.[35]

The importance of economic reasons is also stressed in a study by

Wilfrid Bertrand from 1972. Bertrand surveyed a group of 110 migrants to Jacmel and found that the most frequently cited motive for migration was search for employment. Almost 80 percent of the sample voiced dissatisfaction with life in their area of origin, mainly for lack of economic opportunities, low productivity of the soil, etc.[36]

A study of in-migration to the small towns of Grande Rivière du Nord and Le Borgne in northern Haiti and Chardonnières and Dame-Marie in the south, by Theodore H. Ahlers failed to reveal poverty as a determinant of in-migration. 'Employment and the learning of a trade were conspicuously absent among the motives mentioned,' concludes Ahlers.[37] It appears, however, as if this fact does not contradict the above statements. Among the most important reasons for *out*-migration from these towns figured the need for non-agricultural employment.[38] The explanation, according to Ahlers, seems to be that there are two streams of migrants coming out of rural areas: (1) 'those from rural areas of above average wealth seeking educational opportunities, wage employment, and the status of urban residence'; (2) 'those from poorer households who are forced to seek immediate non-agricultural employment.'[39] Because of the lack of employment opportunities in the smaller towns Ahlers encountered mainly the first group in his survey. The poor peasants had to bypass the small towns and go directly to some of the bigger cities, notably Port-au-Prince, to find employment. They could hardly expect to be successful, however. According to official statistics (see Table E.5) almost 290,000 new jobs would have had to be created between 1950 and 1971 to cover the increase in the active population. This proved to be an impossible task for the economy. According to the census results of 1950 and 1971, open unemployment increased from 40,200 to 245,700 i.e. by 205,500, and more than 50 percent of this increase took place in the *Département de l'Ouest*, i.e. basically in the capital.[40] Another calculation also based on census figures is shown in Table E.6. Coming from the same source as Table E.5, these figures convey an entirely different picture to that given by the employment estimates. According to these figures, open unemployment seems to have increased by only 60,000 persons. However, this figure is an understatement. The largest increase in employment has taken place in the commercial sector, which together with services accounts for almost 70 percent of the total increase. This increase is more apparent than real. As we saw in Chapter 5, it is mainly due to the fact that an additional 127,000 women have been classified as active in the commercial sector. Presumably, only a fraction of this figure represents an actual shift from rural to urban occupations while the rest is due to difficulties of classification of female activities — a notoriously difficult problem in less developed economies. Moreover, a large number of those classified as working in the service sector are not likely to have particularly productive employment. They work there for lack of better alternatives.[41]

Table E.5: Increase in Active Population 1950-71 (1000s)

Active population (15 years and above) 1971	1,993.3
Active population (15 years and above) 1950	1,704.5
Increase in active population 1950-71	288.8

Source: CONADEP (1976), Table A-4.

Table E.6: Absorption of Labor outside the Agricultural Sector 1950-71

Active population (15 years and above) 1971	1,954,153	
Active population (15 years and above) 1950	1,705,139	
Increase in active population 1950-71		249,014
Employment increase 1950-71:		
a) extractive industries	452	
b) manufacturing	55,317	
c) public utilities	349	
d) construction and public works	7,665	
e) commerce (including banking and insurance)	135,634	
f) transport and communications	5,405	
g) services	20,575	
h) unclassified activities	30	
i) military service	4,625	
Total employment increase outside agriculture 1950-71		230,052

Sources: Population working in agriculture and manufacturing 1950: Brand (1965), p. 44. Rest of table: CONADEP (1976), Table A-6.

The rate of out-migration from rural areas by all probability has increased in the 1950s and the 1960s. Increasing numbers leave the countryside every year to seek a living in the cities or outside Haiti.

Epilogue

Few studies of the reasons for this exodus have been made, and even fewer offer any quantitative evidence, but it is difficult to escape the conclusion that one of the most important determinants of the out-migration is the standard of living in rural Haiti. The conditions confronting the migrants in the cities or outside the country have been sufficiently documented to suggest that these appear favorable only when compared to the conditions in the countryside itself.

The Politico-economic Stranglehold

Broadly speaking, the drama of underdevelopment in rural Haiti is the result of the interaction of two sets of actors: one economic, the other political. This interaction, as we have seen several times in the foregoing, is of a complex nature, but basically the economic component is responsible for the slowly declining per capita incomes, while the political component constitutes the most important obstacle to efficient positive action against poverty and deprivation in the rural sector.

The basic problem for the Haitian peasant is one of scarcity of resources; land and capital, in relation to the size of the population that has to be fed. Each year witnesses a deterioration of the balance between the rural population and the means at its disposal to satisfy its basic needs. As the population grows, the supply of agricultural land shrinks. This process of population growth and soil destruction is cumulative. Changes in the factor endowment interact with changes in relative prices to increase the rate of erosion, and as time elapses, the process accelerates, pushing the peasant sector towards some type of long-run equilibrium with decidely Malthusian characteristics.

There is little that the peasants themselves can do to prevent their incomes from falling. Erosion control is infrequently practiced in Haiti, and the peasants have little incentive to introduce the measure. The erosion process involves externalities, and it does not therefore necessarily pay the individual peasant to attempt erosion control unless his fellow peasants do the same thing. Quite probably, all the incentives work in the direction of precluding measures that would keep the soil productive for longer periods.

The effects of erosion could also in principle be counteracted if the peasants could compensate for the declining availability of land by increasing the amount of capital employed in the production process, or if they could acquire new technologies which would permit them to choose between more productive techniques than does the traditional technological setting. Neither capital formation nor technological change, however, takes place to any noticeable extent in the peasant sector.

The peasants are caught in the logic of the cumulative process. As long as the population grows, cumulation will continue to depress per capita incomes, and the peasants cannot stop and reverse the process. The main obstacle is that they are too poor to be able to afford the costs and savings required to accumulate the necessary capital and to undertake the necessary changes in technology. This should have been done generations ago. Today, the cumulative process has already proceeded too far to be stopped by unco-ordinated individual action.

If individual action is inefficient, the government must then step in and see to it that the necessary efforts are made to prevent cumulation from dragging the economy into a Malthusian situation. Nothing of this sort has ever happened in Haiti. In spite of the compelling fact that agriculture has always constituted the very backbone of the Haitian economy, the Haitian governments have traditionally done next to nothing to improve the lot of the peasants. The gulf between the peasant and his government is abysmally wide. Haiti has never possessed a government with a broad popular backing. The country has always been governed by small cliques who in no way have identified themselves with the peasant masses. The history of Haiti is the history of clique infighting for the spoils of the presidential office. Economic development has never been a political goal in Haiti. Instead, a never-ending stream of kleptocracies who could think of little else than filling their pockets have squandered the available funds in their attempts to gain or retain the presidency.

The peasants for their part have never managed to organize themselves enough to participate actively in the political process and have a word in decisions regarding economic policy. They have been content to have as little as possible to do with the government and its representatives. The government in turn, opted for *laissez-faire* in agriculture. Weakened by the constant fights for power and lacking the political will to set the country on the road to development, the Haitian governments came to regard the peasants as little else than a source of the taxes which formed the main part of the incomes of the governing cliques.

Haiti's history has been strongly conditioned by this separation of an elite (and near-elite) group from the peasant masses. The peasants have remained on the land, strenuously toiling to eke out a meager living. The upper classes have concentrated on fighting for political power which would make it possible for them to live a comfortable life. Both groups have succeeded — to the detriment of the peasants. Time has run away from the Haitian peasantry. When the masses at a very early date in history were delivered from slavery and were converted into a class of freeholders who could cultivate their land with relatively little intervention from outside groups, they were unfortunately also drawn into a state of political lethargy which still continues. Inaction for more than a century has made the Haitian peasant incapable of making his voice heard.

It has frequently been contended that the Haitian peasant is subject to direct exploitation by absentee landowners, intermediaries and usurious moneylenders. We have shown that this is not the case. The Haitian economy is basically a competitive economy, and the imperfections prevailing are not primarily a result of monopolistic or monopsonistic practices in commodity or factor markets. The peasant is not being exploited by any of the traditional villains of the rural economy. Instead, his main enemy is the government. The governments of Haiti have not only been passive when it comes to reaching the peasants with positive measures, but have also subjected the latter to taxation without any kind of representation. Whatever surplus the peasant sector has managed to produce has not been tapped by absentee landlords, foreign capitalists, monopsonistic or monopolistic middlemen or extortionist moneylenders. It has been tapped by the governments in the form of taxes.*

Peasant passivity is not the only explanation of why the masses have remained outside politics for more than a century and why they have not been able to make the governing cliques spend on their welfare. The Haitian countryside is run in a tightly military and autocratic fashion which leaves no room for grass-roots democracy. The peasants are kept in ignorance by a rural school system which basically works as a strongly discriminatory filter and through which few rural youths

---

*This is extremely important from the policy point of view. A policy based upon conventional radical wisdom could for example be one aimed at shortening the chain of intermediaries in agricultural marketing by establishing a government marketing board. Such a measure would, however, presumably *reduce,* not increase, peasant welfare. The main effect would be to put the *Madam Sara* out of business (provided that the board works). Hence, the measure is not Pareto sanctioned. Also, it is highly questionable whether the government marketing board would be able to handle the marketing as efficiently as the existing system, i.e. whether it would be able to perform the same services at a lower cost to the economy. Given the amount of corruption prevailing in public administration, the probability is low. Finally, if this corruption spreads to the marketing board as well, exploitation of the peasants may *increase,* not decrease. If the aim is to increase peasant welfare, a reduction of e.g. the coffee tax or increased spending on agriculture is to be preferred.

manage to pass — a school system which is geared to the need for domination by the upper classes and which does not meet the interest of the peasants. They have seen few alleviating changes in the fields of disease and malnutrition. As long as the agricultural sector produces enough to meet the demands of the governing classes, no real intervention will take place in rural Haiti. The peasants are left to solve their problems without aid. Changes are merely token in character and are hardly ever motivated by a desire on the part of those in power to change rural living conditions. The dilemma facing the peasants is that they cannot do without aid. They are caught in an economic stranglehold with strongly negative cumulative tendencies, and this process is given free reign by politicians who are concentrated on the maximization of their own personal incomes and welfare — not on that of the peasants. This fatal combination of economics and politics is slowly killing the peasant economy.

Three Important Development Issues

The present book cannot and does not pretend to provide a concrete solution of Haiti's problem or to the problems of its agricultural sector. This is for obvious reasons. By now, it should be clear that virtually everything has gone wrong in peasant agriculture and that virtually everything is in desperate need of change. Drawing on our analysis it is easy to enumerate areas for action. Any such enumeration would be trivial, however, and would not lead Haiti any closer to economic development. The number of problems is so large and the interconnections between the problems are so complex and far-reaching that monumental human and material resources would be needed for a result. Resources on this scale are simply not available and probably never will be available. Resources are scarce, and we must therefore concentrate on finding priority areas where the impact of change on development will be largest and where action would lead to further changes in other areas.

The first step when it comes to determining these areas, is to focus the attention on the most important issues to be resolved. Only if and when these issues are fully understood will it be possible to begin a discussion of more concrete measures which can help the rural population. This is how far we intend to go in the present book. We will point to three such 'key' issues here, and we will also argue that one of these issues constitutes a bottleneck in the development process. Before that bottleneck has been removed, it does not make much sense to discuss the technicalities of development planning. These three issues are

Erosion

The Haitian peasant sector presents evident signs of being an economy which has failed to adapt to increased population pressure. It possesses most of the usual characteristics of overpopulation in relation to the available resources and technology.[42] The average farm size is extremely small. Holdings are not consolidated but often spread out in two or more scattered plots. Farm incomes are on the decline. The existing technology is backward. Most serious, however, is the increasing destruction of the soil. Unless an end can be put to this process, Malthusian checks will undoubtedly begin to work to establish a precarious equilibrium between population and resources.

Any attempt to improve the rural technology must therefore include soil conservation measures as an integrated part. Landesque capital can substitute for land but not to an unlimited extent. In the long run, the natural resource base must not be destroyed. This is true even if the solution to Haiti's economic problems should happen to lie in industrialization. Most of the basic foodstuffs have to be produced in the country. To have a manufacturing sector which is not supported by a domestic agriculture capable of producing a surplus in excess of what is consumed in rural areas is not a realistic proposition.

The land resources have to be conserved if agriculture is to survive in Haiti. The topsoil must be prevented from being washed away from the hillsides by the heavy tropical downpours. Soil protection is a fundamental issue in Haitian development. Unless there is land, there will be no development. This simple truth has been largely overlooked by development economists. At least, it has not been stressed enough.

Others have been more insistent. Soil conservationists Vernon Gill Carter and Tom Dale, in their book *Topsoil and Civilization*,[43] argue that depletion, exhaustion and destruction of land resources has been one of the major factors (in their opinion the most important one) behind the decline and fall of a number of advanced civilizations at different times and in different regions. The same pattern is distinguishable everywhere:

> How did civilized man despoil his favorable environment? He did it mainly by depleting or destroying the natural resources. He cut down or burned most of the usable timber from the forested hillsides and valleys. He overgrazed and denuded the grasslands that fed his livestock. He killed most of the wildlife and much of the fish and

other water life. He permitted erosion to rob his farm land of its productive topsoil He allowed eroded soil to clog the streams and fill his reservoirs, irrigation canals, and harbors with silt. In many cases, he used or wasted most of the easily mined metals or other needed minerals. Then his civilization declined amidst the despoliation of his own creation or he moved to new land. There have been from ten to thirty different civilizations that have followed this road to ruin (the number depending on who classified the civilizations).[44]

The message of Carter and Dale is clear. It is not permissible to regard the natural resources as given when planning for economic development. The problem is not where and when to apply what quantities and qualities of labor and capital to a constant land endowment. This very endowment changes as well as a result of the actions of man. In Haiti, the time to reverse the destructive trends came a long time ago, but nothing has been done so far. Each day it becomes increasingly difficult to find a solution. Still, a solution has to be found. The very existence of the Haitian population is threatened by the erosion of the natural resource base in agriculture. This is the single most important problem which the Haitian nation faces. All other problems are secondary in their relation to soil destruction.

Anti-peasant Bias

The second key issue to be discussed here is the anti-peasant bias shared by all Haitian governments. In a recent book, *Why Poor People Stay Poor*,[45] Michael Lipton has advanced the thesis that economic and social development in poor countries contains a pronounced 'urban bias':

Development plans are nowadays full of 'top priority for agriculture'. This is reminiscent of the pseudo-egalitarian school where, at mealtimes, Class B children get priority, while Class A children get food. We can see that the new agricultural priority is dubious from the abuse of the 'green revolution' and of the oil crisis (despite its much greater impact on industrial costs) as pretexts for lack of emphasis on agriculture: 'We don't need it,' and 'We can't afford it,' respectively. And the 60 to 80 per cent of people dependent on agriculture are still allocated barely 20 per cent of public resources; even these small shares are seldom achieved; and they have, if anything, tended to diminish. So long as the elite's interests, background and sympathies remain predominantly urban, the countryside may get the 'priority' but the city will get the resources. The farm sector will continue to be squeezed, both by transfers of resources from it and by prices that are turned against it. Bogus justifications of urban bias will continue to earn the sincere, prestige-conferring, but misguided support of visiting 'experts' from industrialised countries and international agencies. And development will be needlessly painful, inequitable and slow.[46]

The interests of the city are systematically pushed to the detriment of the rural population. The same type of patterns as those indicated by Lipton are operative in Haiti. In the present work, we have not dealt systematically with the urban part of the Haitian economy, so the term 'urban' bias needs to be employed with extreme caution. What we *do* know, however, is that a strong bias exists in Haiti against the agricultural sector: an anti-peasant bias.

This bias shows up in a number of ways. Almost 80 percent of the Haitian population live in rural areas and are hence directly or indirectly dependent on agriculture for their living. Agriculture accounts for more than 40 percent of the value of the gross domestic product as of recently, and has contributed far larger shares earlier. In spite of this, the agricultural sector has received on average less than 10 percent of total government expenditure. Development plans for agriculture have virtually always lacked substance. The projects undertaken in the rural sector have been inadequately prepared. Plan targets have not been fulfilled. Aid to agriculture has only been token.

Development funds have gone elsewhere. Agriculture has received very little in the form of rural credit and technical assistance, for example, while the peasants have had to contribute to financing government ventures of a dubious nature outside the rural economy. The tax structure has been concentrated on products which are either produced or consumed by the peasants, while products consumed by the urban elite groups have largely escaped taxation. Similarly, it has not been in the interest of the ruling urban elites and near-elites to levy taxes e.g. on income, or at least not to see to it that such taxes are actually paid.

The countryside is starved of public health facilities and medical care. Consultation with popular herbalists and *houngans* is the most common way of 'curing' diseases in the countryside, while modern facilities are heavily concentrated to the capital. Little attention has been paid to the problem of widespread malnutrition in rural districts.

Other efforts at rural 'development' present directly negative aspects. The educational system is strongly biased against the peasants. The quality and quantity of education provided is low. The rural children are taught in a language which is eminently foreign to them. The system stresses examination. Taken together this means that extremely few rural children ever manage to complete the entire course of primary education, and those who do often migrate to the cities in search for urban jobs. The rural educational system does not work as a mechanism for formation of human capital which might have been useful in agriculture but as a discriminatory filter which breeds ignorance and docility in the countryside.

Any strategy which seriously aims at economic development and which does not amount to mere lip service in a country like Haiti must benefit not only the upper classes of the population living in urban areas but the poor rural majority as well. The pronounced anti-peasant bias pervading economic policy and development efforts must be removed. One can never escape from the fact that Haiti is a *peasant* nation. The most important part of its economy builds on peasant production, and peasant production must be turned into one of the *real* (not token) priority areas for politicians and planners. To attempt development without including the peasants among its beneficiaries is tantamount to attempting no development at all. So far, there has been no scope for mass migration into urban areas. The urban economy can only swallow some of the *increase* of the rural population, let alone absorb enough people to alleviate the population pressure on the land. The Haitians cannot close their eyes to the importance of the countryside. For urban life to exist, the countryside must produce a surplus of food. For foreign exchange to be earned, the peasants must grow coffee. However, the capacity of the countryside to do both things is decreasing due to increasing erosion — but also due to the anti-peasant bias of the governments. A minimum condition for future economic development in Haiti is that this is openly realized. Those in power, i.e. those responsible for the future welfare of the nation, must correct the anti-peasant bias and give agriculture the priority it deserves and must have.

Politics

Anti-peasant bias makes itself felt as misallocation of development resources, but this misallocation is only the result of bias. The source of bias must be sought elsewhere. Anti-peasant bias is primarily a 'state of mind'[47] and the mind is that of the Haitian government. Haiti in economic terms represents an extreme case of underdevelopment, but the main difficulty when it comes to suggesting economic solutions and desirable development strategies lies not in how to make use of the available battery of development measures. Rather it resides in the

Epilogue

political blocking of any sensible strategy. In this sense anti-peasant bias is a state of mind.

It is certainly true that Haiti would face serious development problems with *any* type of government. The economic structures outlined in the foregoing cannot be abolished by a mere change in politics. Even a government which committed all the available resources to economic and social development would have problems. Beginning from a level as low as that prevailing in Haiti at the present time presents a formidable task to politicians and planners. Development can probably only be achieved in a very long-run perspective. However, it is not realistic to believe that development can be achieved without deep-seated political changes. Christopher K. Clague has pointed to the possibility of concentrating on development policies which require as little government intervention as possible.[48] However, such a strategy will yield very marginal results, if indeed it can be implemented at all, since it precludes all action where the government must necessarily play the leading role. A more fundamental objection to this type of strategy is that the possibilities of implementation are small. It is not possible to prescind from the fact that Haiti is a sovereign nation with its own government. That government exists *de facto* – for better or for worse – and a development strategy which does not take this into account is doomed to fail. The government can block any type of strategy which it deems undesirable given its preferences.

Unfortunately, these preferences are dubious. As we have argued at length, the Haitian governments have lacked all identification with the peasantry. They have been anti-peasant in their outlook. 'Development' goals have been defined from a narrow, egoistic viewpoint where only the welfare of the political 'ins' has been maximized. No attention has been paid to commonly accepted norms of development. To reach these egoistic goals, the peasants have been sacrificed. Funds have been mobilized with the aid of the peasantry, but these funds have never found their way back into the rural economy. A number of corrupt and inefficient kleptocrat cliques have maintained themselves at the expense of the masses. This too is a common pattern in the Third World. In a comparative retrospective study of development experience Göran Ohlin makes the following observations:

> It is not difficult for foreign observers to list weaknesses and mistakes that continue to mar economic policies in many developing countries, but often these are primarily due to the rigidities of the internal political situation. It would be dangerously wrong to dismiss

the political problem as a mere obstacle to the implementation of the policies which technocrats and economic experts find advisable. Yet it often is just that, as the result of a pervasive tension between power and development. Governments with a precarious political base are naturally wedded to the status quo and are not given to visions of development and social change with vast and unpredictable consequences. Without political stability and efficiency, economic planning will not matter much, no matter how brilliant. Political crisis accounts for several of the extreme cases of stagnation...

What has been demonstrated is that countries can, from the most varied base of departure, be mobilized into growth rates of 6-10% when they are not torn by political dissent, ridden with corrupt and inefficient administration, or paralyzed in such matters as taxation, exchange rate policy, land reform and education.[49]

Haiti very clearly belongs to the group of countries referred to by Ohlin, where the political situation must be blamed for much of the failure to develop economically. The history of the country speaks eloquently on this point. Haiti has always been ruled by governments lacking a sincere desire to change a situation which works neatly to their own benefit. History teaches us that privileged groups do not give up their privileges voluntarily. The Haitian government stands between any development strategy and the peasants. With this type of government it becomes utterly meaningless to discuss what a strategy for economic development should look like technically. Incompetence, self-interest and corruption make it fairly certain that a given means does not lead to the well-intentioned calculated aim. The main obstacle to economic development in Haiti has always been its governments.

A Look at the Future

The Haitian peasant economy is sliding towards the abyss. Per capita incomes are slowly falling in rural areas, but to a certain extent this fall is mitigated by migration out of Haiti. The cumulative interaction between population growth and soil destruction works in a subdued manner thanks to the fact that some of the rural population has been able to leave the countryside temporarily or permanently.

How long this emigration will be able to restrict the effects of the cumulative process is uncertain. Most of the emigration is already illegal. This restricts the scope for further emigration, for if it is perceived that the inflow of Haitians somehow constitutes a threat in any of the recipient countries, measures to put an end to immigration may quickly follow. Should this happen, the negative effects of population growth may rapidly gain momentum. The domestic economy will be faced with an additional burden consisting of those who would otherwise have emigrated and perhaps also of Haitians repatriated from abroad. In the absence of a sufficiently large and viable non-agricultural sector, virtually the entire absorption of this increase will have to take place in the agricultural sector. The land resources will be subject to further strain. The rate of erosion will increase cumulatively. Per capita incomes will fall perhaps to the point where cumulation becomes strong enough to trigger off Malthusian checks on a larger scale. The extent of malnutrition and nutritionally related diseases will then increase. Larger numbers of people (mainly children) will die of starvation. The population will be forced to adapt its size to the shrinking available resources.

The above is not a utopian scenario. Considering the already low levels of incomes and consumption prevailing in rural Haiti, little may be required to push the peasant sector off its path into a dramatically faster cumulative process. This may be complemented by other undesirable changes. Certain concentration mechanisms may begin to operate as well. Landlessness so far is not believed to be a major problem in the Haitian countryside. However, should the decline of per capita incomes continue, and especially if the possibilities of migration are drastically curtailed, we may arrive at a situation where concentration of landownership may begin to develop. When the peasants see their incomes fall too much, they may have to increase their indebtedness and take longer loans in order to ensure the satisfaction of the basic needs of their families. Quite probably this will lead to a concentration of land in the hands of a smaller portion of the population than before. Increasing indebtedness often is accompanied by an increased use of land as a collateral, and this in turn may mean that the ownership of land is gradually transferred from peasants to moneylenders — to wealthier peasants or to members of the non-peasant community — in case the peasants are unable to pay back their loans.[50] The likelihood of this occurrence increases as per capita incomes, consumption and production capacity decrease among the peasants.

Concentration of landownership means that a class of landless laborers will be created — a class which is dependent on the landowing class for work and incomes. The landless workers will probably also experience difficulties when it comes to obtaining work the entire year, since the need for farm labor arises mainly during the peak seasons.[51]

As the concentration of land resources proceeds, the door to employment of the classic mechanisms of exploitation is opened. The landless become increasingly dependent on the landowners for work and credit, and perhaps also for buying everyday necessities. The Haitian economy will then have closed the circle of irony from exploitation of labor in a plantation system based on slavery, via increasingly declining farm size and increasing fragmentation of holdings back to some type of large-scale farms or latifundia based on employment of landless agricultural laborers working under onerous conditions.

The above may sound ludicrous, but I am afraid it is not. It is hard to think of any better way than rapidly decreasing incomes when it comes to altering the distribution of assets in the direction of increased inequality. There are few things that man will not do to stay alive, and seen in this perspective, pledging one's land may be a relatively minor sacrifice. However, this fact does not make increasing concentration more palatable. Rather, it points to the dramatic need for change. This change must take two forms. The peasant population must be provided with alternative employment to alleviate the pressure on the land. The surplus population must be channelled into other sectors where productive work is to be found, but in addition, the peasant sector itself must be developed, especially in the short run, before a sufficient number of secondary and tertiary activities are available. The question of which development strategy to employ in Haiti is not one of agriculture versus non-agriculture. Both sectors must be included, but before any development can take place, the political will to do away with the anti-peasant bias of the past must exist. Will it, ever?

Notes

1. See Chapter 6 for an analysis of this process.
2. Anglade (1974), p. 78.
3. Griffin & Enos (1970), pp. 59-60. Cf. Holly (1955), pp. 43-4 and Moral (1959), note, p. 40.
4. Anglade (1974), pp. 77-9. Cf. also Ahlers (1977), pp. 4-5.
5. Thomas (1971), p. 524.
6. Castor (1971), p. 84.
7. Millspaugh (1931), note, p. 143.
8. Castor (1971), p. 84.
9. Moral (1959), p. 41.
10. Cf. Leyburn (1966), p. 271; Logan (1968), p. 145.
11. Moral (1961), p. 70.
12. Castor (1971), pp. 84-5.
13. Moral (1961), p. 70.
14. Cf. Thomas (1971), p. 524.
15. Leyburn (1966), p. 271.
16. Cf. Chapter 6.

Epilogue

17. Wingfield (1966), p. 97.
18. Zuvekas (1978), pp. 99-100.
19. Ibid., p. 101.
20. Wingfield (1966), pp. 99-100, 101. Cf. Laguerre (1976:1), p.9.
21. Wingfield (1966), p. 101.
22. For an account, see Riou (1976), pp. 277-81.
23. Wingfield (1966), p. 102.
24. Cf. Piore (1975), p. 42.
25. Zuvekas (1978), p. 100.
26. Cf. Dominguez (1976), pp. 14-15.
27. Saint Surin (1962), p. 6.
28. IHS (1975:2), p. 2.
29. Zuvekas (1978), note, p. 98.
30. Brand (1965), p. 28.
31. Moral (1959), pp. 37-8. Cf. Brand (1965), pp. 29-30.
32. However, one such study, undertaken by Theodore H. Ahlers at the Fletcher School of Law and Diplomacy is under way.
33. Moral (1959), p. 39.
34. Wingfield (1966), p. 86.
35. Ibid., pp. 89-90.
36. Quoted by Ahlers (1977), p. 7.
37. Ibid., p. 16.
38. Ibid., pp. 16-17.
39. Ibid., p. 41. Cf. also Moral (1959), pp. 39-40 and Wingfield (1966), p. 86.
40. CONADEP (1976), Table A-4.
41. Cf. Griffin (1969), pp. 59-60.
42. Grigg (1976), pp. 154-61.
43. Carter & Dale (1974).
44. Ibid., p. 8.
45. Lipton (1977). Cf. also Lipton (1968:2).
46. Lipton (1977), pp. 17-18.
47. Ibid., p. 63.
48. Rotberg & Clague (1971), Chapter 9.
49. Ohlin (1977).
50. Myrdal (1968), pp. 1039-47.
51. Cf. Grigg (1976), pp. 156-68 for comparative empirical evidence regarding this type of concentration mechanisms.

BIBLIOGRAPHY

Abbot, J.C. 'The Development of Marketing Institutions, in Herman M. Southworth & Bruce F. Johnston (eds), *Agricultural Development and Economic Growth*. Ithaca, 1967

Adelman, Irma & Morris, Cynthia Taft. 'A Factor Analysis of the Interrelationship between Social and Political Variables and Per Capita Gross National Product', *Quarterly Journal of Economics*, vol. 79, 1965

Adelman, Irma & Morris, Cynthia Taft. *Society, Politics and Economic Development. A Quantitative Approach*. Baltimore, 1967

Adelman, Irma & Morris, Cynthia Taft. 'Performance Criteria for Evaluating Economic Development Potential: An Operational Approach', *Quarterly Journal of Economics*, vol. 82, 1968:1

Adelman, Irma & Morris, Cynthia Taft. 'An Economic Model of Socio-Economic and Political Change in Underdeveloped Countries', *American Economic Review*, vol. 58, 1968:2

Adelman, Irma & Morris, Cynthia Taft. 'Factor Analysis and Gross National Product: A Reply', *Quarterly Journal of Economics*, vol. 84, 1970

Adelman, Irma & Morris, Cynthia Taft. *Economic Growth and Social Equity in Developing Countries*. Stanford, 1973

Ahlers, Theodore H. *Report on the Statistical Analysis of Migration Data Collected in Survey of Four Haitian Small Towns*. Mimeo, Fletcher School of Law and Diplomacy, Medford, 1977

Akerlof, George A. 'The Market for "Lemons". Quality Uncertainty and the Market Mechanism', *Quarterly Journal of Economics*, vol. 84, 1970

Allen, G.R. 'The World Fertilizer Situation', *World Development*, vol. 5, 1977

Amano, Akihiro. 'Factor Endowment and Relative Prices: A Generalization of Rybczynski's Theorem', *Economica*, vol. 30, 1963

Anglade, Georges. *L'espace haïtien*. Montréal, 1974

Arrow, Kenneth J. *Essays in the Theory of Risk-Bearing*. Amsterdam, 1971

Arrow, Kenneth J. 'Higher Education as a Filter', *Journal of Public Economics*, vol. 2, 2973

Ayal, Eliezer B. 'The Impact of Export Taxes on the Domestic Economy of Underdeveloped Countries', *Journal of Development Studies*, vol. 1, 1965

Bachman, Kenneth L. & Christensen, Raymond P. 'The Economics of Farm Size', in Herman M. Southworth & Bruce F. Johnston (eds) *Agricultural Development and Economic Growth*. Ithaca, 1967

Bairoch, Paul. *The Economic Development of the Third World since 1900*. London, 1975

Baker, Chester B. 'Role of Credit in the Economic Development of Small Farm Agriculture', in AID *Spring Review of Small Farmer Credit: vol. XIX. Small Farmer Credit. Analytical Papers*. Washington, DC, 1973

Balassa, Bela A. 'Success Criteria for Economic Systems', *Yale Economic Essays*, vol. 1, 1961

Baldwin, Robert E. & Weisbrod, Burton A. 'Disease and Labor Productivity', *Economic Development and Cultural Change*, vol. 22, 1974

Balogh, Thomas. *The Economics of Poverty*. New York, 1966

Balogh, Thomas & Streeten, Paul P. 'The Coefficient of Ignorance', *Bulletin of the Oxford University Institute of Economics and Statistics*, vol. 25, 1963

Bardhan, P.K. & Srinivasan, T.N. 'Crop-sharing Tenancy in Agriculture: A Theoretical and Empirical Analysis', *American Economic Review*, vol. 61, 1971

Barlow, Robin. 'The Economic Effects of Malaria Eradication', *American Economic Review*, vol. 57, 1967

[Barskett, James] *History of the Island of St Domingo, from its First Discovery by Columbus to the Present Period*. London, 1818

Bastien, Rémy. *La familia rural haitiana*. México D.F., 1951

Bastien, Rémy. 'Haitian Rural Family Organization', *Social and Economic Studies*, vol. 1, 1961

Bastien, Rémy. 'Vodoun and Politics in Haiti', in *Religion and Politics in Haiti*. Washington, DC, 1966

Bauer, Peter T. *West African Trade: A Study of Competition, Oligopoly, and Monopoly in a Changing Economy*. Cambridge, 1964

Baumol, William J. *Economic Theory and Operations Analysis*. Second edition. Englewood Cliffs, NJ. 1965

Bazile, Robert. 'Quelques aspects de la démographie en Haiti', in *Research and Resources of Haiti. Papers of the Conference on Research and Resources of Haiti*. New York, 1969

Becerra de la Flor, J. César & Abarbanel, Shlomo. *Proyectos de*

desarrollo rural integral. Su evaluación como generadores de empleo. I. Proyecto integral de desarrollo agrícola de la planicie de Cul-de-Sac. "Expansión Bas Boen", Haiti. Mimeo, Organización de los Estados Americanos, Estado de Israel, Port-au-Prince, 1974
Becker, Fary S. *Human Capital. A Theoretical and Empirical Analysis, with Special Reference to Education.* New York, 1964
Beghin, Ivan. 'Le problème de l'alimentation et de la nutrition en Haïti', *Conjonction*, no. 99, 1965
Beghin, Ivan. Fougère, William & King, Kendall W. 'Enquête clinique sur l'état de nutrition des enfants préscolaires de Fond-Parisien et de Ganthier (Haïti): juin 1964', *Annales de la Société belge de Médecine tropicales*, vol. 45, 1965. Reprinted in OEA Institut Interaméricain de l'Enfant: *Recommendations et travaux du Séminaire National de Nutrition d'Haïti. Port-au-Prince. 30 mai au 4 juin 1965.* Montevideo, 1965
Beghin, Ivan, Fougère, William & King, Kendall W. *L'alimentation et la nutrition en Haïti.* Paris, 1970
Bellegarde, Dantès. *Pour une Haïti heureuse II: Par l'éducation et le travail.* Port-au-Prince, 1929
Bellegarde, Dantès. *Un Haïtien parle.* Port-au-Prince, 1934
Bellegarde, Dantès. *La nation haïtienne.* Paris, 1938
Belli, Pedro. 'The Economic Implications of Malnutrition: The Dismal Science Revisited', *Economic Development and Cultural Change*, vol. 20, 1971
Bengoa, José María. *Priorities in Public Health Nutrition Programs.* VIIe Congrès International de Nutrition, Hambourg, 1966
Benoit, Pierre V. *Cent cinquante ans de commerce extétieur d'Haïti 1804-1954.* Port-au-Prince, 1954:1
Benoit, Pierre V. *Evolution budgétaire et développement économique d'Haïti.* Port-au-Prince, 1954:2
Berg, Alan, portions with Miscat, Robert J. *The Nutrition Factor. Its Role in National Development.* Washington, DC, 1973
Berg, Elliot J. 'Major Issues of Wage Policy in Africa', in A.M. Ross (ed). *Industrial Relations and Economic Development.* London, 1966
Berry, Paul. *Writing Haitian Creole: Issues and Proposals for Orthography.* Croton-on-Hudson, 1964
Berry, Paul. 'Literacy and the Question of Creole', in *Research and Resources of Haiti Papers of the Conference on Research and Resources of Haiti.* New York, 1969
Bhaduri, Amit. 'On the Formation of Usurious Interest Rates in

Backward Agriculture', *Cambridge Journal of Economics*, vol. 1, 1977
BID Banque Interaméricaine de Développement. *Possibilités d'investissement et développement du secteur rural en Haïti*. Washington, DC, 1974
BID Banco Interamericano de Desarrollo. *Progreso económico y social en América Latina. Informe anual 1975.* Washington, DC, 1975
BIHCAI. *Bulletin de l'Institut Haïtien de Crédit Agricole et Industricl* Port-au-Prince
Bird, Mark, B. *The Black Man: or Haytian Independence. Deduced from Historical Notes, and Dedicated to the Government and People of Haiti.* New York, 1869
Blaise, Franck. *Le problème agraire à travers l'histoire d'Haïti.* Port-au-Prince, no date
Blaug, Mark. *An Introduction to the Economics of Education*, London, 1970
Boeke, J.H. *Economics and Economic Policies of Dual Societies.* New York, 1953
Bohannan, Paul & Dalton, George (eds). *Markets in Africa*. Evanston, 1962
Boisgris, Oscar. 'Enseignement rural', *Bulletin du Bureau d'Ethnologie*, no. 3, 1944
Bordes, Ary. 'Facteurs culturels et nutrition infantile', in OEA, Institut Interaméricain de l'Enfant: *Recommandations et travaux du Séminaire National de Nutrition d'Haiti. Port-au-Prince. 30 mai au 4 juin 1965.* Montevideo, 1965:1
Bordes, Ary. 'Les milieux haïtiens face aux problèmes de la grossesse, de la naissance et de l'enfance', in OEA, Institut Interaméricain de l'Enfant: *Recommandations et Travaux du Séminaire National de Nutrition d'Haïti. Port-au-Prince. 30 mai au 4 juin 1965.* Montevideo, 1965:2
Bosch, Juan. 'Haití, Duvalier y América', in Pierre-Charles, Gérard. *Radiografía de una dictadura − Haití bajo el régimen del Doctor Duvalier.* México D.F., 1969
Boserup, Ester. *The Conditions of Agricultural Growth. The Economics of Agrarian Change under Population Pressure.* London, 1965
Bottomley, Anthony. *Factor Pricing and Economic Growth in Underdeveloped Rural Areas.* London, 1971
Bourguignon, Erika E. 'Class Structure and Acculturation in Haiti', *Ohio Journal of Science*, vol. 52, 1952
Bowles, Samuel. 'Unequal Education and the Reproduction of the Social Division of Labor', in Martin Carnoy (ed). *Schooling in a*

Corporate Society. New York, 1975
Bowles, Samuel & Gintis, Herbert. 'The Problem with Human Capital Theory — A Marxian Critique', *American Economic Review*, vol. 65, 1975
Brand, Willem. *Impressions of Haiti*. The Hague, 1965
Brewster, John, M. 'The Machine Process in Agriculture and Industry', *Journal of Farm Economics*, vol. 92, 1950
Brisson, Gérald. *Les relations agraires dans l'Haïti contemporaine*. Mimeo, México D.F. (?), 1968
Brookins, Oscar T. 'Factor Analysis and Gross National Product: A Comment', *Quarterly Journal of Economics*, vol. 84, 1970
Brown, Jonathan. *The History and Present Condition of St Domingo, Volume I*. Philadelphia, 1837:1
Brown, Jonathan. *The History and Present Condition of St Domingo Volume II*. Philadelphia, 1837:2
Brummitt, W.C. & Culp, J.E. *Fertilizer Use in Haiti*. Mimeo, Tennessee Valley Authority, Muscle Shoals, no date
Brutus, Edner. *Instruction publique en Haiti 1492-1945*. Port-au-Prince, 1948
BTS Institut Haïtien de Statistique: *Bulletin Trimestriel de Statistique*. Port-au-Prince
Callear, Diana. 'The Stagnation of Peasant Agriculture in Haiti', BA dissertation, University of East Anglia, Norwich, 1977
Cantave, Romane. 'L'artisanat rural', in République d'Haïti. Secrétairerie d'Etat des Affaires Sociales: *Actes du Deuxième Congrès National du Travail. 21-30 avril 1969. Tome II:* Port-au-Prince, 1969
Carnoy, Martin. *Education as Cultural Imperialism*. New York, 1974
Carnoy, Martin. 'Education and Economic Development: The First Generation', in Manning Nash (ed). *Essays on Economic Development and Cultural Change in Honor of Bert F. Hoselitz*. Supplement to *Economic Development and Cultural Change*, vol. 25, 1977
Carter, Vernon Gill & Dale, Tom. *Topsoil and Civilization*. Revised edition, Norman, 1974
Casimir, Jean. 'Aperçu sur la structure économique d'Haïti, *América Latina*, vol. 7, 1964
Casimir, Jean. 'Aperçu sur la structure sociale d'Haïti', *América Latina*, vol. 8, 1965
Castor, Suzy. *La ocupación norteamericana de Haiti y sus consecuencias*. México D.F., 1971

Chatelain, Joseph. *La banque nationale. Son histoire – ses problèmes.* Port-au-Prince, 1954

Chayanov, Alexander V. *The Theory of Peasant Economy.* Daniel Thorner, R.E.F. Smith & Basile Kerblay (eds). Homewood, 1966

Cheung, Stephen N.S. 'Transaction Costs, Risk Aversion and the Choice of Contractual Arrangements', *Journal of Law and Economics* vol. 12, 1969

CHISS Centre Haïtien d'Investigation en Sciences Sociales. 'Les mécanismes d'adhésion des femmes primipares et multipares vis-à-vis de la planification familiale', *Les Cahiers de CHISS*, vol. 9, 1975

CIAP Inter-American Economic and Social Council (IA-ECOSOC), Inter-American Committee on the Alliance for Progress (CIAP), CIAP Subcommittee on Haiti December 19 to 21 1966, Washington, DC: *Domestic Efforts and the Needs for External Financing for the Development of Haiti.* Washington, DC, 1966

CIAP Consejo Interamericano Económico y Social (CIES). Comité Interamericano de la Alianza para el Progreso (CIAP). Décimocuarta reunión del CIAP, 22 y 23 de énero de 1968, Washington, DC. *El caso de Haití.* Washington, DC, 1968:1

CIAP Conseil Economique et Social Interaméricain (CESI). Comité Interaméricain de l'Alliance pour le Progrès (CIAP). Sous-comité du CIAP sur Haïti. Réunion du 29 janvier au 2 février 1968, Washington, DC. *L'effort interne et le financement externe réquis pour le développement d'Haïti.* Washington, DC, 1968:2

CIAP Inter-American Economic and Social Council (IA-ECOSOC) Inter-American Committee on the Alliance for Progress (CIAP), CIAP Subcommittee on Haiti. March 17 to 21 1969, Washington, DC. *Domestic Efforts and the Needs for External Financing for the Development of Haiti.* Washington, DC, 1969

CIAP Organization of American States. Inter-American Economic and Social Council. Inter-American Committee on the Alliance for Progress. CIAP Subcommittee on Haiti. June 10 to 15 1971, Washington, DC. *Domestic Efforts and the Needs for External Financing for the Development of Haiti.* Washington, DC, 1971

CIAP Organisation des Etats Américains. Conseil Economique et Social Interamérican, Comité Interaméricain de l'Alliance pour le Progrès. Sous-Comité du CIAP sur Haïti. 22-25 février 1972, Washington, DC. *L'effort national et le financement nécessaire au développement d'Haïti.* Washington, DC, 1972

CIAP Organization of American States. Inter-American Economic and Social Council. Inter-American Committee on the Alliance for

Progress. CIAP Subcommittee on Haiti. 19-22 February 1974, Washington, DC. *Domestic Efforts and the Needs for External Financing for the Development of Haiti.* Washington, DC, 1974

CIDA Comité Interaméricain de Développement Agricole. *Inventaire de l'information de base pour la programmation du développement agricole en Amérique Latine. Haïti.* Washington, DC, n.d.

Clague, Christopher K. *Economic Stagnation in Haiti, 1804-1915.* Mimeo, Department of Economics, University of Maryland, College Park, 1970

Clark, Colin & Haswell, Margaret R. *The Economics of Subsistence Agriculture.* Third edition, London, 1967

Code Rural et conseils communaux. Législation communale et rurale. Port-au-Prince, 1929

Cohen, Kalman J. & Cyert, Richard M. *Theory of the Firm: Resource Allocation in a Market Economy.* Englewood Cliffs, NJ, 1965

Cole, Hubert. *Christophe, King of Haiti.* New York, 1970

Comhaire, Jean. 'The Haitian "Chef de Section"', *American Anthropologist*, vol. 57, 1955

Comhaire, Jean. 'The Haitian Peasant and His Government', in Sidney W. Mintz (ed.). *Selected Papers on Economic and Social Aspects in Haiti.* Third part, Mimeo, New Haven, no date

Comhaire-Sylvain, Jean & Suzanne. 'Urban Stratification in Haiti', *Social and Economic Studies*, vol. 8, 1959

Comhaire-Sylvain, Suzanne & Jean. 'A Statistical Note on the Kenscoff Market System, Haiti', *Social and Economic Studies*, vol. 13, 1964

CONADEP République d'Haïti. Conseil National de Développement et de Planification. *Le Démarrage (edition technique).* Port-au-Prince, 1963

CONADEP République d'Haïti. Conseil National de Développement et de Planification. *Plan d'action économique et sociale 1968-1969.* Port-au-Prince, no date

CONADEP République d'Haïti. Conseil National de Développement et de Planification. *Plan d'action économique et sociale 1970-1971.* Port-au-Prince, do date

CONADEP République d'Haïti. Conseil National de Développement et de Planification. *Bases et priorités des programmes sectoriels. Période quinquennale 1971-1976* Port-au-Prince, no date

CONADEP République d'Haïti. Conseil National de Développement et de Planification: Haïti *L'assistance externe dans le secteur agricole.* Mimeo, Port-au-Prince, 1974

CONADEP République d'Haïti. Conseil National de Développement et de Planification: *Programme des travaux d'infrastructures économiques et sociales à forte intensité de main-d'oeuvre.* Port-au-Prince, 1976

Constitution Pan American Union. General Secretariat, Organization of American States. *Constitution of Haiti 1964.* Washington, DC, 1968

COPALE Conseil Permanent d'Action de Libération Economique de la République d'Haïti. *Le Démarrage.* Port-au-Prince, 1963

Correa, Hector. *The Economics of Human Resources.* Amsterdam, 1963

Correa, Hector. *Population, Health, Nutrition, and Development* Lexington, 1975

Courlander, Harold. *The Drum and the Hoe: Life and Lore of the Haitian People.* Berkeley, 1960

Courlander, Harold. 'Vodoun in Haitian Culture', in *Religion and Politics in Haiti.* Washington, DC, 1966

Crassweller, Robert D. 'Darkness in Haiti', *Foreign Affairs*, vol. 49, 1971

Crassweller, Robert D. *The Caribbean Community, Changing Societies and US Policy.* New York, 1972

CRN Centre de Recherches en Nutrition, Université Laval, Québec *Programme d'Assistance Alimentaire en Haïti, Volume I: Principes directeurs et stratégie. Rapport presenté à l'Agence Canadienne de Développement International.* Québec, 1975

CUNA Credit Union National Association, Inc. *Untitled memorandum* Mimeo, Washington, DC, 1976

Cyert, Richard M. & March, James G. *A Behavioral Theory of the Firm.* Englewood Cliffs, NJ, 1963

Dale, George A. *Education in the Republic of Haiti.* Washington, DC, 1959

Darmstadter, Joel & Landsberg, Hans H. 'The Economic Background', in Raymond Vernon (ed.). *The Oil Crisis.* New York, 1976

DARNDR Département de l'Agriculture, des Ressources Naturelles et du Développement Rural. *Rapport de la Commission Nationale pour la Conservation des Resources Naturelles Renouvelables.* Port-au-Prince, 1960:1

DARNDR Département de l'Agriculture, des Ressources Naturelles et du Développement Rural. *Projet de loi sur la conservation des ressources naturelles renouvelables.* Port-au-Prince, 1960:2

DARNDR Département de l'Agriculture, des Ressources Naturelles et du Développement Rural. *Rapport annuel du Service de l'Enseignement Rural. Année scolaire 1968-1969.* Damien, no date

DARNDR Département de l'Agriculture, des Ressources Naturelles et du Développement Rural. *Bilan des réalisations du secteur agricole, exercice 1974-75.* Mimeo, Damien, no date

DARNDR Département de l'Agriculture, des Ressources Naturelles et Développement Rural Unité de Programmation/ Secrétariat Technique: *Plan quinquennal du secteur agriculture 1976-1981.* Port-au-Prince, 1976

Dartigue, Maurice. 'L'oeuvre d'éducation rurale du gouvernement du président Vincent 1931-1936', *La Relève*, nos. 9-10-11, 1936

David, Paul A. *Technical Choice, Innovation and Economic Growth. Essays on American and British Experience in the Nineteenth Century.* Cambridge, 1975

Davis, H.P. *Black Democracy: The Story of Haiti.* Second edition, New York, 1929

Davis, Ralph. *The Rise of the Atlantic Economies.* Ithaca, 1973

Debbasch, Yvan. 'Le marronage: Essai sur la désertion de l'esclave antillais', *L'Année Sociologique*, vol. 3, 1961, 1962.

Debien, Gabriel. 'Le marronage aux Antilles Françaises au XVIIIe siècle', *Caribbean Studies*, vol. 6, 1966

Denis, Lorimer & Duvalier, François. *Le problème de classes à travers l'histoire d'Haïti.* Port-au-Prince, 1948

Denison, Edward F. *The Sources of Economic Growth in the United States and the Alternatives before Us.* New York, 1962

Denison, Edward F. *Why Growth Rates Differ. Postwar Experience in Nine Western Countries.* Washington, DC, 1967

Département de l'Economie Nationale. Bureau de Recensement. *Recensement général de la République d'Haïti (Population, habitation, agriculture) août 1950. Instructions aux énumérateurs.* Port-au-Prince, 1950

Département de la Justice. *Code Rural Dr. François Duvalier.* Port-au-Prince, 1963

Département de la Santé Publique. République d'Haïti. *Rapport annuel bio-statistique du Service de la Santé Publique 1948.* Port-au-Prince, 1953

Département de la Santé Publique. République d'Haïti. *Rapport annuel bio-statistique du Service de la Santé Publique 1949.* Port-au-Prince, 1954

Département de la Santé Publique et de la Population. Section de Statistique. *Rapport de la Section de Statistique sur les differentes activités des établissements de santé du Service de la Santé Publique durant les exercises 1968/1969 et 1969/1970.* Port-au-Prince, 1972

Département de la Santé Publique et de la Population. Section de Statistique. *Notification des cas de maladies infectieuses et parasitaires enregistrés pour l'année 1974*. Mimeo, Port-au-Prince, 1974

Deren, Maya. *The Voodoo Gods*. Frogmore, St Albans, 1975. Title of the original: *Divine Horsemen*

De Ronceray, Hubert. 'Quelques réflections sur le problème de la stratification sociale en Haïti', *Cahiers du CHISS*, vol. 2, 1968.

De Ronceray, Hubert & Petit-Frère, Serge. 'Projet expérimental sur le bilinguisme créole-français au niveau de l'enseignement primaire en Haïti (Bilan de la première année 1974-1975)', *Les Cahiers du CHISS*, vol. 9, 1975.

Despeignes, Mimose. *Le service social et le problème de la nutrition en Haïti*. Port-au-Prince, no date

DeYoung, Maurice. *Man and Land in the Haitian Economy*. Gainesville, 1958

DeYoung, Maurice. 'Class Parameters in Haitian Society', *Journal of Inter-American Studies*, vol. 1, 1959

Diebold, P.B. 'Review of Ester Boserup: The Conditions of Agricultural Growth: The Economics of Agrarian Change under Population Pressure', *Economic Development and Cultural Change*, vol. 16, 1968

Diederich, Bernard & Burt, Al. *Papa Doc: Haiti and Its Dictator*. London, 1969

Diederich, Bernard & Burt, Al. 'Epilogue (1971)', in *Papa Doc: Haiti and Its Dictator*. Harmondsworth, 1972

Domínguez, Ramiro. *Communicación en el contexto rural haitiano*. Mimeo, Institut Interaméricain des Sciences Agricoles (IICA), Port-au-Prince, 1976

Dominique, Gladys. 'Aspect qualitatif et quantitatif de la consommation alimentaire' in OEA Institut Interaméricain de l'Enfant. *Recommandations et travaux du Séminaire National de Nutrition d'Haïti. Port-au-Prince. 30 mai au 4 juin 1965*. Montevideo, 1965

Donner, Wolf. *Agricultural Development Regions as Instruments for Spatial Agricultural Planning*. Mimeo, Département de l'Agriculture, des Ressources Naturelles et du Développement Rural, Port-au-Prince, 1975

Dorfman, Robert, Samuelson, Paul A. & Solow, Robert M. *Linear Programming and Economic Analysis*. New York, 1958

Dorsainvil, J.-C. *Manuel d'histoire d'Haïti*. Port-au-Prince, no date

Dorville, René. *Inventaire des techniques améliorées d'emmagasinage de grains comestibles en Haïti*. Mimeo, Département de l'Agriculture, des Ressources Naturelles et du Développement Rural, Port-au-Prince, 1974

Dorville, René. *Quelques aspects particuliers des contraintes de l'agriculture haitienne.* Mimeo, Département de l'Agriculture, des Ressources Naturelles et du Développement Rural, Port-au-Prince, 1975:1

Dorville, René. *Perspectives d'une politique de l'emploi dans le secteur rural d'Haïti.* Mimeo, Département de l'Agriculture, des Ressources Naturelles et du Développement Rural, Port-au-Prince, 1975:2

Dorville, René. *Production et commercialization des légumes en Haïti.* Mimeo, Institut Interamérican des Sciences Agricoles (IICA), Port-au-Prince, 1975:3

Dorville, René & Dauphin, Franklin. *Enquête sur la production agricole de l'arrondissement du Cap-Haïtien.* Mimeo, Département de l'Agriculture, des Ressources Naturelles et du Développement Rural, Port-au-Prince, 1974

Dossous, Raoul. 'Rapport de la Sous-Commission pour l'Assistance Technique, Financière et Sociale', in Secrétairerie d'Etat des Affaires Sociales: *Actes du Deuxième Congrès National du Travail, 21-30 avril 1969. Tome II.* Port-au-Prince, 1969

Douglas, Paul H. 'The American Occupation of Haiti, I'. *Political Science Quarterly*, vol. 42, 1927

Due, John F. *Indirect Taxation in Developing Economies. The Role and Structure of Customs Duties, Excises, and Sales Taxes.* Baltimore, 1970

Duplan, Verdy. *Equivalents des unités de mesure et emballages utilisés pour le transport des produits agricoles.* Mimeo, Institut Interamérican des Sciences Agricoles (IICA), Port-au-Prince, 1975:1

Duplan, Verdy. *Commercialisation des intrants agricoles en Haïti.* Mimeo, Institut Interaméricain des Sciences Agricoles (IICA), Port-au-Prince, 1975:2

Duplan, Verdy & LaGra, Jerry. *Analyse du système de taxation des produits agricoles dans les marchés haïtiens.* Mimeo, Institut Interaméricain des Sciences Agricoles (IICA), Port-au-Prince, 1974

Duplan, Verdy & LaGra, Jerry. *Transport des produits agricoles vers Port-au-Prince.* Mimeo, Institut Interaméricain des Sciences Agricoles (IICA), Port-au-Prince, 1975

Duvalier, François. *Oeuvres essentielles, Volume III La révolution au pouvoir (Première partie).* Port-au-Prince, 1967:1

Duvalier, François. *Le premier Griot, le Dr. François Duvalier, huitième Président à Vie de la République soumet au peuple haïtien le bilan de dix années de gestion. 22 octobre 1967*. Port-au-Prince, 1967:2

Duvalier, François. *Oeuvres essentielles, Tome I. Eléments d'une doctrine*. Third edition, Port-au-Prince, 1968:1

Duvalier, François. *Oeuvres essentielles, Tome II: La marche à la présidence*. Third edition, Port-au-Prince, 1968:2

Duvalier, François. *Mémoires d'un leader du Tiers Monde. Mes négociations avec le Saint-Siège ou Une tranche d'histoire*. Paris, 1969

Duvalier, Jean-Claude. Secrétairerie d'Etat de la Coordination et de l'Information: *Le grand message du 2 janvier 1973 a la nation de Son Excellence Monsieur Jean-Claude Duvalier, Président à Vie de la République*. Port-au-Prince, no date

Duvigneaud & Figaro. Secrétairerie d'Etat de la Coordination et de l'Information (Service d'Information et de Documentation) (S.E. Frédéric Duvigneaud & S.E. Georges J. Figaro). *Rapport de la commission d'enquête sur les dépossessions des paysans de la Vallée de l'Artibonite*. Port-au-Prince, 1958

Dwinelle, J.H., Sheldon, A.J., Rein, C.R. & Sternberg T. 'Evaluation of Penicillin in the Treatment of Yaws', *American Journal of Tropical Medicine,* vol. 27, 1947

L'effort du gouvernement dans le domaine de l'éducation nationale. Port-au-Prince, no date

Efron, Edith. 'The "New Movement" in Haiti', *Caribbean Quarterly*, vol. 4, 1955

Erasmus, Charles John. 'Agricultural Changes in Haiti: Patterns of Resistance and Acceptance', *Human Organization*, vol. 2, 1952

Estimé, Jean-Robert. *Contribution à l'élaboration d'une politique agricole en Haïti*. Mimeo, Faculté des Sciences Agronomiques de Gembloux, Gembloux, 1972

FAO. Programme Elargi d'Assistance Technique FAO. *Rapport au gouvernement d'Haïti sur la politique forestière et sa mise en oeuvre*. Rome, 1955

FAO Food and Agriculture Organization of the United Nations *Production Yearbook,* vol. 26, Rome, 1972

Fatton, Bernard. *Eléments d'information sur la production et la commercialisation du sisal en Haïti*. Mimeo, Institut Interaméricain des Sciences Agricoles (IICA), Port-au-Prince, 1975

Feder, Ernest. *The Rape of the Peasantry. Latin America's Landholding System*. Garden City, 1971

Finck, Arnold. 'The Fertility of Tropical Soil under the Influence of Agricultural Land Use', in *Applied Sciences and Development, A*

Biannual Collection of Recent German Contributions Concerning Development through Applied Sciences. Vol. 1. Tübingen, 1973

Firth, Raymond. *Malay Fishermen: Their Peasant Economy.* London, 1946

Fisher, Irving. *The Theory of Interest.* New York, 1930

Fleischmann, Ulrich. *Aspekte der sozialen und politischen Entwicklung Haitis.* Stuttgart, 1971

Folsom, Robert S. 'Haitian Economy', unpublished PhD Thesis, Revised, Fletcher School of Law and Diplomacy, Medford, 1954

Foster, George M. 'Introduction: What Is a Peasant?' in Jack M. Potter, May N. Diaz & George M. Foster (eds). *Peasant Society. A Reader.* Boston, 1967

Foster, Philip J. 'The Vocational School Fallacy in Development Planning', in C. Arnold Anderson & Mary Jean Bowman (eds). *Education and Economic Development.* Chicago, 1965

Fouchard, Jean. *Les marrons de la liberté.* Paris, 1972

Fougère, William & King, Kendall W. 'Capitulation as a Key Ingredient to Eradication of Severe Malnutrition in Children', *Environmental Child Health*, vol. 21, 1975

Franklin, James. *The Present State of Hayti (Saint Domingo) with Remarks on its Agriculture, Commerce, Laws, Religion, Finances, and Population, etc. etc.* London, 1828

Frederiksen, Harald. 'Malaria Control and Population Pressure in Ceylon', *Public Health Reports*, vol. 75, 1960

Frederiksen, Harald. 'Determinants and Consequences of Mortality Trends in Ceylon', *Public Health Reports*, vol. 76, 1961

Freire, Paulo. *Pedagogy of the Oppressed.* New York, 1970

Friedmann, John R.P. 'Development Planning in Haiti: A Critique of the UN Report', *Economic Development and Cultural Change*, vol. 4, 1955

Frisch, Ragnar. 'Dynamic Utility', *Econometrica*, vol. 32, 1964

Fuchs, Victor R. 'The Contribution of Health Services to the American Economy', *Millbank Memorial Fund Quarterly*, vol. 44, 1966. Reprinted as 'The Output of the Health Industry', Michael H. Cooper & Anthony J. Culyer (eds). *Health Economics.* Harmondsworth, 1973

Galíndez, Jesús de. *La era de Trujillo. Un estudio casuístico de dictadura hispanoamericana.* Buenos Aires, 1962

García Zamor, Jean-Claude. *La administración pública en Haití.* Guatemala, 1966

Gates, William B., Jr. *Some Observations on Economic Development and Haiti*. Mimeo, Williams College, Williamstown, 1959:1

Gates, William B., Jr. *The Haitian Coffee Industry*. Mimeo, Williams College, Williamstown, 1959:2

Gates, William B., Jr. *The Haitian Cotton and Cotton Textile Industries*. Mimeo, Williams College, Williamstown, 1959:3

Gayoso, Antonio. 'A Typology of Small Farmer Credit Programs', in *AID Spring Review of Small Farmer Credit: Vol. XIX. Small Farmer Credit. Analytical Papers*. Washington, DC, 1973

Gédéon, Michaele Amédée, Lamothe, Fayla D. & Haverberg, Linda N. *Prevalence of Protein-Calorie Malnutrition in Haiti: Comparison of the Jelliffe Survey of 1958 and the AFOB Vitamin A Survey of 1975*. Mimeo, Bureau de Nutrition, Port-au-Prince, 1976

Geertz, Clifford. *Agricultural Involution. The Progress of Ecological Change in Indonesia*. Berkeley, 1970

Georgescu-Roegen, Nicholas. 'Process in Farming versus Process in Manufacturing: A Problem of Balanced Development', in Ugo Papi & Charles Nunn (eds). *Economic Problems of Agriculture in Industrial Societies*. London, 1969

Georgescu-Roegen, Nicholas. *The Entropy Law and the Economic Process*, Cambridge, Mass., 1971

Giles, Antonio. *Evaluation des résultats obtenus par l'IDAI au point de vue de crédit agricole. Programme de crédit agricole pour la période 1973/1976. Schéma du rapport d'évaluation d'activités*. Mimeo, Institut Interaméricain de Sciences Agricoles (IICA), Port-au-Prince, 1973

Gillette, Cynthia & Uphoff, Norman. 'The Credit Connection: Cultural and Social Factors Affecting Small Farmer Participation in Credit Programs' in *AID Spring Review of Small Farmer Credit: Vol. XIX. Small Farmer Credit. Analytical Papers*. Washington, DC, 1973

Gingras, Jean-Pierre O. *Duvalier, Caribbean Cyclone. The History of Haiti and Its Present Government*. New York, 1967

Gintis, Herbert. 'Education, Technology, and the Characteristics of Worker Productivity', *American Economic Review*, vol. 61, 1971

Girault, Christian & LaGra, Jerry. *Caractéristiques structurelles de la commercialisation interne des produits agricoles en Haïti*. Mimeo, Institut Interaméricain des Sciences Agricoles (IICA), Port-au-Prince, 1975

Girod-Chantrans, Justin. *Voyage d'un Suisse dans différentes colonies d'Amérique*. Neuchâtel, 1785.

Gisser, Micha. 'Schooling and the Farm Problem', *Econometrica*, vol. 33, 1965

Golding, E.W. *The Investigation of Wind Power Possibilities in Haiti*, Mimeo, United Nations, New York, 1956

Gómez, Carlos J. *Haiti. Family Planning and Maternal and Child Health Program 1974-1978*. Mimeo, Pan American Health Organization, Washington, DC 1974

Good, Richard, Lent, George E. & Ojha, P.D. 'Role of Export Taxes in Developing Countries', *IMF Staff Papers*, vol. 13, 1966

Gould, J.D. *Economic Growth in History. Survey and Analysis*. London, 1972

Green, H.A. John. *Consumer Theory*. Harmondsworth, 1971

Griffin, Keith. *Underdevelopment in Spanish America. An Interpretation*. London, 1969

Griffin, Keith. *The Green Revolution: An Economic Analysis*. Geneva, 1972

Griffin, Keith. *The Political Economy of Agrarian Change. An Essay on the Green Revolution*. Cambridge, Mass., 1974

Griffin, Keith B. & Enos, John L. *Planning Development*. London, 1970

Grigg, D.B. 'Population Pressure and Agricultural Change', in *Progress in Geography*, vol. 8. London, 1976

Griggs, Earl Leslie & Prator, Clifford H. (eds). *Henry Christophe and Thomas Clarkson. A Correspondence*. Reprinted edition, New York, 1968

Guerra y Sánchez, Ramiro. *Sugar and Society in the Caribbean. An Economic History of Cuban Agriculture*. New Haven, 1964

Guha, Ashok. 'Factor and Commodity Prices in an Expanding Economy', *Quarterly Journal of Economics*, vol. 77, 1963

Hall, Robert Burnett. 'The Société Congo of the Ile à Gonave', *American Anthropologist*, New series, vol. 31, 1929

Harbison, Frederick. 'The Prime Movers of Innovation', in C. Arnold Anderson & Mary Jean Bowman (eds). *Education and Economic Development*. Chicago, 1965

Harbison, Frederick H. & Myers, Charles A. *Education, Manpower and Economic Growth*. New York, 1964

Hardouin, A.C. 'Haiti. A Study in Regression', *Mexico Quarterly Review*, vol. 2, 1963

Hartman, Moshe. 'Typology of Countries by Labor Force Participation Patterns', *Economic Development and Cultural Change*, vol. 25, 1977

Hartwell, R.M. 'The Economic History of Medical Care', in Mark Perlman (ed.). *The Economics of Health and Medical Care. Proceed-*

ings of a Conference held by the International Economic Association at Tokyo. London, 1974

Harvey, William Woodis. *Sketches of Hayti; From the Expulsion of the French, to the Death of Christophe*. London, 1827

Hayami, Yujiro & Ruttan, Vernon W. 'Factor Prices and Technical Change in Agricultural Development: The United States and Japan, 1880-1960', *Journal of Political Economy*, vol. 78, 1970

Henderson, James M. & Quandt, Richard E. *Microeconomic Theory. A Mathematical Approach*. New York, 1958.

Herskovits, Melville J. *Economic Anthropology. The Economic Life of Primitive Peoples*. New York, 1952

Herskovits, Melville J. *Life in a Haitian Valley*. New York, 1971

Hicks, Albert C. *Blood in the Streets. The Life and Rule of Trujillo*. New York, 1946

Hirshleifer, J. *Investment, Interest, and Capital*. Englewood Cliffs, NJ, 1970

Hoetink, Harmannus. 'Over de Sociaal-Raciale Structuur van Haiti', *Tijdschrift van het Koninklijk Nederlandsch Aardrijkskundig Genootschap*, vol. 78, 1961

Holly, Marc Aurèle. *Agriculture in Haiti. With Special Reference to Rural Economy and Agricultural Education*. New York, 1955

Honorat, Jean-Jacques. *Enquête sur le développement*. Port-au-Prince, 1974

Huberman, Leo & Sweezy, Paul M. *Socialism in Cuba*. New York, 1969

Hubert, Giles A. 'Some Problems of a Colonial Economy: A Study of Economic Dualism in Haiti', *Inter-American Economic Affairs*, vol. 3, 1950

Huizer, Gerrit. *Peasant Rebellion in Latin America*. Harmondsworth, 1973

Hunter, Guy. *Modernizing Peasant Societies. A Comparative Study in Asia and Africa*. New York, 1969

Huxley, Francis. *The Invisibles. Voodoo Gods in Haiti*. New York, 1969

IBRD International Bank for Reconstruction and Development. International Development Association. *Current Economic Position and Prospects of Haiti. May 3 1972*, Washington, DC, 1972

IBRD International Bank for Reconstruction and Development International Development Association. *Current Economic Position and Prospects of Haiti. April 18 1974*. Washington, DC, 1974

ICA United States of America Operations Missions to Haiti. *The ICA Program in Haiti*. Port-au-Prince, 1961

IFS. International Monetary Fund. *International Financial Statistics*.
IHS. République d'Haïti, Département des Finances et des Affaires Economiques. Institut Haïtien de Statistique. *Guide économique de la République d'Haïti*. Port-au-Prince, 1964
IHS. Institut Haïtien de Statistique. Département des Finances et des Affaires Economiques. *Guide économique de la République d'Haïti*. Port-au-Prince, 1971
IHS. Institut Haïtien de Statistique. Département de Finances et des Affaires Economiques. *Résultats préliminaires du recensement général de la population, du logement et de l'agriculture (septembre 1971)*. Port-au-Prince, 1973
IHS. Département des Finances et des Affaires Economiques. Institut Haïtien de Statistique. *Comptes nationaux et projections macro-économiques*. Port-au-Prince, 1974
IHS. Institut Haïtien de Statistique. Départment des Finances et des Affaires Economiques. *Enquête socio-économique (avril 1970) Premiers resultats*. Port-au-Prince, 1975:1
IHS. République d'Haïti. Institut Haïtien de Statistique. *Fiche statistique de la République d'Haïti*. Port-au-Prince, 1975:2
IHS. Institut Haïtien de Statistique. Département des Finances et des Affaires Economiques. *Recensement général de la population, du logement et de l'agriculture de 1971. Manuel d'instructions aux énumérateurs*. Port-au-Prince, no date:1
IHS. Institut Haïtien de Statistique. *Projection de la population totale d'Haïti de 1950-1986*. Port-au-Prince, no date:2
IICA. Institut Interaméricain des Sciences Agricoles de l'OEA, *Contrôle de l'érosion au Morne l'Hôpital, pour la protection de la ville de Port-au-Prince*. Mimeo, Port-au-Prince, 1974:1
IICA. Inter-American Institute of Agricultural Sciences. *Commercial Activities in Rural Haiti: A Community-Centered Approach*. Mimeo, Port-au-Prince, 1974:2
IICA. Département de l'Agriculture, Ressources Naturelles et du Développement Rurale/COCEA (République d'Haïti). Banque Interaméricaine de Développement – BID. Institut Interaméricain des sciences Agricoles de l'OEA. *Rapport final. Projet intégré d'éducation rurale en Haïti. Volume I.* Port-au-Prince, no date
ILO. International Labour Office. 'Women in the Labour Force', *International Labour Review*, vol. 77, 1958
James, Cyril L.R. *The Black Jacobins: Toussaint L'Ouverture and the San Domingo Revolution*. Second edition. New York, 1963
Jean, Rodrigue. *Classes sociales et sous-développement en Haïti*. Ville St-Laurent, 1974

Jelliffe, Derrick B. & Jelliffe, E.F. Patricia. 'The Nutritional Standard of Haitian Children', *Acta Tropica*, vol. 18, 1961

Johnson, E.A.J. *The Organization of Space in Developing Countries.* Cambridge, Mass., 1970

Johnson, Harry G. *The Two-Sector Model of General Equilibrium.* London, 1971

Jones, Graham. *The Role of Science and Technology in Developing Countries.* London, 1971

JWK International Corporation. *Agricultural Policy Studies in Haiti: Coffee.* Mimeo, Département de l'Agriculture, des Ressources Naturelles et du Développement Rural, Damien, 1976:1

JWK International Corporation. *Agricultural Policy Studies in Haiti: Cotton.* Mimeo, Département de l'Agriculture, des Ressources Naturelles et du Développement Rural, Damien, 1976:2

JWK International Corporation. *Agricultural Policy Studies in Haiti: Sisal.* Mimeo, Département de l'Agriculture, des Ressources Naturelles et du Développement Rural, Damien, 1976:3

JWK International Corporation. *Agricultural Policy Studies in Haiti: Meat.* Mimeo, Département de l'Agriculture, des Ressources Naturelles et du Développement Rural, Damien, 1976:4

JWK International Corporation. *Agricultural Policy Studies in Haiti: Mangoes.* Mimeo, Département de l'Agriculture, des Ressources Naturelles et du Développement Rural, Damien, 1976:5

Kaldor, Nicholas. 'A Model of the Trade Cycle', *Economic Journal*, vol. 50, 1940

Kamarck, Andrew M. *The Tropics and Economic Development. A Provocative Inquiry into the Poverty of Nations.* Baltimore, 1976

KCA. Keesing's Contemporary Archives

Kerblay, Basile. 'Chayanov and the Theory of Peasantry as a Specific Type of Economy', in Teodor Shanin (ed.). *Peasants and Societies.* Harmondsworth, 1971

Kilby, Peter, 'Farm and Factory: A Comparison of the Skill Requirements for the Transfer of Technology', *Journal of Development Studies*, vol. 9, 1972

Kindleberger, Charles P. *Foreign Trade and the National Economy.* New Haven, 1962

King, Dwight Y. & Weldon, Peter D. 'Income Distribution and Levels of Living in Java, 1963-1970', *Economic Development and Cultural Change*, vol.25, 1977

King, Kendall W. 'Nutrition Research in Haiti' in *Research and Resources of Haiti. Papers on the Conference on Research and Resources of Haiti.* New York, 1969.

King, Kendall W., Foucauld, Jean, Fougère, William & Severinghaus, Elmer L. 'Height and Weight of Haitian Children', *American Journal of Clinical Nutrition*, vol. 13, 1963

Klipstein, Frederick A., Samloff, I. Michael & Schenk, Eric A. 'Tropical Sprue in Haiti', *Annals of Internal Medicine*, vol. 64, 1966

Korngold, Ralph: *Citizen Toussaint*. London 1945

Kravis, Irving B. 'International Commodity Agreements to Promote Aid and Efficiency: The Case of Coffee', *Canadian Journal of Economics*, vol. 1, 1968

Kroeber, Alfred L. *Anthropology*. New York, 1948

Kuznets, Simon. *Modern Economic Growth. Rate, Structure, and Spread*. New Haven, 1966

Labour and Welfare Department, *François Duvalier Labour Code*. Port-au-Prince, 1961

Lacerte, Robert K. 'The First Land Reform in Latin America: The Reforms of Alexander Pétion. 1809-1814', *Inter-American Economic Affairs*, vol. 28, 1974/75

LaGra, Jerry, Charleston, Wesner & Fanfan, Guy. *Prix des produits agricoles dans les marchés haïtiens*. Mimeo, Institut Interaméricain des Sciences Agricoles (IICA), Port-au-Prince, 1975

LaGra, Jerry & Duplan, Verdy. *Enquête sur le transport des produits agricoles à l'entrée et à la sortie du Cap-Haïtien*. Mimeo, Institut Interaméricain des Sciences Agricoles (IICA), Port-au-Prince, 1975

LaGra, Jerry, Fanfan, Guy & Charleston, Wesner. *Les marchés publics d'Haïti*. Mimeo, Institut Interaméricain des Sciences Agricoles (IICA), Port-au-Prince, 1975

Laguerre, Michel. 'The Failure of Christianity among the Slaves of Haiti', *Freeing the Spirit*, vol. 2, 1973:1

Laguerre, Michel. 'The Place of Voodoo in the Social Structure of Haiti', *Caribbean Quarterly*, vol. 19, 1973:2

Laguerre, Michel. 'An Ecological Approach to Voodoo', *Freeing the Spirit*, vol. 3, 1974:1

Laguerre, Michel. 'Voodoo as Religious and Revolutionary Ideology', *Freeing the Spirit*, vol. 3, 1974:2

Laguerre, Michel. *Les associations traditionelles de travail dans la paysannerie haïtiens*. Mimeo, Institut Interaméricain des Sciences Agricoles (IICA), Port-au-Prince, 1975

Laguerre, Michel S. *Migration et vie paysanne en Haïti*. Mimeo, Institut Interaméricain des Sciences Agricoles (IICA), Port-au-Prince, 1976:1

Laguerre, Michel S. *Le sangue haïtien: un système de crédit rotatoire*. Mimeo, Institut Interaméricain des Sciences Agricoles (IICA), Port-au-Prince, 1976:2

Lamothe, Camille. *Contribution à la vulgarisation de la pensée coopérative.* Port-au-Prince, 1958

Lamothe, Fayla & Haverberg, Linda. *Report of a Nutritional Evaluation Survey of Children between the Ages of 0-6 Years in Bombarde, DesForges, and L'Arbre*, Mimeo, Bureau de Nutrition, Port-au-Prince, 1976

Laroche, René. 'Rapport de la Sous-Commission pour la Coopération: La coopérative, moteur du développement rural en Haïti', in Secrétairerie d'Etat des Affaires Sociales. *Actes du Deuxième Congrès National du Travail. 21-30 avril 1969.* Port-au-Prince, 1969

Laroche, Victor. 'Infection et malnutrition infantiles en Haïti', in OEA. Institut Interaméricain de l'Enfant. *Recommandations et travaux du Séminaire National de Nutrition d'Haïti. Port-au-Prince. 30 mai au 4 juin 1965.* Montevideo, 1965

Latortue, François. 'Considérations sur la main-d'oeuvre haïtienne', in *Research and Resources of Haiti Papers of the Conference on Research and Resources of Haiti.* New York, 1969

Larose, Serge. *L'exploitation agricole en Haïti. Guide d'étude.* Montréal, no date

Latortue, Gérard R. 'Haiti: Chaotic and Corrupt', *The Nation*, 21 Nov. 1966:1

Latortue, Gérard R. 'Tyranny in Haiti', *Current History*, vol. 51, 1966:2

Latortue, Gérard R. 'Political Crisis in Haiti', *New World*, vol. 3, 1967

Latortue, Gérard R. *Current Trends in Public Administration in Haiti.* Mimeo, Inter-American University of Puerto Rico, Arecibo, no date

Laurent, Garvey & Alphonse, Donasson. 'Etude socio-économique de la Vallée de Camp-Perrin, Plaine de Cayes-Haïti', *Bulletin Agricole*, vol. 5, 1956

Lebeau, Francis. *Rural Sector Assessment of the Republic of Haiti*, Mimeo, US/AID, Port-au-Prince, 1974

Leibenstein, Harvey. *A Theory of Economic-Demographic Development.* Princeton, 1954

Leibenstein, Harvey. *Economic Backwardness and Economic Growth. Studies in the Theory of Economic Development.* New York, 1957

Léon, Rulx. *Les maladies en Haïti.* Port-au-Prince, 1953

Lepkowski, Tadeusz. *Haiti. Tomo I.* La Habana, 1968 1

Lepkowski, Tadeusz: *Haiti, Tomo II.* La Habana, 1968:2

Lewis, W. Arthur. 'Economic Development with Unlimited Supplies of Labour', *Manchester School of Economic and Social Studies*, vol. 22, 1954

Lewis, W. Arthur. *The Theory of Economic Growth.* London, 1955

Leyburn, James, G. 'The Making of a Black Nation', in George Peter Murdock (ed.). *Studies in the Science of Society*. New Haven, 1937

Leyburn, James G. *The Haitian People*. Revised edition, New Haven, 1966

Lindbeck Assar. 'The Efficiency of Competition and Planning', in Michael Kaser & Richard Portes (ed). *Planning and Market Relations*. London, 1971

Lipton, Michael. 'The Theory of the Optimising Peasant', *Journal of Development Studies*, vol. 4, 1968:1

Lipton, Michael. 'The Theory of the Optimising Peasant', *Journal of Development Studies*, vol. 4, 1968:2

Lipton, Michael. 'Strategy for Agriculture: Urban Bias and Rural Planning', in Paul Streeten & Michael Lipton (eds). *The Crisis of Indian Planning. Economic Planning in the 1960s*. London, 1968:2

Lipton, Michael. *Why Poor People Stay Poor. A Study of Urban Bias in World Development*. London, 1977

Lobb, John, 'Caste and Class in Haiti', *American Journal of Sociology*, vol. 46, 1940

Locher, Uli. *The Internal Market System for Agriculatural Produce in Port-au-Prince*. Mimeo, Institut Interaméricain des Sciences Agricoles (IICA), Port-au-Prince, 1974

Logan, Rayford W. 'Education in Haiti', *Journal of Negro History*, vol. 15, 1930

Logan, Rayford W. *Diplomatic Relations of the United States with Haiti 1776-1891*. Chapel Hill, 1941

Logan, Rayford W. *Haiti and the Dominican Republic*. London, 1968

Long, Millard F. 'Interest Rates and the Structure of Agricultural Credit Markets', *Oxford Economic Papers*, vol. 20, 1968:1

Long, Millard F. 'Why Peasant Farmers Borrow', *American Journal of Agricultural Economics*, vol. 50, 1968:2

Long, Millard F. 'Conditions for Success of Public Credit Programs for Small Farmers', in *AID Spring Review of Small Farmer Credit: Vol. XIX. Small Farmer Credit. Analytical Papers*. Washington, DC, 1973

Long, Millard F. *Agricultural Credit*. Mimeo, International Bank for Reconstruction and Development. Washington, DC, 1974

Luce, R. Duncan & Raiffa, Howard. *Games and Decisions. Introduction and Critical Survey*. New York, 1957

Lundahl, Mats. 'Rantesatserna på de informålla kreditmarknaderna i u-länderna', in Mats Lundahl & Bo Södersten (eds). *Utvecklingsekonomi I: Underutverklingens mekanismer*. Stockholm, 1974

Lundahl, Mats. 'Les obstacles au changement technologique dans

l'agriculture traditionelle haïtienne', *Conjonction*, no. 135, 1977
Lutz, Friedrich A. *The Theory of Interest*, Dordecht, 1967
Mackenzie, Charles. *Notes on Haiti. Made during a Residence in that Republic. Volume One.* London, 1830:1
Mackenzie, Charles. *Notes on Haiti, Made during a Residence in that Republic. Volume Two.* London, 1830:2
McKinnon, Ronald I. *Money and Capital in Economic Development.* Washington, DC, 1973
MacLeod, Murdo J. 'The Haitian Novel of Social Protest', *Journal of Inter-American Studies*, vol. 4, 1962
McPherson, W.W. & Johnston, Bruce F. 'Distinctive Features of Agricultural Development in the Tropics', in Herman M. Southworth & Bruce F. Johnston (eds). *Agricultural Development and Economic Growth.* Ithaca, 1967
Magloire, Auguste. *L'erreur révolutionnaire et notre état social.* Port-au-Prince, 1909
Malenbaum, Wilfred. 'Health and Productivity in Poor Areas', in Herbert E. Klarman (ed.) with the assistance of Helen H. Jaszi. *Empirical Studies in Health Economics.* Baltimore, 1970
Malinowski, Bronislaw. *Argonauts of the Western Pacific. An Account of Native Enterprise and Adventure in the Archipelagoes of Melanesian New Guinea.* New York, 1961
Manigat, Leslie F. *Haiti of the Sixties, Object of International Concern.* Washington, DC, 1964
March, James G. & Simon, Herbert A., with the collaboration of Guetzkow, Harold. *Organizations.* New York, 1958
Mason J. & Cavalié, P. 'Malaria Epidemic in Haiti following a Hurricane', *American Journal of Tropical Medicine and Hygiene*, vol. 14, 1965
Meegama, S.A. 'Malaria Eradication and Its Effort on Mortality Levels', *Population Studies*, vol. 21, 1967
Meier, Gerald M. & Baldwin, Robert E. *Economic Development: Theory, History, Policy.* New York, 1957
Melhorn, Kent C. *L'hygiène en Haïti. Un rapport pour l'année fiscale 1928-29.* Port-au-Prince, 1930
Mellor, John W. 'Increasing Agricultural Production in Early Stages of Economic Development: Relationships, Problems, and Prospects', *Indian Journal of Agricultural Economics*, vol. 17, 1962
Mellor, John W. *The Economics of Agricultural Development.* Ithaca, 1966
Mellor, John W. 'Toward a Theory of Agricultural Development', in Herman M. Southworth & Bruce F. Johnston (eds). *Agricultural Development and Economic Growth.* Ithaca, 1967

Métraux, Alfred. *Le vaudou haitien.* Paris 1958
Métraux, Alfred in collaboration with Berrouet, E. & Comhaire-Sylvain, Jean & Suzanne. *Making a Living in the Marbial Valley (Haiti).* Paris, 1951
Millspaugh, Arthur C. *Haiti under American Control 1915-1930.* Boston, 1931
Mintz, Sidney W. 'Internal Market Systems as Mechanisms of Social Articulation', in *Proceedings of the 1959 Annual Spring Meeting of the American Ethnological Society.* Seattle, 1959
Mintz, Sidney W. 'Peasant Markets', *Scientific American,* vol. 203, 1960:1
Mintz, Sidney W. 'A Tentative Typology of Eight Haitian Marketplaces', *Revista de Ciencias Sociales,* vol. 4, 1960:2
Mintz, Sidney W. 'Le système du marché rural dans l'économie haïtienne', *Bulletin du Bureau d'Ethnologie,* vol. 3, 1960:3
Mintz, Sidney W. 'Pratik: Haitian Personal Economic Relationships', in *Proceedings of the 1961 Annual Spring Meeting of the American Ethnological Society.* Seattle, 1961:1
Mintz, Sidney W. 'Standards of Value and Units of Measure in the Fond-des-Nègres Market Place, Haiti', *Journal of the Royal Anthropological Institute,* vol. 91, 1961:2
Mintz, Sidney W. 'The Employment of Capital by Market Women in Haiti', in Raymond Firth & Basil S. Yamey (eds). *Capital, Saving and Credit in Peasant Societies.* Chicago, 1964
Mintz, Sidney W. 'Introduction to the Second Edition' in Leyburn, James G. *The Haitian People.* Revised edition, New Haven, 1966:1
Mintz, Sidney W. 'The Caribbean as a Socio-Cultural Area', *Cahiers d'histoire mondiale,* vol. 9, 1966
Mintz, Sidney W. 'History and Anthropology: A Brief Reprise', in Stanley L. Engerman & Eugene D. Genovese (ed). *Race and Slavery in the Western Hemisphere: Quantitative Studies.* Princeton, 1975
Mirville, Solon. *L'école primaire et la lutte contre l'analphabétisme en Haïti.* Port-au-Prince, 1959
Le Moniteur. Journal officiel de la République d'Haïti. Numér extraordinaire. Budget de fonctionnement et de développement de l'exercice 1974-1975. 1 October 1974
Le Moniteur. Journal officiel de la République d'Haïti. Numéro extraordinaire. Budget de fonctionnement et de développement de l'exercice 1975-1976. 29 September 1975
Montague, Ludwell Lee. *Haiti and the United States 1714-1938.* Durham, 1940

Montgomery, George. 'Education and Training for Agricultural Development', in Herman M. Southworth & Bruce F. Johnston (eds). *Agricultural Development and Economic Growth*. Ithaca, 1967

Moore, O. Ernest. *Haiti: Its Stagnant Society and Shackled Economy, A Survey*. New York, 1972

Moral, Paul. 'La culture de café en Haïti: des plantations coloniales aux "jardins" actuels', *Cahiers d'Outre-Mer*, vol. 8, 1955

Moral, Paul. *L'économie haïtienne*, Port-au-Prince, 1959

Moral, Paul. *Le paysan haïtien (Etude sur la vie rurale en Haïti)*. Paris, 1961

Moreau de Saint-Méry, Médéric-Louis-Elie. *Description topographique, physique, civile, politique et historique de la partie Française de l'isle Saint-Domingue*. New edition, 3 volumes, Paris, 1958.

Morose, Joseph P. 'Pour une réforme de l'éducation en Haïti', PhD thesis, Université de Fribourg, 1970

Murray, Gerald F. 'The Evolution of Haitian Peasant Land Tenure: A Case Study in Agrarian Adaptation to Population Growth', PhD thesis, Columbia University, New York, 1977

Murray, Gerald F. & Alvarez, Maria D. *The Marketing of Beans in Haiti. An Exploratory Study*. Mimeo, Institut Interaméricain des Sciences Agricoles (IICA), Port-au-Prince, 1973

Musgrave, Richard A. *The Theory of Public Finance*. New York, 1959

Mushkin, Selma J. 'Health as an Investment', *Journal of Political Economy*, vol. 70, 1962. Reprinted in Michael H. Cooper & Anthony J. Culyer (eds). *Health Economics*, Harmondsworth, 1973

Myrdal, Gunnar. *Monetary Equilibrium*. London, 1939

Myrdal, Gunnar. *An American Dilemma, The Negro Problem and Modern Democracy*. New York, 1944

Myrdal, Gunnar. *Economic Theory and Under-Developed Regions*. London, 1957

Myrdal, Gunnar. *Asian Drama. An Inquiry Into the Poverty of Nations*. New York, 1968

Myrdal, Gunnar. *The Challenge of World Poverty. A World Anti-Poverty Programme in Outline*. Harmondsworth, 1971

Nafziger, E. Wayne. 'A Critique of Development Economics in the US', *Journal of Development Studies*, vol. 13, 1976

Nath, S.K. *A Reappraisal of Welfare Economics*. London, 1969

Nelson, Richard R. 'A Theory of the Low-Level Equilibrium Trap in Underdeveloped Economies', *American Economic Review*, vol. 46, 1956

Newbery, David M.G. *Cropsharing Tenancy in an Equilibrium Model*.

Paper delivered to the European Meeting of the Econometric Society. Oslo 28-31 August 1973

Newbery, David M.G. 'The Choice of Rental Contract in Peasant Agriculture', in Lloyd G. Reynolds (ed.). *Agriculture in Development Theory*. New Haven, 1975:1

Newbery, David M.G. 'Tenurial Obstacles to Innovation', *Journal of Development Studies*, vol. 11, 1975:2

Newman, Peter. 'Malaria Control and Population Growth', *Journal of Development Studies*, vol. 6, 1970

Nicholls, David. *Economic Dependence and Political Autonomy. The Haitian Experience*. Montreal, 1974

Nicolas, Schiller. 'Déboisement et reboisement en Haïti', *Service National de la Production Agricole et de l'Enseignement Rural*, Bulletin no. 16, 1938

Nisbet, Charles. 'Interest Rates and Imperfect Competition in the Informal Credit Market of Rural Chile', *Economic Development and Cultural Change*, vol. 16, 1967

Nisbet, Charles T. 'Moneylending in Rural Areas: Some Examples from Colombia', *The American Journal of Economics and Sociology*, vol. 30, 1971

Nisbet, Charles T. 'Informal Lenders as Suppliers of Development Credits to Small Farmers in Developing Countries: Attractive or Deceptive Alternatives', in *AID Spring Review of Small Farmer Credit: Volume XV. Small Farmer Credit, Informal Credit*. Washington, DC, 1973

Noël, Pierre. 'Recent Research in Public Health in Haiti', in *Research and Resources of Haiti. Papers on the Conference on Research and Resources of Haiti*. New York, 1969

Nurkse, Ragnar. *Problems of Capital Formation in Underdeveloped Countries*. Oxford, 1953

OAS. Inter-American Commission on Human Rights. *Report on the Situation Regarding Human Rights in Haiti*. Mimeo, Washington, DC, 1963

OEA. Secrétariat Général, Organisation des Etats Américains. *Haïti, Mission d'assistance technique integrée*. Washington, DC, 1972

OEA. Office des Finances Publiques. *Mission en Haïti. Rapport de l'assistance technique dans le domaine fiscal, juillet 1971-juin 1973*. Washington, DC, 1974

OEA-CEPAL-BID. Mission Conjointe OEA-CEPAL-BID en Haïti. *Rapport général présenté au Gouvernement de la République d'Haïti*. Washington, DC, 1962

Ohlin, Göran. *Development in Retrospect*. Paper presented at a conference at Houston, Texas, 3-5 February 1977. Mimeo, no date.

ONAAC. Office National d'Alphabétisation et d'Action Communautaire. *Plan d'action 1969-74 (2e édition, revue et corrigée en fonction du déroulement de plan)*. Port-au-Prince, 1969

ONEC. Département de l'Education Nationale. Office National d'Education Communautaire. *Guide national d'alphabétisation des adultes*. Port-au-Prince, 1962

Oshima, Harry T. 'Food Consumption, Nutrition, and Economic Development in Asian Countries', *Economic Development and Cultural Change*, vol. 15, 1967

Palmer, Ingrid. *Food and the New Agricultural Technology*. Geneva, 1972:1

Palmer, Ingrid. *Science and Agricultural Production*. Geneva, 1972:2

Palmer, Ernest Charles. 'Land Use and Landscape Change along the Dominican-Haitian Border', PhD thesis, University of Florida, Gainesville, 1976

Parry, J.H. *The Establishment of European Hegemony: 1415-1715. Trade and Exploration in the Age of the Renaissance*, Third edition, New York, 1966

Parry, J.H. *The Spanish Seaborne Empire*. New York, 1969

Parry, J.H. & Sherlock, P.M. *A Short History of the West Indies*. Second edition, New York, 1968

Paul, Edouard C. *L'alphabétisation en Haïti*. Port-au-Prince, 1965

Paul, Edouard C. *L'alphabétisation en Haïti, II (Approche fonctionelle)*. Port-au-Prince, 1970

Paul, Emmanuel C. 'Le travail collectif traditionel en Haïti', *Bulletin du Bureau d'Ethnologie*, Serie 3, 1959

Paul, J. Harland & Bellerive, Athèmas. 'A Malaria Reconnaissance of the Republic of Haiti', *Journal of the National Malaria Society*, vol. 6, 1947

P & D. *Planification et Développement. Bulletin du Conseil National de Développement et de Planification (CONADEP)*. Port-au-Prince

Pearse, Andrew. 'Metropolis and Peasant: The Expansion of the Urban-Industrial Complex and the Changing Rural Structure', in Teodor Shanin (ed). *Peasants and Peasant Societies*. Harmondsworth, 1971

Petersen, William. *Population*. Second edition, New York, 1969

Pettigrew, Robert L. *The Story of Fort Liberty and the Dauphin Plantation*. Richmond, 1958

Pierre-Charles, Gérard. *La economía haitiana y su vía de desarollo*.

México. D.F., 1965
Pierre-Charles, Gérard. *L'économie haïtienne et sa voie de développement.* Paris, 1967
Pierre-Charles, Gérard. *Haití: radiografía de una dictadura – Haití bajo el régimen del doctor Duvalier.* México D.F., 1969:1
Pierre-Charles, Gérard. 'El proceso acumulativo del subdesarollo: las sociedades en retroceso', *Boletín uruguayo de sociología,* vol. 8, 1969:2
Pierre-Charles, Gérard. 'Situación económica y perspectivas de desarrollo en Haití', *Pensamiento crítico,* no. 51, 1971
Pierre-Louis, Fritz. 'Les sources d'énergie en Haïti' *Conjonction,* no. 129, 1976
Piore, Michael J. 'Impact of Immigration on the Labor Force', *Monthly Labor Review,* vol. 98, 1975
Plan quinquennal. *Plan quinquennal 1971-1976. Secteur agriculture.* Port-au-Prince, no date
PNUD. Programme des Nations Unies pour le Développement. *Rapport au gouvernement d'Haïti sur bases pour une planification agricole.* Rome, 1971
Prescott, Nicholas M. 'Schistosomiasis and Development', *World Development* vol. 7, no. 1, 1979
Prest, A.R. *Public Finance in Developing Countries.* Second edition, London, 1972
Price-Mars, Jean. 'Classe ou caste? Etude sur "The Haitian People" (Le peuple haïtien) de James G. Leyburn', *Revue de la Société d'Histoire et de Géographie d'Haïti,* vol. 13, 1942
Price-Mars, Jean. *De Saint-Domingue à Haïti. Essai sur la culture, les arts et la littérature.* Vire, 1959
Price-Mars, Jean. *Ainsi parla l'oncle,* Nouvelle édition, Ottawa, 1973
QER. The Economist Intelligence Unit Ltd. *Quarterly Economic Review of Cuba, Dominican Republic, Haiti, Puerto Rico.* London
Rao, C.H. Hanumantha. 'Uncertainty, Entrepreneurship, and Sharecropping in India', *Journal of Political Economy.* vol. 79, 1971
Rawson, Ian G. & Berggren, Gretchen: 'Family Structure, Child Location and Nutritional Disease in Rural Haiti', *Environmental Child Health,* vol. 19, 1973
Rayner, A.C. 'The Use of Multivariate Analysis in Development Theory: A Critique of the Approach Adopted by Adelman and Morris', *Quarterly Journal of Economics,* vol. 84, 1970
République d'Haïti. Secrétairerie d'Etat des Rélations Extérieures. *Rapport fait à S.E. le Président de la République par les membres*

de la *"Mission de bonne volonté" a Washington, D.C. (U.S.A.) décembre 1946-mars 1947.* Port-au-Prince, no date
République d'Haiti. *Données chiffrées pour le XVIIIème Séminaire de la Nutrition de l'Enfant et de la Famille.* Port-au-Prince, 1975
République d'Haiti. *Priorités de la planification et projections quinquennales. Volume I.* Port-au-Prince, no date
Reutlinger. Shlomo. 'Malnutrition: A Poverty or a Food Problem?', *World Development,* vol. 5, 1977
Reutlinger, Shlomo & Selowsky, Marcelo. *Malnutrition and Poverty. Magnitude and Policy Options.* Baltimore, 1976
Reynolds, Lloyd G. 'Agriculture in Development Theory: An Overview', in Lloyd G. Reynolds (ed.) *Agriculture in Development Theory.* New Haven, 1975
Ricardo, David. *Principles of Political Economy and Taxation.* Harmondsworth, 1971
Riou, Roger. *Adieu la Tortue.* Paris, 1976
Robart, Guy. L'écolologie: ses applications à la forêt, en France, en Haiti', *Conjonction,* no. 129, 1976
Rodman, Selden. *Haiti: The Black Republic.* New York, 1961
Rosenberg, Nathan. 'Introduction', in Nathan Rosenberg (ed.). *The Economics of Technological Change.* Harmondsworth, 1971
Rosenstein-Rodan, Paul N. 'Problems of Industrialization of Eastern and South-Eastern Europe', *Economic Journal,* vol. 53, 1943
Rosenstein-Rodan, Paul N. 'Disguised Unemployment and Underemployment in Agriculture', *Monthly Bulletin of Agricultural Economics and Statistics,* vol. 6, 1957
Rostow, W.W. *The Stages of Economic Growth. A non-Communist Manifesto.* Cambridge, 1960
Rotberg, Robert I. with Clague, Christopher, K. *Haiti: The Politics of Squalor.* Boston, 1971
Roumain, Jacques. *Masters of the Dew.* New York, 1947
Roumasset, James A. *Rice and Risk, Decision Making among Low-Income Farmers.* Amsterdam, 1976
Ruttan, Vernon W. 'Technology Transfer, Institutional Transfer, and Induced Technical and Institutional Change in Agricultural Development', in Lloyd G. Reynolds (ed.). *Agriculture in Development Theory.* New Haven 1975.
Rybczynski, T.M. 'Factor Endowment and Relative Commodity Prices', *Economica,* vol. 22, 1955.
Saint Clair, Paul & Dauphin, Franklin. *Résultats de l'enquête sur les exploitations agricoles de l'arrondissement du Cap-Haïtien.* Mimeo,

Département de l'Agriculture, des Ressources Naturelles et du Développement Rural, Port-au-Prince, 1975
St John, Spencer. *Hayti, or the Black Republic.* Second edition. London, 1889
Saint-Louis, René A. *La présociologie haïtienne ou Haïti et sa vocation nationale.* Ottawa, 1970
Saint Surin, Jacques. *Indices démographiques et perspectives de la population d'Haïti de 1950 à 1980.* Port-au-Prince, 1962
Salgado, Antoine. *Problèmes de succession dans l'arrière-pays.* Port-au-Prince, 1967
Sansom, Robert L. *The Economics of Insurgency in the Mekong Delta of Vietnam,* Cambridge, Mass., 1970
Satcunanathan, S. *Non Conventional Energy Resources for the West Indies.* Mimeo, University of the West Indies, St Augustine, 1976
Satcunanathan, S. *Report on Identification and Assessment of Conventional and Non Conventional Energy Resources of Haiti.* Mimeo, University of the West Indies, St Augustine, 1977
Saul, John S. & Woods, Roger. 'African Peasantries', in Teodor Shanin (ed.). *Peasants and Peasant Societies.* Harmondsworth, 1971
Schaedel, Richard P. *An Essay on the Human Resources of Haiti.* Mimeo, US/AID, Port-au-Prince, 1962
Schmidt, Hans. *The United States Occupation of Haiti, 1915-1934.* New Brunswick, 1971
Schoelcher, Victor. *Colonies etrangères et Haïti: Résultats de l'émancipation anglaise.* Vol. II. Paris, 1843
Schramm, Wilbur, Coombs, Philip H., Kahnert, Friederich & Lyle, Jack. *The New Media: Memo to Educational Planners.* Paris, 1967
Schultz, Theodore W. *The Economic Organization of Agriculture.* New York, 1953
Schultz, Theodore W. 'Investment in Human Capital', *American Economic Review,* vol. 51, 1961
Schultz, Theodore W. *The Economic Value of Education.* New York, 1963
Schultz, Theodore W. *Transforming Traditional Agriculture.* New Haven, 1964
Schultz, Theodore W. *Economic Crises in World Agriculture.* Ann Arbor, 1965
Schuman, Howard, Inkeles, Alex & Smith, David H. 'Some Psychological Effects and Noneffects of Literacy in a New Nation', *Economic Development and Cultural Change,* vol. 16, 1968
Schumpeter, Joseph A. *Capitalism, Socialism, and Democracy,* Third

edition, New York, 1950

Scitovsky, Tibor. *Welfare and Competition*. Revised edition, London, 1971

Sebrell, W.H. Jr.; Smith, Sam C.; Severinghaus, Elmer L.; Delva, Hubert; Reid, B.L.; Olcott, H.S.; Bernadotte, Jean; Fougère, William; Barron, George P.; Nicolas, Gabriel; King, Kendall W.; Brinkman, G.L. & French, C.E. 'Appraisal of Nutrition in Haiti', *American Journal of Clinical Nutrition*, vol. 7, 1959

Segal, Aaron, with the assistance of Earnhardt, Kent C. *Politics and Population in the Caribbean*. Rio Piedras, 1969

Selowsky, Marcelo & Taylor, Lance. 'The Economics of Malnourished Children: An Example of Disinvestment in Human Capital', *Economic Development and Cultural Change*. vol, 22, 1973

Sen, Amartya K. *Choice of Techniques. An Aspect of the Theory of Planned Economic Development*. Second edition, Oxford, 1962

Sen, Amartya: *Employment, Technology and Development*. Oxford, 1975

Service Technique. République d'Haïti. Service Technique du Département de l'Agriculture et de l'Enseignement Professionnel. *Bulletin No. 8. Rapport annuel 1925-1926*. Port-au-Prince, no date

Service Technique. République d'Haïti. Service Technique du Département de l'Agriculture et de l'Enseignement Professionnel. *Rapport annuel. Bulletin No. 9 1926-1927*. Port-au-Prince, 1928

Service Technique. République d'Haïti. Service Technique du Département de l'Agriculture et de l'Enseignement Professionnel. *Bulletin No. 13: Rapport annuel 1927-1928*. Port-au-Prince, 1929:1

Service Technique. République d'Haïti. Service Technique du Département de l'Agriculture et de l'Enseugnement Professionnel. *Bulletin No. 17-A: Rapport annuel 1928-29*. Port-au-Prince, 1929:2

Service Technique. République d'Haïti, Service Technique du Département de l'Agriculture et de l'Enseignement Professionnel. *Bulletin No. 24: Rapport annuel 1929-1930*. Port-au-Prince, 1930

Shanin, Teodor. 'The Peasantry as a Political Factor', *Sociological Review*, vol. 14, 1966. Reprinted in Teodor Shanin (ed.): *Peasants and Peasant Societies*, Harmondsworth, 1971

Shanin, Teodor. 'Introduction', in Teodor Shanin (ed.): *Peasants and Peasant Societies*. Harmondsworth, 1971

Shoup, Carl S. 'Production from Consumption', *Public Finance*, vol. 20, 1965

Shoup, Carl S. *Public Finance*. London, 1969

Simon, Julian L. 'The Positive Effect of Population Growth on Agricultural Saving in Irrigation Systems', *Review of Economics and Statistics*, vol. 57, 1975

Simpson, George Eaton. 'Haitian Peasant Economy', *Journal of Negro History*, vol. 25, 1940

Simpson, George Eaton. 'Haiti's Social Structure', *American Sociological Review*, vol. 6, 1941

Singh, Shamsher; de Vries, Jos; Hulley, John C.L. & Yeung, Patrick. *Coffee, Tea and Cocoa: Market Prospects and Development Lending*. Baltimore, 1977

Smith, Adam. *The Wealth of Nations, Volume One*. London, 1970

SNPA & ER. République d'Haïti. Service National de la Production Agricole et de l'Enseignement Rural. *Rapport annuel 1933-1934. Bulletin No. 4*. Port-au-Prince, 1935

SNPA & ER. République d'Haïti. Service National de la Production Agricole et de l'Enseignement Rural. *Bulletin No. 15: Rapport annuel Exercises 1936-37 et 1937-38*. Port-au-Prince, 1939

SNPA & ER. République d'Haïti. Département de l'Agriculture. Service National de la Production Agricole et de l'Enseignement Rural. *Bulletin No. 27: Rapport annuel Exercise 1939-1940*. Port-au-Prince, no date

Södersten, Bo. *A Study of Economic Growth and International Trade*. Stockholm, 1964

Södersten, Bo. *International Economics*. New York, 1970

Solo, Robert. 'The Capacity to Assimilate an Advanced Technology', *American Economic Review*, vol. 56, 1966

Spector, Robert M. 'W. Cameron Forbes and the Hoover Commissions to Haiti', PhD thesis. Boston University, 1961.

Spring Review. *AID Spring Review of Small Farmer Credit: Volume XV: Small Farmer Credit. Informal Credit*. Washington, DC, 1973:1

Spring Review. *AID Spring Review of Small Farmer Credit: Volume XIX. Small Farmer Credit. Analytical Papers*. Washington, DC, 1973:2

Statistical Abstract of Latin America. Kenneth Ruddle & Mukhtar Hamour (eds). *Statistical Abstract of Latin America 1970*. Los Angeles, 1971

Stein, Jerome L. 'Oligopoly in Risk-Bearing Industries with Free Entry', *Economica*, vol. 30, 1963

Stigler, George J. *The Theory of Price*. Revised edition, New York, 1952

Stiglitz, Joseph E. 'Incentives and Risk Sharing in Sharecropping', *Review of Economic Studies*, vol. 41, 1974

Stiglitz, Joseph E. 'The Theory of "Screening", Education, and the Distribution of Income', *American Economic Review*, vol. 65, 1975

Street, John M. *Historical and Economic Geography of the Southwest Peninsula of Haiti*. Mimeo, University of California, Berkeley, 1960

Streeten, Paul. *Obstacles to Development*. Budapest, 1967

Streeten, Paul. *The Frontiers of Development Studies*. New York, 1972

Stuart, M.A. (Republic of Haiti, National Public Health Service). *The Health of Haiti. A Review of the Fiscal Year 1929-1930*. Port-au-Prince, 1930

Stycos, J. Mayone. 'Haitian Attitudes Toward Family Size', *Human Organization*, vol. 23, 1964

Swan, Trevor W. 'Circular Causation', *Economic Record*, vol. 38, 1962

Swerling, Boris C. *International Control of Sugar 1918-1941*. Stanford, 1949

Sylvain-Bouchereau, Madeleine. 'La classe moyenne en Haïti', in Theo R. Crevenna (ed.). *Materiales para el estudio de la clase media en la América Latina*. Washington, DC, 1951.

Tanzi, Vito. 'Export Taxation in Developing Countries: Taxation of Coffee in Haiti', *Social and Economic Studies*, vol. 25, 1976

Thomas, Hugh. *Cuba. The Pursuit of Freedom*. New York, 1971

Thorner, Daniel. 'Peasant Economy as a Category in Economic History' in *Deuxième Conférence Internationale d'Histoire Economique, Aix-en-Provence, 1962, vol. 2*. La Haye, 1962, reprinted in Teodor Shanin (ed.). *Peasants and Peasant Societies*. Harmondsworth, 1971

Timoshenko, Vladimir P. & Swerling, Boris C. *The World's Sugar. Progress and Policy*. Stanford, 1957

Tinnermeier, Ronald L. 'Technology, Profit, and Agricultural Credit', in *AID Spring Review of Small Farmer Credit: Vol. XIX, Small Farmer Credit. Analytical Papers*. Washington, DC, 1973

Titmuss, Richard M. & Abel-Smith, Brian assisted by Lynes, Tony. *Social Policies and Population Growth in Mauritius*. London, 1961

Titus, Henec. 'La mortalité infantile en Haïti' in OEA Institut Interaméricain de l'Enfant. *Recommendations et travaux du Séminaire National de Nutrition d'Haïti. Port-au-Prince. 30 mai au 4 juin 1965*. Montevideo, 1965

Trouillot, Henock. 'La république de Pétion et le peuple haïtien', *Revue de la Société Haïtienne d'Histoire, de Géographie et de Géologie*, vol. 31, 1960

Trouillot, Henock. *Economie et finances de Saint-Domingue*. Port-au-Prince, 1965

Tun Wai, U. 'Interest Rates Outside the Organized Money Markets of Underdeveloped Countries', *IMF Staff Papers*, vol. 6, 1957

Turnham, David assisted by Jaeger, Ingelies. *The Employment Problem in Less Developed Countries. A Review of Evidence*. Paris, 1971

Turnier, Alain. *Les Etats-Unis et le marché haïtien*. Montréal, 1955

Uchendu, Victor C. 'Some Principles of Haggling in Peasant Markets', *Economic Development and Cultural Change*, vol. 16, 1967

UNCTAD. United Nations Conference on Trade and Development. *Handbook of International Trade and Development Statistics*. New York, 1976

Underwood, Frances W. 'The Marketing System in Peasant Haiti', in Sidney W. Mintz (ed.). *Papers in Caribbean Anthropology*. New Haven, 1960

Underwood, Frances W. 'Land and Its Manipulation among the Haitian Peasants', in Ward H. Goodenough (ed.). *Explorations in Cultural Anthropology. Essays in Honor of George Peter Murdoch*. New York 1964

UNESCO. *L'expérience témoin d'Haïti. Première phase 1947-1949*. Paris, 1951

UNESCO. *Haïti: Analyse et perspectives pour une nouvelle éducation*. Paris, no date

Union Nationaliste. *Dépossessions*. Port-au-Prince, 1930

United Nations. *Mission to Haiti. Report of the United Nations Mission of Technical Assistance to the Republic of Haiti*. Lake Success, 1949

United Nations. *Economic Survey of Latin America 1973*. New York, 1975

United Nations. *Statistical Yearbook 1975*. New York, 1976

US/AID Département d'Etat, Agence pour le Développement International. *Haïti – Amélioration des petites plantations*. Mimeo, US/AID, Washington, DC, 1974

US Department of Health. Office of International Health, Division of Planning and Evaluation. *Syncrisis: The Dynamics of Health. An Analytic Series on the Interactions of Health and Socioeconomic Development VI: Haiti*. Washington, DC, 1972

US, Department of State. *Third Annual Report of the American High Commissioner at Port-au-Prince, Haiti: 1924*. Washington, DC, 1925

Vaizey, John. *The Economics of Education*. London 1962

Valdman, Albert. 'The Language Situation in Haiti', in *Research and Resources of Haiti. Papers of the Conference on Research and Resources of Haiti*. New York, 1969

Vallès, Marie-Thérèse. *Les idéologies coopératives et leur applicabilité en Haïti.* Paris, 1967

Velie, Lester. 'The Case of Our Vanishing Dollars in Haiti', *Reader's Digest*, vol. 80, 1962

Victor, René. *Recensement et démographie.* Port-au-Prince, 1944

Viélot, Klébert. 'L'enseignement primaire en Haïti', in *Research and Resources of Haiti. Papers of the Conference on Research and Resources of Haiti.* New York, 1969

Vieux, Serge. 'Les problèmes de la fonction publique haïtienne et les perspectives de recherche dans ce domaine', in *Research and Resources of Haiti. Papers of the Conference on Research and Resources of Haiti.* New York, 1969

Vincent, Sténio. *Efforts et résultats.* Port-au-Prince. 1938

Webster, Cyril C. & Wilson, Peter N. *Agriculture in the Tropics.* London, 1966

Weeks, John. 'Uncertainty, Risk and Wealth and Income Distribution in Peasant Agriculture', *Journal of Development Studies*, vol. 7, 1970

Weisbrod, Burton A., Andreano, Ralph L., Baldwin, Robert E., Epstein, Erwin H. & Kelley, Allen C. with the assistance of Helminiak, Thomas W. *Disease and Economic Development. The Impact of Parasitic Diseases in St Lucia.* Madison, 1973

Weisbrod, Burton A. & Helminiak, Thomas W. 'Parasitic Diseases and Agricultural Labor Productivity', *Economic Development and Cultural Change*, vol. 25, 1977

Welch, Finis. 'Education in Production', *Journal of Political Economy* vol. 78, 1970

Werleigh, Georges-Emmanuel & Duplan, Verdy. *Système de commercialisation interne des produits agricoles au Cap-Haïtien, Haïti.* Mimeo, Institut Interaméricain des Sciences Agricoles (IICA), Port-au-Prince, 1975

Wharton, Clifton, R. Jr. 'Marketing, Merchandising, and Moneylending: A Note on Middleman Monopsony in Malaya', *Malayan Economic Review*, vol. 7, 1962

Wharton, Clifton R., Jr. 'Education and Agricultural Growth: The Role of Education in Early-Stage Agriculture', in C. Arnold Anderson & Mary Jean Bowman (eds). *Education and Economic Development.* Chicago, 1965

Wicksell, Knut. *Lectures on Political Economy. Volume II. Money.* London, 1935

Wingfield, Roland. 'Haiti, A Case Study of an Underdeveloped Area',

PhD thesis, Louisiana State University, Baton Rouge, 1966
Wingfield, Roland & Parenton, Vernon J. 'Class Structure and Class Conflict in Haitian Society', *Social Forces*, vol. 62, 1965
Wirkus, Faustin & Dudley, Taney. *The White King of La Conave*. New York, 1931
Wolf, Eric R. 'Types of Latin American Peasantry: A Preliminary Discussion', *American Anthropologist*, vol. 57, 1955. Reprinted in George Dalton (ed.). *Tribal and Peasant Economies*. Garden City, 1967.
Wolf, Eric R. *Peasants*. Englewood Cliffs, NJ, 1966
Wood, Harold A. 'Physical Influences on Peasant Agriculture in Northern Haiti', *Canadian Geographer*, vol. 5, 1961
Wood, Harold A. *Northern Haiti: Land Use, and Settlement*, Toronto, 1963
Wood, Marie V. 'Agricultural Development and Rural Life in Haiti, 1934 to 1953', PhD thesis. The American University, Washington, DC, 1955
Woodring, Wendell P., Brown, John S. & Burbank, Wilbur S. *Geology of the Republic of Haiti*. Port-au-Prince. 1924
Yotopoulos, Pan A. & Nugent, Jeffrey B. *Economics of Development: Empirical Investigations*. New York, 1976
Zuvekas, Clarence, Jr. *An Annotated Bibliography of Agricultural Development in Haiti*. Mimeo, US/AID, Washington, DC, 1977
Zuvekas, Clarence, Jr. *Land Tenure, Income, and Employment in Rural Haiti: A Survey*. Mimeo, US/AID, Washington, DC, 1978

INDEX

actual expense loans 508-9
Adelman, Irma 316
administration, Haitian: corruption in 23; inefficiency of 22, 24, 25, 197, 615; in nineteenth century 22; wages and salaries of 24
adult: alphabetization 479; education 460, 465, 472, 473, 480, 481, 568; literacy 479, 480, 485, 486n; malnutrition 25, 417-21
affranchis 320, 322, 324, 355; discrimination against 321
AFL-CIO labor federation 346
Agency for International Development, US (AID) 181, 309
agrarian structure 17, 32, 37, 48-55, 81, 503
agricultural colonies 303
agricultural cycle 86-7
agricultural extension service 536, 614-16
agricultural involution 250-4
agriculture: capital in 81, 623; exports, share of 11; foreign assistance programs in 572; GDP, share of 11, 641; importance of 97; labor force in 11; lack of assistance for 299; marketing 37; per capita incomes in 11, 222; production methods 76-80; public investment in 310, 311; stagnation in 18; tax income from 263; techniques 17; technological regression in 28, 80; unemployment in 86; yields in 80
agronomists 614-15
Ahlers, Theodore H. 633
Akerlof, George A. 533n
Alexis, Nord 332
alphabetization 472, 477, 479
Alvarez, Maria D. 33, 125, 149, 153, 154, 156, 168
An American Dilemma 91, 92, 93
anemia 413, 415, 417, 420
Anglade, Georges 623
anti-erosion legislation 228-30
anti-peasant bias 29, 639, 640-2, 646
arable land 58-61
arithmetical literacy 460

army 271, 323, 324, 326, 375-83; expenditure on 24, 271, 366, 377, 379, 400; neutralization 344
arrondissements 629, defined 629n
Arrow, Kenneth J. 454, 456, 601n
Artibonite valley 374; scheme 306-7, 308, 309, 310, 342-3, 604
artisanry 87
Asian Drama 92, 93, 434
assets, sale and repurchase of 515-18
Association des Exportateurs de Café (ASDEC) 138, 139
Auguste, Tancrède 333
autonomous agencies 381-3
avocados 47, 126, 209, 419, 420

bagasse 202
Bahamas, Haitian emigration to 627-8
Balch, Emily Green 266
Balogh, Thomas 453, 454
bananas 40, 43-4, 218, 569, 570; disease 67; exports 18, 47, 307, 339, 341, 566; prices 216; production 206
Banque Commerciale 381
Banque Nationale de la République d'Haiti 331-2, 370, 372n, 381, 382, 522
Barbot, Clément 345, 381
Bas-Boën project 586, 591
Batista, Fulgencio 338, 348
beans 40, 47, 78, 125, 126, 154, 210, 236; marketing 33, 157; prices 219; production 206; yields 80
beef 17, 40, 44-5
Beghin, Ivan 109, 110, 414, 416, 418, 419
Bellegarde, Dantès 463
Benoit, Pierre V. 378n
Berg, Alan 433
Bertrand, Wilfrid 633
'big push' 93
biological waste 201, 202
birth rates 109, 433, 434
blindness 413
blood, export of 349
bocors 353, 430, 608

685

686 Index

Boeke, J.H. 31
Boisrond-Canal, President 367
Bolívar, Simón 271
boll-weevil, Mexican 43, 67, 218, 303
Bon Dieu 352
bonds, series A and C 373
Borno, Louis 338
Bosch, Juan 100
Boserup, Ester 574-6, 592
Bottomley, Anthony 523n
Bowles, Samuel 454, 456
Boyer, Jean-Pierre 366, 562;
    agricultural policy 298, 299; army
    under 378; *Code Rural* 375;
    corruption under 328; educational
    policy 461, 462 and n, 495; fall of
    265, 323, 326, 329, 357, 386, 398;
    GNP decline under 268; land
    reform 264, 297, 327; money
    issue by 368
'brain drain' from rural areas 492
Brand, William B. 191n2, 530, 629,
    630
Brandt, Osvald G. 347
Brazil wood, exports 196
breast feeding 108, 413, 414n, 416,
    420
Brevet Elémentaire 490
Brisson, Gérald 32, 52n1
Brown, John S. 198
Brown, Jonathan 375, 376
Brussels Sugar Convention 281
budget (1885-6), agriculture's share of
    299
bulking, and bulk breaking, of
    agricultural goods 149, 154-5
Bureau de Crédit Agricole (BCA)
    539-40
Bureau de Crédit Rural Supervisé
    (BRCS) 539
Bureau of Internal Revenue 395
Burns, L. Vinton 199, 211

cabbage 154
cacos 33, 334, 336, 338, 356, 379,
    383, 400, 567; defined 271, 331;
    pacified 463
cadastral survey 48
café: décortique 133n; *pilé* 133n;
    rat 62n; *triage* 564
Caisses Populaires 541
Calixte, Col. Démosthènes Pétrus 338
calories: average intake 109, 110, 118,
    418-19, 420; decline in consump-
    tion 109, 118; deficit 439, 599;
    gainful consumption 441; physical
    activity, effect on 441
Cambronne, Luckner 347, 348, 349
Canada, Haitian emigration to 628
capital: accumulation 188; and
    marketing 32; and technical
    progress 69; choice 22, 256;
    formation 82, 503, 504, 552,
    623; input, in agriculture 81;
    problems, of Haiti 271; require-
    ments for crops 259; scarcity, as
    reason for land reform 270
Caribbean Mills wheat plant 439
Carnoy, Martin 454, 493
carreau, defined 49n2
carrots 154
Carter, Jimmy 349
Carter, Vernon Gill 639-40
Casimir, Jean 52n1
caste system, in Haiti 494
Castor, Suzy 626
Castro, Fidel 627
Catholics 318, 326, 353, 354;
    schools 462, 470, 471 and n,
    476, 485
censuses 189, 190, 205; quality of
    189, 191, 1753: 190;
    1918-19: 190-1; 1950: 32, 48,
    49, 50, 52, 55, 71, 75, 191, 192,
    205, 472, 473, 480, 496, 630;
    1960 (planned): 191; 1971: 50,
    51 and n, 52, 60, 70, 75, 189,
    192, 205, 478, 480, 596, 630
Central Agricultural School, Damien
    568, 569
centralization of administration
    388, 400
*Centre Haitien d'Investigation en
    Sciences Sociales* (CHISS) 487
*Centres d'Education Integrée pour
    le Développement Rural*
    (CEIDER) 480
Certificat d'Etudes Primaires 490
Chadbourne plan 282
Challenge of World Poverty 358
charcoal 20, 21, 87, 188, 194, 198,
    200, 204
Charleston, Wesner 33
chefs de section 350-1, 545, 598
child malnutrition 443, 446;
    physiological consequences 411-17
child mortality 427
Choice of Techniques 293
Christophe, Henry 73, 113, 267, 271,
    272, 323, 326, 327, 353, 561,

Index

562; agricultural policy 63n1, 261-3, 270, 560; and education 324, 461; and technological change 558-9; army under 375; death 263, 269, 275, 328, 386; land reform 263n; tax policy 392
circular and cumulative causation 21, 37, 100, 188
Clague, Christopher K. 17, 33, 102, 191, 366n, 376, 466, 543-4, 571, 584, 596; and economic development 643
clairin 114, 198
class system, Haitian 31, 319-50, 454-5
clearing of fields 76-7
climate of Haiti 38
coal 201-2
cocoa 40, 42-3, 78, 113, 229, 256; disease 67; exports 17, 259; labor requirements 236; prices 216; production 206; yields 80
coconuts, pests and diseases 68
Code du Café 305, 571
Code Napoléon 278, 287
Code Noir 321, 324
Code Rural: 1826: 228, 264, 275, 298, 350; 1864: 228, 229, 336, 350, 352n; 1957: 350, 351n; *François Duvalier* 229
coffee 39, 62, 65, 78, 113, 236, 603; disease 67; exports 17, 32, 40-1, 44, 81, 134-45, 209, 229, 259, 262, 303, 304-5, 569, 571; marketing 19, 133-45; plantations 559-60; prices 19, 143-8, 332, 564, 566; production 86, 133n, 206, 570-1; quota 305; study on 33; taxation 140, 142, 216, 244n, 268; technical efficiency 145; washing 571, 582n3; yields 80
collateral 511, 523; land as 517-18
collusion between buyers and sellers 127, 129, 138
colons 321
commodity markets, imperfections in 128
Commonwealth Sugar Agreement 283
communes 629; defined 629n
communications 357, 581, 617
competition in markets 533
complementaries 69, 613
conscientização 493
Conseil National de Développement *et de Planification* (CONADEP) 66, 105, 200n1, 310, 311, 312
constitution of Haiti: 1918: 266, 271; 1935: 339, 1964: 389
consumption: credit 28; loans 28, 509, 515, 516, 547, 551
co-operative credit unions 541
co-operatives 29, 307; lack of 595-8, 617
corn 17, 40, 45, 77, 78, 79, 125, 126, 210, 236; pests and diseases 67; prices 219; production 206; storage 68-9; yields 80
Correa, Héctor 412, 414
corruption in administration 25, 298, 308, 310, 327-50, 357, 358, 365, 375
corvée 73, 264, 272, 273, 336, 398, 561
cotton 32, 40, 62, 78, 79, 126, 236, 218, 256, 262, 569; disease 67; exports 17, 43, 259, 262, 265, 366, 567 and n1; harvesting 87; prices 216, 299, 567, 603; production 206; Stoneville 7-A variety 43, 218; yields 80
coumbites 77, 78, 102, 110-18, 358, 580, 595, 597, 598; as social activities 116-18; changing character of 19; origin 111n, 112-13; proper 114, 115, 116, 117
Courlander, Harold 106, 573, 598n
credit, and agricultural development 585
Crédit Général 367
Creole language 317, 484-8; alphabetization 472, 477; in adult education 473; in primary education 487; orthography 472, 474, 486
crops: labor requirements 236; rotation 78-9; sharing 275
cryptostegia 305
Cuba: loan to Haiti 348; migration to 373, 624-5, 626, 627; sugar production 258, 273, 274, 281, 282, 283
Cumberland, W.W. 371, 474n1
cumulative processes 18-19, 20, 25, 91-120, 221, 255, 636, 644
Cyert, Richard M. 606, 608

Dahomey 112-13

Dale, Tom 639-40
Dartiguenave, Sudre D. 190, 338
David, Paul A. 591
death rates 433, 434
debt, foreign 24, 271-2; consolidation into American hands 375; creation of 366-70; liquidation 372-5, 399
debt service 24, 366-73, 377
deforestation 20, 195, 200, 228-30
de moitié system 50 and n
demonstration farms 569, 571, 601
Département de l'Agriculture, des Ressources Naturelles et du Développement Rural (DARNDR) 615
départements 629; defined 629n
depots 148-9, 161
Depression 24, 303
Descourtilz, Michel-Etienne 572
Dessalines, Jean-Jacques 73, 113, 267, 272, 323, 324, 353, 561; agricultural policy 261, 270, 560; and education 324, 461; army under 375; death 261, 325; land reform 268; tax policy 392
development plans: five-year 307-8, 311-12; one-year 311; two-year 309, 310
de Young, Maurice 32, 54, 123
diarrhea 426-7
Direction Générale de l'Education des Adultes 472
disease 25-6; and population growth 433-4; as obstacle to technological change 29, 606; economic effects 431-48; in Hispaniola 258; situation, 1915-75 421-30
dissaving by peasants 508n
domination through education 503
Domingue, Michel 330; spy system 378
Dominican Republic 45, 60n, 76, 99, 100, 198, 201, 271, 303-4, 376, 377, 378; and technological change 572; government expenditure in 406; migration to 346, 373, 624-5, 626, 627; sugar industry in 282, 346
Donner, Wolf 211
Dorfman, Robert 187
Dorville, René 125, 126, 154, 585
double debt 366-8; liquidated 368
draft animals 581, 591-2, 593
droughts 207, 311, 352, 446, 504, 599 601
Duplan, Verdy 33
duration ratio 434-44
Duvalier family 343-50; fortune 345-6, 349
Duvalier, François 318, 338, 343-50, 351, 354, 387; agricultural policy 307-10, 311; and education 474-9; army and police under 344, 380-1, 382, 400; corruption under 345, 356, 389; death 312, 383, 388
Duvalier, Jean-Claude 348-50; agricultural policy 312
Duvalierville 347
dynamic (technological and economic) efficiency 187-8

Economic Commission for Latin America (ECLA) 385
economic development, stage models 557
economic efficiency 128, 187; defined 127
economies of scale in agriculture 279, 280
Edgeworth-Bowley box diagram 221-3
education 23, 26, 227, 317, 322, 324, 326, 409, 453-97; and class structure 454; and direct knowledge 458; and economizing behavior 456; and extension process 613; and farm management 456-8; and political structure 335; and risk aversion 610; creation of attitudes through 492-3; discrimination in 490-7, 623, 641; domination through 482-95; filter approach to 454; in late nineteenth century 462-3; lack of, as obstacle to technological change 29, 606-16, 618; spillover effects 609; *see also* rural education
Education as Cultural Imperialism 493
efficiency ratio 435-44
elementary process of production 577-9
elite 15, 16; and education 317, 466; and peasants 23, 73-4, 297, 317-54, 355, 636
emigration from Haiti 627-8, 644-5
employment 75-6; agricultural 97; ratio 435-44

Index

energy: need for 189; sources 188; 200-4
Enos, John L. 624
Enquête socio-économique 192
Erasmus, Charles John 31, 590, 594, 595, 601, 608, 609
erosion 20-2, 29, 37, 55, 81, 96, 187-254, 255, 312, 409, 639-40, 645; and composition of output 204-23; and development 639; control 20, 21, 223-30, 255, 635; summary of process 194-5
escouades 111, 112, 114, 115, 116, 117, 596
essential oils 11, 17, 40, 44, 204n
estates 32, 256, 266-7, 298; break-up 365
Estimé, Dumarsais 318, 340, 343, 473, 571; agricultural policy 306-7; and education 472-3; and *Garde* 340, 380; corruption under 339, 341; debt liquidation by 373
Estimé, Jean-Robert 33
Euler's theorem 238
examinations, as educational filter 490, 491, 497, 642
excise duties 396
exploitation of peasants 17, 20, 37, 49, 81, 121; by moneylenders 529-34; defined 128-31
export and subsistence goods, relative price 214-23, 231, 242-9, 255
Export-Import Bank 305, 306, 309, 342
export markets, state of, as cause of land reform 274-5
export products 17, 21, 37, 40-5, 47, 81, 188, 194, 205, 265, 302-3, 567; marketing 123, 133-45, 187, 207, 208; output 209; prices 218; production 206
export taxes 25, 142, 392, 396, 503, 504, 646
extension: agents 546-7, 569, 596, 609, 612; costs 28, 549-50; education 227, 458, 613, 614; personnel, untrained 551; service, lack of 227
external diseconomies 224

factor combination, of peasant agriculture 54-5
fallow and crop rotation 78-80, 592
family: farms 14, 37; labor 87; planning 193; size 530

famine 446-7
Fanfan, Guy 33
farming, large-scale, obstacles to 277-88
farm management 456-8
farm schools (*fermes-écoles*) 464-5, 471
farm size 22, 50-2, 256-89, 591; as obstacle to technological change 590-4
Fatton, Bernard 33
fermage 268, 273, 323-4, 334, 356, 398, 561, 565; abolition 263, 365; defined 261, 323
fertilizers 57, 63-4, 280, 559, 584, 585, 599
Fignolé, Daniel 341
figue-banane 43, 44
firewood 20, 188, 195, 200, 230
Firth, Raymond 13
Fisher, Irving 226-7, 513, 587; theory of interest 513-35
fishing 87
Fleischmann, Ulrich 33
floods 311, 352, 504, 599
flow factors in agricultural production 577-9
Folsom, Robert S. 31
food: consumption credit 441; consumption redistribution within families 442-3; outlays 20, 106, 107, 418, 505; production 99, taboos 416
Food and Agriculture/Organization (FAO) 198, 312, 417; Freedom from Hunger Campaign 417
Forbes commission 335, 372
forced labor see *corvée* and *fermage*
forest products, export 20, 194, 195-8
forest reserves 198-9
formal credit 504; failure of 541-51
formal credit institutions 551; interest rate in 511-12
formal credit markets, defined 535n
formal credit sources 535-51
Fougère, William 109, 110, 414, 418, 419
France 24, 272, 303, 366; 1825 treaty with Haiti 323, 375, 379
Franklin, James 559
freedom of entry in marketing 20, 156-8
Freeman, George F. 466
Freire, Paulo 493
French: as educational filter 484-8

49 491, 497; mastery of, by elite 484
French Revolution 190
fruits 17, 39, 40, 47-8, 104, 126, 229, 416
Fuchs, Victor R. 410
fuel 200, 204
fund factors in agricultural production 577-9
funerals 117
fustic, exports 196

Garde d'Haïti 336, 338, 339, 340-1, 379, 380, 383, 400
gastro-intestinal diseases 25, 426-7, 431, 432
Gates, William B. Jr 32, 136, 137, 139, 570
gathering, of plants etc 87
Geertz, Clifford 250-4
Geffrard, Fabre 377, 566-7; agricultural policy 299; and education 462; army under 378; corruption under 329-30, 368; fall of 271; land reform 265
Gendarmerie d'Haïti 336, 379, 422, 423; expenditure on 379-80
General Receiver 337
gens de couleur 320
geology 16, 201, 569
Georgescu-Roegen, Nicholas 577, 578n, 581
geothermal energy 201, 203
gérants 275
Giles, Antonio 86, 88, 538n
Gillette, Cynthia 544
Gintis, Herbert 454, 456
Girault, Christian 33
Girod-Chantrans, Justine 561
glacis 133n, 141, 237
Gómez criteria 106-7, 108, 109, 412n, 415
government: and agriculture 23, 29, 53, 230, 255, 297-364; and peasants 636; as obstacle to technological change 598, 618, 643, 644; as source of wealth 298, 327-50; credit sources 280; economic action 81; expenditure 25, 365-86; land 52, 265; revenue structure 24-5, 386-98; tax policy 221; views of, in nineteenth century 324
grandes écoles nationales 461
grands blancs 320, 322

grappillage 121, 285; defined 121n
gravitational energy 201, 202, 203
grazing land 79
Green Revolution 582; capital-using bias 584
Griffin, Keith 582, 584, 624
gros habitants 507, 530
gross domestic product (GDP): agriculture's contribution to 11, 97; per capita 18, 102, 103
gross national product (GNP), fall in nineteenth century 265, 398
Guadeloupe, Haitian emigration to 628
Guerra y Sánchez, Ramiro 280, 282
Guerrier, Philippe 265
guildives 198, 216

habitations 39, 47
haggling 20, 163-6
Haitian Agricultural Corporation (HACOR) 42
Haitian American Corporation (Plantation Dauphin) 42, 52, 266, 267, 280, 284-5, 286, 287, 604n
Haitian American Sugar Company (HASCO) 41, 52, 185, 202, 203, 216, 266, 267, 280, 282, 283, 284, 287
Haitian-American treaty (1915) 371
haitianization 100; of educational system 467-73
Haitian land, foreign ownership prohibited 266, 271
Haitian Meat and Provision Company (HAMPCO) 44-5
Haiti, divided by civil war 325
Haiti, The Politics of Squalor 250
Hartwell, R.M. 447
harvesting 78, 81, 86-7
healers 430, 431
health 409-51; defined 410-11; facilities 25
herbalists (*doktè-fèy*) 25, 429, 431, 641
heroin smuggling 349
Herskovits, Melville J. 16n, 31, 55, 111, 112, 569-70
hired labor 87
Hispaniola, Spanish rule in 256, 258-9
Hitler, Adolf 321
Holly, Marc Aurèle 31, 68, 471

Index

Honorat, Jean-Jacques 33
hookworm 402, 423
Hoover, Herbert 335, 372, 465
houmfors 354
houngans 352, 353, 354, 358, 431, 597, 641; as popular doctors 430
Huberman, Leo 273
Hubert, Giles A. 31, 286
Huizer, Gerrit 604n
human capital: and income 503; and technological change 618; approach to education 453, 455-61, 481, 495-6, 503, 642
humanities, in school system 26
Hunter, Guy 596
hurricanes 207, 343, 599; Cleo 207, 311; Flora 207, 311, 425; Hazel 207, 308, 343; Inez 207, 311
Huxley, Francis 318n1
hydroelectric energy 203
Hyppolite, Florvil 299, 332

ill health: among schoolchildren 483; as obstacle to technological change 618
illiteracy 29, 472, 478, 480, 609; in rural areas 463, 596; rate 26, 496, 596
imperialism 100
imported products, consumed by peasants 125
import taxes 25, 392-8
income: and food outlay 505; falling 18, 27, 28, 91-120, 213, 222, 453, 482, 503; Fisher's definition 513n; size 514-15; tax 25; uncertainty, as determinant of time preferences 517-19
indemnity, of 1825 24, 272, 366, 375
Indians, of Hispaniola 189
indigo 256; exports 259, 262
indivisibilities 28, 69; and credit 587-90; and plows 29, 590-4, 617; as obstacle to technological change 29, 585-98, 617
infant mortality 427
inflation 523
informal credit 504, 511-25, 545, 552; market, defined 511n
information, lack of, as obstacle to technological change 29, 606-16
infrastructure skills 458-60
inheritance laws 22; as cause of land subdivision 278, 287

inherited debts 509
innovation: and education 227; defined 558; erosion control as 227; in agriculture 574-80, 616; resistance to 28-9, 557-622
insecticides 67-8, 69, 280
'inside' lenders 532, 533, 534
Institut de Développement Agricole et Industriel (IDAI) 43, 309, 537, 548, 615; supervised credit scheme 537-9, 543-4, 549-50; underutilized lending capacity 539, 547
Institut Haïtien de Crédit Agricole et Industriel (IHCAI) 307, 309, 536-7, 547, 548
Institut Haïtien de Promotion du Café et des Denrées d'Exportation (IHPCADE) 64, 218, 540, 615
Institut Haïtien de Statistique 71, 192, 483
insurance, lack of, in rural areas 599-600
intensity ratio 435-44
Inter-American Committee on the Alliance for Progress (CIAP) 311, 382, 474-5
Inter-American Development Bank (IDB) 312, 385, 479, 481, 537, 612
Inter-American Institute of Agricultural Sciences (IICA) 33, 147n; survey of market places 150, 184, 185
interest rates: as obstacle to technological change 587-90, 617; in rural credit markets 27, 122, 442, 504, 511-53; paid by banks 522-3
intermediaries 19, 20, 637; as lenders 503; in marketing subsistence crops 145-9
International Coffee Agreement 215
International Commission of Jurists 345, 347
International Co-operation Administration, US (ICA) 309
interplanting 77
intestinal parasites 25, 421, 422, 426, 431, 465
intra-uterine devices 193
investment: and yaws eradication; role in Fisherian theory of interest 520-3
involution, agricultural 21, 189, 250-4
iron deficiency 25, 415

irrigation 41, 64-7, 270, 299, 309, 584, 585, 588, 590n2
Jaeger, Ingelies 439, 440
Java 22, 250-4
Jean, Rodrigue 52n1
Jefferson, Thomas 274
Jelliffe, Derrick B. and E.F. Patricia 106, 107, 108, 415, 416
jet airport 346
J.G. White Engineering Corporation 373
Johnson, D. Gale 579n
Jones, Graham 611
JWK International Corporation 33

kêkay 125
Kennedy, John F. 309
kerosene 201
Kindleberger, Charles P. 566
King, Kendall W. 109, 110, 414, 418, 419, 426, 446
kleptocracies 357, 400, 636
koutché 169
kwashiorkor 109, 415 and n2

labor: abundance, as obstacle to large farms 279-80; efficiency ratio 434-44; productivity, decline during nineteenth century 562-3; scarcity during nineteenth century 272-3; supply, 'unlimited' 593n
laboresque capital 279, 294, 295; defined 293
labor force: as production factor 70-6, 81; growth 37, 255
La Gra, Jerry 33
la grande culture 261, 269, 277, 288, 325
Laguerre, Michel S. 34, 114
lakou 600; defined 600n2
lambi 111, 112
land: and erosion 21; classification 57; ownership by peasants 13, 17, 23, 37, 48, 516; productivity and prices during nineteenth century 562-3; purchase/rent 504, 507; savings in 505, 507; scarcity 17, 55, 188, 592, 616, 624, 635; tenure 34, 37
landesque capital 279, 280, 287, 294, 295, 639; defined 293
landholdings: large 52; scattered 52-4, 81
landless workers 37, 645, 646
land/man ratios 75-6
landowners 17, 38, 81, 503, 646

land redistribution 22, 38, 198, 264, 356, 358, 365
land reform 17, 22, 23, 28, 53, 256, 398, 576n1; as political instrument 269-70; causes of 268-88
land titles 29; as obstacle to technological change 603-5
language 23; French v. Creole 26
la petite culture 266
large-scale agriculture, disappearance of 22
latifundia 14, 37, 81, 259, 646; polarization with minifundia 532
Lebeau, Francis 541n
Leconte, Cincinnatus 333
Le Démarrage 310
leisure, preference for 73-4, 592-3
'lemons', in rural credit markets 533, 548; defined 533n
Lescot, Elie 354, 358, 380; agricultural policy 304-6, 571; and education 469; corruption under 339, 341; debt policy 373
Lewis, W. Arthur 279n, 504, 593n
Leyburn, James G. 16, 17, 31, 33, 71, 74, 112, 180, 330, 376
lignite 202
lignum vitae, exports 195
linguistic dualism 484, 485
Lipton, Michael 640-1
literacy 324, 480; and extension education 458-60, 607
livestock, as savings 505, 508
loans, foreign: Export Import Bank 373; Inter-American Development Bank 479; 1825: 272, 366, 375, 1874: 24, 367; 1875: 24, 272, 367, 368; 1896: 24, 272, 368; 1910: 24, 272, 368; 1922-5: 371, 373; series A, B and C 370, 371
loans, internal 368-9, 399
loas 352, 353, 506, 608
Locher, Uli 33, 161
Logan, Rayford W. 462n
logwood, exports 195, 196, 197, 332, 566
luxury goods, taxes on 395
Lycée Pétion 461

Mackenzie, Charles 461
'Madame Sarahs' 68
Madam Sara 71, 147-74, 181-2, 184, 185, 582, 637n; as lenders 511-13, 523, 524, 526, 528-9, 530, 600;

Index

capital requirements 156-7; defined 147; origin of term 147n
Magloire, Paul 341-3, 389; agricultural policy 307-8; and education 473-4; and *Garde* 341, 380; corruption under 345, 356; fall of 343
mahogany, exports 195, 196, 197, 566
malanga 46, 126, 210, 236
malaria 25, 421, 422, 423, 427, 427, 431, 465; campaign against 425-6, 432
malnutrition 412, 413, 414, 415, 417-21, 533, 641; among preschool children 19, 25, 108, 109, 413-21; among women 413-14, 420; and emigration 645; and population growth 434; and ratios 439-44; and schooling 412-13, 483, 491; as obstacle to technological change 29, 606; degrees (first, second and third) 412 and n, 414; economic effects 431-48
Malthusian situations 96, 100, 189, 221, 255, 355, 446, 635, 636, 639, 645
mambos 352, 353
mandats 331
mangoes 47 and n, 126, 209, 419, 420
Manigat, Leslie 342
manioc 17, 40, 46, 69, 79, 126, 210, 236; prices 219; production 206; yields 80
manufactures, tax on 244n
manure 63
marasmus 109, 415 and n2
Marbial valley 49, 50, 52n2, 63, 68, 70, 117, 148, 152, 509-10, 517n, 603; rural education project 306, 473-4
March, James G. 606, 608
marginal productivity of nutrition (MPN) 440-2
market: information 20, 127, 164; places 32, 33, 149-51; taxes 146, 166n2; women 19
market conditions, as obstacle to large farms 280
market economy, importance in Haiti 123-4
marketing: of agricultural goods 121-86, 188; efficiency 171-4, 187; inefficiency 166; process 88, 503
maroons 623

marronage 261, 320-1, 323; defined 320
Martinique, Haitian migration to 628
mass communication in education 459
McConnell-Laubach orthography 472, 474, 486
measures and weights 162-3
meat, as peasant product 126
mechanization of agriculture 273, 279, 287
medical facilities 424, 427-31
Mellor, John W. 557
men, trading by 146
methane gas 202
Métraux, Alfred 31, 47, 49, 50, 70, 77, 78, 117, 152, 153, 506, 517n, 603
middle class 318, 319, 340, 344, 399
middlemen's profit margins: in coffee industry 140-5; in marketing subsistence crops 152-6
migration 29, 192, 623-35, 644-5
military: expenditure in twentieth century 375-83; rule in rural areas 23, 299, 545, 561, 598, 637
millet 45n, 77, 125; yields 80
Millspaugh, Arthur 191, 357, 464
mineral deficiencies 411
minifundia 14, 22, 50, 54, 81, 256, 398
Mintz, Sidney W. 32, 33, 53-4, 125n, 146, 153, 162, 166, 385, 508, 528, 597n
Mirebalais valley 55, 569-70
mixed cultivation 77-8
money 19, 39; lending 523, 552, 637, 645; supply 368
monopolistic middlemen 121-79
monopoly 126, 637; as determinant of interest rates 529-34; in peasant markets 19, 27
monopoly power: of lenders 532; sources of 131-3
monopoly power: of lenders 532; sources of 131-3
monopoly profits 531-4; and interest rates 534; defined 530; due to lack of information 532-3
monopoly rent, and education 454
monopsonistic middlemen 121-79
monopsony 126, 637; in peasant markets 19

monopsony power: of lenders 532; sources of 131-3
Moore, O. Ernest 33, 305, 485n1, 521, 522
Moral, Paul 16-17, 32, 49, 50-1, 58n, 87, 136, 156, 162, 517, 603, 626; and agricultural techniques 572-3; and deforestation 196, 199; and Marbial project 474; and migration 631
Moreau de Saint Méry, Médéric Louis-Elie Elie 189, 195, 320, 321
mornes 188
Morris, Cynthia Taft 316
mothercraft centers 448
Moton commission 465-6
Mouvement de Rénovation Nationale (MRN) 347
Mouvement des Ouvriers et Paysans (MOP) 341
mulattoes 320-7
multicropping 574, 576, 580, 592, 593
Murray, Gerald F. 33, 34, 125, 149, 153, 154, 156, 168
Myrdal, Gunnar 18, 316, 358, 434, 453, 460; and education 483n; and rural problem 91-2

Napoleonic Wars, impact on Haitian trade 274
'Nassaumen' 627
National Railroad 369, 371
necessities, taxes on 395-6
négritude 340, 343
Nicolas, Schiller 210, 211
Nisbet, Charles 523n
Noël, Pierre 425n
non-price competition in marketing crops 20, 166-71
normal schools 472, 475
nuclear energy 201, 203
nurses 429
nutrition 19, 409, 601; and agricultural production 434-46; and birth rates 433; and migration 433-4; and population growth 433-4; deterioration 110, 420, 433, 434, 442, 446; low equilibrium trap 440

Office National d'Alphabétisation et d'Action Communautaire (ONAAC) 479
Office National d'Education Communautaire (ONEC) 477-9
Ohlin, Göran 643-4
oil prices 20
oligopolistic, and oligopsonistic, middlemen 121-79
onions 154, 156
opportunity cost: of moneylending 521, 523, 534; of schooling 482, 483, 484, 490
Oreste, Michel 333, 463
organic matter, as obstacle to technological change 577, 616
Organisme de Développement de la Vallée de l'Artibonite (ODVA) 540 and n
Organization of American States (OAS) 33, 57, 60, 66, 385, 586
Oshima, Harry T. 442
'outside' lenders 533
overmilitarization of Haiti 24, 74, 271, 375-83, 399

pacotilleuses 147n
Palmer, Ernest Charles 34
paper money 368
Parenton, Vernon J. 530
participation ratio 434-44
pastoral lands 188, 194, 209
patente 141, 142, 156; defined 134
Paul, Edouard C. 462n
pays nouveau 623
peas 17, 40, 47, 126, 236; production 206
peasant: consumption goods 19; debt 122; economy 13-18; incomes 507; output 205-23; *Weltanschauung* 298, 350, 352-4
peasants: as risk averters 617; attachment to soil 505-7; capital resources 504; defined 13-16; food outlays by 418
Péligre hydroelectric dam 203
Péralte, Charlemagne 336
Pères Oblats 541
perfect competition, 28, 145; defined 127
pesticides 67-8, 280
Pétion, Alexandre: agricultural policy 262, 267, 559; and education 461, 462n; army under 375; economic liberalism 268; GNP decline under 268, 298; land reform 22, 256, 263-4, 268, 297, 298, 326, 327, 334, 355, 358, 560, 567n1; taxation under 268

petits blancs 320
petroleum 201-2
petty trade 149-50, 152, 155
physicians 429-30
Pierre-Charles, Gérard 32, 52n1, 100, 102, 510n
piti mi 45n, 585-6
plaçage 506; defined 507
planning 307-13, 355
plantains 17, 40, 43, 47, 126, 210; prices; production 206
plantations 22, 38, 40, 81, 256, 259, 297, 565, 646; break-up 54, 255, 273, 398, 561-2; capital equipment for 28; restoration after independence 259-63, 275, 298; specialization by 562
planting 71, 77, 81, 87
plants 18, 62, 69; diseases 67
plows 14, 29, 62, 63nn, 581 and n, 590-4, 617; introduced by Christophe 63n1, 559
pois 47
police, expenditure on 24, 366, 379-83, 400
political marginalization of peasants 23, 319-54, 398, 494, 636
politics 81; and economics 314-17; as main obstacle to development 642-4
Polvérel, Etienne 260n
population decline (1790-1805) 272
population density 55, 60 and n, 61; optimum 574
population growth 25, 55, 80, 188, 189-94, 200, 204-5, 255, 279, 635; and agricultural innovation 28, 574-6; and deforestation 197; and erosion 20, 37, 81, 221; and migration 624, 645
population of Haiti 628
Port-au-Prince: bicentennial exhibition 341; rainfall in 64
Port Dauphin 285
potatoes 154
Poté-Colé project 309, 310, 540 and n
poverty, and marketing of agricultural goods 121-86
pratik 32, 137, 166-71, 511; and credit; defined 166
precautionary loans 508-9
price changes, and erosion 214-23
Price-Mars, Jean 536n, 487-8
price setting in market places 161-6
'prisoner's dilemma' 21, 224-5, 231

private schools 462, 469-71, 472, 477, 478, 485
process, and product, innovations 558
production: in line 578-9, 580; in parallel 578-9; loans 27, 28
production methods 17, 54, 81; in peasant sector 18
property rights 516; and land reform 275-6
property taxes 392
Prosper, Marcaisse 342
prostitution 632
protein, average intake 418-19
protein-calorie malnutrition (PCM) 411, 414-21
Protestant schools 469-71, 476
pruning 78
public administration, efficiency of 387-91
public debt 302, 370-1, 373
public finance, Haitian 24-5, 365-406; aim of 386-7
public health service, reorganization of 423
public servants: method of appointment 389; salaries and working hours 390
pupils in rural schools, characteristics of 482-4

racial prejudice, American against Haitians 466-7
Railroad, National 369, 371
rainfall 28, 64-6, 76, 113, 195, 210; as obstacle to technological change 579-80, 617
Rameau, Septimus 330, 368
rate of time preference 226-7, 231, 513-20, 531, 534, 552; determination 514-19
reafforestation 200
Régie du Tabac 381, 382, 383, 393
regional market places 150-1
relative factor prices, as obstacles to technological change 28, 582-5, 591-5, 617
religion 23
research, government sponsored 611-13
revendeuses 147-71; capital requirements 157; defined 148
revolutions, in Haiti 23
riboflavin deficiency 415, 417, 420
rice 17, 40, 46, 62, 126, 236, 572;

prices 219; production 206; yields 80
Riché, Jean-Baptiste 329
risk: and formal credit 548, 549; as determinant of interest rates 27, 523-6, 534; as determinant of time preferences 517-19, 535; as obstacle to technological change 29, 599-606, 617; faced by lenders 534, 535; minimizing 548; peasant aversion to 600-3, 617
Rockefeller, Nelson A., visit to Haiti 311
Rodman, Selden 63n
root crops 46
Rostow, W.W. 557
Rotberg, Robert I. 17, 33, 102, 191, 250, 251, 328, 341, 345, 376, 466
Roumain, Jacques 187
roundworm 422
Royal Bank of Canada 522
Roy, Eugène 38
rural credit 641; demand for 508-10; problems 503-55
rural credit market 442, 504; entry to 530-3
rural education in Haiti 461-501; discrimination in 26, 484, 490-7; financial aspects 467, 468, 475
rural government, local 350-2
rural incomes, falling 18, 20, 21, 26, 37, 81, 91-120, 623, 645
rural labor force, growth of 204-5, 207
rural nutrition 106-10
rural savings 504-8
rural settlement pattern 483, 597
rural-urban migration 29, 433, 434
Russell, John H. 300
Ruttan, Vernon W. 612
Rybczynski, T.M., theorem 21, 209, 213-14, 235-42, 279n
Ryswick, Treaty of 257

Saget, Nissage 270, 330, 368
Saint-Domingue 40, 41, 43, 73, 195-6, 256, 258, 274, 334, 461, 560, 573; plantation economy 22, 266, 267; slave society 23, 319-22, 616
St John, Sir Spenser 329, 330, 332, 377, 378n
Saint Martin, migration to 628
Saint Surin, Jacques 110, 191, 628
Salnave, Sylvain 270, 330, 378

Salomon, Lysius 266, 270, 299, 378, 567
Sam, Guillaume 334
Sam, Simon 299, 332, 333
Samuelson, Paul A. 187
sangues 511, 529
sanitation 417
savings 22, 27, 101, 503, 504, 522, 523; and capital formation 551; and yaws eradication 438; deposits 521
sawah 251, 252
Schaedel, Richard P. 33, 505n, 530
Schmidt, Hans 466
Schoelcher, Victor 560
schools 26, 469-71, 472; attendance at 465, 471, 472, 473; as educational filter; quality 26
Schultz, Theodore W. 96, 453, 557, 607, 610n
search activities 606-10
Sebrell, W.H. 419, 420
sections rurales 350; defined 629n
seeds 18, 62, 69, 81, 504, 505, 584, 603; yields 585, 601, 605
sékrétè 169; defined 159
semi-rural markets 150
Sen, Amartya K. 22, 256, 279, 293, 590
Service Coopératif Interaméricain de Production d'Aliments (SCIPA) 572
Service National de la Production Agricole et de l'Enseignement Rural (SNPA & ER) 384-5
Service National d'Eradication de Malaria (SNEM) 425
Service Technique du Département de l'Agriculture et de l'Enseignement Professionel: agricultural activities 303, 569, 614-16; educational system 300, 302, 335, 464-7, 494, 611, 614; salaries and wages 384, 468n
sharecropping 13, 49, 50, 79, 227, 603
Shoup, Carl S. 440, 441
Simon, Antoine 333
Simon, Julian L. 574n2
Simpson, George Eaton 31, 570
sisal 17, 22, 40, 42, 267, 280; prices 216, 284, 285, 288; production 33, 206, 288; world market 284-6
slavery 23, 73, 189, 258, 273, 319-21,

Index   697

324, 357, 398, 485, 560; abolition 365; economic life in 259; uprisings against 320
small farms 261; creation of 263-6
Smith, Adam 268, 576, 581, 582
Smoot-Hawley tariff 282
social mobility in Haiti 318
Société Haitiano-Américaine de Développement Agricole (SHADA) 42, 267, 287, 305, 354, 604n
sociétés de travail 114, 115, 116, 596; as social activities 116-18
soft state, in Haiti 23, 326-34, 358, 391; defined 326-7
solar energy 201, 203-4
Solow, Robert M. 187
Somoza, Anastasio 338
Sonthonax, Léger-Félicité 260n
sorghum 17, 40, 45 and n, 46, 78, 126, 236, 585-6; prices 219; production 206; storage 69; yields 80
Soulouque, Faustin 270, 271, 329, 354, 377, 378; and education 462 and n; debt payment by 367
sous-marins 134, 136
sowing 77, 86, 87
Spaniards 256, 258
Spéculateurs 19, 121, 134-45, 396, 512; as lenders 511-13, 524, 526, 528, 529, 530, 532, 600
spoils system 298, 357, 383, 389-90, 399, 636
spy system 377, 378
squatting 22, 198, 265, 272, 275, 276, 277, 286, 325
Standard Fruit and Steamship Company 218, 286, 303, 307, 339, 341
starvation 601, 604, 645
Stiglitz, Joseph E. 454
storage, of crops 68-9
Street, John M. 32, 446
Streeten, Paul 95, 96, 454
student riots 465
subsistence economies 14-15
subsistence products 14, 17, 37, 39, 40, 45-88, 188, 194, 205, 207, 208, 603; harvesting 86; marketing 19, 123, 145-71, 187; output 209; pests and diseases 67; prices 218, 219; taxation 244n
sugar 22, 40, 126, 236, 256-63, 270, 273; exports 17, 22, 262, 265, 366; harvesting 87; marketing 283-4;

prices 22, 216, 274, 280, 281, 282, 283; production 206, 281, 283, 561; quota, in US 283; supply elasticity 282-3; tariffs 282; world market 280-4; yields 80
survival algorithm 601
sweet potatoes 17, 40, 46, 126, 236; pests and diseases 68; prices 219; production 206
Sweezy, Paul M. 273

Tainos 123
Tanzi, Vito 397-8
taxation 16n, 21, 228, 347; inefficient administration 25, 388-9, 400; of peasants and peasant products 15, 24, 327, 334, 395-6, 545, 637, 641
teachers 26; as educational filter 488-9, 491; quality 26; salaries 464, 468-9, 476
technological change 28, 31, 38, 188, 194, 409, 481, 503; and assistance for agriculture 572; and credit 543, 549-51, 552; defined 558; during American occupation 567-70; resistance to 544, 546, 557-618
technological efficiency 20, 128, 145, 187; defined 127
technological inefficiency 130, 131
technological progress 82
technological stagnation, in peasant sector 558-67, 623, 635
technology: economically irrelevant 584, 587; low-yielding 507; peasant-biased 584; ultra-superior 584
tè cho and *tè frèt* 39, 46, 53, 86, 125
temperature, in Haiti 38, 39
tenant farming 13, 37, 49-50, 79, 227, 603
tetanus neonatorum 25, 426, 427, 431
Théodore, Davilmar 333
Theory of Economic Growth 504
Thorner, Daniel 15
threshold farm size 591
ti maché 149-50, 153
time, as obstacle to technological change 577-80
Tinnermeier, Ronald L. 573n, 584
tobacco 569
tonton macoutes 310, 347, 348, 354; defined 344; numbers 381

698 Index

tools, used in agriculture 18, 62, 69, 78, 81, 504, 505, 509, 575
topography 58-9, 122; and land scarcity 81; as obstacle to technological change 581-2, 617
Topsoil and Civilization 639-40
tourist industry 537
Toussaint l'Ouverture 73, 113, 270, 272, 561; agricultural policy 260-1, 262, 267, 270, 323, 560; centralized rule 323, 324; land reform 263; tax policy 392
tractors 581, 591
trade outside market places 168-71
transaction costs: as determinant of interest rates 523, 527-9; for moneylenders 534; in land market 27, 516-17, 520
Transforming Traditional Agriculture 557
transport 28, 357, 581, 582, 617; as obstacle to competition 20, 180-6
treasury notes 522
tree felling 21, 188, 223-4, 230
triage 141
Tripartite mission to Haiti 385
trucks 155, 184n
Trujillo, Rafael Leónidas 303, 338, 339; massacre of Haitians by 626
tuberculosis 25, 421, 422, 423, 426, 431
Tun Wai, U 511 and n, 524-5
Turnham, David 439, 440
Tuskegee Institute 464, 465

unavailability of large land tracts, as obstacle to large farms 286-7
underdevelopment, economic and political interaction in 635
Underwood, Frances W. 32, 149
unemployment: disguised 18, 86-8; seasonal, in agriculture 86, 88
Union Nationaliste 301
United Fruit Company 266, 624
United Nations 540; mission to Haiti 31, 181, 385, 424, 571, 611, 614
United Nations Children's Fund (UNICEF) 425
United Nations Educational Scientific and Cultural Organization (UNESCO) 31, 306, 307, 473-4
United States: aid to Haiti 310-11; coffee quota 306; Financial Advisor in Haiti 337, 371, 395, 464; Haitian emigration to 628; Point Four Program 571-2
United States Marines 339, 463, 466, 567; control of elections 335; creation of *Garde* 336, 400; massacre of peasants 465; salaries 379
United States occupation of Haiti 23, 265, 271, 297, 299-302, 399, 462; administrative reforms by 23, 336-7, 356; and agriculture 282, 299, 398; and education 338, 480, 481-2; and plantations 266-7, 286; and taxation 395; creation of police 74; debt management 24, 370-2, 373; disease during 421-3; economic development under 299-302; failure to foster democracy 334-8, 474; military rule 299; public health service, reorganization 423; technological change during 567-70
Uphoff, Norman 544
urban: bias 640, 641; markets 151; population 55, 56
usury 552; legislation, absence of 531n

vagabondage 352n
vegetables 39; marketing 154
vegetation, of Haiti 38
vente à réméré 517
vicious circles 18, 100, 101
'viejos' 626
Vincent, Sténio 302, 307, 338, 339, 372, 373, 380; agricultural policy 302-4; and coffee exports 571; and education 468-71; land reform 517
vitamin deficiency 25, 411, 413, 415, 419-20, 421
vocational education 26, 458, 480, 491-2; during American occupation 463-7
voodoo 12, 318, 353, 354, 358, 598n; as obstacle to technological change 24, 597-8; ceremonies 117; clergy 24, 25, 352, 430

wages and salaries 70, 74, 366; of public employees 24, 383-6
Wainwright, Joseph 211
Walras' law 244

wars of liberation 22, 24, 43, 270, 322
Washington, Booker T. 464, 467
Wealth of Nations 576
weaning 416
Webster, Daniel 377
weeding 78
West Africa 112, 113, 124
Wharton, Clifton R. Jr 132, 456
whipworm 422
Why Poor People Stay Poor 640
Wicksell, Knut 18, 91
Wilberforce, William 461, 559
Wilson, Woodrow 379
wind energy 201, 203
Wingfield, Roland 33, 101, 102, 105, 426, 530, 631-2
Wolf, Eric R. 15
women: in labor force 71-4, 205; trading by 146-7
wood: export 200; for fuel 194, 198-200, 204
wood cutting, peasant 204, 205, 255
Wood, Harold A. 52, 301, 506, 582n1
Wood, Marie V. 32, 70
Woodring, Wendell P. 198
work effort, inadequate after peak seasons 442
working population, in Haiti 70-5
World Bank 181, 382n, 383
World Health Organization (WHO) 411, 425

yams 17, 40, 46, 80, 126, 210
yaws (*pian*) 25, 307, 421-2, 427, 431, 445; and malnutrition 444-6; campaigns against 423, 424-5; eradication 434, 443; effects on ratios 436-9
yields in agriculture 18, 80, 81

Zamor, Oreste 333
zinglins 271, 377
Zuvekas, Clarence Jr 34